Ala

a travel survival kit

Jim DuFresne

Alaska – a travel survival kit

4th edition

Published by
    Lonely Planet Publications
    Head Office: PO Box 617, Hawthorn, Vic 3122, Australia
    Branches: PO Box 2001A, Berkeley, CA 94702, USA
                    10 Barley Mow Passage, Chiswick, London W4 4PH, UK
                    71 bis rue du Cardinal Lemoine, 75005 Paris, France

Printed by
    Singapore National Printers Ltd, Singapore

Photographs by
    Camp Denali (CD), Jim DuFresne (JD), Carl Palazzola (CP), Donna Pietsch (DP), Robert Strauss (RS),
    Deanna Swaney (DS), National Park Service (NPS)
    Front cover: Icy Bay – Kayakers, Gulf of Alaska Islands (Horizons Photo Library, Ernest Manewal)
    Back cover: Totem, Ketchikan (Carl Palazzola)

Illustrations by
    John Svenson on pages 31, 34, 90, 92, 160, 267, 324, 338, 385

First Published
    June 1983

This Edition
    July 1994

National Library of Australia Cataloguing in Publication Data

DuFresne, Jim
    Alaska – a travel survival kit.

    4th ed.
    Includes index.
    ISBN 0 86442 213 X.

    1. Alaska – Guidebooks.
    I. Title. (Series: Lonely Planet travel survival kit)

917.98045

text © Jim DuFresne 1994
maps © Lonely Planet 1994
photos © photographers as indicated 1994
climate charts compiled from information supplied by Patrick J Tyson, © Patrick J Tyson, 1994

Jim DuFresne

Jim is a former sports and outdoors editor of the *Juneau Empire* and the first Alaskan sportswriter to win a national award from Associated Press. He is presently a freelance writer, specializing in outdoor and travel writing. His previous books include *Tramping in New Zealand* (Lonely Planet Publications) and wilderness guides to Isle Royale, Voyageurs and Glacier Bay national parks.

From the Author

Thanks go to artist mountaineer John Svenson for his illustrations for this book. John has lived in Alaska for over two decades and his woodcuts, water colors and illustrations have appeared in national outdoor magazines as well as art galleries throughout the Northwest. During the summer, he works as a climbing guide, and though his trade has taken him to the summits of four continents, Alaska has always remained his inspirational mecca.

My deepest appreciation goes to my old Juneau housemates Jeff and Sue Sloss and a legion of Lonely Planet travellers who went to Alaska with this book in hand and then took the time to drop me a line. They include:

Kevin and Glenys Hammer, Joan and Don Bailey, Helen Pfeiffer, John Pocock and Fiona Robertson of Australia, John Inglis and Laura McFarland, Chris Wethern, Karen Cooper and Marc Dyer, Lisa Raffel and Scott Smith, Sean Bandon, Keith Judson and Bruce Ohlson of the USA, Armando D Berardinis of Italy, Yvonne and Roger Esch of the Netherlands, Katherine of New Zealand and, Stuart McKenchnie. N D Lowe and N J Terkelsen of the UK.

I received considerable assistance from Carla Sullivan of the Fairbanks Convention & Visitor Bureau, Connie Taylor of the Cordova Chamber of Commerce, Suzi Bock of the Matanuska-Susitna Visitor Bureau, Ken Morris of the Anchorage Convention & Visitors Bureau.

Also lending me a hand were Dave Vickery of the Bureau of Land Management, Linda Mickle of the Alaska Marine Highway System, Carol Waddell of Reeve Aleutian Airways, John Beiler of the Alaska Division of Tourism, Bill Ehrlich of Alaska Airlines, Janet Swanson of Alaska Railroad, and Ike Waits of Wild Rose Guidebooks.I deeply appreciate my equipment sponsors Patagonia, MSR, Kelty, Vasque Boots and Dana Packs.

Most of all I thank my traveling partners and those Alaskans who put me up for a night; Tim and Racheli Feller of Anchorage, Lisa Taylor and Peter Brondz of Bird Creek, Phoebe Riches of Australia. There was Jack and Eileen Hughes and their wonderful sauna in Homer, Sandra Stimson, Rita Gittins and Ed Fogels in Anchorage, Gary Benson of Sourdough Outfitters in Bettles.

An extra dose of appreciation goes out to Carl Palazzola of California and Donna Pietsch of Minnesota and that endless sun of a summer spent in Alaska. In the end this book was made possible By John Barton and Carl Walter, two wilderness Klepper kayak fanatics. Is there a better boat for adventure than the Klepper? Is there a better place to paddle one than Alaska?

From the Publisher

This edition of Alaska was edited at the Lonely Planet office in Australia by Frith Pike. Rachel Black was responsible for design, cartography and some illustrating.

Tamsin Wilson designed the cover. Thanks also to Chris Lee Ack, Paul Clifton and Rachel Black for their cartographic computer pioneering and to Greg Herriman (assistance with mapping), Trudi Canavan (illustrations) and Ann Jeffree (assistance with the index).

Warning & Request

Things change – prices go up, schedules change, good places go bad and bad places go bankrupt – nothing stays the same. So if you find things better or worse, recently opened or long since closed, please write and tell us and help make the next edition better!

Your letters will be used to help update future editions and, where possible, import-ant changes will also be included as a Stop Press section in reprints.

We greatly appreciate all information that is sent to us by travellers. Back at Lonely Planet we employ a hard-working readers' letters team to sort through the many letters we receive.

The best ones will be rewarded with a free copy of the next edition or another Lonely Planet guide if you prefer. We give away lots of books, but, unfortunately, not every letter/postcard receives one.

Contents

Map Legend

BOUNDARIES

International Boundary
Internal Boundary
National Park Boundary
Arctic Circle
Latitudes & Longitudes

ROUTES

Highway
Major Road
Unsealed Road or Track
City Street
Railway
Walking Track
Bike Track
Ferry Route
Canoe Route
Cable Car or Chairlift

AREA FEATURES

Park, Gardens
National Park
State Park, County Park
Reservation
Wilderness Area
Built-Up Area
Pedestrian Mall
Cemetery
Glacier

HYDROGRAPHIC FEATURES

Coastline
River, Creek
Intermittent River or Creek
Lake, Intermittent Lake
Swamp
Canal

SYMBOLS

✪ CAPITAL	National Capital	
◎ Capital	State Capital	
▨ CITY	Major City	
● City	City	
● Town	Town	
● Village	Village	
■	..Hotel, Pension (Places to Stay)	
▼	Restaurant (Places to Eat)	
♊	Pub, Bar (Places to Drink)	
✉ ☎	Post Office, Telephone	
❶ ❸	Tourist Information, Bank	
⊖ ℗	Transport, Parking	
⛫ ⛨	Museum, Youth Hostel	
⊞ Å	Caravan Park, Camping Ground	
† ⊟ †	Church, Cathedral	
☾ ✿	Mosque, Synagogue	
⚘ ⚘	Buddhist Temple, Hindu Temple	

✚ ★	Hospital, Police Station	
✈ ✝	Airport, Airfield	
▣ ✿	Swimming Pool, Gardens	
◈ ☕	Shopping Centre, Cafe	
▲ ⚐	Monument, Golf Course	
←	One Way Street	
⛬	Archaeological Site or Ruins	
⛉ ▣	Castle, Tomb	
⌒ ⌂	Cave, Hut or Chalet	
▲ ※	Mountain or Hill, Lookout	
⛯ ⚓	Lighthouse, Shipwreck	
)(⌐	Pass, Spring	
Ancient or City Wall		
Rapids, Waterfalls		
Cliff or Escarpment, Tunnel		
Railway Station		
Bridge		

Note: not all symbols displayed above appear in this book

Introduction

It isn't the mountains, sparkling lakes or glaciers that draw travelers to Alaska every year but the magic in the land; an irresistible force that tugs on those who dream about the north country.

No area in the USA possesses the mystical pull that this land has. It ignites the imagination of people who live in the city but long to wander in the woods. Its mythical title of the 'Final Frontier' is as strong today as it was in the past when Alaska's promise of adventure and the lure of quick wealth brought the first invasion of miners to the state. Today, they have been replaced by travelers and backpackers but the spirit of adventure is still the same.

Travellers, drawn to Alaska by its colorful reputation, are stunned by the grandeur of what they see and often go home penniless. There are mountains, glaciers and rivers in other parts of North America but few are on the same scale or as overpowering as those in Alaska. To see a brown bear rambling up one side of a mountain valley or to sit in a kayak and watch a five-mile-wide glacier continually calve ice off its face are experiences of natural beauty that permanently change your way of thinking.

If nature's handiwork doesn't effect you, then the state's overwhelming size will. Everything in Alaska is big, that is everything except its population. There are 550,000 residents and almost half of them live in one city, Anchorage. Yet the state is huge at 591,004 sq miles which makes it a fifth of the size of the USA; as big as

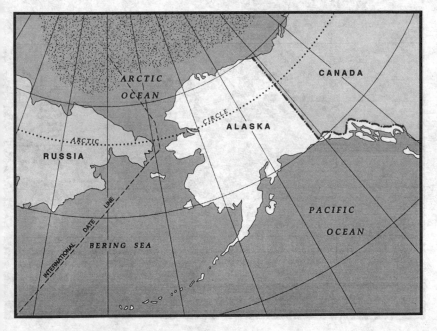

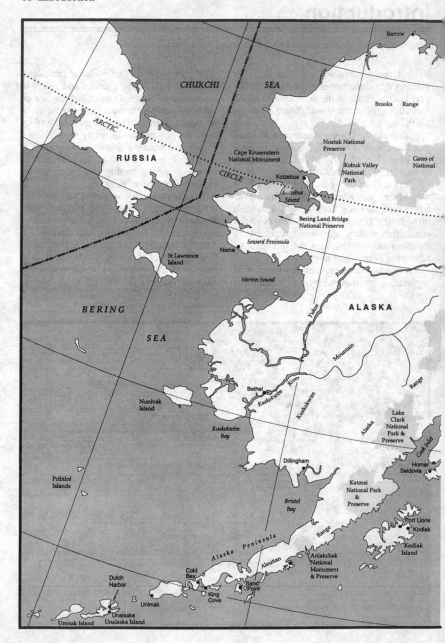

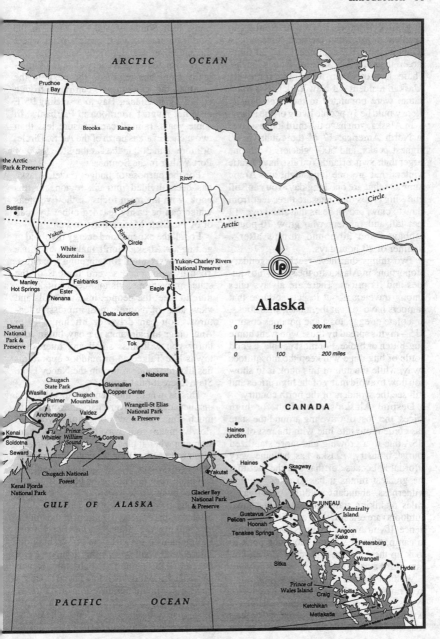

England, France, Italy and Spain put together; bigger than the next three largest states in the USA combined; or 120 times larger than the US state of Rhode Island. There is more than a sq mile for every Alaskan resident – if New York City's Manhattan were populated to the same density there would be 16 people living on the island.

In Alaska, you have the third longest river in North America; 17 of the country's 20 highest peaks; and 5000 glaciers, with one larger than Switzerland. You also have Arctic winters that are one long night and Arctic summers that are one long day. You can still find king crabs that measure three feet from claw to claw, brown bears that stand over 12 feet tall and farmers who grow 70-pound cabbages and 30-pound turnips after a summer of 20-hour days.

Two things that have reached legendary proportions in Alaska are the state's mosquitoes and its prices. There are always tales among travelers about insects so large that campers have to beat them back with sticks; or a plate of eggs, toast and potatoes costing $15 – myths spread by those who went home bug-bitten or broke. For most people, a good bottle of bug dope will keep the mosquitoes away, while the aim of this book is to show you how to avoid many of the high prices and still see the wonders of the north country.

Despite Alaska's reputation for high prices, the cost of traveling around the state has come more into line with the rest of the USA due to a growing and more stabilized tourist industry. Alaska has become very affordable because of that and the fact that the greatest things it has to offer – prime wilderness, abundant wildlife, clear water, miles of hiking trails (in general the great outdoors) are either free or cost little to experience. If you are low on funds but are willing to camp, hike or sit on a mountain peak to soak up the sunshine and scenery, then you can afford a trip to Alaska.

Within the state, which ranges 1400 miles from north to south and 2400 miles from east to west, are several regions each as distinctive as the countries in Europe, making up Alaska's character. You can begin your travels in the rainy, lush Southeast and end them in the Arctic tundra – a vast, treeless plain where the sun never sets during the summer.

The weather and scenery change dramatically from one region to the next. In the summer, the temperatures can range from a cool 50°F in Glacier Bay to a sizzling 95°F on a hot August afternoon in Fairbanks. In some years, rainfall can measure less than two inches in areas north of the Arctic Circle, or more than 300 inches at the little town of Port Walter in the Southeast.

For the purpose of budget travel, Alaska has been divided into six regions in this book, with the main focus on the five areas which can be easily reached either by road or by the State Marine Ferry system.

For all the expense and energy involved in getting to Alaska, don't make your trip a seven-day/six-night fling through five cities. To truly appreciate several regions of the state, or even one, visitors need to take the time to meet the people, hike the trails and view some of nature's most impressive features. You can drive or hitchhike from Anchorage to Fairbanks in a day, but in your hurry you will miss small and interesting towns like Talkeetna or outdoor opportunities like the canoe routes in the Nancy Lake State Recreational Area.

This is where independent travel has a distinct advantage over a package tour – with much time and few obligations, you can slowly make your way through the state, stopping when it pleases you and moving on when it doesn't. Often a quaint little village or sea port will be especially inviting and you can pitch your tent along the beach for a few days or even a few weeks.

Many travelers who have less than three weeks to spare spend it entirely in the Southeast, taking the State Marine Ferry from Bellingham in the US state of Washington. Those who want to see the Southeast and then move further north to Fairbanks, Denali National Park and Anchorage need at least a month and should possibly plan on returning from Anchorage by air. Any less time would be a rush job through a land where one simply cannot afford to hurry.

With an increasing number of nonstop flights being offered today from such cities as Reno, Detroit and Minneapolis, it's possible, and affordable, to fly to Anchorage and complete a tour of that city, Denali National Park and Fairbanks in three weeks.

But what's important is to keep in mind that ever-increasing popularity of Alaska has not only stabilized the tourist industry but also made Alaska a painfully crowded destination at times. Today travelers are shocked to head into the Kenai Peninsula area and find campground after campground filled in July. Denali National Park can be a zoo in August and often finding a bed in towns like Valdez and Seward at the height of the tourist season is a near impossible task. There are times when the George Parks Hwy between Anchorage and Fairbanks is just an endless line of RVers heading south.

The solution to that is to pack in more days to escape further off the beaten path and to try to make as many arrangements in advance of your trip as possible, especially if you plan to visit such popular areas as Denali or Katmai national parks or hope to secure passage for your vehicle on the state ferry system. (There isn't a day that goes by during the summer without a motorist being stunned to find out in Valdez that you need a reservation to transport a car to Whittier.)

One last thing for those, who have seemingly been dreaming forever about Alaska. It's wise to start your trip at the beginning of the summer in case you want to extend your stay another month or even longer. One of the most common stories among residents is how somebody came to visit Alaska for six weeks and ended up staying six years. Once there, Alaska is a hard land to leave.

Facts about Alaska

HISTORY

Alaska's history is a strange series of spurts and sputters, booms and busts. Although today Alaska is viewed as a wilderness paradise and an endless source of raw materials, it has often in the past been regarded as a frozen wasteland, a suitable home only for Inuit and polar bears. When some natural resource was uncovered, however, a short period of prosperity and exploitation followed: firstly there was sea-otter skins; then gold, salmon and oil; and most recently, untouched wilderness. After each resource was exhausted, some would say raped, the land slipped back into oblivion.

The First Alaskans

The first Alaskans migrated from Asia to North America from 30,000 to 40,000 years ago during an ice age that lowered the sea level and gave rise to a 900-mile land bridge spanning Siberia and Alaska. The nomadic groups were not bent on exploring the new world but on following the animal herds that provided them with food and clothing. Although many tribes wandered deep into North and South America, four ethnic groups – the Athabascans, Aleuts, Inuit and the coastal tribes of Tlingits and Haidas – remained in Alaska and made the harsh wilderness their homeland.

The First Europeans

The first written record of the state was made by Virtus Bering, a Danish navigator sailing for the tsar of Russia. Bering's trip in 1728 proved that America and Asia were two separate continents, and 13 years later, commanding the ship *St Peter*, he went ashore near Cordova to become the first European to set foot in Alaska.

Bering and many of his crew died from scurvy during that journey, but his lieutenant (aboard the ship *St Paul*) sailed all the way to the site of present-day Sitka before turning around. Despite all the hardships, the survivors brought back fur pelts and tales of fabulous seal and otter colonies – Alaska's first boom was under way. Russian fur merchants wasted little time in overrunning the Aleutian Islands and quickly established a settlement on Kodiak Island. Chaos followed as bands of Russian hunters robbed and murdered each other for furs while the peaceful Aleutian Indians, living near the hunting grounds, were almost annihilated.

By the 1790s, Russia had organized the Russian-American Company to regulate the fur trade and ease the violent competition. However, tales of the enormous wealth to be gained in the Alaskan wildlife trade brought representatives of several other countries to the frigid waters. Spain claimed the entire North American west coast, including Alaska, and sent several explorers to the Southeast region. These early visitors took boat loads of furs but left neither settlers or forts, only a few Spanish names.

The British arrived when Captain James Cook began searching the area for the mythical Northwest Passage between the Pacific and Atlantic oceans. From Vancouver Island, Cook sailed north to Southcentral Alaska in 1778, anchoring at what is now Cook Inlet for a spell, before continuing on to the Aleutian Islands, Bering Sea and even the Arctic Ocean. The French sent Jean de La Perouse, who in 1786 made it as far as Lituya Bay on the southern coast of Alaska. But it was Cook's shipmate, George Vancouver, returning on his own in the 1790s who finally charted the complicated waters of the Southeast's Inside Passage. Aboard his ship, HMS *Discovery*, Vancouver surveyed the coastline from California to Alaska's Panhandle, producing maps so accurate they were still being used a century later.

After depleting the fur colonies in the Aleutians, Alexander Baranof, who headed the Russian-American Company, moved his territorial capital from Kodiak to Sitka in the Southeast. After subduing the Tlingit Indians in his ruthless manner, he proceeded to build a stunning city, 'an American Paris in Alaska' with the immense profits from furs. At one point, Baranof oversaw, or some would say ruled, a fur empire that stretched from Bistol Bay to northern California but when the British began pushing north into Southeast Alaska, he built a second fort near the mouth of the Stikine River in 1834. That fort, which was named St Dionysius at the time, eventually evolved into the small lumbering and fishing town of Wrangell.

When a small trickle of US adventurers began to arrive, four nations had a foot in the Panhandle of Alaska: Spain and France were squeezed out of the area by the early 1800s while the British were reduced to leasing selected areas from the Russians.

The Sale of Alaska

By the 1860s, the Russians found themselves badly overextended. Their involvement in Napoleon's European wars, a declining fur industry and the long lines of shipping between Sitka and the heartland of Russia were draining their national treasury. The country made several overtures to the USA for the sale of Alaska and fishers from Washington State pushed for it.

The American Civil War delayed the negotiations and it wasn't until 1867 that Secretary of State William H Seward, with extremely keen foresight, signed a treaty to purchase the state for $7.2 million – less than two cents an acre. By then the US public was in an uproar over the 'Frozen Wasteland'. Newspapers called it 'Seward's Ice Box' or 'Walrussia', while one senator heatedly compared Alaska to a 'sucked orange' as little was left of the rich fur trade.

On the Senate floor, the battle to ratify the treaty lasted six months before the sale was approved. On 18 October 1867, the formal transfer of Alaska to the Americans took place in Sitka, while nearby Wrangell, a town both the Russians and the British controlled at one time, changed flags for the third time in its short existence.

Alaska remained a lawless, unorganized territory for the next 20 years, with the US Army in charge at one point and the navy at another. This great land, remote and inaccessible to all but a few hardy settlers, remained a dark, frozen mystery to most people. Eventually its riches were uncovered one by one. First it was whales, taken mostly in the Southeast and later in the Bering Sea and the Arctic Ocean.

Next the phenomenal salmon runs were tapped, with the first canneries being built in 1878 at Klawock on Prince of Wales Island. Both industries brought a trickle of people and prosperity to Alaska.

Gold

What brought Alaska into the world limelight, however, was gold. The promise of quick riches and the adventure of the frontier became the most effective lure Alaska ever had. Gold was discovered in the Gastineau Channel in the 1880s and the towns of Juneau and Douglas sprang up overnight, living off the very productive Treadwell and Alaska-Juneau mines. Circle City in the Interior suddenly emerged in 1893 when gold was discovered in nearby Birch Creek. Three years later, one of the world's most colorful gold rushes took place in the Klondike of the Yukon Territory (Canada).

Often called 'the last grand adventure', the Klondike gold rush took place when the country and much of the world was suffering a severe recession. Thousands of people quit their jobs and sold their homes to finance a trip through Southeast Alaska to the newly created boom town of Skagway. From this tent city, almost 30,000 prospectors tackled the steep Chilkoot Trail to Lake Bennett, where they built crude rafts to float the rest of the way to the goldfields; an equal number of people returned home along the route, broke and disillusioned.

The number of miners who made a fortune was small, but the tales and legends that emerged were endless. The Klondike stampede, though it only lasted from 1896 to the early 1900s, was Alaska's most colorful era and earned Alaska the reputation of being the country's last frontier.

Statehood

By the 1900s, the attention of the miners shifted from the Klondike to Nome and then to Fairbanks, a boom town that was born when Felix Pedro discovered gold 12 miles north of the area in l902. The gold mines and the large Kennecott copper mines north of Cordova also stimulated the state's growth and the 1900 census estimated the state's population to be 60,000, including 30,000 non-indigenous people. Alaskans, who moved their capital from Sitka to Juneau that year, began to clamor for more say in their future. The US Congress first gave them a nonvoting delegate to Washington in 1906 and then assisted in setting up a territorial legislature that met at Juneau in 1913. Three years later, the territory submitted its first statehood bill to Congress.

Statehood was set aside when many of Alaska's residents departed south for high-paying jobs that were created by WW I. Ironically, it took another war, WW II, to push Alaska firmly into the 20th century.

The USA experienced its only foreign invasion on home soil when the Japanese attacked the Attu Islands and bombed Dutch Harbor in the Aleutian Islands during WW II. Congress and military leaders panicked and rushed to develop and protect the rest of Alaska. Large army and air-force bases were built throughout the state at places including Anchorage, Fairbanks, Sitka, Whittier and Kodiak and thousands of military personnel were sent to run them. But it was the famous Alcan (also known as the Alaska Hwy) that was the single most important project of the military build-up. The 1520-mile road was a major engineering feat and became the only overland link between Alaska and the rest of the USA.

At the time, Japan and Germany, allied with Italy, looked all but unbeatable while the only countries with sufficient resources and armies to confront the aggressors (Britain, the Soviet Union and the USA) had but one common border – the Bering Strait, that narrow neck of water separating Alaska and Siberia. There was both a need to supply military hardware to Russia and to protect America's north-west flank, neither of which could be accomplished by sea after Japan bombed Pearl Harbor in December 1941.

An overland route, far enough inland to be out of range of airplanes carried by Japanese aircraft carriers, was the obvious answer. The US Army Corps of Engineers were sent to build the wilderness route and used seven regiments, three of which were Black, to finish the project at breakneck pace. In eight months and 12 days, the soldiers felled trees, put down gravel and built pontoon bridges until the Alcan was opened on 25 October 1942.

The road was built by the military but it was the residents who benefited as it stimulated the development of Alaska's natural resources. The growth lead to a new drive for statehood to fix what many felt was Alaska's status of '2nd-class citizenship' in Washington, DC. Early in 1958, Congress approved a statehood act which Alaskans quickly accepted, and on 3 January l959, President Dwight Eisenhower proclaimed the land the 49th State of the Union.

The Modern State

Alaska entered the 1960s full of promise and then disaster struck: the most powerful earthquake ever recorded in North America (registering 9.2 on the Richter scale) hit Southcentral Alaska on Good Friday morning in 1964. More than 100 lives were lost and the damage was estimated at $500 million. In Anchorage, office buildings sank 10 feet into the ground and houses slid more than 1200 feet off a bluff into Knik Arm. A tidal wave virtually wiped out the entire community of Valdez. In Kodiak and Seward, 32 feet of the coastline slipped into the Gulf of Alaska, while Cordova lost its entire harbor as the sea rose 16 feet.

If the natural catastrophe left the newborn state in a shambles, then it was a gift from nature that rushed it to recovery and beyond. Alaska's next boom took place in 1968 when Atlantic Richfield discovered massive oil deposits underneath Prudhoe Bay in the Arctic Ocean. The value of the oil doubled after the worldwide Arab oil embargo of

1973 but the oil couldn't be touched until there was a pipeline to transport it to the warm-water port of Valdez. The pipeline, in turn, couldn't be built until the US Congress, which still administered most of the land, settled the intense controversy between industry, environmentalists and Native Alaskans with historical claims.

The Alaska Native Claims Settlement Act of 1971 was an unprecedented piece of legislation that opened the way for a group of oil companies to undertake the construction of the 789-mile pipeline. The oil began to flow in 1977, but during the brief years of pipeline construction Anchorage developed into a fully fledged modern city and Fairbanks burst at the seams as the transport center for much of the project. Along with four-digit weekly salaries, there was an astronomical rise in prices for basic items such as housing and food in Fairbanks, which some residents feel never came down with the wages.

In the end, however, oil has given Alaska an economic base that is the envy of many other states; Alaskans enjoy the highest per-capita income in the country. The state's budget is in the billions and legislators in Juneau have transformed Anchorage into a stunning city with sports arenas, libraries and performing-arts centers, while virtually every Bush town has a million-dollar school. From 1980 to 1986, this state of only a half million residents generated revenue of $26 billion. For most Alaskans it was hard to see beyond the gleam of the oil dollar.

Their first rude awakening came in 1986 when world oil prices dropped. Their second dose of reality was even harder to swallow when in March 1989 the biggest oil spill in US history occurred in their state. The accident occurred after the *Exxon Valdez*, a 987-foot Exxon Oil supertanker, rammed Bligh Reef a few hours out of the port of Valdez. The ship spilled almost 11 million gallons of North Slope crude into the bountiful waters of Prince William Sound and then the oil quickly spread 600 miles from the grounding. Alaskans and the rest of the country watched in horror as the spill quickly

became far too large for booms to contain the oil. Within months, miles of tainted coastline began to appear throughout the Gulf of Alaska as currents dispersed streamers of oil and tar balls.

State residents were shocked as oil began to appear from the glacier-carved cliffs of Kenai Fjords to the bird rookeries of Katmai National Park, and from lonely Cook Islet beaches to the salmon streams on Kodiak Island. The spill eventually contaminated 1567 miles of shoreline; scientists estimated between 300,000 and 645,000 birds were killed, while the 1013 sea otters found dead in the oil represented only 20% of the total killed.

> The clean-up last summer and the natural cleansing process this winter have led to a remarkable improvement in the condition of the shoreline.
> **The 1989 Annual Report of Exxon Corporation**

> Spend all day cleaning one huge rock and the tide comes in and covers it with oil again. Spend a week wiping and spraying the surface, but pick up a rock and there's four inches of oil underneath.
> **Walter Meganack, Alutiig Village Chief**

> Don't be upset. We'll pay for everything.
> **Exxon Representative to the Homer Oil Spill Response Center**

Valdez experienced another boom as the center of the clean-up effort which employed 10,000 workers, 800 boats and 45 oil skimmers. But the best this highly paid army could do was scrape 364 miles of shoreline before the on-coming winter weather shut down the effort in September. Only 14% of the oil was ever recovered by the crews. The rest either evaporated, sank to the bottom of the sea or broke down into components and chemicals on the beaches or in the water.

Exxon walked away from the country's worst oil spill after agreeing to a $900 million settlement to the US and Alaska governments.

In the end, many Alaskans felt betrayed by Big Oil, the very companies that had fed them so well in the past. The unfortunate event may be just the latest round in Alaska's greatest debate – that concerning the exploitation of the wilderness. The issue moved to center stage when industry, conservationists and the government came head to head over a single paragraph in the Alaska Native Claims Settlement Act, known simply as 'd-2', that called for the preservation of 80 million acres of Alaskan wilderness. To most residents this evoked the entire issue of federal interference with the state's resources and future.

The resulting battle was a tug of war about how much land the US Congress would preserve, to what extent industries such as mining and logging would be allowed to develop, and what permanent residents would be allowed to purchase. The fury over wilderness reached a climax when, on the eve of his departure from office in 1980, President Jimmy Carter signed the Alaska Lands Bill into law, setting aside 106 million acres for national parks and preserves with a single stroke of the pen.

The problems of how to manage the USA's remaining true wilderness areas are far from over. Oil-company officials, already preparing for the day the Prudhoe Bay fields run dry, have been eyeing other wilderness areas such as the Arctic National Wildlife Refuge (ANWR) and Bristol Bay, home of Alaska's greatest salmon runs. The ANWR also fell victim to the Persian Gulf War and President George Bush's background as a Texas oilman. The Bush administration pushed hard to open up a portion of this 1.5-million acre refuge to drilling after the Gulf War with Iraq made gas prices sky rocket. But environmentalists, especially the National Wildlife Federation, held their ground until November 1991 when the US Senate killed a bill that would have allowed offshore drilling in the ANWR and made it easier to build a gas pipeline across the refuge.

All this alarms environmentalists who say pipelines, oil drills and the activity associated in removing the oil will forever disrupt one of the last true wilderness areas on earth – not just a park or a bay but a complete ecosystem. Others doubt that environmentalists can continue to win this battle in a state where 85% of the revenue comes from the oil industry.

Also at the core of the issue are both 'locking up the land' and federal interference in the lives of Alaskans. Largely as the result of their remoteness, Alaskans have always been extremely independent, resenting anyone who traveled north with a book of rules and regulations. To most Alaskans, Washington, DC, is a foreign capital.

Today's Alaskans tend to be young (the median age is between 26 and 28 years) and spirited in work and play. They are individualistic in their lifestyles, following few outside trends and adhering only to what their environment dictates. They are lovers of the outdoors, though they don't always seem to take care of it, and generally extend a warm welcome to travelers. Occasionally you might run into an Alaskan who is boastfully loud while spinning and weaving tales of unbelievable feats while slapping you on the back. In this land of frontier fable, that's not being obnoxious – that's being colorful.

GEOGRAPHY
Southeast
Also known as the Panhandle, Southeast Alaska is a 500-mile coastal strip that extends from Dixon Entrance, north of Prince Rupert, to the Gulf of Alaska. In between are the hundreds of islands (including Prince of Wales Island, the third largest island in the USA) of the Alexander Archipelago and a narrow strip of coast separated from Canada's mainland by the glacier-filled Coastal Mountains.

Winding through the middle of the region is the Inside Passage waterway, the lifeline for the isolated communities as the rugged terrain prohibits road building. High annual

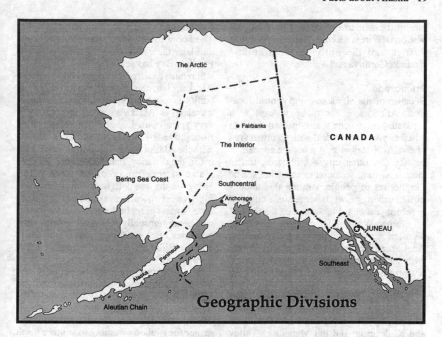

The Arctic

Fairbanks

The Interior

CANADA

Bering Sea Coast

Southcentral

Anchorage

JUNEAU

Peninsula

Southeast

Alaska

Geographic Divisions

Aleutian Chain

rainfall and mild temperatures have turned the Southeast into rainforest which is broken up by majestic mountain ranges, glaciers and fjords that surpass those in Norway.

The area has many small fishing and lumbering towns as well as the larger communities of Ketchikan, Sitka and Juneau (the state capital considered by many to be the most scenic city in Alaska). Other highlights of the region include the wilderness areas of Glacier Bay, Admiralty Island, Misty Fjord and Tracy Arm, and the White Pass Railroad built in the days of the Klondike gold rush. Because the State Marine Ferry connects the Southeast to Bellingham (USA) and Prince Rupert (Canada), it is the cheapest and often the first area visited by travelers.

Southcentral

This region curves 650 miles from the Gulf of Alaska, past Prince William Sound to Kodiak Island. Like the Southeast, it is a mixture of rugged mountains, glaciers, steep fjords and virgin forests, and includes the Kenai Peninsula, a superb recreational area for backpacking, fishing and boating. To the south-west is Kodiak Island, home to much of Alaska's crab industry and the Kodiak bear, the largest species of brown bear in the state. To the east of the Kenai Peninsula is Prince William Sound, a bay that is famous for the Columbia Glacier and College Fjord and is still a mecca for kayakers and adventurers despite the Exxon oil spill.

The weather along the coastline can often be rainy and stormy but the summers are usually mild and have their share of sunshine. The peninsula is served by road from Anchorage and by the State Marine Ferry which crosses Prince William Sound and runs to Kodiak.

Highlights of the region are the historical and charming towns of Homer, Seward, Cordova and Hope, while backpackers will find many opportunities for outdoor adventure in the wilderness areas of the Chugach National Forest, Kenai National Wildlife Refuge and the outlying areas around Kodiak, Cordova and Valdez.

Anchorage
Because of the city's size and central location, Anchorage has to be viewed as a separate region: one that is passed through whether you want to deal with an urban area or not. At first glance, Anchorage appears to be like any other city – billboards, traffic jams, fast-food restaurants and what seems like hordes of people. Among this uncontrolled urban sprawl, however, is a city that in recent years has blossomed on the flow of oil money. While older cities in the Lower 48 often worry about decaying city centers, Anchorage has transformed its city center with such capital projects as a sports arena, performing-arts center and 122 miles of bike paths.

Anchorage also has a feature most other cities don't have – wilderness at its doorstep. The nearby Chugach State Park, Turnagain and Knik arms, and the Matanuska Valley (home of the softball-size radishes) make Anchorage an area worth spending a little time in, if for no other reason other than you'll have to arrive in, depart from or pass through it at some stage.

The Interior
This area includes three major roads – the George Parks, Glenn and Richardson highways – that cut across the center of the state and pass a number of forests, state parks and recreational areas, including Denali National Park & Preserve, Alaska's number one attraction. The heartland of Alaska offers warm temperatures in the summer and ample opportunities for outdoor activities in some of the state's most scenic and accessible areas. With the Alaska Range to the north, the Wrangell and Chugach mountains to the south and the Talkeetna Mountains cutting through the middle, the Interior has a rugged appearance matching that of either Southeast or Southcentral Alaska but without much of the rain and cloudy weather.

Fairbanks
The boom town of both the gold-rush days and later the construction of the pipeline to Prudhoe Bay has settled down a little, but it still retains much of its colorful and hardcore Alaskan character. A quick trip through Fairbanks is often a disappointment to most travelers, as Alaska's second largest city is very spread out. Located in the flat valley floor formed by the Tanana and Chena rivers, with the Alaska Range and Mt McKinley far off in the distance, Fairbanks lacks the dramatic setting many other areas offer. However, the true delights of this freewheeling frontier town are revealed if sufficient time is spent here. In the summer, Fairbanks can be an unusually warm place with temperatures often reaching from 80° to 90°F, and the midnight sun only setting for a few hours.

The surrounding area, especially the White Mountains, Circle, Eagle and the Dalton Hwy to Prudhoe Bay, has some of the most interesting backcountry areas accessible by road. Fairbanks is also the transport center for anybody wishing to venture north of the Arctic Circle or into the Brooks Range, site of many national parks and wildlife refuges.

The Bush
This region covers a vast area that includes the Brooks Range, Arctic Alaska, Western Alaska on the Bering Sea, and the Alaska Peninsula and Aleutian Islands which make up the out-reaching western arm of the state. The Bush is larger than the other five regions put together and is separated from them by great mountains and mighty rivers.

Occasionally, there are ways of beating the high cost of getting to the far reaches of the state, but for the most part traveling to the Bush involves small chartered aircraft, or 'bush planes'. These aeroplanes are a common method of travel through much of the state but, unfortunately, are prohibitively expensive for many budget travelers.

Except for the larger communities of Nome, Kotzebue and Barrow, independent travel in Bush villages is difficult unless you have a contact. If you have just stepped off a chartered aeroplane, the small and isolated villages may appear closed, unfriendly and have very limited facilities.

For those who do make an effort to leave the roads, Bush Alaska offers a lifestyle that is rare in other areas of the USA and, for the most part, is unaffected by the state's booming summer tourist industry. Climate in the summer can range from a chilly 40°F in the treeless and nightless Arctic tundra to the wet and fog of the Bering Sea coast, where the terrain is a flat land of lakes and slow-moving rivers.

CLIMATE & THE 24-HOUR DAY

It makes sense that a place as large and diverse as Alaska would have a climate to match. The effects of oceans surrounding 75% of the state, the mountainous terrain and the low angle of the sun give Alaska an extremely variable climate and daily weather that is famous for being unpredictable.

The Interior can top 90°F during the summer, yet six months later in the same region the temperature can drop to -60°F. Fort Yukon holds the state record for maximum temperature at 100°F in June 1915, yet it once recorded a temperature of -78°F.

For the most part, Southeast and Southcentral Alaska have high rainfall with temperatures that only vary 40°F during the year. Anchorage, shielded by the Kenai Mountains, has an annual rainfall of 15 inches and averages from 60° to 70°F from June to August. Juneau averages 57 inches of rain or snow annually, while Ketchikan gets 154 inches a year, most of which is rain, as the temperatures are extremely mild even in the winter.

Residents will tell you, however, that averages don't mean a thing. There have been summers when it has rained just about every day, and there have been Aprils when every day has been sunny and dry. A good week in Southcentral and Southeast Alaska during the summer will include three sunny days, two overcast ones and two when you will have to pull your rain gear out or duck for cover.

In the Interior and up around Fairbanks, precipitation is light but temperatures can fluctuate by more than 100°F during the year. In the summer, the average daytime temperature can range from 55° to 75°F with a brief period in late July to early August where it will top 80°F or even 90°F. At night, temperatures can drop sharply to 45°F or even lower, and freak snowfalls can occur in the

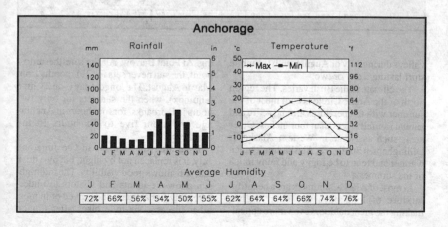

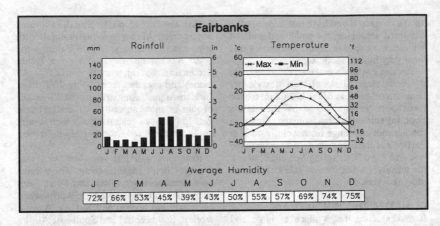

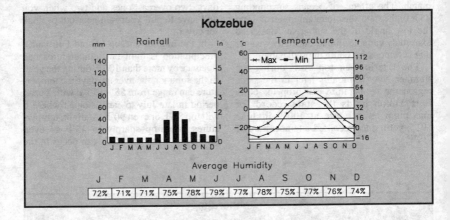

valleys during July or August, with the white stuff lasting a day or two.

The climate in the Bush varies. The region north of the Arctic Circle is cool most of the summer with temperatures around 45°F, and annual rainfall is less than four inches. Other areas such as Nome in Western Alaska or Dillingham in Southwest Alaska aren't much warmer and tend to be foggy and rainy much of the summer.

In most of Alaska, summers are a beautiful mixture of long days and short nights, making the great outdoors even more appeal-ing. At Point Barrow, Alaska's northernmost point, the sun never sets for 2½ months from May to August. The longest day is on 21 June (equinox), when the sun sets for only two hours in Fairbanks, for four hours in Anchorage and from five to six hours in the Southeast.

Even after the sun sets in late June and July, it is replaced not by night, but by a dusk that still allows good visibility. The midnight sun allows residents and visitors to undertake activities at hours undreamed of in most other places – six-mile hikes after dinner, bike rides at 10 pm or softball games at midnight. It also causes most people, even those with the best window shades, to wake up at 4 or 5 am.

No matter where you intend to travel or what you plan to do, bring protection against Alaska's climate. This should include warm clothing, rain gear and a covering if you are camping out. Alaska's weather is unpredictable and often changes when least expected – don't be left out in the cold.

FLORA & FAUNA

From the road, most visitors see more wildlife in Alaska than they do in a lifetime elsewhere. From the trail, such encounters are often the highlight of the entire trip; you can spot an animal, watch it quietly and marvel at the experience when the creature moves on leisurely.

Moose & Deer

Moose are a improbable-looking mammal; long-legged to the extreme, short-bodied, with a huge rack and a drooping nose. Standing there, they look uncoordinated until you watch them run, or better still, swim – then their speed and grace is astounding. They are the largest member of the deer family in the world and the Alaskan species is the largest of all moose. A newborn weighs in at 35 pounds and can grow to more than 300 pounds within five months. Cows range from 800 to 1200 pounds and bulls from 1000 to over 1500 pounds.

In the wild, moose may reach more than 20 years in age and often travel from 20 to 40 miles in their effort to find their main forage of birch, willow, alder and aspen saplings. In the spring and summer, you often encounter them feeding in lakes and ponds with that huge nose below the water as they grab for aquatic plants and weeds.

The population ranges from an estimated 120,000 to 160,000 animals and historically moose have always been the most important game animal in Alaska. Athabascan Indians survived by utilizing the moose as a source of food, clothing and implements while market hunting boomed in the 19th century,

with professional hunters supplying moose meat to mining camps. Today some 35,000 Alaskans and nonresidents annually harvest 9000 moose or a total of five million pounds of meat during the hunting season.

Moose are widespread throughout the state and range from the Stikine River in Southeast to the Corville River on the Arctic slope. They're most abundant in the second-growth birch forests, timberline plateaus and along major rivers of Southcentral and the Interior. Moose are frequently sighted along the Alcan, and Denali National Park is an excellent place to watch them. But the best place to see the biggest moose is the Kenai Peninsula, especially if you take time to paddle the Swanson River or Swan Lake canoe routes in Kenai National Wildlife Refuge. The refuge even maintains a Moose Research Center 50 miles from Soldotna where visitors can often see the animal.

The Sitka black-tailed deer is a native to the coastal rainforests of Southeast Alaska but its original range has since been expanded to the Prince William Sound and Kodiak Island. The deer is a favorite target of hunters but is not the source of meat that the moose is. The largest dressed, the black-tailed weighs 212 pounds but most does weigh an average of 100 pounds and bucks, 150 pounds.

The summer coat is reddish-brown and replaced by gray in the winter. The antlers are small, normal development is three points on each side, and its tail is indeed black. Sitka black-tailed deer respond readily to calls. Most 'calls' are a thin strip of rubber or plastic between two pieces of wood held between the teeth and blown on. It produces a high-pitched note simulating a fawn's cry and can stop a deer in its tracks and turn it around. Some old time hunters can make the call by simply blowing on a leaf.

Caribou

Caribou, of which there are an estimated 600,000 living in Alaska's 13 herds, are more difficult to view as they travel from the Interior north to the Arctic Sea. Often called the 'nomads of the north', caribou range in

Bull Caribou

weight from 150 pounds to more than 400 pounds for a large bull. They migrate hundreds of miles annually between their calving grounds, rutting areas and winter area. In the summer, they feed on grasses, grass-like sedges, berries and small shrubs of the tundra. In the winter, they eat a significant amount of lichen called 'reindeer moss'.

The principal predators of caribou are wolves and some packs on the North Slope have been known to follow caribou herds over the years, picking off the young, old and victims of disabling falls caused by running in tightly massed herds. Bears, wolverines, foxes and eagles will also prey on calves while every year several thousand nonresident hunters come to Alaska in search of a bull. The caribou, however, are most important to the Inuit and other Native Alaskans who hunt more than 30,000 a year in their subsistent lifestyle.

The best place for the average visitor to see caribou is Denali National Park, where they are occasionally seen from the park road. But perhaps one of the greatest wildlife encounters left in the world today is the migration of the Western Arctic herd of barren ground caribou, North America's largest at 300,000 animals. The calving area of the herd is along the North Slope and in late August many of the animals begin to cross the Noatak River on their journey southward. During that time the few visitors lucky enough to be on the river are often rewarded with an awesome experience of watching 20,000 or more caribou crossing the tundra towards the Brooks Range.

Mountain Goats & Dall Sheep

The mountain goat is the single North American species of the widespread group of goat-antelopes. All are characterized by short horns and a fondness for the most rugged alpine terrain. Although Captain Cook obtained goat hides in the 1700s, very little was known about the animal due to its remote habitat.

Although goats are often confused with dall sheep, they are easily identified by their longer hair, black horns and deep chest. They are quite docile, making them easy to watch in the wild, and their gait, even when they're approached too closely, is a deliberate pace. In the summer, they are normally found in high alpine meadows, grazing on grasses and herbs, and in the winter they often drop down to the tree line. In Alaska, they range throughout most of the Southeast, north and west into the coastal mountains of Cook Inlet as well as the Chugach and Wrangell moun-

Dall Sheep

tains. Good places to spot them include Glacier Bay National Park, Wrangell-St Elias National Park and from many of the alpine trails in Juneau. But you have to climb to spot them.

Dall sheep are more numerous and widespread than mountain goats. They number close to 80,000 in Alaska and are found principally in Alaska, Wrangell, Chugach and the Kenai mountain ranges. Often sheep are spotted in Denali National Park when the bus crosses Polychrome Pass on its way to Wonder Lake.

Rams are easy to spot by their massive curling horns which grow throughout the life of the sheep, unlike deer antlers which are shed and regrown annually. The horns, like claws, hooves and your fingernails, grow from the skin and as rams mature the horns continue their ever-increasing curl, reaching a three-quarters curl in four to five years and a full curl in seven years.

It's spectacular to watch two rams in a horn-clashing battle but, contrary to popular belief, they are not fighting over a female, just for social dominance. Dall sheep do not clash as much as their big-horn cousins to the south but you can spot the activity throughout the summer and into fall. The best time to spot rams and see them clash is right before the rut, which begins in November. At that time they are moving among bands of ewes and often encountering other unfamiliar rams.

Bears
Bears and visitors to Alaska have this love-hate relationship. Nothing makes you more afraid in the backcountry than the thought of encountering a bear, but you would hate leaving the state without see a bear in the wild. After a handful of bear encounters, most people leave with a healthy respect replacing that frightening fear of these magnificent animals. There are three species of bear in Alaska – brown, black and polar bears – with brown bears having the greatest range.

At one time brown and grizzly bears were listed as separate species but now both are classified as *Ursus arctos*. The difference isn't so much genetics but size. Browns live along the coast where abundant salmon runs help them reach a large size (often exceeding 800 pounds) while the famed Kodiak brown bear has been known to stand 10 feet tall and tip the scales at 1500 pounds. Grizzlies are browns found inland, away from the rich salmon runs, and normally a male ranges in weight from 500 to 700 pounds. Females weigh half to three-quarters as much.

The color of a brown bear could be anything from an almost black through to blond and resemble a black bear in appearance. One way biologists tell them apart is to measure the upper rear molar – seriously. The length of the crown of this tooth in a brown is always more than an inch and a quarter. Perhaps a better way is to look for the prominent shoulder hump, easily seen behind the neck when a brown bear is on all fours.

Brown bears occur throughout Alaska except for some islands in the Frederick Sound in the Southeast, the islands west of Unimak in the Aleutian chain and some Bering Sea islands. There are more than 40,000 brown bears in Alaska and the most noted place to watch them is McNeil River, where a permit is needed in advance. Brown bears are also commonly seen in Denali National Park, on Admiralty Island in the Southeast and in Wrangell-St Elias National Park.

Though black bears are the most widely distributed of the three bear species in America, their range is more limited in Alaska than that of their brown cousin. They usually are found in most forested areas of the state but not on the Seward Peninsula, or north of the Brooks Range or on many large islands, most notably Kodiak and Admiralty.

The average male weighs from 180 to 250 pounds and can range in color from black to a rare creamy white color. A brown or cinnamon black bear is often seen in Southcentral Alaska, leaving many backpackers confused about what the species is. Beyond measuring that upper rear molar, look for the straight facial profile to confirm it's a black bear.

Both species are creatures of opportunity

when it comes to eating. Bears are omnivorous and common foods include berries, grass, sedge, salmon runs and any carrion they happen to find in their travels. Browns occasional fill the role of predator but only in the spring when the young are most vulnerable.

Bears don't hibernate, rather they enter a stage of 'dormancy', basically a deep sleep while denning up during the winter. Browns and black bears enter their dens usually in November or December and re-emerge in April or May. In the more northern areas of the state, some bears may be dormant for as long as seven or eight months a year.

Polar bears have always captured our interest because of their large size and white color but plan on stopping at the zoo in Anchorage if you want to see one in Alaska. (Polar bears occur only in the Northern Hemisphere and almost always in association with Arctic sea ice. They fall under the jurisdiction of only five nations: Russia, Norway, Denmark (Greenland), Canada and the USA, and past studies have shown there is only limited denning of polar bears along the north Alaska Coast.)

A male usually averages between 600 and 1,200 pounds but occasional tops 1,400 pounds. Adaptations to a life on the sea ice by polar bears include a white coat with water-repellent guard hairs and dense under fur, specialized teeth for its carnivorous diet primarily of seals, and hair almost completely covering the bottom of its feet.

Wolves

While the wolf is struggling in numbers throughout most of the USA, its natural distribution and numbers still seem to be unaffected by human undertakings in Alaska. In fact, expanding wolf packs caused the Alaska Board of Game to schedule an aerial kill of 700 wolves in a 43,000-acre region between Anchorage and Fairbanks in 1993 because 'some hunters feel they are being shortchanged'. The hunter-verus-wolf controversy is hardly a new one but this time environmental groups moved it into the international spotlight with a boycott that

Wolf

threatens the state's tourism industry. Governor Wally Hickel changed his position and cancelled the airborne hunt.

Throughout history no animal has been more misunderstood than the wolf. Alaska has roughly 8000 wolves scattered in packs throughout the state except for some islands in Southeast, Prince William Sound and the Aleutian chain. Unlike the hunters, who seek out the outstanding physical specimens, wolves can usually only catch and kill the weak, injured or young thus strengthening the herd they are stalking. A pack of wolves is no match for a healthy 1,200-pound moose.

Most adult males average from 85 to 115 pounds in weight and could have a pelt that ranges from gray, black, off-white, brown, yellow or even have tinges approaching red. Wolves travel, hunt, feed and operate in the social unit of a pack and are very much carnivores. In the Southeast their principal food is deer, in the Interior it's moose and in Arctic Alaska it's caribou.

Even if you're planning to spend a great deal of time away from the road wandering in the wilderness, your chances of seeing wolves are rare. You might, however, find evidence of them either in their dog-like tracks, their howls at night or the remains of a wild kill.

Other Mammals

In the lowlands, hikers have a chance to view red fox, beaver, pine marten, snowshoe hare, pounds – 100-pound beavers have been recorded in Alaska.

Marine Mammals

The most commonly spotted marine mammals are seals, often seen basking in the sun on an ice floe. There are three species of seal in Alaska but most visitors will encounter only harbor seals, the only seal whose range includes the Southeast, Prince William Sound and the rest of the Gulf of Alaska. The average weight of a male is 200 pounds – reached on a diet of herring, flounder, salmon, squid and small crabs.

The other two species, ringed and bearded seals, occur for the most part in the northern Bering, Chukchi and Beaufort seas where sea ice forms during the winter. Although travel on land or ice is laborious and slow, seals are renowned divers. During a dive their heartbeat may slow from a normal 55 to 120 beats per minute to 15. This allows them to stay under water for more than five minutes, often reaching depths of 300 feet or more. Harbor seal dives of 20 minutes or longer have been recorded by biologists.

Porpoises and dolphins are also commonly seen, even from the deck of the State Marine ferry. Harbor porpoises are often sighted but occasionally ferry travelers are treated to a pod of killer whales, or Orcas, whose high black and white dorsal fin makes them easy to identify from a distance. Orcas, which can exceed 20 feet in length, are actually the largest member of the dolphin family, which also includes the beluga or white whale. Belugas range in length from 11 to 16 feet and often weigh more than 3000 pounds, traveling in herds of more than 100. Their range includes the Arctic waters north of Bristol Bay but also Cook Inlet, where most visitors will spot them, especially in Kenai, where there is a beluga observation area.

The two most common whales seen in coastal waters are the 50-foot long humpback, with its hump-like dorsal fin and long flippers, and the smaller minke whale. Other marine mammals include sea lions, sea otters and walruses.

Red Squirrel

red squirrel, and on very rare occasions wolverines. Around lakes and rivers you have a good chance of spotting land otters and beavers. Both are found throughout the state with the exception of the North Slope, and are large animals. Otters range from 15 to 35 pounds; beavers weigh between 40 and 70

Beaver

The best known destination for witnessing marine mammals, particularly whales, is Glacier Bay National Park in the Southeast. If you can spare a few days to kayak the glaciated sections of the bay, your chances of seeing a whale will be increased greatly. Kayak and boat tours in Prince William Sound, particularly around Kenai Fjords National Park out of Seward, should result in encounters with marine mammals. Just a trip on the state ferry from Seward to Kodiak will provide an opportunity to see a colony of sea lions.

Salmon

The salmon runs (when thousands of fish swim upstream to spawn) are another of Alaska's most amazing sights and are common throughout much of the state. From late July to mid-September, many coastal streams are choked with salmon. You won't see just one here and there, but thousands – so many that they have to wait their turn to swim through narrow gaps of shallow water. The salmon are famous for their struggle against the current, their magnificent leaps over waterfalls, and for covering stream banks with carcasses afterwards. There are five kinds of salmon in Alaska: sockeye (also referred to as red salmon), king (chinook), pink (humpie), coho (silver) and chum.

Birds

More than anything, Alaska is a haven for winged wildlife. Biologists have identified 437 species of bird in the state and only 65 of them are accidental visitors. The Pribilof Islands in the Bering Sea attract birders (they no longer call themselves bird-watchers) from around the world. If you can't afford that, just visit Potter Marsh south of Anchorage, a sanctuary that attracts more than 100 species annually.

The most impressive bird in Alaska's wilderness is the bald eagle, whose white tail and head and a wingspan that often reaches eight feet has become the symbol of a nation. While elsewhere the bird is on the endangered list, in Alaska it thrives in strong numbers. The eagle can be sighted almost

Bald eagle

daily in most of the Southeast and is common in Prince William Sound. It also migrates once a year in a spectacle that exceeds even the salmon runs. As many as 1500 bald eagles gather along the Chilkat River north of Haines from late October to December. They come to feed on the late chum-salmon run and create an amazing scene during the bleakness of early winter. Bare trees, without a leaf remaining, support 80 or more white-headed eagles, four or five to a branch.

The state bird of Alaska, however, is the ptarmigan, a cousin of the prairie grouse. The species is found throughout the state in high treeless country and birds are easy to spot during the summer as their wings remain white while their head and chest turn brown. In the winter they have pure white plummage.

If you're serious about birding while traveling the state, the best bird book to pick up is *Guide to the Birds of Alaska* by Robert H Armstrong (Alaska Northwest Books, 22026 20th Ave SE, Bothell, WA 98021; 344 pages, $19.95). The guide indexes 372 species and includes color photos and field identification marks.

Flora

The flora of Alaska, like everything in the state, is diverse, changing dramatically from one region to the next. There are 33 native species of trees, the fewest of any state in the USA, and only 12 of these are classified as large trees (more than 70 feet in height). Not surprisingly, nine of these species are found in the coastal regions of Southeast and Southcentral Alaska.

In these areas, mild temperatures in winter and summer and frequent rains produce lush coniferous forests of Sitka spruce (the state tree) and western hemlock. Any opening in the forest is often a bog or filled with alder or spiny devil's club, a mildly poisonous plant that often results in a rash on contact. The tree line is often at an altitude between 2000 and 3000 feet where thick alder takes over until finally giving way to alpine meadows.

In the Interior, the large area of plains and hills between the Alaska Range and the Brooks Range is dominated by boreal forest of white spruce, cottonwood and paper birch, while on north-facing slopes and in moist lowlands you'll find a stunted forest of scrawny black spruce. Continue traveling north and you'll enter a zone known as taiga, characterized by muskeg, willow thickets and more stunted spruce, before entering the tundra of the Arctic coastal region.

The Arctic tundra is a bizarre world, a treeless area except for a few small stands on gravel flood plains of rivers. Plant life hugs the ground – even willow trees that only grow six inches in height still produce pussy willows. Other plants, including grasses, mosses and a variety of tiny flowers, provide a carpet of life for a short period in July and August despite little precipitation and a harsh climate.

Tundra can make for tough hiking for those who travel this far north in Alaska. Wet and moist tundra is underlain by permanently frozen ground known as permafrost. The tundra thaws in the summer but remains waterlogged because the permafrost prevents drainage. The caribou get around these soggy conditions because their dew claws and spreading cleft hooves help support their weight on the soft ground. Hikers are not so lucky.

Wild Berries Perhaps the flora that interests hikers and visitors most are Alaska's wild berries. Blueberries are found throughout much of the state while in the Southeast you'll encounter huge patches of huckleberries and salmonberries. Other species include blackberries, raspberries, highbush cranberries and strawberries. If you plan to feast on berries, take time to learn which ones are inedible. The most common poisonous one is the baneberry, found in the Southeast and the Interior, which often appears as a white berry.

GOVERNMENT

The government sector in Alaska is very strong, especially in Juneau, the capital city. Statewide, one in every three people is paid for government work, while in Juneau it's estimated that two-thirds of the residents work for either the federal, state or city government. The result is a lopsided pay scale with workers in the private sector rarely having a salary comparable with government workers.

All this government is most obvious when the state legislature and its army of aides and advisors convene in Juneau for the annual session. From across Alaska, 40 state representatives and 20 state senators arrive and take up temporary residence in the city until April to draw up a budget, spend the oil money and pass bills. Potential legislation is then passed onto the governor, who either signs it into law or vetoes the measures. The best way to understand Alaska's state politics and its colorful history is to join one of the free tours offered at the Alaska State Capitol in Juneau.

Alaska, like three other states in the USA, has only one US state representative and two US senators because of its small population. Local government consists of 1st, 2nd and 3rd-class boroughs and cities along with hundreds of unincorporated villages, the category that most Bush communities fall into. Although the populations may be small, many cities and boroughs can be quite large in area. Juneau, with more than 3000 sq miles within its jurisdiction, is the largest city in the country land-wise.

ECONOMY

Alaska's economy is fuelled by oil, not by the television show *Northern Exposure* as some tourists may think. Oil and gas revenues annually account for almost 90% of the gross state product. Because of Prudhoe Bay, the largest oil field in North America, Alaska is behind only Texas as the country's top oil producer, accounting for more than 20% of US production. Although the oil industry accounts for only a fraction (less than 10%) of the state's workforce, it's made Alaska the richest state in the country. The average annual income of an Alaskan exceeds $21,000 compared with less than $12,000 nationally. Nor do Alaskans pay many taxes. Thanks to North Slope crude, there are no state taxes on income, sales or inheritance. Overall, Alaskans pay the lowest taxes in the USA. *Money Magazine* said that in 1992 the average two-income family paid more than $10,000 in state taxes in New York, but only $1,632 in Alaska.

Alaskans even get a dividend back from the state based on the earning of the Permanent Fund. Set up in 1976 when Prudoe Bay oil began to flow, the money in this account is a percentage of mineral (but mainly oil) revenues, and can only be used for investment, not to operate the state government. That prevents state legislators from squandering it every session on pork-barrel projects in their home district. The fund amounts to billions and the interest it earns is returned to residents annually as a dividend that has exceeded $1,000 in some years. With Prudhoe Bay oil almost 75% recovered, you can understand the concern many Alaskans have about their economy in the future. Not only the petroleum industry, but many residents themselves, are pushing for oil exploration and drilling in the Arctic National Wildlife Refuge.

Commercial fishing is the second largest industry in the state as the Alaskan fleet contributes almost 25% of the country's annual catch, including nearly all canned salmon produced in the USA. The more than 200 million pounds of salmon represents a third of the Alaskan catch while shellfish make up another 20%. In recent years, however, many of the fisheries have been teetering on collapse. The summer of 1993 was an especially bad season with fishermen blamingthe Exxon oil spill for weak runs. In the Yukon River, the chum salmon run was so weak, the state cancelled all seasons including those for Native Alaskans with subsistence rights to the fish.

Tourism is the state's third largest industry and it's growing steadily. Although the Exxon oil spill took a $20-million bite out of what the visitor to Alaska spent in 1989, the industry has since fully rebounded from the mishap, thanks in part to the popularity of *Northern Exposure*, the TV series based on fictional Cicely (actually filmed in the state of Washington). In 1991, around 556,000

Alaska's Permanent Fund

Nothing amazes visitors to Alaska more than a resident telling them that the state *actually gives them money* every year just for living there. The annual checks date back to 1976 when residents approved a constitutional amendment for an Alaska Permanent Fund, money set aside from a percentage of all mineral lease royalties. Prudhoe Bay oil made this fund so lopsided that in 1980 the state legislature created a Permanent Fund dividend payment program, handing out the interest the fund earned based on years of residency.

But that year the US Supreme Court threw out program, claiming it discriminated against short-term residents. In 1982, a new program was passed in which the fund's earning are divided equally among residents who have lived in Alaska six months before applying for the benefit. There's a complicated formula to figuring out the payment but usually it ranges between $800 and $1000 a year.

In 1991 the Permanent Fund was at $11.6 million and if it was a Fortune 500 company, it would be in the top five percent for income earned. It's estimated by the year 2000 the fund will be earning more revenue for the state than Prudhoe Bay and it is already the largest pool of money in the USA. ■

visitors came to Alaska and spent more than $300 million.

Mining continues its long history in the state as there are almost 30,000 active federal mining claims, the vast majority of them lode and placer claims. Although gold holds the lure of riches, zinc is actually the state's most valuable non-fuel mineral. Alaska is the top zinc producing state in the country with the newly developed Red Dog Mine, 90 miles north of Kotzebue, the largest such operation in the world. Alaska is the only state that produces platinum and it ranks second in USA for gold production and third for silver.

Other industries that contribute to the economy include logging and, to a very small degree, commercial farming which takes place almost exclusively in the Matanuska Valley around Palmer and the Tanana Valley between Fairbanks and Delta. These areas are home of the 70-pound cabbages and softball-size radishes but the top agricultural product for Alaskan farmers is milk.

POPULATION

Alaska, the largest state in the USA, has the second smallest population (after only Wyoming) but it is the most sparsely populated. Permanent residents, not including the large influx of seasonal workers in the fishing and tourist industries, number 550,000 in a state of 591,004 sq miles. There is more than a sq mile for every resident but Alaska is even less sparse when you consider that more than half of its population lives in the Anchorage Bowl area.

It is estimated that only 30% of the state's population were born in Alaska while 25% have moved there in the last five years. This means that the average resident is young (aged between 26 and 28 years), mobile and mostly from the US west coast. Inuit and other indigenous groups make up only 15% of the total population while ethnic groups of Japanese, Filipinos and Blacks represent less than 5%.

The five largest cities in Alaska are Anchorage (population 237,907), Fairbanks (population 77,720), Juneau (population 30,000), Kodiak (population 15,575) and Ketchikan (population 13,828).

PEOPLE & CULTURE

Long before Bering's journeys to Alaska, other groups of people had made their way there and established a culture and lifestyle in one of the world's harshest environments. The first major invasion, which came across the land bridge from Asia, was by the Tlingits and the Haidas (who settled throughout the Southeast and British Columbia), and the Athabascans (a nomadic tribe which lived in the Interior). The other two major groups were the Aleuts of the Aleutian Islands and the Inuit (Eskimos) who settled on the coast of the Bering Sea and the Arctic Ocean; both groups are believed to have migrated only 3000 years ago but were well established by the time the Europeans arrived.

The Tlingit and Haida cultures were advanced, as the tribes had permanent settle-

Tlingit Man

ments including large clan houses. They were noted for their excellent woodcarving, most notably poles, called *totems*, that can still be seen today in most Southeast communities. The Tlingits were spread throughout the Southeast in large numbers and occasionally went as far south as Seattle in their large dugout canoes. Both groups had few problems gathering food, as fish and game were plentiful in the Southeast.

Not so for the Aleuts and the Inuit. With much colder winters and cooler summers, both groups had to develop a highly effective sea-hunting culture to sustain life in the harsh regions of Alaska. This was especially true for the Inuit, who could not have survived the winters without their skilled ice-hunting techniques. In the spring, armed with only jade-tipped harpoons, the Inuit stalked and killed 60-ton bowhead whales in skin-covered kayaks called *bidarkas* and *umikaks*.

The Aleuts were known for some of the finest basket weaving in North America, using the highly prized Attu grass of the Aleutian Islands. The Inuit were unsurpassed carvers of ivory, jade and soapstone; many support themselves today by continuing the art.

The indigenous people, despite their harsh environment, were numerous until the White people brought guns, alcohol and disease that destroyed the Native Alaskans' delicate relationship with nature and wiped out entire villages. At one time, there were an estimated 20,000 Aleuts living on almost every island of the Aleutian chain. It took the Russians only 50 years to reduce the population (mainly through forced labour) to less than 2000. The whalers who arrived at Inuit villages in the mid-1800s were similarly destructive, introducing alcohol that devastated the lifestyles of entire villages. Even when the 50th anniversary of the Alcan was celebrated in October 1992, many Native Alaskans and Canadians called the event a 'commemoration' and not a 'celebration' due to the things that the highway brought (disease, alcohol and a cash economy) that further changed a nomadic lifestyle.

Today, there are more than 85,000 indigenous people (half of which are Inuit) living in Alaska. They are no longer tribal nomads but live in permanent villages ranging in size from less than 30 people to 3200 in Barrow, the largest center of indigenous people in Alaska.

Most indigenous people in the Bush still depend on some level of subsistence, but today their houses are constructed of modern materials and often heated by electricity or oil. Visitors are occasionally shocked when they fly hundreds of miles into a remote area only to see TV antennas sticking out of cabins, community satellite dishes, people drinking Coca-Cola or children listening to the latest songs on their boom box.

All indigenous people received a boost in 1971 when Congress passed the Alaska Native Claims Settlement Act in an effort to allow oil companies to build a pipeline across their traditional lands. The act created the Alaska Native Fund and formed 12 regional corporations, controlled and administered by the local tribes, that invested and developed the $900 million and 44 million acres received for their historical lands.

Today, all indigenous people hold stock in their village corporations and receive dividends when there's a profit. Although a few have floundered and lost money, one of them, Sealaska of Juneau, has done so well managing its lands and investing its funds that the corporation has been ranked among the 500 largest companies in the USA in terms of assets.

To give Native Alaskans time to understand capitalism and private ownership, a concept that was completely foreign to their ancestors, the Settlement Act stated that stock couldn't be sold until 1991. In that year, after two decades of waiting, the indigenous population could do what they wanted with their corporation's stock. (These corporations still control millions of acres in Alaska, including mineral rights and timber.) Many indigenous Alaskans fear that their culture will die at the hands of monetary greed. 'Young people look at land in the White sense, as real estate', said one Native

Top: Arctic poppies, Chugiak (DS)
Left: Fall birch colours, Nancy Lake, Susitna Valley (DS)
Right: Fall foliage, Smith Lake, Susitna Valley (DS)

Top: Dungeness crab (CP)
Left: Husky (RS)
Right: Bald eagle fishing in the Deshka River, Susitna Valley (DS)

Alaskan leader, 'they will be offered a good price, they'll sell it and then the land will be gone'.

In a campaign against stock sales, some corporations are promoting 'spirit movements', a return to traditional values and heritage. Smaller villages isolated in the Bush have even gone a step further by demanding 'tribal sovereignty': the right to bypass state and federal laws to control their taxation, education, fish and game regulations, law enforcement and other traditional government functions. In recent years, state attorneys have been in court contesting half a dozen cases involving tribal sovereignty and more are expected as the issue of poaching versus subsistence heats up.

Although the lifestyle of indigenous people has changed drastically, economic opportunities remain as limited as ever in the remote areas. In the north-west region of the state, poverty has lead many Inuit hunters to poach walruses for their valuable ivory. Modern hunting tools make this easy: dogsleds, paddles and harpoons have long since given way to snowmobiles, outboard motors and assault rifles.

The Marine Mammal Protection Act prohibits most walrus hunting except for subsistent hunters who kill for their own

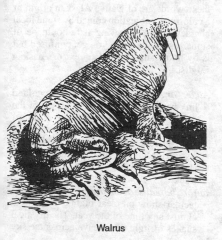

Walrus

food and ivory. But in recent years agents of the US Fish & Wildlife Service have cracked down with investigations that have turned up drugs-for-ivory operations and wanton waste with hunters slaughtering walruses and dumping headless carcasses into the Bering Sea.

Native leaders counter that this represents a small percentage of their people and that it is the tourist dollar, in the form of big game hunting guides and wilderness fishing camps, which is pushing for an end to subsistence as a way of life.

ARTS

Alaska's indigenous people are renowned for their traditional arts and crafts primarily because of their ingenious use of the natural materials around them which in the case of many groups, like the Inuit, was often limited. Roots, ivory tusks, birch bark, grasses and soapstone were used creatively to produce ceremonial regalia and other art work.

Thanks to a flourishing arts market, prompted by the increased tourism to the state, Native Alaskan arts have become an important slice of the economy in many Bush communities. The Inupiat and Yup'ik Inuit, with the fewest resources to work with, made their objects out of sea-mammal parts; and their ivory carving and scrimshaw work is world renowned. The Aleuts of the Aleutian Islands are known for their bentwood hats and visors; the Athabascan Indians make decorative clothing with elaborate beadwork; and the Tlingit, Haida and Tsimshian of Southeast Alaska are among the carvers who ranged south into British Columbia and Washington and were responsible for the great totems and clan houses.

But perhaps no single item represents indigenous art better than Alaskan basketry. Each group produces stunning baskets in distinctive styles based solely on the materials at hand. Athabascans of the Interior weave baskets from willow roots or produce them from birch bark. The Tlingits use cedar bark; the Inuit use grasses and baleen, a glossy hard material that hangs in slats from the jaw of certain species of whales.

The Aleuts are perhaps the most renowned basket weavers. Using rye grass, which grows abundantly in the Aleutian Islands, the Aleuts are able to work the pliable and very tough material into tiny, intricately woven baskets. The three styles of Aleut baskets (Attu, Atka and Unalaska) are named after the islands on which they originated. These baskets carry a steep price whenever they are sold on the open market.

The best known examples of the Native Alaskan craft skills are the totems of Southeast Alaska. Although most tourists envision totems as freestanding poles, totemic art is also used on houses and other clan structures. Totem poles are carved from huge cedar trees and are used to preserve family history or make a statement about a clan. Often they were raised during a 'potlatch', a ceremony in which a major event was held drawing clans from throughout the region. The totem was erected to commemorate the event.

Totems

There probably isn't a community in Southeast Alaska without a totem or two. But Ketchikan has the most impressive collections of them at both Totem Heritage Center in town and Saxman Totem Park and Totem Bight State Park out of town.

RELIGION

For the most part every religion that mainstream America practices in the Lower 48 can be found in Alaska. One of the most interesting, however, is represented by the Russian Orthodox Church, the most enduring aspect of a unique period in Alaska's history. After Russian merchants and traders had decimated indigenous populations in the mid to late 18th century, missionaries arrived as Russia's answer to the brutal subjugation.

They managed to convert the indigenous people of Southwest, Southcentral and Southeast Alaska to a new religious beliefs that are as strong today as they ever were. One only has to look at the familiar onion domes of the Russian Orthodox churches in communities such as Juneau, Sitka, Kodiak or Unalaska to realize this.

ALASKAN ENGLISH

English is spoken all across Alaska but it is tinted with Alaskan words and phrases that make it almost a tongue of its own. Most of these words are of Native Alaskan origin or a colorful combination coined by some local character. The following list should be of some assistance when you get confused but is by no means a complete text of Alaskan English.

Alcan (or Alaska Hwy) – The only overland link between the state and the rest of the country. Although the highway is almost completely paved now, completing a journey across this legendary road is still a special accomplishment that earns you a slash mark on the side of your pick-up truck.

aurora borealis (or northern lights) – A spectacular show on clear nights, possible at almost any time of the year. The mystical snakes of light that weave across the sky from the northern horizon are the result of gas particles colliding with solar electrons. The northern lights are best viewed from the Interior, away from city lights, between late summer and winter.

bidarka – a skin-covered sea kayak used by the Aleuts

blanket toss – an activity originating with the Inuit in which a hunter was tossed into the air with a skin to search for whales offshore

blue cloud – what Southeasterners call a break in the clouds

break-up – A phrase applied to rivers when the ice suddenly begins to disintegrate and flows downstream. Many residents also use it to describe spring in Alaska when the rains come, the snows melt and everything turns to mud and slush.

bunny boots – large, oversized and usually white plastic boots used extensively in subzero weather to prevent the feet from freezing

The Bush – Any area in the state either not connected by road to Anchorage or which does not have a State Marine Ferry dock in town

cabin fever – A winter condition in which cross-eyed Alaskans go stir-crazy in their one-room cabins because of too little sunlight and too much time spent indoors

cache – A small hut or storage room built high off the ground to keep supplies and spare food away from roaming bears and wolves. The term, however, has found its way onto the neon signs of everything from liquor stores to pizza parlours in the cities.

capital move – The political issue that raged in the early 1980s which concerned moving the state capital from Juneau closer to Anchorage. The issue was buried somewhat in a 1982 state election when residents rejected the funding for the move north.

cheechako – Tenderfoot, greenhorn or somebody trying to survive their first year in Alaska.

chum – Not your mate or good buddy but a nickname for the dog salmon

clearcut – A hated sight for environmentalists, this is an area where loggers have cut every tree, large and small, leaving nothing standing. A traveler's first view of one, often from a state ferry, is a shocking sight.

d-2 – A phrase that covers the lands issue of the late 1970s, pitting environmentalists against developers over the federal government's preservation of 100 million acres of Alaskan wilderness as wildlife reserves, forests and national parks.

developers – Those residents of Alaska who favor development of the state's natural resources and land through such endeavors as logging and mining, as opposed to preserving it in national parks.

Eskimo ice cream – A traditional food made of whipped berries, seal oil and snow

fish wheel – A wooden trap that scoops salmon or other large fish out of a river into a holding tank by utilizing the current as power

freeze-up – That point in November or December when most rivers and lakes ice over, signaling to Alaskans that their long winter is here in earnest

glacier fishing – Picking up flopping salmon along the Copper River in Cordova after a large calving from the Child's Glacier strands the fish during the August spawning run. Practised by both bears and people and neither one needs a state fishing license to do so.

greenies – A nickname for environmentalists and others who celebrated the passage of the Alaska Lands Bill

humpie – A nickname for the humpback, or pink salmon, the mainstay of the fishing industry in the Southeast

ice worm – A small, thin black worm that

thrives in glacial ice; made famous by a Robert Service poem

Iditarod – The 1000-mile sled-dog race held every March from Anchorage to Nome. The winner completes the course in under 14 days and takes home $50,000.

Lower 48 – the way Alaskans describe continental USA

moose nuggets – hard, smooth little objects dropped by moose after a good meal. Some enterprising resident in Homer has capitalized on them by baking, varnishing and trimming them with evergreen leaves to sell during Christmas as Moostletoe.

mukluks – lightweight boots of seal skin trimmed with fur, made by the Inuit

muskeg – the bogs in Alaska where layers of matted plant life float on top of stagnant water – a bad place to hike or pitch a tent

no-see-um – nickname for the tiny gnats found throughout much of the Alaska wilderness, especially in the Interior and parts of the Brooks Range

outside – to residents, any place that isn't Alaska

permafrost – permanently frozen subsoil that covers two-thirds of the state

petroglyphs – ancient rock carvings

potlatch – a traditional gathering of indigenous people held to commemorate any memorable occasion

qiviut – the wool of the musk ox that is often woven into garments

scat – any animal droppings but usually used to describe that of a bear. If it is dark brown or bluish and somewhat square in shape, a bear has passed by. If it is steaming, the bear's eating blueberries around the next bend.

solstice – the first day of summer on 21 June and winter on 21 December. In Alaska, however, solstice is synonymous with the longest day of the year, a celebration in most towns.

sourdough – any old timer in the state, who some say is 'sour on the country but without enough dough to get out'. More recently arrived residents believe anybody who has survived an Alaskan winter qualifies as a sourdough. The term also applies to a 'yeasty' mixture used to make bread or pancakes rise.

stinkhead – an Inuit 'treat' made by burying a salmon head in the sand. Leave the head to ferment for up to 10 days, then dig it up, wash off the sand and enjoy!

Southeast sneakers – also known as Ketchikan tennis shoes, Sitka slippers, Petersburg pumps and a variety of other names. These are the tall, reddish-brown rubber boots that Southeast residents wear when it rains and often when it doesn't.

taku wind – Juneau's sudden gusts of wind that may exceed 100 mph in the spring and fall. Often the winds cause another strange phenomenon – horizontal rain which, as the name indicates, comes straight at you instead of falling down on you. In Anchorage and throughout the Interior, these sudden rushes of air over or through mountain gaps are called 'williwaws'.

tundra – often used to refer to the vast, treeless Arctic plains

ulu – a fan-shaped knife that indigenous people use to chop and scrape meat, now the gift shops use them to lure tourists

Facts for the Visitor

VISAS & EMBASSIES

If you are traveling to Alaska from overseas there are one or two things you need depending on your nationality: a passport (except for US and Canadian citizens who only need a driver's license or voter registration card) and at least one visa, possibly two. Obviously a US visa is needed, but if you're taking either the Alcan (also called the Alaska Hwy) or the State Marine Ferry from Prince Rupert in British Columbia then you will also need a Canadian visa. The Alcan begins in Canada, requiring travelers to pass from the USA into Canada and back into the USA again.

Travelers from western Europe and most Commonwealth nations do not need a Canadian visa and can get a six-month travel visa to the USA without too much paperwork or waiting. Visitors from the UK, Australia and New Zealand don't even need a visa to enter the USA if they plan to stay less than 90 days, have a return ticket and complete a visa wavier form and an arrival/departure card. All visitors must have an onward or return ticket to enter the USA and sufficient funds to pass into Canada. Those arriving at the Canadian border with less than $250 will most likely be turned back.

A word of warning: overseas travelers should be aware of the procedures to re-enter the USA. Occasionally visitors get stuck in Canada without the necessary papers to enter Alaska after passing through the Lower 48. Canadian immigration officers often caution people who they feel might have difficulty returning to the USA.

Vaccinations are not required for either country and only people who have been on a farm during the previous 30 days will be detained by immigration officials.

Customs

Travellers are allowed to bring all personal goods (including camping gear or hiking equipment) into the USA and Canada free of duty, along with food for two days and up to 50 cigars, 200 cigarettes and 40 ounces of liquor or wine. What you can't ship around on the airlines is the white gas in your backpacker's stove. Empty it out before you get to the airport as there are steep penalties if you get caught with fuel of any kind in your luggage.

There are no forms to fill out if you are a foreign visitor bringing any vehicle into Alaska whether it is a bicycle, motorcycle or a car; nor are there forms for hunting rifles or fishing gear. Hunting rifles (handguns and automatic weapons are prohibited) must be registered in your own country and you should bring proof of this. There is no limit to the amount of money you can bring into Alaska but anything over $5000 must be registered with customs officials.

Keep in mind that there are endangered species laws prohibiting transporting products made of bone, skin, fur, ivory etc through Canada without a permit. Import and export of such items into the USA is also prohibited. If you have any doubt about a gift or item you want to purchase, call the US Fish & Wildlife Service office in Anchorage at (907) 786-3311.

Hunters and anglers who want to ship home their salmon, halibut or the rack of a caribou can easily do so. Most outfitters and guides will make the arrangements for you which include properly packaging the game. In the case of fish, most towns have a storage company that will hold your salmon or halibut in a freezer until you are ready to leave Alaska. When frozen and packed in dry ice, seafood can usually make the trip to any city in the Lower 48 without spoiling.

Foreign Consulates

There are no embassies in Alaska but there are more than a dozen foreign consulates offices in Anchorage to assist overseas travelers with unusual problems. They include:

Belgium, 1031 West 4th Ave, Room 400, Anchorage, AK 99501-5995; (☎ (907) 276-5617)

Denmark, 601 West 5th Ave, Suite 700, Anchorage, AK 99501-2221; (☎ (907) 276-7401)

Finland, 550 West 64th Ave, Anchorage, AK 99518-1700; (☎ (907) 562-3326)

France, 2804 West Northern Lights Blvd, Anchorage, AK 99517-3305;(☎ (907) 248-2804)

Germany, 425 G St, Suite 650, Anchorage, AK 99501-2176;(☎ (907) 274-6537)

Japan, 550 West 7th Ave, Suite 701, Anchorage, AK 99510-3559 (☎ (907) 279-8428)

Korea, 101 West Benson Blvd, Suite 304, Anchorage, AK 99503-3997 (☎ (907) 561-5488)

Norway, 333 M St, Suite 405, Anchorage, AK 99501-1902; (☎ (907) 263-9102)

Sweden, the corner of Northern Lights Blvd and C St, (PO Box 100600), Anchorage, AK 99510-0600;(☎ (907) 265-2927)

UK, 3211 Providence Dr, Room 362, Anchorage, AK 99508-4614; (☎ (907) 786-4848)

MONEY & COSTS

Alaskans use the same currency as the rest of the USA, American dollars (US$), only they tend to use a little more of it. The state is traditionally known for having the highest cost of living in the country, though places like southern California, and San Francisco and New York City have caught up with Alaska if not surpassed it. There are two reasons for the high prices in Alaska: the long distances needed to transport everything and the high cost of labor.

To buy a dozen eggs in Fairbanks will cost your more than in other parts of the USA (from around $1.50 to $1.90, but to walk into a café and have two eggs cooked and served is where the high prices slap you in the face like a July snowfall. In the restaurants, not only are the transport costs added to the price, but so are the high salaries of the chef, waitress and busboy who put them sunny-side up on your table. Also keep in mind that tourism in Alaska has basically a three-month season. If the prices seem inflated, they have to be to cover the other nine months when many restaurants, motels and other business are barely scrapping by.

The trick to budget travel, or beating the high prices, is to either travel out of season or avoid the labor cost. If you just can't get yourself to take a vacation in Fairbanks in

February when it is -40°F then try to avoid the labor cost. Buy your own food in a market and cook it at the hostel or camp site. Use public transport or better still hitchhike; sleep in campgrounds and enjoy your favorite brew around a campfire at night. It is the restaurants, bars, hotels and taxi companies, with their inflated peak-season prices, that will quickly drain your money pouch.

A rule of thumb for Alaskan prices is that they are lowest in Ketchikan and increase gradually as you go north. Overall, the Southeast is generally cheaper than most places in the Interior or elsewhere because barge transport from Seattle (the supply center for the area) is only one to two days away. Barges arrive weekly in Southeast Alaska, bringing all the necessities of life but fresh food such as bread and milk is frozen before shipping. If you walk into a store and find all the milk half-frozen, don't be alarmed – the barge just arrived.

Anchorage and to a lesser extent Fairbanks are the exceptions to the rule as they have competitive prices due to their large populations and business communities. Anchorage, which also receives most of its goods on ocean-going barges, can be extremely affordable if you live there, outrageous if you are a tourist. Gas prices often hover around $1.15 a gallon and apples in a supermarket could cost less than 90c a pound. But it's hard to find a motel room under $80 and the price of other tourist-related services, such as taxis and restaurants, seem to be inflated as well.

When traveling in the Bush, on the other hand, be prepared for anything. The cost of fresh food, gasoline or lodging can be two or three times what it is anywhere else in the state. It is here that the tales of $25 breakfasts were conjured up, and in some isolated Bush villages these stories might not be too mythical.

On average, a loaf of bread will cost from $2 to $2.50, a can of tuna fish from 90c to $1.60, apples from $1 to $2 per pound and a hamburger anywhere from $2 per pound in the large cities to over $4 per pound in outlying communities. Generally the cost of dairy products, even in Anchorage, will get you to swear off them forever or at least until the end of your trip. A gallon of milk will be priced anywhere from $3.75 to over $5 while in Bettles it's $8 a gallon. When buying fresh fruit and vegetables take the time to look over them closely, especially in small town markets. It is not too uncommon to buy a stalk of celery and later discover the middle of it is spoiled.

The cost of gas is surprisingly reasonable, far cheaper than it is in Canada. A gallon in Anchorage will cost anywhere from $1.10 to $1.30 while in many secondary cities, such as Seward and Valdez it will cost $1.40 or so. Only at some deserted station will you pay more than $2 a gallon. A single room in the cheapest motels or hotels costs from $50 to $60 per night while many state and federal campgrounds charge $6 per tent site and privately owned campgrounds charge anywhere from $10 to $15 a night.

An inexpensive restaurant in Alaska is one where two people can have breakfast, coffee and leave a tip for under $15. For dinner, it's a challenge for two travelers to leave most restaurants, apart from fast-food chains, for under $25. If you need to obtain your main meal at a restaurant, look for the many places that now serve lunch buffets until late in the afternoon. Chinese restaurants (every major town has one) are notorious for this. Often until 3 pm you can enjoy an all-you-can-feed-on feast of fried rice, chow mein and egg rolls for under $7.

The National Bank of Alaska (NBA) is the largest bank in the state with offices in almost every village and town on the heavily traveled routes. The NBA can meet the needs of most visitors and, though opening hours vary from branch to branch, you can usually count on their being open from 10 am to 5 pm Monday to Friday with evening hours on Wednesday and Friday. The popular brands of travelers' cheques are widely used around the state and many merchants also accept Canadian money, though they usually burn you on the exchange rate.

Note All prices quoted in this book are in US dollars unless otherwise stated. The follow-

ing currencies convert at these approximate rates:

A$1	=	$0.72
UK£1	=	$1.49
C$1	=	$0.75
NZ$1	=	$0.58
DM1	=	$0.59

Credit Cards

There are probably cases of a store or a hotel in some isolated Bush community somewhere in Alaska that doesn't accept any type of credit card, but not many. Like in the rest of the USA, Alaskan merchants are geared and willing to accept just about all major credit cards. Visa and MasterCard are the most widely accepted cards by far but American Express and Discovery are not far behind.

Bring along a gasoline credit card if you already have one and plan to do quite a bit of driving. If you don't have one, it's not necessary. Tesoro is one of the most widespread chains of gasoline stations in Alaska and has its own form of plastic money. But practically all stations, Tesoro included, will accept one of the big four cards mentioned above.

You might also consider bringing your ATM card from home to access automatic teller machines in Alaska as a way of receiving funds. The National Bank of Alaska, which has offices throughout the state, is connected to both the Plus and Cirrus ATM networks. Chances are that any bank in the USA is connected to one or the other.

In short, having some plastic money is good security for the unexpected on any major trip and some travelers say it's now even better to take a credit card than haul a wad of travelers' checks. But don't leave home without knowing how to report a lost or stolen card and your bank's procedure for replacing it while you're on the road.

Tipping

Tipping in Alaska, like in the rest of the USA, is expected. The going-rate for restaurants, hotels and taxi drivers is about 15%.

WHEN TO GO

Because most travelers like to avoid minus-degree temperatures, Alaska's traditional travel season has been from June to August with the peak season from early July to mid-August when visiting places like Denali National Park or the Kenai Peninsula can be a dismal experience due to crowds. The reality of the situation is there are an awful lot of tourists trying to see Alaska in a very short period of time.

Consider traveling during part of the 'shoulder season'. May and September offer not only mild weather but also a good chance for off-season discounts with motels and transportation. Often the difference between a winter and summer motel rate is $25 or more. If you arrive early or stay late, just make sure you equip yourself for some cold, rainy weather.

Arriving in Alaska in late April is a possibility in the Southeast but in much of the Interior you could still be running into spring break-up, a time of slush and mud. Stay in October and in the Southeast and Southcentral regions – you're guaranteed rain most of the time, while in the Interior and Fairbanks there will be snow.

In recent years, the state has been actively promoting winter travel in Alaska. Guiding companies that offer dog-sled trips are on the increase and a new downhill ski resort will soon appear next door to Anchorage's Alyeska Ski Resort. But I don't know, I've lived through a handful of Alaskan winters and I can think of other places to visit in January and February.

WHAT TO BRING
Clothes

With nights that freeze and days that fry, layering is the only way to dress for Alaskan summers without having to take a pair of shipping containers. It's an accepted fact in the north country that several light layers of clothing are warmer than a single heavy one. With layers you trap warm air near the body to act as an insulation against the cold. Layers are also easy to strip off when the midday sun begins to heat up.

Instead of a heavy coat, pack a long-sleeved jersey, or woollen sweater, and a wind-breaker/parka; they are easier to pack and more versatile for Alaska's many changes of weather. A woollen hat and mittens are necessary items to fend off the cold night air, freak snowfalls or the chilly rain of the Southeast. Leave the umbrellas at home and instead take a waterproof nylon jacket with a hood for rain protection, and a pair of rain pants if your plans include day hikes or wilderness expeditions.

The number of luxury restaurants, hotels and entertainment spots is growing in the large Alaskan cities; even in Juneau there is now a bar with a dress code which amused the residents when it began in 1984. Along with the proper dress, these places have high prices. For the most part, Alaska is still a land of jeans, hiking boots (or brown rubber boots in the Southeast) and woollen shirts – the acceptable attire for the vast majority of restaurants, bars and hotels throughout this state. If you are going to backpack around the north on a budget, there is no reason to take anything that isn't comfortable, functional in the harsh environment, and easy to pack and wash.

There is no need to buy a pair of the brown rubber boots that you'll see throughout the Southeast, but you should wax or 'grease' your boots to protect your feet from rain and the wet brush on the trail. The new ultralight boots on the market today are fine for most of the hikes described in this book but not all. If your plans include glacier walking and serious ascents into the mountains, traditional all-leather boots (that feel like cement blocks on your feet) are still required footwear.

It is best to avoid anything with goose-down filling such as jackets or sleeping bags, as wet feathers tend to clump and lose most of their insulating power. Polyester fiber is the most common filling used by Alaskans.

Camping & Expedition Equipment

If you plan on extended trips into the wilderness, you will need to have suitable equipment such as a tent, a sleeping bag, a camp stove, maps and a compass. For more specific information about what equipment to take, see the What to Bring section in the Wilderness chapter.

TOURIST OFFICES
The first place to write to while planning your adventure is the Alaska Division of Tourism (Dept 901, PO Box 110801, Juneau, AK 99811; ☎ (907) 465-2010, fax (907) 586-8399) where you can request a copy of the *Alaska State Vacation Planner*, a 120-page annually updated magazine.

Travel information is easy to obtain once you are on the road as almost every city, town and village has a tourist contact center whether it be a visitors bureau, chamber of commerce or a hut near the ferry dock. These places are good sources of free maps, information on local accommodation, and directions to the nearest campground or hiking trail.

BUSINESS HOURS
Banks and post offices in Alaska are generally open from 9 am to 5 pm from Monday to Friday. Other business hours are variable but many shops are open until 10 pm during the week, from 10 am to 6 pm Saturday and from noon to 5 pm on Sunday.

HOLIDAYS & FESTIVALS
Alaskans do their fair share of celebrating, much of it during the summer. One of the biggest celebrations in the state is the Summer Solstice on 21 June, the longest day of the year. Fairbanks holds the best community festival, with a variety of events including midnight baseball games (played without the use of artificial light) and hikes to local hills to view the midnight sun. Nome stages a week-long Midnight Sun Festival while Barrow stages a 'Sun will not set for 83 days' Festival and many towns have unofficial celebrations.

Independence Day (4 July) is a popular holiday around the state when the larger communities of Ketchikan, Juneau, Anchorage and Fairbanks sponsor well-planned events. Perhaps even more enjoyable during

this time of year is a visit to a small settlement such as Gustavus, Seldovia or McCarthy, where you cannot help but be swept along with the local residents in an afternoon of old-fashioned celebrating that usually ends with a square dance in the evening.

Salmon and halibut derbies that end with cash prizes for the heaviest fish caught are regular events around the coastal regions of Alaska, with Juneau and Seward having the largest. Although most travelers are ill prepared to compete in such fishing contests, watching the boats returning to the marina with their catch makes for an interesting afternoon.

State fairs, though small compared to those in the Lower 48, are worth attending if for no other reason than to see what a 70-pound cabbage looks like. The fairs all take place in August and include the Alaska State Fair at Palmer, the Tanana Valley Fair at Fairbanks, the Southeast State Fair at Haines and smaller ones at Kodiak, Delta Junction and Ninilchik.

Regional Festivals & Celebrations
The regional festivals and celebrations in Alaska include:

April
Alyeska Spring Carnival, Girdwood
Alaska Folk Festival, Juneau
Tanner Crab Roundup, Unalaska
Piuraagiaqta Spring Festival, Barrow
May
Little Norway Festival, Petersburg
Miner's Day Celebration, Talkeetna
Crab Festival, Kodiak
Polar Bear Swim, Nome
Prince William Sound Regatta of Ships, Whittier, Cordova and Valdez
June
Summer Music Festival, Sitka
Nenana River Days, Nenana
Renaissance Festival, Anchorage
Nalukataq (Whaling Festival), Barrow
Summer Solstice, Fairbanks
Midnight Sun Festival, Nome
All Alaska Logging Championships, Sitka
Whitewater Weekend, Valdez
Alaska Renaissance Festival, Anchorage
Great Tanana River Raft Classic, Fairbanks

July
> *Moose Dropping Festival*, Talkeetna
> *Mount Marathon Race*, Seward
> *Summer Arts Festival*, Fairbanks
> *Golden Days*, Fairbanks
> *Soapy Smith's Wake*, Skagway
> *Forest Fair*, Girdwood
> *Bear Paw Festival*, Chugiak/Eagle
> *Summer Festival*, North Pole
> *Bluegrass Festival*, Palmer
> *Progress Days*, Soldotna
> *Alaska State Fair*, Delta Junction

August
> *Blueberry Festival*, Ketchikan
> *Tanana Valley Fair*, Fairbanks
> *Southeast Alaska State Fair*, Haines
> *Founders' Day Festival*, Houston
> *Kenai Peninsula State Fair*, Ninilchik
> *Scottish Highland Games*, Eagle River
> *St Herman's Pilgrimage*, Kodiak

September
> *Oktoberfest*, Fairbanks
> *Great Bathtub Race*, Nome
> *Taste of Homer*, Homer
> *State Fair & Rodeo*, Kodiak
> *Equinox Marathon*, Fairbanks
> *Trading Post Potato Festival*, Willow

October
> *Alaska Day Celebration*, Sitka and Haines
> *October Arts Festival*, Petersburg

Tourist offices can provide exact dates and further information on various events.

State Holidays
The state holidays for Alaska include:

1 January
> *New Year's Day*
16 January
> *Martin Luther King Day*
16 February
> *President's Day*
30 March
> *Seward's Day*
March-April
> *Easter*
25 May
> *Memorial Day*
4 July
> *Independence Day*
7 September
> *Labor Day*
12 October
> *Columbus Day*
18 October
> *Alaska Day*

11 November
> *Veteran's Day*
16 November
> *Thanksgiving*
25 December
> *Christmas Day*

POST & TELECOMMUNICATIONS
Planning to write home or to friends? Send your mail 1st class by sticking a 29c stamp on the envelope or by using a 45c airgram for overseas destinations. Surface mail, slow anywhere in the USA, can take up to a month moving to or from Alaska.

To receive mail while traveling in Alaska, have it sent c/o General Delivery to a post office along your route. Although everybody passes through Anchorage (zip code 99510), it's probably better to choose smaller towns like Juneau (99801), Ketchikan (99901), Seward (99664), Tok (99780) or Delta Junction (99737). Post offices are supposed to keep letters for 10 days before returning them, although smaller places may keep letters longer, especially if your letters have 'Please Hold' on the front written in big red print. If you are planning to stay at hostels, theirs are the best addresses to leave with letter writers.

For travelers, especially those from overseas, tripping through Canada into Alaska, it's best to wait if you can until you're in the USA to mail home packages. Generally you'll find the US postal service is half the cost and twice as fast as its Canadian counterpart.

Telegrams, cablegrams and mailgrams can be sent anywhere from Alaska through Western Union by calling (800) 325-6000. Money transfers can also be sent and usually received in 15 minutes at any Western Union branch office in the state. Call the same 800 number to locate the nearest office.

Telephone
Telephone area codes are simple in Alaska: the entire state shares 907 expect Hyder which uses 604.

ELECTRICITY
Voltage in Alaska is 110/120 V – the same as everywhere else in the USA.

LAUNDRY

Virtually every town with more than 100 residents in Alaska has a laundromat, the place to go to clean your clothes or take a shower. A small load of clothes is going to cost from $2 to $2.50, plus you'll need another 50c to dry them in the dryer. A shower and clean towel is around $3. You'll find many hostels and a few motels also provide laundry facilities for a fee.

TIME

In 1983, Alaska reduced its time zones from four to two in an effort to help commerce and communications between its cities. With the exception of four Aleutian Island communities and Hyder, a small community on the Alaska/British Columbia border, the entire state shares the same time zone, Alaska Time, which is one hour earlier than Pacific Standard Time – a zone in which Seattle (Washington) falls.

When it is noon in Anchorage, it is 9 pm in London, 4 pm in New York and 7 am the following day in Melbourne, Australia.

WEIGHTS & MEASURES

Alaska uses the imperial system of measurement. Weight is measured in ounces (oz) and pounds (lb), volume is measured in pints and gallons, and length in inches, feet, yards and miles etc.

A conversion table is provided at the back of this book for people more comfortable with metric measurement.

BOOKS

The following publications will aid travelers heading north to Alaska. A few of the more popular ones can be found in any good bookstore but most are available only in Alaska or by writing to the publisher. A good alternative, however, is to write to Wild Rose Guidebooks, an Anchorage-based distributor of more than 50 Alaskan guides and maps for travel, fishing, camping and natural history as well as recreational books for hikers, backpackers and kayakers. Send for their catalogue by writing to Wild Rose Guidebooks, PO Box 240047, Anchorage,

AK 99524. A list of hiking and wilderness guidebooks can be found in the Books section of the Wilderness chapter.

Travel Guides

The Milepost (Alaska Northwest Books, 22026 20th Ave SE, Bothell, WA 98041; 640 pages, $16.95), unquestionably the most popular travel guide, is put out every year. While it has good information, history and maps of Alaska and western Canada, its drawbacks include its large size – at eight by 11 inches it is impossible to slip into the side pocket of a backpack – and that it is written for travelers who are driving. Listings of restaurants, hotels and other businesses are also limited to advertisers.

The Alaska Wilderness Milepost (Alaska Northwest Books, 22026 20th Ave Southeast, Bothell, WA 98041; 454 pages, $14.95) used to be a slim section in *The Milepost* but it has now been split into a guidebook of its own by the publisher. It is perhaps the most comprehensive guide to Bush Alaska, the parts of Alaska that can't be reached by road, as it covers more than 250 remote towns and villages. Its smaller format, six by nine inches, also makes it easier to store in a pack.

Adventuring in Alaska by Peggy Wayburn (Sierra Club Books, 530 Bush St, San Francisco, CA 94108; 375 pages, $10.95) is a good general guidebook to the many new national parks, wildlife preserves and other remote regions of Alaska. It also contains excellent 'how-to' information on undertaking wilderness expeditions in the state, whether the mode of travel is canoeing, kayaking or hiking.

Alaska's Southeast: Touring the Inside Passage by Sarah Eppenbach (Globe Pequot Press, PO Box 833, Old Saybrook, CT 06475; 308 pages, $12.95) offers some of the most comprehensive accounts of the Southeast's history and culture, although it lacks detailed travel information. It does a superb job giving you a feeling for each town and area of the Panhandle.

The Inside Passage Traveler by Ellen Searby (Windham Press, Box 1332, Juneau, AK 99802; 208 pages, $12.95) is another travel guide devoted to the Southeast as written by a former State Marine Ferry crew member. It is mediocre overall and offers little more than what you can get from brochures and the US Forest Service's *Opportunity & Recreation Guide* on every state ferry.

Alaska's Parklands, The Complete Guide by Nancy Simmerman (The Mountaineers, 1011 SW Klickitat Way, Suite 107, Seattle, WA 98134; 336 pages, $16.95) is the encyclopaedia of Alaska wilderness, covering over 110 state and national parks and wilderness areas. It lacks detailed travel information and guides to individual canoe and hiking routes but does a thorough job of covering the scenery, location, wildlife and activities available in each preserve.

The Alaska Highway: An Insider's Guide by Ron Dalby (Fulcrum Publishing, 350 Indiana St, Golden, CO 80401; 204 pages, $15.95) is a personal alternative to *The Milepost* as guide to the Alaska Hwy. Dalby, a former editor of *Alaska Magazine*, provides information which lacks the detail of *The Milepost* but is long on stories he has gathered driving the legendary road to the north.

General

Alaska by James A Michener (Fawcett Books, New York, NY) – whether you love or hate him as an author, just about everybody agrees that James Michener leaves no stone unturned in writing about a place. He usually begins with the creation of the mountains and rivers, and 1000 pages later brings you to the present; his novel of Alaska is no different. Michener actually spent three summers in Sitka researching the book and the result is an overview of the state's history that few books can provide. It's a bit wordy for my literary taste but many others rave about the book.

Coming into the Country by John McPhee (The Noonday Press, 19 Union Square West, New York, NY 10003; 438 pages, $9.96) takes a mid-1970s look at Alaska in a book that is 600 pages shorter and considerably lighter than Michener's effort. McPhee's experiences included a kayak trip down the Kobuk River in the Brooks Range, living in the town of Eagle for a while and spending time in Juneau during the height of the capital move issue. All of the stories provide an excellent insight into the state and the kind of people who live there.

Alaska's Brooks Range by John Kauffmann (The Mountaineers, 1011 SW Klickitat Way, Suite 107, Seattle, WA 98134; 192 pages, $14.95) is a guidebook but also gives an in-depth profile of what the author says is the world's last, great unspoiled wilderness. Kauffmann, who spent 20 years with the National Park Service and was chief planner for the Gates of the Arctic National Park, explores the geography, history natural inhabitants and the conservation effort to protect this untamed territory.

Facts About Alaska (Alaska Northwest Books, 22026 20th Ave SE, Bothell, WA 98021; 224 pages, $8.95) is an Alaska almanac, covering just about every topic imaginable, from what a 'potlatch' is to the state's heaviest snowfall (974.4 inches). Topics are arranged alphabetically and each subject is a snippet of background information and interesting facts.

City Visitor Guides

Various large and small newspapers around the state put out special visitors' guides at the beginning of the summer. All are filled with local history, information, things to do and trails to hike in the area where the newspaper circulates. The guides are free and are usually found at numerous locations (restaurants, bars, hotel lobbies) around town. If you write to them, most newspapers will send you a copy of the publication before you depart, though they may charge you a small handling and shipping fee. The various cities in Alaska that have newspaper guides are:

Anchorage
    Visitors Guide, Anchorage Daily News, PO Box 149001, Anchorage, AK 99514
Fairbanks
    Interior & Arctic Alaska Visitors' Guide, Fairbanks Daily News Miner, PO Box 710, Fairbanks, AK 99707

Haines
> *Haines Sentinel*, Chilkat Valley News, PO Box 630, Haines, AK 99827

Homer
> *Homer Tourist Guide*, The Homer News, 3482 Landing St, Homer, AK 99603

Juneau
> *Juneau Guide*, Juneau Empire, 235 2nd St, Juneau, AK 99801

Ketchikan
> *Ketchikan Visitors' Guide*, Ketchikan Daily News, PO Box 7900, Ketchikan, AK 99901

Kodiak
> *Kodiak Visitors' Guide*, Kodiak Daily Mirror, 1419 Selig St, Kodiak, AK 99615

Petersburg
> *Viking Visitor Guide*, Petersburg Pilot, PO Box 930, Petersburg, AK 99833

Skagway
> *Skagway Alaskan*, The Skagway News, PO Box 1898, Skagway, AK 99840

Sitka
> *All About Sitka*, Sitka Daily Sentinel, PO Box 799, Sitka, AK 99835

Valdez
> *Valdez/Cordova Visitors' Guide*, Valdez Vanguard, PO Box 157, Valdez, AK 99686

Wrangell
> *The Wrangell Guide*, Wrangell Publishing Inc, PO Box 798, Wrangell, AK 99929

MAPS

Drivers often swear that *The Milepost* has the best set of road maps you can obtain for Alaska. But an even more detailed collection of maps can be found in the *Alaska Atlas & Gazetteer* (DeLorme, PO Box 298-7200, Freeport, MA 04032; (☎ (800) 227-1656); 156 pages, paperback, $19.95). This atlas contains more than 100 maps that cover the state and includes some other unique features like an index of physical landmarks (want to find a certain mountain? Just look it up in the index). Its drawbacks, especially for backpackers and others living out of a suitcase, is its size – 11 by 15 inches.

When driving, I find the road maps in the free publications handed out at every visitors center to be more than adequate to get you from one town to the next. When trekking in the backcountry and wilderness areas, the USGS topographicals (scale 1:63,500) are worth the $2.50 per quad you pay for them. You can purchase them at the Public Lands

Information centers in Anchorage, Tok and Fairbanks (see the regional chapters for addresses and phone numbers), but they tend to carry only the maps for their area of the state. It's best to stop at the main USGS offices in Alaska either in Fairbanks (Federal Building at 101 12th Ave) or Anchorage (Gambell Building on the Alaska Pacific University campus). These USGS sales offices have topos and other maps to cover the complete state.

MEDIA

After 77 years, the *Anchorage Times* published its final edition on 3 June 1992 and then folded, ending one of the great newspaper wars in the USA. The decades-long struggle with its arch rival *Anchorage Daily News* was lost despite the *Times* being purchased in 1989 by cash-rich VECI International, Alaska's largest oil field service company, and being converted from an afternoon to a morning paper.

Today there are still more than 30 daily, weekly and trade newspapers in Alaska, though most contain eight pages of local news, softball scores and advertising. The largest daily in the state with a circulation of almost 61,000 is the *Anchorage Daily News*, a top-rate newspaper that captured the Pulitzer Prize in the 1970s with its stories on the Trans-Alaska Pipeline.

The next biggest daily and an equally fine paper is the *Fairbanks Daily News Miner* while the largest paper in the Southeast is the *Juneau Empire*, though it only recently added a Sunday edition. The *Seattle Post-Intelligencer* is flown into the Southeast daily and the usual news magazines, *Time* and *Newsweek*, are available, though they are a week old by the time they reach the newsstand.

Driving around the state? You'll find a wide range of radio stations throughout Alaska, a lot of them playing country music. If possible, search for a public radio station, like Homer's KBBI (AM 890). A daily staple for most of them is 'bushlines' when messages are passed back and forth to isolated residents on the airwaves. It provides an interesting glimpse of life in Alaska. Where else could you hear, 'Ben, meet me at the cabin Tuesday. I'll have a chainsaw and the dog', but in rural Alaska.

FILM & PHOTOGRAPHY

The most cherished items you can take home from your trip are pictures and slides of Alaska's powerful scenery. Much of the state is a photographer's dream and your shutter finger will be tempted by mountain and glacier panoramas, bustling waterfronts and diverse wildlife encountered during paddling and hiking trips. Even if you have never toted a camera before, seriously consider taking one to Alaska.

A small, fixed-lens, so-called 'no-mind' (just point and shoot!) 35-mm camera is OK for a summer of backpacking in the north country. A better step up, however, is to purchase a 35-mm camera with a fixed zoom lens. The Nikon Zoom-Touch 500 series is such a camera, providing a lens that zooms from a 35-mm wide angle to an 80-mm telephoto. The camera is still compact and easy to use but will greatly increase your variety of shots.

If you want to get serious about photography you need a full 35-mm camera with a couple of interchangeable lenses and maybe even a second body. To photograph wildlife in its natural state, a 135-mm or larger telephoto lens is needed to make the animal the main object in the picture. Just remember any lense larger than 135 mm will probably also require a tripod to eliminate camera shake, especially during low-light conditions. A wide-angle lens of 35 mm, or better still a 28-mm one, adds considerable dimension to scenic views while a fast (f1.2 or f1.4) 50-mm 'normal' lens will provide more opportunities for pictures during weak light. If you want simplicity, check out today's zoom lenses. They are much smaller and compact than they have been in the past and provide a sharpness that's more than acceptable to most amateur photographers. A zoom from 35 mm to 105 mm would be ideal.

Keep in mind the rainy weather that you'll encounter on your trip; a waterproof camera bag is an excellent investment, especially if a great deal of your time will be spent in the woods. When flying to and around Alaska, pack your film in your carry-on luggage and have it hand-inspected. Security personnel at US airports are required by law to honor such requests and are usually very accommodating if you have the film out and ready. I've only met a handful who made me uncap all 48 rolls of film I was hauling along. Scanning machines are supposed to be safe for film, but why take the chance? Remember the higher the speed of film, the more susceptible it is to damage by scanners.

Many photographers find that Kodachrome (ASA 64 or ASA 100) is the best all-around film, especially when you're photographing glaciers or snowfields where the reflection off the ice and snow is strong. A few rolls of high-speed film (ASA 200 or 400) are handy for nature photography as the majority of wildlife will be encountered at dusk and dawn, periods of low light. Bring all your own film if possible; in the large cities and towns it will generally be priced around $8 to $10 for a roll of Kodachrome (36 exposures), while in smaller communities you may have a hard time finding the type of film you want.

HEALTH
Predeparture Preparations
Health Insurance The cost of health care in the USA is extremely high and there's no exception in Alaska. A travel insurance policy to cover theft, loss and medical problems is therefore a wise idea. There is a wide variety of policies and your travel agent will have recommendations. The international student travel policies handled by the Student Travel Association (STA) or other student travel organizations are usually good value. Some policies offer lower and higher medical expenses options but the higher one is chiefly for countries like the USA which have extremely high medical costs. Check the small print.

• Some policies specifically exclude 'dangerous activities' such as motorcycling and even trekking. If such activities are on your agenda, you don't want that sort of policy.

• You may prefer a policy which pays doctors or hospitals directly rather than you having to pay on the spot and claim later. If you do have to claim later, make sure you keep all documentation. Some policies ask you to call back (reverse charges) to a center in your home country where an immediate assessment of your problem is made.

• Check if the policy covers ambulances or an emergency flight home. If you have to stretch out you will need two seats and somebody has to pay for them!

Medical Kit A small, straight-forward medical kit is a wise thing to carry, especially if you plan to venture away from populated areas. A possible kit list includes:

• Paracetamol (called acetominophen in North America) – for pain or fever
• Antihistamine (such as Benadryl) – useful as a decongestant for colds, for allergies, to ease itching from insect bites or stings, or to help prevent motion sickness
• Antibiotics – useful if you're traveling in the wilderness, but they must be prescribed and you should carry the prescription with you
• Kaolin and pectin preparation (Pepto-Bismol), and Imodium or Lomotil – for bouts of giardia or stomach upsets
• Rehydration mixture – for treatment of severe diarrhoea, this is particularly important if traveling with children
• Antiseptic, Mercurochrome and antibiotic powder, or similar 'dry' spray – for cuts and grazes
• Calamine lotion – to ease irritation from bites or stings
• Bandages and Band-aids – for minor injuries
• Scissors, tweezers and a thermometer – mercury thermometers are prohibited by airlines
• Insect repellent, sunscreen, suntan lotion, chap stick and water purification tablets
• Space blanket – to be used for warmth or as an emergency signal

Water Purification

Tap water in Alaska is safe to drink but it is wise to purify surface water that is to be used for cooking and drinking. The simplest way of purifying water is to boil it thoroughly. Technically this means boiling it for 10 minutes, something which happens very rarely! Remember that at high altitude water boils at a lower temperature, so germs are less likely to be killed.

If you cannot boil water, it can be treated chemically. Chlorine tablets (Puritabs, Steritabs or other brand names) will kill many but not all pathogens. Iodine is very effective in purifying water and is available in tablet form (such as Potable Aqua), but follow the directions carefully and remember that too much iodine can be harmful.

If you can't find tablets, tincture of iodine (two percent) or iodine crystals can be used. Two drops of tincture of iodine per quart of clear water is the recommended dosage; the treated water should be left to stand for 30 minutes before drinking. Iodine crystals can also be used to purify water but this is a more complicated process, as you have to first prepare a saturated iodine solution. Iodine loses its effectiveness if exposed to air or damp so keep it in a tightly sealed container. Flavored powder (Kool Aid) will disguise the taste of treated water and is a good idea if you are traveling with children.

If you are trekking in the wilderness, all this can be handled easily by investing in a high-quality filter. Filters such as First Need or MSR's Waterworks are designed to take out whatever you shouldn't be drinking, including *Giardia lamblia* (see following). They cost between $45 and $80 which is well worth it.

Water from glacial rivers may appear murky but you can drink it, if necessary, in small quantities. The murk is actually fine particles of silt scoured from the rock by the glacier and drinking too much of it has been known to clog up internal plumbing.

Medical Problems & Treatment

Giardia Giardiasis commonly known as Giardia and sometimes called 'beaver fever', is caused by an intestinal parasite *(Giardia lamblia)* present in contaminated water. The symptoms are stomach cramps; nausea; a bloated stomach; watery, foul-smelling diarrhoea and frequent gas. Giardia can appear several weeks after you have been exposed to the parasite. The symptoms may disappear for a few days and then return; this can go on for several weeks. Metronidazole, known as Flagyl, is the recommended drug, but it should only be taken under medical supervision. Antibiotics are of no use.

Sunburn & Windburn Sunburn and windburn should be primary concerns for anyone planning to spend time bushwalking or traveling over snow and ice. The sun will burn you even if you feel cold and the wind will cause dehydration and skin chafing. Use a good sunblock and a moisture cream on exposed skin, even on cloudy days. A hat provides added protection, and zinc oxide or some other barrier cream for your nose and lips is recommended for people spending any time on the ice or snow.

Reflection and glare off the ice and snow can cause snow blindness, so high-protection sunglasses should be considered essential for any sort of glacier visit.

Hypothermia Perhaps the most dangerous health threat in the Arctic regions is hypothermia. Hypothermia occurs when the body loses heat faster than it can produce it and the core temperature of the body falls. It is surprisingly easy to progress from very cold to dangerously cold due to a combination of wind, wet clothing, fatigue and hunger, even if the air temperature is above freezing point.

It is best to dress in layers – silk, wool and some of the new artificial fibers are all good insulating materials. A hat is important, as a lot of heat is lost through the head. A strong, waterproof outer layer is essential, as keeping dry is vital. Carry basic supplies, including food containing simple sugars to generate heat quickly and lots of fluid to drink.

Symptoms of hypothermia are exhaustion, numb skin (particularly toes and fingers), shivering, slurred speech, irrational or violent behavior, lethargy, stumbling, dizzy spells, muscle cramps and violent bursts of energy. Irrationality may take the form of sufferers claiming they are warm and trying to take off their clothes.

To treat hypothermia, first get the patient out of the wind and/or rain, remove their clothing if it's wet and replace it with dry, warm clothing. Give them hot liquids – not alcohol – and some high-calorie, easily digestible food. This should be enough for the early stages of hypothermia, but if it has gone further it may be necessary to place victims in warm sleeping bags and get in with them. Do not rub patients, place them near a fire or remove their wet clothes in the wind. If possible, place a sufferer in a warm (not hot) bath.

Motion Sickness Since a great deal of travel in Alaska is done by boat and much of the overland travel is over rough, unsurfaced roads, motion sickness can be a real problem for those prone to it.

Eating lightly before and during a trip will reduce the chances of motion sickness. If you are prone to motion sickness, try to find a place that minimizes disturbance – near the wing on aircrafts, close to midships on boats and near the center of buses. Fresh air or watching the horizon while on a boat usually helps; reading or cigarette smoke doesn't. Commercial antimotion-sickness preparations, which can cause drowsiness, have to be taken before the trip commences; when you're feeling sick it's too late. Ginger is a natural preventative and is available in capsule form.

Rabies Rabies is found in Alaska, especially among small rodents such as squirrels and chipmunks in wilderness areas; it is caused by a bite or scratch from an infected animal. Any bite, scratch or even lick from a mammal should be cleaned immediately and thoroughly. Scrub with soap and running water, and then clean with an alcohol solution. If there is any possibility that the animal is infected, medical help should be sought immediately. Even if the animal is not rabid, all bites should be treated seriously as they can become infected or can result in tetanus. A rabies vaccination is now available and should be considered if you are in a high-risk category – for instance, handling or working with animals.

WOMEN TRAVELERS

Perfumes or scented cosmetics, including deodorants, should not be worn in areas where you are likely to encounter bears as the smell will attract them. Women who are menstruating should also be cautious.

Women should also be alert to the dangers of hitchhiking, especially when they are traveling alone – use common sense and don't be afraid to say no to lifts.

DANGERS & ANNOYANCES

There are many dangers and annoyances associated with the Alaskan wilderness; these range from problems with bears and insects to the dangers of blue-water paddling – for more information on these topics see the Wilderness chapter.

WORK

Opportunities for astronomical wages for jobs on the Trans-Alaska Pipeline and other high-paying employment are, unfortunately, either exaggerated or nonexistent today. Except for brief hiring booms, like during the Exxon oil spill clean-up, the cold reality is that Alaska has one of the highest unemployment rates in the country, averaging 11% annually and often reaching 20% during the winter.

Many summer travelers arrive thinking they will get work on a fishing boat after hearing of someone earning $10,000 in six weeks by getting a percentage of the catch on a good boat. After discovering they lack the deck-hand experience necessary for any kind of position on a fishing vessel, they end up cleaning salmon in a cannery for $6 per hour.

July is the month to be hanging around the harbors looking for a fishing boat desperate for help and the best cities to be in are Kodiak, Cordova and Dillingham. Boats from these places work fish runs in Prince William Sound and Bristol Bay or Ketchikan, Petersburg and Pelican in the Southeast. Most canneries (many of which are based in the Seattle area) fill their summer employment needs during the winter. If you really want to work in a cannery instead of touring Alaska, contact them by February. Otherwise just show up during the season and hope they are hiring. Finding work is possible as most cannery positions don't require experience and burnouts are common in this trade.

Other summer employment in Alaska is possible but be realistic about what you will be paid and look in the right places. In the USA, workers are required to have a social security number, a birth-right for anybody born in the country. For foreigners and others who don't have a social security card, the law stipulates that you apply for a green card, which involves a long bureaucratic process that rarely can be accomplished in a summer.

If you lack the proper documentation, then search out tourist-related businesses such as hotels, restaurants, bars and resorts which need additional short-term help to handle the sudden influx of customers. The smaller the business, the more likely the employer will pay you under the table. Other cash-paying jobs, whether house cleaning or stocking shelves, can sometimes be found by checking bulletin boards at hostels or the student unions at the various University of Alaska campuses.

If you do have your number, check out the regional offices of the US Forest Service and national parks, which also hire a large number of temporary workers during the summer. But be aware that these federal agencies, like many canneries, recruit their workers during the winter and have little if anything to offer someone passing through in June or July.

In short, those people whose sole interest is working for a summer in Alaska rather than traveling should begin looking the winter before. Start by contacting regional offices of the US Forest Service, national parks or the chambers of commerce in fishing communities such as Petersburg, Kodiak or Cordova. You can also get some information from the Alaska State Employment Service (PO Box 3-7000, Juneau, AK 99802) though it tends to do everything it can to discourage outsiders from seeking jobs in Alaska.

The other option is volunteer work. Although you won't get a wage, you are often provided with room and board and get to work in a spectacular setting. Most volunteer positions are with federal or state agencies. The Bureau of Land Management (BLM) uses almost 300 volunteers annually, people who do everything from office work and maintaining campgrounds to even working on the famous Iditarod Trail. For more information on volunteer work with the BLM begin in the winter by writing to BLM-Alaska (Public Affairs, 222 West 7th Ave, Anchorage, AK 99513).

The US Forest Service maintains the largest volunteer program in the state, each year recruiting hundreds of people and providing their room and board and, at times, even transportation costs. Begin in the winter by writing to US Forest Service (Pacific Northwest Region, Volunteer Coordinator, PO Box 3623, Portland, OR 97208). From there write to the individual area offices around the state (see the Wilderness chapter for addresses).

You might also consider contacting the Student Conservation Association during the winter. The non-profit New Hampshire-based organization places more than 1000 college students and adults annually in expense-paid internships which allow the volunteers to live and work with professionals in the conservation and natural resources field. Many of these positions are in Alaska. Write to SCA (PO Box 550, Charlestown, NH 03603) or call (603) 543-1700.

ACCOMMODATIONS
Camping
Bring a tent – then you will never be without inexpensive accommodation in Alaska. There are no cheap bed & breakfast places (B&Bs) like those in Europe and the number of hostels is limited but there are state, federal and private campgrounds from Ketchikan to Fairbanks. Nightly fees range from $3 for the walk-in Morino Campground in Denali National Park to $15 per tent in some of the more deluxe private campgrounds.

It is also a widely accepted practice among backpackers to just wander into the woods and find a spot to pitch a tent. With the exception of Anchorage, Fairbanks and one or two other cities, you can walk a mile or so from most towns and find yourself in an isolated wooded area. It may not be an 'officially designated camp site', but if backpackers are clean and orderly, locals are more than happy to overlook this fact.

Your tent should be light (under five pounds) and come complete with a good rain fly; if it has been on more than its fair share of trips, consider waterproofing the rain fly and tent floor before you leave for Alaska. The new free-standing dome tents work best, as in many areas of the state the ground is rocky and difficult to sink a peg into. Along with the tent, bring a thin foam sleeping pad (not a bulky air mattress); it will soften the hard ground and help you keep warm by putting a layer of insulation between your sleeping bag and the moisture that will seep through the tent floor. The Thinsulite pad is the Rolls Royce of sleeping pads and after a summer of sleeping on the ground in Alaska, you'll think the $60 or $70 you paid for it was the best investment you ever made. Thinsulite even makes a set of straps that turns your pad into a lounge chair, an excellent accessory to have in camp after hiking all day.

Hostels
The once-struggling Alaska Council of American Youth Hostels is now a lot more stable and most of its 12 hostels scattered around the state have been in operation for years at the same location. The mainstays of the system are the hostels in Anchorage, Juneau, Ketchikan, Sitka, Haines, Delta Junction and Tok. The first hostel you check into is the best source of information on which hostels are open and which need reservations in advance. You should always plan reserving your bed at Anchorage, Juneau and Ketchikan.

The hostels range from a huge house in Juneau (four blocks from the capitol building) with a common room with a fireplace, cooking facilities and showers to remote Bear Creek Camp in Haines and a church basement in Ketchikan. Perhaps the most important hostel for many budget travelers is the Anchorage International (AYH) Hostel, which recently moved closer to the city center and the bus terminal.

The hostel fees range from $5 to $12 for a one-night stay, more if you are a nonmember. Some hostels accept reservations and others don't; each hostel's particulars will be discussed later in this guide. Be aware that hosteling means separate male and female dormitories, house parents, chores assigned for each day you stay and curfews. Also, the hostels are closed during the day – even when it rains. The hostels are strict about these and other rules such as no smoking, drinking and illegal drugs. Still, hostels are the best bargains for accommodation in Alaska and the best place to meet other budget travelers and backpackers.

For more information on Alaska's hostels before you depart on your trip, write to or call Hostelling International – Anchorage (☎ (907) 276-3635 or 276-7772 for a machine message), 700 H St, Anchorage, AK 99501.

Backpacker's Hostels Long overdue, Alaska is finally getting some offbeat hostels that offer cheap bunkroom accommodations but without all the rules and regulations of an official youth hostel. Check them out in Anchorage, Fairbanks and Homer. More are sure to spring up in the near future.

B&Bs

It is now possible to stay in a B&B from Ketchikan to Anchorage, Cordova, in Fairbanks, and all the way to Nome and Bethel. What was once a handful of private homes catering to travelers in the early 1980s is now a network of hundreds. One B&B owner estimated there are now more than 1000 such places in Alaska with several hundred in Anchorage alone.

For travelers who want nothing to do with a sleeping bag or tent, B&Bs can be an acceptable compromise between sleeping on the ground and high-priced motels and lodges. Some B&Bs are bargains and most have rates below that of major hotels. Still, B&BS are not cheap and you should plan on spending anywhere from $50 to $100 per couple per night for a room.

Some B&Bs are in small, out-of-the-way communities such as Angoon, Gustavus, McCarthy or Talkeetna where staying in a private home can be a unique and interesting experience. All recommend making reservations in advance but it is often possible, in cities like Anchorage, Juneau and Fairbanks where there are many B&Bs, to obtain a bed the day you arrive by calling around. Many visitors centers now have sections devoted entirely to the B&Bs in their area and even courtesy phones for booking a room. Details about B&Bs will be covered in the regional chapters. For more information before your trip or to make reservations contact the following statewide B&B associations in Alaska:

Southeast Alaska
  Alaska Bed & Breakfast Association, PO Box 21890, Juneau, AK 99802; (☎ (907) 586-2959)
Statewide
  Alaska Private Lodging, 4631 Caravelle Dr, Anchorage, AK 99520; (☎ (907) 248-2292). Send $3 for a descriptive directory.
  Stay with a Friend, 3605 Arctic Blvd, Suite 173, Anchorage, AK 99503; (☎ (907) 278-8800). Send a SASE (self-addressed stamped envelope) for a brochure or $2 for a descriptive directory.
  Accommodations in Alaska, PO Box 110624, Anchorage, AK 99511; (☎ (907) 345-4279 or 345-4761). Send a large SASE for a brochure.
Fairbanks
  Fairbanks Bed & Breakfast, PO Box 74573, Fairbanks, AK 99707; (☎ (907) 452-4967)
Kodiak
  Kodiak Bed & Breakfast Service, 308 Cope St, Kodiak, AK 99615; (☎ (907) 486-5367)

Roadhouses

Roadhouses, found along the highways, are another option. The authentic roadhouses that combine cabins with a large lodge/ dining room are slowly being replaced by modern motels, but some places can still offer rustic cabins and sleep from two to four people for $40 to $70 per night. A few of the roadhouses, those with a roaring blaze in the stone fireplace and an owner who acts as chef, bartender and late-night storyteller, are charming. A classic roadhouse and one of the state's oldest is located in Copper Center.

Hotels & Motels

Hotels and motels are the most expensive lodgings you can book. Although there are a few bargains, the average single room in an 'inexpensive' hotel costs from $40 to $50 and a double costs from $50 to $60 (these are the places down by the waterfront with shared bathrooms). Better hotels in each town will be even more costly, with Anchorage's best places charging close to $150 per night.

The other problem with hotel and motels is that they tend to be full during much of the summer. Without being part of a tour or having advance reservations, you may have to search for an available bed in some cities. In small villages, you could be out of luck as they may only have one or two places to choose from.

Wilderness Lodges

These are off the beaten path and you usually require a bush plane or boat to reach them. The vast majority of places need advance booking and offer rustic cabins with saunas and ample opportunities to explore the nearby area by foot, canoe or kayak (they provide the boats). The lodges are designed for people who want to 'escape into the wilderness' without having to endure the 'hardship' of a tent, freeze-dried dinners or a small camp stove. The prices range from $150 to $250 per person per day and include all meals.

FOOD

The local supermarket will provide the cheapest food whether you want to live on a diet based on fruit and nuts or cook full meals at a hostel. The larger cities will have several markets which offer competitive prices and a good selection of fruit and vegetables during the summer.

While strolling down the aisles also keep an eye out for fresh Alaskan seafood, especially in Southeast and Southcentral markets. Local seafood is not cheap but it is renowned throughout the country for its superb taste. The most common catches are king salmon steaks at $5 to $6 per pound, whole Dungeness crab at $4 to $5 per pound and prawns, which are large shrimp, at $8 to $9 per pound. The larger markets will also have halibut, smoked salmon and cooked king crab.

Alaska is no longer so remote that the US fast-food (and cheapest) restaurants have not reached it. Back in the late 1970s only Anchorage and Fairbanks had a McDonald's. Now you can order a Big Mac in Ketchikan, Juneau and Kodiak, Homer and Eagle River while other chains such as Pizza Hut, Burger King, Wendy's and Taco Bell are almost as widespread. There is even a Dairy Queen in Kotzebue and a Baskin Robbins Ice Cream Shop on the island of Attu at the end of the Aleutian Island chain.

Although these fast-food outlets are cheap, if for no other reason than you don't have to leave a tip, their prices still reflect the high cost of living in Alaska as a Big Mac will cost you between $2.25 and $2.50, a hamburger 89c and a small serve of French fries 95c.

Much of the state, however, is safe from the fast-food invasion and the smaller towns you pass through will offer only a local coffee shop or café. Breakfast, which many places serve all day, is the best bargain; a plate of eggs, toast and hash browns will cost from $4 to $6 while a cup of coffee will cost from 75c to $1.

An influx of Oriental people immigrating to Alaska has resulted in most mid-size towns having at least one Chinese restaurant if not two. Some towns, like Homer (population 3900) support three. All of these places have a lunch buffet that runs from 11 am to 3 pm or so and is an all-you-can-eat affair that costs from $5 to $7. Eat a late lunch here and you can make it through to breakfast the next morning.

One popular eating event during the summer in most of the state, but especially the Southeast, is the salmon bake – a dinner costs from $14 to $18 but it is worth trying at least once. The salmon is caught locally, grilled, smothered with somebody's home-made barbecue sauce and often served all-you-can-eat-style. One of the best bakes is in Juneau, next to the Last Chance Mining Museum, where the cost of the meal includes your first beer, live entertainment and beautiful mountain scenery. There is another excellent salmon bake in Fairbanks.

DRINKS
Coffee
Espresso Shops The coffee craze that began in Seattle and the Northwest has extended into Alaska. Espresso shops are everywhere, even in towns as small as McCarthy you can find somebody with an espresso machine. In Anchorage, there are dozens of these places. People from the West Coast will feel at home. Those from other parts of the country will be confused. In that case, here is a quick guide to ordering coffee in an espresso shop:

Espresso – a heavy, dark coffee generally served in small cups. Most places, however, serve 'doubles' in a regular coffee mug. The cost will range from $1 to $1.50.

Cafe latte – espresso with steamed milk mixed with it and foamed milk on top. It's a delightfully, rich drink that generally costs from $2 to $3 a cup.

Cafe au lait – regular coffee mixed with steamed milk

Cappuccino – espresso that is just topped off with foamed milk and cinnamon. You can expect to pay from $1.50 to $2.

Flavored coffee – espresso or cafe latte that has a shot of Torani. The results are coffees that range from raspberry to hazelnut in flavor.

Alcohol
The legal drinking age in Alaska is 21 years and only the churches outnumber the bars. Except for 70 Native Alaskan towns like Bethel or Angoon, where alcohol is prohibited, it is never very difficult to find an open bar or liquor store. That and the long, dark winters explains why Alaska has the highest alcoholism rate per capita in the USA, especially among the indigenous people. Bar hours vary but there are always a few places

that open their doors at 9 am and don't close until 5 am.

Bars in the larger cities vary in their décor and many offer live entertainment, music and dancing. The bars in smaller towns are good places to have a brew and mingle with people from the fishing industry, loggers or other locals passing through. All serve the usual US beer found in the Northwest (Miller, Rainier, Olympia) and usually one or two places have that fine Canadian brew, which is usually darker and richer than US beer, charging around $3 for a 12 ounces bottle. There is also Alaska Ambler from a Juneau brewer that is now seen all over the state. It's good but will usually cost you a $1 per bottle. In summer, don't be alarmed if you walk into a bar for a couple of beers with the sun still up and walk out while it's rising again, missing the night entirely.

DRUGS
At one time marijuana was technically legal in Alaska when it was used in the privacy of your home. The legalization came about in 1975 after the state Supreme Court ruled that the health threat from marijuana was insufficient to warrant government intrusion on the privacy of residents. For 16 years, Alaskans showed their fierce individual character and distrust of government regulations as Alaska was the only state in the country where you could legally smoke pot.

That all changed in November 1991 when the voters approved a new drug law that made possession of small amounts of marijuana a misdemeanor punishable by up to 90 days in jail and a $1000 fine. Even when marijuana was legal, Alaska was never a paradise for potheads. Marijuana was extremely hard to find and was usually quite expensive, often costing three times what it might sell for elsewhere in the USA. The Alaska Civil Liberties Union has vowed to challenge the new law but regardless of the status of pot in Alaska, it is foolhardy for any visitor to carry it when hitchhiking or driving along the Alcan as you have to pass through the close inspection of immigration officers at two borders. The use of other drugs is also against the law and results in severe penalties, especially for cocaine which is heavily abused in Alaska.

ENTERTAINMENT

You won't find Broadway in Alaska or stadium rock concerts. But the state does have a lively arts community that organizes events that are both affordable and well worth a evening out. Many theater groups feast on the summer tourists by offering plays that combine music, a little local history and a lot of comedy. These events staged in bars, the Lions Clubs and hotels and generally range in admission from $5 to $10 a show. The two shows not to be missed are the 'Days of '98 Show' in Skagway and the show at Ester's Malamute Saloon.

THINGS TO BUY

As far as things to buy go, Alaska abounds with gift shops, with items often much too tacky for my taste. Native Alaskan carving, whether in ivory, jade or soapstone, on the other hand, is exquisite and highly prized, thus expensive. A six-inch craving of soapstone, a soft stone that indigenous people in western Alaska carve and polish, runs from $120 to $300 depending on the carving and the detail. Jade and ivory will cost even more.

Moose nuggets will be seen from one end of the state to the other. But even if they are varnished, you have to wonder who is going to wear ear rings or a necklace made of the scat of an animal. More interesting, and much more affordable than gold nugget jewelry, is what is commonly called Arctic opal. The blue and greenish stone was uncovered in the Wrangell Mountains in the late 1980s and now is set in silver in a variety of ear rings, pins and other pieces.

Want a keepsake T-shirt or jacket? Avoid the gift shops in Anchorage and Fairbanks and head for the bookstores at the University of Alaska campuses which have an interesting selection of clothing that you won't find anywhere else.

HIGHLIGHTS OF ALASKA

There is much to do and see in Alaska. The following are my favorite 10 attractions, but there are many others. Twenty-two outstanding wilderness trips are listed in the Trekking and Paddling sections of the Wilderness chapter. If you have less than three weeks to spend in the state consider either riding the state ferry and visiting three towns in depth (Juneau, Sitka and possibly Haines or Skagway) or flying to Anchorage and driving the Glenn and Richardson highway loop through Valdez with a side trip to Denali National Park.

1. Riding the shuttle bus along the Denali National Park & Preserve road to view the wildlife (Interior chapter)
2. Taking a passage on one of the special State Marine Ferry runs from Kodiak to Dutch Harbor on the Alaskan Peninsula (Bush chapter)
3. Flying into a US Forest Service cabin for a few days (Wilderness chapter)
4. Viewing the northern lights from the University of Alaska campus in Fairbanks (Fairbanks chapter)
5. Traveling to Tenakee Springs aboard the State Marine Ferry and soaking in the village's hot springs (Southeast chapter)
6. Taking a glacier cruise on Prince William Sound, either to Kenai Fjords, College Fjord or taking the State Marine Ferry past Columbia Glacier (Southcentral chapter)
7. Taking in the show and Robert Service poetry at the Malamute Saloon in Ester (Interior chapter)
8. Riding the White Pass & Yukon Route from Skagway (Southeast chapter)
9. Viewing the Midnight Sun on or near 21 June (the summer solstice) from Eagle Summit off the Steese Hwy (Fairbanks chapter)
10. Traveling to and spending a night in McCarthy (Southcentral chapter)

Getting There & Away

Many travelers from the Lower 48 mistakenly think that a trip to Alaska is like visiting another state of the USA. It isn't; getting to the north country is as costly and complicated as traveling to a foreign country. Plan ahead and check around for the best possible deal on airline flights or bus tickets.

If you are coming from the US mainland, there are three ways of getting to Alaska: by the Alcan (also known as the Alaska Hwy), the Inside Passage waterway, or flying in from a number of cities. If you are coming from Asia or Europe, it is no longer as easy to fly direct to Anchorage, via the polar route. Many international airlines, British Airways and Japan Air Lines to name but two, have dropped their service to Anchorage in recent years. Now most international travelers come through a variety of gateway cities including Seattle, Los Angeles, Detroit and Vancouver to pick up a second flight to Anchorage.

AIR

The quickest and easiest (but unfortunately the most expensive) way to reach Alaska is to fly there. A number of major US domestic carriers and international airlines offer regular service to Alaska, primarily to Anchorage International Airport. As a result of the deregulation of the US airline industry, fares tend to fluctuate wildly due to airline ticket wars and travel promotions. Following is a list of sample fares but it is well worth the effort to check out all possibilities before purchasing a ticket.

Tickets generally fall into two basic types: regular fares, which no budget traveler would ever be caught purchasing; and Advance Purchase Excursion (Apex) or 'Supersavers' as they are known domestically that require round-trip tickets to be booked 14 to 30 days in advance and have a maximum number of days you can stay. The US domestic airlines also offer a special price to passengers traveling on Tuesday and

Wednesday – off-peak days for the airline industry and many have off-season rates for those who travel between December and May.

Anchorage International Airport

The vast majority of visitors to Alaska fly into Anchorage International Airport. International flights arrive at the North Terminal, domestic at the South Terminal and there is complimentary shuttle service between the two terminals and all the various parking lots. The People Mover bus departs from the South Terminal for downtown Anchorage (see the Anchorage chapter) and most of the car rental companies also have rental counters here. You'll find taxis at both terminals.

The airport has the usual services of any major center including gift shops, restaurants, bars, banks of pay phones, ATM money machines, currency exchange and baggage storage at $3 a day per bag (ground level of South Terminal; ☎ (907) 248-0373).

The following airlines have scheduled service into and out of Anchorage. The numbers are either local Anchorage numbers or toll-free numbers good for anywhere in the USA:

Aeroflot (☎ 248-8400)
Alaska Airlines (☎ (800) 426-0333)
China Airlines (☎ 248-3603)
Continental (☎ (800) 525-0280)
Delta Airlines (☎ (800) 221-1212)
ERA Aviation (☎ (800) 426-0333)
Hawaiian Airlines (☎ (800) 367-5320)
Korean Air (☎ 243-3329)
MarkAir (☎ (800) 478-0800)
Morris Air (☎ (800) 444-5660)
Northwest Air (☎ (800) 225-2525)
PenAir (☎ (800) 448-4226)
Reeve Aleutian Airways (☎ 243-4700)
United Airlines (☎ (800) 241- 6522)

To/From the Lower 48

Domestic air fares are constantly moving up and down and will vary greatly with the season, the days you want to travel, the length of stay and how rigid the ticket is in terms of changes and refunds after being purchased. Each airline has its own requirements and restrictions that come with discount tickets and these should be examined carefully, especially terms regarding the length of stay. Many tickets allow you to stay in Alaska from three months up to a year. Some allow a stay of 21 days or less which makes it challenging when you're planning a pair of week-long treks into the Alaska wilderness.

It can not be stressed enough that you shop around and keep your eyes and ears open for fare specials when planning your trip. The air fare to Alaska is far more affordable than it was 10 or 15 years ago and occasionally now you can pick up a round-trip ticket from the US Midwest or East Coast to Anchorage for under $500. But the reality is, most of those 'economy fares' either have tight restrictions, are for off-season travel or have such a limited number of seats available that it's a minor miracle when you reserve one. In the end, the summer travel season in Alaska is short and demand for seats on the plane is high. This is when the airlines must make their profit and they can't do that by offering economy fares during July.

Seattle (Washington) is the traditional departure point within the USA for air travel to Alaska, but now you can book a nonstop flight to Anchorage from a number of cities including San Francisco, Salt Lake City, Detroit, Minneapolis, Portland, and Honolulu. Northwest flies round-trip nonstop between Minneapolis and Anchorage for $550 on an advance purchase ticket and $650 for a similar ticket from Detroit. Delta Airlines flies from Salt Lake City to Anchorage for a round-trip fare of $652. Hawaiian Airlines has a nonstop flight from Honolulu on Friday for $549 round-trip to Anchorage. United Airlines has a daily, one-stop flight but with no change of planes from Chicago to Anchorage for $600. Continental offers the same service, one-stop flight with no change of planes, from Houston to Anchorage (that is $672 if booked 14 days in advance). Other cities with one-stop, no-change-of-plane flights included Cincinnati, New York and Dallas (Delta), Los Angeles, San Jose and Oakland (Alaska Airlines), Memphis (Northwest), Washington, DC and Philadelphia (United Airlines).

Flights that change planes in Seattle are offered from an even greater number of cities including Boise, Atlanta, Denver, Los Angeles, Las Vegas, New Orleans, New York, Oakland, Sacramento, Reno, Boston, San Diego, Houston, Dallas and Chicago to name a few.

Alaska Airlines is by far the largest carrier of travelers to Anchorage with 12 daily flights from Seattle as compared to four for United, three for Delta and two for Northwest. During the off season and shoulder seasons (May and September) Alaska Airlines has non-refundable return fares from Seattle to Anchorage for as low as $335. The only requirement is that you book 21 days in advance, stay over at least one Saturday and return within a year. Similar return fares between Seattle and Juneau are $345, and between Seattle and Fairbanks $335. During the profitable summer season you can add another $100 to $150 to that ticket. The other companies also charge around $450 for an advance-purchase ticket between the two cities.

The US domestic airlines can be contacted on the following toll-free numbers for information on fares and schedules:

Alaska Airlines (☎ (800) 426-0333)
Delta Airlines (☎ (800) 221-1212)
United Airlines (☎ (800) 241-6522)
Northwest Airlines (☎ (800) 225-2525)
Hawaiian Airlines (☎ (800) 367-5320)

In short, air travel is the best way to go if you plan to spend three weeks or less touring Alaska or have the funds to afford the flight. But if you are planning to spend a month or the entire summer venturing through the state, you see more and pay less by combining the State Marine Ferry out of Bellingham with a bus ride into the rest of the state from Haines.

Making Your Connection
Based on the size of the airport and how efficient it is in handling and moving passengers, here's what the clockwatchers at Alaska Airlines recommend as the minimum connection time between flights:

Connection City	Domestic	International	
	Departing/Arriving	Departing	Arriving
Anchorage	25 min	60 min	120 min
Bellingham	20 min	–	–
Boise	15 min	–	–
Juneau	15 min	–	–
Ketchikan	15 min	–	–
Los Angeles	20 min	30 min	90 min
Oakland	20 min	–	–
Portland	25 min	–	–
San Diego	20 min	40 min	90 min
San Francisco	25 min	40 min	80 min
San Jose	20 min	35 min	60 min
Seattle	30 min	40 min	65 min
Spokane	20 min	–	–

To/From Canada

Canadian Airlines does not service Alaska but will fly you to Seattle where you can pick up a domestic US carrier for the second leg of your journey. Round-trip fare from Toronto to Seattle, for a ticket purchased 14 days in advance, is C$558.

The airline also has three flights a day during the summer from Vancouver to Whitehorse (the Yukon Territory) where you could then pick up a connecting flight on Air North to Juneau. Round-trip, advance purchase ticket from Vancouver to Juneau is C$550. You can contact Canadian Airlines toll-free at (800) 663-0010 from British Columbia, (800) 263-6133 from Toronto's 416 area code, (800) 268-4910 from anywhere else in Ontario and (800) 426-7000 in the USA.

Air North also has flights that connect Whitehorse with Fairbanks. Round-trip tickets, purchased seven days in advance, cost US$323 while the airlines' Klondike Explorer Pass is US$470. This allows unlimited air travel for 21 days between the five cities its serves: Juneau, Whitehorse, Dawson City, Old Crow and Fairbanks. In Alaska call Air North at (800) 764-0407; in northern British Columbia and the Yukon Territory call (800) 661-0407.

To/From the UK

British Airways no longer flies into Anchorage. The airline does have nonstop flights from London (Heathrow) to Seattle where you can pick up a domestic carrier to continue north. The lowest fare is US$712 and the ticket must be booked 21 days in advance and your stay in the USA can not exceed 45 days.

Delta Airlines also has a London-to-Anchorage flight that begins at Gatwick Airport and changes planes in Cincinnati. A round-trip APEX fare is US$729. Both Northwest (Gatwick) and United Airlines (Heathrow) offer similar flights.

To/From Continental Europe

The most common route to Anchorage from Europe is to head west with a stop in New York and then Seattle. From Paris, Continental offers a daily flight to Anchorage that changes planes in Houston and then makes an additional stop before reaching Alaska. A round-trip fare, purchased 14-days in advance, is US$1213. Northwest also has a daily Paris-to-Anchorage flight, that changes planes in Detroit (don't worry, the airport is 15 miles from the city). Round trip fare is US$1058 but the ticket must be booked 21 days in advance, can only be used in July and August and the maximum stay in Alaska would be 21 days. You also have to travel between Monday and Thursday.

Similar flights can also be arranged from Frankfurt through Delta and Northwest and United Airlines. Northwest charges US$1417 for a round trip with a 21-day advance purchase ticket but allows you to stay up to three months. Travel must take place between Monday and Friday. Flying with Delta costs slightly more at around US$1600.

To/From Asia

There are four daily flights and a variety of others from Tokyo to Anchorage. None is direct, nonstop flights but several fly into Seattle or Los Angeles and then on to Alaska. Keep in mind the fares with US-based airlines like Northwest and Delta fluctuate wildly with the rise and fall of the dollar against the yen.

Northwest flies into Seattle and onto Anchorage daily. They require you to purchase the ticket within 24 hours of making the reservation but do not have advance purchase requirement on it. The round-trip fare is US$1813. Delta offers a daily flight that changes at Salt Lake City and has the same requirements as Northwest. The round-trip fare is US$1550.

Japan Air Lines has discontinued its service to Anchorage nor does it fly into Seattle. On JAL the best you can do is fly to San Francisco for $1943 round trip and then pick up an Alaska Airlines flight to Anchorage.

There is also daily service from Seoul to Anchorage which is far cheaper than departing from Tokyo. United Airlines offers a daily flight with a change of planes at San Francisco. Or you can fly nonstop four days a week with Korean Air. Their round-trip fare is US$1370 and requires only a four-day advance purchase.

There is also nonstop service between Taipei, Taiwan and Anchorage with China Air and daily service with United Airlines with a change of planes in San Francisco.

To/From Australia & NZ

In Australia, STA and Flight Centres are major dealers in cheap air fares. They have branches in all the major cities. Otherwise, check the travel agents' ads in the Yellow Pages and ring around. QANTAS Airways has flights from Sydney to Los Angeles with connections on Alaska Airlines to Anchorage. Several excursion (round-trip) fares are available. A return advance purchase ticket will cost from A$2270 return depending on the duration of your stay in Alaska and the time of year you travel. The US government tax on the ticket is an additional A$32.60.

Most flights between the USA and New Zealand are to/from the USA's west coast. Most go through Los Angeles but some also arrive and depart from San Francisco. With Air New Zealand one-way fares cost from NZ$1349.

Round-the-World Tickets

Round-the-World tickets allow you to fly on the combined routes of two or more airlines in one direction for a more economic journey around the globe. Several major airlines, including TWA and Continental, offer such tickets but unfortunately Anchorage is not one of the possible stopovers.

OVERLAND – THE ALCAN

What began in April 1942 as an unprecedented construction project during the heat of WW II ended eight months later as the first overland link between the Lower 48 and Alaska, known formally as the Alaska-Canada Military Hwy and affectionately as the Alcan. Today, the Alcan (also known as the Alaska Hwy) is a road through the vast wilderness of north-west Canada and Alaska. It offers a spectacular drive enjoyed by thousands of travelers each summer who take their time to soak up the scenery, wildlife and clear, cold streams along the way.

For those with the time, the Alaska Hwy is a unique way to travel north. The trip is an adventure in itself; the 1520-mile road is a legend among highways and to complete the journey along the Alcan is a feather in any traveler's cap. *Mile 0* of the Alcan is at

Dawson Creek in British Columbia, while the other end is at Delta Junction (although some residents of Fairbanks will debate that).

The Alcan is now entirely asphalt-paved, and although sections of jarring potholes, frost heaves (the rippling effect of the pavement caused by freezing and thawing) and loose gravel still prevail, they offer nothing like the rough conditions it was famous for 10 or 15 years ago. The era of lashing spare fuel cans to the side of the car and gasoline stations every 250 miles is also gone. Food, gas and lodging can be found every 20 to 50 miles along the highway, with 100 miles being the longest stretch between fuel stops.

There are several ways to get to the Alcan: you can begin in the US states of Washington, Idaho or Montana and pass through Edmonton or Jasper in Alberta or Prince George in British Columbia, Canada. There are also several ways of traveling the highway: bus, car, a combination of State Marine Ferry and bus or the cheapest of all – hitchhiking.

Bus – the Alcan

A combination of buses will take you from Seattle via the Alcan to Anchorage, Fairbanks, Skagway or Haines for a moderate cost. There are no direct bus services from the Lower 48 to Alaska; travelers have to be patient as services here are more limited than in the rest of the country. But by using buses, the cost of reaching Alaska is cheap compared to flying or taking the State Marine Ferry.

Greyhound The closest you can get to Alaska on this giant of bus companies is Whitehorse in British Columbia and this involves purchasing two tickets. You begin at the Greyhound station in the center of Seattle on the corner of 8th Ave and Stewart St where you can buy a one-way ticket to Vancouver for $22. The bus departs at least three times a day, more often if the demand is high during the summer. Call the station (☎ (206) 628-5530) to double-check exact departure days and times. You switch to a

Greyhound Lines of Canada bus at Pacific Central Station on Main St in Vancouver, and continue your journey north with a two-hour layover at Prince George in British Columbia and another at Dawson Creek. The bus departs at 8.30 am on Monday, Wednesday and Friday and you arrive in Whitehorse at 5.15 am, 44 hours later – beat to hell most likely. But it's hard to travel any cheaper. One-way fare from Vancouver to the Yukon capital is only C$280.

When planning your trip, keep in mind that most Greyhound special offers, such as Ameripass (unlimited travel for seven days), do not apply to Yukon or Alaska destinations. Greyhound does not maintain a toll-free US telephone number anymore.

There is also more pleasant way to reach Alaska than spending two days on a Greyhound Bus. Once in Vancouver, you can also pick up a ticket to Prince Rupert, where you can then hop on the delightful Alaska state ferries. There are two buses a day, at 8.30 am and 8 pm, and they arrive in Prince Rupert 25 hours later. One-way fare is C$157. Call Greyhound of Canada (☎ (604)662-3222) for more information.

Alaskon Express Once you've reached Whitehorse, you change to an Alaskon Express bus for the next leg of the journey. Gray Line of Alaska operates these buses from May to September, from either Westmark Whitehorse, 2288 2nd Ave, or the Greyhound Bus Terminal at the north end of 2nd Ave.

Buses depart the Yukon capital for Anchorage on Tuesday, Wednesday, Friday and Sunday at noon; stay overnight at Beaver Creek in the Yukon and then continue to Anchorage the next day, reaching the city at 7 pm. You can also get off the bus earlier at Tok, Glennallen or Palmer. On Monday, Tuesday, Thursday and Saturday buses depart Whitehorse at noon for Haines, reaching the Southeast Alaska town and ferry terminal port at 6.30 pm.

As a testimony to the popularity of the Chilkoot Trail, an Alaskon Express bus departs daily from Whitehorse at 4.30 pm for

Skagway, stopping along the way to pick up backpackers coming off the popular trek and reaching the Alaskan town two hours later.

You can also go overland to Fairbanks, something that was hard to do in the past. An Alaskon Express bus departs at noon on Tuesday, Wednesday, Friday and Sunday for Fairbanks with a stopover in Beaver Creek. A nice thing about these buses is that you can flag them down along the road or in a small town, which is good if you have been sitting around for most of the morning trying to thumb a ride out of a town like Haines Junction. Can you imagine doing that to a Greyhound bus in the Lower 48?

The one-way fare from Whitehorse to Anchorage is $179, to Fairbanks $149, Haines $76 and to Skagway $52; keep in mind that these fares do not include lodging at Beaver Creek. In Whitehorse, call (403) 667-2223 for current bus information. If you are still in the planning stages of your trip, call the toll-free US number for Gray Line of Alaska, (800) 544-2206; by January they can provide schedules, departure times and rates for the following summer.

Alaska Direct Busline Much smaller and slightly cheaper than Gray Line's Alaskon Express is Alaska Direct Busline based out of Anchorage. On Tuesday, Friday and Sunday an Alaska Direct bus departs Whitehorse at 7 am, reaching Tok around 3 pm where you can continue on to Fairbanks or transfer to a bus for Anchorage.

The one-way fare from Whitehorse to Tok is $80, to Fairbanks is $120 and Anchorage is $145. In Alaska or the USA call Alaska Direct at (800) 770-6652, in Whitehorse call (403) 668-4833. Make sure you call to find out what hotel the pick-up point is that summer or even if the company is still in business.

Norline Coaches This was the Canadian bus company that used to provide the final link between Whitehorse and Alaska but now it runs between Whitehorse and Dawson City to the north. From June to September, buses depart from the White-

horse bus terminal on Monday, Wednesday and Friday at 9 am and cover the 335 miles to Dawson City, arriving at 3.30 pm. The bus then turns around and repeats the trip the same day, arriving at Whitehorse at 10.30 pm, when during the summer this far north there's still daylight. The one-way fare is C$72.76.

While many feel this is the more scenic and adventurous route into Alaska, there is no bus transport beyond Dawson City and the hitch across the border through Chicken and down to Tok can be a long wait at times. For current rates and schedules call Norline on (403) 668-3355.

AlaskaPass
A concept which has been hugely popular in Europe for years arrived in the North Country in 1989 when a small company in Haines (of all places) organized nine major carriers and offered an unlimited travel pass. AlaskaPass Inc, now with headquarters in Seattle has put together the only all-inclusive ground transportation pass that will get you from Washington through Canada into Alaska and even as far north as Dawson City in the Yukon for a set price.

You purchase your pass, choosing the number of days you want to travel, then armed with the schedules of various carriers, make your own reservations or arrangements. The carriers include Alaska State Ferry, Greyhound of Canada, Island Coach Lines, British Columbia Rail and British Columbia Ferries to move you from Bellingham or Vancouver north. You can continue on Alaskon Express, Gray Line of Alaska, Norline Coaches or the Alaska Railroad to reach Alaska and travel around the state. Each time you pick up a ticket you just flip them your AlaskaPass.

On the plus side, you can save money with such a pass. On the down side you have to plan carefully to do so and the pass does not include any air travel. The passes are offered for either continuous or flexible travel which allows travel on a number of days during a time period. The latter is a much better choice as it leaves you time to enjoy an area or take side trips before moving on.

The eight-day pass is $449 but there is a $50 surcharge if you use it in Bellingham to board the Alaska State Ferry. The 15-day pass is $599, the 22-day $729 and the 30-day $849. Still better over the long haul is the 12/21-day pass (travel 12 out of 21 days) for $629 and the 21/45 for $899. There are discounts for children, aged between three and 11 years, and for an off-season pass for travel from October to April.

You can purchase a pass ahead of time from most travel agents or directly from the company by calling (800) 248-7598.

Driving the Alcan

Without a doubt, driving your own car to Alaska allows you the most freedom. You can leave when you want, stop where you feel like it and pretty much make up your itinerary as you travel along. It's not exactly cheap driving to Alaska, and that's not even considering the wear and tear and thousands of miles you'll clock up on your vehicle. The final bill will depend on where you're coming from, where you stay at night (campground, cabins or a lodge) and what you eat (food prepared by yourself or from cafés along the way).

If you're contemplating this car trip, remember that the condition of your tires is most important. The Alcan may be paved but it's constantly under repair and stretches of frost heaves and pot holes are common, especially on the Canadian side; worn tires don't last long here. Even your spare, and you *must* have one, should be fairly new. You should also avoid the newer 'space-saver' spares, and carry a full-size spare as your extra tire.

Windshield wipers are another important item. Replace them before you depart and carry an extra set along with a gallon of solvent for the windshield-washer reservoir. Dust, dirt and mud make good visibility a constant battle while driving. Also bring a jack, wrenches and other assorted tools, spare hoses, fan belts, a quart of oil or two, even an extra headlight or air filter is not being too extreme. Carry them and hope you never have to use them.

Some travelers use an insect screen, others put plastic headlight covers or a wire-mesh screen over the headlights, and others place a rubber mat or piece of carpet between the gas tank and securing straps. All this is to protect the vehicle from the worse danger on the road – flying rocks that are kicked up by truck-and-trail rigs passing you.

By far the worst problem on the Alcan and many other roads in Alaska and the Yukon is dust – that's why even on the hottest days you see most cars with their windows up. To control dust in a RV or trailer, reverse the roof vent on your rig so it faces forward. Then keep it open a few inches while driving, creating air pressure inside to combat the incoming dust.

Those traveling the route in small or compact vehicles often face another common problem – overloading the car. Stuffing the trunk and the backseat and then lashing on a car-top carrier just to take along extra boxes of macaroni-and-cheese dinners could do you in, miles from anywhere. It's been said that the biggest single cause of flat tires and broken suspension systems along the Alcan is an overloaded car.

Since almost 80% of the Alcan is in Canada, it's best to brush up on the metric system (either that or have a conversion chart taped to the dashboard). On the Canada side you'll find kilometer posts (as opposed to the mileposts found in Alaska) are placed every five km with the zero point in Dawson Creek, of course.

With more than 1000 vehicles passing through this town enroute to Alaska daily during the summer, it's the one place where you might want to book a room or a camp site in advance. From there you'll find the traffic and travelers will spread out more and this happens the further north you go. Most Alcan veterans say 300 miles a day is a good pace – one that will allow for plenty of stops to check out scenery or wildlife.

The best stretch? That's tough but some will argue it's the 330 miles from Fort Nelson (British Columbia) to Watson Lake, in the

Yukon. This is the day you cross the Rockies and along with the hairpin turns and granite peaks, you'll enjoy panoramas of the mountains; rest areas overlooking Summit Lake and a good chance of spotting wildlife, especially if you leave early in the morning.

It's always good to have Canadian currency on hand to purchase gasoline and not have to depend on the small stations along the way to cash your travelers' cheques for you. One or two of the major gasoline credit cards (see Credit Cards in the Facts for the Visitor chapter) come in handy, especially if you have a major breakdown. The other thing to keep in mind is that Tourism Yukon operates a number of visitor reception centers that provide a wealth of information and maps for drivers. The ones along the Alcan are:

Watson Lake
   Alaska Highway Interpretive Center, at the junction of the Alcan and Campbell St; (☎ (403) 536-7469)
Whitehorse
   Visitor Center near *Milepost 886*, adjacent to the Transportation Museum; (☎ (403) 667-2915)
Haines Junction
   Visitor Center, at Kluane National Park Headquarters; (☎ (403) 634-2345)
Beaver Creek
   Visitor Center, at *Mile 1202* of the Alcan in the heart of Beaver Creek; (☎ (403) 862-7321)

Books If you are planning to drive to and around Alaska, here are four specialized guidebooks that were written to be read as you bump and rattle your way through the north country. The books can be obtained through Wild Rose Guidebooks (☎ (907) 274-0471), PO Box 240047, Anchorage, AK 99525.

Roadside Geology of Alaska by Cathy Connor & Daniel O'Haire (Mountain Press Publishing, Missoula, Montana; 1988, 250 pages, $12.95) does an excellent job of covering the geology of Alaska you see from the road and how it shaped the state's history and development. Every road and sea route is covered, even dead-end roads in the Southeast. Along the way you learn what happened during the Good Friday Earthquake and why

miners turned up gold on the beaches of Nome – not dull reading by any means.

In *The Highway Angler* by Gunnar Pedersen (Wild Rose Guidebooks; 1989, 258 pages, $19.95) the author describes almost 200 streams, rivers, lakes and saltwater fishing spots in Southcentral Alaska that can be reached by a car and fished from the water's edge. Local maps and road mileages are also provided as well as information on inexpensive fishing adventures in the Kenai Peninsula, around Anchorage, in the Matanuska Valley and up the Glenn and Parks highways.

The Alaska Highway: An Insider's Guide by Ron Dalby (Fulcrum Publishing, 350 Indiana St, Golden, CO 80401; 1991, 204 pages, $15.95). It's not *The Milepost*, but this guide to the Alcan is far less commercialized and a much more personal view of the highway from an Alaskan who has traveled it for years. You won't find every campground or gas station listed but you'll find enough to get you there plus his anecdotes are more interesting than the ads in *The Milepost*.

Wildflowers along the Alaska Highway by Verna Pratt (Wild Rose Guidebooks; 1992, 240 pages, $20.00). Written for the amateur botanist, this guide to the wildflowers of the Alcan has species keyed by color and includes 497 color photographs and a check list for each 300-mile section of the road. There are also sections on poisonous and edible plants.

Hitching the Alcan

Hitching is probably more common in Alaska than it is in the rest of the USA and more so on the rural dirt roads such as the McCarthy Rd or the Denali Hwy than the major paved routes. But this doesn't mean it's a totally safe way of getting around. Just because we explain how it works doesn't mean we recommend it. If you are properly prepared and have sufficient time, thumbing the Alcan can be an easy way to see the country, meet people and save money. Many travelers thumb from Los Angeles to Anchorage, Fairbanks or Juneau in seven to

10 days for under $100. I once did it in four days, and that included a half-day wait at Haines Junction. There are, however, many 'dos', 'don'ts' and 'ifs' to hitching the highway.

The Alcan seems to inspire the pioneer spirit in travelers who drive it. Drivers are good about picking up hitchhikers, much better than those across the Lower 48 – the only problem is that there aren't as many of them. In some places along the route you may have to wait 30 minutes or longer before a car passes by. During the summer, the number of vehicles increases significantly, but if you're attempting the trip in early spring or late fall, be prepared to wait hours or even overnight at one of a handful of junctions along the way.

All hitchhikers should be self-sufficient with a tent, some food, water, warm clothing and a good book or two. While in many parts of the country a long wait can make you go stir-crazy, along the Alcan it isn't so bad. In fact, if the weather is good, it is enjoyable to sit out in the wide open land, surrounded by mountains and clean air. Hitchhikers must be patient and not over-anxious to reach their destination. Moving through the USA and southern Canada, you will get the usual short and long rides from one city to the next. Once you make it to Dawson Creek, it will probably only take you one or two longer rides to reach your destination.

Any part of the Alcan can be slow, but some sections are notorious. The worst can be Haines Junction, the crossroads in the Yukon where southbound hitchhikers occasionally have to stay overnight before catching a ride to Haines in Southeast Alaska. Longer waits may also occur if you are heading home in late summer or early fall and thumbing out of Glennallen, Tok or Delta Junction back into Canada and the Lower 48. The same holds true for those trying to hitchhike north from Dawson Creek in spring and early summer. A sign with your destination on it helps, as does displaying your backpack, which tells drivers you're a summer traveler.

The hardest part of the trip for many is crossing the US-Canadian border. Canadian officials usually pull cars over if the passengers are not of the same nationality as the driver, and they will ask to see proof of sufficient funds. Anybody without prearranged transport is required to have $80 per day to travel through Canada or a total of $200 to $250.

The Canadians are not hassling hitchhikers when they do this, they're just making sure that visitors don't get stuck somewhere for a week because they ran out of money. On the way to Alaska, most travelers will have these funds; on the way back, however, it may be difficult if you are at the end of your trip and without money.

Possible solutions are to catch a ride with someone driving the entire way or with a Canadian willing to tell officials you are a friend visiting. Three places to make contacts for a ride back to the Lower 48 are the Anchorage International (AYH) Hostel; the Wood Center in the middle of University of Alaska campus in Fairbanks, which has a noticeboard for students offering or needing rides; and the Chamber of Commerce hospitality center in Tok, where the free coffee pulls in many drivers before they continue into Canada. If you are heading north, the noticeboard outside the tourist office in Dawson Creek is worth checking as it often contains messages from people looking for somebody to help with fuel costs.

With luck, it can take you less than a week to hitchhike from Seattle to Fairbanks or Anchorage, but to be on the safe side, plan on the trip taking from seven to eight days. The route from Seattle to Alaska is good as it is the most direct and has the most traffic to Dawson Creek. This combines hitching along the Interstate 5 in Washington to the Canadian border, the Trans Canada Hwy 1 to Cache Creek, and Hwy 97 north to Dawson Creek and the Alcan.

An alternative to hitching the entire Alaska Hwy is to take the State Marine Ferry from Bellingham in Washington to Haines and start hitching from there, cutting the journey in half but still traveling along the highway's most spectacular parts. Haines, however, is a town of about 1150 people and traffic is light on the road to the Alcan at Haines Junction. It is best to hustle off the ferry and begin thumbing as vehicles unload, so that you can try to catch a driver heading north. Or seek out a lift while you are still on the boat by taping a notice outside the ship's cafeteria or showers.

A couple more 'dos' and 'don'ts' for those attempting this great adventure in hitchhiking. Taking drugs across the border is risky if you are driving and downright foolish when hitchhiking, as both Canadian and US customs officials make it a habit to search hitchhikers. With only a backpack, it's tough to hide drugs in a place where they won't look.

It is also good to have your Canadian money before leaving southern Canada; once hitching, it is hard to stop at a bank. Most businesses along the Alcan take US money, but they either give less than the normal 20 to 30% difference on the exchange rate or give none at all.

Discuss your travel plans with the driver and make sure that you're not let off at some deserted corner. This isn't a major problem if you're self-sufficient, but it's still nice to be near a town when waiting for a ride. No matter when you attempt the highway, make sure you have warm clothing, mittens, boots and a woollen hat; don't underestimate the weather and its ability to turn freezing cold at any time.

Keep in mind that there is a hostel at Tok (no phone) with 10 beds and tent space; call the Tok Visitor Center (☎ (907) 883-5887) for information. There is also a hostel (☎ (907) 895-5074) further along the Alcan near Delta Junction, just off the highway.

Finally, keep a journal. The pages of a notebook are great for making destination signs when you're standing along the road. But more importantly your experience of the Alaska Hwy legend will live on long after you've completed the trip because the road and the people you meet are one-of-a-kind.

SEA
The Inside Passage
From Bellingham As an alternative to the Alcan or to avoid doubling back on the highway, you can travel the Southeast's Inside Passage, a waterway made up of thousands of islands, fjords and mountainous coastlines. To many, the Southeast is the most beautiful area in the state and the Alaska Marine Ferries are the country's best public transport bargain.

The large 'blue canoes' of the State Marine Hwy are equipped with observation decks, food services, bars, lounges and solariums with deck chairs. You can rent a stateroom for overnight trips but most backpackers head straight for the solarium and sleep in one of the deck chairs or on the floor with a sleeping pad. On long-distance hauls from Bellingham, travelers even pitch their dome tents.

With its leisurely pace, travel on the marine ferries is a delightful experience. The midnight sun is warm and, apart from the scenery, the possibility of sighting whales, bald eagles or sea lions keeps most travelers at the side of the ship. This is also an excellent way to meet other independent travelers heading for a summer in the north country.

A big change in the state ferry system occurred in 1990 when Bellingham replaced Seattle as the new southern terminus of the Alaska Marine Hwy. The new terminus includes an information center, ticket office, luggage lockers and an outdoor seating area with a nice view of Bellingham Bay and the surrounding hills. It's 10 minutes north of the Bellingham International Airport in the historic Fairhaven shopping district, 87 miles north of Seattle. From the Interstate 5 Hwy, you depart west on Fairhaven Parkway (exit 250) for 1.1 miles and then turn right onto 12th St where signs will direct you to the terminal at the end of Harris Ave.

The ferries are extremely popular during the peak season from June to August. Reservations are needed for cabin or vehicle space and for walk-on passengers on departures from Bellingham. Space for summer sailings from Bellingham is often filled by April,

Top: The Alaskan Train on the way to Fairbanks (DP)
Bottom: Matanuska Ferry cruising Southeast Alaska (CP)

Top: Kayakers in Katmai National Park (DP)
Bottom: Harding Icefield, Kenai Fjords National Park (DS)

forcing walk-on passengers to wait stand-by for an available spot.

If you plan to depart Bellingham in June or July, it is best to make reservations. The state ferry's reservation office will take written requests any time and telephone requests from the first working day of January for summer sailings. As telephone lines are jammed most of the time after the first day of the year, it is wise to send in a written request as soon as you can figure out your itinerary.

The summer sailing schedule comes out in December and you can obtain one by contacting the Alaska Marine Hwy (☎ (907) 465-3941), PO Box R, Juneau, AK 99811. There is now a toll-free telephone number (☎(800) 642-0066 from the Lower 48) to handle schedule requests and reservations but you'll often find it nonstop busy, forcing you to pay for the call anyway.

The ferries to Alaska stop first at Prince Rupert in British Columbia, and then continue onto Ketchikan in Alaska. Most ferries then depart for Wrangell, Petersburg, Sitka, Juneau, Haines and Skagway before heading back south. A trip from Bellingham to Juneau takes from 2½ to four days depending on the route. Most ferry terminals are a few miles out of town and the short in-port time doesn't allow passengers to view the area without making a stopover.

If you intend to use the ferries to view the Southeast, obtain a current schedule and keep it handy at all times. State ferries stop almost every day at larger centers like Juneau, but the smaller villages may only have one ferry every three or four days and many places won't have a service at all.

There are six ships working Southeast Alaska; four of them are larger vessels that sail the entire route from Bellingham to Skagway. The *Columbia*, *Malaspina*, *Matanuska* and *Taku* all have cabins, lounges, eating facilities and public showers for both walk-on passengers and cabin renters.

The other two ships are smaller, do not have cabins, and serve out-of-the-way villages from Juneau or Ketchikan. In the summer, the *Aurora* sails between Ketchikan, Metlakatla, Hollis, Hyder and Prince Rupert. The *Le Conte* stops at Juneau, Hoonah, Angoon, Sitka, Kake, Tenakee Springs, Skagway, Haines and Petersburg, and makes a special run to Pelican once a month. The *Chilkat*, the original ship of the fleet, is no longer in service during the summer and only operates in the winter when another vessel is in dry dock.

It's important when you book a passage on the state ferry that you have an idea of what ports you want to visit along the route. Stopovers are free but you must arrange them, with exact dates, when you make the reservation or purchase the ticket. By doing so, a Bellingham-to-Haines ticket would then allow you to leave the boat at a handful of cities including Ketchikan, Petersburg and Juneau, at no additional cost. Once on the boat, you can still arrange a stopover but will be charged an additional fee.

If you plan to spend a good deal of time or the entire summer in the region, purchase a ticket to Juneau and then use that as your base, taking shorter trips to other towns on the *Le Conte*. The fare for walk-on passengers from Bellingham to Haines is $230, while the ticket from Bellingham to Juneau is $216.

One way to save money is to take a bus or hitchhike to Prince Rupert in British Columbia where the dramatic mountain scenery begins, and hop on the ferry from there. The fare from Prince Rupert to Haines is $112 and to Juneau $98. Fares for travel within the Southeast include Ketchikan to Juneau $72, Petersburg to Juneau $42, Juneau to Haines $18, Haines to Skagway $12, and Juneau to Angoon $22.

The *Alaska Marine Highway Schedule* is now a magazine with not only departure times and fares but also ads, blurbs on each port and a section entitled 'What to Expect on Board'. Here are a few tips they don't tell you. When boarding in Bellingham, it is best to scramble to the solarium and either stake out a lounge chair or at least an area on the floor. The solarium and observation deck are the best places to sleep as the air is clean and the night-time peace is unbroken. The other place to crash out is the indoor lounges, which can be smoky, noisy or both.

Backpackers are still allowed to pitch free-standing tents outside the solarium and the ferry staff even designated the correct area for doing so. Bring duck tape to attach the tent to the floor but remember that during the busy summer months tents tend to take up more space than two people really need in an already popular and crowded section of the ship.

Food on board is reasonable compared to what you will pay on shore, with breakfast and lunches costing around $6 and dinner $10. Still it's cheaper to bring your own grub and eat it in the solarium or the cafeteria. Some backpackers bring their own tea bags, coffee or Cup-a-Soup and then just purchase the cup of hot water. The pursers, however, do not allow any camp stoves to be used on board and are very strict about enforcing this. Bringing your own liquor is also prohibited as there is a bar aboard the larger ships, but I have yet to see a cruise where a happy traveler isn't handing out beers from an ice-chest in the solarium.

The only thing cheaper than the food on board are the showers. They're free on all ferries except the MV *Tustumena* and then it's only 25c for 10 minutes. It's the best bargain you'll find in Alaska.

There is a tariff for carrying on bicycles or kayaks, but compared to the cost of bringing a car or motorcycle it is very reasonable. The cost is only $37 to take what ferry officials call an 'alternative means of conveyance' from Bellingham to Haines. A bicycle can be a handy way to see at least part of a town without disembarking for a few days, while a summer (or even a lifetime) can be spent using the ferry system to hop from one wilderness kayak trip to another.

All fares listed in the book are for adults (which the Alaska State Ferry people consider to be anybody 12 years and older). You'll find the fares for children aged from six to 11 years about half the price of an adult fare and children under six years travel free. The ferry system also offers discount passes to both senior citizens and disabled persons.

Both are restricted to travel between Alaska ports for when space is available and can be used only for the *Le Conte*, *Aurora*, *Bartlett* and *Tustumena*. Applications for a disabled pass must be filed in advance by writing to: Alaska Marine Highway System, Pass Desk, PO Box 25535, Juneau, AK 99802-5535.

Above all else, when using the Alaska Marine Ferry system, check and double-check the departures of ferries once you have arrived in the Southeast. It is worth a phone call to the terminus to find out the actual arrival and departure times; the state ferries are notorious for being late or breaking down and having their departures cancelled. It's something that happens every summer without fail.

Leaving Prince Rupert If the Alaska State Ferries are full in Bellingham, one alternative is to begin your cruise in Seattle, utilizing two ferry systems before switching to the Alaska line in Prince Rupert.

From Pier 69 in the heart of Seattle off Alaskan Way, catch the *Victoria Clipper* to Victoria on Vancouver Island. During the summer, boats depart four times daily at 7.50, 8.40 and 9.30 am and 2.30 pm for a trip that takes from 2½ to 3 hours. One-way fare for walk-on passengers is $52. For pretrip planning or reservations call (800) 888-2535 when you are in the USA.

Once you land on Vancouver Island, head north to Port Hardy and catch the British Columbia ferry to Prince Rupert. From this Canadian city, there is a much better chance to board the Alaska Marine ferry because there are five vessels that connect Prince Rupert to Southeast Alaska. Port Hardy can be reached by bus from Victoria on Pacific Coast Lines (☎ (604) 385-4411), which leaves once a day at 6.20 am for a one-way fare of C$72. The bus depot is at 700 Douglas St, behind the Empress Hotel in the center of Victoria.

At Port Hardy, the BC ferries dock at Bear Cove, about five miles from town but there is a shuttle van service from the Island Coach Line bus terminal on Main St. At Bear Cove the *Queen of the North* sails to Prince Rupert one day and returns to Vancouver Island the next, maintaining this every-other-day schedule from June to the end of September. The trip is scenic and the daylight voyage takes 15 hours; the one-way fare for walk-on passengers is C$85. The same ship also makes a stop once a week at the isolated town of Bella Bella in British Columbia.

More information and complete schedules for the BC Ferries can be obtained by calling or writing to BC Ferries (☎ (604) 386-3431), 1112 Fort St, Victoria, British Columbia, Canada V8V 4V2. In Vancouver call (604) 669-1211 and in Seattle call (206) 441-6865 for ferry information and reservations.

From Hyder, Alaska Finally, if for some strange reason you can't catch an Alaska State ferry at Prince Rupert, there's one last alternative. Make your way east along the Yellowhead Hwy from Prince Rupert and then head north along the Cassiar Hwy. You travel 99 miles along the scenic Cassiar Hwy and then turn off at Meziadin Lake for Stewart. You can either hitch this route or catch a Greyhound bus to Terrace 91 miles east, from where Seaport Limousine Service (☎ (604) 636-2622) runs a bus (four hours) to Stewart daily from Monday to Friday. Right across the border from the British Columbia town is Hyder, a Southeast Alaska hamlet of about 100 people with a few cafés, bars and gift shops.

During the summer, the Alaska State ferry *Aurora* usually departs from here every Friday at 2 pm for Ketchikan, where you can continue north on one of several other boats. The one-way fare from Hyder to Ketchikan is $36.

Note It is important to double-check the departure time for the Hyder ferry as it may leave on Pacific Time as opposed to Alaska Time.

TOURS
The land of the midnight sun is also the land of the package tour. Every cruise-ship line and sightseeing company loves Alaska and the draw it has on travelers, especially older tourists with lots of disposable income but not a high sense of adventure.

Actually package tours can often be the most affordable way to see a large chunk of Alaska if your needs include the better hotels in each town and a full breakfast every morning. Just keep in mind they move quickly and rarely offer enough extra time to undertake such activities as a wilderness trek or a paddle into Glacier Bay National Park. A thumbnail stretch of just the largest tour companies follows.

Gray Line
You see this company so often throughout the state that it seems like Gray Line practically owns Alaska. Seattle-based Gray Line offers 17 package tours into the Far North, including six that begin and end in Seattle. They begin with the All Alaska Air Tour, an 11-day trip that includes Juneau, Anchorage, Denali, Fairbanks and even part of the Alcan for $2800 per person based on double occupancy – if this is Thursday, this must be Tok.

They also have a number of shorter ones that begin and end in Alaska such as the Denali/Columbia Discovery, seven days from Anchorage that includes Fairbanks, Denali and Columbia Glacier for $1250 per person. Or the just a Columbia Glacier Tour, a two-day bus and cruise-ship journey past the famous glacier for $290 per person. Most of their tours within the state are covered in detail in the regional chapters. If you're interested in a complete package tour throw away this book and call Gray Line at (800) 628-2449 to get their slick brochure.

American Sightseeing
Another biggie in Alaska, this company offers almost 40 itineraries throughout the state. Several begin with a cruise out of Seattle into Southeast Alaska and then continue on to Fairbanks, Denali and Anchorage. Spirit of Alaska is such a trip that runs 13 days and begins at $2649. That doesn't include airfare to Seattle or from Anchorage where the tour ends. Call Alaska Sightseeing at (800) 426-7702.

Knightly Tours

This company offers budget package tours by booking you on the Alaska State Marine Ferry system. Its Taku Tour is seven days out of Bellingham with a return flight from Anchorage to Seattle. Along the way you cruise the Inside Passage on the state ferry and then fly to Anchorage for two days. The cost is $1675 per person. Skip the Anchorage portion and it becomes known as the Katanuska Tour, six-days in Southeast Alaska that begins with a flight out of Seattle and a return to Bellingham on the ferry for $1265.

Knightly Tours also has a wide selection of other tours that cover the state in a fashion similar to Gray Line. For their complete brochure call them at (800) 426-2123.

Green Tortoise

When you include overnight lodging in the price of the tour, this usually sends the price beyond the reach of most budget travelers. The one exception is Green Tortoise Alternative Travel, the company with recycled buses whose seats have been replaced with foam-covered platforms, sofas and dinettes.

When not sleeping on the bus during night drives, Green Tortoise groups use state and federal campgrounds for accommodation and make an effort to include hiking, rafting and other outdoor activities on their itinerary. Food is not included in the fare but the bus travelers pool their funds to purchase goods in bulk and then prepare food in group cook-outs.

On Green Tortoise tours, group interaction is a large part of the experience. Everybody pitches in during meal time and spontaneous volleyball matches or Frisbee games are frequent activities during rest breaks. Beer and wine are allowed on the bus and people are encouraged to bring musical instruments. Although passengers could be any age, the vast majority of people are in their 20s or early 30s.

The company runs a five-week tour through Alaska in July which includes cruising through Southeast Alaska on the State Marine Ferry as well as stops in the Yukon Territory, Fairbanks, Denali National Park, Kenai Peninsula and then returning home along the Alcan. The bus can be picked up in San Francisco (California), Eugene and Portland (Oregon) or Seattle (Washington). The fare ($1500) covers everything except food and side trips. Food is another $250 if you participate in the group kitchen, and almost everybody does.

For more information write to Green Tortoise, Box 24459, San Francisco, CA 94124; or you can call a variety of offices around the USA, including San Francisco (415) 821-0803, Seattle (206) 324-7433 or New York (212) 431-3348.

ARRIVAL/DEPARTURE TAXES

There is a $10 fee for international travelers passing through customs in Anchorage coming from any foreign destination except Canada and Mexico. You, personally, never pay it as the fee is part of the taxes the airlines add onto the purchase of any ticket. When you leave Alaska, there are no additional state or airport departure taxes to worry about.

Getting Around

Touring Alaska on a budget means not departing from the roads and not traveling in areas without a State Marine Ferry dock. Travelers on a strict budget, however, shouldn't worry because although the roads and the marine highway (the cheapest ways to travel) cover only a quarter of the state, this quarter comprises the most popular regions of Alaska and includes the major attractions, parks and cities.

Even if there is a road to your destination, travel around Alaska is unlike travel in any other state in the country. The overwhelming distances between regions, and the fledgling public transport system makes getting around almost as hard as getting there. Any long visit to Alaska usually combines transport by car, bus, marine ferry, train and often a bush plane for access into the wilderness.

AIR
Bush Planes

When you want to see more than the roadside attractions, you go to a dirt runway or small airfield outside town and climb into a bush plane. With 75% of the state not accessible by road, these small single-engine planes are the backbone of intrastate transport. They carry residents and supplies to desolate areas of the Bush, take anglers to some of the best fishing spots in the country and drop off backpackers in the middle of prime, untouched wilderness.

The person at the controls is a bush pilot, someone who might be fresh out of the Air Force or somebody who arrived in Alaska 'way bee-fore statehood' and learned to fly by trial and error. A ride with such a person is not only transport to isolated areas and a scenic overview of the state but it also can include an earful of flying tales – some believable, some not.

Don't be alarmed when you hear that Alaska has the highest number of aeroplane crashes per capita in the country – it also has the greatest percentage of pilots. One in

every 58 residents has a license, and one resident in almost 60 owns a plane. That's six times more pilots and 16 times more planes per capita than any other state in the USA. Bush pilots are safe flyers who know their territory and its weather patterns; they don't want to go down any more than you do.

A ride in a bush plane is essential if you want to go beyond the common sights and see some of Alaska's most memorable scenery. In the larger cities of Anchorage, Fairbanks, Juneau and Ketchikan it pays to check around before chartering. In most small towns and villages, however, you will be lucky if there is a choice. In the following regional chapters, air-taxi services are listed under the town or area from which they operate.

Bush aircraft include float planes that land and take off on water and beach-landers with oversized tires that can use rough gravel shorelines as air strips. Other aircraft are equipped with skis to land on glaciers, sophisticated radar instruments for stormy areas like the Aleutian Islands, or boat racks to carry canoes or hard-shell kayaks.

The fares differ with the type of plane, its size, the number of passengers and the amount of flying time. On the average, a Cessna 185 that can carry three passengers and a limited amount of gear will cost up to $250 to charter for an hour of flying time. A Cessna 206, a slightly larger plane that will hold four passengers, costs up to $300 and a Beaver, capable of hauling six passengers with gear costs between $300 and $400 for an hour of flying time. Keep in mind that when chartering a plane to drop you off at an isolated Forest Service cabin or for a wilderness trek, you must pay for both the air time to your drop-off point and for the return to the departure point.

As a general rule, if one of the domestic carriers, Alaska Airlines or the intrastate carrier MarkAir, has a flight to your destination, it will be the cheapest way of flying there. Alaska Airlines provides the most extensive service for travel within Alaska and there is a huge difference between a one-way fare and a round-trip fare that is purchased 14 days in advance and includes staying over on a Saturday. A sample of Alaska Airlines fares for intrastate flights are Anchorage to Fairbanks one-way $146, round-trip $214; Juneau to Anchorage one-way $222, round-trip $311; Anchorage to Nome one-way $290, round-trip $406; and Anchorage to Kodiak one-way $193 and, get this, an APEX round trip is actually cheaper at $184.

Before chartering your own plane, check out all the possibilities first. Most air-taxi companies have regularly scheduled flights to small towns and villages in six to nine-seater aircraft with single-seat fares that are a fraction of the cost of chartering an entire plane. Others offer a 'mail flight' to small villages. These flights are run on a regular basis with one or two seats available to travelers.

Even when your destination is a Forest Service cabin or some wilderness spot, check with the local air-taxi companies. It is a common practice to match up a party departing from the cabin with another that's arriving, so that the air-charter costs can be split by filling the plane on both runs.

Air travel in small bush planes is expensive, but the more passengers, the cheaper the charter; two people chartering an entire plane, no matter what the distance, is a costly exercise.

Booking a plane is easy and can often be done the day before or at the last minute if need be. Double-check all pick-up times and places when flying to a wilderness area. Bush pilots fly over the pick-up point and if you are not there, they usually return, call the Forest Service and still charge you for the flight.

When flying in and out of bays, fjords or coastal waterways, check the tides before determining your pick-up time. It is best to schedule pick-ups and drop-offs at high tide or else you may end up tramping a half-mile through mud flats.

If a pilot doesn't want to fly, don't push the subject, just reschedule your charter. The pilot is the best judge of weather patterns and can see, or sometimes feel, bad flying conditions when others can't. Always schedule extra days around a charter flight. It's not uncommon to be 'socked in' by weather for a day or two until a plane can fly in. Don't panic, they know you are there. Think of the high school basketball team in the mid-1960s which flew to King Cove in the Aleutians for a weekend game, they were 'socked in' for a month before they could fly out again.

When traveling to small Bush towns, a scheduled flight or mail run is the cheapest way to go. Don't hesitate, however, to charter a flight to some desolate wilderness spot on your own; the best that Alaska has to offer is usually just a short flight away.

BUS

Regular bus services within Alaska are limited, but they are available between the larger towns and cities for independent travelers (as opposed to package tours) at reasonable rates. The only problem is that as one bus company goes under another appears, so the phone numbers, schedules, rates and pick-up points change drastically from one summer to the next. It pays to call ahead after arriving in Alaska to make sure that buses are still running to where you want to go.

Alaskon Express

These buses are the Gray Line motorcoaches which mainly serve travelers needing transport along the last leg of the Alcan from Whitehorse into Haines, Skagway, Anchorage or Fairbanks (see the Alcan section in the Getting There & Away chapter). You can also use the bus line to travel from Anchorage to Glennallen ($60), from Anchorage to Seward ($59), from Anchorage to Fairbanks ($60) or from Delta Junction to Fairbanks ($45).

From Haines, you can book a passage on Alaskon Express for the two-day run to Anchorage which leaves every Tuesday,

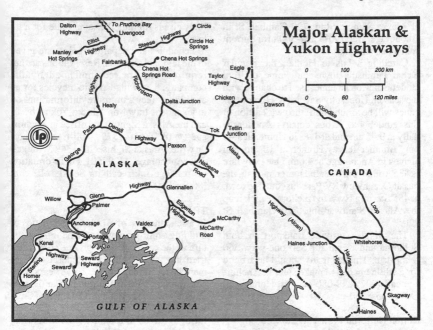

Major Alaskan & Yukon Highways

Wednesday, Friday and Sunday at 8.15 am for $189. The service is offered from mid-May to mid-September and the fare does not include overnight lodging at Beaver Creek. The same is true for Skagway where there is an Alaskon Express bus departing at 7.30 am on the same days, overnighting at Beaver Creek and reaching Anchorage at 7.15 pm. The reverse routes are also possible.

Local passenger boarding points, departure times and phone numbers are given in later chapters. For information or reservations while planning your trip, contact Gray Line of Alaska (☎ (800) 544-2206 – toll-free number), 300 Elliott Ave West, Seattle, WA 98119.

Alaska Direct Bus Line

Alaska Direct offers affordable transportation from Anchorage to the rest of the state on a number of routes. On Monday, Wednesday and Saturday another bus departs Anchorage at 6 am and reaches Haines Junction at 10 pm that night. The next day the bus continues its journey at noon and reaches Haines at 4 pm. One-way fare is $175.

A bus also departs Fairbanks on Monday, Wednesday and Saturday at 9 am, linking up with the run to Haines. One-way fare from Fairbanks to Tok is $40, to Haines $150.

Buses stop at the major hotels in Anchorage for passengers or you can pick them up at the company office at 125 Oklahoma on the north end of town. For more information call Alaska Direct Bus Line at (907) 277-6652 or (800) 770-6652.

Seward & Homer Bus Lines

This company provides services between Anchorage and Seward and in 1992 added a Homer bus line to its schedule. A bus leaves Seward daily at 9 am, reaches Anchorage at noon and then departs at 2.30 pm for the return run, arriving at Seward at 5.30 pm; the one-way fare is $30. Pick up these buses at 1915 Seward Hwy just north of Seward and at Alaska Samovar Inn, 720 Gambell St in Anchorage. Call (907) 224-3608 for current schedules and rates.

Catching a bus to Homer, the popular Kenai Peninsula town and home of Tom Bodette of Motel 6 fame, used to change with the season. Hopefully Seward & Homer Bus Lines will be around until the next edition of this guidebook. A bus departs Anchorage daily at 9.45 am and arrives in Homer at 3.45 pm. Another leaves Homer at 10 am and arrives in Anchorage at 4 pm. One-way fare is $35, round-trip $63. In Homer, pick up the bus at Oceanview RV Park just outside town at 455 Sterling Hwy. In Anchorage pick it up the Alaska Samovar Inn, 720 Gambell St 720.

They'll also provide transport to both Soldotna and Kenai for $30 one-way, $60 round-trip. This company should be around for a while but call to make sure: in Anchorage call (907) 278-0800 and in Homer call (907) 235-8280.

Denali National Park Van Service
A number of small companies offer van transport between Denali National Park and both Anchorage and Fairbanks. They come and go with a great regularly but generally offer the cheapest transport to the popular park and usually get you there well ahead of the train, an important consideration if you are hoping to arrange shuttle-bus rides, campground sites or backpacking permits.

In Anchorage, try Moon Bay Express (☎ (907) 274-6454) which departs daily from the hostel at 8 am and reaches the park at 1 pm. One-way fare is $35, round-trip $60. In Fairbanks, there is Fireweed Express (☎ (907) 488-7928) which departs from the Fairbanks Visitor Center at 8 am, reaches the park at 10.30 am and charges $25 one way.

Alaska-Yukon
This bus company is an arm of Alaska Sightseeing which mainly sells package tours, not seats for independent travelers; their high fares reflect this. Still, you can travel by Alaska-Yukon between Anchorage and Denali ($102), although just about every-body else is running the same route for a lot less.

Schedules and departure points are given in the regional chapters. Reservations are not required but are recommended by the company; they will also ship bicycles for an additional fee. For more information on independent travel on Alaska-Yukon buses call the Alaska Sightseeing office in Anchorage (☎ (800) 666-7375 – toll-free number) or write: Alaska Sightseeing, 349 Wrangell Ave, Anchorage, AK 99501. For information on package tours call its Seattle office at (800) 637-3334.

TRAIN
In a state the size of Alaska, the logistics of building a railroad were overwhelming at the turn of the century; many private companies tried but failed, leading to federal government intervention in 1912. Three years later, construction began on a route from the tent city of Anchorage to the boom town of Fairbanks. The line cut its way over what were thought to be impenetrable mountains, across raging rivers and through a wilderness as challenging as any construction crew had faced in the history of American railroading.

No wonder it took them eight years to build the Alaska Railroad. Today, it stretches 470 miles from Seward to Fairbanks. Despite the state's heavy dependence on air travel, the railroad remains a vital artery in moving people and goods across Alaska's interior. It is so important to Alaskans, that the state purchased the line from the federal government in 1985 for $23.3 million, making it the only state-owned commercial line in the country.

The Alaska Railroad provides a good, though rarely the cheapest, means of transport for travelers, and the scenery on each route is spectacular. You'll save more hitching along the George Parks Hwy, but few travelers, even those counting their dimes, regret booking a seat on the line and viewing one of the world's most pristine wilderness areas from the train's comfortable and, if you're willing to pay a little extra, even gracious carriages.

Anchorage to Fairbanks

The Alaska Railroad operates a year-round service between Fairbanks and Anchorage, and summer services from late May to mid-September between Anchorage and Whittier on Prince William Sound, and from Anchorage to Seward. Although the 114-mile trip down to Seward is a spectacular ride, unquestionably the most popular run is the 336-mile trip from Anchorage to Fairbanks with a stop at Denali National Park. Heading north, the train passes within 46 miles of Mt McKinley at *Mile 279*, a stunning sight from the train's viewing domes on a clear day, and then slows down to cross the 918-foot bridge over Hurricane Gulch, one of the most spectacular views of the trip.

North of the Denali National Park the train hugs the side of the Nenana River Canyon, passes numerous views of the Alaska Range and, 60 miles south of Fairbanks, crosses the 700-foot Mears Memorial Bridge (one of the longest single-span bridges in the world) over the Tanana River. Before the bridge was completed, this was the end of the line in both directions as people and goods were then ferried across the river to waiting cars on the other bank.

From late May to mid-September, two express trains run daily between Anchorage and Fairbanks with stops at Wasilla, Talkeetna, Denali National Park and Nenana. The express trains are geared for out-of-state travelers as they offer vista-dome cars for all passengers to share, reclining seats and a full dining and beverage service. You can also take your own food and drink on board, which isn't a bad idea as dinner on the train can cost between $12 and $15.

The northbound train departs Anchorage daily at 8.30 am, reaches Denali National Park at 3.50 pm and Fairbanks at 8 pm. The southbound train departs Fairbanks at 8 am, reaches Denali National Park at 12.30 pm and Anchorage at 8.30 pm. The one-way fare from Anchorage to Denali National Park is $85, and $115 to Fairbanks; from Fairbanks to Denali it is $45. From late September to mid-May the schedule changes to one train

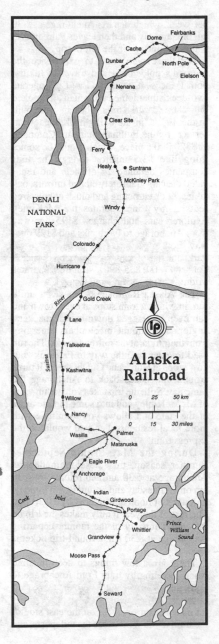

Alaska
Railroad

per week, which departs Anchorage at 8.30 am on Saturday and then leaves Fairbanks at 8 am on Sunday for the return trip.

For those who want to experience the railroad's golden era and travel in luxury, both Princess Tours and Gray Line operate two-deck superdome cars which are hooked onto the end of the train. The cars were built in the 1950s, in the twilight of elegant rail service, by the Pullman-Standard Company at $320,000 a piece, which would be something like $2.5 million today. The tour companies obtained 14 of them and renovated the cars' delicately etched mirrors, oak tables, thick carpeting and plush upholstered seats. Gray Line operates the McKinley Explorer cars and charges $195 one-way from Anchorage to Fairbanks and $129 one-way from Anchorage to Denali National Park; meals, of course, are extra. Princess Tours (☎ (800) 835-8907 – toll free) operates Midnight Sun cars at similar prices.

The Alaska Railroad still makes a 'milk run' in which a train stops at every town and can even be flagged down by backpackers, anglers and mountain climbers emerging from their treks at the railroad tracks. The run used to extend all the way to Fairbanks but now stops at Hurricane Gulch, where it turns around and heads back to Anchorage the same day. Still, the trip takes you within view of Mt McKinley and into some remote areas of the state and allows you to mingle with more local residents than you would on the express train.

During the May to mid-September summer season, this diesel train departs Anchorage at 6.30 am and returns by 4.30 pm on Wednesday and Saturday. On Sunday, it departs at noon and returns by 10.30 pm. The rest of the year it only makes the trip on the first Thursday of the month, departing Anchorage at 8.30 am; a round-trip ticket is $88.

There are a few things to keep in mind when traveling by train from Anchorage to Fairbanks. Arrive at the depot at least 15 minutes before departure as the express trains leave on time. Sit on the east side of the train if you want to see the mileposts, and for the best scenery sit on the west side for the stretch from Anchorage to Denali and then on the east side north of there.

The windows in all carriages are big but taking pictures through them is less than satisfactory due to their distorting curves and the dust on them. To avoid this, step outside to the platform between cars to shoot photos. Railroad and history buffs might be interested in obtaining a copy of the *Ride Guide to the Historic Alaska Railroad* by Laura Zahn & Anita Williams which provides insights along the way and can be purchased at the depot bookstores or through Wild Rose Guidebooks (PO Box 240047, Anchorage, AK 99524).

Finally, it pays to book early on this popular train; in Anchorage call (907) 265-2623. Before your trip call the toll free number, (800) 544-0552 or write to Alaska Railroad, PO Box 107500, Anchorage, AK 99510.

Anchorage to Whittier

There is rail service from Portage and Whittier during the summer. One run is timed to meet the arrivals and departures of the Alaska Marine Ferry, MV *Bartlett*, which crosses Prince William Sound to Valdez on a scenic cruise past the Columbia Glacier.

If you don't have a car, then the first leg is from Anchorage to Portage via a van shuttle service through Eagle Custom Tours. Their office is at 329 F St and the vans depart just around the corner at the Hilton Hotel. Vans depart daily beginning on Memorial Day at 8.30 am and 2.45 and 5.30 pm. One-way fare is $25.

To catch the ferry you need to pick up the 1.20 pm train out of Portage to arrive in Whittier at 2 pm and board the MV *Bartlett* by 2.45 pm. The train then departs Whittier at 3.30 pm and at the other end is an Eagle Custom Tours van waiting to take passengers back to Anchorage. Reservations for the train, ferry and the van are highly recommended as this is a popular excursion. Eagle Custom Tours can be reached by calling (907) 277-6228 or toll-free at (800) 248-3342.

Even if you don't plan to take the marine ferry across Prince William Sound, the trip to Whittier can be a fun day trip as it is a scenic and interesting town. The train ride, although only 40 minutes long, includes two tunnels, one of which is 13,090 feet long. The train shuttle makes several round trips daily; round-trip fare from Portage to Whittier is $16 per passenger and $70 for most cars, which includes driver fare.

There are four runs from Portage on Wednesday and Thursday at 10.15 am and 1.20, 5 and 7.30 pm and six trains during the rest of the week at 7.25 and 10.15 am and 1.20, 5, 7.30 and 10 pm. Tickets for the Whittier shuttle can be purchased from conductors at Portage. No reservations are taken for the rail service between Anchorage and Whittier, but passengers with confirmed ferry tickets have priority on boarding the 1.20 pm train from Portage.

Anchorage to Seward

Some say the ride between Anchorage and Seward is one of the most spectacular train trips in the world, rivaling those in the Swiss Alps or the New Zealand train that climbs over Arthur's Pass in the Southern Alps. From Anchorage, the 114-mile trip begins by skirting the 60-mile-long Turnagain Arm on Cook Inlet where travelers can study the bore tides. After leaving Portage, the train swings south and climbs over mountain passes, across deep river gorges and comes within half a mile of three glaciers: Spencer, Bartlett and Trail. The trip ends in Seward, a quaint town that is surrounded by mountains on one side and Resurrection Bay on the other.

The service is offered daily from late May to early September with a train departing Anchorage at 7 am and reaching Seward at 11 am. It departs Seward the same day at 6 pm and reaches Anchorage at 10 pm; round-trip fare is $75. The Seward run does not include a baggage car, like northbound trains to Denali, and ticket agents will warn you of 'hand-carried luggage only'. But don't despair if you have a hefty backpack or even a Klepper kayak. The train is rarely full and

extra luggage can be stored in the empty seats.

White Pass & Yukon Route

The White Pass & Yukon Railroad, a historical narrow-gauge railroad, was built at the height of the Klondike gold rush in 1898 and connected Skagway to Whitehorse. It was the first railroad to be built in Alaska and at that time the most northern line in North America.

The railroad was carved out of the rugged mountains by workers who, in places, had to be suspended by ropes from vertical cliffs in order to chip and blast the granite away. It followed the 40-mile White Pass Trail from Skagway to Lake Bennett where the miners would build rafts to float the rest of the way to Dawson City on the Yukon River. The line reached Whitehorse in 1900 and by then had made the Chilkoot Trail obsolete.

The railroad also played an important role in building the Alcan during WW II and was then used for transporting ore by mining companies in the Yukon Territory. In 1982, after world metal prices fell and the Canadian mines closed, operation of the White Pass & Yukon Railroad was suspended. But it has always been a popular tourist attraction, especially with big cruise ships, and in 1988, under the name of White Pass & Yukon Route, the railroad resumed limited service.

Today, it's still the incredible ride it must have been for the Klondike miners. The White Pass & Yukon Railroad has one of the steepest grades in North America as it climbs from sea level in Skagway to 2885 feet at White Pass in only 20 miles. The mountain scenery is fantastic, the old narrow-gauge cars intriguing, and the trip is a must for anyone passing through Southeast Alaska.

The train runs from late May to September and offers a one-day summit excursion, a Chilkoot Trail service (see the Trekking section in the Wilderness chapter for details) and a scheduled through-service for travelers who actually want to use it as a means of transport to Whitehorse and the Alcan. Northbound trains depart Skagway daily at 12.45 pm and arrive in Fraser at 2.30 pm, where passengers transfer to buses which arrive in Whitehorse at 6.30 pm (Pacific Time). Southbound buses depart Whitehorse at 8.15 am (Pacific Time), and the train leaves Fraser at 10.25 am arriving in Skagway at noon. The one-way fare from Skagway to Whitehorse is $92.

Knowing the history of this train, reservations wouldn't be a bad idea and can be made before your trip by calling the toll-free number (800) 343-7373, or writing to the White Pass & Yukon Route (☎ (907) 983-2217), PO Box 435, Skagway, AK 99840.

BOAT
State Marine Ferry
In the Southeast, the State Marine Ferry replaces bus services and operates from Juneau or Ketchikan to Skagway, Haines, Hoonah, Tenakee Springs, Angoon, Sitka, Kake, Petersburg, Hyder and Hollis, with an occasional special run to the tiny fishing village of Pelican (see the Inside Passage section in the Getting There & Away chapter for more details).

There are also marine ferry services in Southcentral and Southwest Alaska, where the MV Bartlett and the MV Tustumena connect towns along Prince William Sound and the Gulf of Alaska. The Southwest marine ferry does not connect with the Southeast line, but travelers can get around that by picking up an Alaska Airlines flight from Juneau to Cordova for $176 to continue their ferry trip around the Alaskan coast.

The MV Bartlett sails from Cordova and Valdez to Whittier across Prince William Sound, passing the Columbia Glacier along the way. The MV Tustumena provides a service between Seward, Homer and Seldovia on the Kenai Peninsula; Port Lions and Kodiak on Kodiak Island; and Valdez on the eastern shore of Prince William Sound.

In 1993, the Alaska State Ferry instituted a new direct service from Whittier to Cordova, on board the MV Bartlett. From May to September, the ship makes a round trip between the two sea ports on Monday and Tuesday, leaving Cordova at 6.30 am and arriving at Whittier at 1.30 pm and then turning around for the return trip at 2.45 pm. This makes the charming town of Cordova a delightful side trip from Anchorage as it would be possible to arrive on a Friday and return to Anchorage by Monday.

Also five times during the summer – in mid-May, June, July, August and September – the MV Tustumena also makes a special run to Sand Point, King Cove, Cold Bay and Dutch Harbor at the end of the Alaska Peninsula. The cruise takes three full days from Kodiak and is the cheapest way to see part of Alaska's stormy arm (see the Southwest section in the Bush chapter).

Sample fares for State Marine ferry travel along the Southwest routes for walk-on passengers are:

Valdez to Cordova	$28
Valdez to Whittier	$56
Valdez to Seward	$56
Seward to Kodiak	$52
Homer to Kodiak	$46
Kodiak to Dutch Harbor	$200
Homer to Seldovia	$16

DRIVING
Car Rental
Having your own car in Alaska, as in any other place, provides freedom and flexibility

---

The Business of Ferrying
The Alaska State Marine Ferry is not only a unique way to travel but it's big business to the state itself. The eight vessels travel 3500 miles of waterways, from Dutch Harbor to Ketchikan and almost 30 communities in between, and are responsible for bringing one of every 12 visitors to Alaska, or about 60,000 people in a summer. In 1992, the Alaska State Marine Ferry pumped more than $146 million into the Alaskan economy by carrying a record 415,000 travelers and 111,000 vehicles. ■

that cannot be obtained from public transport. Car rental, however, is a costly way to travel for one person but for two or more people it can be an affordable way to travel out of Anchorage, which has the best car rental rates by far. In Alaska, it isn't the charge per day for the rental but the mileage rate and the distances covered that make it so expensive. Outside Anchorage and Fairbanks, drivers will find gas 20 to 30c per gallon more expensive than in the rest of the USA.

The Alaska tourist boom of the 1980s has produced a network of cheap car-rental companies that offer rates almost 50% lower than those of national firms such as Avis, Hertz and National Car Rental. The largest of these is Practical Car Rental (it used to be Allstar and in Alaska they still refer to themselves as such), which has offices in 10 Alaskan towns including Anchorage, Fairbanks, Kenai, Ketchikan, Petersburg, Wrangell and Sitka. Their rates change from city to city but their branch in Anchorage (☎ (907) 561-0350), at 940 West Interational Airport Rd, offers a daily rate of $29 for a Ford Fiesta with unlimited mileage.

Other companies include Rent-A-Wreck, which has an outlet in Anchorage (☎ (907) 562-5499), at 541 West International Airport Rd. Rent-A-Wreck also has only a $29 daily rate and a weekly rate of $199. But you only get a 100 free miles a day, after that it's 25c a mile. In Fairbanks, there are also Allstar and a Rent-A-Wreck outlets but their rates jump up to $40 a day for a subcompact and 30c a mile. Without question, Anchorage is by far the best place to pick up a long-term rental.

The used cars, though functional, are not pretty and are occasionally stubborn about starting up right away. If there are three or four people splitting the cost, car rental is far cheaper than taking a bus, with all the freedom of a car.

All the used-car rental companies will be listed in the regional chapters under the towns where they maintain offices. Allstar, however, maintains a toll-free number (800) 426-5243 for those who want to reserve a car

in advance of their trip. Call Rent-A-Wreck at (800) 666-9799 toll-free or (907) 562-5499 and U-Save at (800) 272-8728 toll-free or (907) 479-7060.

Motorhome Rental

Want to be a road hog? You can also rent a motorhome in Alaska if that's the way you like to travel. And many people do. RVers flock to the land of the midnight sun in numbers that are astounding. There some roads, like the George Parks Hwy, that are almost nothing but an endless stream of trailers, pop-ups and land cruisers.

More than a dozen companies, almost all of them based in Anchorage, will rent you a motorhome, ranging from 20 to 35 feet in length, that accommodates up to six people. The price can vary from $100 to $150 per day but again you have to consider all the extra charges. Many places offer a 100 free miles per day and 15 to 25 c per mile for any additional mileage.

You also have to pay for insurance and possibly even a 'housekeeping kit' – the pots, pans and sheets you'll need to survive. It's best to anticipate a daily fee of between $150 and $200 and that full-hook-up campgrounds are going to cost you from $15 to $20 a night. Still when divided between four to six people it comes to around $28 to $35 a day per person for both transport and a soft bed at night. Not such a bad deal if you can round up several other people who want to share the same itinerary. Other costs include gasoline, food and camping sites.

You almost have to reserve a motorhome in advance to be insured of securing one when you arrive during the summer. A few of the larger Anchorage rental companies include Alaska Panorama Fleet (☎ (907) 561-8762); Clippership Motorhome Rentals (☎ (800) 421-3456 toll-free); and ABC Motorhome Rentals (☎ (800) 421-7456 toll-free).

BICYCLE

For those who want to bike it, Alaska offers a variety of cycling adventures on paved roads during long days with comfortably cool temperatures. Most cyclists hop on the State Marine Ferry, where they can carry their bike on for an additional fee ranging anywhere from $7 up to $38 for the longest run from Bellingham to Skagway. The individual Southeast communities are good places to gear up for the longer rides up north.

From Haines, you can catch an Alaskon Express bus to Tok or Anchorage in the heart of Alaska. There is no charge for the bike but be prepared to have it stored in the luggage compartment under the bus. You can also take your bike on Alaska Airlines for a $30 excess-baggage fee each way; you don't have to put the bike in a crate, merely hand it over to the ticket officials at the counter.

Summer cyclists have to take some extra precautions in Alaska. There are few towns with comprehensively equipped bike shops so it is wise to carry not only metric tools but also a tube-patch repair kit, brake cables, spokes, brake pads and any other parts that might be needed during the trip.

Due to the high rainfall, especially in the Southeast, waterproof saddle bags are useful, as are tire fenders. Rain gear is a must, and storing gear in zip-lock plastic bags within your side saddles is not being overcautious. Warm clothing, mittens and a woollen hat should be carried, along with a tent and rain tarpaulin.

Some roads do not have much of a shoulder – the Seward Hwy between Anchorage and Girdwood being the classic example – so cyclists should utilize the long hours of sunlight to pedal when the traffic is light in such areas. It is not necessary to carry a lot of food, as you can easily restock every couple of days on all major roads.

Most cyclists avoid gravel, but biking the Alcan (an increasingly popular trip) does involve riding over some short gravel breaks in the paved asphalt. When riding along gravel roads, figure on making 50 to 70% of your normal distance and take spare inner tubes – flat tires will be a daily occurrence.

Mountain bikers, on the other hand, are in heaven with such gravel roads as the Denali Hwy in the Interior, the logging roads on Prince of Wales Island in the Southeast and

the park road in Denali National Park. Mountain bikers are even pedaling the Dalton Hwy to Prudhoe Bay.

The following cities and towns in Alaska have bike shops that offer a good selection of spare parts and information on riding in the local area. However, by the end of the summer many are low on, or completely out of, certain spare parts.

Anchorage
    The Bicycle Shop, 1035 West Northern Lights Blvd; (☎ (907) 272-5219)
    Gary King Sporting Goods, 202 East Northern Lights Blvd; (☎ (907) 279-7454)
    REI Co-op, 1200 West Northern Lights Blvd; (☎ (907) 272-4565)
Fairbanks
    Beaver Sports, 2400 College Rd; (☎ (907) 479-2494)
    Campbell Sports, 609 3rd St; (☎ (907) 452-2757)
Juneau
    Adventure Sports, 2092 Jordan Ave (near Nugget Mall); (☎ (907) 789-5696)
Sitka
    Southeast Diving & Sport Shop, 203 Lincoln St; (☎ (907) 747-8279)
Haines
    Sockeye Cycle, Portage St in Fort Seward; (☎ (907) 766-2869)

The following are the more common long-distance trips undertaken by cyclists during the summer in Alaska.

Anchorage to Fairbanks

This ride can be done comfortably in five to six days along the George Parks Hwy, and is 360 miles of generally flat road with scattered sections of rolling hills. Highlights are the impressive views of Mt McKinley and an interesting side trip into Denali National Park where cyclists can extend their trip with a ride along the gravel park road. Keep in mind the stretch from Anchorage to Denali National Park is busy road with heavy traffic most of the summer. To avoid this, many cyclists take the Alaska Railroad part of the way and then bike the rest; there is an excess-baggage charge for carrying your bicycle on the train.

Anchorage to the Kenai Peninsula

There is an endless number of possible bike trips or combinations of biking and hiking adventures in the Kenai Peninsula. You can also utilize the Southwest runs of the Alaska State Marine Ferry. A common trip is to cycle from Anchorage to Homer, take the ferry to Kodiak, then return via Seward and pedal back to Anchorage.

This is a seven to 12-day trip depending on how much time you spend in Homer and Kodiak; the distance by bike is 350 miles with an additional 400 miles by ferry. Bikes can also be used to hop from one hiking trail to another in some of Alaska's most pleasant backcountry. Or, you can cycle to Portage, combine the rail and ferry transport across Prince William Sound to Valdez and then head north. The Kenai Peninsula can also be a nightmare of heavy traffic for bikers while the Seward Hwy from Anchorage to Girdwood is narrow with little shoulder in many places. The best bet is to begin with a bus trip at least to Portage.

Fairbanks to Valdez

This is perhaps one of the most scenic routes cyclists can undertake and also one of the hardest. The six to seven-day trip follows the Richardson Hwy from Delta Junction to Glennallen and then goes onto Valdez; a total of 375 miles. It includes several hilly sections and tough climbs over Isabel Pass before Paxson, and Thompson Pass at 2771 feet, 25 miles east of Valdez.

New brake pads are a must, along with rain gear and warm clothing, as the long ride downhill from Thompson Pass is often a cold and wet one. From Valdez, you can take a ferry across Prince William Sound and head back to Anchorage, or backtrack to the Glenn Hwy and eventually to Anchorage.

North Star Bicycle Route

This 3400-mile ride is a summer-long adventure that begins in Missoula (Montana) and ends in Anchorage. Along the way you cross the Canadian Rockies, pick up the Alcan in British Columbia, pedal through the Yukon Territory and follow Alaskan highways from Tok to Anchorage.

Although the Alcan is now paved, miles of rough surface still exist due to construction work, making this a trip only for experienced cyclists looking for a grand adventure. The trip can be reduced significantly by either bussing part of the route in Canada (see the Bussing the Alcan section in the Getting There & Away chapter) or by utilizing the State Marine Ferry from Bellingham. It is 446 miles from Haines to Tok, and 328 miles from Tok to Anchorage, a ride that can be done comfortably in five days.

Those interested in this route could pick up bicycle maps from Missoula north to Jasper, Alberta from Bicycle Travel Association (☎ (406) 721-1776), PO Box 8308, Missoula, MT 59807. The two-map set costs $15.95. This nonprofit bicycle travel association also sells several other guides including *The Canadian Rockies Bicycling Guide* ($9.95) that would come in handy for anybody contemplating this once-in-a-lifetime ride.

Cycling Books You might also consider the *Alaska Bicycle Touring Guide* by Pete Praetorius and Alys Culhane (The Denali Press, PO Box 021535, Juneau, AK 99802-1535; 1989, 328 pages, maps, photos, $17.50), which is the first guide put together for touring Alaska on two wheels. It's been called the 'bicycling equivalent of *The Milepost*' for its thorough description of routes throughout the state, including two that go north of the Arctic Circle.

Mountain Bike Alaska by Richard Larson (Glacier House Publications, PO Box 201901, Anchorage, AK 99520; 1991, 120 pages, maps, $14) is a guide to 49 trails for mountain bikers. They range from the Denali Hwy and the Denali park road to many of the traditional hiking trails on the Kenai Peninsula.

The Wilderness

Alaska is many things, but first and foremost it is the great outdoors; you go there for the mountains, the trails, the wildlife and the camping – the adventure of it all. If retrieving the morning newspaper is all the fresh air you can handle, Alaska can be a dull place. But if you're a camper, hiker, backpacker or someone who likes to spend a lot of time at scenic lookouts, the north country has two things for you – extensive wilderness areas and long days to enjoy them in.

Compared to the cost of getting there, the cost of enjoying most of the backcountry is relatively low. Hiking is free and even the most expensive camping fee is cheap compared to what motels will charge. Camping areas vary across Alaska from places with cosy lounges and heated bathrooms to out-of-town clearings.

The different adventures available in Alaska vary as much; you can take a three-hour hike on a well-maintained trail that begins from the center of Juneau or a week-long trek in Wrangell-St Elias National Park where there are no trails at all.

The best way to enter the state's wilderness is to begin with a day hike the minute you step off the State Marine Ferry or depart from the Alcan. Once having experienced a taste of the woods, many travelers forgo the cities and spend the rest of their trip taking long-term adventures into the backcountry to make the most of Alaska's immense surroundings.

THE WILDERNESS EXPERIENCE

Alaska, which covers over 550,000 sq miles, is serviced by only 5000 miles of public highway. Most of the recent tourist boom is centered around these roads and visitors tend to cling to them. Ironically, this causes the state, with all its space, to have its share of over-crowded parks and campgrounds.

Residents of Alaska know this and tend to stay away from heavily touristed places like Denali National Park during the middle of summer. They also know how to escape into the backcountry – those wearing Sierra Club T-shirts call it a 'wilderness experience'. Others throw a backpack together and say they're 'going out the road for a spell'. It's all the same – a journey into the woods, away from the city, neighbors, TV and other signs of human existence. That is the greatest enjoyment Alaska can offer anyone – a week of nothing but nature in all its splendor.

You have to be careful on such adventures. In a true wilderness experience, you are completely on your own. But don't let the lack of communication with the civilized world prevent you from venturing into the wilderness – it's the best part. On an ideal trip, you won't meet another person outside your party, see a boat or hear the hum of a bush plane.

In this perfect tranquillity, all the worries and pressures of day-to-day living are cast aside and you begin to discover yourself in the natural setting. More enjoyment and satisfaction can be derived from a few days in the wilderness than from a three-week bus tour. Some people, once they enter the wilderness, never get it out of their blood.

Local hiking trails and camping areas are covered in the regional chapters. The 23 trips described in this chapter are popular wilderness excursions that backpackers can do on their own if they are properly equipped and have sufficient outdoor experience. These are either maintained trails or natural paddling routes enjoyed by backpackers every year. Some trips cannot provide a true 'wilderness experience' as they are too popular during the summer, but many are in isolated areas and offer a glimpse of pristine backcountry.

Those people who didn't come to Alaska with the right gear or who lack camping knowledge can still escape into the woods and return safely. There are two ways of doing this. The first way is to join a guided expedition where equipment, group organization and knowledge of the area are supplied. Guided expeditions, which cover the state, range from half a day to three weeks and cost between $125 and $175 per person per day (a list of guide companies is given in the Tours section at the end of this chapter). The other way to sample the wilderness, without enduring a 20-mile hike or hiring the services of a tour guide, is to rent a Forest Service cabin.

GENERAL INFORMATION
Who Controls What

With almost three-quarters of the state locked up, it's good to know what federal or state agency administers the land you want to hike on. Almost all of the recreational areas, parks and forests, including the campgrounds and trails in them, are controlled by one of five agencies.

US Forest Service (USFS) This federal bureau handles the Tongass and Chugach national forests which cover practically all of the Southeast and Eastern Kenai Peninsula, including Prince William Sound. The US Forest Service can provide information on the 190 public-use cabins it maintains, along with hiking, kayaking, canoeing and other recreational opportunities in its domain. Most USFS campgrounds charge from $5 to $8 per day, depending on the facilities, and have a 14-day limit. The addresses for the main USFS offices are given in the Accommodation section of this chapter but there are also smaller offices in Craig, Wrangell, Hoonah and Yakutat.

In the Southeast, each USFS office has a copy of the *Southeast Alaska Community Opportunity Guide*, which is put together by the Forest Service and contains information about camping, trails, fishing areas and cabins throughout Tongass National Forest. If you plan to spend any time in a Southeast town, it is well worth your while to venture to the USFS office and thumb through this reference guide.

National Park Service The National Park Service administers Denali, Glacier Bay and Katmai national parks and preserves, all of which have maintained campgrounds and are accessible by either an Alaska Airlines flight or by road. The seven campgrounds in Denali National Park are scattered across the park. Morino Campground at the entrance to the park is a no-frills area for backpackers without vehicles with sites for $3 a night.

Two other national parks, Kenai Fjords and Wrangell-St Elias, also have roads leading into them but their facilities are not nearly as well developed for visitors as the first three national parks mentioned – of course many people consider that a plus. Without the visitor centers, camper van hook-ups, hot showers and expensive lodges, these national parks escape the midsummer crush of tourists that the other parks suffer.

There are three other national parks (Gates of the Arctic, Kobuk Valley and Lake Clark) and three national preserves (Aniakchak National Monument & Preserve, Noatak and Yukon-Charley Rivers national preserves) that are administered by the National Park Service. All of them are only accessible by bush plane or boat and offer no facilities within the park. Most visitors reach them through guide companies which venture into the wilderness areas by raft, kayak or foot.

The National Park Service also maintains numerous national monuments and national historical parks for a total of 54 million acres. For addresses and more information on the individual parks, check the regional chapters. For general information on all parks, contact the main National Park Service offices: Alaska Public Lands Information Center (☎ (907) 271-2737), 605 West 4th Ave, Suite 105, Anchorage, AK 99501-2231; and the National Park Service (☎ (907) 586-7137), 709 West 9th St, Juneau, AK 99801

Bureau of Land Management (BLM) The Bureau of Land Management is the federal agency that maintains much of the wilderness around and north of Fairbanks. It has developed 25 camping areas and a dozen public-use cabins in the Interior as well as two popular trails (Pinnell Mountain and

White Mountain), both off the highways north of Fairbanks. Most of the cabins are in the White Moutains National Recreation Area whose trails are primarily winter routes and often impassable during the summer. Camping, free in most BLM campgrounds, is handled on a first-come-first-serve basis. The cabins are $15 a night and most of them are within 100 miles of Fairbanks.

The BLM offices have good publications on the Taylor Hwy, a secondary road that is an adventure in itself, and national wild rivers such as the Gulkana, Fortymile and Delta. For more information contact the BLM District Office (☎ (907) 474-2200); 1150 University Ave, Fairbanks, AK 99709 or the BLM District Office (☎ (907) 822-3217), PO Box 147, Glennallen, AK 99588.

US Fish & Wildlife Service This arm of the Department of the Interior administers 16 wildlife refuges in Alaska that total more than 77 million acres. The largest, Yukon Delta that surrounds Bethel in Western Alaska, covers almost 20 million acres.

The purpose of wildlife refuges is to protect habitats; visitor use and developed recreational activities are strictly an afterthought. Most of the refuges are in remote areas of the Bush with few, if any, developed facilities – guide companies are the only means by which most travelers visit them. The one exception is Kenai National Wildlife Refuge, which can be reached by road from Anchorage. This preserve has 15 campgrounds, of which the Kenai-Russian River Campground is by far the most popular, and over 200 miles of hiking trails and water routes, including the popular Swanson River Canoe Route.

The Kodiak National Wildlife Refuge, although considerably more remote and more expensive to reach than Kenai, does offer nine wilderness cabins similar to USFS cabins for $15 per night. For more information about individual areas, see the regional chapters. For general information contact the Regional Office (☎ (907) 786-3487), US Fish & Wildlife Service, 1011 East Tudor Rd, Anchorage, AK 99503.

Alaska Division of Parks The Alaska Division of Parks & Outdoor Recreation controls more than 100 areas in the Alaskan state park system, ranging from the 1.5-million-acre Wood-Tikchik State Park, north of Dillingham on Bristol Bay, to small wayside parks along the highway. The areas also include state trails, campgrounds, wilderness parks and historic sites, all maintained by the state.

Among the more popular parks which offer a variety of recreational opportunities are Chugach, Denali State Park south of Mt McKinley, Nancy Lake Recreational Area just south of Willow, Captain Cook State Recreation Area on the Kenai Peninsula and Chilkat State Park south of Haines. Most campgrounds cost $6 a night with a couple of the more popular ones charging $10 a night.

For travelers planning to spend a summer camping in Alaska, a state park camping pass, allowing unlimited camping for a year, is a wise investment at $75. The state parks division also rents out recreational cabins in the Southeast, the Southcentral and the Interior regions for $20 to $25 a night. To obtain an annual Alaska Camping Pass in advance, send a cheque or money order to one of the following offices: Alaska Division of Parks (☎ (907) 561-2020), PO Box 7001, Anchorage, AK 99510, or the Alaska Division of Parks (☎ (907) 465-4563), 400 Willoughby Center, Juneau, AK 99801.

Backpacking

Camping, hiking and backpacking in Alaska are more dangerous than in most other places. The weather is more unpredictable, the climate harsher, and encounters with wildlife a daily occurrence. Unpredictable situations like getting lost, snow storms in the middle of the summer or being 'socked in' by low clouds and fog for days while waiting for a bush plane happen annually to hundreds of backpackers in Alaska.

If you're planning to wander beyond roadside parks, don't take your adventure lightly. You must be totally independent in the wilderness – a new experience for most city dwellers. You need the knowledge and equipment to sit out bad weather, endure an overturned boat or assist an injured member of your party.

The information and suggestions in this chapter are only a guide to backpacking in Alaska, not a complete lesson on surviving the outdoors. For that you should consult a survival manual such as *Walking Softly in the Wilderness* by John Hart (Sierra Club Books). It can not be stressed enough that the most important thing about Alaska wilderness is to be prepared before you enter the woods.

Backcountry Conduct

It is wise to check in with the US Forest Service (USFS) office or National Park headquarters before entering the backcountry. By letting them know your intentions, you'll get peace of mind knowing that someone knows you're out there. If there is no ranger office in the area, the best place to advise of your travel plans is the air charter service responsible for picking up your party.

Do not harass wildlife while traveling in the backcountry. Avoid startling an animal, as it will most likely flee, leaving you with a short and forgettable encounter. If you flush a bird from its nest, leave the area quickly, as an unattended nest leaves the eggs vulnerable to predators. Never attempt to feed wildlife; it is not healthy for you or the animal.

Finally, be thoughtful when in the wilderness as it is a delicate environment. Carry in your supplies and carry out your trash, never littering or leaving garbage to smoulder in a fire pit. Always put out your fire and cover it with natural materials or better still don't light a fire in heavily traveled areas. Use biodegradable soap and do all washing away from water sources. In short, practice low-impact no-trace camping and leave no evidence of your stay. Only then can an area remain a true wilderness.

DANGERS & ANNOYANCES
Drinking Water

Alaska's water is affected by *Giardia lamblia*, or 'beaver fever' as it is known among backpackers. The parasite is found in surface water, particularly beaver ponds, and is transmitted between humans and animals. For information on water purification and how to treat giardia, see the Health section in the Facts for the Visitor chapter.

Water from glacial rivers may appear murky but it can be drunk, if necessary, in small quantities, although drinking too much of it tends to clog up the internal plumbing. The murk is actually fine particles of silt scoured from the rock by the glacier.

Insects

Alaska is notorious for its biting insects. In the cities and towns you have few problems, but out in the woods you'll have to contend with a variety of insects, including mosquitoes, black flies, white-socks, no-see-ums and deer flies. Coastal areas, with their cool summers, have smaller numbers of insects than the Interior. Generally, camping on a beach where there is some breeze is better than pitching a tent in the woods. In the end, just accept the fact that you will be bitten.

Mosquitoes can often be the most bothersome pest. They emerge from hibernation before the snow has entirely melted away, peak in late June and are around until the first frost. It's the female of the species which is after your blood, and they're most active early in the morning and at dusk. Luckily, even a slight wind grounds them. You can combat mosquitoes by wearing light colors, a snug-fitting parka and by tucking the legs of your pants into your socks or boots.

The best protection by far is a high-potency insect repellent; the best contain a high percentage of Deet (diethyltoluamide), the active ingredient. A little bottle of Musk Oil or Cutters can cost $6 or $7 (they contain 100% Deet) but it's one of the best investments you will make.

Unfortunately, repellents are less effective, and some people say useless, against black flies and no-see-ums. Their season runs from June to August and their bite is far more annoying. The tiny no-see-um bite is a prolonged prick after which the surrounding skin becomes inflamed and itches intermittently for up to a week or more. Unlike the mosquito, these insects will crawl into your hair and under loose clothing in search of bare skin.

Thus, the best protection and a fact of life in Alaska's backcountry are long-sleeved shirts, socks that will allow you to tuck your pants into them and a snug cap or woollen hat. You also see many backcountry travelers packing head nets. They're not something you wear a lot, it drives you crazy looking through mesh all day, but when you really need one they are a lifesaver. As they are relatively light to pack and inexpensive, you might as well pack one if you are doing extensive wilderness travel in areas like the Brooks Range or Katmai National Park.

Other items you might consider are bug jackets and an after-bite medication. The mesh jackets are soaked in insect repellent and kept in a zip-lock bag until you wear them and some people say they are the only effective way to keep no-see-ums at bay. After-bite medications contain ammonia and are rubbed on; while this might drive away your tent partner, it does soothe the craving to scratch the assortment of bites on your arms and neck.

Bears

You could spend the entire summer in Alaska without ever seeing a bear, or you could be on an early morning stroll in Juneau and see one scrambling towards the woods a block away from the Governor's Mansion. The fact is, as one ranger put it, 'no matter where you travel in Alaska, you'll never be far from a bear'.

Too often, travelers decide to skip a wilderness trip because they hear a local tell a few bear stories. Your own equipment and outdoor experience should determine whether you take a trek into the woods, not the possibility of meeting a bear on the trail. You have a much better chance of being mugged in Los Angeles than getting mauled by a bear in Alaska. Or, as the Alaska Department of Fish & Game points out, the probability of being injured by a bear is one-fiftieth of the chance of being injured in a car accident on Alaskan highways.

The best way to avoid bears is to follow a few common-sense rules. Bears do not roam the backcountry looking for hikers to maul; they only charge when they feel trapped, when a hiker comes between a sow and her cubs or when they are enticed by food. It is a good practice to sing or clap when traveling through thick bush so you don't bump into a bear. That has happened, and usually the bear feels threatened and has no choice but to defend itself. Don't camp near bear food sources or in the middle of an obvious bear path. Stay away from thick berry patches, streams choking with salmon or beaches littered with bear scat.

Other people attach 'bear bells' all over their backpack, boots and clothing. Bells will alert any bear in the immediate area, but unfortunately will also scare all other wildlife, even the species you want to see. The constant ringing not only eliminates the chances to view animals but blocks out the natural sounds of the woods that ease the mind and fill the soul with wonder.

Leave the pet at home; a frightened dog only runs back to its owner and most dogs are no match for a bear. Set up your 'kitchen' – the spot where you will cook and eat – 30 to 50 yards away from your tent. In coastal areas, many backpackers eat in the tidal zone, knowing that when the high tide comes in all evidence of food will be washed away.

At night try to place your food sacks 10 feet or more off the ground by hanging them in a tree, placing them on top of a tall boulder or putting them on the edge of a rock cliff. In a treeless, flat area, cover up the food sacks with rocks. A bear is not going to see the food bags, it's going to smell them. By packaging all food items in zip-lock plastic bags, you greatly reduce the animal's chances of getting a whiff of your next meal. Avoid odoriferous foods such as bacon or sardines in areas of high concentrations of bears.

And please, don't take food into the tent at night. Don't even take toothpaste, hand lotion, suntan oils or anything with a smell.

If a bear smells a human, it will leave; anything else might encourage it to investigate.

If you do meet a bear on the trail, *do not* turn and run. Stop, make no sudden moves, and begin talking calmly to it. Bears have extremely poor eyesight and speaking helps them understand that you are there. If it doesn't take off right away, back up slowly before turning around and leave the area. A bear standing on its hind legs is not on the verge of charging, only trying to see you better. When a bear turns sideways or begins a series of woofs, it is only challenging you for space – just back away slowly and leave. But if the animal follows you, *stop* and hold your ground.

Most bear charges are bluffs, with the animal veering off at the last minute. Experienced backpackers handle a charge in different ways. Some throw their packs three feet in front of them, as this will often distract the bear long enough for them to back away. Others fire a hand-held signal flare over the bear's head (but never at it) in an attempt to use the noise and sudden light to scare it away. If an encounter is imminent, drop into a fetal position, place your hands behind your neck and play dead.

Some people carry a gun to fend off bear charges. This is a skilled operation if you are a good shot, a foolish one if you are not. With a gun, you must drop a charging bear with one or two shots as it will be extremely dangerous if only wounded. Others are turning to defensive aerosol sprays which contain capsicum (red pepper extract) that cost $40 a piece and have been used with some success for protection against bears.

Art, the pilot for Glacier Bay Airways, pointed and said something but I didn't hear him. The rattle and roar of the small float plane was deafening and despite sitting next to him I couldn't catch his words the first time. The second time he turned to me and shouted it in my ear and it came out loud and clear over the thunder of the propeller.

Black bears!

I followed his outstretched finger and saw a pair of black dots far below us, moving along the shoreline in search of something to eat. Thirty seconds later, Art pointed out another one and then two more before he made a sharp turn and a smooth landing in the west arm of Dundas Bay.

What a welcome committee at Glacier Bay National Park: five bears in Dundas Bay, the starting point for our 15-day journey in this icy wilderness. Five bears and we hadn't even taken our first stroke yet but it turned out to be only the beginning.

After the float plane roared off my paddling partner and I quickly assembled our Klepper kayak and then crammed every inch of its hull with equipment, two weeks of freeze-dried food and ourselves. Then we shoved off.

It was 10.30 am and we hadn't paddled more than a mile and a half when we spotted bear number six meandering across a grassy flat. By the time we pulled into a small cove to make camp that first evening we had spotted six more. All black bears and all of them along the shoreline.

Our timing was perfect; we were witnessing the awakening of bruins throughout the bay. They had a late spring in Southeast Alaska and these bears were coming out of the mountains and heading straight for the lowlands, looking for something to eat after a long winter's nap.

In another week or two, most would retreat deeper into the lush spruce forest inland but right now they all seem to be on the shoreline for the first available food of the summer. We would silently glide by them within 20 or 30 yards and watch them munch down on grass or work at opening a mussel. Most would pick up our scent, stand up to squint at us and then leisurely move on. One big male, who easily tipped the scales past 350 pounds, didn't. He looked at us eye-to-eye, with grass still hanging out of his month, and then kept eating.

In the evening, we paddled the empty Klepper to a stream in the north arm of Dundas Bay to try our luck fishing. Just as we picked up our poles and began to hike towards the mouth, we stopped dead in our tracks. There is the grassy area surrounding the small river, out in the open within several hundred yards of each were four more bears, giving us 16 sightings in one day.

'Maybe they're having a convention', said my partner. Maybe, but we quickly retreated, deciding not to stick around to ask. ∎

These sprays are effective at a range of six to eight yards but must be discharged downwind. If not, you will just disable yourself.

Be extremely careful in bear country, but don't let the bears' reputation keep you out of the woods.

ACCOMMODATIONS
Camping
Choosing a spot to pitch a tent in a campground is easy, but in the wilderness the choice is more complicated and should be made carefully to avoid problems in the middle of the night. Throughout much of Alaska, especially the Interior, river bars are the best place to pitch a tent. Strips of sand or small gravel patches along rivers provide good drainage and a smoother surface than tussock grass on which to pitch a tent.

Take time to check out the area before unpacking your gear. Avoid animal trails (whether the tracks be moose or bear), areas with bear scat, and berry patches with ripe fruit. In late summer, it is best to stay away from streams choked with salmon runs.

In the Southeast and other coastal areas of Alaska, search out beaches and ridges with southern exposures; they provide the driest conditions in these rainy zones. Old glacier and stream outwashes (sand or gravel deposits) make ideal camp sites as long as you stay well above the high-tide line. Look for the last ridge of seaweed and debris on the shore and then pitch your tent another 20 to 30 yards above that to avoid waking up with salt water flooding your tent. Tidal fluctuations along Alaska's coast are among the largest in the world – up to 30 feet in some places.

Forest Service Cabins
Built and maintained by the US Forest Service (USFS), these cabins are scattered throughout the Tongass National Forest (practically the entire Southeast), the Chugach National Forest on the Kenai Peninsula, and different islands and bays in Prince William Sound. For the most part, the cabins are rustic log cabins or A-frames with wood-burning stoves, plywood bunks, pit toilets and often a rowboat if the cabins are on a lake. They are usually near remote lakes or streams, along coastal beaches or above the timberline.

A few cabins can be reached by hiking, but for most a bush plane or chartered boat has to drop you off and then return for you. Staying in the cabins is an ideal way to sneak into the woods and separate yourself from the world without having to undertake rigorous backcountry travel.

Although there are a few free shelters, the vast majority of cabins cost $25 per night to rent but can comfortably hold parties of six or more people. You can reserve the cabins 179 days in advance by sending the total payment and the dates you want to stay to the various Forest Service offices which administer the cabins.

During the summer, the cabins are heavily used by both locals and travelers, and stays are limited to seven consecutive nights per party. In the Chugach National Forest, there is a three-day limit on hike-in cabins from May to August. Some cabins are so popular that the Forest Service holds a lottery among all the reservation requests sent 179 days in advance, in order to determine who will be allowed to occupy the cabins during peak periods of the summer.

The cabins provide excellent shelter from bad weather but you have to bring your own bedding (sleeping bag and ground pad), food and cooking gear, including a small backpacker's stove for when the wood pile is wet.

Other items that come in handy are insect repellent, matches, candles and a topographical map of the surrounding area. The USFS also recommends that any water obtained from nearby lakes should be purified (see the Health section in the Facts for the Visitor chapter for information on water purification and giardia).

Of the 190 USFS public-use cabins, almost 150 of them are in the Southeast and are accessible from Ketchikan, Petersburg, Juneau or Sitka. If you don't make reservations but have a flexible schedule, it is still possible to rent one. During the summer, USFS offices in the Southeast maintain lists of the cabins and dates still available. There are always a few cabins available for a couple of days in the middle of the week, although they will most likely be the remote ones requiring more flying time (and thus money) to reach. The most accessible ones are usually booked solid by the time June rolls around.

In the regional chapters, a description of selected cabins is given under the names of towns they are most accessible from. These cabins are special because they can either be reached in 30 minutes or less by bush plane or have some intriguing feature nearby, such as natural hot springs or a glacier.

For a complete list of cabins in the Southeast, write to the following USFS offices in Alaska, which will forward a booklet describing each cabin in its district along with details about the surrounding terrain and the best way to travel to it.

Chatham Area Supervisor
    204 Siginaka Way, Sitka, AK 99835; (☎ (907) 747-6671)
Forest Service Information Center
    PO Box 1628, Juneau, AK 99802; (☎ (907) 586-8751)
Ketchikan Area Supervisor
    Federal Building, Ketchikan, AK 99901; (☎ (907) 225-3101)
Stikine Area Supervisor
    PO Box 309, Petersburg, AK 99833; (☎ (907) 772-3871)

The Chugach National Forest in Southcentral Alaska has 39 cabins, including seven along the Resurrection Trail and three on the Russian Lakes Trail.

There are also a couple of cabins in the Cordova area that can be reached by foot, but the rest are accessible only by air or boat. For a complete list of cabins and for bookings in the Chugach National Forest, write to the following USFS district offices in Alaska.

Anchorage Ranger District
    201 East 9th Ave, Suite 206, Anchorage, AK 99501; (☎ (907) 271-2500)
Cordova Ranger District
    PO Box 280, Cordova, AK 99574; (☎ (907) 424-7661)

Seward Ranger District
    PO Box 390, Seward, AK 99664; (☎ (907) 224-3374)

BOOKS
A great deal of reference material is available to assist backpackers in finding their way along the trail or to give them a better understanding of the natural world around them. The following books can be found in good Alaskan bookstores or can be obtained directly from Wild Rose Guidebooks, PO Box 240047, Anchorage, AK 99524.

Hiking Guides
55 Ways to the Wilderness in Southcentral Alaska by Nancy Simmerman & Helen Nienhueser (Mountaineer-Books, 306 2nd Ave West, Seattle, WA 98119; 1985, 176 pages, $10.95) is a hiking guide covering popular trails around the Kenai Peninsula, the Anchorage area and from Palmer to Valdez. The text includes maps, distances and estimated trekking times.

15 Hikes in Denali by Don Croner (Wild Rose Guidebooks, PO Box 240047, Anchorage, AK 99524; 1989, 42 pages, $7.95) is a large-format guide which outlines 15 hikes in Denali National Park, ranging from short day hikes to 40-mile treks. This second edition also contains additional information and drawings covering plants, birds and geology of the park. It's a good purchase if you plan an extended trip to the park.

Trekking in Alaska by Jim DuFresne (Lonely Planet Publications, PO Box 617 Hawthorn, Victoria 3122, Australia; 1995, 250 pages, maps, photos. This addition to the Lonely Planet trekking guide series is due out in 1995. The book will cover in detail 40 trails around the state ranging from day hikes to week-long treks. The trails are scattered across Alaska from Ketchikan to Fairbanks, including several routes in Denali National Park.

Alaska Wilderness; Exploring the Central Brooks Range by Robert Marshall (Wild Rose Guidebooks, PO Box 240047, Anchorage, AK 99524; 1989, 175 pages, $12.95) was written and published in the 1930s and then republished in 1989 for the simple reason that the mountains, rivers, passes and terrain of the central Brooks Range have not changed. What Marshall saw and many of the routes he explored are still the popular ones today.

Juneau Trails by the US Forest Service (1985, 60 pages, $3), a little green book, is a bible for Juneau hikers as it describes 26 trails around the capital city – perhaps the best area for hiking in Alaska. The guidebook includes maps, distances, rating of the trails and location of trailheads along with brief descriptions of the route. The book can be obtained at the USFS information center in the Centennial Building on Egan Dr in Juneau, but you have to ask for it.

Sitka Trails by the US Forest Service (72 pages, $3) is similar to *Juneau Trails* and covers 30 hiking trails around Sitka and its nearby coastline. Each trail has a one-paragraph description, a rough map and information on access and special features. Either write ahead of time or stop at Sitka Ranger District, 204 Siginaka Way, AK 99835.

Discover Southeast Alaska with Pack and Paddle by Margaret Piggott (Mountaineer-Books, 306 2nd Ave West, Seattle, WA 98119; 1990, 238 pages, $12.95), a longtime guidebook to the water routes and hiking trails of the Southeast, was out of print for years before the author finally updated the first edition in 1990. The guide thoroughly covers the hiking and paddling routes from Ketchikan to Skagway. Its downfall is the weak, hand-drawn maps. Make sure you pack the topos.

Backcountry Companion for Denali National Park by Jon Nierenberg (Alaska Natural History Association, 605 West 4th Ave, Anchorage, AK 99501; 94 pages, maps, photos, $8.95), is general guide to wilderness trekking in the popular national park. It's not a trail guide, but rather provides short synopses to each of Denali's backcountry zones to assist backpackers to pick the right area to travel in.

Katmai by Jean Bodeau (Alaska Natural History Association, 605 West 4th Ave,

Anchorage, AK 99501; 1992, 206 pages, photos, $14.95) is a general guide to Katmai National Park on the Alaska Peninsula. It will assist you in understanding this special park and help you arrange a trip here but not necessarily lead you through the Valley of 10,000 Smokes.

Paddling Guides

The Coastal Kayaker by Randel Washburne (Globe Pequot Press, Old Chester Rd, PO Box Q, Chester, CT 06412; 1983, 224 pages, $11.95) deals mostly with the art of bluewater kayaking and how to survive in the coastal wilderness of British Columbia and Southeast Alaska. It contains paddling notes and basic maps for seven different areas, including four in the Southeast.

A Guide to Alaska's Kenai Fjords by David Miller (Wilderness Images, Anchor Cove, PO Box 1367, Seward, AK 99664; 1987, 116 pages, $8.95) is a coastal paddling guide to the Kenai Fjords National Park with route descriptions and maps. The author provides an overview of the area plus specific information about protected coves, hikes, fishing tips and protected areas for kayakers to arrange drop-offs and pick-ups.

Glacier Bay National Park: A Backcountry Guide to the Glaciers and Beyond by Jim DuFresne (Mountaineer-Books, 306 2nd Ave West, Seattle, WA 98119; 1988, 144 pages, $8.95) is a complete guide to Glacier Bay's backcountry. Along with introductory material on the park, the book contains information on kayak rentals, transport up the bay and detailed descriptions of water and land routes in this trail-less park; maps are included.

Alaska Paddling Guide by Jack Mosby & David Dapkus (J&R Publishers, PO Box 140264, Anchorage, AK 99514; 1986, 113 pages, $7.95) is a statewide guide which covers 110 possible water trips, many having road access. Descriptions of the journeys are brief but practical, with information such as access points, trip length and a rough map.

The Alaska River Guide by Karen Jettmar (Alaska Northwest Books, 2208 NW Market St, Seattle, WA 98107; 1993, 302 pages, maps, photos, $16.95) is the newest river guide for Alaska, covering more than 100 possible trips with two or three pages of description and a general map. The rivers range from the Chilkat in the Southeast to Colville on the Arctic slope.

General

Guide to the Birds of Alaska is by Robert Armstrong (Alaska Northwest Books, 130 2nd Ave South, Edmonds, WA 98020; 1990, 332 pages, $19.95). To ornithologists, Alaska is the ultimate destination. More than 400 species of birds have been spotted in the state and the above guide has information on identification, distribution and habitat of 335 of them. Along with text, the books contains color photographs of the species, drawings and a bird checklist.

A Guide to Alaskan Seabirds by the Alaska Natural History Association (2525 Gambell St, Anchorage, AK 99503; 1982, 40 pages, $4.95) is a thin guide to the birds that thrive in coastal Alaska. It has excellent drawings for easy identification.

Wild, Edible & Poisonous Plants of Alaska by Dr Christine Heller (Alaska Natural History Association; 88 pages, $2.50), a handy little guide, is an excellent companion on any hike, as it contains both drawings and color photos of Alaskan flora, including edible plants, berries and wild-flowers.

A Guide to Wildlife Viewing in Alaska (Wild Rose Guidebooks; 1983, 170 pages, $12.95), sponsored by the Alaska Department of Fish & Game, describes the best opportunities to view wildlife by regions and seasons. The first chapter explains how to find wildlife and the following chapters cover Alaska's 14 different types of wildlife habitats.

ACTIVITIES
Blue-water Paddling

Blue water in Alaska refers to the coastal areas of the state that are characterized by extreme tidal fluctuations, cold water temperatures and the possibility of high winds and waves. Throughout Southeast and Southcentral Alaska, the open canoe gives way to the kayak, and blue-water paddling is the means of escape into the coastal wilderness.

Don't confuse white-water kayaking with ocean touring. River running in light, streamlined kayaks wearing helmets, wet suits and executing Eskimo rolls has nothing to do with paddling coastal Alaska in ocean-touring kayaks. Every year, hundreds of backpackers with canoeing experience arrive in the north country and undertake their first blue-water kayak trip in such protected areas as Muir Inlet in Glacier Bay National Park or Tracy Arm Fjord, south of Juneau.

Tidal fluctuations are the main concern in blue-water areas. Paddlers should always pull their boats above the high-tide mark and secure them by tying a line to a rock or tree. A tide book for the area should be in the same pouch as the topographical map – paddlers schedule days around the changing tides, traveling with the tidal current or during slack tide for easy paddling. Check with local rangers for the narrow inlets or straits where rip tides or whirlpools might form, and always plan to paddle these areas during slack tides.

Cold coastal water, rarely above 45°F in the summer, makes capsizing more than unpleasant. Even with a life jacket, survival time in the water is less than two hours; without one it is considerably less. Plan your trip to run parallel with the shoreline and arrange your schedule so you can sit out rough weather without missing your pick-up date. If you do flip, stay with the boat and attempt to right it and crawl back in. Trying to swim to shore in Arctic water is risky at best.

Give a wide berth to marine mammals such as sea lions, seals and especially any whales that are seen while paddling. Glacial ice should also be treated with respect. It is unwise to get closer than a half a mile to a glacier face as icebergs can calve suddenly and create a series of unmanageable waves and swells. Never try to climb onto floating icebergs as they are extremely unstable and can roll without warning.

Framed backpacks are almost useless in kayaks; gear is better stowed in duffel bags or small day packs. Carry a large supply of assorted plastic bags, including several garbage bags. All gear, especially sleeping bags and clothing, should be stowed in plastic bags, as water tends to seep in even when you seal yourself in with a cockpit skirt. Other equipment taken along on any blue-water paddle should include an extra paddle, a large sponge for bailing the boat, sunglasses and sunscreen, extra lines and a repair kit of duct tape and a tube of silicon sealant for fiberglass cracks.

River Running

Throughout Alaska's history, rivers have been the traditional travel routes through the rugged terrain and still are today. Many rivers can be paddled in canoes; others, due

to extensive white water, are better handled in rafts or kayaks. If access is available by road, hardshell canoes and kayaks can be used. If not, you might have to arrange for a folding boat, such as a Klepper kayak, or an inflatable canoe or raft. Either that or pay for an additional bush flight so a hardshell can be carried in on the floats.

Alaska's rivers vary from one end of the state to the other but you will find they share characteristics not found on many rivers in the Lower 48. Water levels tend to change rapidly in Alaska. Due to temperature, rainfalls and other factors, a river's depth and character can change noticeably even within a day. Many rivers are heavily braided and boulder-strewn and require a careful eye in picking out the right channel if you don't want to spend most of the day pulling your boat off gravel. And count on there being

River Running

cold water, especially in any glacial-fed river where the temperatures will be in the mid-30s (°F). You can survive flipping your canoe in an Alaskan river but you'll definitely want a plan of action in case you ever do.

North Slope rivers in the Arctic tend to be extremely braided, swift and free flowing by mid-June. They remain high and silty for several weeks after that, but by mid-July even the sea ice is open enough to permit coastal lagoons.

Rivers flowing from the south slope of the Brooks Range are moving by early June and have good water levels through mid-August while rivers in Fairbanks and Interior areas can usually be run from late May to mid-September. Further south around Anchorage and the Southcentral region, the paddling season lasts even longer – from May to September.

Much of the equipment for canoers is the same as it is for blue-water paddlers. You want all gear in dry storage bags, especially extra clothing, sleeping bag and tent. Tie everything into the canoe, you never know when a whirlpool or a series of standing waves will be encountered. Wear a life jacket at all times. Many paddlers stock their life jacket with insect repellent, waterproof matches and other survival gear in case they flip and get separated from their boat.

Always make a float plan before you depart and leave it with either the bush pilot who flies you in or the nearest BLM or US Forest Service office. Most importantly, research the river you want to run and make sure you have the ability to handle whatever class of water it's rated. Descriptions of paddling conditions follow:

Class I – easy
> The river ranges from flatwater to occasional series of mild rapids.

Class II – medium
> The river has frequent stretches of rapids with waves up to three feet high and easy chutes, ledges and falls. The best route is easy to identify and the entire river can be run in open canoes.

Class III – difficult
> The river features numerous rapids with high, irregular waves and difficult chutes and falls that often require scouting. These river are for expe-

rienced paddlers who either use kayaks and rafts or have a spray cover for their canoe.

Class IV – very difficult
> Rivers with long stretches of irregular waves, powerful back eddies and even constricted canyons. Scouting is mandatory and rescues can be difficult in many places. Suitable in rafts or white-water kayaks with paddlers equipped with helmets.

Class V – extremely difficult
> Rivers with continuous violent rapids, powerful rollers and high, unavoidable waves and haystacks. These rivers are only for white-water kayaks and paddlers who are proficienct in the Eskimo roll.

Class VI – highest level of difficulty
> These rivers are rarely run except by highly experienced kayakers under ideal conditions.

Wilderness Fishing

Many people have a 'fish-per-cast' vision of angling in Alaska. They expect every river, stream and lake, no matter how close to the road, to be bountiful but often go home disappointed when their fishing efforts produce little to brag about. Serious anglers visiting Alaska carefully research the areas to be fished and are equipped with the right gear and tackle. They often pay for guides or book a room at remote camps or lodges where rivers are not 'fished out' by every passing motorist.

If, however, you plan to undertake a few wilderness trips, by all means pack a rod, reel and some tackle. It's now possible to purchase a backpacking rod that breaks down into five sections and has a light reel; it takes up less room than soap, shaving cream and wash rag. In the Southeast and Southcentral regions, backpackers can catch cutthroat trout, rainbow trout and Dolly Varden (a fish similar to the other two). Further north, especially around Fairbanks, you'll get grayling, with its sail-like dorsal fin, and arctic char; during August, salmon seem to be everywhere.

If angling is just a second thought, load an open-face spinning reel with light line, something in the four to six-pound range, and take along a small selection of spinners and spoons. After you arrive, you can always purchase the lures used locally, but in most wilderness streams I've rarely had a problem catching fish on Mepps spinners, sizes No 1 to No 3. Other lures that work well are Pixies, Dardevils and Krocodiles.

For fly fishing a No 5 or No 6 rod with a matching floating line or sinking tip is well suited for Dolly Vardens, rainbows and grayling. For species of salmon a No 7 or No 8 rod and line are better choices. For ease of travel, rods should break down and be carried in a case.

Here is a brief synopsis of the most common non-salmon species you find in lakes and streams all summer long roaming Alaska's backcountry.

Rainbow Trout This is without a doubt the best fighting fish and thus the most sought after by most anglers. Fishing from shore in lakes is best in late spring and early summer, just after ice break-up, and again in the fall when water temperatures are cooler. During the height of the summer, rainbows move

into deeper water in lakes and you usually need a boat to fish them.

Fish them at dawn and dusk when on calm days they can be seen surfacing for insects. Turn to spinners, size No 1 to No 3, and flashy spoons but avoid treble hooks (or clip one or two of the hooks on them) as they make releasing fish hard. The workhorse fly is the lake leech, in either purple or olive, fished with a slow retrieve on sinking-tip lines.

Cutthroat Trout The cutthroat picks up its name from reddish-orange slash along the inner edge of the fish's lower jar. Outside Southeast Alaska, most traveling anglers end up casting for resident cutthroats that spend their entire lives in the streams and lakes as opposed to larger anadromous (those migrating upstream) cutthroats that migrate to saltwater where food is more abundant. This trout likes to stay around submerged logs, aquatic vegetation or near other cover and is an aggressive feeder.

In most lakes, you can take them on small spinners, size No 0 up to No 2, but also will hit on larger spoons, especially red-and-white Dardevils. For fly fishing, a floating line with a nine-foot leader and a slowly twitching mosquito-larva fly can be very effective. The best time to fish is early morning and at dusk when light is low and cutthroats are often cruising the shallows for food.

Dolly Varden This is one of the most widespread varieties of fish in Alaska and their aggressive behavior makes them easy to catch. Dolly Varden are often caught near the entrances of streams or along weed beds near shore, making them accessible to backpacking anglers. With spinning gear, use spinners in sizes No 1 and No 2 or small spoons. Fly fishers often use a blue smolt fly on a sinking-tip line and a short leader and use an erratic strip retrieve. Other streamers work as well while a pin-head muddler and a floating line is often used in shallow rivers or when Dolly Varden are holding in shallow water.

Arctic Char A closely related cousin to the Dolly Varden, the arctic char is not quite as wide spread in Alaska. Often anglers will confuse the two species. Arctic char will be encountered predominantly in the Alaska Peninsula and Bristol Bay areas, on Kodiak Island, in some lakes in the Kenai Peninsula and in the Brooks Range and to the north. Spawning male char turn brilliant red or gold with red or orange spots while Dolly Varden are just as brightly colored but only on their lower body. For the most part, anglers use the same tackle and techniques for catching both species.

Grayling There's no mistaking the grayling, its long dorsal fin allows travelers to identify the fish even if they have never hooked one before. Grayling in streams feed at the surface or in mid-water drift and almost exclusively on insects or larvae. In other words, they are a fly fisher's dream. They are extremely receptive to dry flies and rarely are so selective as to choose one pattern over another. Generally small flies (sizes No 16 to No 18) will produce more rises than larger ones. Even if you have spinning gear, tie on a clear plastic bubble four to six feet above a dry fly and fish for grayling with that.

Other Fishing Infomation A nonresident's fishing license costs $50 a year (compared with only $15 for residents) or you can purchase a three-day license for $15 or a 14-day one for $30; every bait shop in the state sells them. The Alaska Department of Fish & Game puts out a variety of material including the *Recreational Fishing Guide*. You can obtain the 72-page guide ($5) by writing to the Department of Fish & Game (☎ (906) 465-4290), PO Box 3-2000, Juneau, AK 99802-2000.

Perhaps the most comprehensive guide to fishing Alaska is the recently released, *Fishing Alaska on Dollars a Day* by Christopher & Adela Batin, available from Alaska Angler Publications (☎ (800) 446-2286 – toll free), PO Box 83550, Fairbanks, AK 99708 for $23.95. It is based on Forest Service cabin accommodation that can be rented for $25 a day. The 338-page guide describes each cabin, fishing in the immediate area and gateway city, and provides good introductory material. The authors suggest that some of Alaska's best sport fishing lies on the doorsteps of the state's 200 recreational cabins.

Watching Wildlife

The BLM says to avoid being disappointed by not seeing wildlife in Alaska the first thing you have to do to not pack high expectations. Every year visitors arrive thinking they will see herds of wildlife, only to go home with a photos of a squirrel that was raiding their picnic table.

To see a variety of wildlife you have to leave the roads, travel into the backcountry and learn how to 'watch wildlife'. Here's what the BLM recommends:

• *Keep your distance.*
Don't try to get too close with camera in hand. Most wild animals react with alarm when approached by humans on foot or in vehicles. Repeated disturbances may cause animals or birds to leave the area for good. Also learn animal behavior patterns that will tip you off when you are too close. Mammals often raise their heads high with ears pointed in the direction of the observer if you are closing in too fast. They might also exhibit signs of skittishness or display aggressive behavior.

You are too close to birds if they also seem skittish or raise their heads to watch you. They may preen excessively, give alarm calls, flush repeatedly or even feign a broken wing when felt threatened by your presence.
• *Don't Hurry.*
The more time you take in the backcountry, the greater the opportunity to observe wildlife. Instead of moving camp every day, set up a base camp and do nothing at dawn or dusk but scan areas for wildlife.
• *Use proper equipment.*
You will see more by carrying high-quality binoculars or even a spotting scope. If you're set on photographing wildlife, make sure you have the telephoto lens, tripod and the right film for low light conditions to deliver those close-up shots.
• *Blend in.*
Wear muted colors, sit quietly and even avoid using scented soaps and perfumes.
• *Look for wildlife signs*
There's added enjoyment in recognizing animals by their tracks, droppings or vocalizations. To do that you might want to carry a field guide or two. Espe-

cially for tracks. An excellent one is *Animal Tracks of Alaska* (Mountaineer-Books, 1011 SW Klickitat Way, Seattle, WA 98134; 120 pages, $5.95).

Wildlife tracks

WHAT TO BRING
Day-Hike Equipment

Too often, visitors undertake a day hike with little or no equipment and then, three hours from the trailhead, get caught in bad weather wearing only a flimsy cotton jacket. Worse still, they suffer a major mishap such as losing the trail and have to spend a long night in the woods without food, matches or warm clothing.

Along with your large, framed backpack, take a soft day pack or rucksack with you to Alaska. These small knapsacks are ideal for day hikes and should contain waterproof clothing, woollen mittens and hat, a knife, high-energy food (like chocolate), matches, map and compass, a metal drinking cup and insect repellent.

Expedition Equipment

For longer treks and adventures into the wilderness, backpackers should double-check their equipment before they leave home, rather than scurry around some small Alaskan town trying to locate a camp stove

or a pair of glacier goggles. Most towns in Alaska will have at least one store with a wall full of camping supplies, but prices will be high and by mid to late summer certain items will be out of stock.

You don't need to arrive with a complete line of the latest Gore-Tex, but then again, that $4.95 plastic rain suit probably won't last more than a few days in the woods. Bring functional and sturdy equipment to Alaska and you will go home after a summer of wilderness adventures with much of it intact.

Clothing Alaska has traditionally been wool country. Wool insulates not only against snow and cold but also against the constant drizzle, which during the summer often leaves hikers wet and susceptible to hypothermia. Even when it's wet, wool will keep you warm, and it dries much faster than cotton.

However, wool is gradually giving way to the new synthetic pile or spun artificial fibres which possess the same qualities; they may even outperform wool under severe wet and cold conditions. The drawback is that the jersey of acrylic piling costs twice as much as a good old woollen jacket. Take your pick but avoid cotton items (jacket, socks and blue jeans) and outerwear that contains goose down, as these things are useless when wet.

On any trip longer than two days you should have two to three pairs of woollen socks, along with woollen mittens and a knitted hat. Taking woollen pants and shirts is not going too far as the weather can change suddenly. Dress in layers – or 'like an artichoke', as residents say – for maximum containment of body heat. Always carry a heavy jersey or jacket for the evenings, and waterproof clothing should be on the top of everybody's pack.

Boots The traditional footwear is the heavy leather hiking boot that has been smeared on the outside with half a can of beeswax. Most recreational backpackers today, however, opt for the new lightweight nylon boots made by sporting-shoe companies like Nike,

Vasque or Hi-Tech. These are lighter to pack and easier on the feet than leather boots, while providing the foot protection and ankle support needed on most trails and wilderness trips when carrying a medium weight pack. Others still turn to leather boots when heavy loads must be shouldered or a trek involves technical mountaineering. Normal tennis shoes are not enough for the trails but are handy to have as a change of footwear at night or for fording rivers and streams.

Tent Coming to Alaska without a lightweight tent is like going to Hawaii without a beach towel. A tent is the biggest cost-saver you can bring. It doesn't have to be fancy, but should have a rain fly which can double as a shade during long summer days when the sun is out long after you've gone to bed. Make sure the netting around the doors and windows is bug proof and will prevent you from turning into a nightly smorgasbord for any mosquito that passes by.

If the tent is more than four years old, waterproof the floor and rain fly before departing on your trip. If you are purchasing a tent for this journey, consider a free-standing dome with a vestibule to keep your equipment dry. Just make sure you know how to pitch it before you leave home.

Sleeping Bag This is a good item to bring whether you plan on camping or not, as it is also very useful in hostels, on board the State Marine Ferry and in seedy hotels when you're not sure what's crawling in the mattress.

There has been many an all-night discussion among backpackers on the qualities of down versus synthetic fibres. What can't be argued about though is down's quality of clumping when wet – in rainy Southeast and Southcentral Alaska, this means trouble during most wilderness trips.

Along with a sleeping bag, bring an insulated foam pad to sleep on – it will reduce much of the ground chill. In the Interior, you will often be sleeping just inches away from permafrost or permanently frozen ground. If you'll be spending a considerable amount of time sleeping in the wilderness, skip the foam and invest in a self-inflating sleeping pad such as the Thermarest. It may cost $60 but once you're out there you'll be thankful for having purchased it.

Camp Stove Cooking dinner over a crackling campfire may be a romantic notion while you're planning your trip, but it is an inconvenience and often a major headache when you're actually on the trail. Bring a reliable backpacker's stove and make life simple in the woods. Rain, strong winds and a lack of available wood will hamper your efforts to build a fire, while some preserves like Denali National Park won't even allow campfires in the backcountry. There are many brands of stove on the market today but ones like MSR Whisper Lite, that can be 'field repaired', are the most dependable you can take along.

Remember, you cannot carry white gas or other camp-stove fuels on an airline flight but just about every small town or park visitor center will stock them.

Map & Compass Backpackers should not only carry a compass into the wilderness but should also have some basic knowledge of how to use it correctly. You should also have the correct US Geological Survey (USGS) map for the area in which you are planning to travel.

USGS topographical maps come in a variety of scales but hikers prefer the smallest scale of 1:63,360, where each inch equals a mile. Canoers and other river runners can get away with the 1:250,000 map. The free maps of Tongass and Chugach national forests produced by the US Forest Service will not do for any wilderness adventure, as they cover too much area and lack the detail that backpackers rely on.

USGS maps cost $2.50 a section for 1:63,360 and $4 for 1:250,00 and can generally be purchased at bookstores, sports shops or camping stores in the last Alaskan town from which you enter the backcountry. However, it is not uncommon for the stores to be out of the maps covering popular areas.

If possible, order your maps ahead of time from the main office, USGS Western Distribution Branch, Denver Federal Center, PO Box 25286 Denver, CO 80225; write first and ask for a free index of maps for Alaska.

Sun Protection Alaska has long hours of sunlight during the summer and the sun's rays are even more intense when they are reflected off snow or water. All backpackers should bring a cap with a visor on it and a small tube of sunscreen to save at least one layer of skin on their nose. If you plan to do any kayaking, canoeing or alpine hiking around snowfields, you should also plan on bringing a pair of dark sunglasses, known by many locals as 'glacier goggles'.

Food You can buy food in almost any town or village at the start of most trips. If traveling to Glacier Bay, Denali or Katmai national parks, don't plan on purchasing your main supply of food at the park headquarters; stock up at the last major town you pass through.

Hiking

The following trips are along routes that are popular and well developed. Backpackers still need the proper gear and knowledge but can undertake these adventures on their own without the services of a guide. Always check with the offices or park headquarters listed for current trail conditions. A few of the trails have US Forest Service (USFS) cabins along the way, but these must be reserved well in advance. Bring a tent on any wilderness trek.

CHILKOOT TRAIL
Denali National Park may be the most popular park in Alaska, but the Chilkoot is unquestionably the most famous trail and often the most used during the summer (more than 2800 hikers followed it in 1992). It is the same route as that used by the Klondike gold miners in the 1898 to 1900 gold rush and walking it is not so much a wilderness adventure as a history lesson.

The well-developed and well-marked trail is littered from one end to the other with artefacts of the era – everything from entire ghost towns and huge mining dredges to a lone boot lying next to the trail. The trip is from 33 to 35 miles long (depending on where you exit) and includes the Chilkoot Pass – a steep climb up loose rocks to 3550 feet, where most hikers use all fours to scramble over the loose rocks. The trail can be attempted by anyone in good physical condition with the right equipment and enough time. The hike normally takes three days, though it can be done in two days by experienced trekkers.

Traditionally one of the more popular highlights of the hike was riding the White Pass & Yukon Railroad back to Skagway. After the service was suspended in 1982, the number of hikers plummeted even though there was bus service for the return. The historic railroad has since resumed its runs and the number of the trekkers increases annually. That's because experiencing the Chilkoot and returning on the White Pass & Yukon Route is probably the ultimate Alaska trek, combining great scenery, a first-hand view of history and an incredible sense of adventure. Best of all, it's affordable even for budget travelers.

Getting Started
The Chilkoot Trail can be hiked from either direction (starting at Skagway or Lake Bennett) but it's actually easier and safer when you start from Skagway/Dyea in the south and climb up the loose scree of the Chilkoot Pass rather than down. Besides there is something about following the footsteps of the Klondike miners that makes this such a special adventure. As gold miners did at the turn of the century, most hikers also arrive at Skagway (the historic gold-rush town) by ferry and spend a day or so walking the wooden sidewalks and purchasing supplies from stores with false fronts. They then continue north along the Chilkoot Trail.

From Skagway, make your way to Dyea,

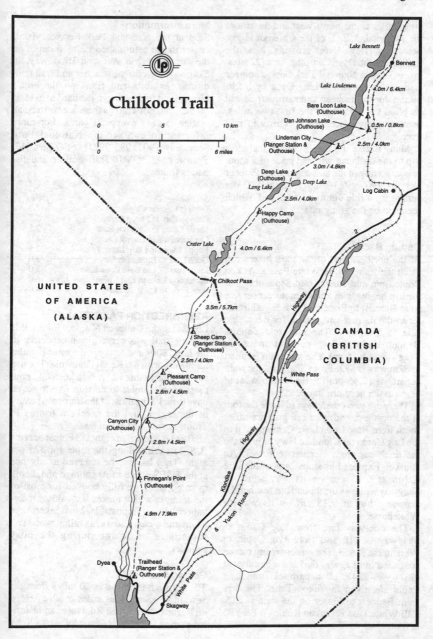

Chilkoot Trail

UNITED STATES
OF AMERICA
(ALASKA)

CANADA
(BRITISH
COLUMBIA)

Lake Bennett

Bennett

Lake Lindeman

4.0m / 6.4km

Bare Loon Lake
(Outhouse)

Dan Johnson Lake
(Outhouse)

0.5m / 0.8km

Lindeman City
(Ranger Station &
Outhouse)

2.5m / 4.0km

3.0m / 4.8km

Deep Lake
(Outhouse)

Deep Lake

Long Lake

Log Cabin

2.5m / 4.0km

Happy Camp
(Outhouse)

4.0m / 6.4km

Crater Lake

Chilkoot Pass

3.5m / 5.7km

Sheep Camp
(Ranger Station &
Outhouse)

2.5m / 4.0km

Pleasant Camp
(Outhouse)

White Pass

2.8m / 4.5km

Canyon City
(Outhouse)

2.8m / 4.5km

Finnegan's Point
(Outhouse)

4.9m / 7.9km

Dyea

Trailhead
(Ranger Station &
Outhouse)

Skagway

White Pass

Klondike & Yukon Route

Highway

0   5   10 km
0   3   6 miles

eight miles to the north-west and the site of the trailhead. *Mile 0* of the Chilkoot is just before the Taiya River crossing. Near the trailhead is the Dyea Camping Area (22 sites, no fee) and a National Park Service ranger station. It's tough reaching Dyea by hitch-hiking due to the steep and narrow road and its blind curves – after the first two miles, there are few places for motorists to pull over.

Many B&Bs and hotels in town include a trip to the trailhead with the price of a room or contact any of the taxi companies. Pioneer Taxi (☎ (907) 983-2623) charges $10 per person for a ride out to the trailhead, which seems to be the going rate.

Getting Back
At the northern end of the trail, hikers can catch the train on the White Pass & Yukon Route from mid-June to mid-September, but the trip begins with a track motorcar service from Bennett to Fraser. At Fraser you transfer to the narrow-gauge train for the scenic ride to Skagway. The motorcar departs Bennett daily at 3.45 pm and arrives in Skagway at 6.15 pm. The fare from Bennett to Skagway is $72. From Skagway, the train departs at 12.45 pm for those who want to begin at the northern trailhead.

There are two other ways to leave the trail at the northern end: you can hike six miles south from Bare Loon Lake Campground to the Log Cabin on Klondike Hwy or just take the track car from Bennett to Fraser. An Alaskon Express bus stops daily at the Log Cabin at 6.15 pm on its way south to Skagway while a northbound bus reaches the warming hut at 9.15 am on its way to Whitehorse.

The one-way fare from Log Cabin to Skagway is $18 and from Log Cabin to Whitehorse is $53. The bus company can be contacted in Skagway during the summer at (907) 983-2241; all departures from Log Cabin are given in Yukon Time. The fare from Bennett to Fraser on the train is $15. Call White Pass & Yukon Route (WP&YR) at (800) 343-7373 toll-free.

More Information
Stop at the National Park Service visitor center in the refurbished railroad depot on the corner of 2nd Ave and Broadway St, Skagway, for current weather and trail conditions, exhibits and films on the area's history, and hiking maps. It's hard to get lost on the Chilkoot Trail as there seems to be an orange marker every 50 yards. For more information contact the National Park Service (☎ (907) 983-2921) at PO Box 517, Skagway, AK 99840. Trail sections and distances follow:

Section	miles
Dyea to Canyon City	7.7
Canyon City to Sheep Camp	5.3
Sheep Camp to Chilkoot Pass	3.5
Chilkoot Pass to Happy Camp	4.0
Happy Camp to Deep Lake	2.5
Deep Lake to Lindeman City	3.0
Lindeman City to Bare Loon Lake	3.0
Bare Loon Lake to Log Cabin	6.0
Bare Loon to Lake Bennett	4.0

RESURRECTION PASS TRAIL
Located in the Chugach National Forest, this 39-mile trail was carved by prospectors in the late 1800s and today is the most popular hiking route on the Kenai Peninsula. The trip can be done in three days by a keen hiker but most people prefer to do it in five to seven days to make the most of the immense beauty of the region and the excellent fishing in Trout, Juneau and Swan lakes.

There is a series of eight US Forest Service (USFS) cabins along the route for $25 per night. They have to be reserved in advance at the USFS office in Anchorage and, being quite popular, are fully booked for most of the summer which makes last-minute reservations almost impossible. Most hikers take a tent and a camp stove, as fallen wood can sometimes be scarce during the busy summer.

Getting Started
The northern trailhead is 20 miles from the Seward Hwy and four miles south of Hope on Resurrection Creek Rd. Hope, an historical mining community founded in 1896 by

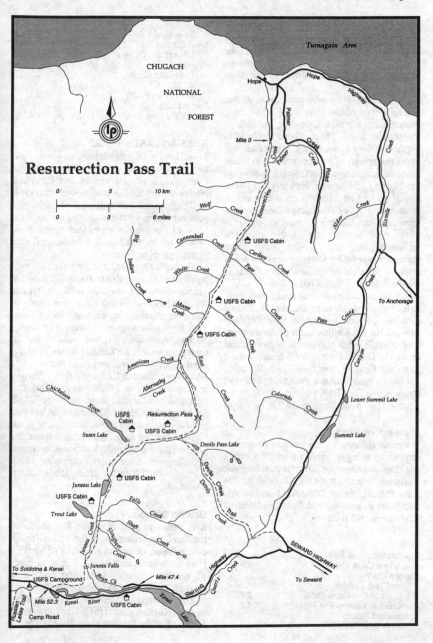

CHUGACH

NATIONAL

FOREST

Turnagain Arm

Hope

Hope Highway

Palmer Creek

Palmer Creek Road

Mile 0

Wolf Creek

Resurrection Creek

Alder Creek

Sixmile Creek

Resurrection Pass Trail

0   5   10 km

0   3   6 miles

Big Indian Creek

Cannonball Creek

USFS Cabin

Caribou Creek

Caribou Pass

White Creek

Moose Creek

Fox Creek

USFS Cabin

Pass Creek

To Anchorage

USFS Cabin

East Creek

American Creek

Abernathy Creek

Canyon Creek

Chickaloon River

Colorado Creek

Lower Summit Lake

USFS Cabin

Resurrection Pass

USFS Cabin

Swan Lake

Summit Lake

Devils Pass Lake

Devils Creek

Devils Creek Trail

USFS Cabin

Juneau Lake

USFS Cabin

Falls Creek

Trout Lake

Shaft Creek

Juneau Creek

Slaughter Creek

Sterling Highway

Quartz Creek

SEWARD HIGHWAY

To Seward

Juneau Falls

Bean Ck

Mile 47.4

To Soldotna & Kenai

USFS Campground

Mile 52.3

Camp Road

Hassan Lakes Trail

Kenai River

USFS Cabin

Kenai Lake

gold seekers, is a charming, out-of-the-way place to visit, but Hope Hwy is not an easy road to hitchhike. It does receive a fair amount of traffic in the summer but still patience is the key as eventually someone will give you a lift.

From Hope Hwy you turn south at the posted Resurrection Pass Trail signs onto Resurrection Creek Rd, passing the fork to Palmer Creek Rd. The southern trailhead is on the Sterling Hwy, near Cooper Landing or 53 miles east of Soldotna and 106 miles south of Anchorage. Hitchhiking is easy on the Sterling and Seward highways in either direction, or you can hop on a Seward & Homer Bus out of Anchorage (see the Bus section in the Getting Around chapter). A quarter of a mile east of the southern trailhead along the Sterling Hwy is the Russian River USFS Campground (84 camp sites, $6 per night for tents) and the trailhead for the Russian Lakes Trail.

An alternative route that avoids traveling to the remote northern trailhead is the Devils Pass Trail, which is posted at *Mile 39* of the Seward Hwy, 88 miles south of Anchorage. The 10-mile path leaves the highway and climbs to Devils Pass at 2400 feet, where it joins the Resurrection Pass Trail. By using the Devils Pass Trail and the lower portion of Resurrection Pass Trail, you can hike from the Seward Hwy to the Sterling Hwy in two days.

More Information
For more information on the trail or reserving cabins along it, contact the USFS office for the Anchorage District: Chugach National Forest (☎ (907) 271-2500), 201 East 9th St, Suite 206, Anchorage, AK 99501. Trail sections and distances (starting from the north) follow:

Section	miles
Resurrection Creek Rd to	
Caribou Creek Cabin	6.9
Caribou Creek to	
Fox Creek Camp site	4.7
Fox Creek to East Creek Cabin	2.8
East Creek to Resurrection Pass	4.9
Resurrection Pass to	
Devils Pass Cabin	2.1
Devils Pass to	
Swan Lake Cabin	4.4
Swan Lake to	
Juneau Lake Cabin	3.3
Juneau Lake to	
Trout Lake Cabin	2.7
Trout Lake to	
Juneau Creek Falls	2.3
Juneau Creek Falls to	
Sterling Hwy	4.4

RUSSIAN LAKES TRAIL
This 21-mile, two-day hike is an ideal alternative for those who do not want to over-extend themselves in the Chugach National Forest. The trail is well traveled, well maintained and well marked during the summer and not too demanding on the legs. Most of the hike is a pleasant forest walk broken up by patches of wildflowers, ripe berries, lakes and streams.

The walk's highlights include the possibility of viewing moose or bears, the impressive glaciated mountains across from Upper Russian Lake or, for those carrying a fishing pole, the chance to catch your own dinner. The trek offers good fishing for Dolly Varden, rainbow trout and salmon in the upper portions of the Russian River, rainbow trout in Lower Russian Lake, Aspen Flats and Upper Russian Lake; and Dolly Varden in Cooper Lake near the eastern trailhead.

If you plan ahead, there are three USFS cabins on the trail for $25 per night but you need to reserve them in advance. One is on Upper Russian Lake, nine miles from the Cooper Lake trailhead. Another is at Aspen Flats, another three miles north-west along the trail or 12 miles from the western trailhead.

Getting Started
It is easier to start from the Cooper Lake trailhead, the higher end of the trail. To reach the trailhead, turn off at *Mile 47.8* of Sterling Hwy onto Snug Harbor Rd. The road leads 12 miles to Cooper Lake and ends at a marked parking lot and the trailhead.

The western trailhead is on a side road marked Russian River USFS Campground at *Mile 52.7* of the Sterling Hwy. Hike 0.9 miles

Russian Lakes Trail

0   2.5   5 km
0   1.5   3 miles

to the end of the campground road to reach a parking lot at the beginning of the trail. There is a $2 fee if you leave a car here. If you're planning to camp at Russian River the night before starting the trek, keep in mind that the campground is extremely popular during the salmon-running season from mid-June to mid-July and fills up with anglers by early afternoon.

More Information

For more information on the trail or to reserve cabins, contact the Anchorage District USFS Office (☎ (907) 271-2500), 201 East 9th St, Suite 206, Anchorage, AK 99501. Trail sections with distances follow:

Section	miles
Cooper Lake trailhead to junction of Resurrection River Trail	5
trail junction to Upper Russian Lake Cabin	4
Upper Russian Lake to Aspen Flats Cabin	3
Aspen Flats to Lower Russian Lake	6
Lower Russian Lake to Russian River Campground	3

JOHNSON PASS TRAIL

In the same area as the Resurrection Pass and Russian Lakes trails, and nearly as popular, is the Johnson Pass Trail, a two-day and 23-mile hike over an alpine pass 1500 feet in elevation. The trail was originally part of the Old Iditarod Trail blazed by prospectors from Seward to the golden beaches of Nome, and later was used as part of the old Seward mail route.

Most of the trail is fairly level, which makes for easy hiking, while anglers will find arctic grayling in Bench Lake and rainbow trout in Johnson Lake. Plan to camp at either Johnson Lake or Johnson Pass, but keep in mind that these places are above the tree line, making it necessary to carry a small stove. There are no cabins on this trail.

Getting Started

The trail can be hiked from either direction. The northern trailhead is at *Mile 64* of the Seward Hwy or 96 miles south of Anchorage; there is a gravel road marked Forest Service Trail No 10 that leads a short way to a parking lot and the trail. The trail goes south over Johnson Pass and then to the shore of Upper Trail Lake before reaching the Seward Hwy again at *Mile 32.5*, just north of the small hamlet of Moose Pass. Hitchhiking to or from either end of the trail is easy during the summer, or arrangements can be made with Seward & Homer Bus Lines (see the Bus section in the Getting Around chapter).

More Information

Because the trail lies in the Chugach National Forest, contact the Anchorage District USFS Office (☎ (907) 271-2500), 201 East 9th St, Suite 206, Anchorage, AK, 99501 for more information and trail conditions. Trail sections and distances follow:

Section	miles
northern trailhead to	
Bench Creek Bridge	3.8
Bench Creek Bridge to Bench Lake	5.5
Bench Lake to Johnson Pass	0.7
Johnson Pass to Johnson Lake	0.6
Johnson Lake to	
Johnson Creek Bridge	5.1
Johnson Creek Bridge to	
Upper Trail Lake	3.7
Upper Trail Lake to	
Seward Hwy	3.6

To Anchorage
Seward Hwy
Stxmile Creek
Granite Creek Guard Station
Centre Creek
Bench Creek

Johnson Pass Trail

Groundhog Creek
Bench Creek
Gleason Ck
Ohio Ck
Bench Lake
Johnson Pass
Johnson Lake

0 2.5 5 km
0 1.5 3 miles

CHUGACH

NATIONAL

FOREST

King Ck
Johnson Creek

To Crater Lake Trail
Moose Pass
Upper Trail Lake
Seward Hwy

COASTAL TRAIL

Caines Head State Recreation Area is a 6000-acre park on Resurrection Bay south of Seward. This area has long been favored by boat and kayak enthusiasts who go ashore to explore the remains of Fort McGilvray and the South Beach Garrison, old WW II outposts that were built as a result of the Japanese attack on the Aleutian Islands. Along with the remains of an army pier, firing platforms and the 'garrison ghost town' at South Beach, the park also has much natural beauty including a massive headland that raises 650 feet above the water and provides sweeping views of Resurrection Bay.

The Coastal Trail is a 4.5-mile one-way hike from Lowell Point to North Beach, where you can continue along old army roads to Fort McGilvray and South Beach. Along the way you pass a walk-in campground, vault toilets and a picnic shelter at Tonsina Point; and a campground, picnic shelter and ranger station at North Beach. This hiking trail makes an excellent overnight trip, combining history with great scenery and a opportunity to climb a spur trail into alpine areas; it's also affordable as the trailhead is an easy walk from Seward.

Getting Started

The trailhead is at the end of Lowell Point Rd, three miles south of Seward's ferry terminal. Before leaving town, purchase a tide book – the 1.5-mile stretch between Tonsina Point and Derby Cove can only be hiked during low tide. Plan to leave Seward two hours before low tide to avoid becoming stranded along the way. Due to steep cliffs along the shoreline, it's not possible to follow the beach from the trailhead to Tonsina Point. The trek to North Beach is a two to three-hour walk at which point you have to stay until the next low tide (12 hours after the last low tide) before returning.

More Information

For a brochure on the park, stop at the Caines Head State Recreation Area office (☎ (907) 224-3434), on the 2nd floor of the City/State Building on the corner of 5th Ave and Adams St in Seward. Sections and distances follow:

Section	miles
northern trailhead to Tonsina Point	1.5
Tonsina Point to North Beach	3.0
North Beach to Fort McGilvray	2.0
North Beach to South Beach	2.5

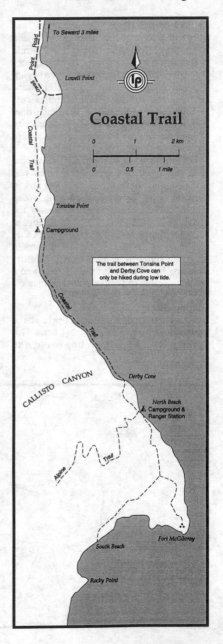

Coastal Trail

The trail between Tonsina Point and Derby Cove can only be hiked during low tide.

CHENA DOME TRAIL

Fifty miles west of Fairbanks in the Chena River State Recreation Area, this 29-mile trail makes for an ideal three-day backpacking trip with you ending up where you began. The trail circles the entire Angel Creek drainage area and for the first three miles cuts through forest and climbs to the timberline. It ends that way as well but the vast majority of the hike follows tundra ridgetops where the route has been marked by rock cairns.

For those who enjoy romping in the alpine area, this route is a treat. Four times you reach summits that exceed 3000 feet and in between you are challenged with steep climbs and descents. Chena Dome is the highest point on the trail, a flat-topped ridge at 4,421 feet that provides awesome views. Other highpoints of the hike are the wildflowers in July; the blueberries in August; wildlife, including bears, at anytime of the year and a public-use cabin that can be rented in advance.

Getting Started

If hiking the loop, it's best to begin at the trailhead at *Mile 50.5* of the Chena Hot Springs Rd. When traveling west, the trailhead is 0.7 miles past Angel Creek Bridge on the left side of the road. The other trailhead is at *Mile 49*. There's no public transportation this way but hitching is easy during the summer as traffic on the road is generally good. Or rent a car in Fairbanks and pay $40 a day while it sits and you hike.

Pack a stove, open fires are not permitted in the area. Also bring an extra quart of water and then replenish it at every opportunity along the trail. For the most part water will be collected from small pools in the tundra and must be treated.

Mosquitoes and gnats can be bad from June to early August, bring powerful insect repellent. And most importantly, obtain the USGS topos for Big Delta D5 and Circle A5 and A6. You'll need them to follow the route in the tundra.

The Angel Creek Cabin makes for a welcome place for spending the third night but plan on reserving it well in advance of leaving for Alaska. Another nice treat is to reserve a room or cabin at Chena Hot Springs Resort for after the trek. There's nothing a like a day or two to soak those tired muscles after rambling for 30 miles in the alpine area.

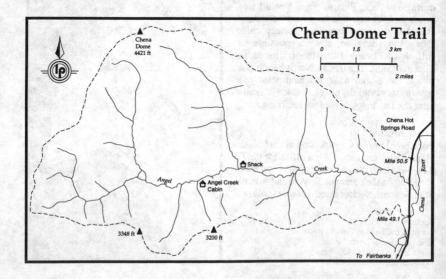

The Wilderness – Hiking 105

More Information
For a trail information sheet or to reserve the Angel Creek Cabin contact Alaska Division of Parks & Recreation (☎ (907) 451-2695), 3700 Airport Way, Fairbanks, AK 99709. Trail sections and distances follow:

Section	miles
Mile 50.5 Trailhead to timberline	3.0
timberline to Chena Dome summit	6.2
Chena Dome to spur to Angel Creek Cabin	13.3
Cabin spur to final descent off ridge	3.5
final descent to *Mile 49* trailhead	3.0

PINNELL MOUNTAIN TRAIL
The midnight sun is the outstanding sight on the Pinnell Mountain Trail, a 27.3-mile trek, 85 miles north-east of Fairbanks on the Steese Hwy. From 18 to 25 June, the sun never sets on the trail, giving hikers 24 hours of light each day. The polar phenomenon of the sun sitting above the horizon at midnight can be viewed and photographed at several high points on the trail, including the Eagle Summit trailhead.

The route is mostly tundra ridgetops that lie above 3500 feet and can be steep and rugged at times. The other highlight of the trip is the wildflowers (unmatched in much of the state) which carpet the Arctic-alpine tundra slopes, beginning in late May and peaking in mid-June. Hikers may spot small bands of caribou along with grizzly bears, rock rabbits and an occasional wolf in the valleys below but you need binoculars to spot any wildlife. The views from the ridge tops are spectacular, with the Alaska Range visible to the south and the Yukon Flats to the north.

Getting Started
The trail is a natural three-day adventure, with backpackers covering eight to 10 miles a day. Most hikers begin at the Eagle Summit trailhead on *Mile 107.3* of the Steese Hwy,

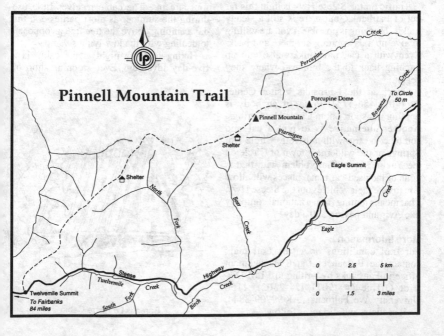

the higher end of the trail. The western end lies at Twelvemile Summit, closer to Fairbanks at *Mile 85* of the Steese Hwy. There are two small shelters built by the Youth Conservation Corps (YCC) which are open to anyone without reservations or fees. They are great places for waiting out a storm or cooking a meal on a windy evening but still bring a tent with good bug netting to sleep in at night.

Snow cover can be expected in May (with patches remaining to June) and mid-September. These patches are good sources of water which is scarce on this trail. Bring at least two quarts of water per person and then refill your supply at either snow patches, springs or tundra pools at every opportunity. Boil or filter all standing water from pools and slow-running springs.

The winds can be brutal in this barren region, as there are no trees to slow the gusts that can come howling over the ridges. Bring a wind screen for your camp stove, otherwise cooking dinner can become a long ordeal.

Traffic on the Steese Hwy is light this far out of Fairbanks, but there is still a steady trickle. Hitching is possible if you are willing to give up a day getting out there and back. Even with a car, most hikers also end up hitching back to the trailhead where they began.

Check at the Fairbanks Visitor Center (☎ (907) 456-5774) to see if anybody is running transport out to Circle Hot Springs. Another alternative is to rent a car and combine the trip with a drive to Circle Hot Springs or the wilderness town of Circle on the Yukon River. The problem with that is none of the used-car rental places will allow you to take their vehicles out the Steese Hwy. That means renting from a national company like Avis and paying $60 a day.

More Information

For trail conditions or a free trail map, contact the Bureau of Land Management office in Fairbanks by writing to BLM District Office (☎ (907) 474-2302), 1150 University Ave, Fairbanks, AK 99709-3844. Trail sections and distances follow:

Section	miles
Eagle Summit trailhead to Porcupine Dome	6.0
Porcupine Dome to 1st YCC shelter	4.0
1st shelter to 2nd YCC shelter	8.0
2nd shelter to Twelvemile Summit	9.5

WHITE MOUNTAINS SUMMIT TRAIL

The Bureau of Land Management (BLM), which maintains the Pinnell Mountain Trail, also administers the White Mountains trail network, which includes Summit Trail. This 22-mile, one-way route was especially built for summer use and includes boardwalks over the wettest areas. The route winds through dense spruce forest, traverses scenic alpine ridgetops and Arctic tundra, and ends at Beaver Creek in the foothills of the majestic White Mountains.

On the banks of the creek is the Borealis-Le Fevre Cabin which can be reserved for $25 a night. Reservations aren't really necessary as the last 2.5 miles of this trail drops off the ridgeline and descends into an muskeg area where hikers must ford up to four streams. The cabin receives little use during the summer as most parties end the day camping above the tree line as opposed to dealing with the low-lying swamp.

Hiking in for a night at the cabin is a five-day adventure. Even stopping short of

Borealis Le Fevre Cabin

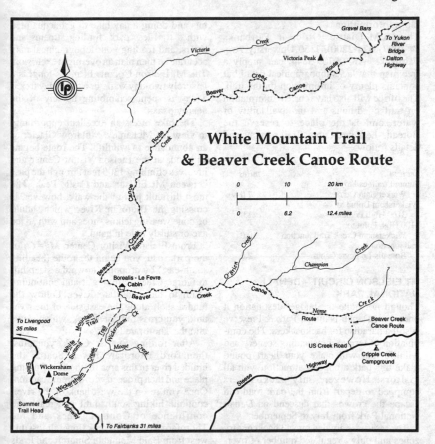

White Mountain Trail & Beaver Creek Canoe Route

0   10   20 km

0   6.2   12.4 miles

the cabin, the hike still requires two or three days to camp near the highest point along the route. The trailhead is at *Mile 28* of the Elliott Hwy, 31 miles north of Fairbanks. As on the Pinnell Mountain Trail, you need to bring water which is scarce in the alpine sections. Highlights of the trek are the views from the top of Wickersham Dome – it's possible to see Mt McKinley, the White Mountains and the Alaskan Range.

Getting Started
Don't confuse the White Mountain Summit Trail (also called Summer Trail), which was

made for hikers, with the Wickersham Creek Trail, that also departs from the trailhead (but leads more to the north-east). The Wickersham Creek or Winter Trail was cut primarily for snow machines, cross-country skiers and people using snow shoes, and leads through swampy, muskeg lowlands.

Stock up with provisions in Fairbanks. The last place you can purchase food and gasoline is at Fox on the junction of the Steese and Elliott highways. There is no public transportation on the Elliott Hwy and the hitching is generally slower than on the Steese Hwy.

More Information

The BLM District Office in Fairbanks (☎ (907) 474-2200), 1150 University Ave, Fairbanks, AK 99709-3844, can supply a free map that lacks topographical detail but contains plenty of information on the trail. The office will also have current information on trail conditions and the availability of water, and is the place to reserve the Borealis-Le Fevre Cabin. Trail sections and details follow:

Section	miles
Summit trailhead to	
Wickersham Dome	7.0
Wickersham Dome to	
3100 High Point	3.0
3100 High Point to	
Wickersham Creek Trail junction	10.0
trail junction to	
Borealis-Le Fevre Cabin	2.0

MT EIELSON CIRCUIT – DENALI NATIONAL PARK

Though not quite the budget destination it once was, Denali National Park & Preserve is still a paradise for backpackers. The combination of terrain, outstanding scenery and wildlife that will make your heart pound make this park a popular attraction with all visitors. However, only backpackers equipped to depart from the park road can escape the crowds that descend on Denali National Park from July to September.

The reserve is divided into 43 backcountry zones and only a regulated number of overnight hikers, usually from two to 12, are allowed into each area with the exceptions of a few unregulated zones west of Wonder Lake. In the height of the summer, it may be difficult to get a permit for the section of your choice and other sections will be closed off entirely when the impact of visitors is too great for the wildlife. The number of visitors tapers off dramatically in late August. Many people consider the end of August to mid-September as the prime time to see the park, as the crowds and bugs are gone and the fall colors are setting in.

There are many treks in the park. If time allows, begin by taking a ride on the shuttle bus and doing a day hike to get acquainted with a trail-less park, fording streams and rivers, and reading your topographical map accurately; then plan an overnight excursion. The Mt Eielson Circuit, 14 miles long, is a leisurely two-day walk, or a three-day trek if a day is spent scrambling up any of the nearby peaks.

The hike offers an excellent opportunity to view Mt McKinley, Muldrow Glacier or an abundance of wildlife. The route begins and ends at the Eielson Visitor Center and involves climbing 1300 feet through the pass between Mt Eielson and Castle Peak. The most difficult part of the walk, however, is crossing the Thorofare River, which should be done wearing tennis shoes and with an ice axe or sturdy pole in hand.

From Eielson Visitor Center, *Mile 66* of the park road, you begin the route (heading south-east) by dropping down the steep hill to Gorge Creek, crossing it and continuing south to the Thorofare River. Follow the tundra shelf along the east side of the river until you cross Sunrise Creek, which flows into the Thorofare River.

After fording Sunrise Creek, you must then ford Thorofare River. Search the braided river in this area for the best crossing place and then proceed with extreme caution. Once you're on the west bank of the river, continue hiking south until you reach the confluence of Contact Creek and the Thorofare River. The creek flows almost due west from Bald Mountain Summit and leads up to the pass between Mt Eielson and Castle Peak. The pass, at an elevation of 4700 feet, is a good place to spend the night, as views of Mt McKinley are possible in clear weather.

From the pass, follow the rock cairns west to pick up Intermittent Creek. The creek leads to the gravel bars of Glacier Creek on the south-west side of Mt Eielson. This section of the river makes for easy hiking or a good camp site for those who want to tackle Mt Eielson from the west side, its most manageable approach. Head north along Glacier Creek until you reach the flood plain with the many braids of Camp Creek and the

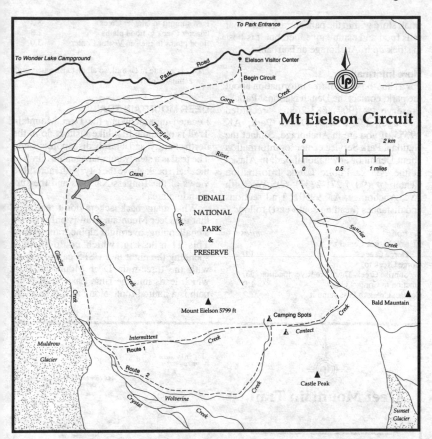

Thorofare River woven across it. Cross the channels and proceed north-east towards the Eielson Visitor Center.

Getting Started

There is information about the park in the Denali National Park section in the Interior chapter. There are several ways of getting to the park from either Fairbanks or Anchorage, including the services offered by a handful of bus companies and the Alaska Railroad (see the Bus and Train sections in the Getting Around chapter).

There is now an entrance fee at Denali; a

$3 pass is good for seven days while an annual permit is $15. Once in the park, many backpackers stay at Morino Campground where a site is $3 a night and then they obtain their backcountry permit from the Visitor Access Center at Riley Creek. Permits are handed out on a first-come, first-serve basis but the zones around the Eielson Visitor Center are extremely popular and, if you arrive in July or early August, you might have a two to three-day wait before obtaining one. Both visitor centers sell topographical maps: the Mt Eielson Circuit is contained on one section – Mt McKinley B-1. There is a small store within the park entrance area that sells food and camp-stove fuel, but it is best to stock up in Anchorage or Fairbanks.

More Information

For a shoe-box full of free information about the park, contact the Denali National Park & Preserve (☎ (907) 683-2686 – recorded message), PO Box 9, Denali Park, AK 99755. If you are in Anchorage, contact the National Park Service center for information about Denali or any national park in Alaska at the Alaska Public Lands Information Center (☎ (907) 271-2737), 605 West 4th Ave, Anchorage, AK 99501. Trail sections and distances (heading south-east) follow:

Section*	miles
Eielson Visitor Center to Gorge Creek	1.0
Gorge Creek to Sunrise Creek-Thorofare River junction	2.0
junction to Contact Creek	1.0
Contact Creek to Pass summit	1.2
Pass summit to Glacier Creek	3.3
Glacier Creek to flood plains	2.5
flood plains to Eielson Visitor Center	3.0

* This is a route not a trail, so all distances are rough estimates only.

DEER MOUNTAIN TRAIL

Located in Ketchikan, the Deer Mountain Trail is often the first hike visitors do in the north country, and it rarely disappoints them. The trail is a steady but manageable climb to the sharp peak above the city, with incredible views of the Tongass Narrows and the surrounding area.

What many backpackers don't realize is that the Deer Mountain Trail is only part of a challenging, overnight alpine trail system. This 11-mile trip, which could include spending the night in a USFS cabin, begins with the three-mile Deer Mountain Trail which leads into the Blue Lake Trail. This path is a natural route along an alpine ridge

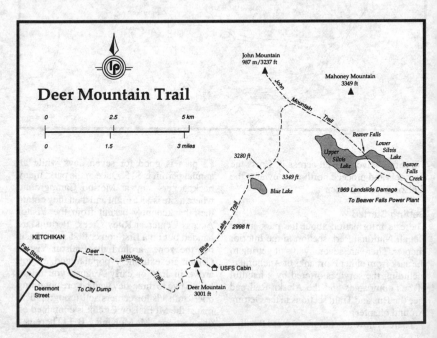

Deer Mountain Trail

extending four miles north to John Mountain. Here, hikers can return to the Ketchikan road system by taking the John Mountain Trail for two miles to Upper Silvis Lake and then following an old access road from the hydroplant on Lower Silvis Lake to the parking lot off Beaver Falls Hwy.

Deer Mountain is a well-maintained and heavily used trail during the summer. Even though it is a steady climb, the hike to the summit is not overly difficult. A quarter of a mile before the summit you pass the junction to Blue Lake and the posted trail to the Deer Mountain USFS Cabin. The cabin, located above the tree line, sleeps eight people and used to be free. But it was improved and now the USFS rents it out for $25 per night. The Blue Lake Trail crosses alpine country with natural but good footing, although in rainy weather it may be difficult to follow. The scenery from the trail is spectacular.

Within two miles from the junction of the Deer Mountain Trail, you arrive at the shore of Blue Lake. This lake, at 2700 feet, is above the tree line in a scenic alpine setting.

If you are going to trek along the John Mountain Trail, it is marked by a series of steel posts and has 20% grades on the first mile from Upper Silvis Lake. After this it then goes through alpine country. The John Mountain Trail is a fairly difficult track to follow and presents hikers with a challenge in reading their topographical maps and choosing the right route.

Getting Started

The trailhead for the Deer Mountain Trail can be reached by following the gravel road from the corner of Fair and Deermount streets in Ketchikan, past a subdivision (to the south-east) towards the city dump. Just before reaching the dump, a trail sign points left to a side road which leads to the trailhead and small parking lot.

To get to the start of the John Mountain Trail, hitchhike 12.9 miles east of Ketchikan along the South Tongass Hwy (also known as the Beaver Falls Hwy) to its end at the power plant. There is a two-mile hike along an old access road from the power plant at the tidewater to the hydroplant on Lower Silvis Lake.

There are a couple of ways to reach the upper lake: one begins on the roof of the lower lake powerhouse, following an old outlet stream course. The John Mountain Trail begins at the old outlet at the western end of the upper lake.

More Information

The cabins and trails are maintained by the US Forest Service, which has its main headquarters and visitor center in the Federal Building on Stedman St in Ketchikan. You can contact them for trail conditions or more information at USFS Office (☎ (907) 225-3101), Federal Building, Ketchikan, AK 99901. Trail sections and distances follow:

Section	miles
Deer Mountain trailhead to	
Deer Mountain Summit	3.1
summit to Blue Lake	2.2
Blue Lake to John Mountain	2.0
John Mountain to Upper Silvis Lake	2.0
Upper Silvis Lake to	
South Tongass Hwy	2.0

PETERSBURG CREEK TRAIL

A short hop across the Wrangell Narrows from the fishing community of Petersburg is Petersburg Creek Trail and the first of four trails that can be combined into a circular hike connecting two US Forest Service cabins. The Petersburg Creek Trail has been brushed and re-marked and now provides backpackers with a wilderness opportunity and access to USFS cabins that don't require expensive bush-plane travel. Both cabins need to be reserved and cost $25 per night.

Petersburg Creek Trail is entirely planked, but those planning to go onto Portage Bay or Salt Chuck should consider carrying a pair of rubber boots or 'Southeast sneakers', as they will encounter wet muskeg areas or stretches flooded out by beaver dams. Also bring a fishing pole, as there are good spots in the creek for Dolly Varden and cutthroat trout. In August and early September, there are large coho-salmon runs throughout the area that attract anglers and bears.

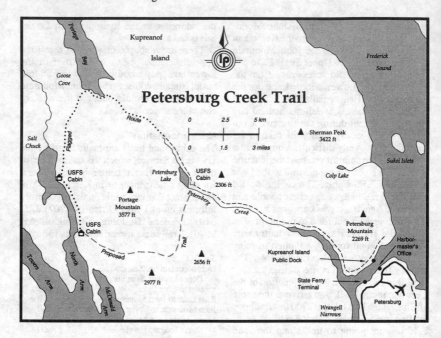

The trek begins across Wrangell Narrows from Petersburg at the Kupreanof Island public dock. From the dock a partial board-walk leads south for two miles past a handful of cabins and then turns north-west up the tidewater arm of the creek, almost directly across Wrangell Narrows from the ferry ter-minal.

A well-planked trail goes from the salt-water arm and continues along the northern side of the freshwater creek to the Petersburg Lake USFS Cabin on the eastern end of the lake. From the cabin, a second trail continues north to Portage Bay, and though some sec-tions might be hard to follow, it is marked with a series of blue diamond-shaped blazes on the trees.

Leading west from the trail to Portage Bay is the trail to Salt Chuck; you definitely need rubber boots to make it through the wet sections on this path. It's the most challeng-ing of the three trails but Salt Chuck East USFS Cabin, an A-Frame with an extended

side, is in a beautiful spot surrounded by mountains. The cabin is equipped with a rowboat and there's good trout fishing nearby. The cabin is often reserved well in advance during the August salmon runs, but it is easy to obtain from mid-June to late July.

Someday the USFS plans to turn this into a circular route by building a trail around the south side of Portage Mountain from Salt Chuck back to the Petersburg Lake USFS Cabin. But that project is continually being postponed due to lack of funds. Most back-packers can handle the trek into Petersburg Lake but to go beyond is a trip for those with experience in wilderness travel.

Getting Started
The only hitch to this trip is getting across Wrangell Narrows to the public dock on Kupreanof Island. The USFS office above the post office in Petersburg provides a list of charter-boat operators and places to rent a skiff. This can be expensive as a boat can cost

as much as $150. The cheapest and probably the easiest way to get across Wrangell Narrows is to hitch a ride with one of the boats that cross the narrows every day.

Go to the skiff float in the North Harbor (Old Harbor) near the Harbormaster's Office on the waterfront and ask around for boats crossing. A small population lives on the other side of the narrows so boats are constantly crossing, though at times you might have to wait a bit. Also try to enquire at the Harbormaster's Office, though at times they tend to discourage this practice.

Those who arrive at Petersburg with their own kayak can paddle to the creek during high tide to avoid much of the hike along the tidewater arm. This is one trip that you'll want good waterproof clothing and rubber boots for. Bring a tent or plan on reserving the cabins at least two months in advance, even earlier if you want to tackle the route in August during the coho-salmon runs.

More Information

The Petersburg District USFS office is on the 2nd floor of the post office along Main St. Make sure you contact the office before embarking to double-check on trail conditions and the status of the new trail from Salt Chuck to Petersburg Lake. Contact them at Petersburg Ranger District (☎ (907) 772-3871), PO Box 1328, Petersburg, AK 99833. Trail sections and distances follow:

Section	miles
Kupreanof Island dock to tidewater arm	2.0
tidewater arm to Petersburg Creek	3.0
trail by creek to USFS cabin	6.5
USFS cabin to Portage Bay	5.5
Portage Bay to Salt Chuck East Cabin	6.0

DAN MOLLER TRAIL

Across the Gastineau Channel from the center of Juneau is the Dan Moller Trail. It was originally built during the 1930s for downhill skiers and at one time had three warming huts and two toll ropes along it. Today, the skiers continue along the North Douglas Hwy to the Eaglecrest Ski Area, while the Dan Moller Trail has become a popular access to the alpine meadows in the middle of Douglas Island.

The trail is 3.3 miles long and leads to a beautiful alpine bowl where the US Forest Service has restored the remaining ski cabin. As with all USFS cabins, you have to reserve it in advance (rental costs $25 per night) but from 10 am to 5 pm it's shared by everybody as a warming hut.

Even if you can't secure the cabin, don't pass up this trail. Camping in the alpine bowl is superb and an afternoon or an extra day can be spent scrambling up and along the

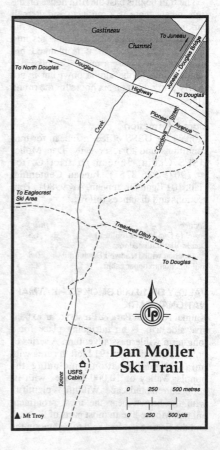

Dan Moller Ski Trail

ridge that surrounds the bowl and forms the backbone of Douglas Island. From the ridge, there are scenic views of Douglas Island, Admiralty Island and Stephens Passage.

Getting Started

The trailhead is 1.5 miles from the Juneau International (AYH) Hostel. You can easily walk to it or catch the minibus to Douglas and get off at Cordova St, which leads to a growth of apartments and condominiums known as West Juneau. From Cordova St, turn left (south-east) onto Pioneer Ave and follow it to the end of the pavement.

The trail begins past the fifth house on the right where there is a trailhead and a small parking area. An old jeep track serves as the first part of the trail before it emerges into open muskeg. Most of it is planked but waterproof boots are a must. The hike is a steady climb to the alpine bowl but is not overly tiring; plan on six hours for the round trip.

More Information

Contact the USFS office in Juneau for trail conditions and to reserve the Dan Moller USFS Cabin: Juneau District Office (☎ (907) 586-8751), Juneau Centennial Hall, 101 Egan Dr, Juneau, AK 99801. Trail sections and distances follow:

Section	miles
hostel to Dan Moller trailhead	1.5
Dan Moller trailhead to junction with Treadwell Ditch Trail	0.8
trail junction to upper cabin	2.5

VALLEY OF 10,000 SMOKES – KATMAI NATIONAL PARK

Katmai National Park & Preserve, an expensive side trip, is an intriguing place for a long-term wilderness adventure. A series of volcanic eruptions in 1912 left the area with unique land formations, including the popular Valley of 10,000 Smokes with its eerie, barren landscape. Wildlife is plentiful, with the brown bear the most prominent animal. Moose live in most parts of the park and the fishing is often said to be among the best in Alaska, as Katmai is an important spawning area for salmon.

The Valley of 10,000 Smokes is the most popular route for backpacking in Katmai, even though none of the famed '10,000 smokes' is active today. It begins with a short trail from Three Forks Overlook Cabin at the end of the park road to Windy Creek on the floor of the valley. A well-defined route then leads 12 miles south-east across the valley to some old cabins on the side of Baked Mountain.

The hike is considered fairly difficult and includes some steep trekking along the foothills of the Buttress Range, followed by a drop down to the River Lethe, a major fording. From the river, you head for the divide between Broken Mountain (3785 feet) and Baked Mountain (3695 feet). You then head south-east to climb the short but steep slope of Baked Mountain to the cabin.

Getting Started

Turn to the Katmai National Park section in the Bush chapter for travel information for getting to and from Katmai National Park, but be prepared to pay around $300 to $400 for a return trip from Anchorage, 290 miles away. The only developed facilities in the park, apart from a couple of expensive wilderness lodges, are at Brooks Camp, the summer headquarters of the park.

At Brooks Camp, there is lodging, a restaurant and a park store which sells limited quantities of freeze-dried food, topographic maps and white gas for camp stoves. The park store also rents tents, canoes, camp stoves and fishing poles among other things. It is best to stock up on food and fishing tackle in Anchorage to avoid emptying your entire money pouch here.

Like Denali National Park, Katmai has a shuttle bus that travels the park road daily but, unlike Denali's free bus, it is operated by a concessionaire. A return trip on the bus costs $60 and a spot should be reserved the night before. Hikers who have a week in the park can skip the bus fare by walking the 23 miles out to Three Forks Overlook from Brooks Camp or take the bus just one-way and pay $30. The weather in the area can be consistently poor even by Alaskan standards; the skies are clear only 20% of the summer and from September onwards strong winds are frequent.

More Information

In Anchorage, contact the Alaska Public Land Information Center (☎ (907) 271-2737), on the corner of 4th Ave and F St, for information about Katmai National Park. If you're planning to visit the park, it is best to write ahead for information to Katmai National Park (☎ (907) 246-3305), PO Box 7, King Salmon, AK 99613. Trail sections and distances follow:

Section	miles
Brooks Camp to Three Forks via Park Rd	23
Three Forks to Windy Creek*	1
Windy Creek to River Lethe via the Buttress Range*	7
River Lethe to Baked Mountain Cabins*	4

* Marked distances are rough estimates only.

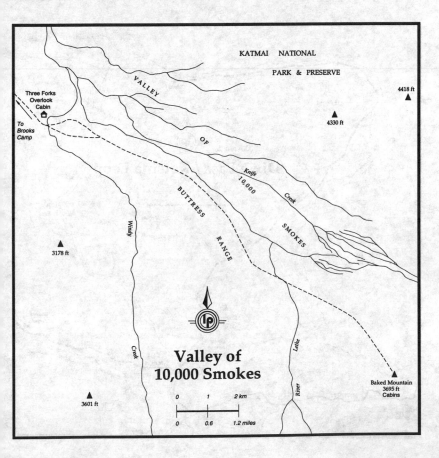

Valley of 10,000 Smokes

DIXIE PASS – WRANGELL-ST ELIAS NATIONAL PARK

Even by Alaskan standards, Wrangell-St Elias National Park is a large tract of wilderness. At 13.2 million acres it's the largest US National Park, contains the most peaks over 14,500 feet in North America and has the greatest concentration of glaciers in the continent. The park is a mountainous wilderness as three mountain chains (Wrangell, St Elias and Chugach) converge here. Wildlife in the park includes dall sheep, three herds of caribou, moose and, of course, lots of bears. The rivers are full of grayling, while trout thrive in the lakes.

The most common trek is to spend a day hiking up to Bonanza Mine or Root Glacier (see the Wrangell-St Elias National Park section in the Southcentral chapter). Dixie Pass offers a longer, more rugged and more authentic wilderness adventure into the interior of this park. The trek up to Dixie Pass and back is 24 miles, but plan to camp there at least one or two extra days to take in the alpine beauty and explore the nearby ridges.

This itinerary requires three or four days and is of moderate difficulty.

The trip begins from McCarthy Rd by hiking 2.5 miles up the Nugget Creek/Kotsina Rd and then another 1.3 miles along Kotsina Rd after Nugget Rd splits off to the north-east. The Dixie Pass trailhead is posted on the righthand side of Kotsina Rd usually as a pile of rocks with a stick in it. It's a definite trail but easy to miss. The route begins as a level path to Strelna Creek, reached in three miles, and then continues along the west side of the creek for another three miles to the first major confluence.

After fording the creek, you continue along animal trails, fording the creek when necessary to avoid rock bluffs. It's five to six miles to the pass and along the way you cross two more confluences and hike through a interesting gorge. The ascent to the pass is a fairly obvious route. Dixie Pass offers superb scenery, good camping and opportunities to spend an extra day or two hiking the ridges.

The vast majority of people backtrack but for the more adventurous, return along the Kotsina Trail Loop. This trail begins by descending the pass and following Rock Creek north 5.5 miles to the Upper Kotsina River drainage area. The route involves hiking along the west side of the creek and then fording it at Pass Creek to avoid a canyon area. Where Rock Creek merges into Kotsina River, you can pick up Kotsina Rd for the final 25 miles back to the Dixie Pass trailhead. In all, the Kotsina Trail Loop is a 45-mile hike that requires from five to seven days and that you have experience in wilderness travel.

Getting Started

Pick up supplies at Glennallen and stop at the park headquarters to fill out a backcountry trip itinerary and obtain your US Geological Survey quadrangle maps (Valdez C-1 and McCarthy C-8). Then arrange travel with Backcountry Connection (☎ (907) 822-5292 in Glennallen) for the trip deep into the park.

The bus departs Glennallen on Monday and Wednesday at 1.15 pm, Thursday, Friday and Sunday at 8 am and Saturday at 10.45

am from the Caribou Motel. The round trip is $110 per person. It's possible to hitch to the trailheads but it could be a long wait to cover the final 13 miles on McCarthy Rd.

Make arrangements to be dropped off and picked up at Nugget Creek/Kotsina Rd, 13.5 miles east of Chitina and then continue onto McCarthy to see more of this great park's wilderness. This trip is affordable and easy to arrange but you still have to be well prepared; it could take several days for help to reach you if you have a mishap. Bears may be present anywhere and stream fording must be attempted with extreme caution. Pack extra food, good waterproof clothing and woollens as the weather can change quickly.

More Information

For more information, contact the Wrangell-St Elias National Park headquarters (☎ (907) 822-5235), PO Box 29, Glennallen, AK 99588. During the summer there is also a ranger station (☎ (907) 823-2205) at Chitina. Trail sections and distances follow:

Section	miles
McCarthy Rd to trailhead	3.8
trailhead to Strelna Creek	3.0
Strelna Creek to Dixie Pass	8.5
Dixie Pass to Upper Kotsina River	5.5
Kotsina River to trailhead via road	25.0

Paddling

MISTY FJORDS

The Misty Fjords National Monument, which encompasses 2.3 million acres of wilderness, lies between two impressive fjords – Behm Canal, 117 miles long, and Portland Canal, 72 miles long. The two natural canals give the preserve its trademark of extraordinarily deep and long fjords with sheer granite walls that rise thousands of feet out of the water. Misty Fjords is named after the rainy weather that seems to hover over it much of the year; the annual rainfall is 14 feet!

But don't let the rain put you off, Misty

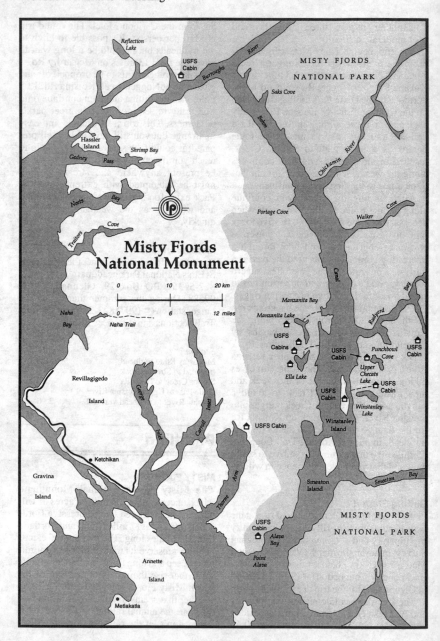

Fjords is an incredible place to spend a few days paddling. Lush forests, dramatic waterfalls plunging out of granite walls and diverse wildlife make the monument a kayaker's delight.

The destination for many kayakers are the smaller but equally impressive fjords of Walker Cove and Punchbowl Cove in Rudyerd Bay, off Behm Canal. The vegetation in this monument area is dense spruce-hemlock rainforest, while the abundant wildlife includes sea lions, harbor seals, killer whales, brown and black bears, mountain goats, moose and bald eagles.

Ketchikan is the departure point for most trips into Misty Fjord. Several tour boats run day trips into the area and there are the usual expensive sightseeing flights on small bush planes. Kayakers can either paddle out of the city (a seven to 12-day trip for experienced paddlers only) or utilize one of the tour boats to drop you off deep in Behm Canal near Rudyerd Bay and protected water.

Those contemplating paddling all the way from Ketchikan have to keep in mind that the currents around Point Alava and Alava Bay are strong and tricky, often flowing in unusual patterns.

Rounding the point into Behm Canal should be done at slack tide, which means leaving the city at high tide. The three to four-mile crossing of Behm Canal should also be done with caution, as northerly winds can create choppy conditions.

The Misty Fjords National Monument, which is administered by the US Forest Service, has 15 cabins (reservations needed, $25 rental fee) and 15 miles of trails. Two of the cabins, at Alava Bay and Winstanley Island, are right on Behm Canal and allow kayakers to end a day of paddling at the doorstep of a cabin. Many of the others are a short hike inland.

Getting Started

Outdoor Alaska, a Ketchikan tour company, offers many services for kayakers to Misty Fjords, including a variety of boat and plane trips into the monument. The company will drop you off and pick you up anywhere in the preserve for $175; a boat leaves on Monday, Wednesday, Thursday, Friday and Sunday. This allows inexperienced paddlers to avoid much of the open water of Behm Canal and to experience only the protected and spectacular areas of Rudyerd Bay or Walker Cove.

For the same fee, they will place your kayak on their tour boat and fly you out to Rudyerd Bay, and then return you to Ketchikan on the tour boat. They also have one-way fares for those who want to paddle all the way back to town.

To rent a kayak contact Southern Exposure Sea Kayaking. This guiding company will rent a double fiberglass kayak for $45 per day and a single for $35 per day for one to three days. Rent it four or more days and the rate drops.

If possible, plan ahead and reserve your kayaks before the summer. Contact Southeast Exposure (☎ (907) 225-8829) at PO Box 9143, Ketchikan, AK 99901. Outdoor Alaska (☎ (907) 225-6044) is at PO Box 7814, Ketchikan, AK 99901.

You cannot do this trip without good rain gear or a backpacker's stove, as wood in the monument is often too wet for campfires. Be prepared for extended periods of rain and have all gear sealed in plastic bags.

Either order your maps ahead of time or hope that the sections you want are in stock at the Tongass Trading Company, 203 Dock St in Ketchikan.

Then take the maps to the USFS office and have somebody point out the camping spots in the area where you are going to paddle. Since much of the monument is steep-sided fjords, good camp sites are scarce in many areas.

More Information

For information or hand-outs on the monument, either visit the USFS office in the Federal Building in Ketchikan or contact the monument office at Misty Fjords National Monument (☎ (907) 225-2148), 3031 Tongass Hwy, Ketchikan 99901. Canoe-route sections and distances follow:

TRACY ARM

Tracy Arm, like Glacier Bay, is another fjord in the Southeast that features tidewater glaciers rumbling and calving icebergs into the water. Unlike Glacier Bay, this wilderness area is not nearly as popular during the summer. It combines steep 2000-foot granite walls rising straight out of the water with cascading waterfalls and a pair of glaciers that sparkle like diamonds on a ring.

The 30-mile arm is no more than half a mile wide at its upper end – ideal conditions for the novice kayaker. Calm water is the norm in Tracy Arm as the steep and narrow fjord walls provide protection from stormy weather and strong winds. Wildlife includes bald eagles, mountain goats, seals, brown and black bears and an occasional whale. Even more interesting is the gallery of icebergs that float past you out to sea.

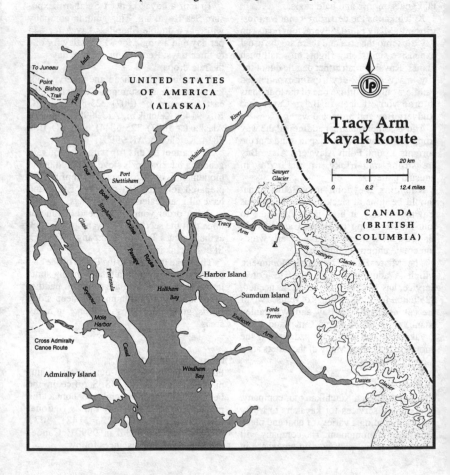

Tracy Arm Kayak Route

Adjoining Tracy Arm, just to the south, is Endicott Arm, a 30-mile fjord that was carved by Dawes and North Dawes glaciers. It is icebergs from these glaciers, some as large as three-story buildings, that often make it into the main shipping lanes of Stephens Passage, creating navigation hazards and delighting travelers on the state ferries.

Extending from Endicott Arm is Fords Terror. This narrow water chasm was named after a US sailor who in 1889 found himself battling surging rapids, whirlpools and grinding icebergs for six terrifying hours when he tried to row out against the incoming tide. Endicott Arm, Tracy Arm and Fords Terror together make up the Tracy Arm-Fords Terror Wilderness Area, a 653,000-acre preserve and a great place for a week's paddling.

Getting Started

The departure point for Tracy Arm is Juneau. Kayaks can be rented for $40/50 a single/double per day from Alaska Discovery (☎ (907) 463-5500), 11798 Glacier Hwy, Auke Bay. As the rental shop is in Auke Bay figure on spending another $25 each way for transportation of the kayaks downtown to Wilderness Swift Charters (☎ (907) 563-4942). The tour boat offers drop-offs and pick-ups at the entrance of the arm for $85 per person. This makes the trip considerably easier as it is a two or three-day paddle in open water to the mouth of Tracy Arm.

It is a pleasant two to three-day paddle from one end of the arm to the other. Most kayakers camp on Harbor Island, near the entrance of Tracy and Endicott arms, for at least one night even though level ground for a tent is difficult to find. The only other camping spots in the first half of Tracy Arm are two valleys almost across from each other, eight miles north along the arm.

Purchase topographic maps from the Big City Bookstore at 100 North Franklin St in Juneau, and head north to the Alaska Discovery rental office at 11798 Glacier Hwy in Auke Bay for tips on the trip and camp-site locations. Also get a tide book, available in town, and plan your paddle with the tides for

an easier trip. To reserve kayaks in advance contact Alaska Discovery (☎ (907) 586-1911) at 234 Gold St, Juneau, AK 99801.

More Information

Tracy Arm Wilderness Area is managed by the US Forest Service, which can be contacted for more information or hand-outs at USFS Juneau District (☎ (907) 789-3111), PO Box 2097, Juneau, AK 99801.

CROSS ADMIRALTY ISLAND

Admiralty Island National Monument, 50 miles south-west of Juneau, is the site of one of the few canoe routes in the Southeast. This preserve is a fortress of dense coastal forest, ragged peaks, and brown bears outnumbering anything else on the island including humans. The island also supports one of the largest bald-eagle nesting areas, and Sitka black-tailed deer can be seen throughout the monument.

The Cross Admiralty Canoe Route is a 32-mile paddle that spans the center of the island from the village of Angoon to Mole Harbor. Although the majority of it consists of calm lakes connected by streams and portages, the 10-mile paddle from Angoon to Mitchell Bay is subject to strong tides that challenge even experienced paddlers.

Avoid Kootznahoo Inlet as its tidal currents are extremely difficult to negotiate; instead, paddle through the maze of islands south of it. Leave Angoon at low tide, just before slack tide so that the water will push you into Mitchell Bay, and keep a watchful eye out for tidal falls and whirlpools. When paddling to Angoon, leave Salt Lake four hours before the slack tide, after high tide.

From the west end of Salt Lake there is a 3.5-mile portage to Davidson Lake, which is connected to Lake Guerin by a navigable stream. Between Lake Guerin and Hasselborg Lake is a 1.7-mile portage followed by a half-mile portage on the east side of Hasselborg Lake to Beaver Lake.

Canoeists can paddle from Beaver Lake to the east end of Lake Alexander, where they can take a 2.5-mile trail to Mole Harbor. This is the most common route followed, but there

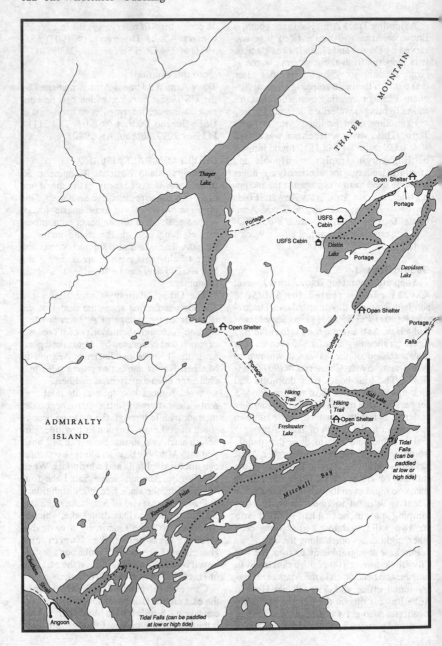

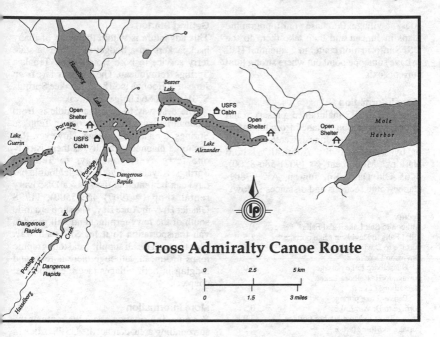

Cross Admiralty Canoe Route

are numerous trails in the area including portages to Thayer Lake and a route along Hasselborg Creek that connects Salt Lake with Hasselborg Lake.

There are good camping spots at Tidal Falls on the eastern end of Salt Lake, on the islands at the south end of Hasselborg Lake and on the portage between Davidson Lake and Distin Lake. The US Forest Service also maintains three-sided shelters (no reservations or rental fee) at the south end of Davidson Lake, at the east end of the Hasselborg Lake portage and at Mole Harbor. Finally, for those who can plan in advance, there are several USFS cabins (reservations needed, $25 per night) along the route, including those on Hasselborg Lake, Lake Alexander and Distin Lake.

Getting Started

Juneau is the departure point for this four to seven-day trip, though you will probably have to pass through the small village of

Angoon, a port of call on the State Marine Highway, which greatly reduces your transport costs as the one-way fare between Juneau and Angoon is $22. The problem is what to do at Mole Harbor, the east end of the trail. You can charter a bush plane to pick up both your party and the boats, but that is an expensive exercise for those on a tight budget.

The best alternative is to backtrack to Angoon and return to Juneau on the state ferry, which charges only $7 for canoes or kayaks which are carried on. This means setting up your trip around the ferry schedule, but the savings are enormous.

Renting a boat for this trip is an even bigger challenge. You can rent a kayak at Alaska Discovery (☎ (907) 463-5500) in Auke Bay but it's a hassle to portage across the trails. The preferred boat is a canoe. In Angoon, Favorite Bay Inn (☎ (907) 788-3123) had a few canoes to rent but that means paddling a return trip to the small Native

Alaskan village. Purchase your topographic maps in Juneau and then take them to the USFS information center in Centennial Hall to have someone point out where strong tidal currents exist.

More Information

This is a USFS-maintained preserve and information can be obtained from the information center in the Juneau Centennial Hall or by writing to the Admiralty Island National Monument (☎ (907) 586-8800), 8465 Old Dairy Rd, Juneau, AK 99801. Canoe-route sections and distances follow:

Section	miles
Angoon to Salt Lake Tidal Falls	10.0
Tidal Falls to Davidson Lake portage	2.5
portage to Davidson Lake	3.5
Davidson Lake to Hasselborg Lake portage	6.0
portage to Hasselborg Lake	1.7
Hasselborg Lake to Beaver Lake portage	2.0
portage to Beaver Lake	0.5
Beaver Lake to Mole Harbor portage	3.0
portage to Mole Harbor	2.5

HOONAH TO TENAKEE SPRINGS

This 40-mile paddle follows the shorelines of Port Frederick and Tenakee Inlet from Hoonah to Tenakee Springs and includes a short portage of a 100 yards or so. You might pass an occasional clear cut, but there are few other signs of civilization along the route once you are beyond the two villages. The area is part of the Tongass National Forest and consists of rugged and densely forested terrain populated by brown bears, which are often seen feeding along the shoreline.

It is important to carry a tide book and to reach the portage at high tide. Boot-sucking mud will be encountered along the portage, but take heart, it is just a short walk over a low ridge to the next inlet. Highlights of the trip include the scenic south shore of Tenakee Inlet with its many bays and coves. The village of Tenakee Springs has a public bath house around its natural hot springs that will soothe any sore muscles resulting from the paddle.

Getting Started

This adventure is within the grasp of many backpackers on a budget as there is a state ferry service to both Hoonah and Tenakee Springs from Juneau. The one-way fare from Juneau to Hoonah is $18 (to Tenakee Springs $20), with a $6 charge for kayaks.

The best way to start the paddle is from Hoonah in order to end the trip in Tenakee Springs, a charming village. However, this has to be planned carefully, as there is only one ferry every four days to Tenakee Springs. Kayaks ($40/50 a single/double per day) can be rented at the Alaska Discovery rental shop (☎ (907) 463-5500), 11798 Glacier Hwy in Auke Bay. The shop is a mile south of the ferry terminal and will provide van transportation to it for $10 each way. Plan to purchase all supplies and topographic maps in Juneau, although there is food and lodging in both villages (see the Southeast chapter).

More Information

For more information about the route or the surrounding area, contact the USFS office in

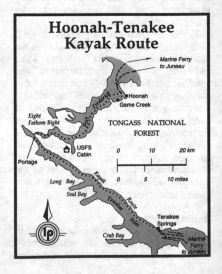

Hoonah-Tenakee Kayak Route

the Hoonah Ranger District (☎ (907) 945-3631), PO Box 135, Hoonah, AK 99829.

JOHN HOPKINS – GLACIER BAY NATIONAL PARK

More than anything else, Glacier Bay is a kayaker's paradise. When you combine the stunning alpine scenery of the Fairweather Mountains, with more than a dozen glaciers and the marine wildlife, you can understand the attraction for blue-water paddlers, despite the high costs of getting there. Those with some extra change in their pocket and a few spare days, can put together a paddle into John Hopkins Inlet, arguably the most spectacular glaciated inlet of the park.

By utilizing the tour boat service, you can be dropped off at Ptarmigan Creek, near the entrance of the inlet. Then spend one or two days exploring this icy wonder and another day to paddle to charming Reid Glacier just around the corner before being picked up and returned to Bartlett Cove. It's even possible to set up camp at Ptarmigan Creek and never move your tent, though at times this popular camping area is a tent city in the middle of the wilderness. To escape the August crowds,

paddle north to the end of Tarr Inlet and camp overnight in full view of Grand Pacific and Margerie glaciers. Just keep in mind that it's a full-day paddle from Ptarmigan Creek to the end of Tarr Inlet.

Getting Started

Once again turn to the Glacier Bay section in the Southeast chapter for general information about Glacier Bay National Park & Preserve. Once at Bartlett Cove, backpackers can stay in the free campground while preparing for their excursion up the bay. Call at the visitor center to obtain a backcountry permit and to purchase the proper topographic maps.

It's best to arrange both kayak rental and tour boat passage in advance. Glacier Bay Sea Kayaks in Gustavus will rent two-person kayaks for $50 a day for one to three days, $40 for four to six days. The price includes paddles, lifevests, spray covers and loading the kayaks on the tour boat. The *Spirit of Adventure* will provide drop-off and pick-up at Ptarmigan Creek from July to mid-September. One-way drop-offs are $88 per person, round-trip $168 per person.

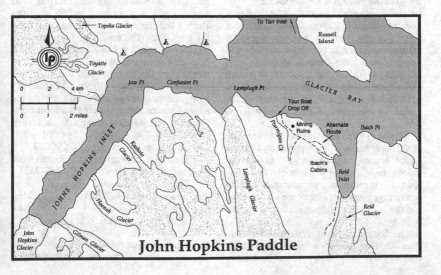

John Hopkins Paddle

You must pack waterproof clothing (pants, parka) and a camp stove. Stock up on supplies in Juneau to avoid having to purchase anything in Gustavus. To reserve a kayak contact Glacier Bay Sea Kayaks (☎ (907) 697-2257) at PO Box 26, Gustavus, AK 99826. This is a good little company and will also take care arranging the boat passage, give suggestions of other possible paddles, even rent you a pair of Southeast sneakers.

More Information

In Juneau, the US Forest Service office in the Centennial Hall supplies information on Glacier Bay along with maps and hand-outs. For information before you depart, contact the National Park Service (☎ (907) 697-2230), Glacier Bay National Park, Gustavus, AK 99826. Route sections and distances follow:

Section	miles
Ptarmigan Creek to Topeka Glacier in John Hopkins Inlet one-way	6.5
Ptarmigan Creek to Reid Inlet round-trip	5.9
Ptarmigan Creek to end of Tarr Inlet	15.0

SWANSON RIVER & SWAN LAKE

In the northern lowlands of the Kenai National Wildlife Refuge there is a chain of rivers, lakes, streams and portages (of course) that make up the Swanson River and nearby Swan Lake canoe routes. The trips are perfect for novice canoeists as rough water is rarely a problem and the portages do not exceed half a mile on the Swan Lake system or one mile in the Swanson River area.

Fishing is good for rainbow trout in many of the lakes and wildlife is plentiful; a trip on either route could result in sightings of moose, bear, beaver or a variety of waterfowl. Both routes are popular trips among Anchorage canoeists as they are well marked and maintained, with open shelters along the way.

The Swanson River system links more than 40 lakes and 46 miles of river, and a one-way trip is 80 miles. It can be a more challenging trip than the Swan Lake paddle, especially when the water is low. The easier Swan Lake route connects 30 lakes with forks of the Moose River; the one-way trip is 60 miles. A common four-day trip on Swan Lake begins at the west entrance of the canoe route and ends at Moose River Bridge on the Sterling Hwy.

Getting Started

To reach either the Swan Lake or Swanson River canoe routes, travel to *Mile 84* of the Sterling Hwy east of Soldotna and turn north on Robinson Lake Rd, just west of Moose River Bridge. Robinson Lake Rd turns into Swanson River Rd and leads to Swan Lake Rd 17 miles north from the Sterling Hwy. East on Swan Lake Rd are the entrances to both canoe systems, with the Swanson River route beginning at the very end of the road. The west entrance for Swan Lake is at Canoe Lake and the east entrance is another six miles beyond at Portage Lake; both are well marked.

During the summer, the Great Alaska Fish Camp, a lodge at *Mile 81.7* of the Sterling Hwy where it crosses the Moose River, rents out canoes and runs a shuttle bus service to the head of Swan Lake Canoe Trail. You conveniently end up back at Moose River Bridge and the camp to eliminate any need for a pick-up. The rental fee for a canoe is $25 per day, and it costs $60 to have your boat and yourself shipped to the western entrance of the trail and $70 to the eastern entrance. The same outfitter also rents out tents, sleeping bags and camp stoves for spur-of-the-moment wilderness adventurers. Contact the Great Alaska Fish Camp (☎ (907) 262-4515; (800) 544-2261 – toll free), PO Box 218, Sterling, AK 99672.

You can also rent canoes in Soldotna from Ronland's Sports Den (☎ (907) 262-7491), PO Box 2861, Soldotna, AK 99669; or in Anchorage from Hugh Glass Backpacking Company (☎ (907) 344-1340), PO Box 110796, Anchorage, AK 99511.

More Information

The visitor center for the Kenai National

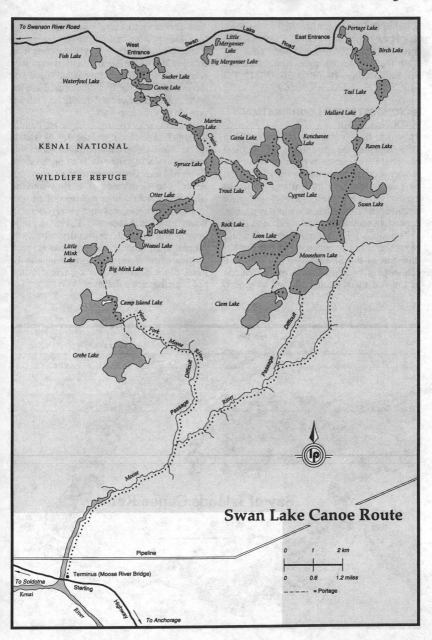

Swan Lake Canoe Route

Wildlife Refuge is at *Mile 97.9* of the Sterling Hwy, two miles south of Soldotna. You can also get information before your trip from the Refuge Manager, Kenai National Wildlife Refuge (☎ (907) 262-7021), PO Box 2139, Soldotna, AK 99669.

SAVONOSKI RIVER LOOP – KATMAI NATIONAL PARK

This route begins and ends at Brooks Camp (the summer headquarters of Katmai National Park) and takes paddlers into more remote sections of the preserve, offering the best in wilderness adventures with out expensive bush plane travel. The complete circuit is an 80-mile, six to eight-day paddle, depending on weather and wind conditions.

The trip is long and moderately difficult. No white water is encountered but the 12-mile run of the Savonoski River can be a challenging paddle because of its braided nature and many deadheads and sweepers.

You also have to carry your boat across a mile-long portage that during most summers is a mud-hole of a trail. The first section from Brooks Camp to the Bay of Islands is especially scenic and well protected at the end where you dip in and out of the Bay of Islands. Here the water is deep and clear and the offshore islands provide superb camp sites.

It takes two to three days to paddle through Naknek Lake and the Bay of Islands to the Lake Grosvenor portage. From this portage, it is a 14-mile paddle along the south shore of Lake Grosvenor to the Grosvenor River. The Grosvenor is a slow-moving clear-water river where paddlers often spot moose, bears, beavers and river otters. It flows into the Savonoski River, a prime brown-bear habitat, especially when the salmon are running. For this reason, park rangers often recommend paddling the 12 miles of the Savonoski in a single day and not camping along the river.

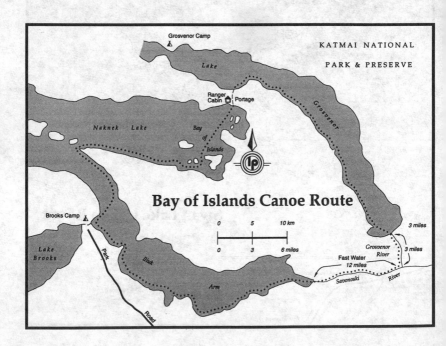

Bay of Islands Canoe Route

Top: Mt Blackburn & Kennicott Glacier, Wrangell-St Elias National Park (DS)
Bottom: Bonanza Mine, Wrangell-St Elias National Park (DS)

Top: Bald eagle over Homer Spit (DS)
Bottom: Russian Orthodox Church at Ninilchik, Kenai Peninsula (DS)

Canoeists also have to keep a sharp eye out for obstructions and sand bars that may develop in the river. The last leg is the 20-mile paddle along the south shore of the Iliuk Arm back to Brooks Camp.

Getting Started

See the Katmai National Park section in the Bush chapter for information on getting to and from the park; also check the section on the Valley of 10,000 Smokes in this chapter for the special backcountry needs of the preserve. Paddlers have to remember that Katmai is famous for its sudden and violent storms, some that last for days. Good waterproof clothing is essential and all gear should be sealed in plastic bags. It is unwise to paddle too far from shore, as it leaves you defenseless against sudden storms or high winds.

Getting a canoe or hard-shell kayak into the park is now possible as there is a jet-boat service from King Salmon to Brooks Camp. But most visitors either haul in a folding Klepper Kayak or rent a canoe from the lodge in Brooks Camp for $30 per day but you can't reserve them in advance.

For more rental information write to Katmailand Inc (☎ (800) 544-0551 – toll free), 4700 Aircraft Dr, Anchorage, AK 99502. Keep in mind the preferred mode of travel on this route is a kayak due to the sudden winds and rough nature of the big lakes. People still paddle it in canoes but generally need to sit out a day or two on every trip due to foul weather.

More Information

For more information about the park or hand-outs covering backcountry travel, contact the park headquarters at Katmai National Park (☎ (907) 246-3305), PO Box 7, King Salmon, AK 99613. Route sections and distances follow:

Section	miles
Brooks Camp to	
Lake Grosvenor portage	30.0
portage	1.0
Lake Grosvenor to Grosvenor River	14.0
Grosvenor River to Savonoski River	3.0
Savonoski River to Iliuk Arm	12.0
along Iliuk Arm to Brooks Camp	20.0

CHENA RIVER

The Chena River is one of the finest rivers for canoeing in the Fairbanks area and a longtime favorite among local residents. It flows through a landscape of rolling forested hills with access to alpine tundra above 2800 feet. The river features no white water and paddlers only have to watch out for the occasional sweeper or log jam.

Wildlife in the area includes brown bears, moose, red foxes, beavers and river otters, while the fishing is excellent for grayling and northern pike. With the Interior's long, hot summer days, this trip can be an outstanding wilderness adventure.

Getting Started

Chena Hot Springs Rd provides access to the river at *Mile 27.9* east of Fairbanks, *Mile 28.6*, *Mile 29.4*, *Mile 33.9* at Four Mile Creek and *Mile 39.6* at North Fork Chena River where there is a state campground (20 sites, $6 fee). From *Mile 39.6* of Chena Hot Springs Rd, the paddle along the river to Fairbanks is a 70-mile trip that can be done comfortably in four to five days.

You can rent canoes from 7 Bridges Boats & Bikes (☎ (907) 479-0751), which set up shop on the north side of the Cushman St Bridge. They rent boats for $30 a day and will probably make you a deal for a week-long rental. More importantly, they will provide transport out along Chena Hot Springs Rd for a $1 a mile. Beaver Sports (☎ (907) 479-2494) at 3480 College Rd in Fairbanks has canoes for rent at $85 per week but you have to worry about getting to the trailhead. Hitchhiking with a canoe is tough, though I've seen several backpackers be successful at it.

The other alternative is to rent a used car in Fairbanks (see the Getting Around section in the Fairbanks chapter), drop off the canoe and hitchhike back to the trailhead after returning the car to Fairbanks.

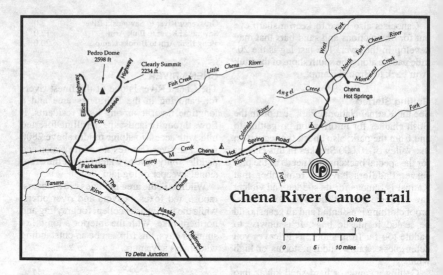

Chena River Canoe Trail

More Information

Much of the river lies in the Chena River State Recreation Area, which is administered by the Alaska Division of State Parks. Contact the Fairbanks office for more information at the Division of Parks (☎ (907) 451-2695), 3700 Airport Way, Fairbanks, AK 99709.

BEAVER CREEK

Travellers with lots of time, a yearning to paddle through a roadless wilderness but not a lot of funds for bush-plane travel, will find Beaver Creek the ultimate adventure. The moderately swift stream, characterized by long clear pools and frequent rapids, is rated Grade I in difficulty and can be handled by novice canoers with previous expedition experience. The Bureau of Land Management (BLM) manages the 111-mile creek, as part of the White Mountains National Recreation Area, where it flows through rolling hills forested in white spruce and paper birch and past the jagged peaks of the White Mountains.

The scenery is spectacular, the chances of seeing another party remote and you'll catch so much grayling you'll probably never want to eat another one after the trip. If you take a day off at Victoria Creek and scale the 5000-foot high Victoria Peak, you should see wildlife such as moose, bears and mountain sheep. You can also spend a night in the Borealis-Le Fevre Cabin, a BLM cabin on the banks of Beaver Creek.

The trip begins from *Mile 58* of the Steese Hwy at Nome Creek where nine times out of 10, due to low water, you'll be forced to line your boat 10 miles to its confluence with Beaver Creek. Most paddlers then plan on seven to 10 days to reach Victoria Creek, a 127-mile trip, where gravel bars nearby are used by bush planes to land and pick paddlers up.

You can avoid the air fare by continuing along Beaver Creek which spills out of the White Mountains into Yukon Flats National Wildlife Refuge where it slows down and meanders through a marshy area. Eventually it flows north into the Yukon River where after two or three days you'll pass under the Yukon River Bridge over Dalton Hwy. This is a 395-mile paddle and a three-week expedition – the stuff great Alaska adventures are made of. See the White Mountain Trail & Beaver

Creek Canoe Route map in the Trekking section of this chapter.

Getting Started

You can rent a canoe at either 7 Bridges Boats & Bikes or Beaver Sports, see the Chena River Canoe Route in this chapter for details. The trick is to arrange transport out to the Steese Hwy and be picked up on the Dalton Hwy – either one is a challenge in logistics. The start of the paddle is at *Mile 58* of the Steese Hwy where a rough 4WD track, US Creek Rd, leads down to Nome Creek. The Yukon River Bridge on the Dalton Hwy is about 175 miles north of Fairbanks.

Try Backcountry Logistical Services (☎ (907) 457-7606) at PO Box 82265, Fairbanks, AK 99708-2265, where you can rent the canoe and put together some transportation, all for a price, of course. Another way to arrange transport is to visit the student center at the University of Alaska (Fairbanks) and seek out somebody looking to earn a few dollars. Even if you have to pay them $75 to drop you off on the Steese Hwy and $100 to haul you out from the Yukon River, it would still be a fraction of a bush-plane fare.

If you do find transport, keep in mind that Steven's Village is half a day's paddle from the Yukon River Bridge on the banks of the river. Spending a night in this small village is a cultural experience in itself and you could use its one radiotelephone to contact your driver and arrange an exact pick-up time for the next day.

You can also check with the Fairbanks Visitor Center for any tour company running trips up the Dalton Hwy.

More Information

For more information contact the Steese-White District of the BLM (☎ (907) 474-2200), at 1150 University Ave, Fairbanks, AK 99709.

TOURS

Guide Companies

Most of Alaska's wilderness is not accessible to the first-time visitor; travelers either don't know about wilderness areas or don't know how to get to them. This is where guide companies are very useful.

Guides are not only for novice, never-put-on-a-backpack campers. Their clients can be experienced backpackers who want to explore the far reaches of Alaska's wilderness but don't have the time or money to put together an expedition on their own. Guides can arrange the many details of a large-scale trip into the backcountry – everything from food and equipment to air charter. They work on the principle that a group of 10 or 12 people can explore an area cheaper than one or two.

Trips can range from a day hike on a glacier to a 12-day raft trip or a three-week ascent of Mt McKinley, and costs range from $150 to more than $200 per day, depending upon the amount of air travel involved. Expeditions usually have five to 12 clients; guide companies are hesitant to take larger groups because of their environmental impact. The tour season is from late May to September, while a select group of companies specialize in winter expeditions of Nordic (cross-country) skiing or dog-sledding.

Guided expeditions cost money, and most budget travelers prefer unguided trips. However, many guide companies offer adventures to areas that are only visited by a few people each year and there is something inviting about that. Although most companies begin taking reservations in April, don't hesitate to call one after you've arrived in Alaska. Often you can score a hefty discount of 30 to 50% in the middle of the summer as guide companies are eager to fill any remaining places on a scheduled trip.

The following is a list of recreational guide companies in Alaska. Don't get them confused with hunting or fishing guides whose main interest is to make sure that their client gets a trophy to hang on the wall of the family room. Also be careful not to confuse expeditions with fishing camps or wilderness lodges. The camps and lodges are established rustic resorts in the wilderness where you spend a week with many of the comforts of home, but see little beyond the immediate area.

Southeast Southeast Exposure (☎ (907) 225-8829), PO Box 9143, Ketchikan, AK 99901, is a Ketchikan guide company that rents kayaks and offers guided trips to Misty Fjords National Monument and Barrier Islands, a wilderness area on Prince of Wales Island. A four-day paddle to the heart of Rudyerd Bay, the most scenic part of Misty Fjords, along with Manzanita Bay and Behm Canal is $630 per person and includes boat transport from Ketchikan. A six-day trip that also includes Walker Cove is $870 per person while an eight-day expedition into Barrier Islands is $1,210.

Alaska Discovery (☎ (907) 586-1911), 234 Gold St, Juneau, AK 99801, was organized in 1972 and today is one of the oldest and largest guide companies in Alaska. They used to operate mainly in the Southeast but have since expanded with raft trips down the Kongakat River in the Arctic National Wildlife Refuge and even hiking expeditions into Russian Far East. Still, kayak trips in Glacier Bay and Russell Fjord, home of Hubbard Glacier, and raft trips down the Tatshenshini River are their specialty. Among their expeditions are a five-day paddle in Glacier Bay for $1,500 per person and a spectacular nine-day Hubbard Glacier adventure for $1550 per person. They also offer a seven-day canoe journey to Pack Creek on Admiralty Island to photograph brown bears for $1250 per person.

Chilkat Guides (☎ (907) 766-2491), PO Box 170, Haines, AK 99827, offers a handful of raft trips from its base in Haines, including a four-hour float down the Chilkat River to view bald eagles. The small guiding company is best known for its raft trips down the Tatshenshini and Alsek rivers. Both are spectacular trips past dozens of glaciers. The 'Tat' is a 10-day float for $1650 per person and the Alsek, which involves helicopter time in bypassing Turnback Canyon, is a 13-day trip for $2125.

Alaska Cross Country Guiding & Rafting

(☎ (907) 767-5522), PO Box 124, Haines, AK 99827, is based in Haines and runs trips around the Chilkat Bald Eagle Preserve. Wildlife photography and hiking trips are supported by raft, canoe and sometimes air boats. The outfitter's best trip begins with a flight to remote mountainous cabins just outside Glacier Bay National Park for a night and then continues with a float down to the Chilkat River back to Haines. This two-day adventure is $452 per person.

Anchorage Area & Southcentral Adventures & Delights (☎ (907) 276-8282 or (800) 288-3134), 414 K St, Anchorage, AK 99501, specializes in sea-kayak adventures in Prince William Sound and Kenai Fjords National Park. A three-day paddle into Resurrection Bay from Seward is $575 per person, a three-day trip into Kenai Fjords is $795. The company also rents kayaks in Seward and can arrange drop-off and pick-up service.

Hugh Glass Backpacking Co (☎ (907) 344-1340), PO Box 110796, Anchorage, AK 99511, is a long-established guide company which offers a wide range of trips into Prince William Sound, Kenai Fjords National Park, the Arctic National Wildlife Refuge, Katmai National Park, Brooks Range, and the Wrangell and St Elias mountains. Trips may include trekking, canoeing, rafting or sea kayaking, and can be designed as photography or fishing adventures. Among its expeditions is a nine-day expedition into Lake Clark National Park that combines hiking with rafting for $1,595 per person.

Alaska River Adventures (☎ (907) 276-3418), Mile 48.2 Sterling Hwy, Cooper Landing, AK 99572, offers guided tours all year round. In summer, they run boating trips from a overnighter along the Kenai River for $149 to three days of white-water paddling through the Talkeetna Canyon and five days on Lake Creek, south of Mt McKinley, for $1695. There are also longer expeditions to the Alagnak River and the Kanektok River in the Bristol Bay region as well as sea kayaking on Prince William Sound and Kenai Fjords (six days/$1795).

CampAlaska (☎ (907) 376-9438), PO

Box 872247, Wasilla, AK 99687, is not quite a true wilderness guide company. They offer van tours that combine camping with day hikes, rafting, canoeing and, of course, sightseeing from the Alaskan highways. CampAlaska also runs a seven-day trip along the George Parks and Richardson highways that includes Denali National Park, Fairbanks and Valdez for $575 per person. A 10-day 'Alaska Range Bike & Hike' trip that includes biking Denali Hwy and hiking in Denali National Park is $1,100 per person.

Alaska Wildtrek (☎ (907) 235-6463), PO Box 1741, Homer, AK 99603, offers guided tours throughout the state from the Brooks Range to the Alaska Peninsula. Directed by Chlaus Lotscher, a German 'transplant' in Alaska, the company caters almost entirely to Europeans, especially Germans.

Mt McKinley & the Interior St Elias Alpine Guides (☎ (907) 277-6867), PO Box 111241, Anchorage, AK 99511, specializes in mountaineering and glacier skiing adventures at Wrangell-St Elias National Park. They also offer a 12-day trip down the Copper River to Cordova and a 11-day backpacking trip around Chitistone Canyon of the Wrangell-St Elias National Park. Many of the trips begin and end in Anchorage and the prices range from $1,900 to $2,200 per person.

Denali Raft Adventures (☎ (907) 683-2234), Drawer 190, Denali Park, AK 99755, offers a variety of day rafting trips down the Nenana River near Denali National Park; some are in calm waters while others involve two hours of white-water rafting. Prices range from $36 to $60 per person for two to five-hour trips. They also have a full-day trip.

Nova (☎ (907) 745-5753), PO Box 1129, Chickaloon, AK 99674, specializes in river rafting. Their trips range from a day run down the Matanuska River for $50 per person to a three-day journey along the Talkeetna River that involves flying to the heart of the Talkeetna Mountains and grade IV white water for $700 per person. The company runs trips to the Kobuk River in the

Brooks Range (10 days for $2,300 per person) and the Cooper River in Wrangell-St Elias National Park (six days for $1,200).

Alaska Back Country Guides Co-op (☎ (907) 479-8907), PO Box 81533, Fairbanks, AK 99708, is based in Fairbanks and offers a variety of backpacking, glacier trekking, rafting and canoeing trips. Among them are canoe trips in the Wrangell-St Elias National Park and throughout the Kenai Peninsula.

Alaska Whitewater (☎ (907) 822-5850), PO Box 12294, Anchorage, AK 99514, has an excellent two-day float down the Tonsina River for $299 per person that features wildlife and the outstanding mountain scenery of the Wrangell-St Elias National Park. There is also a three-day, fly-in trip for $549 on the same river.

Fairbanks & Brooks Range Alaska Fish & Trails Unlimited (☎ (907) 479-7630), 1177 Shypoke Dr, Fairbanks, AK 99701, runs backpacking, kayaking and canoeing trips in the Gates of the Arctic National Park, a photography trip in late fall, spring Nordic ski tours and fishing adventures that include rafting out of the Brooks Range to Bettles.

Arctic Treks (☎ (907) 455-6502), PO Box 73452, Fairbanks, AK 99707, is a family operation that specializes in treks and rafting in the Gates of the Arctic National Park and the Arctic National Wildlife Refuge. A 15-day trip to circumnavigate the highest peak in the western Brooks Range combines backpacking and rafting in the Gates of the Arctic and costs $2500. They also float the Hulahula River through the Arctic North Slope for 10 days for $2450 and offer an eight-day base camp in fall to witness the caribou migration for $2250.

Sourdough Outfitters (☎ (907) 692-5252), PO Box 90, Bettles, AK 99726, runs canoe, kayak and backpacking trips to the Gates of the Arctic National Park, Noatak and Kobuk rivers and other areas. The outfitters also provide unguided trips for individuals who have the experience to make an independent journey but want a guide company to handle the logistics (such as trip planning, transport and canoe or raft rental) of a major expedition. Unguided trips throughout the Brooks Range are priced from $300 to $800 per person depending on the number of people in your party. Guided trips range from an eight-day backpacking trek in the Gates of the Arctic National Park for $1250 per person to a 10-day canoe trip along the Noatak River for $1900 per person and a five-day paddle of the Wild River in the Brooks Range for $1050 per person.

CanoeAlaska (☎ (907) 479-5183), PO Box 81750, Fairbanks, AK 99708, specializes in canoeing trips that teach boating skills and explore scenic rivers. Classes are limited to eight people and rafts are used to support and assist paddlers. Throughout the summer, the guide company runs two-day trips on the Chena River and three-day outings on the Gulkana River. The cost is $125 per person and includes instruction, canoe and paddling equipment, meals and transport.

Southeast Alaska

The north country begins in Southeast Alaska, as do the summer adventures of many visitors to the state, and for good reasons. The Southeast is the closest part of Alaska to continental USA; Ketchikan is only 90 minutes away by air from Seattle or two days on the State Marine Ferry from Bellingham.

The Southeast, affected greatly by warm ocean currents, has the mildest climate in Alaska and offers warm summer temperatures averaging 69°F, with an occasional heat wave that sends temperatures to 80°F. Similarly, the winters are equally mild and subzero day temperatures are rare. Residents who have learned to live with an annual rainfall of 60 to 200 inches call the frequent rain 'liquid sunshine'. The heavy precipitation creates the dense, lush forests and numerous waterfalls most travelers come to cherish.

Travel to and around the Southeast is easy. The Alaska State Marine Ferry system connects this roadless area to Bellingham in the US state of Washington and provides transport around the area, making it the longest (and many think the best) public ferry system in North America. Relaxing three-day cruises through the maze of islands and coastal mountains of the Southeast's Alexander Archipelago are a pleasant alternative to the long and often bumpy Alcan (Alaska Hwy). The state ferry connects 14 ports and services 64,000 residents, of which 75% live in Juneau, Ketchikan, Sitka, Petersburg and Wrangell.

However, the best reason to begin and end your trip in the Southeast is its scenery. Few places in the world have the spectacular views found in the Southeast. Rugged snow-capped mountains rise steeply from the water to form sheer-sided fjords, decorated by cascading waterfalls. Ice-blue glaciers that begin among the highest peaks, fan out into a valley of dark-green Sitka spruce trees, and wilderness waters support whales, sea lions, harbor seals and huge salmon runs.

At one time the Southeast was the heart and soul of Alaska, and Juneau was not only the capital but the state's major city. However, WW II and the Alcan shifted the state's growth to Anchorage and Fairbanks. Today, much of the region lies sleepily in the Tongass National Forest, which at 16 million acres, is the largest national forest in the USA.

In recent years, the Southeast has experienced an incredible boom in summer tourism, but there is still room to breathe. The population density is about 2.5 people per sq mile and will probably stay that way as much of the region is federal monuments and preserves such as the spectacular Glacier Bay National Park & Preserve, Admiralty Island and Misty Fjords national monuments, Klondike National Historical Park, Tracy Arm and Fords Terror wilderness.

More than anywhere else in Alaska, each community in the Southeast clings to its own character, color and past. There is Norwegian-influenced Petersburg and Russian-tinted Sitka. You can feel the gold fever in Skagway, see lumberjacks and fishers in Ketchikan or venture to Juneau for a hefty dose of government, glaciers and uncontrolled growth.

The best way to visit the Southeast is to purchase a ferry ticket from Bellingham to Skagway ($236 one way) with lengthy stops

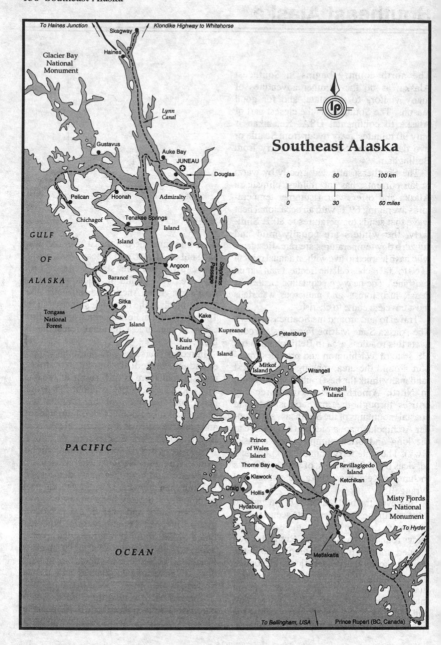

at a handful of towns. To rush from the Lower 48 to Juneau and then fly to Anchorage is to miss some of the best things that Alaska has to offer.

Ketchikan

Ketchikan, otherwise known as the First City, has a population of 13,828 and is on the south-west side of Revillagigedo (ra-vee-ah-ga-GAY-doh) Island, only 90 miles north of Prince Rupert. It is the first stop the state ferry makes in Alaska so tourists pile off the boat for their first look at the north country, and rarely does Ketchikan disappoint them.

The town grew around salmon canneries and sawmills. The first cannery was built in 1883, and at one time Ketchikan was proclaimed the 'Salmon Capital of the World', a title which has since disappeared. A sawmill was built in the center of Ketchikan in 1903, and in 1954 the huge Ketchikan Pulp Mill was constructed at Ward Cove. However, in the 1970s over-fishing nearly collapsed the salmon fisheries while strikes began to mar the logging industry.

Just as Ketchikan began to recover from hard times, the sawmill in the city center was hit by a strike in 1983 that resulted in Louisiana-Pacific's closing the mill. Two years later the historical downtown mill was razed for a parking lot. In 1984, Louisiana-Pacific shut down the Ward Cove Pulp Mill, the area's major employer, for six months, and Ketchikan's population actually decreased during the hard times of the early 1980s.

The city and the people survive, a credit to their frontier image. Although the First City's industries now include government services and tourism, fishing and timber are still its trademark. Fishing provides almost 20% of the city's economy and 230 commercial fishers are based in Ketchikan. The timber industry (consisting of logging, a sawmill and a pulp mill) account for another 14.5% of the jobs. These industries have given the city its rough-and-tumble character

and on a Saturday night Ketchikan bars are full, loud and lively.

If you stay in Ketchikan longer than an hour, chances are good that it will rain at least once, if not several times. The average annual rainfall is 162 inches, but has been known to be more than 200 inches. Despite all the rain, the only people with umbrellas are tourists. First City residents never seem to use them, nor do they let the rain interfere with their daily activities, even outdoor ones, whether it be fishing, hiking or having a softball game. If they stopped everything every time it drizzled, Ketchikan would cease to exist.

Orientation

The city is spread out – it is several miles long and never more than 10 blocks wide. Ketchikan is centered around one road, Tongass Ave, which runs along the shores of Tongass Narrows and sometimes over it, supported by pillars. Crossroads appear mostly in the city center and the area surrounding the state ferry terminal known as West End. There were no traffic signals in Ketchikan until 1984, and the first one was installed despite the objections of many residents. Many businesses and homes are suspended above the water or cling to the hillside and have winding staircases or wooden streets leading to their front doors.

On a clear day – and there are a few during the summer – Ketchikan is a bustling community. It is backed by forested hills and surrounded by a waterway that hums with float planes, fishing boats, ferries and large cruise ships; to the south is the distinctively shaped Deer Mountain. Whether basked in sunshine or painted with a light drizzle, Ketchikan is an interesting place to start an Alaskan summer.

Information
Tourist Offices The Ketchikan Visitor Bureau (☎ 225-6166) on the City Dock can supply general information about Ketchikan and the city bus system. The bureau is open Monday to Friday from 8 am to 6 pm.

For information about hiking trails, cabin

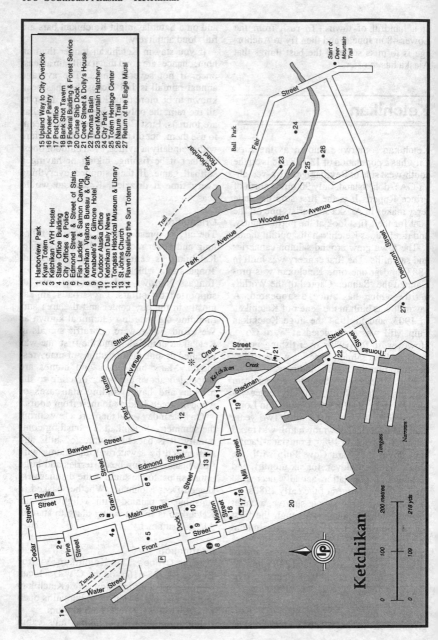

Ketchikan

1 Harborview Park
2 Kyan Totem
3 Ketchikan AYH Hostel
4 State Office Building
5 City Offices & Police
6 Edmond Street & Street of Stairs
7 Fish Ladder & Salmon Carving
8 Ketchikan Visitors Bureau & City Park
9 Annabelle's & Gilmore Hotel
10 Outdoor Alaska
11 Ketchikan Daily News
12 Tongass Historical Museum & Library
13 St Johns Church
14 Raven Stealing the Sun Totem

15 Upland Way to City Overlook
16 Pioneer Pantry
17 Post Office
18 Bank Shot Tavern
19 Federal Building & Forest Service
20 Cruise Ship Dock
21 Creek Street & Dolly's House
22 Thomas Basin
23 Deer Mountain Hatchery
24 City Park
25 Totem Heritage Center
26 Nature Trail
27 Return of the Eagle Mural

reservations or other outdoor opportunities, contact the US Forest Service (USFS) information center (☎ 225-3101) in the Federal Building on the corner of Stedman and Mill streets. It is open from 7.30 am to 4.30 pm weekdays and has information and handouts on activities in the Ketchikan area and a list of cabins still available during the summer. There is also an interesting slide presentation and other displays.

Laundromats & Showers The Highliner Cafe & Laundromat (☎ 225-5308) is at 2703 Tongass Ave while The Matt (☎ 225-0628) is at 989 Stedman St.

If you are camping and need a shower in town, you can head to one of Ketchikan's two public pools at the Valley Park Elementary School (☎ 225-5720), south-east of the city center, or Ketchikan High School (☎ 225-2010) on Baranof Rd in the West End area. Call for opening times and rates. There are also showers at the Highliner Cafe & Laundromat.

Things to See
The best way to explore Ketchikan is on foot with a three-hour, two-mile walk around the city center. Start at the visitors bureau, a brown building on the busy City Dock, and pick up a free *Ketchikan Walking Tour Map* which has a two-mile tour that highlights 27 attractions and takes about two hours to cover. Begin by heading up Mission St and swinging (south-west) over to Mill St, past the site of the Ketchikan Spruce Mill that was demolished in 1985.

Within three blocks, on the corner of Mills and Stedman streets, is the distinctive white **Federal Building** where the US Forest Service maintains its Tongass National Forest Visitor Center on the 1st floor.

By turning right (south-west) on Stedman St, you cross Ketchikan Creek and come to **Creek St**, not so much a street as a boardwalk built on pilings. This was the famed red-light district in Ketchikan for half a century until prostitution became illegal in 1954. During its heyday, Creek St supported up to 30 brothels. The first house, with its

Creek St, Ketchikan

bright red doors and windows, is **Dolly's House**, the parlor of the city's most famous madam, Dolly Arthur.

The house has since been turned into a museum dedicated to this infamous era and is open only when there are tour ships in port – almost daily during summer. For a $2.50 admission fee you can see the brothel, including its bar that was placed over a trapdoor to the creek for quick disposal of bootleg whiskey. There are another 20 buildings on Creek St including small shops and a restaurant. Perhaps the best attraction on this unusual street is free – watching the salmon swim up Ketchikan Creek to spawn.

Across from Creek St (to the south) is **Thomas Basin**, one of three boat harbors in the city. It is impossible to stay in Ketchikan and not spend any time at the waterfront. The lifeblood of this narrow city is found in its collection of boat harbors, float planes and fishing fleets that stretch along the lapping waters of the Tongass Narrows.

Thomas Basin, along with Thomas Street

(another boardwalk built on pilings) is the most picturesque harbor. An hour or so spent at the docks will acquaint you with Ketchikan's fishing fleet and the three kinds of fishing boats – gillnetters, power trollers and seiners. You may even end up at the colorful Potlatch Bar on Thomas St having a brew with someone from the fishing fleet.

Continuing south on Stedman St, you'll pass the large mural, *Return of the Eagle*, on the Ketchikan Community College's Robinson Building. Turn left (east) onto Deermont St. At the beginning of the street is a steep hill, the first of many you will tackle in the Southeast, and at the end is the trailhead for the 3.1-mile climb to Deer Mountain (see the Trekking section in the Wilderness chapter). About halfway up the street to the left is a short road that swings to the **Totem Heritage Center**, where totem poles salvaged from deserted Tlingit communities are brought to be restored to their original condition.

The total collection, the largest in Alaska, numbers more than 30. Five of the poles are on display in the central gallery along with indigenous art and artefacts. There are also lectures, films and a 15-minute guided tour during the summer, usually scheduled around the times when the large cruise ships are in port. The center (☎ 225-5900) is open daily from 8 am to 5 pm in the summer; admission is $2 but it is free on Sunday afternoon.

A bridge from the Totem Heritage Center crosses Ketchikan Creek to the **Deer Mountain Hatchery** (☎ 225-6760), a fascinating place where biologists annually raise 150,000 king salmon and an equal number of coho salmon and then release them into the nearby stream. Observation platforms, outdoor displays and friendly workers provide an interesting lesson in the salmon's life cycle. In July or later, you'll see not only the salmon fry but returning adult fish swimming upstream to spawn.

Next to the hatchery is **City Park**, a quiet spot with numerous small streams, each, it seems, with its own wooden bridge and bench. The park is a pleasant place to escape from the bustling crowds and tour

groups that fill the city when a cruise ship is in town.

From the hatchery head down Park Ave, cross Ketchikan Creek again and on the other side of the road you will soon see the Upland Way stairs. A climb up the stairs takes you to a viewing platform overlooking the city center, Thomas Basin and Creek St. Beyond Upland Way on Park Ave you will arrive at another bridge crossing Ketchikan Creek, with a wooden salmon mounted over a fish ladder at the creek's falls. The ladder enables salmon to reach upstream spawning gravels; it's a magnificent sight when these fish leap against the current during the late-summer migration.

Park Ave curves south towards the city center and ends at Dock St. Near the corner of Park Ave and Dock St is the Centennial Building which houses the **Ketchikan Public Library** and the **Tongass Historical Museum**. The museum features a small collection of local and indigenous artefacts, many of them tied in with Ketchikan's fishing industry; entry costs $1 but is free on Sunday.

Among the more interesting displays is the model of the *Ketchikan Queen*, a seine boat. The museum is open Monday to Sunday from 8 am to 5 pm during the summer. The library is open Monday and Wednesday from 10 am to 8 pm, Tuesday and Thursday to Saturday from 10 am to 6 pm and from Sunday 1 to 5 pm. Just outside the Centennial Building is the 'Raven Stealing the Sun' totem, which was commissioned by the city in 1983.

Head west along Dock St, and alongside the Ketchikan Daily News Building is Edmond St. This is the 'Street of Stairs', as it leads to a system of long staircases. Back along on Dock St, the next crossroad to the west is Main St which leads north to the Ketchikan (AYH) Hostel on the corner of Grant St and to the huge Kyan Totem another block beyond that. If you stay on Dock St and head west, you will return to the City Dock.

Festivals

Ketchikan has three major festivals during the summer, of which the Fourth of July celebration is the biggest and the best. It includes a parade, contests and softball games, an impressive display of fireworks over the channel and a logging show sponsored by the Alaska Loggers Association.

On a smaller scale is the Blueberry Festival that takes place in the lower floor and basement of the State Office Building towards the end of August. The festival consists of an arts & crafts show, singers and musicians, and food stalls that serve blueberries in every possible way.

Places to Stay

Camping There are four public campgrounds in Ketchikan and all of them, except Settler's Cove, are $5 per night for a site and have a 14-day limit. Unfortunately, none of them is close to town.

Settler's Cove (12 sites) is 16 miles north of the ferry terminal and has tables, pit toilets, firewood, a beach area but no hookups. There is a $6 per night charge and a seven-day limit that is enforced.

The other three campgrounds are on Ward Lake Rd. Take North Tongass Hwy four miles north of the ferry terminal to the pulp mill on Ward Cove and then turn right onto Ward Lake Rd. The first campground is *Signal Creek* (25 sites), a mile up the road. It is followed by *CCC Campground* (four sites) a quarter of a mile further up and *Last Chance Campground* (25 sites), another 1.8 miles along Ward Lake Rd.

The entire area is known as the Ward Lake Recreational Area and a night spent here is worth all the effort it takes to reach it. Along with the campgrounds there are four scenic lakes and three trails that dip back into the surrounding lush rainforest.

Hostels The *Ketchikan (AYH) Hostel* (☎ 225-3319) is in the basement of the United Methodist Church on the corner of Grant and Main streets in the center of the city. It's open from Memorial Day (25 May) to Labor Day (7 September) and provides kitchen facilities (50c extra per meal), showers and a space on the floor with a mat to sleep on.

The hostel is interesting because it always seems full with travelers heading north for a long trip. Since Ketchikan is their first Alaskan stop, they fill the recreation room with travel talk and much excitement in the evenings, and often depart the hostel with a traveling partner or having made warm friendships. The fee is $5 per night for hosteling members and $8 per night for nonmembers. If you're arriving at night, call the hostel to check whether space is available.

The *Rain Forest Inn* (☎ 225-9500) is at 2311 Hemlock St, 0.7 miles from the state ferry terminal and half a block from the bus stop on the corner of Tongass Ave and Jefferson St. The Inn offers dormitory bunks for $21 per night and provides showers, laundry facilities and a guest lounge. There are also eight rooms for rent ($45 per night) that accommodate from two to four guests.

B&Bs Check with Ketchikan Bed & Breakfast (☎ 225-8550) to arrange a stay in a private home. Rates begin at $50/60 a single/double, and include breakfast and usually transport from the ferry terminal or airport. You might consider *The Great Alaska Cedar Works* (☎ 247-8287) which at one time was the foreman of a salmon cannery's house. Eleven miles north of the city, it offers two bedrooms and a sleeping loft with a great view of the Inside Passage; rates are $35/55 a single/double, or $25 per person for three or more.

Other B&Bs offer more unusual accommodations. At *Water Street Bed & Breakfast* (☎ 247-0200) you can stay in an older home with a mountain view or a houseboat. The couple live within walking distance of the downtown area at 1508 Water St and charge $50/60 a single/double. *North Tongass Bed & Breakfast* (☎ 225-3273 or toll-free (800) 478-4121) is out the road at Ward Cove and has a two-bedroom apartment nestled in the woods. The place sleeps up to six people and goes for $60 a night for two and $25 for each additional person.

Hotels There is a wide range of hotels in Ketchikan from those catering to cruise-ship tourists to the more dilapidated ones, like the *Union Rooms Hotel* (☎ 225-3580), at 319 Mill St, that survive on the flood of summer workers coming to the city. The *Gilmore Hotel* (☎ 225-9423) at 326 Front St used to be another run-down place before undergoing major renovations, giving it a historical flavor. They still have studio rooms with shared baths but the rates now range from $64 to $90 per night.

There's also *Super 8 Motel* (☎ 225-9088) a half-mile south of the ferry terminal at 2151 Sea Level with rates that begin at $76. From here, the prices at the rest of the hotels jump to $80 per night or more during the summer. Among those to try are the *Best Western Landing* (☎ 225-5166) 3434 Tongass Ave or the *New York Hotel* (☎ 225 0246), a charming eight-room hotel with a waterfront view and located downtown adjacent to Creek St.

Resorts & Lodges There are a number of resorts and 'wilderness lodges' scattered around the Ketchikan area that offer remote locations, full accommodations and the boats, equipment and guides to almost guarantee some fishing success. More often than not, you pay for a 'package stay' that includes room, meals and use of a boat. Prices range anywhere from $1700 for a four-day/three-night stay to more than $2500 for an entire week.

One of the exceptions is *Alaskan Home Fishing Lodge*, 11 miles north of Ketchikan which can be reached by a rental car as opposed to a float plane. Its lodge accommodates 10 guests who have access to a gym and jacuzzi in its wooded rainforest setting. The lodge (☎ (800) 876-0925) offers a three-night package rate of $750 per person during the summer which includes fishing expeditions.

Sixty-two air miles west of Ketchikan on Prince of Wales Island is *Waterfall Resort* (☎ (800) 544-5124 or 225-9461) offering individual cabins, a boarding house, store and lodge in the remote site of an old cannery. Activities range from fishing and hiking to touring the cannery. Rates begin at $2275 per person for three nights/four days

and includes the float plane from Ketchikan, all meals, a room and fishing trips.

Also on the east side of Prince of Wales Island is *Boardwalk Wilderness Lodge*, (☎ (800) 327-9382) 42 air miles from Ketchikan. The lodge holds only eight people and rates begin at $1875 per person for three nights/four days.

Places to Eat

There's a good choice of places to eat in Ketchikan, but all places reflect the expensive Alaskan prices that usually send the newly arrived visitor into a two-day fast. If this is your first Alaskan city, don't fret – it gets worse as you go north!

For breakfast in the city center, there is the *Pioneer Pantry* at 124 Front St, that opens at 7 am and where two eggs, potatoes and toast costs $7. For deli sandwiches or subs check out *Grandeli's* in the Plaza Shopping Mall and be prepared to shell out from $4 to $7. In the back of the Gilmore Mall on Front St is *Annabelle's* for sourdough pancakes in the morning, chowders for lunch and an espresso at night. You'll find the chowder costs $5 a cup and sandwiches from $7 to $10.

The best restaurant for vegetarian dishes and other 'healthy stuff' is *The Five Star Cafe* in the Star Building on Creek Street. Their menu ranges from home-made soups and baked goods to a nice variety of sandwiches, salads, even an espresso bar. Also in the same building is *A&G Mercantile* that sells health foods.

During the summer, the City Dock has several food vendors serving everything from shish kebabs and clam chowder to halibut sandwiches and crepes; most items are under $6 and can be enjoyed while watching the busy waterway and without having to leave a tip.

Ketchikan is one of a handful of communities with a *McDonald's*; it's in Port West Plaza on Tongass Ave between the ferry terminal and the tunnel. *Pizza Mill* at 808 Water St and *Harbor Lights Pizza*, 2531 Tongass Ave, are the places to go for a large pizza with everything on it and a pitcher of beer.

The cheapest way to enjoy Alaskan seafood, is to purchase it in the supermarkets or stop at the *Silver Lining* store at 1705 Tongass Ave, where you can purchase fresh seafood then cook it yourself.

Entertainment

After hiking all day, if you're still raring to go, try the *Bank Shot Tavern* on 127 Main St. The split-level bar has entertainment and dancing nightly during the summer and can be an exceptionally lively place in the true 'bottoms up' fashion.

Another lively place with dance music is the *Sourdough Bar* at the north end of the City Dock. The walls of the bar are covered with rows of photos (all of fishing boats) while ship bells, ring floats and other fishing memorabilia hang from the ceiling.

The longtime fisher's pub is the *Potlatch Bar* on Thomas St just above the Thomas Basin Boat Harbor. Just before you enter the tunnel you'll see the *Arctic Bar*, a quiet little place where you can go for an afternoon brew on a hot summer day. The bar is built on pillars above the water and has an open deck that overlooks Tongass Narrows. Here you can enjoy the sea breeze while watching the float planes take off and land, as Taquan Air is next door and moors its planes at the dock right below the deck. For something quieter, stop in at *Annabelle's* in the Gilmore Hotel for some light entertainment and a beer in the historic décor.

Tours

Need a tour of the city? Ketchikan being the cruise ship port that it is has bundle of different tours you can sign up for. Tour giant *Gray Line* (☎ 225-5930) has a Totem Bight and City tour that lasts 2½ hours and costs $29 per person and a Saxman Native Village Tour for $40 which lasts three hours.

For something cheaper try the local companies. Orca Tours (☎ 225-0411) has a two-hour tour that includes Totem Bight and Creek Street for $10 per person and Ketchikan Local Tours (☎ 225-1989) has a one-hour special that includes a quick (very quick) visit to Saxman Totem Park for $14.

For something a little more natural, call North Wind Expeditions (☎ 225-4751) for a two-hour tour that includes exploring tidepool areas, eagles' nests, salmon spawning upstream in August and a hike in the rainforest. The cost is $29 per person.

Hiking

There is a variety of hiking adventures in the Ketchikan area, but the majority are either out of town or the trailhead must be reached by boat. The one exception is the Deer Mountain Trail, a 3.1-mile climb which begins near the city center and provides access to a US Forest Service cabin ($20 a night, reserve in advance) and two other alpine trails (see the Trekking section in the Wilderness chapter).

Ward Lake Nature Walk This is an easy trail around Ward Lake that begins near the shelters at the far end of the lake. The trail is a 1.3 miles of flat terrain and information signs. To reach the lake, follow North Tongass Hwy seven miles out of the city to the pulp mill on Ward Cove, turn right on Ward Lake Rd and follow it for a mile.

Perseverance Trail This trek is a 2.2-mile walk from Ward Lake Rd to Perseverance Lake through mature coastal forest and muskeg. The view of the lake with its mountainous backdrop is spectacular, while the hiking is easy as the trail consists mainly of boardwalks and steps. The trailhead is 1.5 miles from the start of Ward Lake Rd.

Talbot Lake Trail This trail starts from Connell Lake Rd which is a gravel road that heads east, three miles from the start of Ward Lake Rd. The 1.6-mile trail is a mixture of boardwalk and gravel surface and leads north from the Connell Lake Dam to Talbot Lake, where it ends at private property. The more adventurous, however, can cross a beaver dam at the south end of the lake and hike eastward onto the north ridge of Brown Mountain to eventually reach its 2,978-foot summit. Keep in mind this is steep country with no established trail.

Paddling

Many short and long-term kayak trips begin in Ketchikan and range from an easy paddle in well-protected waters to a week trip to Misty Fjords National Monument and back (see the Paddling section in the Wilderness chapter). Kayaks can be rented from Southeast Exposure (☎ 225-8829) at 507 Stedman St and transported to some areas through Outdoor Alaska (☎ 225-6044). Double kayaks rent for $45 for one to three days, $40 for four days or more. There are also singles available. Before any trip, purchase the topographical map that covers the area from Tongass Trading Company at the north end of City Dock or Murray Pacific at 1007 Water St.

If you just want to try your hand kayaking without the rigors of a overnight paddle on your own, Southeast Exposure has two great paddling tours. The first is a three-hour Waterfront day trip where a guide leads you past the historic downtown area of the city. The cost is $50 per adult and includes all equipment. The second is an extended day trip to a number of areas including Carroll Inlet, George Inlet or Naha Bay. The cost is $60 for six hours of paddling.

Naha River Trail From the end of the North Tongass Hwy, it's an eight-mile paddle to the trailhead for the Naha River Trail, a 6.5-mile path that follows the river and leads to three USFS cabins and two lakes. The trailhead is on Naha Bay, a body of water that leads into Roosevelt Lagoon through a narrow outlet. Kayakers trying to paddle into the lagoon must enter it at high slack tide, as the narrow pass becomes a frothy, roaring chute when the tide is moving in or out. The current in the salt chuck actually changes directions depending on the tide.

The trail is a combination of boardwalk, swing bridges and an uphill walk to Naha River, Jordan and Heckman Lake cabins. All three cabins ($25 per night) must be reserved in advance at the USFS office in Ketchikan. This is an interesting side trip as locals fish these waters for salmon and trout while in August it's often possible to see bears catch-

ing salmon at a small waterfall two miles up the trail from the Roosevelt Lagoon.

Wolf Creek Trail An even easier paddle is the five-mile trip from the end of North Tongass Hwy to the trailhead for the Wolf Lake Trail at Moser Bay. The 2.5-mile trail passes through timber slopes and over muskeg to a three-sided shelter (no reservation or rental fee) at the outlet of Wolf Lake. A steep hill is encountered near the salt water but this should not discourage the average hiker.

George & Carroll Inlets At the end of South Tongass Hwy past Herring Bay, you are already in George Inlet, which makes this three to four-day paddle an easy one in water that is calm most of the time. North winds do occasionally whip down George Inlet but both waterways are protected from southwesterlies, the prevailing winds in the Ketchikan area.

While not on the same dramatic scale as Misty Fjords, the two inlets are scenic and it's an easy way to explore some of Ketchikan's backcountry. The return trip from Herring Bay to the end of George Inlet is a 25-mile paddle.

USFS Cabins

There are 30 cabins in the Ketchikan area; most need to be reserved in advance and cost $25 per day. With the exception of Deer Mountain Cabin, which you can hike to, the rest require charter air time. The following cabins are close to the city, which reduces air-charter time, the biggest cost factor in using them. There are numerous bush-plane operators in Ketchikan; two of the more reliable ones are Taquan Air (☎ 225-9668), 1007 Water St, Ketchikan, AK 99901 and Ketchikan Air Service (☎ 225-6608), 1600 International Airport, Ketchikan, AK 99901.

Alava Bay Cabin This cabin is on the southern end of Behm Canal. It provides ample opportunity for hiking and beachcombing along the coast, freshwater fishing and viewing wildlife such as black bear and Sitka deer. The cabin is 20 air miles from Ketchikan.

Fish Creek Cabin A short trail connects Thorne Bay with the Fish Creek Cabin. You can either paddle to it (a three to four-day trip) or fly in, as it is only 18 air miles from Ketchikan. There is a trail to nearby Low Lake; fishing for cutthroat trout, rainbow trout and Dolly Varden is possible in the creek.

Patching Lake Cabins There are two cabins on Patching Lake, 20 air miles from Ketchikan. At either one there is good fishing for cutthroat trout and grayling.

Getting There & Away

Air Alaska Airlines (☎ 225-2141) flies to Ketchikan with stops at other major Southeast communities as well as Anchorage and Seattle. There are several flights between Ketchikan and Juneau, including one that locals call the 'milk run', as it stops at Petersburg, Wrangell and Sitka and is little more than a series of take-offs and landings. One-way fare from Ketchikan to Juneau is $124, and $110 to Petersburg.

Boat It's an exceptional day when there isn't a ferry departing from Ketchikan for other Southeast destinations or Bellingham. One-way fares from Ketchikan to Wrangell are $22, Petersburg $36, Juneau $72, Sitka $52 and Haines $86.

The state ferry *Chilkat* used to make several runs a day to Metlakatla from Ketchikan but now it only sails during the winter when the other boats are in dry dock. The service to Metlakatla has since been added to the *Aurora* on its trip to Hollis on Prince of Wales Island. The trip runs almost daily during the summer and the one-way fare to Hollis is $18 and to Metlakatla $12.

For exact sailing times call the ferry terminal (☎ 225-6181).

Getting Around

To/From the Airport The Ketchikan airport is on one side of Tongass Narrows and the city is on the other. Years ago there was talk of building a bridge from the airport across the channel to town. That was only talk, and today you hop on the airport ferry that leaves the airport 15 and 45 minutes past the hour to a ramp next to the state ferry terminal. The fare is $2.50 one way for walk-on passengers.

Bus The city bus system consists of small buses that hold up to 30 passengers and follow a circular route from the ferry terminal in the West End to the area south of Thomas Basin, circling back by the Totem Heritage Center and the trailhead to Deer Mountain. The route does not include Saxman Totem Park or anything north of the state ferry terminal. Buses return to each stop every hour; the fare is $1 and hours of operation are 6 am to 6 pm.

The drivers are exceptionally friendly and can often be coaxed into pointing out the town's highlights and giving you tidbits of Alaskan lore. The city buses are a cheap alternative to the expensive Gray Line bus tours of the city.

Car Rental There is always Alaska Car Rental, which rents vehicles for $40 a day with unlimited mileage. For two to four people, this is a good way to spend a day seeing the sights out of town. The rental company operates two offices, one at the airport (☎ 225-2232) and a second in the city center (☎ 225-5123).

AROUND KETCHIKAN

Saxman Totem Park

For a look at the world's largest standing collection of totem poles, head 2.3 miles south of Ketchikan on South Tongass Hwy to Saxman Totem Park. The park's 24 poles were bought here from abandoned villages around the Southeast and were restored or recarved in the 1930s.

At the entrance to the park is the impressive **Sun & Raven totem**, probably the most photographed one in Alaska, and the rest of the park is uphill from there. Among the collection is a **replica of the Lincoln Pole**;

The Rise of Totems

Ironically Europeans both stimulated and then almost ended the art of carving totems by Native Alaskans in the Southeast region. Totems first flourished in the late 18th century after clans had acquired steel knives, axes and other cutting tools through the fur trade with White explorers.

But between 1880 and the 1950s the art form was almost wiped out when a law forbidding potlatches took effect and banned the Native ceremony for which most totems were carved. When the law was repealed in 1951 a revival of the totem carving took place and continues today.

The oldest totems generally are 50 to 60 years old. After they reach this age, the heavy precipitation and acid muskeg soil of Southeast Alaska takes it toll on the cedar pole until the totem tumbles due to the wood rotting. ■

the original is in the Alaska State Museum in Juneau. This pole was carved in 1883 to commemorate the first sighting of white people, using a picture of Abraham Lincoln.

Saxman Totem Park, an incorporated Native Alaskan village of more than 300 residents, also has a community hall and theater where you can see a slide and sound show about the park and Tlingit culture. This cultural center (☎ 225-5163) is open daily in the summer from 9 am to 4 pm. There is also a gift shop, of course, and a tribal house with indigenous artists working on various projects. Dance performances and tours are given regularly at Saxman during the summer; call the cultural center for details.

North Tongass Hwy

Mud Bight is 9.5 miles north of Ketchikan along North Tongass Hwy, past the Ward Creek Recreation Area. This community of float houses is an interesting spot as the dwellings rise and fall with the water to the extent that they are left high on the mud at low tide.

Totem Bight, 10 miles north of Ketchikan, is a state historical park (no entry fee) which contains 14 restored or recarved totems and a colorful community house. Just

as impressive as the totems is the park's wooded setting and the coastline. A viewing deck overlooks the Tongass Narrows. The North Tongass Hwy ends 18 miles north of Ketchikan at Settler's Cove State Campground, another scenic coastal area with a lush rainforest bordering a gravel beach and rocky coastline.

Misty Fjords National Monument

This spectacular national monument, which begins just 22 miles east of Ketchikan, is best noted for its sea cliffs, steep-sided fjords and rock walls that jut 3000 feet straight out of the ocean. Walker Cove, Rudyerd Bay and Punchbowl Cove (the most picturesque areas of the preserve) are reached via Behm Canal, the long, deep inlet that separates Revillagigedo Island from the Coastal Mountains on the mainland.

Wildlife at Misty Fjords includes brown or black bears, mountain goats, Sitka deer, bald eagles and a variety of marine mammals. As the name suggests, the monument can be a drizzly place with an average annual rainfall of 150 inches, but many people think the real beauty of Misty Fjords lies in the granite walls and tumbling waterfalls wrapped in a veil of fog and mist.

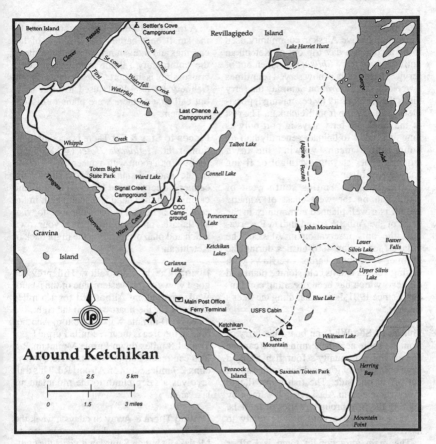

Around Ketchikan

The preserve is popular with kayakers (see the Paddling section of the Wilderness chapter), while less adventurous visitors view it on day cruises or sightseeing flights. Viewing Misty Fjords from a charter plane costs $130 per hour or so with either Misty Fjords Air Outfitters (☎ 225-5155) or Taguan Air Service (☎ 225-9668). The time actually spent viewing the monument is short, however, and the area's peaceful atmosphere is lost when the pilot has to yell at you over the roar of the bush plane.

Tour ships offer a more dramatic perspective of the preserve while letting you view it at a much more leisurely pace. Outdoor Alaska (☎ 225-6044) offers an 11-hour cruise for $140 that departs from Ryus float at the foot of Dock St, Ketchikan. The boat leaves at 8.30 am every Monday, Wednesday, Thursday, Friday and Sunday, and the cruise includes a small breakfast, sandwich buffet lunch and dinner. A shorter seven-hour trip in which you return aboard a bush plane costs $185. If you can plan ahead, the best way to experience Misty Fjords is to rent one of the 15 US Forest Service cabins (reservations needed, $25 per night) in the area.

Metlakatla

This small Native Alaskan community used to be a common day trip out of Ketchikan until the state ferry *Chilkat* was taken out of service. Metlakatla is now served four times a week by the *Aurora*; on Saturday the ferry visits the community twice, making it possible to do a day trip from Ketchikan. The rest of the week the ferry stays in port only as long as it takes to unload, generally half an hour, which means viewing the town requires either staying overnight or flying back to Ketchikan.

Metlakatla, 12 miles south-west of Ketchikan on the west coast of Annette Island, is a well-planned community in the heart of the Annette Island Indian Reservation, the only reservation in Alaska. The village (population 400) bustles during the summer as its boat harbor overflows with fishing vessels and its cold storage plant and cannery, which has been operating continuously since 1901, is busy handling the fleet's catch.

Things to See While on board the ferry or from the shore near the terminal, you can see one of the community's four fish traps, a large collection of logs and wire with a small hut off to one side. The fish traps, illegal everywhere else in Alaska, catch salmon by guiding the fish through a series of funnels, keeping them alive until they're ready to harvest.

The main attraction in town is **Father Duncan's Cottage**, now preserved as a museum. Metlakatla was founded when William Duncan, a Scottish-born minister, led several hundred Tsimshian Indians here from British Columbia in 1887 after a dispute with church authorities. In 1891, Congress granted reservation status to the entire island and under Duncan's supervision the tribe prospered after building a salmon cannery and sawmill. Duncan lived in the cottage until his death in 1918 and it now features the minister's personal artefacts and photographs of turn-of-the-century Metlakatla. The museum is open Monday to Friday from 10 am to noon; admission is $1.

A traditional **Tribal Loghouse**, down by the small boat harbor, has displays of log carvings and indigenous art, and is the site of the community salmon bake whenever a cruise ship is in port. The Annette Island Cannery (☎ 886-4661) used to offer tours but call first as there were plans to discontinue them.

Places to Stay & Eat There is accommodation at the *Metlakatla Hotel* (☎ 886-3456) for $90 for a room with a queen-size bed and in the back a small café overlooks the cannery. Keep in mind the town is 'dry' and camping on the island is discouraged. In the end, it's better and much cheaper to visit Metlakatla on Saturday, bring your own lunch and plan on spending the night back in Ketchikan.

Hiking The hike to Yellow Hill provides good views of the western side of the island. Walk south along Airport Rd for 1.5 miles and look for the boardwalk on the right; it's an easy 30-minute walk to the top. Another hike in the area is the three-mile Purple Lake Trail, 1.8 miles down Purple Mountain Rd. You can reach Purple Mountain Rd by traveling 2.7 miles south on Airport Rd. This trail involves a steep climb to the mountainous lake area.

Getting There & Away Six days a week the state ferry *Aurora* makes a single run to Metlakatla but on Saturday it visits the community twice. The first run departs Ketchikan at 6.15 am, arriving in Metlakatla in about an hour. The second run leaves Metlakatla at 8.45 pm, giving you almost a full day on the island. Since the ferry terminal is only a mile east of town, there's enough time to walk to Metlakatla for an interesting and cheap trip. The one-way ferry ticket from Ketchikan to Metlakatla is $12.

You can also fly to Metlakatla. Taquan Air (☎ 225-9668) provides daily, regularly scheduled flights for around $25 one way.

Hyder

Hyder is a state ferry port at the head of

Portland Canal on the fringe of Misty Fjords National Monument. Nass Indians regularly visited the area to hunt birds, pick berries and more often than not to hide from the aggressive Haida tribes. In 1896, Captain D D Gailland explored the Portland Canal for the US Army Corps of Engineers and built four stone storehouses, the first masonry buildings erected in Alaska, which still stand today.

But Hyder and its British Columbia neighbor Stewart, didn't boom until Yukon gold-rush prospectors began settling in the area at the turn of the century. Major gold and silver mines were opened in 1919 and Hyder, enjoying its heyday, became the supply center for more than 10,000 residents. It's been going downhill ever since and the population has now shrunk to around 90 year-round residents, leading to its title 'the friendliest ghost town in Alaska'.

Because of Hyder's isolation from the rest of the state, and the country for that matter, residents are almost totally dependent on the much larger Stewart (population 2000) just across the Canadian border. They use Canadian money in Hyder, set their watches to Pacific time (not Alaska time), use a British Columbia area code and the children go to school in Canada. All this can make a side trip here a little confusing.

The most famous thing to do in Hyder is drink at one of its 'friendly saloons'. The historic *Glacier Inn* is the best known and features an interior papered in signed bills, creating the '$20,000 Walls' of Hyder. The *First and Last Chance Saloon* is also well known and both bars hop at night.

Stewart has a museum on the corner of 6th and Columbia streets that is open afternoons from Monday to Friday and features local artefacts and mining relics. Or you can head three miles north of town to Fish Creek and watch bears feed on chum salmon runs from late July to September. If you want to kill a day, hitchhike 30 miles east of Stewart on Hwy 37A in British Columbia to Bear Glacier; it can be viewed without even getting out of the car.

Places to Stay In Stewart, there's the *Stewart Lions Campground* ($9 per night) or the *King Edward Hotel* and the *King Edward Motel* (☎ (604) 636-2244). In Hyder, try the *Grand View Inn* (☎ (604) 636-9174) a mile from the ferry terminal where you can get a single/double for $45/50.

Getting There & Away Hyder is a possible side trip from Ketchikan because the ferry *Aurora* departs Ketchikan at 11.45 pm on Thursday and reaches Hyder at 11 am the next day. It then departs Hyder at 2 pm on Friday and reaches Ketchikan at midnight, giving you three hours to explore the town (or drink in the bars). The one-way fare is $36 and the trip includes cruising scenic Portland Canal. If you want to stay overnight, you might have to charter a flight there. Temsco Airlines which used to offer scheduled service once a week between Ketchikan and Hyder has since gone under.

Prince of Wales Island

If time is no problem and out-of-the-way places or different lifestyles intrigue you, then this accessible island with Native Alaskan villages and logging camps can be an interesting jaunt. At 135 miles long and covering more than 2230 sq miles, Prince of Wales Island is the third largest island in the USA after Kodiak and Hawaii.

The island's landscape is characterized by steep forested mountains, deep U-shaped valleys, lakes, salt-water straits and bays that were carved out by glaciers long ago. The mountains rise to 3000 feet and the spruce-hemlock forest is broken up by muskeg and, unfortunately, more clear cuts than most visitors ever dreamed they would see. The 900-mile coastline has numerous bays, coves, inlets and protective islands, making it a kayaker's delight.

You can take the state ferry from Ketchikan to Hollis. From this village (population 475) there is access to a 500-mile network of roads, the most extensive network in the Southeast – in fact more roads than in the rest of the Southeast put together. Some stretches in the center of the island are

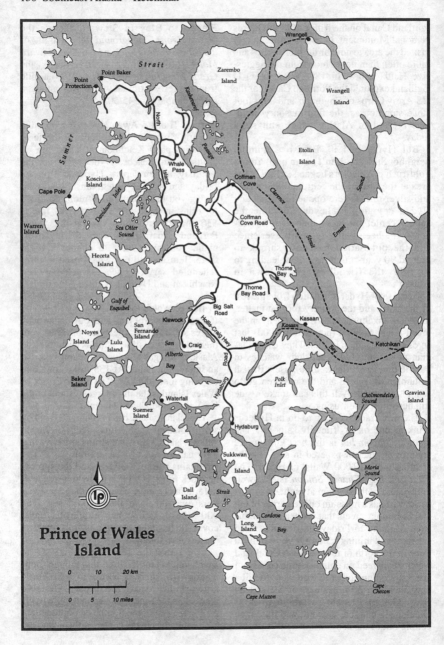

Prince of Wales
Island

now paved but the vast majority are rough dirt roads. The logging roads connect Hollis with remote backcountry and the villages of Craig, Klawock, Thorne Bay and Hydaburg. For someone carrying a bicycle through Alaska, especially a mountain bike, a week on Prince of Wales Island is worth all the trouble of carting the bike around.

Getting There & Away The state ferry *Aurora* makes a daily run, expect on Friday, from Ketchikan to Hollis during the summer, including two trips on Saturday. The one-way fare from Ketchikan to Hollis is $18. Once you're at Hollis, where there are few visitor facilities and no stores or restaurants, getting around the island is a little more difficult.

Prince of Wales Transporter (☎ 755-2348) runs a minivan between Hydaburg and Klawock, stopping at Craig along the way, for $17 one way. Ask the ticket agent at the state ferry terminal as soon as you arrive for information on minivan departures. You can always hitchhike as there is a small amount of traffic to Craig and Klawock after the arrival and departure of each ferry, but keep in mind that almost half the boats arrive after 2 am.

If there are three or four of you, an ideal way to get around is to rent a vehicle at Ketchikan's Alaska Rental (☎ 225-2232 in Ketchikan) and take it over on the state ferry for an additional $21 one way. Or make your way to Klawock on the daily mail flight of Taquan Air (☎ 225-9668 in Ketchikan) and then rent a car at Allstar Rent-A-Car (☎ 755-2524). This allows you to explore the far reaches of the island and to fish the highly productive streams (accessible by road) for cutthroat trout, Dolly Varden and salmon. Two of the 22 US Forest Service cabins, Stanley Creek Cabin and Red Bay Lake Cabin (reservations needed, $25 rental fee), can be reached from the road; check with the USFS information center in the Ketchikan Federal Building for availability.

With a mountain bike you can explore the island and its network of logging roads; there are only 30 miles of gravel-surface roads which stretch from Hollis to Klawock and then south to Craig. The rest are logging roads and their condition depends on the weather and the amount of traffic on them. It's not unusual to find a culvert missing or a section washed out completely and passable only by 4WD vehicles – in other words, a mountain biker's dream come true. The fare to carry a bike over on the ferry is $6 one way but invest another $3 for a copy of the *Prince of Wales Road Guide* that can be purchased at the US Forest Service office in Ketchikan or Craig.

Craig Craig (population 1500), 31 miles south-west of Hollis, is the most interesting community to visit, and on a Saturday night you can rub elbows with loggers and fishers in lively Alaskan fashion at the Craig Inn. The town was founded as a salmon canning and cold-storage site in 1907 and today fishing still accounts for more than half of its employment. Most of the rest of the local workforce is employed in the logging industry which explains the clear cuts around Craig.

Other than a totem pole that washed up on a beach and was erected in front of the old school gym, there are no 'attractions' in Craig. The reason you come here is to experience an Alaskan town that doesn't turn itself inside out for tourists every summer. For information on fishing, hiking and paddling trips, contact the US Forest Service office (☎ 826-3271) on 9th St near the boat harbor; it's open Monday to Friday from 8 am to 4.30 pm.

Camping is permitted in the city park overlooking the ocean. The park is a short hike from town and can be reached by following Hamilton Dr onto Graveyard Island, or just ask any local for directions to the ball field. Other accommodation includes a lodge and *Ruthann's Hotel* (☎ 826-3377) which has 10 rooms from $65 per night, *Haida Way Lodge* (☎ 826-3268) with rates beginning at $85 per night and *TLC Laundry & Rooms* (☎ 826-2966) for a bunkroom bed and shared bathrooms for $30 a night. There are also three restaurants, including *Lacey's*

Pizza in the Thibodeau Mall, closed on Monday and Tuesday but open to 9 pm the rest of the week, and *Thompson House Grocery*. Just want a cold beer? Not to worry. Craig has three bars and three liquor stores.

Klawock   Klawock (population 890) is a Tlingit village 24 miles north-west of Hollis and only six miles north of Craig. The town was the site of the first cannery in Alaska (built in 1878) but is better known today for its collection of 21 totem poles. Totem Park, in the center of the village, features 21 totems that were both replicas and originals that were found in the abandoned Native Alaskan village of Tuxekan in the 1930s.

The best place to stay is half a mile up Big Salt Road at *Log Cabin Campgrounds* (☎ 755-2205) which offers tent space and showers for $5 per night per person and rustic cabins along the beach for $35 per night. They also rent canoes for $18 per day that can be used in either Big Salt Lake or Klawock Lake. Within town there is *Fireweed Lodge* (☎ 755-2930) with rooms for $75 a night and *Dave's Diner* (☎ 755-2986) for the cheapest meals.

Thorne Bay   Thorne Bay (population 600) was established in 1962 when Ketchikan Pulp Company moved its main logging camp here from Hollis. Some say the town still looks like a logging camp but it lies in a picturesque setting 59 miles north-east of Hollis.

Just after turning east on Thorne Bay Road, you pass the relatively new *Eagles Nest Campground* overlooking a pair of lakes. The 11-site facility is also a canoe launching place on Balls Lake and almost a half-mile boardwalk along the shore. The fee is $5 a night. Continuing east, the *Gravely Creek Picnic Area* is reached after 13 miles. The facility has fireplaces, pit toilets and an open shelter. Less than a mile away, the Thorne River offers excellent fishing for cutthroat trout, Dolly Varden, rainbow trout and steelhead. Another scenic spot, just six miles north of Thorne Bay on Forest Rd 30, is *Sandy Beach Picnic Area* with tables, pit toilets and fireplaces. It's a great place to set up camp as there are spectacular views of Clarence Strait.

In Thorne Bay, supplies can be obtained at *Thorne Bay Market* while *McFarland's Floatel* (☎ 828-3335) offers rooms in a large float house that rises and falls with the tides from $60 for a single. They also have beachfront log cabins that sleep four. There is a US Forest Ranger Office (☎ 828-3304) in town for recreational information on the area.

Hydaburg   This town (population 450) was founded in 1911 when three Haida villages were combined. Today, most of the residents are commercial fishers but subsistence is still a necessary part of life. Located 36 miles south-west of Hollis, Hydaburg was only connected to the rest of the island by road in 1983.

This scenic village is known for an excellent collection of restored totems in a park that was developed in the 1930s. It also provides easy access for paddlers into the South Prince of Wales Wilderness, a 90,000-acre preserve.

Lodging and meals are available at *Sanderson's Boarding House* (☎ 285-3244) as well as *Marlene Edenshaw Boarding House* (☎ 285-3254) which charges $65 for a bed and breakfast. There is also a grocery store and gasoline station in town.

Wrangell

The next major town north along the state ferry route is Wrangell (population 2600), a cluster of canneries, shipping docks, lumber mills and logging tugs. The community's claim to history is that it is the only Alaskan fort to have existed under three flags – Russian, British and American. Its strategic location near the mouth of the Stikine River has given it a long and colorful history.

The Russians founded the town when they arrived in 1834 and built a stockade they called Redoubt St Dionysius. The town's purpose then was to prevent encroachment

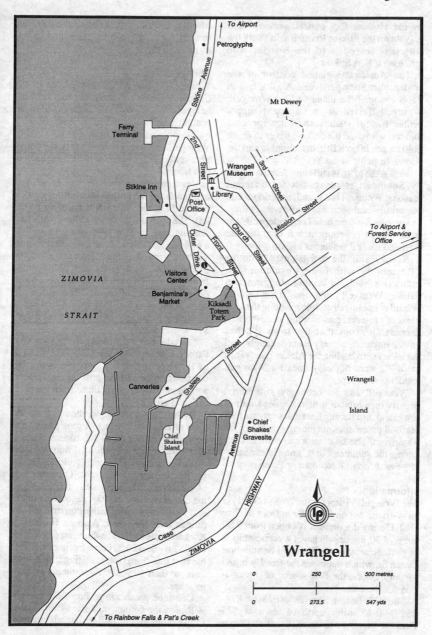

To Airport

Petroglyphs

Stikine Avenue

Mt Dewey

Ferry
Terminal

2nd Street

Wrangell
Museum

Library

Stikine Inn

Post
Office

3rd Street

Mission Street

To Airport &
Forest Service
Office

ZIMOVIA

Outer Drive

Church Street

Front Street

Visitors
Center

Benjamins's
Market

Kiksadi
Totem
Park

STRAIT

Wrangell

Island

Shakes Street

Canneries

Chief
Shakes Island

Chief
Shakes'
Gravesite

Shakes Avenue

ZIMOVIA HIGHWAY

Case

Wrangell

| 0 | 250 | 500 metres |

| 0 | 273.5 | 547 yds |

To Rainbow Falls & Pat's Creek

by the Hudson Bay traders working their way down the Stikine River. But in 1840, the Russians leased it to the British, who renamed it Fort Stikine.

The Americans gained control of the center when they purchased Alaska, and in 1868 changed the name to Fort Wrangell. Wrangell thrived as an important supply center for fur traders and later for gold miners, who used the Stikine River to reach gold rushes in both British Columbia and the Klondike fields in the Yukon.

Today, the town is still considered colorful by Southeast residents but for different reasons. Wrangell is a proud, traditional and sometimes stubborn community that clings to age-old Alaskan beliefs of independence from excess government and of using the land and natural resources to earn a living.

As the rest of the state is pushed into the 21st century with heavy regulations on industries such as mining, logging and fishing, Wrangell often finds itself lagging behind economically while resisting the new ideas of preserving and setting aside the wilderness. It's not that the town lynches environmentalists every Saturday night, but the issues surrounding the Alaska Lands Bill, or 'd-2', were not easy ones for Wrangell residents to accept.

Wrangell has an economy still based heavily on a lumber mill, six miles south of town, and on a fishing fleet that supports four seafood processors, including one along the waterfront. The boat harbor in town is busy during the summer, but it is nowhere near as large as those in Ketchikan or Petersburg.

Information

The Wrangell Visitor Center (☎ 874-3901) is an A-frame hut on Outer Dr in front of City Hall. During the summer it's open from 9.30 am to 4.30 pm or whenever a cruise ship is in port. Nearby is the Wrangell Sentinel on Lynch St, which publishes the free *Wrangell Visitors Guide*, the best source of information for the area.

The US Forest Service office (☎ 874-2323), 0.75 miles north of town at 525 Bennett St, is open from 8 am to 5 pm Monday to Friday. It is the source of information for USFS cabins, trails and campgrounds in the area.

Things to See

Wrangell is one of the few places in the Southeast where the ferry terminal is in the heart of town. If you're not planning to spend a night here, you can still disembark for a quick look around. To get a good view of Wrangell, including a stroll out to the petroglyphs along the shoreline, you'll need about two hours.

Beginning at the state ferry terminal, you can reach the **Wrangell Museum** by going up 2nd St to the large white building on the left. The museum is housed in the town's first schoolhouse, built in 1906 and later used as a morgue and city hall, among other things. The collection features indigenous artefacts, petroglyphs, local relics and photographs from Wrangell's past. There is also a room devoted to the town's artists. The museum is open Monday to Saturday from 1 to 4 pm or whenever a cruise ship is in port; it charges $1 for admission.

Next door to the museum is the **Wrangell Public Library** with several totems in front of it, while diagonally opposite is the US Customs office and the post office. There is a good view of Zimovia Strait from the post-office lawn.

By heading south down the hill from the post office, you come to Front St and the beginning of Wrangell's business district. The eastern (uphill) side of Front St is the historical section with each building featuring its distinctive false front. The other side of the street is a land-fill area – a fire ravaged the center of town in 1952, destroying docks and buildings originally constructed on pilings over the water. Also on Front St is **Kiksadi Totem Park**, which was dedicated in 1987 by Sealaska Native Corporation with the first traditional totem raising in Wrangell in more than 40 years. Four totems are now in place.

Continue south along Front St and you will pass the former mill site of the Alaska Pulp Company. The mill still stands but operations have been moved to another mill six miles south along the Zimovia Hwy. At the old mill, Front St flows into Shakes St, which ends with the cannery and freezing factory of Wrangell Fisheries Inc and Wrangell Fresh Seafood. No tours are available at either place.

Across from the cannery is the bridge to **Chief Shakes Island**, Wrangell's most interesting attraction, about a mile from the ferry terminal. The island, in the town's Inner Boat Harbor, features an impressive collection of totem poles (duplicates of the originals that were carved in the late 1930s) and the **Shakes Community House** (☎ 874-3770). The community house is an excellent example of a high-caste tribal house and contains tools, blankets and other cultural items. It is open at various times to accommodate the cruise ships in town and there is a $1 donation to see it. Call the Wrangell Museum (☎ 874-3770) to find out when a tour is scheduled. Just as impressive as the tribal house is the view of bustling Wrangell Harbor from the island.

From Shakes St (heading north) you can turn right onto Case Ave and follow it for two blocks to Hansen's Boat Shop. Across the street on the hillside is **Chief Shakes' gravesite** enclosed by a Russian-style picket fence topped by two killer-whale totems.

Festivals

The only major event during the summer, other than the local salmon derby, is the Fourth of July celebration. All of Wrangell, like most small Alaskan communities, gets involved in the festival, which features a parade, fireworks, logging show, street games, food booths and a salmon bake in town.

Places to Stay

Camping The nearest campground to town is the *City Park*, 1.8 miles south of the ferry terminal on Zimovia Hwy. This waterfront park is immediately south of the cemetery and city ball field and provides picnic tables, shelters and rest rooms. Camping is free but there is a one-night limit.

Further out of town is the *Shoemaker Bay Recreation Area*, 4.7 miles south of the ferry terminal on Zimovia Hwy and across from the trailhead to the Rainbow Falls Trail. Camping is provided in a wooded area near a creek, and there is a 10-day limit but no fees.

Still further south is *Pat's Creek* at *Mile 10.8* of Zimovia Hwy where it becomes a narrow Forest Service road. There are two dirt roads heading off to the left; the first is to the lake and the second is to the campground, basically just a clear spot that is no longer maintained by the US Forest Service. Near the campground there is a trail along the creek that leads back to Pat's Lake where you'll find good fishing for cutthroat trout and Dolly Varden.

B&Bs If staying in a private home interests you, there is *Clarke Bed & Breakfast* (☎ 874-2125 day, 874-3863 evening) at 732 Case Ave. A bed and a meal in the morning costs $40/50 a single/double. You should call ahead as their rooms are limited. There's also *D&D Bed & Breakfast* (☎ 874-3970) at 120 3rd St.

Hotels There is no hostel and only three hotels in town; the cheapest is the *Thunderbird Hotel* (☎ 874-3322), at 110 Front St, with rooms at $50/59 a single/double. A mile south of town is *Hardings Old Sourdough Lodge* (☎ 874-3613) with 20 rooms, a sauna, steambath and free transport from the ferry or airport. Rooms with meals are $65 per person, with breakfast only $63, room only $55. Still further out of town, four miles south on Zimovia Hwy, is *Roadhouse Lodge* (☎ 874-2334 or 874-2336). The lodge also has a courtesy car and rents bicycles so you can get back into town. Rooms are $50/58 a single/double.

Places to Eat

The cheapest place for a meal is *Diamond C* on Front St, in the Kadin Building. The restaurant is open daily and has the usual fare of egg breakfasts for around $5, sandwiches and hamburgers. Nearer to the ferry terminal and open later at night is *J&W's* at the City Dock, which sells hamburgers and hot dogs while pizza is best purchased at *Maggie's & Sons* on Front St.

The top place to eat, featuring local shrimp and other seafood, is at the *Dockside Restaurant* in the Stikine Inn, with its excellent view of the boat harbor. Dinners here range from $15 to $20 or you can just tackle the salad bar for under $5.

Benjamin's on Outer Dr is the largest supermarket, featuring an in-store bakery and carries ready-to-eat items in its deli. Also, fishers often sell their catch to residents and visitors down at the boat harbors. Shrimp and salmon are the delicacy of the Wrangell fleet.

Entertainment

It is often in the town's bars that the true spirit of Wrangell comes shining through. Mingle with locals at the *Totem Bar* on Front St or with people from the fishing industry at the *Marine Bar* on Shakes St near Chief Shakes Island. During a night run on the ferry, you have time to get off for a beer at the *Stikine Inn Lounge*, which has live music and the only dance floor in Wrangell.

Hiking

Petroglyphs An interesting afternoon can be spent looking for petroglyphs – primitive rock carvings believed to be 8000 years old. The best set lies 0.75 miles from the ferry terminal and can be reached by heading north on Evergreen Rd or, as the locals call it, Old Airport Rd. Walk past Stough's Trailer Court and proceed to a marked wooden walkway. Follow the boardwalk to the beach and then turn right and start walking north towards the end of the island. With your back to the water, look for the carvings on the large rocks.

Many of the petroglyphs are spirals and faces, and there are about 20 in the area but most are submerged during high tide. Check a tide book before you leave and remember that the entire walk takes an hour or two – too long for the state ferry stopover. Gift shops in town, including Norris Gifts, sell 'rubbing kits' that allow you to take images of the carvings home on rice paper but a local archaeologist is currently discouraging the practice as there is evidence that it is damaging the carvings.

Mt Dewey Trail This half-mile trail winds its way up a hill to an observation point overlooking Wrangell and the surrounding waterways. From Mission St, walk a block and turn left at the first corner, 3rd St. Follow the street past a brown and red A-frame house with a white balcony. The trail, marked by a white sign, begins 50 yards past the house on the right. Once you're at the trailhead, the hike is a short one, 15 minutes or so to the top, but it is often muddy. John Muir fanatics will appreciate the fact that the great naturalist himself climbed the mountain in 1879 and built a bonfire at the top, alarming the Tlingits living in the village below.

Rainbow Falls Trail This old trail was rebuilt and extended in 1985 by the US Forest Service. The trailhead for the Rainbow Falls Trail is signposted 4.7 miles south of the ferry terminal on the Zimovia Hwy. The trail begins directly across from the Shoemaker Bay Recreation Area and just before the Wrangell Institute Complex.

From the trailhead it is a mile hike to the waterfalls and then another 2.5 miles to an observation point overlooking Shoemaker Bay on Institute Ridge, where the USFS has built a three-sided shelter. The lower section can be soggy at times so it is best hiked in rubber boots, while upper sections are steep. The views are worth the hike and a pleasant evening can be spent on the ridge. A return trip to the ridge takes four to six hours.

Thoms Lake Trail At the end of the paved Zimovia Hwy is a dirt road, known officially as Forest Rd 6290, that extends 30 miles south along Wrangell Island. On this road, 23 miles south of Wrangell, is the Thoms Lake Trail, which leads 1.2 miles to a state park recreation cabin and a skiff on the lake. Since there is no state park office in

Wrangell, you have to reserve the cabin through the Division of Parks office in Juneau (☎ 465-4563). Keep in mind that this trails cuts through muskeg and during wet weather can get extremely muddy. It is a 1½-hour hike to the cabin.

Long Lake Trail The trailhead for the Long Lake Trail is 27 miles south-east of Wrangell on Forest Rd 6270. This pleasant hike is only 0.6 miles long and is planked the entire way. It leads to a shelter, skiff and outhouses on the shores of the lake. Plan a half hour for the trek into the lake or out.

Highbush Lake Trail This very short (300-foot) path leads to the lake where there's a skiff and oars. Fishing is fair and the surrounding views excellent. The parking lot for the trailhead is 29 miles from Wrangell on Forest Rd 6265 and Forest Rd 50040.

Paddling

The beautiful, wild Stikine River is characterized by a narrow, rugged shoreline and the mountains and hanging glaciers that surround it. It is the fastest navigable river in North America and is highlighted by the Grand Canyon, a steep-walled enclosure of the waterway where churning white water makes river travel impossible. Trips from below the canyon are common among rafters and kayakers; they begin with a charter flight to Telegraph Creek in British Columbia and end with a 160-mile float back to Wrangell.

Travelers who arrive at Wrangell with their own kayak but not enough funds for the expensive charter of a bush plane can undertake a trip from the town's harbor across the Stikine Flats, where there are several US Forest Service (USFS) cabins, and up one of the three arms of the Stikine River. By keeping close to shore and taking advantage of eddies and sloughs, experienced paddlers can make their way 30 miles up the Stikine River to the Canadian border or even further, passing 12 USFS cabins and the two bathing huts at Chief Shakes Hot Springs along the way. But you must know how to line a boat upstream and navigate a highly braided river,

and while in the lower reaches accept the fact there will be a considerable amount of jet-boat traffic.

The USFS office in Wrangell can provide information on the Stikine River, including a very helpful brochure and map entitled *Stikine River Canoe & Kayak Trips*. There are no places in Wrangell to rent a canoe or kayak. If you are without a boat but are still intrigued by the Stikine River, plan to rent one in Juneau.

Guide companies no longer offer boat trips down the Stikine, probably due to a lack of demand. Several charter captains will run up the river but usually only for a day of fishing or sightseeing. Call TH Charters (☎ 874-2085) enquire at the visitor center for a complete list of who's running the river.

USFS Cabins

The 20 USFS cabins in the Wrangell Ranger District are not usually as busy as those around Juneau or Ketchikan. Six of them (Binkley Slough, Koknuk, Little Dry Island, Sergief Island and two on Gut Island) lie on the Stikine River flats, 12 to 15 miles from Wrangell. The cabins can be paddled to or are a 30-minute bush-plane flight.

The most interesting cabin in the area, however, is on the mainland at Anan Bay, 28 air miles from Wrangell. Near the Anan Bay Cabin is a mile trail that leads to a bear observation & photography platform. The observatory is on the creek from Anan Lake and in July and August can be used to safely watch black bears and a few browns feeding on the salmon runs. The cabin is a 50-minute flight from Wrangell or a 31-mile paddle.

Even if you don't have access to the cabin for a night, the Anan Creek Bear Observatory can still be visited and, in late July to early August, a fascinating day can be spent photographing the bears and eagles feeding on the salmon. A number of charter companies including TH Charters (☎ 874-2085) and Aqua Sports (☎ 874-3061 or 874-3811) will take you, via jet boat, to the trailhead. The trips range from five to eight hours long and generally cost $125 per person with four people chartering the boat.

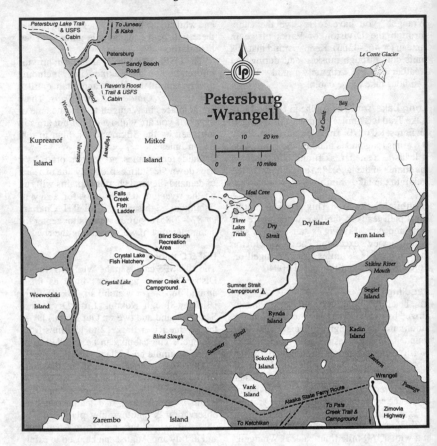

Getting There & Away

Air Alaska Airlines (☎ 874-3308) provides a year-round jet service to Wrangell with a daily northbound and southbound flight. Many claim that the flight north to Petersburg is the 'world's shortest jet flight', since the 11-minute trip is little more than a take-off and landing with the huge aircraft seeming to skim the waterway.

Boat There is an almost daily northbound and southbound ferry service from Wrangell in the summer. The next stop north is Petersburg via the scenic Wrangell Narrows. The

ferry terminal in Wrangell is open 1½ hours before each ferry arrival and from 2 to 5 pm on weekdays. There is also a recorded message (☎ 874-3711) for 24-hour ferry information.

Petersburg

When the state ferry heads north from Wrangell, it begins one of the most scenic and exciting sections of the Inside Passage trip. After crossing over from Wrangell

Island to Mitkof Island, the ferry threads its way through 46 turns of Wrangell Narrows, a 22-mile narrow channel that is only 300 feet wide and 19 feet deep in places. At one point the sides of the ship are so close to the shore that you can almost gather firewood for the evening.

At the other end of this breathtaking journey through the Wrangell Narrows lies Petersburg (population 3620), one of the hidden gems of Southeast Alaska. This busy little town, an active fishing port during the summer, is decorated by weathered boat-houses on the waterfront, freshly painted homes along Nordic Dr (Main St) and the distinctive Devil's Thumb peak and other snow-capped mountains on the horizon.

Peter Buschmann arrived in the area in 1897 and found a fine harbor, abundant fish and a ready supply of ice from nearby Le Conte Glacier. He built a cannery and enticed his Norwegian friends to follow him there, and the resulting town was named after him. Today, a peek into the local phone book will reveal evidence of the strong Norwegian heritage which unifies Petersburg.

1 Petersburg Fisheries
2 Swimming Pool
3 Harbor Bar
4 Harbormaster's Building
5 Pilot Newspaper
6 Hospital
7 Visitors Center
8 Clausen Memorial Museum
9 Helse Heath Foods
10 Alaska State Troopers
11 Scandia House
12 Kito's Kave
13 Forest Service & Post Office
14 Municipal Building
15 Sons of Norway Hall
16 Harbor Lights Pizza

To Sandy Beach Road

Nordic Drive

Petersburg Fisheries

Petersburg

0   150   300 metres

0   150   300 yds

Balder St

Charles W St

Dolphin

Excel

Fram

Gjoa

Haugen

Birch St

Ira

Casino

Nordic Drive

Hammer Slough

Sing Lee Alley

To State Ferry Terminal, Campground & Recreation Area

To Sandy Beach Recreation Area, Airport & Tent City

Petersburg is the youngest community in the Southeast but boasts of having the largest home-based halibut fleet in Alaska, some say the world. The economy has blossomed on fishing and four canneries and two cold-storage plants that draw an army of summer workers from the Lower 48. Several of the canneries are sitting above the water on pilings overlooking boat harbors bulging with vessels and a constant flow of barges, ferries and sea planes. Even at night you can see small boats trolling the nearby waters for somebody's dinner.

This healthy economy explains why Petersburg doesn't go out of its way for tourists, especially those traveling independently and on the cheap. The lack of a youth hostel and viable camping areas near town and what one traveler calls the 'anti-social arrival time of the ferry' (in other words in the middle of the night) often leaves you little choice but to book a $75 room for the night.

Orientation & Information

The town's historic Forest Service Building, on the corner of Fram and 1st streets, has been recently renovated as the Petersburg Visitor Center and is loaded with information on the community and surrounding area. Summer hours are from 8.30 am to 5 pm Monday to Wednesday and Friday, until 6 pm on Thursday, and until 4 pm on Saturday and Sunday.

You can still go to the Chamber of Commerce office (☎ 772-3646) in the Harbormaster's Building at the head of North Boat Harbor on the waterfront for free maps of Petersburg and other hand-outs. The chamber is open from 7.30 am to 5 pm weekdays.

For information about hiking, paddling, camping or reserving cabins, head over to the US Forest Service office (☎ 722-3871) upstairs in the post office on Nordic Dr (Main St). The office is open weekdays from 8 am to 5 pm and the entrance is at the rear of the building. Hikers attempting to cross to Kupreanof Island to tackle Petersburg Mountain or the Petersburg Lake trails should seek a ride at the Skiff Float near the end of the North Boat Harbor.

Across the street from the Harbormaster's Building you'll find the office of the Petersburg Pilot, which publishes the free *Viking Visitor Guide* every summer.

Top: Rafting on the Kenai River, Kenai Peninsula (RS)
Bottom: McCarthy General Store, McCarthy (RS)

Top Left: Eklutna Russian Orthodox cemetery (RS)
Top Right: Fishing boats on Homer Spit, Kenai Peninsula (DS)
Bottom Left: Kennicott ghost town, Wrangell-St Elias National Park (DS)
Bottom Right: The Salty Dawg Saloon on Homer Spit (DP)

Things to See

On the waterfront near the corner of Dolphin St and Nordic Dr is **Petersburg Fisheries**, founded in 1900 by Peter Buschmann and today a subsidiary of Icicle Seafoods of Seattle. On Harbor Way, at the end of Gjoa St, is the long pier that leads out to **Chatham Strait Seafoods**. The canneries, the backbone of the Petersburg economy, are not open to the public and do not offer tours.

Continuing south, Harbor Way passes Middle Boat Harbor and turns into **Sing Lee Alley** (Indian St). This was the center of old Petersburg and much of the street is built on pilings over Hammer Slough. The **Sons of Norway Hall**, begun by Buschmann in 1897 and finished in 1912, is the predominant large white building with the colorful rosemaling, a flowery Norwegian art form.

Hammer Slough provides photographers with the most colorful images of Petersburg. Both Sing Lee Alley and Birch St follow the tidal area and wind past clusters of weathered homes and boathouses suspended on pillars above a shoreline of old boats, nets and crab pots. Sing Lee Alley crosses Hammer Slough and then joins Nordic Dr. To the south, Nordic Dr turns into Mitkof Hwy and heads out past the state ferry terminal; to the north Nordic Dr heads back into the center of Petersburg.

Turn east up Fram St from Nordic Dr to the **Clausen Memorial Museum** on the corner of 2nd St. Outside the museum is the *Fisk*, an 11-foot bronze sculpture commemorating the town's life by the sea. Inside the museum is an interesting collection of local artefacts and relics, most tied in with the history of fishing in Petersburg. Included in the back room is the largest king salmon ever caught – 126 pounds. You'll also see the giant lens from the old Cape Decision Lighthouse. The museum is open daily during the summer from 1 to 4 pm. There is no admission charge but donations are welcome.

From the museum, follow 2nd St north for three blocks to reach the Petersburg High School. Within the same complex is the Roundtree Swimming Pool (☎ 772-3392), a large white building attached to the rear of

Stedmen Elementary School up the hill. A swim in the pool is $2 per person; contact the pool for opening hours.

Festivals

Petersburg puts on its own Fourth of July celebration with the usual small-town festivities. The community's best event, and one that is famous around the Southeast, is the Little Norway Festival, held on the weekend closest to Norwegian Independence Day on 17 May, usually before most tourists arrive. If you are even near the area, hop over to Petersburg for it. The locals dress in old costumes, Nordic Dr is filled with a string of booths and games, and several dances are held in local halls. The best part of the festival is the fish feed, when the town's residents put together a pot-luck feast.

Little Norway Festival, Petersburg

Places to Stay

Camping It is difficult to camp near town. Petersburg has *Tent City* on Haugen Dr, half a mile or a 10-minute walk north-west of the airport. The city-operated campground provides wooden pads, each holding three to five tents, to avoid the wet muskeg. However, the facility was designed primarily for young cannery workers who arrive in early summer and occupy an entire pad by building plastic shelters around them. By the time you come along, there are few, if any, spaces available to pitch a tent.

If you can stake out an area, head down to the police station in the Municipal Building on Nordic Dr and pay the officer in charge your user fee. The cost is $5 per night plus a $25 deposit, although during the last few summers city officials have been rather loose about collecting the deposit.

The other organized campgrounds are designed for motorhomes and RVs. In town, there is *Le Conte RV Park* (☎ 772-4680), a private campground with full hook-ups at $15 a night. Out of town at *Mile 22* of the Mitkof Hwy is the *Ohmer Creek Campground* (15 sites, no fee) with a 14-day limit, and at *Mile 26.8* is the *Sumner Strait Campground* (no fee).

Backpackers have a couple of ways to avoid the lack of budget accommodation in Petersburg. There is no camping within the city limits, and if you pitch a tent at the Sandy Beach Recreation Area, on the corner of Sandy Beach Rd and Haugen Dr three miles north of town, local police will most likely kick you out in the middle of the night.

However, by hiking half a mile beyond the Sandy Beach picnic area and shelter along the shoreline, you can camp on the scenic beach. Bring drinking water and pitch your tent above the high-tide line. You can also camp up along the Ravens Roost Trail which begins near the airport, but you will have to walk more than a mile uphill before finding a site that isn't muskeg.

Another way to avoid expensive accommodation is to rent a used car at Rent-A-Dent Rental (☎ 772-4424) and drive to a campground out of town. The agent for the car rental company is in Scandia House on Nordic Dr, but during the summer it pays to call ahead and reserve a vehicle. Rates are $40 per day.

B&Bs *Jewell's by the Sea* (☎ 772-3620) is an interesting place to stay as the owner has an art gallery and shop on the 1st floor and guests enjoy a spectacular view of the Narrows. The B&B is three blocks north of the ferry terminal and charges $50/60 a single/double. *Gypsy Bed & Breakfast* (☎ 772-4531) features a deck overlooking Hammer Slough and a sauna while *Mountain Point Bed & Breakfast* (☎ 772-9382) has a good view of the Narrows and charges $65/75 a single/double.

Hotels Petersburg is a hard-working fishing community that concentrates on the present rather than trying to package its past for a ship full of visitors. This explains why budget accommodations are nonexistent here.

There is no hostel in Petersburg, although the town desperately needs one, and the one cheap hotel underwent major renovation a few years back and increased its prices. *Scandia House* (☎ 772-4281), on Nordic Dr (Main St) in the center of town, now has a 'European' style and charges $55 for a single without a bath. Even *Narrows Inn* (☎ 772-3434), opposite the ferry terminal and supposedly the 'budget-conscious' lodge, charges $55/65 for a single/double. One of the better hotels is *Tides Inn* (☎ 772-4288) on the corner of 1st and Dolphin streets. Singles/doubles are $65/80 but include a continental breakfast while some rooms have kitchenettes that will help keep you out of those costly restaurants.

Places to Eat

For breakfast, there's the *Homestead Cafe* on Nordic Dr, a longtime favorite. A plate of eggs, potatoes and toast costs $7 while hamburgers are $6 and up. *Harbor Lights Pizza* is diagonally opposite the Sons of Norway Hall on Sing Lee Alley (Indian St) and offers pasta dinners for around $7, entire pizzas for $10, beer and wine along with a good view of the busy boat harbor below it. Want pizza without the view? Try *Pelleritos Pizza* at 1105 South Nordic Dr.

Another interesting place in town is *Helse*

Health Foods & Deli on Sing Lee Alley. The health-food store and restaurant is a pleasant place for tea during a rainy afternoon and features home-made breads and soups, seafood chowder on Friday and specials every night. Hours are from 9 am to 5 pm Monday to Friday and 10 am to 3 pm on Saturday.

Entertainment

To listen to the fisher's woes or to meet cannery workers, there is the *Harbor Bar* on Nordic Dr. For something a little livelier try *Kito's Kave* on Sing Lee Alley (Indian St). This bar and liquor store has live music and dancing most nights after 9 pm. When the boats are in it can be a rowdy place that hops until 2 or 3 am.

Hiking

Frederick Point Boardwalk Near the downtown area is this mile-long boardwalk that begins off Nordic Dr next to Sandy Beach Recreation Area. The trail winds through rainforest, across muskeg and then crosses a salmon stream that is quite a sight during the peak spawning runs in August.

Raven's Roost Trail This four-mile trail begins at the water tower on the south-east side of the airport, accessible from Haugen Dr. A boardwalk crosses muskeg areas at the start of the trail, while much of the route is a climb to beautiful open alpine areas at 2013 feet; some of it is steep and requires a little scrambling. A two-story US Forest Service cabin (reservations needed, $25 per night) is above the tree line in an area that provides good summer hiking and spectacular views of Petersburg, Frederick Sound and Wrangell Narrows.

Petersburg Mountain Trail On Kupreanof Island, this trail ascends 2.5 miles from Wrangell Narrows behind Sasby Island to the top of Petersburg Mountain. There are outstanding views from here, the best in the area, of Petersburg, the Coastal Mountains, glaciers and Wrangell Narrows. Plan on three hours to the top of the mountain and

two hours for the return. To get across the channel, go to the skiff float at the North Boat Harbor (Old Boat Harbor) and hitch a ride with somebody who lives on Kupreanof Island. From the Kupreanof Public Dock, head right on the overgrown road towards Sasby Island.

Petersburg Lake Trail This 6.5-mile trail, just one of a trail system in the Petersburg Creek-Duncan Salt Chuck Wilderness on Kupreanof Island, leads to a USFS cabin (reservations needed, $25 per night). See the Trekking section in the Wilderness chapter for further details.

Three Lakes Trails These four short trails, connecting three lakes and Ideal Cove, are off Three Lakes Rd, a Forest Service road that heads east off Mitkof Hwy at *Mile 13.6* and returns at *Mile 23.8*. Beginning at *Mile 14.2* of Three Lakes Rd is a three-mile loop with boardwalks leading to Sand, Crane and Hill lakes, known for their good trout fishing.

On each lake there is a skiff and a picnic platform. Tennis shoes are fine for the trail but to explore around the lakes you need rubber boots. There is a free-use shelter on Sand Lake. From the Sand Lake Trail there is a 1.5-mile trail to Ideal Cove on Frederick Sound.

Blind River Rapids Boardwalk Starting at *Mile 14.5* of the Mitkof Hwy is this easy mile-long boardwalk that winds through muskeg before arriving at the rapids, a popular fishing spot during the summer.

Paddling

There is a variety of interesting trips in the Petersburg area, most of which are blue-water paddles requiring a week or more to undertake. Kayaks are difficult to come by in Petersburg, and if you're planning a major expedition from this port, you may want to obtain one in Juneau or Ketchikan. You can try Ron Campton of *Alaskan Scenic Waterways* (☎ 772-3777) who runs both daily trips to Le Conte Glacier as well as organizes wilderness excursions and acts as a local booking agent.

You can purchase topographic maps at Diamante (☎ 772-4858) on Nordic Dr, but often in a town this size the map you want is gone. It's best to obtain maps in Ketchikan or Juneau before you arrive. Within Petersburg there are a dozen charter boats that deal mostly in fishing trips, but they can also provide drop-off and pick-up services to remote areas. Contact the chamber of commerce office for a current list of them.

Le Conte Glacier The most spectacular paddle in the region is to Le Conte Glacier, 25 miles east of Petersburg and the southernmost tidewater glacier in North America. From town, it takes three to four days to reach the frozen monument, which includes crossing Frederick Sound north of Coney Island. The crossing should be done at slack tide as winds and tides can cause choppy conditions. If the tides are judged right, it is possible to paddle far enough into Le Conte Bay to camp within view of the glacier.

To skip the paddling but still see the glacier, check with Kupreanof Flying Service (☎ 772-3396) or Nordic Air (☎ 772-3535) for flightseeing trip but expect to split $150 among three passengers for the trip. More worthwhile is a cruise to the glacier with Alaskan Scenic Waterways (☎ 772-3777) or Alaska Passages (☎ 772-3967). Either one would also arrange drop-off and pick-up service for kayakers who don't want to cross Frederick Sound.

Thomas Bay Almost as impressive is Thomas Bay, 20 miles from Petersburg and north of Le Conte Bay on the east side of Frederick Sound. The bay features a pair of glaciers, including Baird Glacier where many paddlers spend a day hiking. The mountain scenery surrounding the bay is spectacular and there are three USFS cabins (reservations needed, $25 per night): Swan Lake Cabin, Spurt Cove Cabin and Cascade Creek Cabin. Consult the local USFS office (☎ 874-2323) about crossing Frederick Sound and the availability of cabins. Pad-

dlers need from four to seven days for the round trip out of Petersburg.

Kake to Petersburg Backpackers can take the state ferry to the Native Alaskan village of Kake and paddle back to Petersburg. This 90-mile route follows the west side of Kupreanof Island through Keku Strait, Sumner Strait and up Wrangell Narrows to Petersburg. The highlight of the trip is Rocky Pass, a remote and narrow winding waterway in Keku Strait that has almost no boat traffic other than the occasional kayaker. Caution has to be used in Sumner Strait, which lies only 40 miles away from open ocean and has its share of strong winds and waves. Plan on seven to 10 days for the trip.

Getting There & Away
Air The Alaska Airlines (☎ 772-4255) milk run through the Southeast provides a daily northbound and southbound flight out of Petersburg. The airport is a mile east of the post office on Haugen Dr.

Boat The State Marine Ferry terminal (☎ 772-3855) is about a mile along Nordic Dr from the southern edge of town. There is usually one northbound ferry arriving daily. Travelers continuing onto Juneau should consider taking the *Le Conte* on Thursday if it fits into their schedule. This ship sails from Petersburg to Juneau but stops at Kake, Sitka, Angoon, Tenakee and Hoonah along the way; the one-way fare is $42.

AROUND PETERSBURG
There are a few sights around Petersburg, although it's debatable whether it's worth the hassle of getting out to see them. Those without transport can either rent a vehicle or contact Tongass Traveler (☎ 772-4837) which offers a two-hour van tour. For $30, Patti Norheim takes you to a shrimp cannery, fish hatchery and a tree farm amongst other things, and then returns you to her home in town where you sit on her deck enjoying wine and a shrimp cocktail. Travelers with their own vehicle who plan to spend some time around Petersburg should pick up a

copy of the *Mitkof Island Road Guide* from the US Forest Service office for $3.

One of the best fishing spots in the area is at *Mile 14.5* of the Mitkof Hwy where a 0.3-mile boardwalk leads through a muskeg meadow to the **Blind River Rapids Recreation Area**. There is a small trail shelter along the river where anglers come to catch Dolly Varden, cutthroat trout and steelhead from mid-April to mid-May, king salmon in June and July, and coho salmon after mid-August.

The **Crystal Lake Fish Hatchery** at *Mile 17.5* of the Mitkof Hwy is a $2.2 million facility used to stock coho, king salmon and trout throughout the Southeast. No formal tours are offered, but hatchery personnel are pleasant and informative. It is open weekdays from 8 am to 4 pm. Nearby in Blind Slough Recreation Area is the **Trumpeter Swan Observatory**, designed to permit sheltered photography and viewing of this majestic bird.

On the way back to town, stop at the **Falls Creek Fish Ladder** at *Mile 13.7* of the Mitkof Hwy, an impressive sight in August when coho and pink salmon leap along its steps. At *Mile 9* of the highway is the **Heintzleman Nursery** operated by the US Forest Service, which includes six greenhouses that produce a million seedlings of Sitka spruce per year. It is open to the public on an informal basis on weekdays from 8 am to 4.30 pm. Like at the hatchery, there is no admission charge.

Kake

Kake is an Indian beachfront community (population 700) on the north-west coast of Kupreanof Island. It is the traditional home of the Kake tribe of the Tlingit Indians and today the community maintains subsistence rights while also running commercial fishing, fish processing and logging enterprises to supplement its economy. Kake is known for having the tallest totem pole in Alaska (and some say the world), a 132-foot carving that was first raised at Alaska's pavilion in the 1970 World's Fair in Osaka, Japan.

The state ferry *Le Conte* stops twice a week at Kake on its run between Petersburg and Sitka. The one-way fare from Petersburg to Kake is $20. Within town, 1.5 miles from the ferry terminal, are three general stores, a laundromat and the *New Town Inn*, where rooms are $52/79 for singles/doubles. Rough logging roads lead south from town and eventually reach scenic Hamilton Bay, 20 miles south-east of Kake.

Unless you want to spend three or four days in Kake, you can fly out on regularly scheduled flights via Wings to Alaska (☎ 785-6466) or LAB (☎ 785-6435) to Juneau or Bellair (☎ 785-6411) to Sitka. One-way fare to either is around $90.

Tebenkof Bay Wilderness Kake serves as the departure point for blue-water trips into Tebenkof Bay Wilderness, a remote bay system composed of hundreds of islands, small inner bays and coves. The return paddle is a scenic 10-day adventure that can lead to sightings of bald eagles, black bears and a variety of marine mammals. Paddlers should have experience in ocean touring and be prepared to handle a number of portages. Kayaks can be rented in either Juneau or Sitka and then carried on board the state ferry to Kake.

The most common route is to paddle south from Kake through Keku Strait into Port Camden, where at its western end there is a 1.3-mile portage trail to the Bay of Pillars. From the Bay of Pillars you encounter the only stretch of open water as you paddle three miles around Point Ellis into Tebenkof Bay. The return east follows Alecks Creek from Tebenkof Bay into Alecks Lake, where there is a 2.3-mile portage trail to No Name Bay. From here paddlers can reach Keku Strait and paddle north to Kake via the scenic Rocky Pass.

Sitka

In a region of Alaska already strong in color and history, Sitka (population 8300) is the gem in a beautiful setting. Facing the Pacific

Ocean, the city is overshadowed to the west by Mt Edgecumbe, the extinct volcano with a cone similar to Japan's Mt Fuji. The waters offshore are broken up by a myriad of small, forested islands that are ragged silhouettes during the sunsets, while to the east the town is flanked by snow-capped mountains and sharp granite peaks. On a clear day Sitka, the only city in Southeast Alaska that actually fronts the Pacific Ocean, rivals Juneau for the sheer beauty of its surroundings.

Along with its natural beauty, Sitka is steeped in history. The Russians may have actually landed in Sitka Sound as early as 1741 after two ships under explorer Vitus Bering became separated in a storm. While Bering himself was sighting in Mt St Elias to confirm the presence of a continent, the other ship was much further south where it sent two longboats ashore in Sitka Sound in search of water. The boats never returned and the Russians wisely departed.

What the sailors undoubtedly encountered were members of two powerful Tlingit tribes: the Kiksadi and the Kogwanton, who over time had developed the most advanced culture of any group of Native Americans in Alaska. The Tlingits were still there in 1799 when the Russians returned and established the first non-indigenous settlement in the Southeast. Alexander Baranof built a Russian fort near the present ferry terminal to continue the rich sea-otter fur trade. He was in Kodiak three years later when Tlingits, armed with guns from British and American traders, overwhelmed the fort, burned it to the ground and killed most of its inhabitants.

Baranof returned in 1804, this time with an imperial Russian Navy warship, and after destroying the Tlingit fort, established a settlement called New Archangel at the present site of Sitka, making it the headquarters of the Russian-American Company. Sitka flourished both economically and culturally on the strength of the fur trade; it was known as the 'Paris of the Pacific' in its golden era.

In 1867, Sitka picked up its present name after the USA took control of the town following the purchase of Alaska. After the territorial capital was transferred to Juneau in 1900, the city fell upon some hard times but boomed again during WW II when a military base was built on nearby Japonski Island. At one time during the war, Sitka had a population of 37,000 military and civilian residents. Today, the city is supported by a pulp mill, fishing fleet, cold-storage plants and several federal agencies that have offices in the area.

However, the town clings to its strong Russian heritage and prides itself on being the cultural center of the Southeast, if not of all Alaska. It seemed only natural to those living in Sitka that when author James Michener decided to write his epic novel *Alaska* he chose their town as his home base to conduct research.

When arriving in Sitka by state ferry, you will sail through the Sergius Narrows, a tight waterway that ships must follow at slack tide. At any other time it is too hazardous for vessels to negotiate the fierce currents caused by the changing of the tides. This often forces the state ferry to take a three-hour stop at Sitka while waiting for the tide and allows travelers a quick view of the city even if they're not disembarking.

The ferry terminal is seven miles north of town, too far to see anything on foot, but Sitka Tours does run a bus tour for those waiting for the ferry to depart. The tour briefly covers the major sites: Sitka National Historical Park, St Michael's Cathedral and Sheldon Jackson College. The cost is $8 per person.

Information

The Sitka Visitor Bureau (☎ 747-5940), in the Centennial Building off Harbor Dr next to the Crescent Boat Harbor, is open from 8 am to 5 pm weekdays. The US Forest Service office (☎ 747-6671), the place to go for trail information, cabin reservations and handouts about enjoying the wilderness, is in a three-story red building on the corner of Siginaka and Katlian streets, across from the Thomas Boat Harbor. The office is open on weekdays from 8 am to 5 pm. Sitka has three state recreation areas; information about

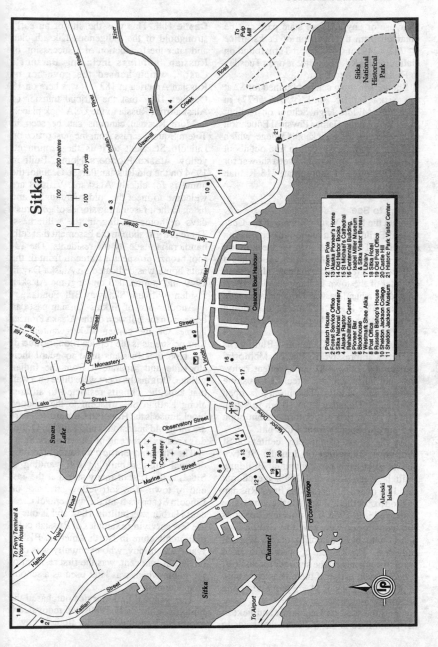

Sitka

0   100   200 yds
0   100   200 metres

To Pulp Mill

Sitka National Historical Park

To Ferry Terminal & Youth Hostel

Swan Lake

Russian Cemetery

Crescent Boat Harbour

Channel

Sitka

Aleutski Island

To Airport

O'Connell Bridge

Gavan Hill Trail

Streets and roads:
River Road
Indian River Road
Sawmill Creek
Indian Creek
Davis Street
Jeff Street
Baranof Street
Monastery Street
Groid Street
De Street
Lake Street
Lincoln Street
Marine Street
Observatory Street
Harbor Drive
Point Road
Halibut Road
Kaltian Street

1   Potlatch House
2   Forest Service Office
3   Sitka National Cemetery
4   Alaska Raptor Rehabilitation Center
5   Pioneer Bar
6   Blockhouse
7   Westmark Shee Atika
8   Post Office
9   Russian Bishop's House
10 Sheldon Jackson College
11 Sheldon Jackson Museum
12 Totem Pole
13 Alaska Pioneer's Home
14 Old Harbor Books
15 St Michael's Cathedral
16 Centennial Building, Isabel Miller Museum & Sitka Visitor Bureau
17 Library
18 Sitka Hostel
19 Old Post Office
20 Castle Hill
21 Historic Park Visitor Center

their use or any Alaskan state park can be obtained from the Division of Parks office (☎ 747-6249) at Old Airport Turnaround on Halibut Point Rd. The office is open Tuesday to Friday from 6 to 8 am.

Showers in town can be obtained for $2 at the Sitka Public Pool (☎ 747-5677) in Blatchley Middle High School on Halibut Point Rd or at the Hames Physical Education Center in Sheldon Jackson College which also has a pool for $3; call to find out about opening hours. You can also get a shower for $2 at Homestead Laundromat, 713 Katlian St, behind Potlatch Motel.

Things to See

Contact the Sitka Visitor Bureau in the Centennial Building for a map of the city listing the points of interest. Also inside the building is the **Isabel Miller Museum** which has a collection of relics from the past, along with a model of the town as it appeared in 1867. Outside is a hand-carved Tlingit canoe made from a single log. The Centennial Building is open from 8 am to 10 pm from Monday to Saturday.

Next door to the Centennial Building is the city's impressive **Kettleson Memorial Library** (☎ 747-8708), an excellent rainy-day spot when you don't feel like sloshing through the puddles. The library is open Monday to Thursday from 10 am to 9 pm, Friday 10 am to 5 pm, Saturday from noon to 5 pm and Sunday from 1 to 5 pm.

At the heart of the city center is **St Michael's Cathedral** on Lincoln St, two blocks west from the Centennial Building. Built between 1844 and 1848, the church stood for over 100 years as the finest Russian Orthodox cathedral in Alaska until fire destroyed it in 1966. The priceless treasures and icons inside were saved by Sitka's residents, who built a replica of the original cathedral. The church is open daily from noon to 4 pm during the summer for visitors. It opens even earlier if there is a cruise ship in port. Donations of $1 are requested upon entering.

Continue west on Lincoln St and next to the post office is the walkway that leads to **Castle Hill**. This was the site of an early stronghold of the indigenous Kiksadi clan and later the foundation of a succession of Russian buildings including Baranof's Castle, which housed the governor of Russian America in 1837. It was here on 18 October 1867 that the official transfer of Alaska from Russia to the USA took place.

More Russian cannons can be seen in Totem Square across from the post office on Lincoln St. Next to it is the prominent, yellow **Alaska Pioneers Home**. Built in 1934 on the old Russian Parade Ground, the home is for elderly Alaskans. Visitors are welcome to meet the 'old sourdoughs' and listen to their fascinating stories of gold-rush days or homesteading in the wilderness. There is a gift shop in the basement that sells handicrafts made by the residents. The 13-foot bronze prospector statue in front of the state home was dedicated on Alaska Day in 1949 and is modelled on longtime Alaskan resident William 'Skagway Bill' Fonda.

Another part of Sitka's Russian past can be seen on the hill west of the Alaska Pioneer Home. On the corner of Kogwanton and Marine streets is the replica **blockhouse** of the type the Russians used to guard their stockade and separate it from the Indian village. Originally, there were three on a wall that kept the Tlingits restricted to an area along Katlian St. Adjacent to the wooden blockhouse is the **Russian Cemetery**. There are more old headstones and Russian Orthodox crosses at the end of Observatory St.

The **Russian Bishop's House**, the only original Russian building still standing in Sitka, is the first of many sights at the east end of town. The soft-yellow structure on Lincoln St across from the west end of Crescent Harbor was built in 1842 and is one of the few surviving examples of Russian colonial architecture in North America. Bishop Ivan Veniaminov, who eventually was canonized St Innocent, was the first resident of the home which was later used as a school, chapel and office.

The National Park Service purchased the building in the early 1980s and renovated it to its 1853 setting. The 1st floor is now a museum dedicated to the building and its Russian occupants, while the 2nd floor has been restored as the bishop's personal quarters and the Chapel of the Annunciation. Hours are from 8.30 am to 5 pm daily in the summer.

Further east along Lincoln St, past the boat harbor, is **Sheldon Jackson College**, where Michener stayed and worked for much of the three summers he spent in Alaska. Among the buildings on campus is the octagonal **Sheldon Jackson Museum**. Constructed in 1895, it's the oldest cement building in Alaska and today houses one of the best indigenous-culture collections in the state.

The artefacts were gathered by Dr Sheldon Jackson, general agent for education, from 1880 to 1900, making the collection the oldest in the state. It features an impressive display of indigenous masks, hunting tools and baskets from such peoples as the Inuit, Tlingit, Haida and Aleut. Hanging from the ceiling, and equally impressive, is the collection of boats and sleds used in Alaska – from reindeer sleds and dog sleds to kayaks and umiaks. The museum (☎ 747-8981) is open daily from 8 am to 5 pm in the summer; admission is $2.

For a lot of visitors, Sitka's most colorful area is **Katlian St**, which begins off Lincoln St at the west end of town. The road is a classic mixture of weather-beaten houses, docks and canneries where there always seem to be fishing boats unloading their catch. Katlian St portrays the sights and sounds of the busy Southeast fishing industry. Even the vacant yards along it reflect dependence on the sea, as they have discarded fishing nets or stacks of crab pots. In short, it is a colorful, bustling place and a photographer's delight.

Sitka's most noted attraction lies further east at the end of Lincoln St, where the National Park Service maintains the **Sitka National Historical Park**. The 107-acre park, half a mile east of the city center, features a trail that winds past 15 totem poles moved here from the Louisiana Exposition in St Louis in 1904 and now standing in a beautiful forest setting next to the sea.

The park is at the mouth of the Indian River where the Tlingit Indians were finally defeated by the Russians in 1804 after defending a wooden fort for a week. The Russians had arrived with a warship and three other ships to revenge a Tlingit Kiksadi clan raid on a nearby outpost two years earlier. But despite their cannons, they did little damage to the walls and, when they stormed the structure with the help of Aleuts, they were repulsed in a bloody battle. It was only when the Tlingits ran out of gunpowder and flint and slipped away at night that the Russians were able to enter the now deserted fort.

Begin at the park's visitor center (☎ 747-6281) where there are displays of Russian and indigenous artefacts, and where carvers demonstrate traditional arts. A mile-long self-guided loop leads past the totems to the site of the Tlingit fort near the Indian River. The fort is long gone but its outline can still be seen and is marked by posts. Admission is free and the visitor center is open daily from 8 am to 5 pm in the summer.

Nearby on Sawmill Creek Rd, just beyond the Indian River Bridge is **Alaska Raptor Rehabilitation Center**. A raptor is a bird of prey and at ARRC you'll see eagles, hawks, owls that are sick or injured and are undergoing treatment intended to enable them to survive again in the wild. There are also more than a dozen bald eagles, the favorite is

named 'Buddy', that can be viewed close up or you can watch the exercise sessions that are staged twice a week in a nearby muskeg areas. Here the birds are secured by a loose line and are encouraged to fly from one stand to the next.

When cruise ships are in, there is often a full tour to the center for $10 per person. Otherwise the ARRC (☎ 747-8662) is usually open daily for visitors. Call ahead for the times and days of practice sessions.

Also at the east end of town and a place of interest mostly to history buffs is the **Sitka National Cemetery**. The plot is off Sawmill Creek Rd, just west of the Public Safety Academy, and can be reached from Sheldon Jackson College along Jeff Davis Rd. The area was designated a national cemetery by past president Calvin Coolidge and includes headstones of Civil War veterans, members of the Aleutian Campaign in WW II and many notable Alaskans.

Festivals
Extending its reputation as the cultural center of the Southeast, the city sponsors the Sitka Summer Music Festival over three weeks in June at the Centennial Building. The emphasis of the festival is on chamber music and brings together professional musicians for concerts and workshops. The highly acclaimed event is popular so it can be hard to obtain tickets to the twice-weekly evening concerts. However, rehearsals, open to the public, are easier to attend and usually free.

A bit of Russian culture is offered whenever a cruise ship is in port during the summer. The New Archangel Russian Dancers take the stage at the Centennial Building then for a half-hour show. It's $4 per person to see the performance of more than 30 dancers in Russian costumes.

Sitka also stages the All-Alaska Logging Championships in late June when the locals compete with outsiders from the Pacific Northwest in such events as chopping, axe tossing, bucking trees with huge chainsaws and tree climbing. A week later is the town's Fourth of July celebration.

On the weekend nearest 18 October, the city holds its Alaska Day Festival by re-enacting the transfer of the state from Russia to the USA with costumes (and even beard styles) of the 1860s. A parade highlights the three-day event.

Places to Stay
Camping The nearest campground to the center of town is *Sealing Cove* (☎ 747-3439), a commercial campground for RVers at Sealing Cove Harbor on Japonski Island. Unfortunately there are no tent sites here. There are two US Forest Service campgrounds in the Sitka area but neither is close to town.

Starrigavan Campground is a 0.7-mile walk north of the ferry terminal at *Mile 7.8* of Halibut Point Rd. The campground (30 sites, $5 per night) is in a scenic setting and adjacent to a saltwater beach and hiking trails. On your way to the area you'll pass Old Sitka State Park, which features lit trails and interpretive displays dedicated to the site of the original Russian settlement.

Sawmill Creek Campground (nine sites) is six miles east of Sitka on Blue Lake Rd off Sawmill Creek Rd and past the pulp mill. Although the area is no longer maintained by the USFS, it provides mountain scenery with an interesting trail to Blue Lake, a good fishing spot. Others find informal camp sites half a mile along Indian River Trail right on the river.

Hostels The *Sitka (AYH) Youth Hostel* (☎ 747-8356) is in the basement of the Methodist Church at 303 Kimsham Rd. Follow Halibut Point Rd north-west out of town and then turn right onto Peterson Rd, a quarter of a mile past the Lakeside Grocery Store. Once on Peterson Rd you immediately veer left onto Kimsham Rd. Registration is from 6 to 11 pm and check-out time is 8 am. There are now kitchen facilities along with a lounge and an eating area. The hostel is open from June to August and the cost is $5 for members and $8 for nonmembers. Shuttle buses from the ferry will often drop you right at the door step.

B&Bs There are many B&Bs in the Sitka area that offer rooms with a good meal in the morning for around $45/55 a single/double. Stop at the Sitka Visitor Bureau for an updated list of them or try *Creek's Edge Guest House* (☎ 747-6484) which overlooks Sitka Sound and Mt Edgecumbe and provides a shuttle service. *Helga's Bed & Breakfast* (☎ 747-5497), right on the beach at 2821 Halibut Point Rd, has five rooms for $50/60 a single/double. The ferry bus will drop you off here on the way to town.

Sitka House Bed & Breakfast (☎ 747-4937), on a hill above St Michael's Russian Orthodox Cathedral at 325 Seward St, features a hot tub on an outdoor deck for $50 or $55 a night. If you have some extra funds and want a unique experience, book a room at the *Rockwell Lighthouse* (☎ 747-3056), the last lighthouse built in Alaska. They will provide the three-minute skiff ride from town and you'll not only get to stay in a lighthouse but will enjoy an excellent view of town and the rugged coastline around it. It's not cheap though at $125 per day.

Hotels There are five hotel/motels in Sitka. The cheapest is the *The Bunkhouse* (☎ 747-8796) at 3302 Halibut Point Rd with four rooms at $32/39 a single/double. A step up is *Potlatch House* (☎ 747-8611), at the end of Katlian St, near the intersection with Halibut Point Rd; the motel has 30 rooms from $67. There's also *Super 8 Motel* (☎ 747-8804), at 404 Sawmill Creek, with rooms beginning at $71 and the town's impressive *Westmark Shee Atika* (☎ 747-6241), right downtown, where you'll spend at least $110 a night.

Places to Eat

Sitka has restaurants suitable for everybody's budget and desire. For breakfast try *Red Rooster Cafe*, behind the Shee Aitka Hotel on Seward St, which serves eggs, toast and potatoes until 3 pm before switching over to barbecue ribs and chicken in the evening. For just coffee in the morning, there is the *Coffee Express* on Lake St, next door to the fire station. It has limited seating inside, opens at 7 am on weekdays and offers a choice selection of coffees and teas and sandwiches for around $6. There's also *Back Door Cafe*, accessed through Old Harbor Bookstore on Lincoln St, for sandwiches and coffee and *Lulu's* nearby for reasonably priced breakfast and hamburgers.

For dinner, try *Los Amigos*, 1305 Sawmill Creek Rd, for Mexican dishes. The *Bayview*, upstairs in the Bayview Trading Center across from Crescent Harbor, has the best hamburgers in Sitka. Although the service can be slow at times, their menu lists 26 varieties of hamburger as well as a variety of fresh seafood. The Bayview also serves beer and wine in a setting which offers every table a view of the boat harbor across the street.

Along Katlian St there is the *Twin Dragon* and *Rockfish Cafe*. Twin Dragon is a Chinese restaurant with greasy décor but good food, especially their fried beef in hot sauce and Mongolian beef. At Rockfish Cafe you can carry out salads, sandwiches and fish and chips. The city's *McDonald's* is a mile out of town on Halibut Point Rd while *Subway* is behind Shee Atika Hotel on Seward St and is open to midnight from Monday to Saturday. The *Raven Room* in the Westmark Shee Atika is a fine restaurant but meal prices are high. Head here in the morning, however, as it is a great place to sip a cup of coffee while watching the sunrise over Crescent Boat Harbor.

Entertainment

Sitka's most interesting night spot is the *Pioneer Bar*, the classic fisher's pub on Katlian St down by the waterfront. The walls are covered with photos of fishing boats and the scoreboard for the pool table often has 'help wanted' messages scrawled across it from fishers looking for black-cod crew or notes from somebody seeking work on a troller. Above the long wooden bar is a large brass bell, but put off the urge to ring it unless you want to buy a round of drinks for the house. Just as crowded after work but with a different clientele is the lounge in the *Westmark Shee Atika*, which draws professionals and office workers for music, dancing and drinking.

Another option at night is to book a passage on the 2½-hour night cruise offered by Silver Bay Harbor Tours (☎ 747-8941). Their boat departs from Crescent Harbor daily at 6 pm for a view of Sitka and its waterfront on Saturday, Sunday and Monday night; the fare is $25 per person.

Tours

Land tours in Sitka include the ferry-stop-over adventure by Sitka Tours (☎ 747-8443) for those waiting for the tide to switch. The two-hour tour includes Sitka National Historical Park, some shopping and the Russian Cathedral for $8. The same company also offers an historical tour ($22 for three hours) which also includes Castle Hill and Russian Bishop's House. To escape into the forest, call Wolf's Alaska Tours (☎ 747-6769) for hikes that range from three hours to the whole day. Group sizes are small and the fee includes lunch and rain gear.

You can also book marine tours in Sitka. Allen Tours (☎ 747-8100) has a three-hour trip to view sea otters 25 miles north of Sitka for $80 per person while Alaska SeaTours (☎ 747-5576) uses a catamaran and rafts to get you close to wildlife for about the same price.

Hiking

Sitka offers superb hiking in the beautiful but tangled forest that surrounds the city. Second only to Juneau for the variety and number of trails that can be reached on foot, Sitka has eight trails which start from its road system and total over 40 miles through the woods and mountain areas. If you're planning to spend time in Sitka, stop at the US Forest Service office and ask for a copy of *Sitka Trails* for $1 which provides information and rough maps of 30 trails in the area.

Indian River Trail This easy trail is a 5.5-mile walk along a clear salmon stream to the Indian River Falls, an 80-foot waterfall at the base of the Three Sisters Mountains. The hike takes you through a typical Southeast rainforest and offers the opportunity to view black bears, deer and bald eagles. The

trailhead, a short walk from the center of town, is off Sawmill Creek Rd just east of the National Cemetery. Pass the driveway leading to the Public Safety Academy parking lot and turn up the dirt road with a gate across it. This leads back to the city water plant where the trail begins left of the pump house. Plan on four to five hours for a round trip to the falls.

Gavan Hill Trail Also close to town is the Gavan Hill Trail which ascends three miles and almost 2500 feet to the Gavan Hill peak. The trail provides excellent views of Sitka and the surrounding area. From the end of the trail, the adventurous hiker can continue onto the peaks of the Three Sisters Mountains.

Gavan Hill is now linked to Harbor Mountain Trail (see the following description) while halfway along the Cross Trail is a free alpine shelter. Built in 1991 by the USFS, the shelter is used on a first-come-first-gets-a-bunk basis and is 3.2 miles from the Gavan Hill trailhead.

From Lincoln St, head north up Baranof St for six blocks to the house at 508 Baranof St past Merrill St. The trail begins just beyond this house and heads to the northeast, reaching Cross Trail within three-quarters of a mile. There is good camping in the alpine regions of the trail, but bring water and a camp stove, as wood and drinking water are not available above the tree line. Plan on three to four hours to hike the trail one way.

Airport Causeway Hike This hike begins in Sitka city center with a 1.8-mile walk across O'Connell Bridge and past the boat harbors on Japonski Island to the airport. From the high arch of the bridge, you get some of the best views of Sitka and the mountains that flank it to the east. At the airport, the hike continues along the airport causeway and extends 1.5-miles into Sitka Sound across Sasedni, Kirushkin and Makhnati islands.

The causeway was built during WW II when the army wanted to provide harbor protection for the naval air station and the city. Along the causeway there is fascinating

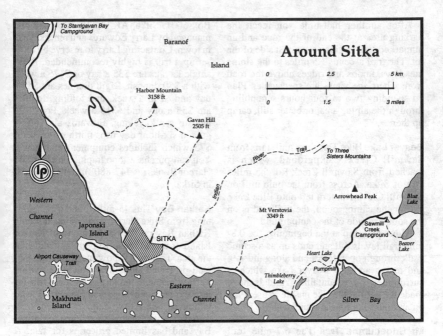

beachcombing for shells and driftwood, and interesting tidal pools to investigate. You can also view the underground bunkers, personnel quarters and gun emplacements on Makhnati Island that were left over from Sitka's military build-up during WW II.

Most people reach the trailhead by boat, and travelers can rent a kayak in Sitka (see the Sitka Paddling section for more details). At times it is also possible to arrange an escort across the airport runway to the beginning of the causeway. When you get to the airport you must contact the airport manager (☎ 966-2960) during work hours, simply scampering across the runway is illegal. Plan on two to three hours for the round trip.

Mt Verstovia Trail This 2.5-mile trail is a challenging climb of 2550 feet to the 'shoulder', a small summit that is the most common end of the trail, although it is possible to climb to 3349 feet, the actual peak of Mt Verstovia. The view from the 'shoulder'

on clear days is spectacular, undoubtedly the best in the area.

The trailhead is two miles east of Sitka along Sawmill Creek Rd. Once you reach the Kiksadi Club on the left, look for the trailhead marked 'Mount Verstovia Trail'. The Russian charcoal pits (signposted) are reached within a quarter of a mile and shortly after that the trail begins a series of switchbacks. Plan on a four-hour round trip to the 'shoulder'. From the 'shoulder', the true peak of Mt Verstovia lies to the north along a ridge that connects the two. Allow an extra hour each way to hike to the peak.

Harbor Mountain Trail This trail is reached from Harbor Mountain Rd, the only road in the Southeast that provides access to a subalpine area. Head four miles north-west from Sitka on Halibut Point Rd to the junction with Harbor Mountain Rd. It is 4.5 miles up the rough dirt road to a parking area and nearby picnic shelter.

After another half-mile you reach the parking area at the end of the road and an unmarked trail begins on the east side of the lot. The trail ascends 1.5 miles to the alpine meadows, knobs and ridges above the road from where the views are spectacular. Plan on spending two to four hours scrambling through the alpine area, or better still, camp up there.

Beaver Lake Hike This short trail starts from Sawmill Creek Campground, which is reached from Sawmill Creek Rd, 5.5 miles east of Sitka. Across from the pulp mill on Sawmill Creek Rd, turn left onto Blue Lake Rd for the campground; the trailhead is on the southern side of the campground.

Although steep at the beginning, the 0.8-mile trail levels out and ends up as a scenic walk through open forest and along muskeg and marsh areas to Beaver Lake which is surrounded by mountains. Vandals have made the skiff at the lake unsafe to use. Plan on an hour hike for the round trip.

Mt Edgecumbe Trail The 6.7-mile trail begins at Fred's Creek USFS Cabin (reservations needed, $25 per night), and ascends to the top of the summit crater of this extinct volcano. Needless to say, the views from the summit are spectacular on a clear day. About three miles up the trail is a free-use shelter (no reservations required).

Mt Edgecumbe lies on Kruzof Island, 10 miles west of Sitka, and can only be reached by boat because large swells from the ocean prevent float planes from landing. Stop at the Sitka Visitors Bureau for a list of local operators who will drop off and pick up hikers for around $70 one way per party. Actual hiking time is from five to six hours one way, but by securing Fred's Creek USFS Cabin you can turn the adventure into a pleasant three-day trip with nights spent in two shelters.

Paddling
Sitka also serves as the departure point for numerous blue-water trips along the protected shorelines of Baranof and Chichagof islands. Baidarka Boats (☎ 747-8996), PO

Box 6001, Sitka, AK 99835, is owned and managed by Larry Edwards and rents kayaks in town. Contacting Larry to reserve boats or set up a trip is highly recommended. Rigid single kayaks are $35 a day or $175 a week with a $50 deposit. Rigid doubles are $45 a day and $245 a week, and folding doubles are $55 a day and $315 a week. For those new to sea kayaking, Edwards also offers guided six-hour day trips north of town for $75 which includes equipment and lunch. You can purchase topographic maps at Old Harbor Books (☎ 747-8808), 201 Lincoln St in Sitka.

Katlian Bay This 45-mile round trip, beginning from Sitka Harbor and ending at scenic Katlian Bay on the northern end of Kruzof Island, is one of the most popular paddles in the area. The route follows narrow straits and well-protected shorelines which are marine traffic channels, making it an ideal trip for less experienced blue-water paddlers who will never be far from help.

A fish buyer is usually anchored in Katlian Bay and has limited groceries for sale. A scenic side trip is to hike the sandy beach from the Katlian Bay around Cape Georgiana to Sea Lion Cove on the Pacific Ocean. Catch the tides to paddle the Olga and Neva straits on the way north and return along Sukot Inlet, spending a night at the USFS cabin on Brent's Beach, if you can reserve it. Plan on four to six days for the paddle.

Shelikof Bay You can combine a 10-mile paddle to Kruzof Island with a six-mile hike across the island from Mud Bay to Shelikof Bay along an old logging road and trail. Once on the Pacific Ocean side you'll find a beautiful sandy beach providing lots of beachcombing and the Shelikof USFS Cabin (reservations needed, $25 per night).

West Chichagof The western shoreline of Chichagof Island is one of the best blue-water trips in Southeast Alaska for experienced kayakers. Unfortunately, the trip involves a float-plane charter, as few paddlers have the experience to be able to paddle the open ocean around Khaz Peninsula that forms a barrier between the north end of Kruzof Island and Slocum Arm. The arm is the southern end of a series of straits, coves and protected waterways that shield paddlers from the ocean's swells and extend over 30 miles north to Lisianski Strait.

With all its hidden coves and inlets, the trip is a good two-week paddle. Those with even more time and some sense of adventure in their hearts could continue another 25 miles through Lisianski Strait to the fishing village of Pelican, where the state ferry stops twice a month in the summer. Such an expedition would require at least two to three weeks but would keep the air charter costs down to a 30-minute flight to Slocum Arm.

USFS Cabins

There are a number of USFS cabins close to Sitka which require less than 30 minutes of flying time to reach. The following cabins, which cost $25 per night, should be reserved in advance through the USFS office in Sitka.

For information on Fred's USFS Cabin, Brent's Beach USFS Cabin and Shelikof USFS Cabin on Kruzof Island (the site of Mt Edgecumbe) see the Sitka Hiking and Paddling sections. Local air-service operators which can handle chartering requests are BellAir (☎ 747-8636) at 475 Katlian St, and Mountain Aviation (☎ 966-2288) in the airport terminal.

Redoubt Lake Cabin This A-frame cabin is at the north end of Redoubt Lake, a narrow body of water south of Sitka on Baranof Island. The cabin is a 20-minute flight from Sitka. You can also reach it by paddling to the head of Silver Bay from town and then hiking along a five-mile trail south to the cabin.

Baranof Lake Cabin This cabin is a favorite among locals, as it has a scenic, mountainous setting on the east side of Baranof Island with a mile trail to Warm Springs Bay. At the bay there is a bathhouse constructed around the natural hot springs which costs $2.50 to use. The cabin is a 20-minute flight from Sitka.

Lake Eva Cabin On Baranof Island, this cabin has a skiff with oars, an outdoor fire pit and a wood stove inside. A trail from the lake outlet, which can be fished for Dolly Varden, cutthroat trout and salmon in late summer, leads down to the ocean. The cabin is a 20-minute flight from Sitka.

White Sulphur Springs Cabin A 45-minute flight to the western shore of Chichagof Island, this cabin is popular with Southeasterners because of the hot springs bathhouse in front of it. The free hot springs are used by cabin renters as well as fishers and kayakers passing through.

Getting There & Away

Air Sitka is served by Alaska Airlines (☎ 966-2266) with flights to Juneau for $85 one-way as well as to Ketchikan for $120 as part of the milk run that connects the city to Wrangell and Petersburg. The airport is on Japonski Island, 1.8 miles west of the town center. On a nice day, it can be a scenic 20-minute walk from the airport terminal over the O'Connell Bridge to the heart of Sitka. Otherwise, the white Airporter minibus of Sitka Tours meets all jet flights and charges $2.50 for a ride to the city hotels; it does not go to the international hostel.

Regularly scheduled flights among the small air charter companies include Sitka to Pelican for $95 one way with Bellair (☎ 747-8636) at 475 Katlian St, and Sitka to Tenakee Springs with Mountain Aviation (☎ 966-2288), in the airport terminal, for $75 one way.

Boat The State Marine Ferry terminal is seven miles north of town on Halibut Point Rd, and there are northbound or southbound departures almost daily. Because of the unusual route the boats must follow to Sitka, it's a good idea to call the ferry terminal (☎ 747-8737) to double-check sailings and departure times.

Passage from Sitka to Juneau is $24, Sitka to Angoon $20, Sitka to Petersburg $24 and Sitka to Tenakee Springs $20. The Ferry Transit Bus (☎ 747-8443) meets all ferries for a trip into town. You can also catch the minibus out to the ferry terminal from the Westmark Shee Atika when it picks up hotel guests.

Getting Around

Car & Bicycle Rental Allstar Rental (☎ 966-2552) can provide a compact vehicle for $39.95 per day with unlimited mileage. The dealer is adjacent to the airport terminal. J&B Bike Rentals (☎ 747-8279) at Southeast Diving & Sports, 203 Lincoln St has bicycles for rent.

Tenakee Springs

What began in the late 1800s as a winter retreat for fishers and prospectors on the east side of Tenakee Inlet has today evolved into a rustic village known for its slow and relaxed pace of life. At the turn of the century the springs were actually enlarged when the locals blasted out the surrounding rock. The Forest Service followed up by building a concrete container around them in 1915 to keep the hot water out and brushed back a path along the shoreline that now serves as the town's main street.

Today Tenakee Springs (population 150) has no roads, cars or running water, and consists mainly of a ferry dock, a row of houses, cabins on pilings and the dirt path behind them. The town's main attraction is still the natural hot springs that send 108°F water bubbling out of the ground. The alternative lifestyle is centered around the public bathhouse at the end of the ferry dock. The building there encloses the principal spring which flows through the concrete bath at seven gallons per minute. Bath hours, separate for men and women, are posted and most locals take at least one good soak per day, if not two.

The Thanksgiving Storm of 1984 hit the Tenakee Springs waterfront hard and demolished a dozen of the buildings on pilings and damaged others. The community has since patched itself up and the relaxed atmosphere has returned to this quaint Chichagof Island hamlet. Tenakee Springs is an interesting and inexpensive side trip, especially if you use the state ferry *Le Conte*'s Friday night run from Juneau, thus saving accommodation expenses.

Places to Stay & Eat

Opposite the bathhouse at the foot of the ferry dock is the *Snyder Mercantile Company* (☎ 736-2205). Started by Ed Snyder in the late 1890s, the store has been in business ever since and in 1976 installed the town's first phone. Snyder's sells limited supplies and groceries, and also rents seven cabins for $30 to $60 per night. To be sure of getting a cabin, you have to reserve them in advance (PO Box 505, Tenakee Springs, AK 99841) and check in during store hours, Monday to Saturday from 9 am to 5 pm. You also need a sleeping bag.

Relatively new in town is the *Tenakee Inn* (☎ 736-9238), a Victorian-style lodge that has beds in a bunkroom with a fireplace, kitchenette and bay windows. It's nice, so is the price – $15 a night or $25 per couple. There are also rooms on the 2nd floor with private baths from $45 to $60 and some rooms even have a private balcony overlooking the water.

There is a chance your ferry will arrive in the middle of the night, in which case it's best to plan on camping out for the first evening. Since much of the land around town was purchased through the Alaska Lands Lottery in the late 1970s, you have to hike out of town a fair way before finding an available spot to camp.

The best place to pitch a tent, if you are planning to stay a few days, is at the rustic campground a mile east of town at the mouth of the Indian River. It's quiet, picturesque and equipped with several tables and a covered picnic shelter. Keep the camp clean, however, to discourage brown bears from investigating your site, especially during the salmon runs in late August.

The town's restaurant is the *Blue Moon Cafe*. Further down the path towards the boat harbor is the *Tenakee Tavern*, the spot to have a brew after your evening soak.

Hiking & Paddling

There is good fishing in the local streams for trout, salmon and Dolly Varden, and day hikes begin at each end of town. The dirt path, dubbed Tenakee Ave, extends eight miles east of town, where it ends at an old cannery on Coffee Cove, and more than seven miles to the west of town, passing a few cabins in either direction.

Tenakee Springs is one end of a common blue-water paddle from Hoonah (see the Paddling section in the Wilderness chapter); obtain supplies and a kayak from Juneau. If, however, you just want to paddle in the inlet for a day, rent kayaks from the Tenakee Inn (☎ 736-9238) for $35 a day.

Whether paddling or hiking along the shore, always keep an eye out for marine mammals such as humpback whales which are commonly sighted in Tenakee Inlet along with orcas, or killer whales, and harbor porpoises. You may also see brown bears while paddling or hiking in the area as Chichagof Island is second only to Admiralty Island in the Southeast for the highest density of bears.

Getting There & Around

The ferry *Le Conte* stops at Tenakee Springs three to four times a week, connecting it to Angoon, Hoonah, Sitka, Juneau and occasionally even Haines and Skagway. Study the ferry schedule carefully to make sure you don't have to stay in the town longer than you want.

For the true budget traveler, the best deal is to take a Friday night ferry out of Juneau, saving on a night's accommodation and arriving in Tenakee Springs at 4 or 5 am on Saturday. It's then possible to catch a middle-of-the-night ferry the following morning that reaches Juneau on Sunday morning, making for a rather unusual two-day but no nights (at least none that you have to pay for) side trip. The one-way fare from Tenakee Springs to Juneau or Sitka is $20.

Wings of Alaska (☎ 789-0790 in Juneau) has flights from Juneau to Tenakee Springs

at 8.30 am and 5.30 pm from Monday to Saturday. The one-way fare is about $60. For getting around the town, you can rent a bicycle at the Tenakee Inn.

HOONAH

As you head north on board the state ferry *Le Conte*, the next stop after Tenakee Springs before reaching Juneau is Hoonah. It is the largest Tlingit village in Southeast Alaska, with a population of almost 900. The Huna, a Tlingit tribe, have lived in the Icy Strait area for hundreds of years and legend tells of their being forced out of Glacier Bay by an advancing glacier. A store was built on the present-day Hoonah site in 1883 and an established community has existed there ever since.

Hoonah's population is roughly 80% indigenous people. The town lacks the charm and friendliness – as well as the public bathhouse – of Tenakee Springs, but it does offer spectacular scenery in the surrounding mountains. The lifestyle is mainly subsistence while the occupation of most residents involves fishing or logging as evidenced by the clear cuts seen from the roads.

The town serves as the beginning of the kayak trip down Port Frederick to Tenakee Inlet (see the Paddling section in the Wilderness chapter).

Things to See

The most photogenic area lies a mile northwest of Hoonah, where the faded red buildings of the old **Hoonah Packing Cannery** serenely guard Port Frederick. There is good fishing for Dolly Varden from this point.

In town, or actually on a hill overlooking Front St, is the **Cultural Center & Museum** which displays indigenous art and artefacts. The center, open Monday to Friday from 9 am to 3 pm, has no admission charge.

Places to Stay & Eat

There is a small grocery store in Hoonah. You can occasionally purchase fresh seafood directly from the *Cold Storage Plant*. You'll find showers and a laundromat at the marina, and accommodation and meals at the *Huna Totem Lodge* (☎ 945-3636), 1.4 miles from the ferry terminal. In town, breakfast, burgers and pizza are available at *Spank's*, open until 8 pm from Monday to Thursday and until 9 pm on Friday and Saturday, and better meals from *Mary's Inn Restaurant*.

There are no official campgrounds but backpackers do not have to walk far out of town to find a suitable spot to pitch a tent. The high school also has a pool with showers; admission is $1.

Hiking & Paddling

Hoonah lies south-east of Glacier Bay National Park across Icy Strait, but the paddle to the preserve is an extremely challenging trip for advanced kayakers only. An overnight kayak trip can be made to the Salt Lake Bay USFS Cabin, 14 miles from Hoonah on Port Frederick.

The cabin is rented out for $25 per night and needs to be reserved, but it is not heavily used. Originally a trapper's cabin, the structure is small but can still sleep four. There is a log-transfer facility across the bay and active logging in the area so be ready for clear cuts.

The **Spassky Trail**, a 3.3-mile walk, begins 3.5 miles east of Hoonah and winds to Spassky Bay on Icy Strait.

The **Pavlof Trail** is a three-mile walk along the Pavlof River, past two fish ladders between the lake and harbor of the same name. During mid to late August, the salmon runs can be impressive here. Originally the trail was accessed only by boat and plane but now you can link up with the trailhead from Forest Development Road 8515. Pick up a copy of *Hoonah Area Road Guide* if you want to go looking for this trail.

There is also *Bear Paw Lake Trail*, 18 miles south of town on Forest Development Road 8508. The short trail leads to Bear Paw Lake which attracts the interests of anglers.

For more information about paddling or hiking in the area, contact the USFS office (☎ 945-3631) at PO Box 135, Hoonah, AK 99829.

Getting There & Away

The *Le Conte* docks in Hoonah three days a week on its route between Tenakee Springs and Juneau. The ferry terminal (☎ 945-3292), half a mile from town, is open two hours before the ferry arrives. Wings of Alaska (☎ 945-3275) and LAB Flying Service (☎ 945-3266) also maintain offices in Hoonah and provide daily services to Juneau.

PELICAN

If you time it right, you can catch a ferry to Pelican, a lively little fishing town on Lisianski Inlet on the north-west coast of Chichagof Island. The *Le Conte* makes a special run to the town twice a month, providing transport from Juneau for only $30 one way.

The town was established in 1938 by a fish packer and named after his boat. Fishing is Pelican's reason for being – it is the closest harbor to the rich Fairweather salmon grounds. Its population of 200 doubles during the summer when commercial fishers and cold-storage workers arrive for the trolling season from June to mid-September.

The town is a photographer's delight as most of it is built on pilings over tidelands and its main street is a wooden boardwalk; there are only two miles of gravel road beyond that. There's *Harbor Bed & Breakfast* (☎ 732-2261) at the top of the fishing ramp where you can get a bed for $65 or rent a kayak for the day. There's also *Rosie's Bar & Grill* (☎ 735-2265) where you can get a burger, a beer or even a bed – there are four rooms for rent upstairs for around $65.

The reason for visiting Pelican is to get a good view of the Southeast's fishing industry and to mingle with trollers and cold-storage workers at Rosie's at night. If you plan to stay over (and don't want to wait two weeks for the next ferry), Wings of Alaska (☎ 789-0790 in Juneau) has daily scheduled flights to Juneau.

Juneau

First appearances are often misleading, and Juneau (population 30,000) is a case in point. Over half the northbound state ferries arrive in the capital city between midnight and 6 am at the Auke Bay Ferry Terminal, 14 miles from the city center, leaving disgruntled backpackers and tired travelers to sleepily hunt for transport and lodging. At this point you might be unappreciative of Juneau, but give it a second chance. Few cities in the USA and none in Alaska are as beautiful as Juneau. Residents claim it is the most scenic capital in the country, while others describe it as a 'little San Francisco'.

The city center, which hugs the side of Mt Juneau, has many narrow streets running past a mixture of new structures, old store-fronts and slanted houses, all held together by a network of staircases. The bustling waterfront features cruise ships, tankers, fishing boats, a few kayakers and a dozen float planes buzzing in and out like flies. Overhead are the snow-capped peaks of Mt Juneau and Mt Roberts, which provide just a small part of the superb hiking found in the area.

Although the Gastineau Channel was a favorite fishing ground for local Tlingit Indians, the town was founded on gold nuggets. In 1880, Sitka mining engineer George Pilz offered a reward to any local chief who could lead him to gold-bearing ore. Chief Kowee arrived with such ore and Pilz sent Joe Juneau and Dick Harris, two vagabond prospectors, to investigate. The first time the prospectors arrived they found little that interested them in Gold Creek. But at Kowee's insistence, Pilz sent the two men back to the Gastineau Channel and this time they hacked their way through the thick rainforest to Snow Slide Gulch, the head of Gold Creek, and found, in the words of Harris, 'little lumps as large as peas and beans'. On 18 October 1880, the two men staked out a 160-acre townsite and almost overnight a mining camp appeared. It was not only the state's first major gold strike but within a year the camp became a small town, the first to be founded after Alaska's purchase from the Russians.

Initially the town was called Harrisburg and then Rockwell, then finally in 1881 the miners met and officially named it after Juneau. The post office was established shortly later and the name has stuck ever since. After the declining whaling and fur trade reduced the importance of Sitka, the capital of Alaska was moved to Juneau in 1906.

Almost 75 years later in 1974, Alaskans voted to move the state's capital again, this time to a small highway junction called Willow that lay in Anchorage's strong sphere of influence. The so-called 'capital move' issue hung over Juneau like a dark cloud, restricting its growth and threatening to turn the place into a ghost town, as 50% of the residents work for the federal, state or local government.

The issue became a political tug-of-war between Anchorage and the Southeast until the voters, faced with a billion-dollar price tag to reconstruct a capital at Willow, defeated the funding in 1982. Although the conflict will probably never go away, the state-wide vote gave Juneau new life and the town boomed in typical Alaskan fashion, literally bursting at its seams.

McDonald's and Burger King's fast-food chains appeared, new office buildings sprang up and apartments and condominiums mush-roomed. The sudden growth was too much too soon for many of the residents, who were disgusted at the sight of wooded hillsides being bulldozed for yet another apartment complex.

The city entered the 1990s with new concerns over growth and development, this time surrounding a growing interest in opening historical mines. By 1989, the Green Creek Mine, the largest silver mine in North America, was opened on Admiralty Island and had a workforce of 260 people who were living in Juneau and traveling daily to the mine via a catamaran. There was also interest in re-opening the Kensington

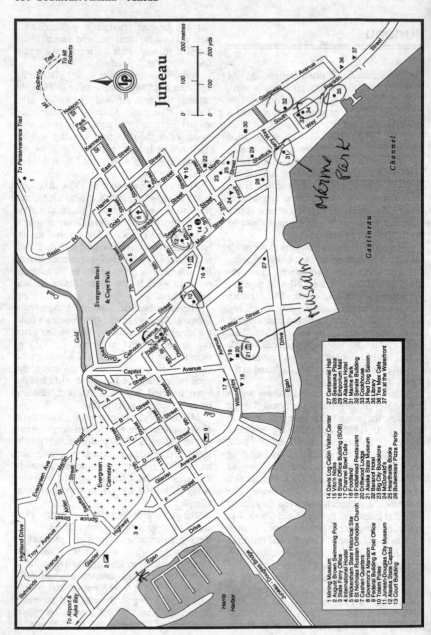

Juneau

1 Mining Museum
2 Augus Brown Swimming Pool
3 State Ferry Office
4 International Hostel
5 Wickersham State Historical Site
6 St Nicholas Russian Orthodox Church
7 Driftwood Lodge
8 Governor's Mansion
9 Federal Building & Post Office
10 Totem Poles
11 Juneau-Douglas City Museum
12 Alaska State Capitol
13 Court Building
14 Davis Log Cabin Visitor Center
15 Vron Nicks
16 State Office Building (SOB)
17 Channel Bowl Cafe
18 Foodland
19 Fiddlehead Restaurant
20 Armadillo Cantina
21 Alaska State Museum
22 Baranof Hotel
23 Big City Bookstore
24 Hearthside Books
25 Bullwinkles' Pizza Parlor
26 Bullwinkles' Pizza Parlor
27 Centennial Hall
28 Sealaska Plaza
29 Emporium Mall
30 Alaskan Hotel
31 Marine Park
32 Senate Building
33 Bootlhouse
34 Red Dog Saloon
35 Library
36 Tex Mex Cafe
37 Inn at the Waterfront

Mine 40 miles north of the city near Berners Bay where engineers believed there was an estimated $855 million worth of gold still lying below the surface.

But the heart of the mining controversy surrounded an effort by a Canadian company to reopen the Alaska-Juneau Mine for gold production. The A-J Mine operated from 1893 until WW II forced its closure due to primarily a shortage of labor. During that time it produced 3.5 million ounces of refined gold or about a fourth of all the lode gold ever taken produced in Alaska. As Echo Bay Exploration began to plot the re-opening of the A-J, environmental concerns swept through Juneau. Plans call for disposing the tailings of the mine in Sheep Creek Valley, the site of a popular hiking trail. But other people are pushing for the project to proceed, seeing the new interest in mining as a way for Juneau to lessen its dependency on government.

Regardless of the unique issues facing this city, travelers will find Juneau to be a fine place offering a variety of accommodation, good restaurants and transport services. It also serves as the departure point for several wilderness attractions, including Glacier Bay National Park and Admiralty Island National Monument.

Orientation

While the city center clings to a mountainside, the rest of the city 'officially' sprawls over 3100 sq miles to the Canadian border, making it one of the largest cities, area-wise, in the USA. There are five sections to Juneau, with the city center being the busiest and most popular area among visitors during the summer. From here, Egan Dr, the only four-lane highway in the Southeast, heads north-west to Mendenhall Valley.

Known to locals as simply 'the Valley', this area contains a growing residential section, much of Juneau's business district and the world-famous Mendenhall Glacier. In the Valley, Egan Dr turns into Glacier Hwy, a two-lane road that takes you to Auke Bay, the site of the State Marine Ferry terminal, more boat harbors and the last spot for

purchasing food or gas to the end of the road at Echo Cove.

Across the Gastineau Channel is Douglas, a small town south-east of Juneau, which at one time was the area's major city. The road north out of this sleepy little town is Douglas Hwy which runs around Douglas Island to the fifth area of Juneau known to locals as North Douglas. Around here you'll find the Eagle Crest Ski Area, many scenic turn-offs, and a lot of cabins and homes (owned by people who work in Juneau but don't want to live in its hustle-bustle) which are half hidden in the trees.

Information

The main visitor center is the Davis Log Cabin (☎ 586-2201), at 134 3rd St, open from 8.30 am to 5 pm Monday to Friday, and during the summer from 10 am to 5 pm on Saturday and Sunday as well. There are also smaller visitor information booths at the Juneau Airport terminal out in the Valley and at the Marine Park on the city waterfront.

For information about cabin rentals, hiking trails, Glacier Bay, Admiralty Island or any outdoor activity in the Tongass National Forest, stop at the information center (☎ 586-8751) in the Centennial Hall at 101 Egan Dr. The center is staffed by both US Forest Service and National Park personnel and is open from 8 am to 5 pm daily in the summer.

For current fishing conditions and local hot spots, the Alaska Fish & Game Department has a fishing hotline on 465-4116. The Alaska Division of State Parks (☎ 465-4563) also has an office in Juneau on the 3rd floor, 400 Willoughby Ave, which is open from 8 am to 4.30 pm Monday to Friday.

Laundromats, Showers & Services Need some clean clothes? Harbor Washboard (☎ 586-1133) at 1114 Glacier Avenue, across Egan Dr from the Small Boat Harbor, is open until 9 pm from Monday to Saturday and until 6 pm on Sunday. The laundromat also has showers. Out in the valley there's Mendenhall Laundromat (☎ 789-2880) at

9101 Mendenhall Road and open until 10 pm daily.

You can also get a shower at the Alaskan Hotel (☎ 586-1000) on Franklin St until 9 pm daily or store baggage there day or night for a small fee.

To kill a rainy afternoon, there's the Juneau City Library (☎ 586-5249) above the parking garage on Marine Way near the cruise ship docks. Open from 11 am to 9 pm from Monday to Thursday and noon to 5 pm Friday to Sunday, the library not only has some good books but also has a great view of the busy channel.

Things to See

Much of your sightseeing time will be spent in the city center, where nothing more than a good pair of walking shoes is needed. Start at the **Marine Park**, a delightful waterfront park across from the Sealaska Building at the southern end of Egan Dr, where there is an information kiosk, open daily from 9 am to 6 pm. Among the hand-outs they offer is a walking-tour map.

The tour leads from the park along Admiralty Way to **South Franklin St**, a historical district that underwent major renovation in 1985. The buildings along this stretch, many dating back to the early 1900s, have since been turned into bars, gift shops and restaurants and are stormed by mobs of visitors every time a cruise ship docks. Heading north-west you will pass an excellent bookstore, Hearthside, a good source of Alaskan literature and material.

At Hearthside, the tour veers left onto Front St and then continues onto Seward St, where it passes the **Davis Log Cabin**, a replica of the first public school in Juneau. The cabin is another information center and houses a small collection of local historical relics and objects.

Swing left (south-west) onto 3rd St and head uphill on Main St where first you'll pass an impressive lifesize bronze sculpture of a bear and then reach the **State Capitol** (☎ 464-4565), though you might not recognize it as such. Built in 1920 as the territorial Federal Building, to many the capitol looks

more like a high school than the Alaskan seat of government. Inside are the legislative chambers, the governor's office and offices for the hundreds of staff members who arrive in Juneau for the winter legislative session. Within the lobby is a visitors desk where free 30-minute tours of the building are offered daily during the summer from 8.30 am to 5 pm; call for exact times.

The walking tour returns to Seward St, climbs one block up and then turns right (north-east) on 5th St to the **St Nicholas Russian Orthodox Church**, probably the most photographed structure in Juneau. The octagonally shaped building was built in 1894, making it the oldest church in the Southeast, and has exhibits of Russian icons, original vestments and religious relics. Tours are conducted during the summer from 9 am to 6 pm Monday to Saturday. Admission is a $1 donation.

You backtrack to the corner of 4th and Main streets to reach the **Juneau-Douglas City Museum** (☎ 586-3572). Housed in the old Memorial Library building, the museum has local artwork, a large custom relief map of the area and audio-visual presentations. But its best exhibits are interpretive displays covering the gold-mining history of Juneau and Douglas. The museum is open from 9 am to 5 pm Monday to Friday and from 11 am to 5 pm Saturday and Sunday; the admission charge is $1.

Across from the museum is the **State Office Building**, or the SOB as it is known locally. Inside the SOB on the 8th floor is the grand court which features a century-old totem pole and a restored 1928 Kimball organ played for office workers and visitors each Friday at noon. The **Alaska State Library** is also off the grand court. The panoramic view of Juneau's waterfront and Douglas Island from the adjoining outdoor balcony is most impressive – an excellent place to have lunch on a sunny day.

Heading west from the SOB, 4th St curves north and becomes Calhoun Ave; in a block it reaches the six-pillar **Governor's Mansion**. Built and furnished in 1912 at a cost of $44,000, the structure has a New

England appearance but is accented by a totem pole, carved in 1940 by Tlingit Indians and presented to the governor as a gift. Tours can be arranged by contacting the Governor's Office (☎ 465-3500).

Behind the Governor's Mansion is Indian St which curves sharply into 9th St. Follow 9th St south-west to the **Federal Building**, where the main post office is on the 1st floor. The Federal Building is at the junction of 9th St and Glacier Ave, a major bus stop where you can pick up buses to the Valley or Douglas. Following Glacier Ave back towards town you will arrive at a bridge over Gold Creek where a memorial plaque has been placed to honor Joe Juneau and Dick Harris, who stumbled upon gold in the icy stream.

Glacier Ave curves east and becomes Willoughby Ave, and in a few blocks you reach Whittier St. Turn right (south) on Whittier St to the **Alaska State Museum**, an impressive white building. This outstanding museum provides Alaskans with a showcase of their past, including artefacts from all four indigenous groups: Athabascan, Aleut, Inuit and north-west coast people. There are also displays relating to the Russian period, major gold strikes in the state, and the Trans-Alaska Pipeline.

By far the most impressive sight is the full-size eagle's nest which sits on top of a tree that is as high as the 2nd floor of the museum. A circular staircase allows you to view the nest from all angles. The museum is open Monday to Friday from 9 am to 6 pm and Saturday and Sunday from 10 am to 6 pm; admission is $2.

From Whittier St you can turn left (east) onto Egan Dr to the **Centennial Hall**, where there is a US Forest Service (USFS) information center (☎ 586-8751). During the summer varied films and slide presentations are shown in the adjoining theater.

Continue east on Egan Dr, and just before reaching the Marine Park you come to the **Sealaska Building**, the headquarters for one of the state's most successful Native Alaskan corporations. Step inside the 1st-floor lobby to view a Haida canoe, Chilkat blankets or

the beautiful tapestry in the Bank of the North that was designed by Rie Munoz, a well-known Juneau artist.

Another attraction downtown is at the top (northern end) of Main St. After climbing the steep street, catch your breath and turn right (west) on 7th St to the **Wickersham State Historical Site**, the historical home of Judge James Wickersham, the pioneer judge and statesman of Alaska. The house was built in 1898 and occupied by the judge who also served as Alaska's first delegate to Congress from 1928 to 1939. For years it was maintained by his granddaughter but in 1985 the state took over the historical site. Inside are photographs, books and other memorabilia from the judge's colorful career. The house is open from noon to 5 pm Sunday to Friday and 10 am to 2 pm Saturday; admission is $1.

Gold

Gold fever and gold mines built Juneau and today mining companies are staging a resurgence in and around the city. There are several interesting and free places which help you gain an idea of what must have been an incredible era in Alaska's history. First head to the Juneau-Douglas City Museum for its exhibit and pick up the *Last Chance Basin Walking Tour* and *Treadwell Mine Historic Trail* brochures.

A hike up Basin Rd, a two-mile walk from the city center will take you to the remains of the compressor house for the Alaska-Juneau Mine on Gastineau Channel. At one time the building was a museum but it closed in 1986. Even so, you can still view the impressive complex of railroad lines, ore cars and repair sheds. To reach the area follow North Franklin St up the hill to its end and turn right (south-east) onto 6th St. Turn immediately left (north-west) on Gold St which turns into Basin Rd. The ruins are half a mile down this scenic road.

At the end of nearby Perseverance Trail (see the Juneau Hiking section) is the **Glory Hole**, a caved-in mine shaft that was connected to the Alaska-Juneau Mine, along with the remains of the **Silver Bowl Basin Mine**.

Perhaps the most interesting areas to explore are the **Treadwell Mine** ruins across the Gastineau Channel near Douglas. From the Capital Transit bus turnaround in Douglas, continue south towards the Sandy Beach Recreation Area, past the softball fields and Douglas Boat Harbor. The beach was made from the tailings of the Treadwell Mine and the old pilings from its shipping dock still stand.

Take one of the staircases from the beach to St Ann's St right above Sandy Beach and follow the street further south to Old Treadwell Rd. The dirt road leads to old foundations, the shells of boarding houses and the mine shaft, another glory hole, of the Treadwell Mining Community. The operation closed down in 1922 after a 1917 cave-in caused the financial collapse of the company. During its heyday at the turn of the century, the mine made Douglas the major city on the channel with a population of 15,000.

Across the channel from Treadwell is the **Alaska-Juneau Mine** on the side of Mt Roberts. The mine closed down in 1944 after producing more than $80 million in gold, then valued at $20 to $35 an ounce. Today, the mine is the center of a controversial plan by a Canadian mining company to reopen it.

Gold Panning There is a natural fascination among visitors passing through the Southeast about gold-rush history and even an interest among many to try gold panning themselves. It has turned out to be quite a recreational activity throughout much of the state the past few years, even giving rise to commercial gold-panning tours.

These tours are not really necessary. Any hardware store in Juneau will sell you a gold pan (black plastic ones are the cheapest and easiest to see those flecks of gold in) and at the US Forest Service information center you can find out all the 'dos and don'ts' to avoid trespassing and jumping any claims. Those really serious about panning for gold

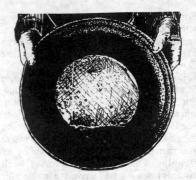

Gold Panning

bring a short shovel, boots, rubber gloves and a small bottle to hold all that gold.

The best public creeks to pan in Juneau are Bullion Creek in the Treadwell Mine area, Gold Creek up by the Last Chance Basin, Sheep Creek on Thane Rd and Salmon, Nugget and Eagle creeks off Egan Dr and Glacier Hwy north of the city center. To spend a day with an 'old sourdough' try the Thane Orehouse (☎ 586-3442) where equipment, hands-on instruction and access to an ore-bearing creek are $6 per person for a whole day of panning.

Glaciers

Juneau is also known as the 'Gateway to the Glaciers'. There are several glaciers in the area including the Mendenhall Glacier, Alaska's famous drive-in glacier. The ice floe is 13 miles from the city center at the end of Glacier Spur Rd. Head out along Egan Dr and at *Mile 9* turn right onto Mendenhall Loop Rd, staying on Glacier Spur Rd when the loop curves north to head back to Auke Bay.

Today, the Mendenhall Glacier flows 12 miles from its source, the Juneau Icefield, and has a 1.5-mile face. On a sunny day it's beautiful, with blue skies and snow-capped mountains in the background. On a cloudy and drizzly afternoon it can be even more impressive, as the ice turns shades of deep blue.

There is an interesting visitor center (☎ 789-0097) at the glacier. It's open from 9 am to 6 pm daily during the summer. Inside is a large relief map of the icefield and glaciers, and audio-visual room with slide presentations and films, and an information desk with trail information. There are several hiking trails in the area, including a half-mile nature trail, the East Glacier Trail or the Nugget Creek Trail (see the Juneau Hiking section).

The cheapest way to see the glacier is to hop on a Capital Transit bus in the city center and get off at the corner of Mendenhall Loop and Glacier Spur roads. The fare is $1 and buses depart from the State Capitol and the Federal Building every half an hour or so. From the Loop Rd, it is another mile to the visitor center. Then there is always hitchhiking, a relatively easy method of travel in Juneau.

On your way out to Mendenhall Valley, look to your right high in the mountains when you pass Lemon Creek to see the remains of the Lemon Creek Glacier. By hiking, you can get a close and uncrowded look at Herbert Glacier on *Mile 27.5* of Glacier Hwy or Eagle Glacier at *Mile 28.4* (see the Juneau Hiking section).

One way to see all the glaciers and the icefield is to splurge on a sightseeing flight. They're not cheap, most cost around $80 per person for a 45-minute flight, but on a clear day can provide a spectacular overview of the icefield. All the air charter companies run them. Wings of Alaska (☎ 789-0790) offer scenic flights during the summer from the International Airport and the Marine Park at the city waterfront when there is a cruise ship in port.

You can also view the icefield and glaciers from a helicopter which includes landing on the sea of ice and spending a few minutes walking around. Gray Line (☎ 586-3773) offers such a tour that lasts 90 minutes. The price to stand on ice? How about $135 per person.

Festivals
Juneau's main festival during the summer is on 4 July when the celebrations include a parade, a carnival, fireworks over the channel, and a lot of outdoor meals from Sandy Beach in Douglas to Juneau's city center. In mid-April there is the week-long Alaska Folk Festival.

Places to Stay
Camping There are some fine campgrounds beyond Mendenhall Valley and a dozen unofficial ones near the city center. *Mendenhall Lake Campground*, one of the most beautiful US Forest Service campgrounds in Alaska, is 13 miles from downtown and five miles south of the Auke Bay Terminal. The campground (60 sites) has a separate seven-site backpacking unit and is on Montana Creek Rd, a dirt road that runs off Mendenhall Loop Rd. The tent sites are alongside a lake and many have spectacular views of the nearby glacier. There is a 14-day limit and the nightly fee is $5 per site.

The other USFS campground, *Auke Village*, is two miles north of the ferry terminal on Glacier Hwy. The area (11 sites) provides shelters, tables, wood and an inter-

Mendenhall Valley

esting beach to walk along. The fee is also $5 per night with a 14-day limit.

The city of Juneau now allows RV parking at the Norway Point Parking Area, near Aurora Basin off Egan Dr downtown, and Savikko Park in Douglas for $5 a night. There are no services or hook-ups at these areas but a trailer dump station and water are available at Savikko Park. There is also *Auke Bay RV Park* (☎ 789-9467), 1.5 miles east of the ferry terminal, a full-service campground that charges $16 per night.

Many backpackers prefer to stay close to the city center and end up hiking along Basin Rd. Where the road crosses Gold Creek there are some flat areas in the bush that serve as good spots to pitch a tent. If you have some time, it is even better to hike the Perseverance Trail off Basin Rd to the Granite Creek Trail and camp in the bowl at the end of this footpath (see the Juneau Hiking section).

Glacier Hwy ends 41 miles north of Juneau at a pleasant spot called Echo Cove. There are no developed facilities here, but it's a nice spot to camp for a while and a favorite among locals. There is usually good offshore salmon fishing in August. Other scenic but undeveloped areas are Eagle Beach on Glacier Hwy, and Fish Creek on North Douglas Hwy.

Hostels In 1985, the *Juneau International (AYH) Hostel* (☎ 586-9559) went from being just another church basement to being one of the best hostels in Alaska. The large yellow house is on the corner of Harris and 6th streets in the colorful Starr Hill neighborhood. Its location is ideal – five blocks from the State Capitol, four blocks from the Mt Roberts Trail and two blocks from Basin Rd and the beginning of the scenic Gold Creek area.

The hostel has cooking and laundry facilities, showers, and a common room with a fireplace. Check-in time is from 5 to 11 pm, check-out is 9 am and reservations are accepted if accompanied by the first night's fee and sent with a self-addressed, stamped envelope. Fees are $8 for hostel members and $11 for nonmembers. For reservations

contact the Juneau International (AYH) Hostel, 614 Harris St, Juneau, AK 99801.

B&Bs Juneau has exploded with bed & breakfast lodging. There are almost two dozen B&Bs and most have rates that range from $40 to $50 for singles and $60 and up for a double. The only problem is securing a room after stepping off the ferry late at night. For that reason, it's wise to book ahead, even a day or two while traveling through the region. An easy way to do this is to contact the Alaska Bed & Breakfast Association (☎ 586-2959) which covers most of the Southeast, including Juneau, of course.

When looking for a B&B, keep in mind that the downtown places will be booked solid for months in advance. But you might find a room and even have a more enjoyable stay at one outside the city. The *Pearson's Pond* (☎ 789-3772) is in the Mendenhall Valley, within walking distance of the famous glacier, and has two suites and a hot tub for guests. Rates begin at $69 a night and climb from there. Even further out is *Lost Cord Bed & Breakfast* (☎ 789-7296), 12 miles from downtown but featuring a private beach on Auke Bay. Rooms rates are $50/55 a single/double but include a courtesy pick-up at the ferry terminal or airport. In North Douglas, try *Blueberry Lodge* (☎ 463-5886) which has five rooms near the Eaglecrest Ski Facility and a great view of the Gastineau Channel. Rates begin at $70.

Hotels Most hotels, especially the downtown ones, tend to be heavily booked during the summer tourist season. The cheapest hotel is the *Inn at the Waterfront* (☎ 586-2050), a small hotel across from the cold-storage plant on South Franklin St. The owners recently redecorated the rooms, but it would still be wise to look before you rent. Rooms rates begin at $35 for a single with a shared bath but the price includes the use of a steam bath.

Cashen Quarters (☎ 586-9863) is a small hotel at 303 Gold St with only four rooms to rent. Each room has a three-quarter size bath and costs $45 a single.

On South Franklin St is the *Alaskan Hotel* (☎ 586-1000) with charming historical décor in its lobby and rooms dating back to 1913 when it was first opened. Singles without bath are $50 a night and the hotel features private sauna rooms and an interesting bar in the back. There is also *Driftwood Lodge* (☎ 586-2280), downtown near the Alaska State Museum. Rooms begin at $62, the motel has a courtesy van that meets the ferry and you can't beat the location. Near the airport is your *Super 8 Motel* (☎ 789-4858) with a van that meets flight and ferry arrivals, and rates that begin at $60. The norm for the majority of the other motels in the Juneau area is $75 to $80 a single.

Places to Eat

Juneau's size allows it to have an excellent range of restaurants that no other Southeast town could possibly support. There are more than 50 in the area with 29 of them in the downtown area, a couple in Douglas and the rest in the Mendenhall Valley.

If you're really hungry, the best bargain for a full dinner during the summer is one of the town's two salmon bakes. The *Gold Creek Salmon Bake* is held in the Last Chance Basin on Basin Rd and is a pleasant walk from the hostel. The salmon bake costs $20 for an all-you-can-eat affair that includes salad, bread, your first beer and salmon that is cooked with a tangy brown sugar sauce. At the outdoor tables you can enjoy the spectacular mountain scenery and there is usually nightly entertainment. You can also catch a free bus to the bake which departs from the Westmark Baranof Hotel daily beginning at 6 pm.

Four miles south of town on Thane Road is the *Thane Ore House Salmon Bake* (☎ 586-3442). The dinner is basically the same except there's no beer and the price is $16 per person. Near the remains of the Alaska Gastineau Mine, the Ore House has a small mining museum and is where *Gold Rush Days Review* is performed by the Janice Holst Dancers (for an additional charge). For times and pick-up points of its free transport vehicle, call the Ore House.

Downtown The cheapest place for breakfast or lunch is the *Federal Building Cafeteria* on the 2nd floor of the Federal Building, which also provides a nice view of the Gastineau Channel for its diners. Open from 7 am to 3.30 pm, the restaurant offers eggs, potatoes, toast and bacon for around $4, and hamburgers and sandwiches for under $3. The nearby *Channel Bowl Cafe*, a local hang-out on Willoughby Ave across from the Foodland Supermarket, is known for large portions and reasonable prices, especially for breakfast. Try the Mt Jumbo, heaped plate of eggs, potatoes and peppers for $6. It will keep you full until dinner.

McDonald's, which now serves breakfast, is on the corner of 2nd and Seward streets diagonally opposite the Sealaska Building. Closer to the international hostel at 299 North Franklin St is *Vito 'n Nicks*, which offers huge cinnamon rolls in the morning for under $3 as well as pizza and pasta dishes in the evening until 9 pm on weekdays and 11 pm Friday and Saturday.

Cheap dinners of pizza or sandwiches can be obtained at *Bullwinkle's Pizza Parlor* across from the State Office Building on Willoughby Ave. Good-sized sandwiches cost between $5 and $8, while nine-inch pizzas begin at $6. There is also wine, a large selection of imported beer, and silent movies shown on the back wall at night.

The best Mexican restaurant in the city center is *Armadillo Tex-Mex Cafe*, at 431 South Franklin St, where you can fill up on huge tostada compuesta, nachos polo loco (crazy chicken) and other Mexican delights all washed down with Alaskan Amber beer. Most dinners are $10 and under. Almost across the street on the 1st floor of the Emporium Mall is the *Heritage Coffee Co & Cafe*, a good spot for an afternoon break, as it serves various coffees, cappuccino, steamed milk and croissants.

Next door to the Red Dog Saloon on South Franklin St is the *Cookhouse* with a soup and salad bar, and an early bird special from 4 to 6 pm. They claim to serve the largest hamburger in Alaska. For $14 you can judge for yourself. For a quick lunch, the street vendors, selling everything from hot dogs to bagel sandwiches, are probably the cheapest way to go. Look for them along Marine Park and elsewhere downtown.

For a complete dinner, if you're not worrying about paying for your ferry ticket to Haines, try the *Fiddlehead Restaurant* on Willoughby Ave. The food is excellent but dinners are priced from $18. The place is another good spot for afternoon tea and freshly baked foods. They occasionally have live folk music at night. *Luna's*, at 210 Seward St, serves excellent Italian where you can have linguine with clams, spinach lasagne or halibut florentine. Pasta dinners range from $9 to $12, seafood is more.

The *Summit Restaurant* (☎ 586-2050), on the main floor of the Inn on the Waterfront, has a menu of gourmet dishes from $16 which are served in a tiny dining room which holds perhaps 15 people. It's an interesting little restaurant, but you have to call ahead to reserve a table.

Juneau's fishing fleet is nowhere near the size of those in Ketchikan or Petersburg, but there are still a number of places to obtain Alaska's delicacies from the sea. In the city center, *Foodland Supermarket* on Willoughby Ave across from the Federal Building has a good selection of local seafood, including salmon, halibut, prawns and crabs' legs. The *Taku Smokehouse*, at 230 South Franklin St in the Marine View Center, specializes in shipping seafood home with visitors.

Finally, as you are strolling around town, look for the occasional fisher selling prawns, crabs and halibut from boats at several spots along the waterfront, including the City Dock on South Franklin St and the Auke Bay Harbor out of town.

Douglas The best restaurant in Douglas is *Beauty & the Feast* next to the Billiken Bar at 916 3rd St. The pub-like restaurant has excellent salads and omelettes.

The Valley A second *McDonald's* is on the corner of Egan Dr and Old Glacier Hwy across from the Nugget Mall. In the Mendenhall Mall, on Mendenhall Loop Rd a short way from the Egan Dr junction, there is a *Taco Bell* and another *Bullwinkle's Pizza Parlor* which has a lunch buffet with all the pizza and salad you can eat.

Jovany's, in the Airport Shopping Center on Glacier Hwy, will serve you huge helpings of lasagne and salad, while in the Nugget Mall there is *Pizza Pizzazz* for pizza, a soup and salad bar and a lunch buffet where for $8 you can spend all afternoon eating. With an entrance outside the mall, it's open to midnight daily.

Entertainment

With a population that is larger, younger and a little more cultured than in most other Southeast towns, Juneau is able to support a great deal more nightlife. The most famous nightspot is the *Red Dog Saloon*, which is mentioned in every travel brochure and the final destination of every tour bus. In 1987, the bar moved to a new location on the corner of Marine Way and South Franklin St but has still managed to retain its Alaskan décor. The bar is interesting with its sawdust floor and relics covering the walls, but the Red Dog is not a place to spend an entire evening drinking unless you can put up with instamatic cameras flashing at the stuffed bear. The best time to go is after 11 pm.

South Franklin St as a whole is Juneau's drinking section. Many places are local hang-outs that will undoubtedly turn you off, which is fine with those leaning against the bar inside. The *Triangle Club*, however, is a pleasant little spot on the corner of Front and South Franklin streets. Although there is limited seating inside, the bar offers widescreen television and a good hot dog to go along with a mug of beer.

Hidden in the back of the *Alaskan Hotel* is a unique bar with an interior and cash register that matches the rest of the hotel's historical setting. Often there is folk or jazz music. Just down the street at the top of the Senate Building, you'll find *The Penthouse*. The bar, which was the first in Juneau to enforce a dress code after 7 pm, has music, dancing and a huge video screen. Many locals beat the code and high prices by stopping by in the afternoon to enjoy a drink and the fine views of Juneau.

A little quieter and at the west end of the downtown area is the *Breakwater Inn* on Glacier Ave, past the high school. The bar is on the 2nd floor and overlooks the Aurora Basin Boat Harbor, an active place in the summer. In the neck of the woods there is also *The Fireweed Room*, upstairs at the Fiddlehead Restaurant at 429 Willoughby Ave, for jazz on the weekends.

On the other side of the channel in Douglas, there are two bars, similar in atmosphere and across the street from each other. *Billikens* and *Louie's* on Douglas Hwy are favorites with locals, especially softball players who hold their games at nearby Sandy Beach Recreational Area.

Another way to spend an evening is soaking in a hot tub or sweating in a sauna, a favorite activity among all Alaskans. The Augustus Brown Pool (☎ 586-5325) next to the high school on Glacier Ave has a large 20-person sauna along with a pool and exercise area. There are various opening hours, including one at night from Monday to Thursday. Admission costs range from $1 to $3 per session.

For a more private evening, rent out one of the hot-tub rooms at the Alaskan Hotel (☎ 586-1000) which are designed for two or three people and include a sauna and shower. The cost is $10 per person per hour and you should call ahead to reserve it.

Hiking

Few cities, if any, in Alaska have the many diverse hiking trails that Juneau has. To spend time here without taking at least a day hike is to miss the area's top attraction.

The US Forest Service maintains 20 trails which are described in its booklet *Juneau Trails*, available for $3, from the information center in the Centennial Hall.

For those who don't feel up to walking the trails on their own, Juneau Parks & Recreation (☎ 586-5226) holds adult hikes every Wednesday, and family hikes along easier trails every Saturday. The hikes begin at the trailhead at 10 am; on Wednesday there is often car-pooling to the trail with hikers meeting at Cope Park, a short walk from the international hostel. Call Juneau Parks & Recreation for more details.

There is also Alaska Rainforest Tours (☎ 463-3466) which offers guided hikes into the surrounding area while supplying transportation, lunch and any equipment that you might need such as rain gear or boots.

Perseverance Trail This trail system off Basin Rd is the most popular one in Juneau and includes the Perseverance, Mt Juneau and Granite Creek trails. Together, the trails can be combined into a rugged 10-hour walk for hardy hikers or an overnight excursion into the mountains that surround Alaska's capital city. To reach the trailhead from the international hostel, take 6th St one block south-west to Gold St which turns into Basin Rd, a dirt road that curves away from the city into the mountains as it follows Gold Creek. After crossing a bridge over the creek look for the posted trailhead on the left.

From the Perseverance Trail it is possible to pick up the Granite Creek Trail and follow the path to the creek's basin, a beautiful spot to spend the night. From here, you can gain access to Mt Juneau by climbing the ridge and staying left of Mt Olds, the huge rocky mountain. Once on the summit of Mt Juneau, you can complete the loop by descending along the Mt Juneau Trail, which joins Perseverance Trail a mile from its beginning.

The hike to the 3576-foot peak of Mt Juneau along the ridge from Granite Creek is an easier but longer trek than the ascent from the Mt Juneau trail. The alpine sections of the ridge are peacefully serene and on a clear day in the summer there are outstanding views.

At the end of the Perseverance Trail, there are gold-mine ruins and the steep-sided Glory Hole. From the trailhead for the Perseverance Trail to the upper basin of Granite Creek is a 3.3-mile one-way hike. From here it is then another three miles along the ridge to reach Mt Juneau.

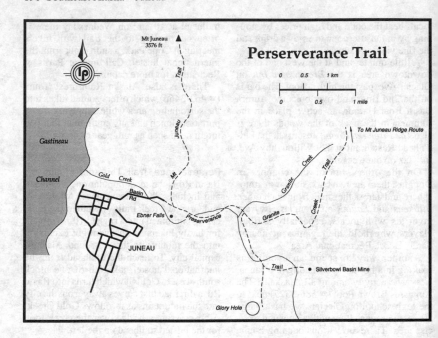

Perserverance Trail

Mt Juneau
3576 ft

Gastineau

Channel

Gold Creek

Basin
Rd

Ebner Falls

Preserverance

JUNEAU

Mt Juneau Trail

Mt
Juneau
Trail

To Mt Juneau Ridge Route

Granite Creek

Granite Creek Trail

Trail

Silverbowl Basin Mine

Glory Hole

Mt Roberts Trail This is the other hike that starts close to the international hostel. The trail is a four-mile ascent to the mountain above the city. The trail begins at a marked wooden staircase at the north-eastern end of 6th St and consists of a series of switchbacks with good resting spots. When you break out of the trees at Gastineau Peak you come across a wooden cross and good views of Juneau, Douglas and the entire Gastineau Channel. The Mt Roberts summit is a steep climb through the alpine brush to the north of the city.

Dan Moller Trail This 3.3-mile trail leads to an alpine bowl at the crest of Douglas Island where there is a USFS cabin (reservations needed, $25 per night). See the Trekking section in the Wilderness chapter for further details.

Treadwell Ditch Trail Also on Douglas Island, this trail can be picked up either a mile up the Dan Moller Trail or just above D St in Douglas. The trail stretches 12 miles north from Douglas to Eagle Crest, although most people only hike to the Dan Moller Trail and then return to the road, a five-mile trip. The path is rated as easy and provides views of the Gastineau Channel while winding through scenic muskeg meadows.

Mt Bradley Trail This 2.6-mile trail begins in Douglas through a vacant lot behind section 300 of 5th St and is a much harder climb than the hikes up Mt Roberts or Mt Juneau. Both rubber boots and sturdy hiking boots are needed as the trail can be muddy in the lower sections before you reach the beautiful alpine areas above the tree line. The climb to the 3337-foot peak should only be attempted by experienced hikers.

Cropley Lake Trail Another trail on Douglas Island is the 1.5-mile route to Cropley Lake. The trail was built primarily for cross-country skiing but in the summer it can be hiked to the alpine lake, which provides good scenery and camping. The start is up Fish Creek Rd, a short way past the Eagle Crest Ski Lodge in a creek gully to the right.

Sheep Creek Trail Southeast of Juneau along Thane Rd is the very scenic Sheep Creek Trail, a three-mile walk into the valley south of Mt Roberts where there are many historic mining relics. The trailhead is four miles from Juneau at a staircase on the gravel spur to a Snettisham Power Plant substation. The trail is relatively flat in the valley, from where you scramble up forested hillsides to the alpine zone. Many hikers follow the power line once they are above the tree line to reach the ridge to Sheep Mountain. It is possible to continue from Sheep Mountain over Mt Roberts and return to Juneau along the Mt Roberts Trail. This is a very long 10 to 12-hour day hike, if attempted.

Point Bishop Trail At the end of Thane Rd, 7.5 miles south-east of Juneau, is this eight-mile trail to Point Bishop, a scenic spot that overlooks the junction between Stephens Passage and Taku Inlet. The trail is flat but can be wet in many spots, making waterproof boots the preferred footwear. The hike makes for an ideal overnight trip as there is good camping at Point Bishop.

East Glacier Trail This trail, the first of several near the Mendenhall Glacier, is a three-mile round trip that provides good views of the glacier from a scenic lookout at the halfway point. The trail begins off the half-mile nature walk near the Mendenhall Glacier Visitor Center.

Nugget Creek Trail Just beyond the East Glacier Trail's scenic lookout is the start of the 2.5-mile Nugget Creek Trail to the Vista Creek Shelter, a free-use shelter that doesn't require reservations. The total round trip to the shelter from the Mendenhall Glacier Visitor Center is eight miles. Hikers who plan to spend the night at the shelter can continue along the creek towards Nugget Glacier, though the route is bushy and hard to follow at times.

West Glacier Trail This is one of the most spectacular trails in the Juneau area. The 3.4-mile trail begins off Montana Creek Rd past Mendenhall Lake Campground and hugs the mountainside along the glacier, providing exceptional views of the icefalls and other glacial features. It ends at a rocky outcrop but a rough route continues from here to the summit of Mt McGinnis, another two miles away. Plan on four to five hours for the West Glacier Trail, an easy hike that can be done in tennis shoes; or plan on a long day if you want to tackle the difficult Mt McGinnis route.

Montana Creek & Windfall Lake Trails These two trails connect at Windfall Lake and can be combined for an interesting 13-mile overnight trip. It is easier to begin at Montana Creek and follow the Windfall Lake Trail out to the Glacier Hwy.

The 9.5-mile Montana Creek Trail, known for its high concentration of bears, begins near the end of Montana Creek Rd, close to the rifle range. The 3.5-mile Windfall Lake Trail begins off a gravel spur that leaves the Glacier Hwy just before it crosses Herbert River, 27 miles north-west of Juneau. Wear rubber boots as either trail can be muddy during the summer, although the worst parts are planked.

Spaulding Trail This trail's primary use is for cross-country skiing, but it can be hiked in the summer if you're prepared for some muddy sections. The three-mile trail provides access to the Auke Nu Trail that leads to the John Muir USFS Cabin (reservations needed, $25 per night rental). The trailhead for the Spaulding Trail is at Glacier Hwy just past and opposite the Auke Bay Post Office, 12.3 miles north-west of Juneau. Check at the information center in the Centennial Building about the availability of the cabin.

Peterson Lake Trail This four-mile trail provides access to good Dolly Varden fishing in both Peterson Creek and Peterson Lake. The trailhead has been moved to avoid private property and is now 20 feet before the *Mile 24* marker on Glacier Hwy, north of the Shrine of St Terese. Wear rubber boots as it can be muddy during the summer. A USFS cabin (reservations needed, $25 per night rental) is at Peterson Lake.

Herbert Glacier Trail This level trail extends 4.6 miles along the Herbert River to Herbert Glacier. The trail is easy, though wet in some places, and the round trip takes four to five hours. The trail begins just past the bridge over Herbert River at *Mile 28* of Glacier Hwy in a small parking lot to the left.

Amalga Trail Also known as the Eagle Glacier Trail, this level route winds 5.5 miles one way to the lake formed by Eagle Glacier, where there is now a USFS cabin (reservations needed, $25 per night rental) 0.8 miles from its face. The view from the Eagle Glacier Cabin is one of the best USFS cabins in the area and well worth the effort of reserving in advance. The trailhead is just beyond the Glacier Hwy bridge across Eagle River, 0.4 miles past the trailhead for the Herbert Glacier Trail. Plan on a round trip of seven to eight hours to reach the impressive Eagle Glacier.

Paddling
Both day trips and extended three to five-day paddles are possible out of the Juneau area in sea kayaks. Boats can be rented from Alaska Discovery at its rental shop (☎ 463-5500) at 11798 Glacier Hwy in Auke Bay. Single hardshells are $40 a day and doubles $50, with discounts for rentals of five days or more. They will also provide drop-off and pick-up service for you and your rental, with rates ranging from $10 to the ferry terminal to $25 to the downtown area.

Topographical maps can be obtained in Juneau at the Foggy Mountain Shop (☎ 586-6780), across from the Baranof Hotel on North Franklin St, or Big City Books (☎ 586-1772), at 100 North Franklin St. The bulletin boards at Foggy Mountain are good to check for used kayaks or canoes for sale. If you have the funds, purchasing and reselling a boat in Juneau is a cheap alternative to renting one for longterm paddles.

If you are unsure about this kayaking thing, Alaska Discovery offers a guided day trip daily during the summer where you get a chance to paddle the coastal islands of Lynn Canal. Tours are limited to 10 people and depart downtown Juneau at 10 am and return at 6 pm. Everything is provided, boats, lifejackets, rubber boots and personal dry bags and the cost is $95 per person. Call Alaska Discovery's main office (☎ 586-1911) to make a reservation.

Auke Bay The easiest trip is to rent a kayak from Alaska Discovery and then just paddle it out and around the islands of Auke Bay. You can even camp on the islands to turn the adventure into an overnight trip.

Taku Inlet This waterway is an excellent four to five-day trip highlighted by close views of Taku Glacier. Total paddling distance is 30 to 40 miles depending on how far you travel up the inlet. It does not require any major crossing, though rounding Point Bishop can be rough at times. It is possible to camp at Point Bishop and along the grassy area south-west of the glacier, where brown bears are occasionally spotted.

Berners Bay At the western end of Glacier Hwy, 40 miles from Juneau, is Echo Cove where kayakers put in for paddles into the protected waters of Berners Bay. The bay, which extends 12 miles north to the outlets of the Antler, Lace and Berners rivers, is ideal for an overnight trip or longer excursions up Berners River.

Oliver Inlet On the north-east coast of Admiralty Island is Oliver Inlet, where a 0.8-mile portage trail connects it to scenic Seymour Canal. The paddle to Oliver Inlet is 18 miles and involves crossing Stephens Passage, a challenging open-water crossing for experienced kayakers only. At the south end of the portage trail from Oliver Inlet is the Seymour

Canal USFS Cabin (reservations needed, $25 per night).

USFS Cabins

Numerous USFS cabins are accessible from Juneau but all are heavily used, requiring reservations as much as 180 days in advance. If you're just passing through, however, check with the USFS information center in the Centennial Building, where the staff maintain a cabin update listing that shows which units are still available and when.

The John Muir, Peterson Lake, Dan Moller and the new Eagle Glacier Cabin, accessible by foot from the Juneau road system; and Seymour Canal Cabin, at the southern end of the portage from Oliver Inlet, have already been mentioned in the Juneau Hiking and Paddling sections. The following cabins are within 30 minutes' flying time from Juneau; the air charter costs range from $200 to $250 per person for return transport. Both Loken Aviation (☎ 789-3331) and LAB Flying Service (☎ 789-9160) can provide air services on short notice.

West Turner One of the most scenic and by far the most popular cabin in the Juneau area, this unit is a 30-minute flight from Juneau on the western end of Turner Lake, where there is good fishing for trout, Dolly Varden and salmon. A skiff is provided.

Admiralty Cove This cabin on a scenic bay has access to Young Lake along a very rough 4.5-mile trail. The unit is a 30-minute flight from Juneau in a tidal area where float planes can land only during high tide. Brown bears frequent the area.

Young Lake There is a USFS cabin at each end of Young Lake, and both cabins are provided with a skiff. The lake offers good fishing for cutthroat trout and land-locked salmon. An overgrown trail connects North Young Lake Cabin with Admiralty Cove. There is no trail between South and North Young Lake cabins.

Getting There & Away

Air Alaska Airlines (☎ 789-0600) has scheduled services to Seattle, all major Southeast communities, Glacier Bay, Anchorage, and Cordova from Juneau daily during the summer. The one-way fare from Juneau to Anchorage is $196. Even better is the $141 fare from Juneau to Cordova which allows you to continue traveling on the state ferries to Valdez, Seward, Homer and Kodiak. Delta Airlines (☎ 789-9771) has daily scheduled flights from Juneau to Anchorage, Fairbanks and Seattle. Both airlines have a ticket office in the Baranof Hotel on South Franklin St.

The smaller air-service companies have a number of scheduled flights to small communities in the area that are considerably cheaper than chartering a plane there. LAB Flying Service (☎ 789-9160) flies to Hoonah for $45 one way and Haines for $60. Wings of Alaska (☎ 789-0790) offers a $60 flight to Tenakee Springs, $76 to Pelican and $75 to Angoon.

On Friday, Tuesday and Sunday evenings, Skagway Air (☎ 789-2006) flies to Haines for $70 and Skagway while Glacier Bay Air (☎ 789-9009) can take you to Gustavus, departure point for Glacier Bay National Park, for $60.

Boat The state ferry arrives and departs from the Auke Bay Ferry Terminal (☎ 789-7453). This is a hassle for budget travelers but it made the city businesses happy when the state ferry quit coming downtown as it opened up another dock to large 'Love Boat' cruise ships, the real money spenders.

There are daily state ferry departures during the summer from Juneau to Sitka for $24, Petersburg $42, Ketchikan $72, Haines $18 and Skagway $24. A smaller ferry, the *Le Conte*, connects Juneau to Hoonah, Angoon and Tenakee Springs. The main ticket office for the ferry (☎ 465-3941) is at 1591 Glacier Ave. You can either call that office or the Auke Bay terminal for ferry information.

Getting Around

To/From the Airport & Ferry Terminal

Transport can be a problem when you arrive at Juneau Airport or the Auke Bay Ferry Terminal. Late-night arrivals heading for the downtown area are best off getting the Mendenhall Glacier Transport bus (☎ 789-5460) that meets all ferry arrivals and Grayline Shuttlebus (☎ 586-3773) that provides a service from the airport. Fares to the city center are $6 from the airport and $6 from Auke Bay Ferry Terminal.

During the day, travelers have more of an option. Hitchhiking is easy in the area, as long as you're not trying to catch a ferry, and avoid thumbing along the four-lane Egan Dr. It is also possible to walk to the nearest public bus stop for a $1 ride into town. From the ferry terminal, walk south along the Glacier Hwy for a little over a mile to Dehart's Grocery Store near the Auke Bay terminal. From the airport, just stroll from the terminal to Airport Mall on Old Glacier Hwy.

Bus

Capital Transit, Juneau's public bus system, runs hourly during the week with alternating local and express services from 7 am until 11.45 pm and 9 am to 6.30 pm on Sunday. The main route circles the downtown area, stopping at the City Dock Ferry Terminal, Capitol Building, the Federal Building, and then heading out to the Valley and Auke Bay Boat Harbor via the Mendenhall Loop Rd, where it travels close to the Mendenhall Lake Campground. There is also a minibus that runs every hour from city stops to Douglas. Fares are $1 each way.

Grab a route map at the city offices on Marine Way or the visitor center; call 789-6901 for more information.

Car Rental

There are almost a dozen car rental places in Juneau for those needing a vehicle – a great way for two or three people to see the sights out of the city or to reach a trailhead. Most agencies either offer unlimited mileage or at least a 100 free miles. Considering all the roads in Juneau don't total much more than 100 miles, you don't need to worry too much about the mileage charge. For a $29 special call Rent-A-Wreck (☎ 789-4111) at 8600 Airport Blvd or Mendenhall Auto Center (☎ 789-1386) in the Valley at 8725 Mallard St. The rest tend to be around $40 a day. Try Allstar Rental (☎ 790-2414), Payless Rentals (☎ 780-4144) or Budget Rent-A-Car (☎ 789-5186).

Tours

Tracy Arm is a steep-sided fjord, highlighted by a pair of tidewater glaciers and a gallery of icebergs that float down the length of it. Fifty miles south-east of Juneau, the fjord makes an interesting day trip. Glacier Spirit (☎ 463-5510) offers both full-day and half-day cruises, where you flight-see one-way and cruise the other. The full-day cruise departs downtown at 8 am and returns at 5.30 pm for $99 per person. Due to the float-plane air time involved, the half-day cruise is $164. Also check into Wilderness Swift Charters (☎ 463-4942) which provides kayaker's drop-off service as well as day trips, and Tracy Arm Glacier Cruises (☎ 586-3311). For something longer, call Alaska Sightseeing (☎ 586-6300) which offers an overnight cruise into Tracy Arm each Sunday at 3 pm for $159 per person.

A number of companies offer city tours through Juneau and the surrounding area for those travelers with limited time. Gray Line (☎ 586-3773) departs from the Baranof Hotel at 127 North Franklin St and offers a 2½-hour Mendenhall Glacier tour for $29. Even better is Mendenhall Glacier Transport (☎ 789-5460) which has a $9, 2½-hour glacier tour that includes a few city sights.

The other popular tour is the float trip down the Mendenhall River. This is not a wilderness experience by any stretch of the imagination, rather a casual raft down a calm river and through a few stretches of short rapids. The three and four-hour float is set up mostly for the cruise ship patrons. Call Gray Line or Alaska Travel Adventures (☎ 789-0052) and expect to pay $75 to $80 per person.

AROUND JUNEAU

Just three miles north of downtown at 2697 Channel Dr is **Gastineau Salmon Hatchery Visitor Center** part of the new $7 million, state-of-the-art Douglas Island Pink & Chum Hatchery (☎ 463-4810). The entire facility is a major producer of salmon for the northern region of Southeast Alaska and is geared up for visitors with underwater viewing windows that allow you to see fish spawning, fish ladders and interpretive displays explaining the lifecycle of salmon and the different hatchery operations. There is even a gift shop that sells salmon leather wallets. The hatchery is close to a bus stop and tours are offered from 10 am to 6 pm Sunday to Friday and noon to 5 pm on Saturday. Admission is $2.50 per person.

Other sights outside the city include the **Alaska Brewing Company** (☎ 780-5866) on Shaune Dr in the Lemon Creek area. Juneau's only brewery, in fact Alaska's only brewery, offers tours from Tuesday to Saturday every half-hour from 11 am to 4.30 pm and a free glass of suds at the end. Stop by or go into any liquor store and purchase its

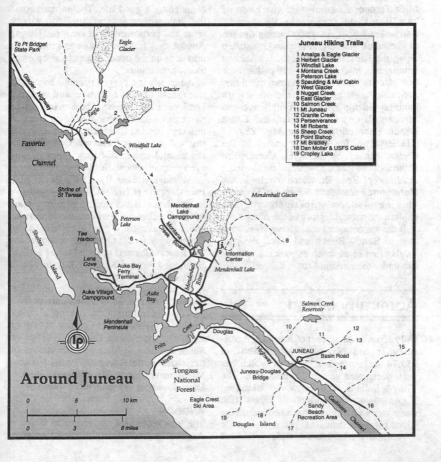

Juneau Hiking Trails
1 Amalga & Eagle Glacier
2 Herbert Glacier
3 Windfall Lake
4 Montana Creek
5 Peterson Lake
6 Spaulding & Muir Cabin
7 West Glacier
8 Nugget Creek
9 East Glacier
10 Salmon Creek
11 Mt Juneau
12 Granite Creek
13 Perseverance
14 Mt Roberts
15 Sheep Creek
16 Point Bishop
17 Mt Bradley
18 Dan Moller & USFS Cabin
19 Cropley Lake

Around Juneau

pale ale or amber beer. Beware, although brewed locally the beer's not cheap at $7 for a six pack.

The **Auke Bay Marine Lab** is 12.5 miles north-west of Juneau and a mile south of the State Marine Ferry terminal. The research facility has a self-guided tour of displays and saltwater tanks and is open from 8 am to 4.30 pm on weekdays. South of the lab on the shores of Auke Lake is the **University of Alaska (Juneau Campus)**, a small college in a beautiful setting. Among the many buildings are a student union and a bookstore.

At *Mile 23.3* of Glacier Hwy is the **Shrine of St Terese**, a natural stone chapel on its own island that is connected to the shore by a stone causeway. As well as being the site of numerous weddings, the island is situated along the Breadline, a well-known salmon fishing area in Juneau. This is perhaps the best place to fish for salmon from the shore.

Scenic viewing points include North Douglas Rd for a look at Fritz Cove and Mendenhall Glacier from afar, and **Eagle Beach Recreation Area** at *Mile 28.6* of Glacier Hwy for stunning views of the Chilkat Mountains and Lynn Canal. Bird enthusiasts should stop at the scenic lookout at *Mile 6* of Egan Dr, which overlooks the **Mendenhall Wetlands & Refuge**. There's a viewing platform with signboards that explain the natural history of the refuge.

If the temperatures soar above 80°F, head over to **Sandy Beach** and watch the pale locals cram in as much suntanning as they can under the midnight sun.

Admiralty Island

Only 15 miles south-east of Juneau is Admiralty Island National Monument, a 955,747-acre preserve, most of which has been designated as a wilderness area. The Tlingit Indians who know the island as Xootsnoowu, 'the Fortress of Bears' (the name was well chosen), have resided on the island for more than 1000 years.

Admiralty Island has a wide variety of wildlife. Bays like Mitchell, Hood, Whitewater and Chaik contain marine mammals such as harbor seals, porpoises and sea lions. Seymour Canal, the island's largest inlet, has one of the highest densities of nesting eagles in the world, and humpback whales often feed in the waterway. Sitka black-tailed deer are plentiful and the streams choke with spawning salmon during August. But more than anything else Admiralty Island is known for its bears.

The island has one of the highest densities of bear in Alaska; it supports more brown bears than people. On Admiralty Island, the bears enjoy a good life. The animals roam the drainage areas, searching for sedges, roots and berries much of the year. During August, they feast on salmon and then settle into dens on the upper slopes to sleep away most of the winter.

Admiralty is a rugged island. The coastal rainforest of Sitka spruce and western hemlock cover the island, broken up only by numerous lakes, rivers and open areas of muskeg. Around 2500 feet, the tree line is reached and beyond that you'll find alpine-tundra and eventually rock outcrops and even permanent icefields.

Although you can fly in for a stay at a US Forest Service (USFS) cabin or an expensive lodge, most visitors to the monument are people looking for a wilderness experience and who take the Cross Admiralty Island Canoe Route (see the Paddling section in the Wilderness Chapter) or spend time paddling Seymour Inlet and Mitchell Bay or one of many other bays.

Before arriving, secure supplies and information in Juneau. Most visitors arrive from Juneau and information can be obtained from the USFS office at Centennial Hall on Egan Dr, the Alaska Discovery office on South Franklin St (they rent the canoes on the island) or the Admiralty Island National Monument office (☎ 586-8800) at 8465 Old Dairy Road out in Mendenhall Valley.

ANGOON

The lone settlement on Admiralty Island is Angoon, a predominantly Tlingit community of 650 residents. Tlingit tribes occupied the site for centuries, but the original village was wiped out in 1882 when the US Navy, sailing out of Sitka, bombarded the indigenous people after they staged an uprising against a local whaling company.

Today, the economy is a mixture of commercial fishing (mainly for halibut and hand-trolling for salmon), and subsistence, while in town the strong indigenous heritage is evident in the painted fronts of the 16 tribal community houses. The old lifestyle is still apparent in this remote community and time in Angoon can be spent observing and gaining some understanding of the Tlingit culture. Tourism seems to be tolerated only because the village is a port-of-call for the state ferry.

Angoon only has three miles of road. The village itself is at one end, perched on a strip of land between Chatham Strait on the west coast of Admiralty Island and turbulent Kootznahoo Inlet which leads into the interior of the national monument. The community serves as the departure point for many kayak and canoe trips into the heart of the monument, including the 32-mile Cross Admiralty Canoe Route to Mole Harbor.

Many people are content to just spend a few days paddling and fishing Mitchell Bay and Salt Lake. Alaska Discovery used to rent canoes in Angoon and actually had them stashed along the route to make portages easier. But they discontinued the service when they dropped the trip as a guided expedition. Today you have to call around to rent a canoe in Angoon; try the Angoon Trading Company (☎ 788-3111) on Kootznahoo Rd, Whalers Cove Lodge (☎ 788-3123) or Dick Powers at Favorite Bay Inn (☎ 788-3123). Before undertaking such an adventure, stop at the US Forest Service office (☎ 788-3166) in the Old City Office Building on Flagstaff Rd in Angoon for information on the tides in Kootznahoo Inlet and Mitchell Bay. The office is open from 8 am to 5 pm Monday to Friday. The tides here are among the strongest in the world; the walk between the airport and the town allows you to view the turbulent waters at mid-tide.

Places to Stay & Eat

By far the best place to stay in Angoon is the *Favorite Bay Inn* (☎ 788-3123) in Dick Powers' large, rambling home two miles from the ferry terminal. A bed and a hearty breakfast is $49/89 for a single/double. *Kootznahoo Lodge* (☎ 788-3501), with 10 rooms for $66/75 a single/double, is on Kootznahoo Rd.

Angoon is a dry community and the only café in town is a hang-out for teenagers at night. Groceries and limited supplies can be picked up at the *Angoon Trading Company* (☎ 788-3111) on Kootznahoo Rd. It might also be a place to rent canoes though this seems to change from summer to summer. There are also supplies at the *Seaside Store* on Chatham St but it's best to come with a full supply of your own food.

Getting There & Away

There are approximately three southbound and two northbound ferries a week stopping at Angoon on the run from Sitka to Juneau during the summer. The one-way fare to Angoon is $22 from Juneau and $20 from Sitka. The ferry terminal is three miles from town.

Wings of Alaska (☎ 788-3530 in Angoon) has daily flights to Juneau for $75. Bellair, the Sitka air charter company, also has an office in Angoon (☎ 788-3501) and has scheduled flights between the two towns for about the same fare as flying to Juneau.

PACK CREEK BEAR REFUGE

On the eastern side of Admiralty Island, spilling into Seymour Canal, is Pack Creek. To the north of it is Swan Cove and to the south is Windfall Harbor. All three areas have extensive tide flats that draw a large number of bears to feed, thus making them favorite spots to observe and photograph the animals.

As Pack Creek has been closed to hunting since the mid-1930s, several bears have become used to the presence of humans. The bears are most abundant in July and August when the salmon are running, and most visitors are boaters who go ashore to view the

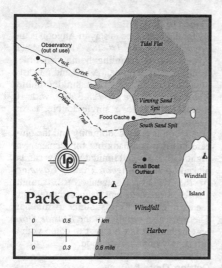

Pack Creek

Observatory (out of use)

Pack Creek

Pack Creek Trail

Food Cache

Tidal Flat

Viewing Sand Spit

South Sand Spit

Small Boat Outhaul

Windfall Island

Windfall Harbor

0   0.5   1 km

0   0.3   0.6 mile

animals and then camp somewhere else. At Pack Creek, you watch the bears from the Viewing Sand Spit, while a mile-long trail leads back to an old observatory. There are camp sites south of a small boat outhaul or, better yet, on the east side of Windfall Island. There is also a free three-sided shelter at Windfall Harbor. If you're contemplating

this trip, first check with the USFS office in Juneau. The number of bear/human incidents has increased in the last few years along with the number of visitors to the refuge. In 1981, 100 people visited the area; in 1987, visitor numbers topped 900. There has been talk of either curtailing people in the area or introducing a permit system such as the one used at McNeil River State Game Sanctuary, Alaska's most famous bear-watching area.

Pack Creek is an adventure for experienced backpackers who are used to encountering bears in the wilderness. The bears may be used to humans but they are far from tame. Reportedly a few of them have been fed human food and they occasionally approach visitors in search of more.

A food cache is provided near the South Sand Spit as you should never enter the area with food in your pack. Do not leave the Viewing Sand Spit into the meadow to get closer to the bears. Stay on the spit, wait for the bears to move into range and use a telephoto lens for close-up shots.

Getting There & Away

Experienced kayakers can rent a boat from Alaska Discovery (☎ 463-5500) in Juneau and paddle to the refuge. The run down

Brown Bears

Gastineau Channel and around Douglas Island isn't bad, but the Stephens Passage crossing to reach Oliver Inlet has to be done with extreme care and a close eye on the weather. From the inlet, the Alaska Division of Parks & Outdoor Recreation operates the Oliver Inlet tramway that can be used to cross the a mile-long portage into Seymour Canal. At the south end of the portage is the Seymour Canal Cabin (reservations needed) that can be rented for $25 per night by calling the State Division of Parks office (☎ 465-4563) in Juneau.

You can also arrange to be dropped off and picked up by any of the air charter companies in Juneau (see the Juneau Getting There & Away section); it's about a 30-minute flight from Juneau. There is one camp site south of Pack Creek from where it is possible to hike north to the Viewing Sand Spit area. Alaska Discovery also offers guided trips into the area, including a one-day tour. This trip includes flying over to Admiralty Island and then paddling canoes to Pack Creek, where you spend the day watching bears before returning to Juneau. The cost is $245 per person. Call the downtown Alaska Discovery office (☎ 586-1911) about this or multi-days trips into the area.

Glacier Bay

Sixteen tidewater glaciers spilling out of the mountains and filling the sea with icebergs of all shapes, sizes and shades of blue have made Glacier Bay National Park & Preserve an icy wilderness renowned throughout the world.

When Captain George Vancouver sailed through the ice-choked waters of Icy Strait in 1774, Glacier Bay was little more than a dent in a mountain of ice. Less than a century later, John Muir made his legendary discovery of Glacier Bay and found that the end of the bay had retreated 20 miles from Icy Strait. Today, the glacier that bears his name is 60 miles from Icy Strait and in its rapid retreat has revealed plants and animals which have fascinated naturalists since 1916.

Apart from having the world's largest concentration of tidewater glaciers, Glacier Bay is the habitat for a variety of marine life, including whales – the humpbacks being by far the most impressive and acrobatic as they heave their massive bodies out of the water in leaps known as breaching. Adult humpbacks can often grow to 50 feet and weigh up to 37 tons. Other marine life includes harbor seals, porpoises, killer whales and sea otters, while other wildlife includes brown and black bears, wolves, moose, mountain goats and over 200 species of birds.

Glacier Bay is a park of contrasts. It is an area of lush spruce/hemlock forests, bare shores recently exposed by glaciers, steep fjords up bay, the flat terrain around Gustavus and an inlet full of icebergs. It's also site of a controversy that's brewing between the tourist industry, most notably the cruise ship lines, and environmentalists. To the operators of the huge 10-story cruise ships, Glacier Bay is the jewel that attracts customers to these high-priced trips. To others, these floating resorts are the cause of the humpback whales' leaving the park while bringing smog – a big city problem – to the middle of the wilderness.

After the number of whales dropped dra-

Killer Whale

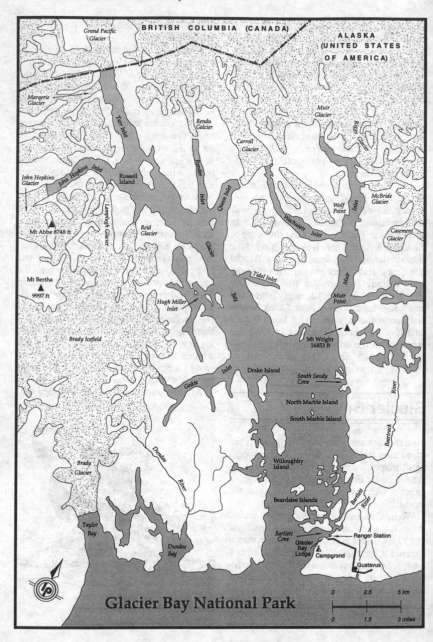

Glacier Bay National Park

matically in 1978, the National Park Service reduced ship visits from 103 to 79 during the three-month season. But during the 1980s the number of cruise ships increased to the current 107. Now the industry is lobbying US Congress (the US way of getting what you want) to increase that by 68% to 180 a year or two a day during the season. Among the more bizarre problems the ships bring is smog, created when they park for an hour or so in front of a glacier and an air inversion leaves a haze hovering over the ice. In 1992, the state fined three cruise lines for repeated violations of air-pollution laws.

To kayakers and backcountry users, such a ship (a hotel on water, with 1000 passengers waving from the railing and a public-address system announcing happy hour) passing by is an eyesore and an invasion of the natural peace. In an effort to separate the groups, the National Park Service has designated Muir Inlet, or the East Air, as wilderness waters prohibiting the large boats to sail there.

The park is many things to many people, but to no one is it a cheap side trip. Of the 216,000 annual visitors, over three-quarters arrive aboard a cruise ship and never leave the boat. The rest are a mixture of tour-group members who head straight for the lodge and backpackers who wander towards the free campground. Plan on spending at least $300 for a trip from Juneau to Glacier Bay, but remember that the cost per day drops quickly after you've arrived.

GUSTAVUS

The park is serviced by a small settlement called Gustavus, an interesting backcountry community of 220 residents. Among the citizens of Gustavus is a mixture of professional people – doctors, lawyers, former government workers and artists – who have decided to drop out of the city rat race and live on their own in the middle of the woods. Electricity only arrived in the early 1980s, and in most homes you still have to pump the water at the sink or build a fire before you can have a hot shower.

There is no 'town center' in Gustavus; the town is merely an airstrip left over from the military build-up of WW II and a road to Bartlett Cove, known to locals as 'the Road'. They refer to every other road and dirt path in the area as 'the Other Road' regardless of which one they are talking about. Along the Road there is little to see, as most cabins and homes are tucked away behind a shield of trees. The heart of Gustavus is the bridge over the Salmon River; near it is the town's park, the Gustavus Inn and the only grocery store in the area.

Places to Stay & Eat

The Gustavus Inn (☎ 697-2254) is a charming family homestead lodge that recently added six more rooms; it now has 16 rooms and space for 26 people. The inn is mentioned in every travel book and brochure on Alaska and rooms are hard to obtain at the last minute. Nightly rates are $120 per person and include meals. The inn is really known for its gourmet dinners which include home-grown vegetables and entrées (main courses) of local seafood such as salmon, crab, halibut and trout served family style. Dinners cost $25 per person and you have to call ahead for a space at the table.

Another fine place is the *Glacier Bay Country Inn* (☎ 697-2288) which offers a room and three meals a day for $99. A cheaper alternative for lodging in Gustavus is the *Salmon River Cabins* (☎ 697-2245) on a road that heads north-east just before you cross the Salmon River Bridge from the airport. Cabins are $40 per night and can accommodate up to four people. Each has a wood-burning stove and a gas camp stove for cooking. Bicycles can be rented for $5 a day.

Puffin Bed & Breakfast (☎ 697-2260) has four cabins near the Salmon River that begin at $40, along with a laundromat and bicycles for guests. Other homes with lodging include *Goode River Bed & Breakfast* (☎ 697-2241), a spacious log home and *Glacier Bay Bed & Breakfast* (☎ 697-2241). To rent a rustic log cabin out in the woods with no running water, thus no flush toilets (how Alaskan can you get!), call *Beyond Goode River* (☎ 697-2241).

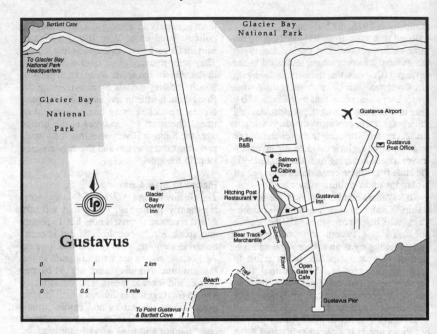

Just north of the Salmon River Bridge is the *Hitching Post*, with a limited menu of hamburgers and sandwiches. Or head south on the road to the dock to reach the *Open Gate Cafe* with a deli-style bakery and sandwiches. Try to avoid buying too much from *Bear Track Merchantile*, the small grocery near the bridge.

BARTLETT COVE

Bartlett Cove is the park headquarters and includes the Glacier Bay Lodge, a restaurant, a visitor center, a campground and the main dock where the tour boats depart for excursions up the bay. The cove lies within the Glacier Bay Park but is still 40 miles south (and another high-priced trip) of the nearest glacier. At the foot of the dock is the park's visitor center where you can obtain backcountry permits, seek out information or purchase a variety of books or topographic maps that cover the park.

Places to Stay

The campground is free and always seems to have space. It is a quarter of a mile south of the Glacier Bay Lodge (see following) in a lush forest just off the shoreline. It provides a bear cache, eating shelter and pleasant surroundings in which to pitch a tent. Coin-operated showers are available in the park, but there is no place that sells groceries or camping supplies.

Glacier Bay Lodge (☎ (800) 622-2042) has 55 rooms that cost $126 per night for a double. It also offers dormitory bunks at $20 a night but the campground is still a better place to spend the night. In the evening, there is a crackling fire in the lodge's huge stone fireplace while the adjoining bar usually hums with an interesting mixture of park employees, visitors, backpackers and locals from Gustavus. Nightly slide presentations, ranger talks and movies held upstairs cover the natural history of the park.

Hiking

Glacier Bay is a trail-less park, and in the backcountry foot travel is done along river banks, on ridges or across ice remnants of glaciers. The only developed trails are in Bartlett Cove.

Forest Trail This mile-long nature walk begins and ends near the Bartlett Cove Dock and winds through the pond-studded spruce/hemlock forest near the campground. There are daily ranger-led walks along this trail; enquire at the lodge.

Bartlett River Trail This 1.5-mile trail begins just up the road to Gustavus, where there is a posted trailhead, and ends at the Bartlett River estuary. Along the way it meanders along a tidal lagoon and passes through a few wet spots. Plan on two to four hours for the three-mile return trip.

Point Gustavus Beach Walk This walk along the shoreline south of Bartlett Cove to Point Gustavus and Gustavus provides the only overnight trek from the park headquarters. The total distance is 12 miles while the walk to Point Gustavus, an excellent spot to camp, is six miles. Plan on hiking the stretch from Point Gustavus to Gustavus at low tide, which will allow you to ford the Salmon River as opposed to swimming across it. Point Gustavus is an excellent place to sight killer whales in Icy Strait.

Paddling

Glacier Bay offers an excellent opportunity for people who have experience on the water but not a lot as kayakers. By utilizing the tour boat it is possible to skip the long and open paddle up the bay and enjoy only the well-protected arms and inlets where the glaciers are.

Kayaks with skirts, paddles, life vests and foot-controlled rudders can be rented from Glacier Bay Sea Kayaks (☎ 697-2257), but reservations are strongly recommended for trips in July and August. Write to them before you leave at: Glacier Bay Sea Kayaks, PO Box 26, Gustavus, AK 99826. The rigid

double kayaks cost $50 per day up to three days, $40 a day up to six days and $35 a day for longer rentals.

Transport is on the *Spirit of Adventure* which departs daily at 7 am and will put you ashore at Muir Point, Ptarmigan Creek (near the entrance of John Hopkins Inlet) or Blue Mouse Cove on the west side of the bay. The most dramatic glaciers are in the West Arm, but surprisingly many paddlers prefer Muir Inlet due to the lack of cruise ships and tour boats in that arm. Plan on a week to paddle from Muir Point up the arm and return to the pick-up point, from eight to 10 days for a drop-off in the West Arm with a return paddle to Bartlett Cove.

Transport fares for kayakers (above and beyond your boat rental) are $88 per person for a one-way drop-off and $168 return. If you're going to spend this much money, purchase the multi-drop pass which means, for an additional $24, you can be picked up and dropped off at another location. Then make sure you have enough time to enjoy this wonder in ice.

For paddlers who want to avoid the tour-boat fares but still long for a kayak adventure, there are the Beardslée Islands. While there are no glaciers to view, the islands (a day's paddle from Bartlett Cove) offer calm water, protected channels and pleasant beach camping. Wildlife includes black bears, seals and bald eagles, while the tidal pools burst with activity at low tide. The islands make for an ideal and easy three-day paddle.

Alaska Discovery also offers single-day guided trips that begin and end at Bartlett Cove. They supply the kayaks, lifevests, rubber boots, paddles and rain gear. You supply $95. The paddles are only to Beardslee Islands, and not the glaciers, and it's best to reserve a spot on the trip at the Juneau office (☎ 586-1911).

Getting There & Away

The only way to get to Glacier Bay from Juneau is to fly. There is no state ferry terminal at Gustavus and the commercial cruise-ship service was discontinued in

1990. The cheapest flight is with Alaska Airlines that departs Juneau daily at around 8 am and 5 pm for the 15-minute trip to Gustavus; the round-trip fare is $88.

The *Glacier Express* that used to run from Juneau to Gustavus is no longer operating but check at the visitor center to see if somebody else hasn't picked up this service. Glacier Bay Airways (☎ 697-2249 in Gustavus, 789-9009 in Juneau) also flies daily to Glacier Bay with a round-trip ticket at $120.

Once at Gustavus Airport, you are still 10 miles from Bartlett Cove, the park headquarters. The Glacier Bay Transportation Company has a bus service that meets all airline flights, but at $8.50 a seat you might consider hitchhiking. Thumbing along the road is not too bad as there is always a small stream of traffic shuffling between Gustavus and the park headquarters.

The other way to reach Glacier Bay is to book a total package tour out of Juneau, which usually includes return air fares and boat passage up the bay to view the glaciers. Such packages are offered by Alaska Sightseeing (☎ (800) 426-7702 or stop at their desk in Juneau's Baranof Hotel). They have a three-day, two-night cruise from Juneau into the West Arm on the *Spirit of Glacier Bay* for $499 and another that includes Tracy Arm for $595 for four days/three nights. You can also contact Glacier Bay Yacht Tours (☎ 586-6835), which will fly you over to Glacier Bay, put up in the lodge for a night and reserve you a spot on park boat for $357 per person from Juneau.

Tour Boats In preparation for the day when Muir Inlet will no longer have any true tidewater glaciers, the *Glacier Bay Explorer* was withdrawn from service in 1989. The other park tour boat, *Spirit of Adventure*, was switched to a day trip up the West Arm of Glacier Bay as opposed to Muir Inlet. It's a little ironic, perhaps, but Glacier Bay's most famous tourist attraction, the glacier Muir made famous, is slowly melting back into the mountains.

The *Spirit of Adventure*, a 220-passenger catamaran, departs Bartlett Cove for an eight-hour trip up the West Arm daily at 7 am. It returns at 4.30 pm where a waiting bus will whisk you away in time to catch the Alaska Airlines flight back to Juneau. The tour of the West Arm glaciers, the reason you've spent so much money to get here, is another $142. But that includes lunch – what a deal!

Haines

Haines (population 1150) lies in the upper (northern) reaches of the Inside Passage and is an important access point to the Yukon Territory (Canada) and Interior Alaska. While the town itself may lack the charm of Sitka or Petersburg, the surrounding scenery is stunning. Travelers who arrive on the state ferry will see Lynn Canal, the longest and deepest fjord in North America, close in on them. There's a mad scramble to the left side of the boat when the US Forest Service guide on board announces the approach of Davidson and Rainbow glaciers to the west.

Once in town, mountains seem to surround you on all sides. To the west, looming over Fort Seward, are the jagged Cathedral Peaks of the Chilkat Mountains; to the east is the Chilkoot Range; and standing guard behind Haines is Mt Ripinsky.

Haines is 75 miles north of Juneau on a wooded peninsula between the Chilkat and Chilkoot inlets. Originally it was a stronghold of the wealthy Chilkat Tlingit Indians who called the settlement Dtehshuh, meaning 'end of the trail'. The first White person to settle was George Dickinson of the Northwest Trading Company who arrived in 1878 and was followed by missionaries and a trickle of other settlers. Eventually, of course, the gold prospectors stampeded through the town.

In 1897, Jack Dalton, a gun-toting entrepreneur, turned an old Indian trade route into a toll road for miners seeking an easier way to reach the Klondike. He charged $2 per head of cattle. The Dalton Trail quickly became a heavily used pack route to mining districts north of Whitehorse, and Dalton himself reaped the profits until the White Pass & Yukon Railroad in Skagway put him out of business in 1900.

The army established Alaska's first permanent post at Haines in 1903 and named it Fort William H Seward after the secretary of state who negotiated the purchase of the state. It was renamed Chilkoot Barracks in 1922 to avoid confusing it with the town of Seward and for the next 20 years was the only army post in Alaska. The fort was used as a rest camp during WW II and from there

soldiers moved on to various points in the state where they formed the nucleus of new army installations. By 1946, the fort was deactivated and declared surplus.

WW II also led to the construction of the Haines Hwy, the 159-mile link between the Southeast and the Alcan (Alaska Hwy). By 1942, the Japanese had captured two Aleutian islands and were headed, many believed, towards a land war in Alaska. Military planners, seeking a second link to the sea and another possible evacuation route, chose to connect Haines to the Alcan. Construction

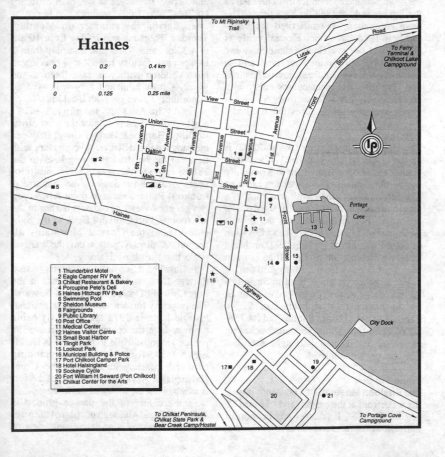

Haines

```
0        0.2        0.4 km
0     0.125        0.25 mile
```

To Mt Ripinsky Trail

To Ferry Terminal & Chilkoot Lake Campground

View Street

Union Avenue

Portage Cove

City Dock

1 Thunderbird Motel
2 Eagle Camper RV Park
3 Chilkat Restaurant & Bakery
4 Porcupine Pete's Deli
5 Haines Hitchup RV Park
6 Swimming Pool
7 Sheldon Museum
8 Fairgrounds
9 Public Library
10 Post Office
11 Medical Center
12 Haines Visitor Centre
13 Small Boat Harbor
14 Tlingit Park
15 Lookout Park
16 Municipal Building & Police
17 Port Chilkoot Camper Park
18 Hotel Halsingland
19 Sockeye Cycle
20 Fort William H Seward (Port Chilkoot)
21 Chilkat Center for the Arts

To Chilkat Peninsula, Chilkat State Park & Bear Creek Camp/Hostel

To Portage Cove Campground

began two months after the Alaska Hwy was completed and engineers merely followed Jack Dalton's trail. The route through the mountains is so rugged it would be 20 years before US and Canadian crews even attempted to keep the 'Haines Cut-off Road' open during the winter and, up until the early 1970s, a radio check system was used to make sure cars made it through. By the 1980s the Haines Hwy was paved and today more than 50,000 travelers in cars, RVs and buses follow it annually.

Logging and fishing have been the traditional industries of Haines, but in the 1970s the town became economically depressed as the lumber industry fell on hard times. The town's remaining sawmill filed for bankruptcy in 1984, but by then Haines' residents had already begun to swing their economy towards tourism. Haines survived and is becoming a major Southeast tourist destination. The town has spectacular scenery with comparatively dry weather (only 53 inches of rain annually) and is accessible by road.

Information

The Haines Visitor Center (☎ 766-2202) is on the corner of 2nd Ave and Willard St in Haines and is open from 8 am to 8 pm daily during the summer. The center has racks of free information, along with rest rooms, a small message board and a used-book exchange. For information on the town's three state parks, head to the Alaska Division of State Parks office (☎ 766-2292) on Main St above Helen's Shop. The office is open Monday to Friday from 8 am to 4.30 pm.

For a shower in town, head to Susie Q's Laundromat near the eastern end of Main St by the boat harbor; showers cost $1.50. There is also the Haines Public Pool (☎ 766-2666) open for various sessions, including early-bird swims and late-night sessions. The cost per session is $4.

Things to See

The **Sheldon Museum** (☎ 766-2366) is near the waterfront at the eastern end of Main St, just off Front St. It features a collection of indigenous artefacts and relics from Haines'

pioneer and gold-rush days, including the sawn-off shotgun Jack Dalton used to convince travelers to pay his toll. Twice a day the museum also shows *Last Stronghold of the Eagles*, an excellent movie by Juneau film-maker Joel Bennett about the annual gathering of bald eagles. Admission is $2 and the museum is open from 1 to 4 pm daily.

Across Front St from the museum, the **Small Boat Harbor** bustles during the summer with fishers and pleasure boats. A walk up Main St will take you through the heart of the Haines' business district. South along 3rd Ave from Main St is the post office, and across the street is the public library (☎ 766-2545). In the summer, the library is open during the summer on Monday, Tuesday, Thursday and Friday from 10 am to 4.30 pm and 7 to 9 pm; Saturday from 1 to 4 pm and Sunday from 2 to 4 pm. If you have children with you, take them to the library's story hour and they will have an opportunity to mingle with local kids.

Follow 3rd Ave south and turn left (southeast) onto the first road past the post office to **Tlingit Park** near Portage Cove. Between the park and Front St is an old **cemetery** with many of the headstones dating back to the 1880s, marking the graves of Haines' pioneers. Across Front St along the shoreline is **Lookout Park**, a vantage point where you can get good views of the boat harbor to the left (north), Port Chilkoot Dock to the right (south) and the Coastal Mountains all around. A display points out the various peaks that rise above Haines.

Follow Front St south as it curves around Portage Cove and turn uphill (east) at the Port Chilkoot Dock to reach **Fort Seward**. The old army fort was designated a national historical site in 1972 and is slowly being renovated. In the center of the fort are the parade grounds, while to the north is Building No 53, formerly the commanding officers' quarters and today, the Hotel Halsingland. A walking-tour map of the fort is available in the lobby of the hotel.

In the center of the parade ground is **Totem Village**. Although not part of the original fort, it provides an interesting view of two tribal houses, totem poles and a Yukon trapper's cabin. Also in Fort Seward is the **Alaskan Indian Arts Skill Center** (☎ 766-2160) in the former post hospital and the **Chilkat Center for the Performing Arts** – a refurbished cannery building and the site of nightly productions from the Chilkat Dancers and Lynn Canal Community Players. The skill center features indigenous artists carving totems, masks and war clubs or weaving Chilkat blankets; many of these items are available for purchase. The center is open from 9 am to noon and from 1 to 5 pm Monday to Saturday during the summer.

Art Galleries In the past few years, Haines has slowly become a commune for artists in the same way that Homer attracts the creative souls of Southcentral Alaska. With Haines' spectacular surroundings, it is not hard to understand why. The visitors center publishes a guide to galleries, and local artists some of whom work and display their art in their homes. It also puts out a Totem Trail brochure to guide you around town for a look at Haines' totem poles.

In the middle of Fort Seward's parade ground is **Sea Wolf Art Studio** (☎ 766-2266), which features the work of Tresham Gregg, one of Haines' better known indigenous artists, who is involved mostly in wood carving and making prints of Tlingit designs.

Nearby on Beach Rd is the **Art Shop** (☎ 766-2491), a small red gallery that was formerly the Port Chilkoot telegraph office. It now holds an impressive display of art including the prints of John Svenson, known throughout the Northwest as Alaska's foremost mountain illustrator. Other galleries worth stopping at are **Chilkat Valley Arts** (☎ 766-2990) on the corner of 2nd Ave and Willard St and the **Northern Arts Gallery** (☎ 766-2850) opposite. Near the visitor center is **The Whaler Rider** (☎ 766-2540) which often has artists carving in the shop.

New in 1993 for Haines is **Dalton City** near the state fair grounds. The 1890's gold rush town is the result of Hollywood's arriving here in 1989 and building a set to film Jack London's classic *White Fang*. Ironi-

cally, with no movie theater in town, residents either had to take a ferry to Juneau to watch the film or wait two years until it arrived at the local video rental shop. Future plans for Dalton City call for a Klondike Saloon, a logging museum, a turn-of-century print shop, and daily demonstrations including gold panning, sled dogs and on-site artists. It will, no doubt, take a few years to get all this off the ground. Stop in at the visitor's center or call the Southeast Alaska State Fair (☎ 766-2476) for more information on hours and what's available.

Festivals
Like every other Alaskan town, Haines has a Fourth of July celebration, but its biggest festival is the Southeast Alaska State Fair. Held in mid-August, the event includes parades, dances, livestock shows and exhibits that draw participants from all Southeast communities and its famous pig races. Coinciding with the state fair is the Bald Eagle Music Festival that brings together more than 50 musicians for five days of blues and bluegrass music.

Places to Stay
Camping Haines has several state campgrounds; the closest to town is *Portage Cove* (nine sites, $6). This scenic beach campground for backpackers and cyclists is only half a mile south-east of Fort Seward or two miles from the center of town and has water and pit toilets. Follow Front St south (which becomes Beach Rd as it curves around the cove near Fort Seward) and the campground is at the end of the gravel road. Five miles north of the ferry terminal on Lutak Rd is *Chilkoot Lake State Park* (32 sites, $8). The campground, which offers picnic shelters and good fishing for Dolly Varden, is on Chilkoot Lake, a turquoise-blue lake surrounded by mountain peaks.

If you have some spare time in Haines, spend the night at *Chilkat State Park* (33 sites, $6), seven miles south-east of Haines on Mud Bay Rd. The park, situated towards the end of the Chilkat Peninsula, has good views of Lynn Canal and of the Davidson and Rainbow glaciers that spill out of the mountains into the canal. There are hiking trails and fishing nearby. Within town, you can pitch your tent at *Port Chilkoot Camper Park* (☎ 766-2755) for $7 a night. The private campground is in Fort Seward behind the Hotel Halsingland and has showers for $1.50. Other RV campgrounds include *Eagle Camper Park* (☎ 766-2335) on Union St, *Haines Hitch-up RV Park* (☎ 766-2882) on the corner of the Haines Hwy and Main St, and *Oceanside RV Park* (☎ 766-2444) down by the waterfront. All offer full hook-ups.

Hostels *Bear Creek Camp & Hostel* (☎ 766-2259) is 2.5 miles south of town. From the post office, follow 3rd Ave south onto Mud Bay Rd near Fort Seward. After a half-mile veer left onto Small Tract Rd and follow it for 1.5 miles to the hostel. There is room for 20 people in the hostel's dorms; the cost is $10 per night for hosteling members and $12 for nonmembers. There are also tent sites for $3.25 per night (shower included) and cabins that sleep up to four people for $30 per night. Open year round, the camp has a wood stove and cooking facilities but is definitely on the rustic side. It appeals to some, but for many travelers of late it has been a dismal experience staying there.

B&Bs The *Summer Inn Bed & Breakfast* (☎ 766-2970), at 247 2nd Ave four miles from the ferry terminal, has a number of bedrooms from $55 per night, most with a good view of Lynn Canal. There are sourdough pancakes for breakfast with your ham and eggs. Within the military complex, there's *Fort Seward Bed & Breakfast* (☎ 766-2856) in the former home of the army's surgeon where rooms with shared baths are $62/72 for singles/doubles. Also in Fort Seward is *Officers' Inn Bed & Breakfast* (☎ 766-2000 or (800) 542-6363), where rooms with shared bath are $40/50 a single/double.

Hotels In Haines there are six hotels and lodges of which the *Fort Seward Lodge* (☎ 766-2009), the former Post Exchange in the fort, is the cheapest with rooms that begin at $40. Also in the former fort is *Hotel Halsingland* (☎ 766-2000 or (800) 542-6363) where singles/doubles cost $64/67, while near the entrance on Mud Rd is *Mountain View Motel* (☎ 766-2900 or (800) 478-2902) with rooms with kitchenettes at $54/59 a single/double. In town, there is *Thunderbird Motel* (☎ 766-2131 or (800) 327-2556) with singles/doubles for $58/68 and, a mile out along Haines Hwy, the *Eagle's Nest Motel* (☎ 766-2891) where rooms begin at $60.

Places to Eat

The popular place for breakfast among locals is the *Chilkat Restaurant & Bakery*, on the corner of Main St and 5th Ave, which opens at 7 am. A plate of eggs, potatoes and toast is $6, and you can get coffee and a warm muffin for around $2. On Friday night they have an all-you-can eat Mexican dinner for $12.

The *Commander's Room* in Fort Seward's Hotel Halsingland provides a historical setting (with a nice view of the surrounding mountains) in which to eat. The cost of breakfast is similar to the Chilkat Restaurant & Bakery and the portions are filling. At night, the restaurant serves a variety of seafood including prawns, scallops and salmon, with dinners for around $18. The best breakfast value in town is at the *Bamboo Room*, on the corner of 2nd Ave and Main St, where a plate of pancakes and coffee costs $5.

For deli-type sandwiches or pizza by the slice try *Porcupine Pete's* deli across from the Bamboo Room on 2nd Ave, while the best pizza in town is at the *Pizza Cutter* within the Fogcutter bar, near the eastern end of Main St. Locally caught seafood ends up on a variety of menus in Haines. The town's salmon bake, *Port Chilkoot Potlatch*, takes place nightly from 5 to 8 pm at Totem Village in the center of Fort Seward. For $18 per person you can enjoy all the grilled salmon, salad and baked beans you can handle in one sitting.

To take some salmon or crab back to your camp site, go to *Howsers Supermarket*, a distinctive store front with the large moose antlers on Main St. The food market, which is open daily, usually has a good selection of whatever is being caught in the area as well as a deli for just-made sandwiches and a salad bar.

Entertainment

For beer on tap and to rub elbows with the locals, stop at the *Fogcutter* on Main St or the *Pioneer Bar* next to the Bamboo Room on the corner of 2nd Ave and Main St. Both spots can get lively and full at night as Haines is a hard-drinking town. For somewhere a little quieter where you can watch the traffic in the bay, there is the *Harbor Bar* next to the Small Boat Harbor at the eastern end of Main St.

Other activities at night include performances by the Chilkat Dancers in full Tlingit costume at the Chilkat Center for the Performing Arts in Fort Seward. The performances start at 8 pm on Monday, Wednesday and Saturday; the admission charge is $7. On Friday and Sunday at 8 pm you can see the melodrama *Lust for Dust*, performed by the Lynn Canal Community Players during the summer; tickets are $7.

Hiking

There are two major trail systems near Haines. South of town are the Chilkat Peninsula trails which include the climb to Mt Riley; north of Haines is the path to the summit of Mt Ripinsky. Stop at the visitor center in town before hiking and pick up its brochure, *Haines is for Hikers*, which describes the trails in more detail.

Mt Ripinsky Trail The trip to the 3563-foot summit of Mt Ripinsky (also known as the South Summit) is an all-day hike (taking from six to eight hours) with a sweeping, uninterrupted view almost from Juneau to Skagway. The route which includes Peak 3920 and a descent from (7 Mile Saddle to Haines Hwy is either a strenuous 10-hour journey for experienced hikers or an overnight trip.

To reach the trailhead, follow 2nd Ave north to Lutak Rd (the road to the ferry terminal) and past the fire station. Leave Lutak Rd when it curves right and head up the hill on Young St. Turn right along an old, buried pipeline and follow it for a mile to the start of the trail, just as the pipeline heads downhill to the tank farm.

The trail crosses a pair of streams, passes by an old reservoir and then ascends steadily through spruce and hemlock, reaching open muskeg at 1300 feet. After a second climb you come to Johnson's Creek at 2500 feet where there is drinking water and impressive views of the Southeast's snowcapped mountains all the way to Admiralty Island. From here, the route goes from dwarfed hemlock to open slope where there is snow until late summer.

The North Summit has a benchmark and a high wooden surveyor's platform. You can camp in the alpine area between the two peaks and then continue the next day by descending the North Summit and hiking west along the ridge to Peak 3920. From here you can descend to 7 Mile Saddle and then to the Haines Hwy, putting you seven miles north-west of town. This is a 10-mile loop and a challenging overnight hike where the trail is steep in places and easily lost. The views, however, are spectacular.

Battery Point Trail This 2.4-mile trail is a flat walk along the shore to Kelgaya Point where there is a primitive camp site and a vault toilet. At Kelgaya Point, you can cut across to a pebble beach and follow it to Battery Point. The trail begins a quarter of a mile beyond Portage Cove Campground at the end of Beach Rd. Plan on about two hours for the return hike.

Mt Riley Trails This climb to a 1760-foot summit is considerably easier than the one to Mt Ripinsky, but it still provides good views in all directions, including Rainbow and Davidson glaciers. One trail up the mountain begins at a junction almost two miles up the Battery Point Trail out of Portage Cove Campground. From here, you hike 5.5 miles over Half Dome and up Mt Riley.

Another route, closer to town, begins at the end of FAA road which runs behind the Officers' Row in Fort Seward. From the road's end, follow the water-supply access route for two miles to a short spur which branches off to the right and connects with the trail from Mud Bay Rd. The hike is 3.8 miles one way and prevents you from having to find the three-mile ride out to Mud Bay Rd, the site of the third trailhead to Mt Riley. The trailhead off Mud Bay Rd is posted and this route is the steepest but most direct to the summit. Plan on five to six hours for a return hike to the summit.

Seduction Point Trail The trail begins at Chilkat State Park Campground and is a 6.5-mile, one-way hike to the point that separates Chilkoot and Chilkat inlets. The trail swings between inland forest and beaches and provides excellent views of Davidson Glacier.

If you have the equipment, it can be turned into an excellent overnight hike by setting up camp at the cove east of Seduction Point. Carry in water and check the tides before departing as the final stretch along the beach after David's Cove should be walked at low or mid-tide. The entire round trip takes most hikers from nine to 10 hours.

Rafting
Haines is also the departure point for numerous raft trips in the area. Chilkat Guides (☎ 766-2491) offers a four-hour float down the Chilkat River that provides plenty of opportunity to view bald eagles and possibly brown bears; there is little white water. The guide company runs the trip daily beginning at the Art Shop on Beach Rd in Fort Seward. The cost is $70 for adults and $30 for children.

On a much greater scale of adventure is the 11-day raft trip down the Tatshenshinin-Alsek River system from Yukon Territory to the coast of Glacier Bay. Haines serves as the departure point for this river trip which is unmatched by any other Alaskan raft trip for its scenic mix of rugged mountain ranges and dozens of glaciers. Both Chilkat Guides and

Alaska Discovery (☎ 586-1911) run the trip which costs around $1700 per person.

Getting There & Away
Air There is no jet service to Haines, but several charter companies run regularly scheduled north and southbound flights. The cheapest service, Wings of Alaska (☎ 766-2030), has four daily flights to Juneau for $60, and four flights to Skagway for $35. Also check with Haines Airways (☎ 766-2646) or LAB Flying Service (☎ 766-2222). Any of them will arrange a sightseeing flight over Glacier Bay National Park; the park is only a 10-minute flight from Haines. With Haines Airways a 60 to 70-minute flight is $85 for adults and $63 for children. On a clear day it's money well spent.

Bus From Haines you can catch buses north to Whitehorse, Anchorage or Fairbanks. Alaskon Express has a bus departing Haines at 8.15 am Tuesday, Wednesday, Friday and Sunday that overnights at Beaver Creek and then continues on to Anchorage, reaching the city at 7.15 pm the following day. The fare from Haines to Anchorage is $189 and does not include lodging.

On the same runs you can also make connections at either Haines Junction or Beaver Creek for Fairbanks, Whitehorse or Skagway, though why anybody would want to ride a bus instead of a ferry to Skagway is beyond me. The one-way fare to Fairbanks is $165, Glennallen $160 and Whitehorse $76. The bus picks up passengers at Hotel Halsingland and the Wings of Alaska office (☎ 766-2030) on 2nd Ave.

There is also Alaska Direct Busline (☎ (800) 770-6652) which on Tuesday, Friday and Sunday departs at 6 am for the four-hour trip to Haines Junction. At Haines Junction you can pick up their buses to Fairbanks, Anchorage or Whitehorse, though you might have to wait around a bit. This company changes its times and pick-up locations almost annually. Call to get the latest information. One-way fare from Haines to Haines Junction is $50. Another $100 will get you all the way to Fairbanks.

Boat State ferries arrive and depart almost daily from the terminal (☎ 766-2111) in Lutak Inlet north of town. The one-way fare north to Skagway is $12 and south to Juneau is $18.

Haines Taxi runs a ferry shuttle bus (☎ 766-3138), meets all arrivals, and for $5 will take you the four miles into town. The bus also departs town 30 minutes before each ferry arrival and stops at the Hotel Halsingland, the Art Shop in Fort Seward and near the visitor center in town before heading out to the ferry terminal.

For a day trip to Skagway, contact Haines-Skagway Water Taxi (☎ 766-3395). The 40-passenger boat departs twice daily, the first at 8 am and then again at 5 pm, from the boat harbor in the heart of Haines; round-trip fare is $29, one-way is $18. Tickets can be purchased in advance on board the MV *Sea Venture* at the Haines Small Boat Harbor between noon and 4 pm.

Car Rental To enjoy the sites out the road, especially to visit the Chilkat Bald Eagle Preserve on your own, there are five car-rental agencies in Haines. Surprisingly the most affordable is Hertz operating out of the Thunderbird Motel (☎ 766-2131) which has some compacts for $35 a day and 40c a mile. There is also Eagle Nest Motel (☎ 766-2891) with vehicles at $42 a day and 100 free miles.

Bicycles & Kayaks Sockeye Cycle (☎ 766-2869) on Portage St in Fort Seward rents both mountain bikes and road bikes by the hour, day or even weekly as well as selling parts and renting kayaks. The shop also offers bike tours that range from one hour to one-day journeys or will arrange van transport to those who want to cycle on their own.

AROUND HAINES
Alaska Chilkat Bald Eagle Preserve
In 1982, the state reserved 48,000 acres along the Chilkat River to protect the largest known gathering of bald eagles in the world.

Each year from October to January, more than 3500 eagles congregate here to feed on chum salmon. They come because an upswelling of warm water prevents the river from freezing and encourages the late run of salmon. It's a remarkable sight, hundreds of birds along the banks of the river sitting in the bare trees that line the river, with often six or more birds to a branch.

The eagles can be seen from the Haines Hwy, where lookouts allow motorists to park and view the birds. The best view is between *Mile 18* and *Mile 22* of the Haines Hwy and

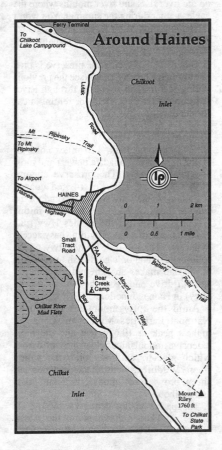

you really have to be here after November to enjoy the birds in their greatest numbers. Unfortunately, most travelers have long departed Alaska by then. Still there are more than 200 resident eagles which can be spotted throughout the summer.

The state park office in Haines can provide a list of state-permitted guides who conduct tours into the preserve. Among them is Alaska Nature Tours (☎ 766-2876) which conducts three-hour tours in the morning and afternoons, based on the cruise-ship schedules. The tours cover much of the scenery around the Haines area but often concentrate on the river flats and river mouths where the eagles gather during the summer. You won't view thousands of birds, but groups generally see several dozen eagles during the day. The tour is $45 per person.

Other ways of seeing the preserve is on a raft through Chilkat Guides (see the previous rafting section), on a jet boat through River Adventures (☎ 766-2050), or renting a car for the day.

Kluane National Park

Kluane National Park, 120 miles north of Haines, is one of Canada's newest and most spectacular parks. The preserve encompasses 8649 sq miles of rugged coastal mountains in the south-western corner of the Yukon Territory. There are no roads in this wilderness park but the Haines Hwy runs along its eastern edge, providing easy access to the area. The 159-mile Haines Hwy, which follows Jack Dalton's gold-rush toll road, is paved and makes an extremely scenic and smooth drive ending at the Alcan (Alaska Hwy) in Haines Junction.

Amid the lofty mountains of Kluane National Park lies Mt Logan, Canada's highest peak at 19,636 feet and the most extensive nonpolar icefield in the world from which glaciers spill out onto the valley floors. Wildlife is plentiful and includes dall sheep, brown bears, moose, mountain goats and caribou.

The park's visitor center (☎ (403) 634-2251), in Haines Junction on the Alcan (Alaska Hwy), is open from 8.30 am to 9 pm daily in the summer. Along with displays and a free slide show covering the area's natural history, the center can provide you with information, backcountry permits and topographic maps for overnight hikes into the park.

The main activity in Kluane is hiking, and trails consist primarily of old mining roads, animal trails or natural routes along river beds or ridges. The trailheads for eight routes are located along the Haines and Alaska highways. For those who want to view the park but not hike in it, Burwash Lodge, near the north end of Kluane Lake, offers 90-minute sightseeing flights for groups of four at $120 per person.

Alsek Pass Trail This 15-mile trail is a flat walk along an old abandoned mining road most of the way. It begins six miles west of Haines Junction at Mackintosh Lodge and ends at Sugden Creek.

Auriol Trail This 12-mile loop which begins 3.8-miles south of Haines Junction is a good day hike. The trail passes several vantage points which provide sweeping views of the area. A primitive campground along the way can be used to turn the walk into an overnight excursion.

Cottonwood Trail This 53-mile loop begins at the Kathleen Lake Campground, 12 miles south of Haines Junction. It ends at Dezadeash Lodge off the Haines Hwy. The route runs along old mining roads that require some climbing and fording of streams. Wildlife, especially brown bears, is plentiful on this four-day hike.

Slims River Trail This 16-mile trail is one of the most scenic in the Kluane National Park as it passes old mining relics and ends at Observation Mountain, which you can scramble up for a view of the spectacular Kaskawulsh Glacier. The trailhead is 40 miles west of Haines Junction near a park information centre.

Skagway

Skagway (population 800), a place of many names, much history and little rain, is the northern terminus of the state ferry. The town lies in the narrow plain of the Skagway River at the head of the Lynn Canal and, at one time or another, has been called Skaguay, Shkagway and Gateway to the Golden Interior. It is also known as the Home of the North Wind, and residents tell visitors that it blows so much here you'll never breathe the same air twice.

But Skagway is also one of the driest places in what is often the soggy Southeast. While Petersburg averages over 100 inches of rain a year and Ketchikan a drenching 154 inches, Skagway only gets 26 inches of rain annually.

Much of Skagway is within the Klondike Gold Rush National Historical Park which extends from Seattle to Dawson in the Yukon Territory. The National Park Service is constantly restoring the old shop fronts and buildings so the town looks similar to the boom town it was in the 1890s, when the gold rush gave birth to Skagway.

The town and the nearby ghost town of Dyea were the start for over 40,000 gold-rush stampeders who headed to the Yukon by way of either the Chilkoot Trail or the White Pass Trail. The Chilkoot Trail, which started from Dyea, was the most popular as it was several miles shorter. The White Pass Trail, which began in Skagway and was advertised as a 'horse trail', was brutal. In the winter of 1897-98, some 3000 pack animals were driven to death by over-anxious owners and the White Pass was called the 'Dead Horse Trail'.

In 1887, the population of the town was two; 10 years later 20,000 people lived there and the gold-rush town was Alaska's largest city – a center for saloons, hotels and dance halls. Skagway became infamous for its lawlessness. For a time, the town was held under the tight control of Jefferson Randolph 'Soapy' Smith and his gang who conned and swindled naive newcomers out of their money and stampeders out of their gold dust. Soapy Smith was finally removed from power by a mob of angry citizens in a gunfight between him and city engineer Frank Reid. Both men died in the fight and Smith's reign as the 'uncrowned prince of Skagway' ended, having lasted only nine months.

At the height of the gold rush, Michael J Heney, an Irish contractor, convinced a group of English investors that he could build a railroad over the White Pass Trail to Whitehorse. Construction began in 1898 with little more than picks, shovels and blasting powder, and the narrow-gauge railroad reached Whitehorse, the Yukon capital, in July 1900. The construction of the White Pass & Yukon Railroad was nothing short of a superhuman feat, and the railroad became the focal point of the town's economy after the gold rush and during the military build-up of WW II.

The line was shut down in 1982 but was revived in 1988 to the delight of backpackers walking the Chilkoot Trail and cruise-ship tourists. Although the train hauls no freight, its rebirth was important to Skagway as a tourist attraction. Today, Skagway survives almost entirely on tourism as bus tours and more than 200 'Love Boat' cruise ships visit to turn this village into a modern-day boom town every summer. When two or three ships arrive on the same day, this is where Alaska can really get crowded. Keep in mind that Skagway has to make a living in three months but if the throngs of tourists are still too much for you, skip this town and depart the Southeast through Haines.

Information

For information on the Chilkoot Trail, local trails and camping, contact the National Park Service Visitor Center (☎ 983-2921) on the corner of Broadway St and 2nd Ave. For any other information, visit the Skagway Visitor Bureau (☎ 938-2854) in the City Hall on the corner of Spring St and 7th Ave. It's open from 8.30 am to 5 pm Monday to Friday. From May to September the bureau operates a visitor information center in the Arctic

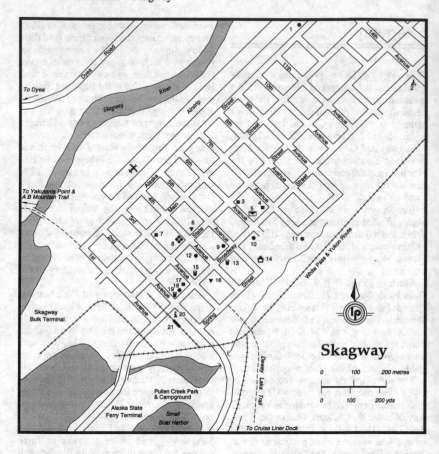

Skagway

Convention Hall, the driftwood building on Broadway St, that is open from 8.30 am to 5 pm daily.

Things to See

Unlike most Southeast towns, Skagway is a delightful place to arrive at aboard the state ferry. The dock and terminal are at the southwestern end of Broadway St, the main avenue in town. You step off the ferry right into a bustling town where half the people are dressed as if they are trying to relive the gold-rush days while the other half are obviously tourists off the luxury liners.

Near the dock, on the corner of Broadway St and 2nd Ave, is the National Park Service (NPS) office and visitor center in the White Pass & Yukon railroad depot. The visitor center is open from 8 am to 6 pm daily and features displays, slide shows and the movie *Days of Adventure, Dreams of Gold*, shown every hour. The 30-minute movie is narrated by Hal Holbrook and is the best way to slip back into the gold-rush days; other gold-rush programs begin at 10 am. The center also has walking tours of the historical city center daily at 11 am and 3 pm.

A seven-block corridor along Broadway

1	Air Terminal
2	Hanousek Park Campground
3	Irene's Inn
4	Skagway Inn
5	Post Office
6	Corner Cafe
7	Skagway (AYH) Home Hostel
8	Fairway Market
9	Laundromat
10	Eagle's Hall
11	City Hall & Trail of '98 Museum
12	Sports Emporium
13	Moe's Frontier Bar
14	Moore's Cabin
15	Sweet Tooth Saloon
16	Sourdough Cafe
17	Golden North Hotel
18	Arctic Brotherhood Hall
19	Red Onion Saloon
20	White Pass & Yukon Railroad Depot & NPS Office & Vistor Center
21	Train Station

St, part of the historical area, contains the restored buildings, false fronts and wooden sidewalks of Skagway's golden era. Diagonally opposite the NPS office is the **Arctic Brotherhood Hall**. The hall is hard to miss as there are about 20,000 pieces of driftwood tacked to the front of it, making it one of the most distinctive buildings in Alaska and probably the most photographed. The hall was recently taken over by the Skagway Visitors Bureau and, along with a ton of local information, features a multimedia show *Skagway at War* and a photo exhibit on the same subject. The film is shown in the hall at various times during the day from 8.30 am to 5 pm; admission is $2.50 for the film but also includes a ticket to the city museum.

Near the corner of 3rd Ave and Broadway St is the **Mascot Saloon**, the latest renovation project completed by the National Park Service. Built in 1898, the Mascot was one of just 70 saloons during Skagway's heyday as 'the roughest place in the world'. On the 1st floor are exhibits depicting the old saloon at the height of the gold rush while the NPS maintains offices on the 2nd floor; admission is free. Just up Broadway St at 5th Ave is the

Corrington Museum of Alaska History (☎ 983-2580). This private museum in the back of a gift shop covers the state's history, beginning with the Bering Land Bridge, on 40 pieces of scrimshaw, hand-carved ivory from walrus tusks. There is a $1 admission fee.

A block south-east of the museum on 5th Ave is **Moore's Cabin**, the oldest building in Skagway. Captain William Moore and his son built it in 1887 when they staked out their homestead as the founders of the town. Moore had to move his home to its present location, however, when gold-rush stampeders overran his homestead. The National Park Service has since renovated the building and in doing so discovered that the famous Dead Horse Trail that was used by so many stampeders actually began in the large lawn next to the cabin. Though a half-mile from the bay today, a century ago an occasional high tide reached this far up the valley. No more, however, as the Skagway area raises about an inch a year due to glacial rebound of the land.

At the south-eastern end of 7th Ave is the **City Hall**; upstairs is the **Trail of '98 Museum**. They are housed in a granite building that was built in 1900 as McCabe College and later served as a US Court until the city obtained it in 1956. The museum is open daily in the summer from 9 am to 5 pm and charges $2 for admission. The money is well spent, however, as the museum is jammed with gold-rush relics including many items devoted to the town's two leading characters, 'Soapy' Smith and Frank Reid. You can purchase a copy of the 15 July 1898 *Skagway News* that described all the details surrounding the colorful shoot-out.

For visitors who become as infatuated as the locals over Smith and Reid, there is the walk out to the **Gold Rush Cemetery**. From the ferry terminal, it is a 2.5-mile stroll to the graveyard north-east along State St, which runs parallel to Broadway St. Follow State St until it curves into 23rd Ave and look for the sign to Soapy's grave across the railroad tracks. A wooden bridge along the tracks leads to the main part of the cemetery, the site of many stampeders' graves and the plots of Reid and Smith. From Reid's gravestone, it is a short hike uphill to the lovely **Reid Falls** which cascade 300 feet from the mountainside.

In 1898, Skagway's rival city, **Dyea**, at the foot of the Chilkoot Trail, was the shortest route to Lake Bennett where stampeders began their float to Dawson City. After the White Pass & Yukon Railroad was completed in 1900, Dyea quickly died. Today it is little more than a few old cabins, the pilings of Dyea Wharf and Slide Cemetery, where 47 men and women were buried after perishing in an avalanche on the Chilkoot Trail in April 1898.

Dyea Rd, a scenic drive, winds nine miles from Skagway to the ghost town but is filled with hairpin turns that are a headache for drivers of camper vans. **Skagway Overlook**, a scenic turn-off with a viewing platform, is 2.5 miles out of town along the Dyea Rd. The overlook offers an excellent view of Skagway, its waterfront and the peaks above the town. Just before crossing the bridge over the Taiya River, you pass the Dyea Camping Area (22 sites), a free campground where a NPS ranger is stationed in the summer to assist hikers on the Chilkoot Trail which starts near the campground.

Festivals

Skagway's most unusual celebration is when locals and the cast of the Days of '98 show celebrate Soapy Smith's Wake on 8 July with a hike out to the grave and a toast of champagne, often sent up by Smith's great grandson from California. The Fourth of July celebrations feature a foot race, parade and fish feed. The town holds an equally entertaining Solstice Party on 21 June, highlighted by a street dance on Broadway St. The Dyea Dash run, held on the last Saturday in August, is from Dyea to Skagway. It ends with each person who finishes receiving a T-shirt.

Places to Stay

Camping The city manages two campgrounds that serve RVers and backpackers.

On the corner of Broadway St and 14th Ave is *Hanousek Park*, which provides tables, pit toilets and water for $8 per tent site. Near the ferry terminal is *Pullen Creek Park Campground* (33 sites) on the waterfront by the Small Boat Harbor. Designed primarily for RVers, sites with electricity cost $15 per night. This is also the place to go for a shower ($1).

For an informal but scenic camp site, go to the picnic area along Yakutania Point, two miles from the ferry terminal. Head northwest (left) on 1st Ave, cross the air strip and suspension bridge over Skagway River and then head west (left) along the path on the other side of the river. The path follows the river and leads to a picnic area that includes tables, grills and even a covered shelter. Nine miles north of Skagway is the free *Dyea Camping Area* (22 sites) which is operated on a first-come-first-to-set-up basis. There are vault toilets, tables and fire places but no water.

Hostels The *Skagway (AYH) Home Hostel* (☎ 983-2131), a very pleasant and friendly place to stay, is a half-mile from the ferry terminal on 3rd Ave near Main St. Reservations are advised – call the hostel or write to the Home Hostel, Box 231, Skagway, AK 99840. The hostel has 15 beds ($10 for members, $15 for nonmembers), along with a kitchen and baggage storage area. Check-in time is from 5 to 10.30 pm but the hostel will also accommodate late ferry arrivals if you contact them in advance.

B&Bs The *Skagway Inn* (☎ 983-2289 or (800) 478-2290) is in a 1897 Victorian home on the corner of Broadway St and 7th Ave. The B&B serves a filling meal in the morning, is within walking distance of the downtown sights and provides a free ride to the trailhead of the Chilkoot Trail. Best of all the rates are reasonable; $45/52 a single/double. There is also *Gramma's Bed & Breakfast* (☎ 983-2312), on the corner of 7th Ave and State St, with four rooms at the same rate.

Hotels *Irene's Inn* (☎ 983-2520), on Broadway St at 6th Ave, is the cheapest place with singles (with shared baths) from \$35 per night and doubles for \$50. The *Golden North Hotel* (☎ 983-2294), Alaska's oldest hotel on the corner of Broadway St and 3rd Ave, has some triple rooms for \$80 and quads for \$85.

Sergeant Preston's Lodge (☎ 983-2521), on 6th Ave between Broadway and Main streets, has rooms from \$60 a night and the *Westmark Inn* (☎ 983-6000 or (800) 544-0970), on 3rd Ave between Broadway and Spring streets, has backpacker accommodations in an adjacent facility with rates from \$49 to \$75 and provides a courtesy van to the Chilkoot Trail for guests. Keep in mind that getting a hotel room in Skagway during the summer is extremely difficult without advance reservations.

Places to Eat

For breakfast there is the *Sweet Tooth Saloon* near the ferry terminal on Broadway St or *Corner Cafe* on the corner of 4th Ave and State St.

A full breakfast at either place ranges from \$5 to \$7 while the Corner Cafe serves halibut and other Alaskan seafood and when the weather is nice has seating outside. There is also *Prospector's*, on the corner of 4th Ave and Broadway St, for soughdough pancakes and waffles served until 3 pm or *Sourdough Cafe*, on Broadway St between 3rd and 4th avenues, for those looking for quantity not so much quality. They serve an all-you-can-eat spaghetti dinner for \$9.

A better deal to splurge on is the breakfast buffet at the *Bonanza Bar & Grill* at the Westmark Hotel and then you can fast for the rest of the day.

Irene's Inn now has a bakery and espresso bar while there is always the *Fairway Market,* on the corner of 4th Ave and State St, for those camping or staying at the hostel.

The *Skagway Sports Emporium*, on 4th Ave between Broadway and State streets, sells freeze-dried food for hiking trips, along with topographic maps and limited camping equipment.

Entertainment

For a town with only 700 permanent residents, there's a lot to do in Skagway at night. On the corner of Broadway St and 2nd Ave is the town's most unique bar, the *Red Onion Saloon*, which frequently features folk music. This former brothel that was built in 1898 is now a gold-rush saloon in the tradition of Juneau's Red Dog Saloon. There are even mannequins leering down at your from the 2nd story to depict those turn-of-the-century working girls. The place really hops when cruise ships are in, as the ships' bands often hold a jam session for locals in the bar.

Moe's Frontier Bar down the street can also be a lively spot, especially late at night, as can the *Golden North Hotel Lounge*, which offers the cheapest way to drink – beer by the pitcher.

Skagway has the best melodrama in the Southeast. Gambling for prizes and drinking begins in the back room of the *Eagle's Hall,* on the corner of Broadway St and 6th Ave, every night at 8 pm. This is followed at 9 pm by the lively production of *Skaguay in the Days of '98* which covers the gold-rush days of the town and the full story of 'Soapy' Smith in a truly entertaining manner. It is \$12 for both the play and preshow entertainment.

Hiking

The Chilkoot Trail (see the Trekking section in the Wilderness chapter) is probably the most popular hike in Alaska, but there are other good treks around Skagway. There is no US Forest Service (USFS) office in Skagway, so for trail conditions and other information contact the National Park Visitor Center (☎ 983-2921) on the corner of Broadway St and 2nd Ave.

Dewey Lake Trail System This series of trails leads east of Skagway to a handful of alpine and subalpine lakes, waterfalls and historical sites. From Broadway St follow 3rd Ave south-east to the railroad tracks. On the east side of the tracks are the trailheads to Lower Dewey Lake, 0.7 miles; Icy Lake, 2.5 miles; Upper Reid Falls, 3.5 miles; and Sturgill's Landing, 4.5 miles.

Plan on taking an hour for the return hike to Lower Dewey Lake where there are picnic tables, camping spots and a trail that circles the lake. At the northern end of the lake is an alpine trail that ascends steeply to Upper Dewey Lake, 3.5 miles from town, and Devil's Punchbowl another 0.7 miles south of the upper lake. The hike to Devil's Punchbowl is an all-day trip or an ideal overnight excursion, as the views are excellent and there is a free-use USFS shelter on Upper Dewey Lake that does not require reservations.

A B Mountain Trail Also known as the Skyline Trail, this route ascends 5.5 miles to the 5100-foot summit of A B Mountain, named for the A B that appears on its south side in the form of a snow-melt every spring. The trailhead is on Dyea Rd about a mile from Skagway via the Skagway River footbridge off the north-west end of 1st Ave. The trail is steep and requires a full day to complete.

Denver Glacier Trail This trail begins at *Mile 6* of the White Pass & Yukon Route and heads up the East fork of the Skagway River for two miles. Near the ruins of an old miner's cabin, the trail swings south and continues another 1.5 miles up the glacial outwash to Denver Glacier. This part is overgrown with brush and is tough hiking.

Laughton Glacier Trail At *Mile 14* of the White Pass & Yukon Route is a short hike to a USFS cabin (reservations, rental $25 per night). The trailhead is at Glacier Station, an old rail depot, and from here it is a two-mile trek to Laughton Glacier, an impressive hanging glacier between 3000-foot walls of the Sawtooth Range. The alpine scenery from the windows of this cabin is worth all the hassle of reserving it in advance. On both this and the Denver Glacier trail, book train drop-off and pick-up with the White Pass & Yukon Route.

Getting There & Away
Air There are regularly scheduled flights from Skagway to Juneau, Haines and Glacier Bay with LAB Flying Service (☎ 983-2471), Wings of Alaska (☎ 983-2442), and Skagway Air (☎ 983-2218) which generally offers the cheapest fares. Expect to pay $85 one-way to Juneau and $60 to Haines.

Bus Northbound travelers will find that scheduled buses are the cheapest way to travel other than hitchhiking. Alaskon Express has a bus departing at 7.30 am daily that arrives in Whitehorse at 11.30 am. On Tuesday, Wednesday, Friday and Saturday, you can continue to Beaver Creek where the bus stops overnight and connections can be made to Anchorage or Fairbanks. Purchase tickets and board the bus at the Westmark Hotel (☎ 983-2241) on 3rd Ave between Broadway and Spring streets. The one-way fare from Skagway to Anchorage is $199, to Fairbanks $189 and Whitehorse $52.

Train It is now possible to travel to Whitehorse on the White Pass & Yukon Route with a bus connection at Fraser (British Columbia). The northbound train departs the Skagway depot daily during the summer (from late May to September) at 12.45 pm, reaching Fraser at 2.30 pm. You then board a bus and arrive in Whitehorse at 6.30 pm. The one-way fare is $92, quite a bit more than the bus but the ride on the historic, narrow-gauge railroad is worth it. Purchase tickets at the railroad depot (☎ 983-2217).

Boat The state ferry (☎ 983-2229) departs daily during the summer from the terminal and dock at the south-west end of Broadway St. There are lockers in the terminal but the building is only open three hours prior to the arrival of a ferry and while the boat is in port.

There is also the Haines-Skagway Water Taxi which sells tickets at the Pullen Creek RV Park Office (☎ 983-2083) on Congress Way. The 40-passenger ship departs the Skagway Small Boat Harbor twice daily for Haines with the first run at 10 am and the second at 7 pm. Round-trip fare is $29 and one-way is $18.

Hitchhiking Hitchhiking, the cheapest form of transport, is possible along the Klondike Hwy if you are patient and are hitching when a state ferry pulls in. Backpackers contemplating hitchhiking north would do better, however, if they bought a $12-ferry ticket to Haines and hitchhiked along the Haines Hwy instead as it has considerably more traffic.

Getting Around

There is a taxi and bus service out to Dyea and the trailhead for the Chilkoot Trail (see the Trekking section in the Wilderness chapter), or you can hitchhike to the trail – possible because a stream of hikers goes out there daily in summer.

Tours Without a doubt the most spectacular tour from Skagway is the Summit Excursion on the White Pass & Yukon Route. The three-hour journey begins at the railroad depot where you board the 1890 parlour cars for the trip to White Pass along the narrow-gauge line built during the height of the 1898 Klondike gold rush.

This is only a small portion of the 110-

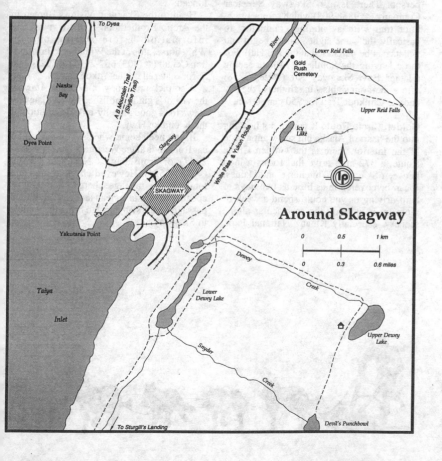

Around Skagway

mile route to Whitehorse but it contains the most spectacular scenery including crossing Glacier Gorge and Dead Horse Gulch, viewing Bridal Veil Falls and then making the steep climb to White Pass at 2885 feet, 20 miles from Skagway. The tour is offered twice a day at 8.45 am and 1.15 pm. Tickets are $72 per person and can be purchased at the railroad depot (☎ 983-2217).

Both Alaska Sightseeing (☎ 983-2828) and Gray Line (☎ 983-2241) offer two-hour tours of the city that include Gold Rush Cemetery, the historical district and Skagway Overlook. Tickets are $17 per person. There is also Skagway Streetcar Company (☎ 983-2908) which offers a two-hour tour with a 'singing conductor' to basically the same sights. Tours begin and tickets can be purchased at the AB Hall. For those leaving the Southeast without seeing Glacier Bay, Skagway Air (☎ 983-2218) offers one-hour sightseeing flights of the bay and the Chilkoot Trail for $50 per person.

Golden Circle Route If you're not heading into the heart of Alaska but still want a taste of the interior, there is the Golden Circle Route, a 372-mile drive that forms a loop between Skagway, Whitehorse and Haines. It can be covered in as little as two days of hard driving or you could spend a week or more on it to enjoy the spectacular alpine scenery, especially Kluane National Park,

the numerous campgrounds and the eagles of the Chilkat River north of Haines.

The 100-mile Klondike Hwy, from Skagway to Whitehorse, is particularly scenic as it parallels the White Pass Trail and then passes Emerald and Kookatsoon lakes near Carcross where there is a handful of campgrounds.

From Whitehorse you get to drive a 105-mile portion of the Alaska Hwy and then head south back into Alaska at Haines Junction on the Haines Hwy. The State Marine ferry would then complete the loop with transport back to Skagway or a return to Juneau.

Head to the Skagway Visitors Bureau in the Arctic Brotherhood Hall for maps and information before staring out. In Whitehorse, stop at the Whitehorse Information Center (☎ (403) 667-2915) at 302 Steele St for material on the Yukon capital.

Also pick up a copy of *Skaguay Alaskan* the visitor's guide published by the Skagway News for a good mile-by-mile description of the Klondike Hwy.

If you need some wheels, you can rent a car from Avis at the Westmark Hotel (☎ 983-2247) or from Eagles Nest Car Rental (☎ 983-2523). However, check around and total up the mileage charge. It might be cheaper to rent in Juneau and pay additional passage on the state ferry to bring the vehicle to Skagway.

Southcentral Alaska

Upon reaching Haines, most independent travelers continue their Alaskan adventure by heading north through Canada's Yukon Territory to the Alcan (Alaska Hwy). They drive, hitchhike or bus the famous highway to the state's interior, viewing Denali National Park and possibly Fairbanks before heading south towards Anchorage (see the Getting Around chapter).

For travelers who were enchanted by the Southeast and the Alaska Marine Hwy and want to avoid the long days on the Alcan (Alaska Hwy), there is a pleasant and cheaper alternative from Juneau. For less than the cost of a Haines-to-Anchorage bus ticket, you can fly on Alaska Airlines from Juneau to Cordova ($176), another remote coastal fishing town.

From Cordova you can jump on the southwest system of the Alaska State Marine Ferry to explore Southcentral Alaska to the west. Known by many as the Gulf Coast region, this area is really a continuation of Alaska's rugged coastal playground that begins in Ketchikan.

Both Southeast and Southcentral Alaska boast spectacular scenery with glaciers, fjords and mountain ranges half buried by icefields and covered at the base by lush forest; both areas are also affected by the Japanese Current causing a wet but mild climate. Fishing is an important industry to these regions and the state ferry is one of the main modes of transport.

However, Southcentral (the region around Prince William Sound and the Gulf of Alaska) has one important feature that the Panhandle (Southeast) doesn't have – roads and traffic between many of the towns. This alone makes the Southcentral one of the cheapest, most accessible and most popular areas in the state to visit.

With half of Alaska's population just to the north in Anchorage, the Southcentral's Kenai Peninsula is a haven for RVers, anglers and tour groups. There are dozens of trails and water routes throughout the peninsula, but because of its accessibility you may have to hike a little longer or climb a little higher to achieve the wilderness solitude so easily obtained in the Southeast.

Southcentral can be divided into three main areas. Prince William Sound, with its communities of Cordova, Valdez and Whittier, is characterized by towering mountains, glaciers and abundant marine wildlife. To the west of the sound is the Kenai Peninsula and the towns of Seward, Kenai, Soldotna and Homer. This great forested plateau, bounded by the Kenai Mountains and the Harding Icefield to the east, is broken up by hundreds of lakes, rivers and streams, making it an outdoor paradise for hikers, canoeists and anglers.

To the south-west is Kodiak Island and the city of Kodiak, the home of the largest fishing fleet in Alaska. Though often caught in the rainy and foggy weather created on the Gulf of Alaska, Kodiak has a rugged beauty and isolated wilderness areas few visitors make an effort to venture into.

YAKUTAT

On the flight to Cordova there is a stopover at Yakutat (population 520), the most northern Southeast community. The town is isolated from the State Marine Ferry because of the turbulent nature of the Gulf of Alaska.

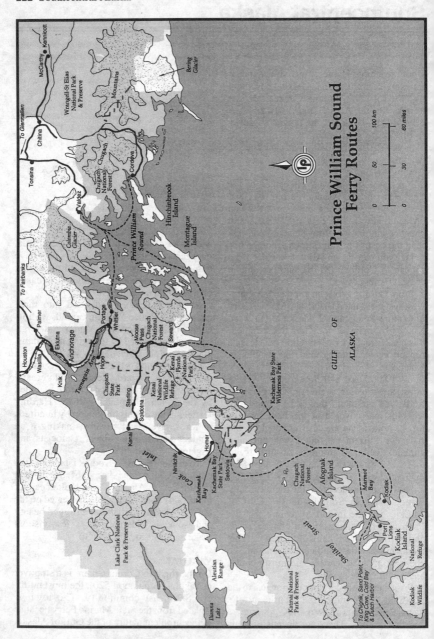

Prince William Sound Ferry Routes

For travelers on a tight schedule, there is no reason to stop over in Yakutat but those who do will find the scenic setting of the Tlingit village stunning, even if the visitor facilities are limited and expensive.

The town is surrounded by lofty peaks, including Mt Elias at 18,114 feet to the west and Mt Fairweather at 15,388 feet to the east. North-west of Yakutat is the large Malaspina Glacier.

Yakutat has three lodges, the cheapest being the *Ponderosa Inn* (☎ 443-2368) with rooms from $65, a handful of restaurants and cafés, and two grocery stores. Camping is possible at *Cannon Beach*, a picnic area near town that is administered by the US Forest Service (USFS). The main attraction in the area is the Malaspina Glacier, which can be viewed from sightseeing flights offered by Gulf Air Taxi (☎ 784-3240), the local air-charter operator based at the airport. Other visitors come to beachcomb the miles of sandy beach that surround Yakutat, searching for Japanese glass balls blown onshore by the violent Pacific storms.

USFS Cabins

The USFS, which maintains an office at Yakutat Airport, administers 11 cabins in the area along with the Russell Fjord Wilderness to the north-east. None of the cabins is on the fjord or near Hubbard Glacier – the advancing ice floe that made world news when it reached Gilbert's Point in June 1986 and basically turned Russell Fjord into a fresh-water lake by cutting it off from Disenchantment Bay. Within a few months the pressure of the rising water broke the ice dam and Hubbard Glacier began to retreat. Other than on a quick sightseeing flight, the only way to see the glacier and the amazing scene of it calving during mid-tide is through an Alaska Discovery guided expedition.

Five of the 11 USFS cabins in the area can be reached from Forest Hwy 10 that extends east from Yakutat. It is best to rent the cabins from the USFS office in the Juneau Centennial Hall (☎ 586-8751 in Juneau) when you pass through the capital city. Rental information can also be obtained at the Yakutat USFS

office (☎ 784-3359) in the Flight Service Building at the airport in Yakutat or by contacting USFS, PO Box 327, Yakutat, AK 99689.

Situk Lake This cabin is on the forested south-eastern shore of the lake and provides excellent fishing for salmon and steelhead trout as well as good viewing of brown bears, moose, otters and bald eagles. It can be reached by a five-mile trail that begins east of the bridge at *Mile 9* of Forest Hwy 10.

Situk Weir Travelers who raft down the Situk River end up at Situk Landing, a large parking lot eight miles from town along Lost River Rd. A quarter-mile trail leads from the parking area to the Situk Weir USFS Cabin. The cabin provides excellent fishing for salmon, Dolly Varden and trout in the mouth of the Situk River. For some good beachcombing, the beaches along the Gulf of Alaska can be reached along a two-mile path.

Harlequin Lake This cabin is a 30-mile drive from Yakutat along Forest Hwy 10. The unit offers excellent fishing and views of Harlequin Lake and the massive icebergs from Yakutat Glacier. A trail leads south four miles from the cabin to Middle Dangerous USFS Cabin.

Prince William Sound

Prince William Sound, the northern extent of the Gulf of Alaska, rivals the Southeast for the steepest fjords and the most spectacular coastlines and glaciers. The sound is a marvelous wilderness area of islands, inlets, fjords, lush rainforests and towering mountains. Flanked to the west by the Kenai Mountains and to the north and east by the Chugach Mountains, Prince William Sound covers 15,000 sq miles and has abundant wildlife, including whales, sea lions, harbor seals, otters, eagles, dall sheep, mountain goats and, of course, bears.

Mountain Goat

Another trait the sound shares with the Southeast is rain – lots of rain. There's an average of well over 100 inches of rain per year, with the fishing town of Cordova receiving 167 inches annually. Summer temperatures range from 54° to 70°F.

At center stage of Prince William Sound is the Columbia Glacier. The bluish wall of ice, named after New York's Columbia University, is one of the most spectacular tidewater glaciers on the Alaskan coast, as it covers 440 sq miles. The glacier's face is three miles wide and in some places it is 262 feet high.

When passing the glacier by boat, the stunning scene includes hundreds of seals sunning on the ice pack, a backdrop of mountains and usually the thunder of ice calving off its face – sometimes induced by the ship's captain who sounds the horn in front of it. When the Columbia Glacier calves icebergs into the sea, there's an explosion of ice and water that few onlookers ever forget.

Travelers who take the Alaska Airlines jet to Cordova can continue their journey across

Prince William Sound by the Alaska Marine Ferry. At Valdez, you have the option of returning to the road, but most travelers elect to stay on the state ferry to Whittier on the west side of the sound as this section of the marine highway includes passing the Columbia Glacier. From Whittier, there is a rail service to Anchorage (see the Getting Around chapter), and from Valdez you can reach Anchorage by bus.

CORDOVA

Nestled between Orca Inlet and Lake Eyak and overshadowed by Mt Eccles, Cordova is a beautiful little fishing town on the east coast of Prince William Sound and a place worth the extra time and expense needed to visit it due to the isolated nature. Like towns in the Southeast, Cordova is inaccessible by road.

The community has 2600 permanent residents but its population doubles during the summer with fishers and cannery workers because the town's economy is centered around its fishing fleet and fish-processing plants. The area around Cordova is an outdoor paradise, and the town is a jumping-off point to 14 USFS cabins; some good alpine hiking; and the Copper River Delta, a staging and nesting area for millions of birds each year.

The area was first settled by nomadic Eyak Indians who were drawn down the Copper River by the enormous salmon runs and abundance of shellfish. Early US fishermen built a cannery here in 1889 but modern-day Cordova was born when Michael J Heney, the builder of the White Pass & Yukon Railroad from Skagway to Whitehorse, arrived in 1906. At that point he had decided to transform the summer cannery site into the railroad terminus for his line from the Kennecott copper mines near McCarthy. Construction of the Copper River & Northwestern Railroad began that year and was completed in 1911 – another amazing engineering feat by the 'Irish Prince' that cost $23 million to build.

Within five years, Cordova was a boom town with more than $32 million worth of

Top: Fall in Eagle River valley (DS)
Bottom: Sea kayaking in Blackstone Bay, Prince William Sound (DS)

Top: Ice crystals, Eagle River, Chugach State Park (DS)
Bottom: South Fork Valley, Harmony Mountains, Chugach State Park (DS)

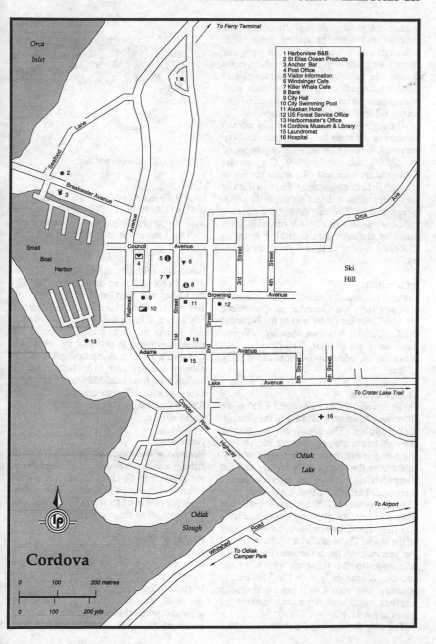

To Ferry Terminal

Orca
Inlet

1 Harborview B&B
2 St Elias Ocean Products
3 Anchor Bar
4 Post Office
5 Visitor Information
6 Windsinger Cafe
7 Killer Whale Cafe
8 Bank
9 City Hall
10 City Swimming Pool
11 Alaskan Hotel
12 US Forest Service Office
13 Harbormaster's Office
14 Cordova Museum & Library
15 Laundromat
16 Hospital

Seafood Lane

Breakwater Avenue

Small
Boat
Harbor

Council Avenue

Ski
Hill

Browning Avenue

Railroad 1st Street 2nd Street 3rd Street 4th Street

Adams

Avenue

Lake Avenue 5th Street 6th Street

To Crater Lake Trail

Copper River Highway

Odiak
Lake

To Airport

Odiak
Slough

Whitshed Road

To Odiak
Camper Park

Cordova

0   100   200 metres

0   100   200 yds

copper ore passing through its docks. The railroad and town prospered until 1938, when labor strikes and the declining price of copper permanently closed the Kennecott mines. The railroad ceased operations and Cordova turned to fishing, its main economic base today, which is why the 1989 Exxon oil spill devastated the town.

Although most of the halibut and salmon swimming beneath the oil appear to have survived, the mishap cancelled or postponed the fishing seasons in 1989. Commercial fishing boats were left idle, while stories of lifelong fishermen breaking down in tears as they steered their boats through the slick were common. The only saving grace for the industry was that Exxon was forced to lease many of the commercial fishing boats at $3400 a day or more to assist with the clean-up.

Information
General information about Cordova can be obtained from the Chamber of Commerce (☎ 424-7260) on 1st St next to the National Bank of Alaska; it is open Monday to Thursday from 9 am to noon. The chamber also maintains an information booth at the ferry office.

Things to See
On the corner of Adams Ave and 1st St is the **Cordova Museum & Library** in the Centennial Building. The small but interesting museum has displays on marine life, including a rare leatherback turtle caught nearby, relics from the town's early history and the Kennecott mine, Russian artefacts and a three-seater bidarka (kayak-style boat).

In the evening at 7.30 pm or when the state ferry is in port, the museum shows an excellent film, *The Cordova Story*, on the history of the town. There is also a visitor center at the entrance of the museum. There's free admission to the museum which, in the summer, is open daily from 1 to 5 pm except Monday, and from 7 to 9 pm on Thursday and Saturday. The library has more extended hours in the evening.

The **City Swimming Pool** (☎ 424-7200)

Dungeness crab

is on Railroad Ave in a brown building next to City Hall. Built in 1974, the Olympic-size pool is open to the public at various times. Call for a list of the session times and activities.

North on Railroad Ave from the pool is the **Small Boat Harbor**, the real center of activity in Cordova during the summer. In 1984, the harbor was doubled in size to 845 slips, and it is now one of the five largest harbors in the state. It hums with the activity of boats and fishers between season openings and when the fleet is in town on the weekends. Cordova's fleet is composed primarily of salmon seiners and gillnetters, and the season runs from mid-May into September. Dungeness and Tanner crabs are harvested for a few months during the summer and later in the winter.

Festivals
Because of the economic importance of the fishing season, no events are planned during the summer in Cordova other than a small Fourth of July celebration. The town's biggest event is its Iceworm Festival in mid-February, when there is little else to do.

Places to Stay
Camping There is no hostel in Cordova. The closest campground is the *Odiak Camper Park* (☎ 424-6200), half a mile from town on Whitshed Rd next to the recently covered and landscaped dump site. The gravel campground is primarily for RVers and charges $5 per night, but water, showers and restrooms

are available. Unofficial spots for pitching a tent are on the bluffs across from the ferry terminal or up 6th St at the ski hill.

B&Bs Quite a few B&Bs have popped up in the past few years: when this book was being researched there were five operating around town. Check with the visitor center for a current list of B&Bs as they often change, and expect to pay between $45 and $55 per person for a room. One of the oldest B&Bs, *Oystercatcher* (☎ 424-5154), is on the corner of 3rd St and Council Ave. Also in town are *Otter B'Here* (☎ 424-5863) with a double room for $55 on Breakwater Ave and the *Harborview Bed & Breakfast* (☎ 424-5356) on Observation Ave with singles for $50. Further out of town is *Queen's Chair* (☎ 424-3000) near the Powder House Inn along the Copper River Hwy with a view of Eyak Lake. Doubles are $60 a night and the hosts will pick you up in town or at the ferry.

Hotels Of the four hotels in town, the *Alaskan Hotel & Bar* (☎ 424-3288) on 1st St is the cheapest. A single room with a shared bath costs $35 a night, while singles with a bathroom are $45. The Alaskan, like all hotels in Cordova, is booked solidly through most of the summer. The *Cordova Hotel* (☎ 424-3388), on 1st St between Adams and Browning avenues, has higher rates with doubles at $65, while the *Prince William Sound Motel* (☎ 424-3201), on the corner of 2nd St and Council Ave, has rooms from $80. Then there is the *Reluctant Fisherman Inn* (☎ 424-3272), on the corner of Railroad and Council avenues, usually booked solidly during the summer despite the cost of rooms beginning around $100 a night.

Places to Eat
The *Windsinger Cafe* on 1st St behind the Club Bar has breakfast beginning at 6 am, home-made soups and quick bites to eat (they have a take-away window). Try the *OK Restaurant* near the museum for Chinese food with main meals ranging from $13 to $16, and *Baja Taco Wagon*, in a converted school bus on Nicoloff Ave near the new boat harbor, for cheap Mexican food. The *Ambrosia*, also on 1st St, specializes in pizza and Italian food with dinners around $15, while the *Killer Whale Cafe* in the Orca Book & Sound Store is a delicatessen with good desserts, espresso and a view of the harbor.

For a more expensive meal with a view, try the restaurant in the *Reluctant Fisherman* which overlooks the harbor and specializes in seafood. *The Powder House*, a little way from town at *Mile 1.5* of the Copper River Hwy, is a bar that serves sandwiches, chilli and barbecue dinners and has a deck overlooking Eyak Lake.

Places to pick up your own supplies include *Davis Super Foods*, a supermarket on 1st St and *St Elias Ocean Products* on Seafood Lane near the Small Boat Harbor for seafood.

Entertainment
The Powder House Bar, which earns its name because it lies on the site of the original Copper River & Northwestern Railroad powder house, is a fun place that features folk, bluegrass and country music at night. If you happen to be there on a rare evening when it isn't raining, there is a deck outside overlooking Eyak Lake.

In town, there is the *Club Bar* on 1st St with music nightly or the *Anchor Bar*, on Breakwater Ave across from the Small Boat Harbor, for those who want to mingle with the fishers. The *Alaskan Hotel Bar* on 1st St usually has live music.

Hiking & USFS Cabins
There are a number of hikes and cabins (reservations needed, $25 per day rental) accessible from the Cordova road system. Before venturing into the surrounding area, hikers should first stop at the US Forest Service office (☎ 424-7661) on the corner of Browning Ave and 2nd St to pick up an assortment of free trail maps. Seaman's Hardware on 1st St sells topographic maps of the area.

Mt Eyak Ski Hill After quick scramble up the ski hill at the end of 6th Ave, hardy hikers can spend a day climbing from here to the top of Mt Eyak and down the other side to Crater Lake.

Crater Lake Trail This 2.5-mile hike begins on Eyak Lake, about half a mile beyond the Municipal Airfield on Eyak Lake Rd. The trail ascends steeply but is easy to follow as it winds through lush forest. At the top, it offers panoramic views of both the Copper River Delta and Prince William Sound. Plan on two to four hours for the round trip from the road to the open country around Crater Lake. Once at the lake, you can continue with a 5.5-mile ridge route to Power Creek Trail. The entire loop would be a 12-mile trek or an ideal overnight backpack.

Lydic Slough Trail & Eyak River Cabin At *Mile 7.1* of Copper River Hwy is Lydic Slough Trail, which leads three miles along the Copper River Flats to a cabin (reservations needed, rental $25 a night) on the Eyak River. The Eyak River offers excellent trout and salmon fishing as well as opportunities to view moose, brown bear and a wide range of waterfowl.

McKinley Lake Trail The 2.5-mile McKinley Lake Trail begins at *Mile 21.6* of Copper River Hwy and leads to the head of the lake and the remains of the Lucky Strike gold mine. Two cabins, McKinley Lake and McKinley Trail (reservations needed, rental $25 a night), are on this path, making them accessible by foot from the highway.

Pipeline Loop Trail At *Mile 21* of Copper River Hwy is this 1.8-mile trail past several small lakes. The trail provides access to good fishing holes for grayling and trout, and merges into the McKinley Trail that can be followed back to make something of a loop. The entire walk provides excellent views of the surrounding Chugach Mountains but the muskeg areas can be very wet in places and rubber boots are recommended.

Sheridan Mountain Trail This trail starts at the end of Sheridan Glacier Rd, 17 miles

south-east of town. Most of the 1.9-mile, one-way trail is a moderate climb that passes through mature forests before breaking out into an alpine basin. The view of mountains and Sheridan and Sherman glaciers from the basin is a stunning sight, and it only gets better when you start climbing the surrounding rim. During a dry spell, hiking boots are fine for the walk, otherwise you might want to tackle this one in rubber boots as well.

Saddlebag Glacier Trail This trail is accessed via a firewood-cutting road, at *Mile 25* of the Copper River Hwy. It's an easy walk of three miles through cottonwoods and spruce until you emerge at the outlet of Saddlebag Lake. The view is outstanding as the namesake glacier is at the far end of the lake and surrounded by peaks and cliffs. Often you can spot mountain goats residing here.

Getting There & Away

Air Alaska Airlines (☎ 424-7151) makes a daily stop at Cordova on its run from Seattle to Anchorage. The one-way fare for the short flight to Anchorage is $72. Wilbur's Flight Service (☎ 424-5695) provides a daily commuter service from Cordova to Valdez and Anchorage as well as the usual sightseeing flights and transport to USFS cabins.

Boat During the summer, the MV *Bartlett* stops daily at Cordova and twice on Friday and Monday, making a day trip possible from Valdez with a night spent on the ferry each way, not a bad deal if you're counting your dimes and nickles. You would leave Valdez at 11.45 pm the night before, arrive in Cordova at 5.30 am on Monday or Friday and then catch an outgoing boat at 12.30 am that evening. The fare from Cordova to Valdez is $28; it's $56 to Whittier. The ferry terminal (☎ 424-7333) is north of town on Railroad Ave.

Getting Around

To/From the Airport All jets arrive and depart from Cordova Airport, 12 miles from town on Copper River Hwy. The Airporter bus (☎ 424-3284) greets all arrivals and charges $5 for the trip into town. You can catch the bus at the major hotels in town for a ride out to the airport.

AROUND CORDOVA
Copper River Hwy

There are more than 50 miles of road extending out from Cordova, most of it centered around the Copper River Hwy. Built on the old railroad bed to the Kennecott mines, the road was originally going to connect Cordova with the Richardson Hwy and the rest of Alaska. Construction was halted in 1964 after the Good Friday Earthquake damaged the existing roadbeds and bridges, knocking out the fourth span of the famous Million Dollar Bridge in front of Childs Glacier.

Things to See Today, the highway provides access to the **Copper River Delta**, a huge area of tidal marshes and outwashes, and a birder's paradise. Millions of birds or waterfowl including arctic terns, dusty Canada geese, trumpeter swans, great blue herons and bald eagles,use it as a nesting and staging area during the summer. A drive along the highway at dawn or dusk can provide views of moose, brown bears, beavers and porcupines, while on rare occasions a lynx or wolverine can be seen from the roadside.

The wildlife is so abundant in this area that in 1962, the US Forest Service, the US Fish & Wildlife and the state agreed to manage 33,000 acres of the delta as a game and fish habitat. The refuge has since been enlarged to 2.3 million acres and, in 1972, the delta on the east side of the Copper River Hwy was closed to off-road vehicles.

The area provides access to hiking (see the Cordova Hiking & USFS Cabins section), wildlife, bird-watching, rafting on swift glacial rivers and angling. The streams and rivers along the highway are renowned for their fishing and can provide the ultimate angling experience – fishing an isolated stretch of river with mountains around you and wildlife just beyond the next bend. Sockeye salmon fishing begins in mid-June and peaks around 4 July. Coho salmon run

from August to September, and cutthroat trout and Dolly Varden can be caught throughout the summer and fall.

The highway also provides access to a handful of glaciers that flow out of the Chugach Mountains. The first is the **Sheridan Glacier**, which you can view from the bridge over the Sheridan River 15 miles from Cordova or three miles beyond the Cordova Airport. One mile before the bridge, the Sheridan Glacier access road leads 4.3 miles to the north, ending at a picnic table with a partial view of the ice floe. From here there is a one-mile trail to the dirt-covered glacial moraine.

Several other glaciers can be seen spilling out of the mountains; by far the most impressive is **Childs Glacier** to the west of the Million Dollar Bridge, 48 miles from Cordova. A short side road leads from the highway to within 200 yards of the spectacular glacier's face. Periodic calving from the glacier almost stops Copper River's downstream momentum. From the Million Dollar Bridge you can view Childs Glacier, less than a mile downstream or **Miles Glacier**, five miles upstream.

Nearby you'll find a 15-foot-high viewing platform with an interpretive display on the history of the bridge and the start of the Childs Glacier Trail. The 1.2-mile trail follows an old road along the Copper River, passing superb views of the glacier. It ends at the Child's Glacier Recreation Area, featuring picnic tables, restrooms, and more interpretive displays and short trails.

At least a day should be spent exploring the Copper River Hwy, or take more if you want to include some time fishing and hiking. Stop at the USFS office in Cordova and pick up a copy of the brochure *Copper River Delta* which includes a map and milepost listings of every trailhead, undeveloped camp sites, wildlife-viewing areas and streams to toss a lure into.

Getting Around The only problem in experiencing this area is transport. Hitching along the Copper River Hwy is slow going and renting a car in Cordova is expensive, if you can even obtain a vehicle. Both the Imperial Cab Company (☎ 424-3201) and the Reluctant Fisherman Inn (☎ 424-3272) rent vehicles for $75 per day and 75c a mile, making a single-day journey to Childs Glacier (a $150 affair) – worth it if there are three or more people sharing the expenses.

Footloose Tours (☎ 424-5356) offers a six-hour tour out to the Million Dollar Bridge for $35 per person, a minimum of four people per trip, and is by far the most reasonable way to see this road. Footloose uses a 25-passenger bus and serves a box lunch at the Childs Glacier Recreation Area. If you arrive with a Klepper kayak or a raft, the company will provide shuttle service for those who want to float the Copper River from either the Million Dollar Bridge or Flag Point at *Mile 27* of the highway. The cost is $20 per person or $80 a trip.

Also check with Copper River Express (☎ 424-5463) which also offers five-hour tours to the glacier for the same price. Then there is Whiskey Ridge Cycle Shop (☎ 424-3354) on Breakwater Ave. It rents mountain bicycles for $10 a day and if you have three spare days an excellent bike trip can be managed, highlighted by day hikes and glacier watching.

VALDEZ

In the heart of Prince William Sound and less than 25 miles east of the Columbia Glacier is Valdez, the most northerly ice-free port in the western hemisphere and the southern terminus of the Trans-Alaska Pipeline. The town and port were named after a Spanish naval officer by Spanish explorer Don Salvador Fidalgo in 1790. Valdez boomed in 1897-98 when 4000 gold-seekers arrived looking for what was being advertised in the Lower 48 as the 'All American Route' to Alaska's Interior and the Klondike gold fields. Talk about truth in advertising – what they found was a few tents set up above the tide line and one one of the most dangerous routes to the Klondike.

Also known as the Valdez Trail, the route included a trek over two glaciers, beginning with the Valdez Glacier, as the key to crossing the Chugach Mountains. It was a suicidal trip at best and hundreds of lives were lost due to falls in crevasses, snowblindness and hypothermia. In the spring of 1899, Captain William Abercrombie arrived to find a devastated group of men, most of whom had scurvy and were short of supplies never having anticipated a lack of them in Valdez. The army captain soon set up a hospital and made arrangements for supplies and then began surveying a better route to the interior. It was Abercrombie who found Keystone Canyon and Thompson Pass as a much more suitable place to cross the Chugach range. Eventually the gold miner's trail was improved into a wagon trail and then was paved in the 1920s to become the Richardson Hwy.

Valdez prospered briefly with a few mines of its own and as outpost for the army. But by the early 1900s the town began a long decline when, in a bitter fight, it lost the Copper River & Northwestern Railroad to Cordova despite blasting tunnels in Keystone Canyon in anticipation of a line.

In 1964, Valdez lost even more than its role as the main cargo route to Interior Alaska. In four short minutes, the Good Friday Earthquake demolished the city. All of Valdez's history is dated either before or after the devastating catastrophe, as the city was one of the worst hit in Alaska with the epicenter only 45 miles to the west of town. The earthquake caused the land to ripple like water, a 4000-foot slice of waterfront to slide into the harbor and produced massive tidal waves that left few buildings undamaged in the town.

Afterwards, the residents voted to rebuild their city at a new site on more stable ground. The old town lies four miles east of Valdez on Richardson Hwy, but all that remains today is a vacant field and a plaque dedicated to those who lost their lives during the frightful event.

Valdez regained its role as the gateway to the Interior when it was chosen as the terminus of the Trans-Alaska Pipeline. Work began in 1974 and the $9 billion project was completed in 1977; the first tanker was filled

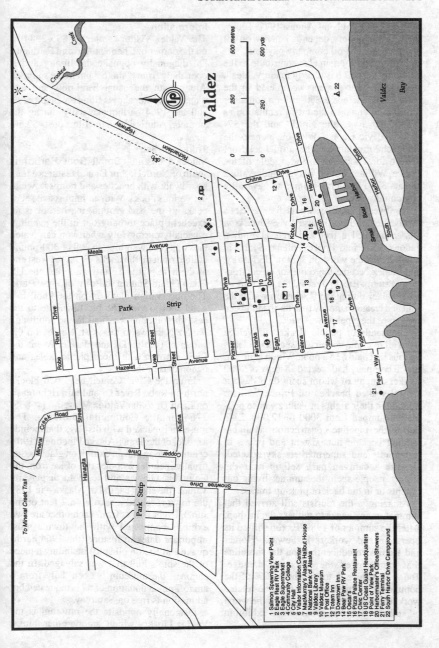

Valdez

Richardson Highway

Crooked Creek

Valdez Bay

Small Boat Harbor

Chitna Drive

Meals Avenue

Park Strip

Hazelet Avenue

Park Strip

Mineral Creek Road

To Mineral Creek Trail

Harbor Drive

North Drive

Kobuk Drive

Egan Drive

Galena Drive

Clifton Avenue

Fidalgo Drive

Ferry Way

Robe River Drive

Lowe Street

Parker Drive

Fairbanks Drive

Hanagita Street

Klutina Drive

Copper Drive

Snowmee Drive

1 Salmon Spawning View Point
2 Eagle Rest RV Park
3 Eagle Supermarket
4 Community College
5 City Hall
6 Visitor Information Center
7 MacMurray's Alaska Halibut House
8 National Bank of Alaska
9 Valdez Library
10 Valdez Museum
11 Post Office
12 Totem Inn
13 Downtown Inn
14 Bear Paw RV Park
15 Oscar's
16 Pizza Palace Restaurant
17 Civic Center
18 US Coast Guard Headquarters
19 Point of View Park
20 Harbormaster's Office/Showers
21 Ferry Terminal
22 South Harbor Drive Campground

500 metres
500 yds
0 250
0 250

with the black gold on 1 August 1977. Today, the city's economy depends heavily on oil and the taxes the oil company pays out.

Fishing and tourism also contribute to the economy, but oil has clearly made Valdez a rich city. Major projects completed in the early 1980s include a $50-million container terminal to enhance the city's reputation as the 'Gateway to the North' and the $7-million Civic Center. With oil money, the Chugach Mountains as a beautiful backdrop, and an ideal location in the middle of the Prince William Sound playground, Valdez and its 3700 residents seemed to have all a city could want.

However, a price was paid for the city's involvement in the oil industry when the *Exxon Valdez* rammed a reef and spilt 11 million gallons of oil into Prince William Sound in 1989. It was the worst oil spill in US history, and Valdez became the center of an environmental storm. Exxon directed the oil clean-up from Valdez during the first summer after the spill and created a money rush that hadn't been seen since the pipeline was built.

Thousands of people flocked to Valdez from all over the country in search of clean-up jobs that paid $15 an hour. Within a month, the oil company had created an army of 9000 workers, many of whom spent their days at the oil-soaked beaches on Prince William Sound but their nights in Valdez whose population jumped from 3000 to 12,000. Like during the pipeline construction, available lodging became nonexistent and prices in restaurants and supermarkets skyrocketed. Despite a caravan park set up near the airport, people spent the summer living out of tents or in the back of pick-up trucks.

Amazingly, the tourists still arrived that summer, many eager to witness the mishap. After the summer of 1989, Exxon shifted its operation and workers to Seward, Homer and Kodiak to concentrate on the shoreline that experienced the worst oil damage. Today in Valdez, a town where 30% of the population is employed in pipeline-related work, the only memorial to one of the worst oil spills in the country is a small exhibit in the museum.

Information

The Valdez Visitor Center (☎ 835-2984) is on the corner of Chenega Ave and Fairbanks Dr, diagonally opposite the library and is open daily from 8 am to 8 pm in the summer. Along with the usual hand-outs and city maps, the center shows films on the pipeline and the 1964 earthquake daily during the summer. Admission to the films costs $2.50.

Things to See

Valdez's bustling **Small Boat Harbor** is south of North Harbor Dr and features a long boardwalk with benches and ramps down to the various docks. With an impressive set of peaks in the background, the harbor is an excellent place to hang out in the evening, especially during July when you can watch lucky anglers weighing in 200 or 300-pound halibut right on the docks. From the west end of the harbor it is a short walk past the US Coast Guard Station to **Point of View Park**. The observation platform on the knoll is a good spot to view the old town site to the east, the pipeline terminal to the south and Valdez Narrows to the west. Nearby on the corner of Fidalgo Dr and Hazelet Ave is the **Civic Center** with more picnic tables and panoramas of the area.

From the Civic Center, head two blocks north on Robe River Dr and turn right (east) on Egan Dr to the **Valdez Museum** (☎ 835-2764) in the Centennial Building. The museum is packed with displays that include a model of the Trans-Alaska Pipeline, a 19th-century saloon bar, an exhibit on glaciers that usually includes a cooler full of ice from the Columbia Glacier and a photo display on Valdez (the snow capital of Alaska – in 1989 the town received a record 46.7 feet of the stuff). Right across from each other are two exhibits connected with the town's most important dates in history (the 1964 earthquake and Exxon oil spill) including a piece of the ship's hull that was salvaged. In the summer, the museum is open daily from 8 am to 7 pm; a donation of $2 is requested but admission is free on Saturday.

Diagonally opposite the museum is the **Valdez Library** which, among other things, runs a book and magazine swap for travelers on its lower floor. The library is open Monday to Thursday from 10 am to 8 pm, and on Friday and Saturday from 10 am to 6.30 pm. To reach **Prince William Sound Community College**, follow Chenega Ave north from the museum and turn right (east) on Pioneer Dr. The small campus, a division of the University of Alaska, has three huge wooden carvings that are part of Peter Toth's collection of 50 sculptures dedicated to the Native Americans.

Pioneer Dr runs east into Richardson Hwy, and half a mile to the north is the **Salmon Spawning View Point** on Crooked Creek. The wooden platform, the site of the old hatchery, is a good spot to watch salmon spawn in July and August.

Festivals
Valdez has both a Fourth of July celebration and an end-of-summer festival called Gold Rush Days. The five-day festival takes place in mid-August and includes a parade, bed races, dances, a free fish feed and a portable jailhouse that is pulled throughout town by locals who go about arresting people without beards and other innocent bystanders.

Places to Stay
Camping Valdez, the city of wealth and beauty, desperately lacks cheap accommodations for backpackers and a good public campground. Within town, there is *South Harbor Drive Campground*, a gravel area on the southside of the Small Boat Harbor. This is, for the most part, a facility for the seasonal cannery workers with tent pads and vault toilets. It's maintained by the Valdez Parks & Recreation Department (☎ 835-2531) and the nightly fee is $5. Out of town, is the *Valdez Glacier Campground* (101 sites) almost six miles from town past the airport on Airport Rd. There is a fee of $7 a night for a site in an area that tends to attract the local teenagers. Valdez Glacier Campground isn't too bad, at least you get a private wooded site, but both places lack the charm of the state campgrounds you've been passing along the highway all day.

A better deal are the private campgrounds in town. Downtown Valdez is full of RV campgrounds, you'll be amazed how they pack them in around the harbor. Two of the commercial campgrounds, however, also cater to those who arrive with a tent. *Bear Paw RV Campground* (☎ 835-2530), just off the Small Boat Harbor, has sites for $12 a night in a special wooded area just for tents. It's a small knob above the City Dock and includes its own shower and laundry building. *Eagle Rest RV Park* (☎ 835-2373), on the corner of Pioneer Dr and the Richardson Hwy, also has tent sites for $12 a night that includes showers and a laundry room.

In recent years, Valdez has begun to restrict unauthorized camping within the city, especially on the hill overlooking the waterfront across Chitna St. The best place for an unauthorized camp site is to hike a mile up Mineral Creek Rd.

B&Bs There are almost 20 B&Bs in and around town charging around $55/65 a single/double. They change often but the Visitor Center has a speed-dial phone outside with a bulletin board listing all the current B&Bs and their rates. Just pick a home and push a button. Or try *Mineral Creek Bed & Breakfast* (☎ 835-4205), a cedar log cabin with a sauna, and mountain bikes to ride back into town. There's also the *Lake House* (☎ 835-4752), away from town and near an alpine lake, with rooms for $60/70 a single/double.

Hotels Rates in the city's six motel/hotels range from $80 a night for singles in the *Valdez Motel* (☎ 835-4444), at 112 Egan Dr, to $120 at the top-of-the-range *Westmarks*. The best deal is *Downtown Inn* (☎ 835-2791 or (800) 478-2791 in Alaska only) which calls itself a B&B but in reality is a more of a hotel with 25 rooms. The inn is at 113 Galena Dr, near the post office, and has some rooms with shared bathrooms that begin at $65 a double. You also get a filling breakfast in the morning and there is a coin-operated washer and drier that are half the price of the local laundromat. Keep in mind rooms are not easy to obtain for anybody who has just stepped off the ferry. Call ahead if you can.

Places to Eat

What used to be a Tastee Freez is now *Oscar's* and definitely a step up. On North Harbor Dr across from the Small Boat Harbor, the restaurant has eggs-toast-potatoes for $5, hamburgers for $4 and, perhaps its best deal, home-made chowder served in a sourdough bread bowl for $3.75. More local seafood can be enjoyed at *Mac-Murray's Alaska Halibut House*, on the corner of Meals Ave and Fairbanks Dr across from Village Inn, the closest thing Valdez has to a fast-food place. The restaurant has a salad bar and serves a fish and chip basket of halibut for $5.75 or catch-of-the-day (take your chances as to what they caught that day) for $3.90.

A little classier than the local hamburger joint is *Mike's Palace* on North Harbor Dr. The place specializes in pasta and local seafood, especially halibut, and dinners cost from $9 to $15, but you can pick up a small pizza that will easily feed two or three people for under $10. A short walk from the Small Boat Harbor is *Fu Kung* at 207 Kobuk St. The Chinese restaurant is in an old military hut but you wouldn't know it from the inside and the food is excellent. Dinners run from $8 to $13 but come before 2.30 pm and get a better deal with their lunch special: main dish, soup, fried rice and egg roll for $6.75. *Totem Inn* (☎ 835-4443), on the corner of Kobuk and Chitna drives, runs a salmon bake if you haven't had your fill of them yet.

Eagle's, on the corner of Pioneer Dr and Meals Ave, has the cheapest supermarket prices in town along with a salad-hot soup-and-taco bar, where $5 will get you a taco salad that will keep you filled until morning. They also serve breakfast in take-away trays from 6 to 10 am and for under $3 (unheard of almost anywhere else in Alaska) you can get your eggs, toast and hash browns.

Entertainment

Among the places you may want to try are *Sugarloaf Saloon* at the Village Inn, on the corner of Meals Ave and Richardson Hwy, for something classier or the *Harbor Club Bar* next door to Mike's Place if you want to hang out with fishermen.

There are usually numerous activities, including traveling theater groups, that perform at the Civic Center (☎ 835- 4440) during the summer. The Prince William Sound Community College also runs a live theater that taps into the tourism season and sells its tickets at the Visitor Center (☎ 835-2984).

Hiking

In an area surrounded by mountains and glaciers, you would think that there is good hiking around Valdez, but this is not the case. There are few developed trails in the area (though many are now being proposed), so reaching much of the surrounding alpine country requires considerable hacking through thick bush. There is no US Forest Service office in Valdez and no nearby cabins.

Mineral Creek Trail The best walk away from town is the old road along Mineral Creek and the one-mile trail from its end to the old Smith Stamping Mill. The road can be in poor condition at times but most cars can usually manage it without bottoming out too many times.

To reach the trailhead, follow Hazelet Ave north 10 blocks from Egan Dr to Hanagita St and turn left (west); then turn right (north) onto Mineral Creek Rd. The road bumps along for 5.5 miles and then turns into a mile-long trail to the old stamping mill. Following the trail beyond the mill at Brevier Creek also requires considerable bush hacking. If you are hiking the entire road, the trip up the lush green canyon can be a pleasant 13-mile adventure that requires five to six hours.

Solomon Gulch Trail A newer trail is located across from the Solomon Gulch Fish Hatchery on Dayville Rd, off the Richardson Hwy. This 1.3-mile trail is a steep, uphill hike that quickly leads to splendid views of the

Valdez Port and the city below. It ends at Solomon Lake, the source of 80% of Valdez's power.

Goat Trail

The oldest trail in the area is Goat Trail, which originally was an indigenous route and then was discovered by Captain Abercrombie in his search of safe passage to the interior. Today you can pick up the posted trailhead at *Mile 13.5* of the Richardson Hwy, just past Horseshoe Falls in Keystone Canyon. The trail twists and turns for five miles as it follows the Lowe River until it stops at the original bridge over Bear Creek.

Rafting & Kayaking

Lowe River This glacial river cuts through the impressive Keystone Canyon and is a few miles outside Valdez. Lowe River has become a popular float trip during the summer. Keystone Adventures (☎ 835-2606 or (800) 328-8460) offers day trips on the river, carrying passengers six miles through white water and past the cascading waterfalls that have made the canyon famous. The guide company runs the 1½-hour trip five times daily (beginning at 10 am and ending with a run at 6 pm) and charges $30 per person for the scenic adventure.

Shoup Bay This bay off Valdez Arm is the location of a retreating tidewater glacier of the same name and is the destination of a popular overnight trip by kayak. The glacier features two tidal basins and is a well-protected area of icebergs, with harbor seals and other sea life. It's about 10 miles to the bay and another four miles up to the glacier but take a tide book. You must enter the bay two hours before the incoming tide to avoid swift tidal currents. Anadyr Adventures (☎ 835-2814), sets up shop and rents kayaks off North Harbor Dr across from the Small Boat Harbor where you can launch from. Singles are $45 a day, doubles $65 and there is a discount if you rent for more than two days. They also run a day trip to the glacier that begins with a drop-off at the bay. The cost is $135 per person.

Columbia Glacier

This is the largest tidewater glacier in Prince William Sound and a spectacular spot to spend a few days kayaking among the crackling ice and watching seals and other wildlife. To paddle the open water from Valdez Arm to the glacier is for experienced paddlers only. All others arrange a drop-off and pick-up with one of the many tour boats that run cruises to the glacier such as Stan Stephens Cruises (☎ 835-4731 or (800) 992-1297). Many kayakers paddle Heather Bay to view the ice and camp on Heather Island. Rent a boat from Anadyr Adventures (☎ 835-2814) which also offers day trips to the glacier for $162 per person or overnight paddles for $238, for a minimum of four people.

Getting There & Away

Air Alaska Airlines, through its contract carrier ERA Aviation (☎ 835-2636), provides three flights from Monday to Friday and two on Saturday and Sunday between Valdez and Anchorage from the Valdez Airport, five miles from town on Airport Rd. The one-way fare is $80. MarkAir (☎ 835-5147) also services Valdez.

Bus Gray Line's Alaskon Express buses (☎ 835-2357), operating out of the Westmark Hotel, departs Valdez at 8 am Tuesday, Thursday, Friday and Sunday and reaches Anchorage at 6 pm that night. One-way fare is $89. You can also get off at Glennallen and pick up a connecting Gray Line bus to just about anywhere in the state, including Fairbanks for $137.

Backcountry Connection (☎ 822-5292 or (800) 478-5292 in Alaska only) also provides transportation out of town and departs from the Visitor Center. The van departs at noon Monday and Friday and reaches Glennallen at 3 pm or makes a connection to put you in McCarthy at 5.30 pm. One-way fare to Glennallen is $40 and to McCarthy $72. You can also check into Caribou Express (☎ 278-5776 in Anchorage) which departs Valdez at 3.20 pm on Wednesday, Friday and Sunday for a return trip to Anchorage, reaching the city at 10.35 pm.

One-way fare is $75. Call for pick-up locations as this company moves around a lot.

Boat Taking the Alaska State Marine Ferry is by the far the cheapest way to view the Columbia Glacier and generally you can get almost as close to the thick ice pack as you would with most private tours. There is also a US Forest Service naturalist on board pointing out sea otters, seals and sea lions and giving programs during the trip on the natural history of glaciers. Just keep in mind that private tours spend a great deal more time at the ice pack and observing wildlife – the state ferry, on the other hand, has a schedule to keep.

The one-way Valdez to Whittier fare is $56. The state ferry also connects Valdez to Cordova ($28), Seward ($56), Homer ($136) and Kodiak ($96), since both the MV *Bartlett* and MV *Tustumena* call at Valdez. Between the two ships there are runs to Whittier four times a week, three weekly sailings to Cordova and a weekly run to Seward, Homer and Kodiak. The ferry terminal (☎ 835-4436) in Valdez is at the southern end of Hazelet Ave and reservations for these popular runs are strongly recommended. If you don't have a confirmed space for you and your car, you can try your luck on standby. For the 7.15 am run to Whittier, the ferry terminal opens at 4.30 am and it's best to get there as early as you can to be at the front of the line of stand-by vehicles. Normally there is enough extra space for two or three cars.

Bicycle There is an excellent paved bike path that begins downtown near and extends several miles out along Richardson Hwy. Eagle Rest Campground (☎ 835-2373) has single-speed bicycles available for rent.

AROUND VALDEZ

The **oil pipeline terminal**, the heart and soul of Valdez, lies across the bay on Dayville Rd, eight miles from town along Richardson Hwy. Dayville Rd is interesting as it branches off the highway and hugs the mountainside passing several eagle nests and the scenic **Solomon Gulch**.

The **Copper Valley Hydro Project** which supplies power for both Valdez and Glennallen has been completed at Solomon Gulch. Across the road is the **Solomon Gulch Hatchery**, which has a self-guided interpretive walk open to visitors from 8 am to 5 pm daily. Admission is $1. Dayville Rd ends at the terminal's visitor center and a bronze monument dedicated to the construction workers who built the pipeline.

The terminal is nothing short of remarkable as it contains over 15 miles of pipeline, 18 oil-storage tanks and four tanker berths. Oil is pumped out of Prudhoe Bay on the Beaufort Sea in northern Alaska and travels 800 miles south through the pipeline to the terminal, where it is either stored or loaded into tankers. It is estimated that there are 9.6 billion barrels of oil under the North Slope and 1.7 million barrels flow out of the pipeline into tankers every day at the terminal.

Displays at the visitor center explain all this, and for many it's enough to stare at the facility from the entrance gate and then head back. If you want a closer look, Alyeska runs a free two-hour tour that departs from the visitors center at the airport several times daily. The tours are very popular with the RV crowd so bookings (☎ 835-2686) are recommended. You begin with a movie and then board a 25-seat bus for the trip to the terminal. Along the way you pass through a security check that's tougher than what you experience at most airports and you only step off the bus twice. Despite being total PR for big oil companies, the tour is interesting and unless you're a founding member of Greenpeace, you can't help but be a little impressed with all the security measures and safeguards they carefully follow here, especially in the wake of the *Exxon Valdez* oil spill.

COLUMBIA GLACIER

Columbia Glacier is the second largest tidewater glacier in North America and spills 40 miles out of the Chugach Mountains and ends with a three-mile-wide face.

Most travelers view this magnificent tidewater glacier while crossing Prince William

Sound to or from Valdez. The MV *Bartlett* is the only State Marine ferry that passes a tidewater glacier and provides the cheapest way to sail between Whittier and Valdez. Because the glacier has been rapidly retreating for almost 10 years, it's difficult for any boat to get close to the face and subsequently there is now little difference between the state ferry and the other cruise ships as far as the distance they travel up the bay. It's just too clogged with ice.

Privately-run cruise ships do spend considerably more time at the ice pack, threading their way through the icebergs, where you can often observe seals basking under the sun. At best the MV *Bartlett* turns up the bay and slows down but keeps chugging along and for many people, that's all the glacial fix they need. Regardless of whether you are close to the 300-foot face or not, this sea of ice with the Columbia Glacier filling up the background is still an awesome sight and a photographer's delight.

Stan Stephens Charters (☎ 835-4731 or (800) 922-1297) operates three boats and offers daily cruises throughout the summer. A five-hour tour departs at 7 am and costs $61 per person. An eight-hour lunch cruise departs at 9.30 am and a similar dinner cruise departs at 1.30 pm. Both cost $87 per person. Stop at Bear Paw RV Park to purchase tickets or make reservations.

Also check with Glacier Charter Service (☎ 835-5141) which runs the *Lu-Lu Belle* and maintains an office on Kobuk Dr behind Totem Inn. The boat departs at 2 pm daily and during the height of the tourist season adds an 8 am cruise as well. The boat features a full bar and the cost of the five-hour cruise is $55 per person. Gray Line (☎ 835-2357), operating out of the Westmark Hotel, offers a $69 cruise which includes a champagne lunch or a round-trip to Whittier, past the Columbia twice, for $85.

The Columbia Glacier being the kind of tourist attraction that it is, you'd expect several other tour boats to be competing for your money pouch. They are. Smaller operators come and go but it might pay to shop around by walking the docks of the Small

Boat Harbor one night or carefully checking brochures at the Visitor Center.

RICHARDSON HIGHWAY TO GLENNALLEN

The section of the Richardson Hwy from Valdez to Glennallen is an incredibly scenic route that includes canyons, mountain passes, glaciers and access to the massive Wrangell-St Elias National Park. Hitchhiking is fairly easy during the summer, making it convenient to stop often and enjoy the sights and campgrounds along the way.

The highway begins in the center of Valdez, but *Mile 0* is near the site of old Valdez, as the mileposts were erected before the Good Friday Earthquake and were never changed. The junction with Dayville Rd, which leads to the pipeline terminal, is 6.9 miles from town, and at this point Richardson Hwy swings north.

At *Mile 13* you reach **Keystone Canyon** with its many waterfalls and unusual rock formations high above the road. In the next mile, two magnificent waterfalls appear, first the Horsetail and then the Bridal Veil half a mile down the highway. The canyon wall is so sheer that the waterfalls appear to be cascading straight down and actually spray the road with mist.

At *Mile 14.8* of Richardson Hwy, the northern end of the canyon, there is an abandoned hand-drilled tunnel that residents of Valdez began but never finished when they were competing with Cordova for the railroad to the Kennecott mines. A historical marker briefly describes how nine companies fought to develop the short route from the coast to Kennecott copper mines, leading to the 'shootout in Keystone Canyon'.

The **Trans-Alaska Pipeline** can be seen at *Mile 20.4*. The short loop road to the first camping area, *Blueberry Lake State Recreation Site*, is at *Mile 24* of Richardson Hwy. The recreational area offers 10 sites and four covered picnic shelters in a beautiful alpine setting with lofty peaks surrounding it. Often during the summer all the sites will be taken by RVers but it's easy for backpackers to find a spot to pitch their tent near the trails.

There's good fishing in the nearby lakes for rainbow trout. In Summit Lake these fish can reach 18 inches long and are usually caught with flies, small spinners or salmon eggs. There is no camping fee here but beware if you are spending the night because you are above the tree line and the weather can be windy and foul at times.

The highway continues to ascend until it reaches **Thompson Pass** at *Mile 26*. There are several scenic turn-offs near the pass (elevation 2771 feet) which in early summer is covered in wildflowers. This spot also holds most of Alaska's snowfall records, including 62 inches of snow in a 24-hour period in December 1955. That's the reason for the L-shaped poles along the highway. The snow is so deep here in the winter, snowplows need the poles to guide them over the pass.

At *Mile 28.6* of Richardson Hwy is the turn-off to the **Worthington Glacier State Recreation Area**, where it is possible to drive to the glacier's face on a short access road. Within this state recreation area are outhouses, picnic tables and a large covered viewing area.

Mile-long Worthington Glacier View Trail begins at the parking lot and follows the crest of the moraine. It's a scenic hike that follows the edge of the glacier, and the walk should be done with caution. Never hike on the glacier itself. Thompson Pass and the surrounding area above the tree line are ideal for tramping, as hikers will have few problems climbing through the heather.

The pipeline continues to pop into view as you travel north on Richardson Hwy and at one point it passes beneath the road. The next campground, the *Little Tonsina River State Recreation Site* (10 sites, $6 per night), appears at *Mile 65*. None of the sites is on the Little Tonsina River but a path leads down to the water where anglers will find fishing for Dolly Varden good most of the summer. The *Squirrel Creek State Campground* (14 sites, $6 per night) is at *Mile 79.4* of Richardson Hwy and offers a scenic little camping area on the banks of the creek. There are fishing opportunities for grayling and rainbow trout

in Squirrel Creek, the reason, no doubt, why the campground is often filled. Nearby is a roadhouse for meals, while across the street is a small gas station and supplies.

The Edgerton Hwy junction that leads to the heart of the Wrangell-St Elias National Park is three miles past the campground while a lookout over **Willow Lake** is at *Mile 87.6*. The lake can be stunning on a clear day with the water reflecting the Wrangell Mountains, the 100-mile chain that includes 11 peaks over 10,000 feet. The two most prominent peaks visible from the lookout are Mt Drum, 28 miles to the north-east, and Mt Wrangell, Alaska's largest active volcano, to the east. Mt Wrangell is 14,163 feet high and on some days a plume of steam is visible from its crater.

The Richardson Hwy now bypasses **Copper Center** (population 449) which used to be at *Mile 101*. You now have to make a special effort to see the small village but you shouldn't hesitate. This town is a classic, especially compared with that dusty trailer park known as Glennallen to the north.

At the turn of the century, Cooper Center was an important mining camp for the thousands of prospectors eyeing the gold fields in the Yukon and later in Fairbanks. Near the bridge over the Klutina River is the *Copper Center Lodge* (☎ 822-3245), which began in 1897 as the Blix Roadhouse and was the first lodge built north of Valdez. The lodge still serves as a roadhouse today. You can get a delicious plate of sourdough pancakes, reputedly made from century-old starter. The dining room is open from 7 am to 9 pm; rooms range from $55 to $65.

Next door is the **George Ashby Museum**, open from 1 to 5 pm Monday to Friday and Friday evening from 7 and 9 pm, no admission fee. Inside the log cabin are mining artefacts from the Kennecott mines as well as the record moose rack for Alaska. It's hanging over the door and, with a spread of almost 70 inches, you pray it doesn't fall when you leave. Also check out the Copper Center City Hall, it's good for a laugh.

Copper Center has gas; a store for supplies; a post office and the *Silver Fox Drive*

Inn, an old bus that serves everything from hamburgers to tacos for under $5. Before you return to Richardson Hwy, you pass the **Wrangell-St Elias National Park Visitor Center**. During the summer the center is open to 6 pm daily and is the place to go for topo maps, trip suggestions and to leave your backpacking itinerary. Even if you don't plan to enter the park's backcountry, the center has a few displays and a small viewing area where they show videos on the area.

Just north of the town on Richardson Hwy is the **Chapel on the Hill**, built in 1942. During the summer, the log chapel features a short slide presentation on the history of the Copper River Basin area; admission is free.

At *Mile 115* is the major junction between the Glenn and Richardson highways. The Richardson Hwy continues north to Delta Junction and eventually Fairbanks (see the Interior chapter). The Glenn Hwy (see the Interior chapter) heads west to Glennallen, a short distance away, and onto Anchorage.

WRANGELL-ST ELIAS NATIONAL PARK

This national park, created in 1980, stretches north 170 miles from the Gulf of Alaska. It encompasses 13.2 million acres of mountains, foothills and river valleys bounded by the Copper River on the west and Canada's Kluane National Park to the east. Together, Kluane and Wrangell-St Elias national parks make up almost 20 million acres and the greatest expanse of valleys, canyons and towering mountains in North America, including the continent's second and third highest peaks.

This area is a crossroads of mountain ranges. To the north are the Wrangell Mountains; to the south, the Chugachs; and thrusting from the Gulf of Alaska and clashing with the Wrangells are the St Elias Mountains. There are so many mountains and so many summits in this rugged land that, as the park brochure says, 'you quickly abandon the urge to learn their names'.

Spilling out from the peaks are extensive icefields and over 100 major glaciers – some of the largest and most active in the world. The Bagley Icefield near the coast is the largest subpolar mass of ice in North America. The Malaspina Glacier, which spills out of the St Elias Range between Ice Bay and Yakutat Bay, is larger than the state of Rhode Island.

Wildlife in Wrangell-St Elias National Park is more diverse and plentiful than in any other Alaska park. Species in the preserve include moose, black and brown bears, dall sheep, mountain goats, wolves, wolverines, beavers, and three of Alaska's 11 caribou herds live there.

The Richardson Hwy borders the northwest corner of the park and two rough dirt roads lead into its interior. The most popular access road by far is the McCarthy Rd with the historic mining towns of McCarthy and Kennicott, serving as something of a visitor's area into the park. Whereas in the early 1980s a few hundred people would venture across the Kennicott River into McCarthy, today that many will show up on a good weekend and in 1993 both towns attracted more than 20,000 visitors.

Despite the rebirth of McCarthy, Wrangell-St Elias is still a true wilderness park with few visitor facilities or services beyond the highway. An adventure into this preserve requires time and patience rather than money, but it can lead to a once-in-a-lifetime experience.

Information

The park's main headquarters (☎ 822-5235) is at *Mile 105* of Richardson Hwy, 10 miles before the junction with the Glenn Hwy. The office is open from 8 am to 6 pm daily during the summer and rangers can answer questions about the park as well as supply various hand-outs and rough maps of the area. During the summer, rangers are stationed in a log cabin visitor center in Chitina (☎ 823-2205), at the end of Edgerton Hwy. There is also a ranger stationed in Nabesna but in 1992, the ranger station 'mysteriously' caught on fire and burnt down, an indication of the strong sentiments of locals against the National Park Service and the rules the federal agency uses in an effort to preserve the land.

Kennicott

In 1900, a pair of sourdough miners named Jack Smith and Clarence Warner stumbled up the east side of the Kennicott Glacier until they arrived at a creek and found traces of copper. They named the creek Bonanza and was it ever – the entire mountainside turned out to hold some of the richest copper ever uncovered. In the Lower 48, mines were operating on ore that contained only two percent copper. Here the veins would average almost 13% and some as high as 70%.

Eventually, a group of East Coast investors bought the existing stakes and formed the Kennecott Copper Corporation, named after a clerical worker misspelt 'Kennicott'. First the syndicate built their railroad, 196 miles of rails through the wilderness, including the leg that is now the McCarthy Rd and Cordova's famous 'Million Dollar Bridge'. The line cost $23 million before it even reached the mines in 1911.

Then they built the company town of Kennicott, a sprawling red-painted complex that included offices, the crushing mills, bunkhouses for the workers, company stores, a theater, wooden tennis courts and a school, all perched on a side of a mountain above the Kennicott Glacier. From 1911 until 1938, the mines operated 24 hours a day, produced 591,000 tons of copper and reported a net profit of more than $100 million.

Then in November 1938 faced with falling world prices for copper; an uncertainty of how long the veins would play out; and, most of all, a possible labor strike; the company managers decided to close the operation. They made the decision one night and then the next morning told the workers the mine was shut down and that they could stay or leave but that in two hours the last train out of Kennicott was leaving. The disgruntled miners left in what has to be one of the greatest exoduses from a town in the USA.

With the exception of two large diesel engines, everything was left behind and Kennicott was this perfectly preserved slice of US mining history. Unfortunately, when the railroad bed was converted to a road in the 1960s, Kennicott also became the biggest help-yourself hardware store in the country. Locals were taking windows, doors and wiring; tourists were picking the town clean of tools, spikes anything they could haul away as a souvenir.

Despite the pillage, Kennicott is still an amazing sight for most travelers. The mill where the ore was crushed and the copper concentrated, towers above the surrounding buildings and still has tram cables leading up to the mountain mines. The rest of the buildings, including bunkhouses, train depot, worker's cottages and power plant, sit perched above the Kennicott Glacier with peaks around.

Keep in mind that most, if not all, the buildings are privately owned and it is illegal to enter them. Eventually several of the larger ones, the mill and power plant among others, will probably be acquired and renovated by the NPS but that will take years. Until then, you have to be content with strolling through the center of town and admiring the mining history by peeping through the windows.

You can reach Kennicott from McCarthy by either walking the railroad grade, now the main road, or hiking up the Old Wagon Rd. The Wagon Rd is more of a trail for hiking or mountain bikes and is picked up from the main road at a junction marked with a 'To Glacier' sign. Either way it's a five-mile trek up. Keep in mind there is also van service in McCarthy and it's always possible to hitch a ride up as during the summer there is a trickle of traffic between the two towns.

McCarthy

With the exception of a lodge in Kennicott, all services are located in the mountainous hamlet of McCarthy, a scenic and funky little town. Year-round population ranges from eight to 12 people depending on who is sticking out the winter but during the summer it swells to around 100. Once you've crossed the Kennicott River on the tram, follow the road to the McCarthy River that now can be crossed on a footbridge. On the other side the road leads a half-mile to the **McCarthy & Kennicott Museum**, an old railroad depot that features old photographs and a few mining artefacts dating back to the mining days, along with a small coffee shop that serves giant muffins in the morning. From the museum take the right fork into the town of McCarthy, the left fork is the main road to Kennicott.

Kennicott was a company town, self-contained and serious. McCarthy, on the other hand, was created in the early 1900s for the miners as a place of 'wine, women and song'. In other words, it had several saloons, restaurants and a red light district in its heyday when it had several hundred residents, its own newspaper and school. Today both O'Neill's Hardware Store and MotherLode Power House (the site of St Elias Alpine Guides) had been listed on the National Register of Historical Places.

Places to Stay & Eat

The cheapest of accommodations is to camp along the west side of the Kennicott River before crossing over on the tram. There are vault toilets but not piped-in water. On the weekends it can get crowded and dusty here.

It hard to camp around either McCarthy or Kennicott due to private ownership of most of the land. Accommodations in McCarthy change almost seasonally so it pays to walk around to see if anybody is renting out a cabin or has started up a B&B. For an affordable bunk, stop at the *McCarthy Country Store* which has four bunks in a cabin out the back for $20 a night.

Just down the street is the *McCarthy Lodge* (☎ 333-5402), full of mining relics and photographs of the era, and the place to get a bed, meal, shower or a cold beer in a frosty mug. The main lodge has a dining room where full dinners cost $17 and a lively bar with $3.75 beers. A lot for a beer maybe, but, hey, they're cold! Showers are $5 so skip the shower and have a beer. Across the street the lodge runs *Ma Johnson's Hotel*, built in 1916 as a boarding house and today totally renovated with rooms beginning at $95 a night.

In Kennicott there is *Kennicott Glacier Lodge* (for advance reservation call (800) 582-5128 outside Alaska and (800) 478-2350 within the state) which offers beds, running water and electricity starting at $119 but most rooms are $129. They also have a dining room and for $210 you can get bed, meals and a guided walk of the mines. Even if you don't stay here, hike up in the morning and have breakfast on the long front porch. The meal is $9 but includes eggs, sourdough pancakes and sausage along with pitchers of juice and coffee, all enjoyed with a spectacular view of peaks and glaciers.

Hiking

Root Glacier From Kennicott, it's a 2.5-mile round trip past the mine ruins to Root Glacier, a sparkling white and blue floe of ice. Hike west of the town and continue west past an unmarked junction to the mines, reached in less than a quarter mile. Along the way you cross Jumbo Creek, where you will find a plank upstream for an easy ford in normal water conditions. Many people will climb the glacier upon reaching it but extreme caution should be used if you are inexperienced and lack the proper equipment (crampons, ice axe) for walking on ice.

Bonanza Mine Trail One of the best hikes from Kennicott is the alpine trek to Bonanza Mine. It's a round trip of almost seven miles to the mine and a steep uphill walk all the way. Plan on three to four hours to hike up if the weather is good and half that time to get back down. The trail is actually a rough dirt road to the tree line and is picked up just west of town at a junction that makes a sharp 180° turn up the mountain. Once above the tree line, a three-hour climb for most people, the view is stunning and you can clearly see the mountain valley where the mine still sits on the slope. To reach the mine, you have to scramble up a scree slope to the remaining bunkhouse, and shafts and tram platform.

There is water once you reach the top but carry at least a quart if the day is hot. For those who want to skip the long haul up but still enjoy the alpine portion of the hike, check at the Kennicott Lodge to see if anybody is driving hikers up. Normally a local will run you up to the tree line for $15 one-way or $20 round-trip. From there it's still a good 90-minute trek to the mine.

Rafting

Kennicott River Beginning near the glacier itself, rafting companies float the Kennicott River on half-day trips that features Class III white water. Copper Oar (☎ 522-1670 in Glennallen) maintains a small office on the west side of the river near the tram platform. The company offers a two-hour run down the Kennicott for $40 per person.

Nizina River For a full-day float, rafting companies combine the Kennicott with the Nizina and a portion of the Chitina River and then return you to McCarthy via a bush plane for a view of the mountains from above. The highpoint of the day is the run through the vertical-walled Nizina River Canyon. St Elias Alpine Guides in the MotherLode Power House has a full-day Three-Rivers trip for $195; Copper Oak prices theirs at $175.

Getting There & Away

Bus Hitching McCarthy Rd is not nearly as challenging as it was 10 years ago but it still can be a long wait at times. The alternative is Backcountry Connection (☎ 822-5292). The small tour company departs Caribou Motel on Glenn Hwy in Glennallen at 1.15 pm on Monday and Wednesday, 8 am on

Thursday, Friday and Sunday and 10.45 am on Saturday for the five-hour trip to McCarthy. It stays at McCarthy for a couple of hours and then returns that evening. One-way fare is $55. On Friday, they will also run a van that departs at 2 pm from McCarthy to Valdez. One-way fare for this trip is $72.

Once you're in McCarthy, you can pick up a ride to Kennicott from either McCarthy Air or Wrangell Mountain Air which maintain log cabin offices in town. Both run vans up to the company town for $4 per person.

Car Edgerton Hwy and McCarthy Rd combine to provide a 92-mile route into the heart of Wrangell-St Elias National Park, ending at the tram across the Kennicott River to McCarthy.

The 32-mile Edgerton Hwy, fully paved, begins at *Mile 82.6* of Richardson Hwy and ends at Chitina. The town, which has 40 or so permanent residents, is the last place to purchase gas and to get a reasonably priced meal (that's 'reasonably' by Alaskan standards). Backpackers can camp along the three-mile road south to O'Brien Creek or beside Town Lake within Chitina. The best spot, however, is to stop 10 miles before you reach Chitina at *Liberty Falls State Recreation Site*. The campground has only three, maybe four, sites for RVs but there are another half-dozen spots for tents, including four tent platforms right along rushing Liberty Creek. There is no piped-in water here but there is thundering Liberty Falls within the campground. Best of all the facility is free.

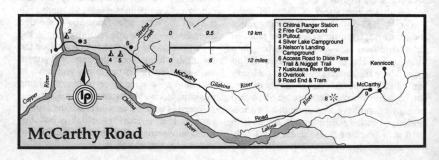

1 Chitina Ranger Station
2 Free Campground
3 Pullout
4 Silver Lake Campground
5 Nelson's Landing Campground
6 Access Road to Dixie Pass Trail & Nugget Trail
7 Kuskulana River Bridge
8 Overlook
9 Road End & Tram

McCarthy Road

There is also a small campground with eight free sites next to the Copper River Bridge that is maintained by the Alaska Department of Transportation and used primarily by dipnetters who descend on Chitina in July and August to scoop up reds and king salmon. Within Chitina there is a NPS ranger station, open from 8 am to 5 pm daily during the summer, and Spirit Mountain Artworks, a delightful gallery that also plugs flats for $7 a tire or patches them for $12. Art Koeninger loves his art but he undoubtedly makes a living repairing tires the McCarthy Rd chews up.

There is also a grocery store, post office and two restaurants in town. Try *Chitina Cafe*, a good place to stop before the long drive out to McCarthy. The interior has – what else – miner's décor. Prices range from $5 to $10 for breakfast and $7 for a hamburger. Try the home-made biscuits and gravy for $5, guaranteed to keep you fueled until you've pulled the tram to McCarthy.

From Chitina, McCarthy Rd – a rough dirt road that is not regularly maintained – follows the abandoned Copper River & Northwest Railroad bed that was used to transport copper from the mines to the coast at Cordova. It leads 60 miles or so further east to the Kennicott River. Your $29-a-day rental car can usually travel this stretch during the summer, but plan on three to four hours for the trip and if it's been raining hard don't plan it at all.

The road starts two miles west of Chitina and the first few miles offer spectacular views of the Chugach Mountains, the east-west range that separates the Chitina Valley lowlands for the Gulf of Alaska with peaks averaging 7000 to 8000 feet in height. You'll also cross the mighty Copper River where it possible to see a dozen fish wheels or, if your timing is right, hordes of dipnetters. Just before *Mile 9* there is a pullout on the north side of the road that provides access to the half-mile trail to Strelna Lake. The lake is stocked with rainbow trout and silver salmon that anglers entice during the summer with salmon eggs.

Two commercial campgrounds with very limited services, gas not being one of them, are quickly passed and then at *Mile 13.5* you come to the access road to the trailheads for the Dixie Pass, Nugget and Kotsina trails (see the Hiking section in the Wilderness chapter), across from the Strelna Airstrip. For an interesting night or a unique perspective on the NPS, head up the access road a couple of miles and book a bed at the *Strelna Zephyr Bunkhouse*. Sandy Casteler and her family run the quaint log cabin accommodations and inside you'll find four bunks, a wood-burning stove but no running water or electricity – they don't have it, why should you? Bunks are $25 a night.

At *Mile 17* of McCarthy Rd is the Kuskulana River Bridge. This historic railroad bridge was built in 1910 with a 525-foot span across an impressive gorge that rises 238 feet above the river. From the time the road was opened to cars in the 1960s until the 1980s, this narrow, three-span railroad bridge was known as 'the biggest thrill on the road to McCarthy'. In 1988, however, the structure was completely upgraded by the state when they added guard rails and replanked it. Although it is no longer quite as thrilling, the view of the steep-sided canyon and rushing river from the middle of the bridge is mind-boggling, well worth the time to park at one end and walk back across it.

Two more bridges are crossed at *Mile 28.5* and *Mile 44* and at the first one you can still admire an impressive railroad trestle that was abandoned in the 1930s and left standing. At *Mile 57.3*, you come to an overlook on the south side of the road with a view of the town of McCarthy and glimpse of Kennicott Glacier through the forest of spruce and poplar.

To continue the final mile to McCarthy you have to use the hand-pulled trams erected by the state when the bridge was washed out in 1978. Only the first tram is necessary as a footbridge has been erected over the McCarthy River. Both are open platforms with two benches facing each other and appear to a normal person as if they hold two people at time. But not to the locals and not on Friday evening when there could be an hour wait to cross over on the tram. At times like these four or five people, with backpacks, will cram onto the tram, two of them hanging onto the outside. Others, waiting at each end, will pull them across. It's a crazy scene and pure McCarthy where 'everyday is Saturday once you cross over on the tram'.

Tours Several small air companies fly daily service between McCarthy and Glennallen. Ellis Air (☎ 822-3363 or (800) 478-3368) departs the Gulkana Airstrip at 9.45 am daily, arriving in McCarthy at 11 am and then turns around and heads back. One-way fare is $56. Wrangell Mountain Air (☎ 345-1160 or (800) 478-1160) also has daily service between McCarthy and Glennallen and even Chitina.

Getting Around
For a guided walk through Kennicott search out Chris Richards, the town's only legally registered voter. The year-round resident lives across the street from the Kennicott Glacier Lodge and has a call box along the street as Kennicott-McCarthy Wilderness Guides. He provides a colorful 1½-hour tour of the mines for $12.50 per person as well as giving you an idea of what it's like to live in a one-person town in the winter (he reads a lot). The tour is well worth it.

St Elias Alpine Guides (☎ 277-6867 in Anchorage) located in the MotherLode Power House offers a variety of day trips out of McCarthy including a three-hour historical tour of the area for $25 per person. If you just want to wander through Kennicott on your own, stop at the McCarthy Museum and for $1 pick up a copy of its *Walking Tour of Kennicott*.

If the day is clear, splurge on a flightseeing tour of the surrounding mountains and glaciers. Both McCarthy Air and Wrangell Mountain Air offer a wide range of scenic flights, with a 30-minute flight beginning at around $35. But if you do fly, invest in an hour flight at $60 per person, giving you enough air time to fly around 16,930-foot Mt Blackburn and volcanic Mt Wrangell.

Mountain Biking Those old mining roads and trails are tough on vehicles but are great for mountain bikes, turning McCarthy into something of a biker's paradise. Both locals and travelers take to the wide-tired bikes as a means of getting around the area as mountain bikes clearly outnumber cars here. If you have your own bike, you can bring it across on the tram by hanging it on a pair of hooks on the outside, praying all the way across that the wind doesn't blow it into the river below. If not, or you can't bear to ship your $800 bike like that, then St Elias Alpine Guides rents Diamond Back mountain bikes for $25 a day.

WHITTIER
On the day the military was cutting the ribbon that marked the completion of the Alcan (Alaska Hwy), the army was also having a tunnel 'holing through' ceremony outside Whittier. WW II and the Japanese invasion of the Aleutian Islands brought the US military searching for a second warm-water port in Southcentral Alaska, one that would serve as a secret port. Whittier was chosen because it was well hidden between the high walls of the Passage Canal Fjord in which it lies, and for the consistently bad weather that hangs over it.

Work began immediately on two tunnels through the Chugach Mountains that would connect the port to the main line of the Alaska Railroad. The tunnels, though overshadowed by the Alcan, were another amazing feat of engineering. The first was drilled through almost a mile of solid rock, while the second, begun simultaneously from the other side of the mountain, required carving a route 2.5 miles long. When General Simon Buckner blasted open the second tunnel during the 'holing through' ceremony in 1942, the two tunnels missed perfect alignment by an eighth of an inch.

Whittier owes both its existence and its skyscraper appearance to the military. After WW II, the port remained a permanent base due to the Cold War, and tall concrete buildings were constructed to house and serve the personnel. One building, the Begich Towers, is 14 stories tall. Nearby, the massive Buckner Building once housed 1000 people and had a bowling alley, a theater, cafés, a hospital, a pool and a jail. These skyscrapers look strange but their upward-pointing design greatly reduced the need for removal of snow which some winters exceeds 14 feet.

The army declared the Whittier Post unnecessary in 1960 but maintained it until 1968, in part because of the extensive damage the town suffered from the Good Friday Earthquake. The quake caused more than $5 million in damage while 13 people died here and the harbor was destroyed by a tidal wave. Whittier was incorporated in 1969 and in 1973 the city bought seven military buildings and 97 acres for $200,000. Begich Towers was quickly converted into 198 condominiums and located the city offices on the 1st floor and the community on the 2nd floor.

Today, the Begich Towers is where 60% of Whittier's 344 residents live and on the first two floors you'll find a laundromat, convenience store, beauty salon, post office, even a church. Since the military has left, Whittier has survived with some fishing, tourism, and as a port of call for both the Alaska State Marine Ferry and the Alaska Railroad.

Things to See

The vast majority of travelers stay in Whittier only long enough to board the train to Anchorage or the ferry to Valdez. Although the town itself is nothing to brag about, even appearing dismal to many, the surrounding area is a scenic blend of mountains and glaciers and, on a rare clear day, an interesting spot to layover for the afternoon.

As soon as you disembark from the train, you will spot the new **Whittier Visitor**

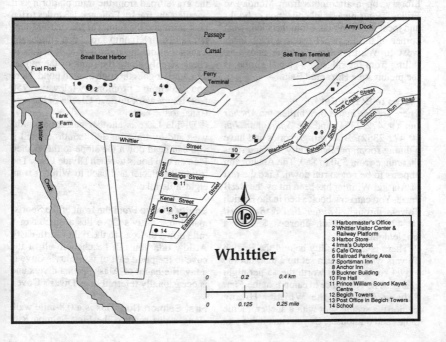

Whittier

| | 0 | 0.2 | 0.4 km |

| | 0 | 0.125 | 0.25 mile |

1 Harbormaster's Office
2 Whittier Visitor Center & Railway Platform
3 Harbor Store
4 Irma's Outpost
5 Cafe Orca
6 Railroad Parking Area
7 Sportsman Inn
8 Anchor Inn
9 Buckner Building
10 Fire Hall
11 Prince William Sound Kayak Centre
12 Begich Towers
13 Post Office in Begich Towers
14 School

Center (☎ 472-2379), housed in a rail car donated by the Alaska Railroad. It's part visitor center and part gift shop but the staff are friendly and will point you in the right direction. Due north is the **Small Boat Harbor** with fishing boats, private craft and the numerous tour vessels that work the Columbia Glacier route between Whittier and Valdez.

There is also a small museum in town on the 1st floor of the Begich Towers, down the hall from the post office. The **Whittier Historical Museum** is open from 1 to 5 pm Wednesday to Friday. It looks like a garage sale more than a museum and contains mostly historic photos and maritime specimens. Its most interesting display is a mounted wolf fish that a six-year-old girl caught while fishing in Prince William Sound. The mouth of this rare fish is filled with sharp teeth and molars used to eat shellfish and, on occasion, to attack people.

Also in the Begich Towers is the **Whittier Library**, open afternoons from Monday to Friday, featuring a small collection of books and local memorabilia. From the south-west corner of the Begich Towers, a track leads west to Whittier Creek, while above it, falling from the ridge of a glacial cirque, is the picturesque **Horsetail Falls**.

Places to Stay & Eat

There are two hotels in Whittier: the *Anchor Inn* (☎ 472-2354) and the *Sportsman Inn* (☎ 472-2352). Both sell groceries and have a dining room, public laundry, bar and rates that range from $50 to $60. The Anchor Inn appears to be not so run down. Like the rest of Alaska, Whittier has been hit by the B&B craze. You can now book a bed in the Begich Towers through *Whittier Bed & Breakfast* (☎ 472-2396) which charges $35/50 a single/double.

There is a RV facility behind the Begich Towers where you can set up a tent, but the gravel surface is not worth the $5 per night charge. The best place to camp is at the *First Salmon Run* (see the Whittier Hiking section), a scenic spot with a shelter, picnic tables and outhouses. Or you can pitch a tent just about anywhere near town by walking into the bush and away from the road.

For hamburgers, there is the *Hobo Bay Trading Company*, while the east end of the Small Boat Harbor has been developed into something of strip mall – Whittier style. Here you'll find among the gift shops, information booth and reindeer pen, *Irma's Outpost* where $6 will get you a hamburger or corned beef sandwich. Nearby is the quaint *Cafe Orca* for fresh pastries and a cup of gourmet coffee or espresso, while between the two places is *Tsunami Trading Co* for beer and pizza. Take your choice.

Hiking

Portage Pass Trail This makes a superb afternoon hike as it provides good views of Portage Glacier, Passage Canal and the surrounding mountains and glaciers. Even better, hike up in the late afternoon and spend the evening camping at Divide Lake.

To pick up the trailhead, walk west along the gravel road from the train platform as it parallels the tracks. Follow it 1.3 miles to the tank farm and the tunnel at Maynard Mountain, and turn left onto a road that crosses the tracks. Follow the right fork as it begins to climb steeply along the flank of the mountain, until it goes through a small pond. Here you can climb a promontory (elevation 750 feet) for views of Portage Glacier or Passage Canal to the east.

Divide Lake is another half-mile southwest and by traveling left (south) around it you can head down the slope to the glacier. Plan on two hours to reach Divide Lake. The trip to the glacier and back to Whittier is an eight-mile hike.

Smitty's Cove From the front of the Sportsman Inn, Smitty's Cove lies a quarter of a mile down the road to the right (north-east). At low tide you can beachcomb all of the cove to the point east of it. Smitty's Cove is a favorite haunt of Alaska scuba divers and is occasionally referred to as Diver's Cove.

First Salmon Run This is a 0.8-mile walk along a dirt road to the First Salmon Run

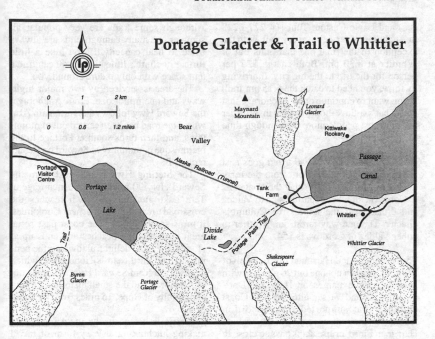

Portage Glacier & Trail to Whittier

Picnic Area, so named because of the large king and silver salmon runs in the creek in June and late August.

From the north-east corner of the Buckner Building behind the Sportsman Inn, follow the road that leads up the mountain, staying to the right at the first fork and to the left at the second fork. The road leads into the picnic area, where you can cross a bridge over the stream and continue another three miles to Second Salmon Run. This walk, along what is known as Shotgun Cove Rd, is exceptionally scenic as you can see Billings Glacier most of the way.

Kayaking

Whittier is a prime location for sea kayakers as it is practically surrounded by glaciated fjords and inlets. *Prince William Sound Kayak Center* (☎ 562-2866 in Anchorage and 472-2452 in Whittier) operates out of Whittier during the summer and can outfit you with a kayak rental and gear. The center

is not a shop here but rather is located in a fenced-in storage area just off Glacier St a block down from Begich Towers. It's best to make arrangements in advance at Anchorage as often the boats are rented out during the summer. A single kayak is $35 a day or $150 a week, a double is $55 a day or $220 a week. They'll also shuttle people out to Smitty's Cove or First Salmon Run for $5 per person.

Getting There & Away

There are two ways of getting out of Whittier and neither one is by road. To go west you take the Alaska Railroad; to head east you take a boat.

Train There are four trains departing Whittier on Wednesday and Thursday, and six trains the rest of the week. The one-way fare from Whittier to Portage is $13. Once in Portage you can take a shuttle bus to Anchorage. Two bus lines provide this transport, Caribou Express (☎ 278-5776 in Anchorage) and Eagle Custom Tours (☎ 277-6228 in Anchorage), servicing every train with the exception of the final one that pulls out of Whittier at 8.30 pm. Both charge $25 per person for the trip to the big city. If arriving by ferry, you need to catch the 6.15 pm train if you want to continue on to Anchorage that day. That's a three-hour layover in Whittier and for most people more than enough time for this town.

Boat The state ferry MV *Bartlett* goes east six times a week at 2.45 pm from the ferry dock. On Monday and Friday the boat sails to Cordova, all other departures go to Valdez and cruise near the impressive Columbia Glacier. The one-way fare from Whittier to either Valdez or Cordova is $54.

Tours College and Harriman fjords, north of Whittier, contain not one but 26 glaciers with such academic names as Harvard, Dartmouth, Yale and Vassar, after the East Coast colleges that supported the expedition leading to their discovery. On the way to Harriman Fjord, cruise ships pass so close to a kittiwake rookery that you can see the eggs of the black-legged birds in their nest.

Various tour boats which sail out of the Small Boat Harbor in Whittier offer day cruises to this icy world, including the *Klondike*, a high-speed catamaran operated by Phillips Tours (☎ 276-8023 in Anchorage or (800) 544-0529). The 110-mile return trip lasts almost six hours and costs $119 per person; it's cheaper if you take the tour before mid-June. In Whittier, contact the visitor center for tickets and names of other tour boats operating.

Kenai Peninsula

Because of its diverse terrain, easy accessibility and close proximity to Alaska's largest city (Anchorage), the Kenai Peninsula has become the state's top recreational area. It is well serviced, well developed and, unfortunately, well used during the summer.

Although some trails are very popular all summer and many campgrounds are always filled to near capacity, if you hike a little further or climb a little higher you can find a tent space with only nature around you.

The area is serviced by two major highways and one minor one. From Anchorage, the Seward Hwy follows the Turnagain Arm where the road has been carved out of mountains, and then turns south at Portage to the picturesque community of Seward on Resurrection Bay.

The Sterling Hwy heads west from the Seward Hwy 90 miles out of Anchorage at Tern Lake Junction. When it reaches the crossroad town of Soldotna, near Cook Inlet, it turns south, follows the coast past some great clam-digging beaches and ends up at Homer, the most delightful town on the peninsula. The third road is Hope Hwy, which heads north from Seward Hwy, 70 miles out of Anchorage, to the small historical mining community of Hope, 16 miles from the junction.

Traffic is heavy on the main highways, making hitchhiking an easy form of travel during the summer. The area is connected to the rest of Prince William Sound by the state ferry MV *Tustumena* which runs from Cordova and Valdez across the sound to Seward, over to Homer and then south to Kodiak. Alaska Airlines, through its contract carrier, also provides regularly scheduled services between Anchorage and Kenai, Homer and Kodiak.

SEWARD HIGHWAY

Travelers from Whittier should think twice before immediately rushing back to Anchorage. From Portage it's easy traveling down the Seward Hwy and into the heart of the Kenai Peninsula, Alaska's outdoor playground. The highway stretches for 127 miles and is another scenic gem in the state's fledgling system of roads.

The first section of the Seward Hwy from Anchorage, *Mile 127*, to Portage Glacier, *Mile 79*, is covered in the Anchorage chapter. When heading south, keep in mind that the mileposts along Seward Hwy show distances

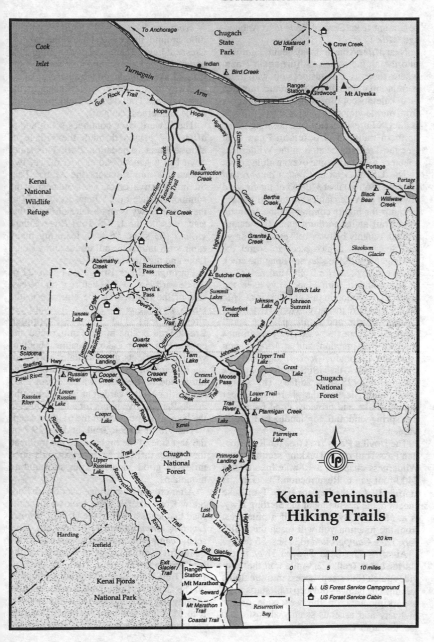

Kenai Peninsula Hiking Trails

△	US Forest Service Campground
⌂	US Forest Service Cabin

beginning from Seward, *Mile 0*, to Anchorage, *Mile 127*.

Near *Mile 68* the highway begins climbing into the alpine region of **Turnagain Pass**, where there is a roadside stop with litter barrels and toilets. In early summer, this area is a kaleidoscope of wildflowers ranging from purple violets to reds. Just past *Mile 64* is the US Forest Service sign pointing to the northern trailhead of **Johnson Pass Trail** (see the Trekking section in the Wilderness chapter), a 23-mile route over an alpine pass.

The USFS *Granite Creek Campground* (18 sites, $6 fee) is at *Mile 63* of the Seward Hwy and provides tables, water and a place to camp for hikers coming off the Johnson Pass Trail at its northern end. This campground, roughly halfway between Anchorage and Seward, is a nice place to spend the evening. Most of the sites are along the creek which can be fished for Dolly Varden.

The junction with Hope Hwy (see the Hope Hwy section in this chapter) is at *Mile 56.7*. From here the paved Hope Hwy heads 18 miles north, and a mile past the small hamlet of Hope. Seward Hwy continues south of this junction, and at *Mile 46* you cross the Colorado Creek Bridge and the short side road to the USFS *Tenderfoot Creek Campground* (28 sites, $6 fee). This scenic campground lies on the shores of Upper Summit Lake and provides good fishing in the spring and fall for landlocked Dolly Varden.

The **Devil's Pass Trail** (see the Resurrection Pass Trail in the Trekking section of the Wilderness chapter), a 10-mile hike over a 2400-foot gap to Resurrection Pass Trail, is at *Mile 39.4* of the Seward Hwy. Tern Lake Junction, the beginning of the Sterling Hwy, is at *Mile 37*. By driving half a mile west from the junction you will reach the USFS *Tern Lake Campground* (33 sites, $6 fee).

At *Mile 33* of the Seward Hwy is the **Carter Lake Trail**, a 2.3-mile trail that provides quick (but steep) access into subalpine terrain. The path, an old jeep trail, starts from a parking area on the west side of the highway and ascends steeply almost 1000 feet to Carter Lake.

From the lake, a trail continues another mile around the west side of the lake to Crescent Lake. There is good camping at the end of Carter Lake. Half a mile south of the Carter Lake trailhead on the other side of the highway is the southern trailhead to the Johnson Pass Trail (see the Trekking section in the Wilderness chapter).

The Seward Hwy continues south and at *Mile 29.4* passes through the village of **Moose Pass** (population 200). This small town has a general store, post office, two restaurants and sponsors the Moose Pass Summer Festival on the weekend nearest the summer solstice on 21 June. At *Mile 24* of the Seward Hwy is an obscure dirt road that leads west to the USFS *Trail River Campground* (63 sites, $6 fee), featuring many camp sites among the tall spruce along Kenai Lake and the Lower Trail River.

Ptarmigan Creek Bridge is at *Mile 23* of the Seward Hwy. Right before it on the east side of the highway is the entrance to the USFS *Ptarmigan Creek Campground* (26 sites, $6 fee). The 3.5-mile **Ptarmigan Creek Trail** begins in the campground and ends at Ptarmigan Lake, a beautiful body of water that reflects the mountains surrounding it. A four-mile trail continues around the north side of the lake, which offers good fishing for Dolly Varden at its outlet to the creek. Plan on five hours for a return hike to the lake, as some parts of the trail are steep.

The **Victor Creek Trail**, at *Mile 19.7* on the east side of the highway, is the trailhead for a fairly difficult path that ascends three miles to good views of the surrounding mountains.

After crossing the bridge over South Fork Snow River at *Mile 17.2*, look west for the road that leads a mile to the USFS *Primrose Landing Campground* (10 sites, $6). This scenic campground is on the east end of the beautiful Kenai Lake and contains the trailhead to the Primrose Trail (see the Lost Lake Trail in the Seward Hiking section).

The **Grayling Lake Trail**, a two-mile hike to Grayling Lake, has side trails that connect it to Meridian and Leech lakes, a beautiful spot with good views of Snow River Valley.

All three lakes have good fishing for grayling. The trailhead is in a paved parking lot at *Mile 13.2* on the west side of the Seward Hwy.

SEWARD

Seward (population 3000) is a pretty little town flanked by rugged mountains on one side and the salmon-filled Resurrection Bay on the other. It's the only town on the eastern side of the Kenai Peninsula and was founded in 1903 when Alaska Railroad surveyors needed an ice-free port to serve as the ocean terminal for the rail line. The first spike was driven in during 1904 and the line was completed in 1923.

During that time, Seward prospered as it served as the beginning of the Iditarod Trail to Nome and thousands of prospectors stampeding their way through town. Dog teams were used to haul supplies and mail along this 1200-mile route and return with the gold. In 1910, one of the largest shipments of Nome gold arrived when miner Bob Griffis mushed his dogs into Seward with his own armed guards. Griffis' gold bags would have been worth more than $6 million today.

Like most towns in Southcentral Alaska, Seward began a new era of history in 1964 after the Good Friday Earthquake (or Black Friday as Alaskans call it) caused fires and tidal waves that destroyed 90% of the town. At one point, a 3500-foot stretch of waterfront slid into the bay and Seward was completely cut off from the rest of the state.

Today, the only reminder of the natural disaster is at the public library on the corner of 5th Ave and Adams St across from City Hall, where the slide show, *Seward is Burning*, is shown from Monday to Saturday at 2 pm. It covers the earthquake through the eyes of residents who witnessed it.

The town has completely rebuilt its fine Small Boat Harbor and waterfront facilities with a $10 million dock designed to be earthquake proof. Most of the area's residents either work at Seward Fisheries (the largest halibut-receiving station on the US west coast), fish, or are connected with the Seward

Marine Center, a ship-repair facility, and the town's growing maritime industry.

Information

Head over to the Seward Railroad Car on the corner of 3rd Ave and Jefferson St. Built as a dining car by Pullman Company in 1916, today it houses the Chamber of Commerce Information Cache (☎ 224-3094), where you can pick up maps, information or a walking-tour map of the city. Inside you'll still find the original lunch counter and stools where you can sit back, enjoy a 25c cup of coffee and ask the local volunteer questions. The center is open daily in the summer from 11 am to 5 pm.

The Kenai Fjords National Park Visitor Center (☎ 224-3175) in the Small Boat Harbor has displays, information and a slide show on the nearby park. The center is open daily during the summer from 8 am to 7 pm. For information on Chugach National Forest trails, cabins and campgrounds, go to the US Forest Service Ranger Station (☎ 224-3374) on the corner of 4th Ave and Jefferson St. And for information on Caines Head State Park, head to the Alaska Division of Parks & Outdoor Recreation office (☎ 224-3434) on the 2nd floor of the City/State Building on the corner of 5th Ave and Adams St. Both the state parks and US Forest Service offices are open Monday to Friday from 8 am to 5 pm.

Things to See

From the Seward Railroad Car on 3rd Ave, the houses on the left are known as **Millionaires Row** and are the first stop on the local walking tours. They were built around 1905 by railroad officials and bankers who had just arrived in the newly created town. Nearby on the corner of Jefferson St and 3rd Ave is the **Resurrection Bay Historical Museum**, open daily from 11 am to 5 pm. The museum features artefacts and photographs of the 1964 earthquake, including a clock that stopped the instant the disaster struck. There are also exhibits on the Russian era in Resurrection Bay when a shipyard was established in 1793, and Seward's role in the Iditarod Trail. The admission charge is $1.

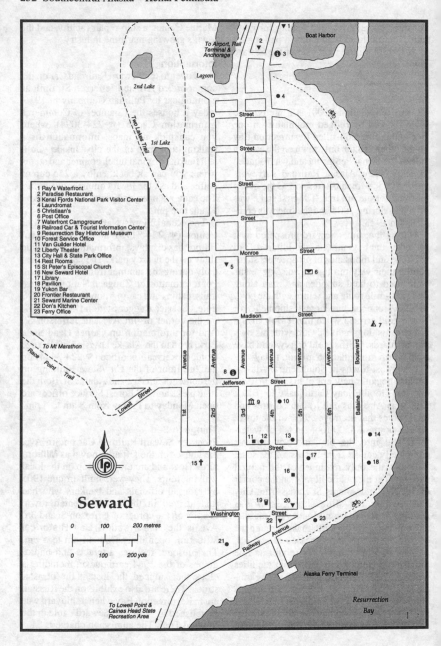

1 Ray's Waterfront
2 Paradise Restaurant
3 Kenai Fjords National Park Visitor Center
4 Laundromat
5 Christiaan's
6 Post Office
7 Waterfront Campground
8 Railroad Car & Tourist Information Center
9 Resurrection Bay Historical Museum
10 Forest Service Office
11 Van Gilder Hotel
12 Liberty Theater
13 City Hall & State Park Office
14 Rest Rooms
15 St Peter's Episcopal Church
16 New Seward Hotel
17 Library
18 Pavilion
19 Yukon Bar
20 Frontier Restaurant
21 Seward Marine Center
22 Don's Kitchen
23 Ferry Office

Seward

Head west to 1st Ave and follow it south to Lowell St to see the start of the trail to Mt Marathon (see the Seward Hiking section) and then continue east onto Adams St, where on the corner of 2nd Ave is **St Peter's Episcopal Church**. Built in 1906, the church contains the famous mural of the Resurrection by Dutch artist Jan van Emple who used Alaskan models and the nearby bay as the backdrop.

South on the corner of 3rd and Railway avenues is the **Seward Marine Education Center**, operated by the University of Alaska. The center has aquariums featuring live Alaska marine specimens as well as interesting displays and films on the sea life so important to the state. If you haven't witnessed a whale yet, you'll get a good idea of how large they are as a skull of a minke whale fills the middle of the room. Hours are from 10 am to noon and 1 to 5 pm during the summer. Admission is $1.

The **Seward Library** (☎ 224-3646) is on the corner of 5th and Adams avenues and besides the daily showing of the earthquake movie at 2 pm ($1.50), it often sponsors a used-book sale during the summer. Stock up on some good paperbacks. Hours are from noon to 8 pm Monday to Friday and until 6 pm on Saturday.

Not included on the tour but equally interesting is the **Small Boat Harbor** at the northern end of 4th Ave. The place hums during the summer with fishing boats, charter vessels and a large number of sailboats. It has also developed into a separate business district for Seward, especially as far as restaurants are concerned. The heart of the district is the Harbormaster's Office outside which, displayed in a square, is a pair of huge sea anchors and an equally impressive pile of chain. Nearby is the **Kenai Fjords National Park Visitor Information Center** (☎ 224-3175). The center has both a book shop and a few displays on the park. Most impressive is the video (on how the Exxon oil spill affected the park) they show it in a small theater. At the back there are restrooms as well as picnic tables and a free sighting scope overlooking the harbor and the bay – it's a nice place to enjoy lunch.

Festivals

Seward holds two events each summer that have become popular with Alaskans throughout the Southcentral. The Fourth of July celebration is a big event in Seward, highlighted by the annual Mt Marathon Race, which draws runners from around the state. The city's most famous event, however, is the Silver Salmon Derby on the second Saturday of August. First prize is in the thousands of dollars for the largest salmon caught. Other events on derby weekend include the Silver Salmon Run and softball tournaments.

Places to Stay

Camping Seward is one of the few towns in Alaska that has an excellent and affordable campground right in the heart of its downtown area. The Waterfront Campground, managed by the city's Parks and Recreation Department (☎ 224-3331), is along Ballaine Blvd, overlooking the bay. Most of it is open gravel parking for RVers, but you'll also find a grassy tent area that even has a few trees and shrubs. There is a day-use area with grills, picnic tables and small shelters while running through the campground is a paved bike path. Best of all it's $5 a night for tents, $6 for RVers.

Forest Acres Campground is two miles north of town on the west side of Seward Hwy and has a $4.25 fee and a 14-day limit. Further out of town still, but free, is the 12-site *Exit Glacier Campground*, a National Park Service facility for tents only, nine miles out at the end of Exit Glacier Rd.

If camping and looking for a shower, there's always the Harbormaster's Office, but a cleaner and closer place to the Waterfront Campground is Seward Laundry (☎ 224-5727), on the corner of 4th Ave and B St near the Small Boat Harbor. Showers, including towel and soap, are $3.

Hostels If you don't have a tent and sleeping bag, cheap accommodation can be tough to find in Seward. There's *Snow River Youth Hostel*, but it's near Primrose State Campground 16 miles north of town on the Seward

Hwy. The home hostel has 14 beds, a kitchen, laundry facilities, a storage area but no phone. The rate is $10 a night and it almost always gets high marks from travelers.

B&Bs The dining car information center has a wire rack full of B&B brochures. Grab a few and try your luck but expect rates to run from $55 to $65 a night. Downtown there is *Seward Waterfront Lodging* (☎ 224-5563) adjacent to the ferry terminal and *Harborview B&B* (☎ 224-3217) on the corner of 3rd Ave and C St.

For more interesting places to stay, head away from the town (isn't that always the case?). Three miles north of town on Salmon Creek Rd is *The Farm B&B* (☎ 224-5691) which has a wide variety of accommodations. Rooms in the remodeled farmhouse range from $65 to $85 a night for two people. But there are also sleeping cottages for $75 a night, complete with decks and the House Boatel, that sleeps four people for $40 a night. At the beginning of Exit Glacier Rd are several inns and B&Bs, including *Creekside Bed & Breakfast* (☎ 224-3834) with cabins, tent sites and sauna, all overlooking Clear Creek.

Hotels None of the hotels in town is cheap. The best motel in the Small Boat Harbor area is *Breeze Inn* (☎ 224-5237) with singles/doubles at $81/92. *Murphy's Motel* (☎ 224-8090) nearby has singles/doubles for $75/85 a night, and the *Marina Motel* (☎ 224-5518) just up the highway offers rooms in the same range but neither are as nice as Breeze Inn.

Downtown there is *Taroka Inn* (☎ 224-8687), on the corner of 3rd Ave and Adams St, where rooms begin at $75 but include kitchenettes. One of the nicest places to stay in Seward is the *Van Guilder Hotel* (☎ 224-3525), at 307 Adams St. Built in 1916 and operated as a hotel since 1921, the Van Gilder was placed on the National Register of Historical Places in 1980 and since has been restored to its original Edwardian charm. It has a few 'pension rooms' for $50 a night while double rooms with private bath

start at $85. Keep in mind that a last-minute room is hard to secure in Seward at the height of the summer season.

Wilderness Lodges A delightful side trip from Seward is *Kenai Fjords Wilderness Lodge* (☎ 224-5271), on Fox Island in Resurrection Bay. Accommodations are rustic cabins and each package includes a night's lodging, transport over and back from Seward and use of a boat to sight seabirds and other wildlife. Meals are not included but there are kitchens in the cabins. The cost per person for the overnight package is $190 and $45 for each additional night.

Places to Eat
Downtown *Don's Kitchen* at 405 Washington St is open 24 hours and probably has the cheapest breakfast fare; breakfasts begin at $4 and the Yukon Scrambler for $5.25 will keep you going until late in the afternoon. They also have a halibut dinner for $9. For a big hamburger that will only set you back $4 and a 25c cup of coffee, try the *Main Street Cafe* on the corner of 4th Ave and Washington St.

For something nicer, try the *Frontier*, across Washington St from Don's, where you can enjoy a view of the bay from any table. A late lunch of fresh pasta and seafood can be had for $8, dinners begin at $12. The *Harbor Dinner Club* is an upscale restaurant across 5th Ave from Hotel Seward, has good seafood and often 'inflation-fighter' specials for under $10.

Want Chinese? The *Peking Chinese Restaurant* is on the corner of 4th Ave and Jefferson St and is open until 10 pm daily. For a Mexican burrito, a pizza with everything or fish and chips, head to *Niko's* at 133 4th Ave. If it's Greek or Italian you're craving, *Apollo* on 4th Ave has both with pasta dinners beginning at $9 and a gyro plate priced at $12. They also serve Alaskan seafood and Mexican dinners. Hey, you have to make a living.

Small Boat Harbor This is home for Seward's cheap eats. *Shake n' Dog* has hot dogs from $2 to $3.50. Near the national park information center is *Paradise Restaurant* for 'Chinese fast food'. It's fast and not that bad and best of all it's filling. Dinners run from $5 to $6. *The Depot*, near the small shelter where the train drops you off, has sandwiches and hamburgers that begin at $5 and a pleasant solarium area overlooking the harbor. Or pick up whole, cooked Dungeness crabs at the *Seafood Market* next to Shake n' Dog for $5 a pound and enjoy it at the picnic tables behind the Kenai Fiords Visitor Center. Finally, there's *Ray's Waterfront* overlooking the boat harbor for excellent seafood, including fresh oysters, salmon and halibut. It's one of Seward's nicer restaurants with prices to match.

For something a little more healthier than milkshakes and fried food, try *Le Barn Appetit* on Resurrection Rd past the first bridge. This health food store, B&B and bakery has deli sandwiches, crêpes, fresh baked bread, quiche and other good things to eat.

Entertainment

Feel like pinning a few dollars to the ceiling? Head over to *Yukon Bar* on the corner of 4th Ave and Washington St – Seward's most lively bar. You can order one of 20 imported beers or try a Yukon ice tea for $7. From Wednesday to Saturday they somehow pack a band in and offer live music. Just down the street is the competition, *Tony's Bar*, which has live music on Friday and Saturday but not as much character. If you don't like either one of these places there's another half-dozen bars on 4th Ave.

Liberty Theater (☎ 224-5418), a great little movie theater on Adams St next door to the Van Gilder Hotel, shows movies nightly. The Seward Museum also has evening slide programs on Monday, Wednesday and Friday at 7 pm on either the history of Seward or the Iditarod Trail. Admission is $1.

Hiking

For information on the hikes in and around the Seward area, stop at the US Forest Service office (☎ 224-3374) on 4th Ave between Adams and Jefferson streets. The office is also the place to check out the availability of cabins in the Seward area.

Race Point Trail The most popular trail near the town center is the trek towards the top of Mt Marathon, the mountain that sits behind the city. The route is well known throughout Alaska. In 1909, two sourdough miners wagered how long it would take to run to the top and back and then dashed off for the peak.

After that, it became an official event at the Seward Fourth of July celebrations and today attracts hundreds of runners with an equal number of spectators who line the streets to watch them race. The fastest time is 43 minutes and 23 seconds, set in 1981. Most runners come down the mountain in less than 10 minutes, usually by sliding halfway on their behinds.

Hikers, on the other hand, can take their time and enjoy the spectacular views of Seward and Resurrection Bay. The hiker's trail begins at the end of Monroe St but is overgrown and hard to find at times. The runner's trail begins at the west end of Jefferson St (also known as Lowell St) up the Lowell Canyon. The trailhead is marked and is in a small gravel pit just past a pair of water tanks.

Scramble up the ridge to the right of the gully, and for fun return through the gully's scree. You never really reach Mt Marathon's summit, though you do reach a high point (known as Race Point) at 3022 feet on the broad east shoulder. Plan on three to four hours for the three-mile round trip.

Two Lakes Trail This easy one-mile loop goes through a wooded area and passes two small lakes at the base of Mt Marathon. Begin the hike near the first lake behind the Alaska Vocational & Training Center on the corner of 2nd Ave and B St. Near the start of the trail is a scenic waterfall.

Resurrection River Trail This 16-mile trail, built in 1984, is the last link in a 70-mile system across the Kenai Peninsula from Seward to Hope. This continuous trail is broken only by the Sterling Hwy and provides the best long-term wilderness adventure on the Peninsula, leading hikers through a diversity of streams, rivers, lakes, wooded lowlands and alpine areas.

The southern trailhead for the Resurrection River Trail is eight miles up the Exit Glacier Rd that leaves the Seward Hwy at *Mile 3.7* (see the Kenai Fjords section in this chapter). The northern trailhead joins the Russian Lakes Trail (see the Trekking section in the Wilderness chapter), five miles from Cooper Lake or 16 miles from the Russian River Campground off Sterling Hwy. The hike from Seward Hwy to Sterling Hwy is a 40-mile trip, including walking up Exit Glacier Rd.

There are two USFS cabins (reservations needed, $25 per night) along the trail; the Resurrection River USFS Cabin is 6.5 miles from the southern trailhead and the Fox Creek USFS Cabin is another 1.5 miles beyond it. Check with the USFS office in Seward about availability of the cabins and the best places to camp along the trail, as good sites are scarce.

Lost Lake Trail At *Mile 5.2* of Seward Hwy, this seven-mile trail to the alpine lake is one of the most scenic hikes the Kenai Peninsula has to offer in midsummer. The trailhead is marked in a parking area west of the highway and the beginning of the trail is a rough logging road. At 1.5 miles, a winter trail, designed primarily for snowmobiles, branches off to the right. The final two-miles of the trail are above the tree line and the lake is a glorious place to spend a night.

An option to returning is to continue around the east side of Lost Lake to the Primrose Trail, another USFS-maintained route. This eight-mile trail leads through alpine country and ends at Primrose Campground at *Mile 17.2* of Seward Hwy. Plan on seven to 10 hours for the return trip to Lost Lake and bring a camp stove because there is no wood near the lake.

Caines Head State Recreation Area This 6,000-acre preserve lies along the shore of Resurrection Bay, 5.5 miles south of Seward. It's the scenic site of an abandoned WW II fort and includes military ruins and 650-foot headlands that rise above the water for sweeping views of the bay and the mountains around it.

Facilities around the North Beach include shelters, toilets, camp sites and a ranger station that is staffed through most of the summer. You can explore this coastline either by boat, kayak or on foot beginning at the end of Lowell Rd (see the Coastal Trail in the Trekking section of the Wilderness Chapter for more information).

The trailhead into the park is a three-mile walk south of Seward on Lowell Rd. Even if you're not up for an overnight backpacking trip, the hike to Tonsina Point is a round-trip of only three miles and is fairly easy. At the point, you can view the salmon spawning up Tonsina Creek if it's July or early August or hike along the bay through a ghost forest whose stark trunks were created by the Good Friday Earthquake.

Kayaking

Kayaks can be rented from *Alaska Treks & Voyages* (☎ 224-3960) in the Small Boat Harbor for $30/40 a day for singles/doubles. The company also offers guided day trips which include morning kayaking instructions and then a paddle that departs and returns from Lowell Point three miles south of town. The cost is $95 per person. The company also has an overnight tour from Seward for $395 and a three-day tour for $575.

Getting There & Away

Bus Seward Bus Lines (☎ 224-3608) provides a daily service to Anchorage during the summer, with a bus departing from a small depot at 1915 Seward Hwy at 9 am. The bus departs Anchorage at 2.30 pm for the return trip to Seward; the one-way fare is $30. The bus company also has connecting vans to Soldotna, Kenai and Homer.

Top: Nugget Pond at Camp Denali with Mt McKinley behind (CD)
Bottom: Horned Puffins, Kenai Fjords National Park (NPS)

Top: Small boat harbour, Seward (DS)
Bottom: Trans-Alaska Pipeline workers monument, Valdez (DS)

Train The Alaska Railroad resumed passenger services to Seward in 1987 for the first time since the 1950s and now makes a daily run to the city from Anchorage. Trains leave Seward at 6 pm daily and reach Anchorage at 10 pm after traveling a spectacular route that includes glaciers, steep gorges and rugged mountain scenery. Even when departing at 6 pm, you can still view the scenery thanks to those long Alaskan days. The one-way fare is $40 and the service is offered from late May to early September. There's no depot in Seward so you need to call the Anchorage terminal (☎ 265-2494) for more information.

Boat The state ferry terminal (☎ 224-5485) is on the waterfront near the corner of 5th and Railroad avenues. Ferries arrive in Seward twice a week, on Thursday and Friday, from Kodiak or Valdez and depart for the same communities before continuing onto other Southcentral ports. The fare to Valdez is $56, to Kodiak $52 and to Homer $94. The trip to Valdez includes passing the Columbia Glacier. The boat to Kodiak Island passes the Stellar sea lions on the Chiswell Islands near the mouth of Resurrection Bay and nearby Bear Glacier.

Getting Around

Trolley To get around town, the Seward Trolley (☎ 224-7373) has a service that extends from the ferry terminal north past the railroad terminal for $1 per ride or $3 for a day pass. It runs from 7 am to 8 pm and stops at the library, museum, Harbormaster's Office and campgrounds.

Bicycle Seward has a nice bike path that begins in the Waterfront Campground and extends out towards Exit Glacier Rd. Rent bikes at Grizzly Bicycle Rentals (☎ 224-3960), in the Small Boat Harbor next to Alaska Treks & Voyages. The shop is open from 9 am to 6 pm and has mountain bikes for $8 an hour and $32 a day and road bikes for $7 an hour and $25 a day. You'll need a mountain bike if you're planning to ride out to Exit Glacier.

KENAI FJORDS NATIONAL PARK

Seward serves as the departure point for most trips into the Kenai Fjords National Park. The park, created in 1980, was thrust into the news during the Exxon oil spill. It covers 587,000 acres and consists mainly of the Harding Icefield, the rugged coastline where tidewater glaciers calve into the sea, and the offshore islands.

The Exxon oil spill had an impact on the park two weeks after the tanker struck the reef in Prince William Sound. But much of the coastline was spared from heavy damage as favorable winds kept the bulk of the initial oil from striking the shore. Still, there was damage and the park staff, determined not to let the public forget the heavy price of our oil dependency, has since created a series of oil spill exhibits in their visitor center in the Small Boat Harbor.

With its abundance of marine wildlife and glaciers, Kenai Fjords is a major tourist attraction, but unfortunately not an inexpensive one. That's why easy-to-reach Exit Glacier is its main attraction, drawing more than 100,000 visitors each summer.

For the adventurous, there is Harding Icefield. One of the largest icefields in North America, it remained undiscovered until the early 1900s when a map-making team realized several coastal glaciers belonged to the same massive system. The icefield is 50 miles long and 30 miles wide and in some places 200 inches deep. Eight glaciers reach the sea from it, while Exit Glacier is a remnant of a larger one that once extended into Resurrection Bay.

Hikers can reach the edge of the icefield, via the Harding Icefield Trail, but experienced mountaineers, equipped with skis, ice axes and crampons, are the only ones who can explore the 300 sq mile of ice. The many deep fjords, the broken coastline and rich marine life also make the park a blue-water paddler's dream, though kayakers have to either paddle the sections exposed to the Gulf of Alaska to reach it or pay for a drop-off.

To the vast majority of visitors, however, the national park is either a quick trip to Exit

Glacier or a splurge on a tour boat cruise to the coastal glaciers that set them back $90 to $120 each.

Information

The Kenai Fjords National Park Visitor Center (☎ 224-3175) is on 4th Ave in Seward near the Harbormaster's Office and the Small Boat Harbor. It is open daily from 8 am to 7 pm and has exhibits and slide programs as well as books for sale and hand-outs on the park. There is also a ranger station at Exit Glacier, which is staffed and open daily during the summer from 10 am to 5 pm daily.

Exit Glacier

The three-mile-long Exit Glacier is fast becoming a frozen tourist attraction, ranking right up there with Portage Glacier and Juneau's Mendenhall. It picked up its name when explorers, crossing the Harding Icefield, found the glacier a suitable way to 'exit' the ice and mountains. It's believed that at one time the glacier extended all the way to Seward and today it is still active, only now it's retreating into the mountains.

You and hundreds of RVers reach the ice on Exit Glacier Rd which leaves the Seward Hwy at *Mile 3.7* at a posted junction. The road first parallels the heavily braided Resurrection River, providing access to some unofficial but great camping spots on the surrounding gravel bars. Within seven miles you pass the trailhead to the Resurrection River Trail (see the previous Hiking section) and then cross a bridge over the river that was built only in 1985. At this point the view of the glacier fills your windshield and dominates the scenery for the remaining two miles.

At the end of the road there's the 12-site campground, a large parking area, a whole row of pit toilets and the ranger station. Inside you'll find a few displays and books for sale as well as the answers to any questions you might have. A ranger-led nature walk departs the station daily at 2 pm for a short hike around the glacier. Every Saturday at 8 am, there is a ranger-led trek up to the

Harding Icefield that lasts a good part of the day.

A paved, wheelchair-accessible trail leads a quarter mile to the overlook of the glacier and information shelter. To continue further you have to take to the trails with the vast majority of people hiking the Lower Loop Trail so they can have their picture taken in front of the bluish ice.

Hiking

Nature Trail A half-mile nature trail departs from the ranger station and winds through cottonwood forest, alder thickets and along old glacial moraines before emerging at the information shelter. It's a great way to return from the glacier if you're not up to facing the mass of humanity on the paved trail.

Exit Glacier Trails A network of loops provides close access to the ice itself from the information center. The Lower Loop Trail is an easy half-mile walk to the outwash plain in front of the ice. All around there's warning signs telling you to stay away from the face due to the danger of falling ice. Despite the signs, people are so insistent to touch the ice or have their picture taken next to it, the park often posts a ranger out there to keep them away.

The Upper Loop Trail departs off the first loop and climbs steeply to an overlook at the side of the glacier before returning. Both trails make for a hike not much more than a mile in length and sections may be closed at times due to falling ice. Don't skip the short spur to Falls Overlook, a scenic cascade off the upper trail.

Harding Icefield Trail Besides the nature trail from the ranger station to Exit Glacier, the only other developed hike in the glacier area is the trek to Harding Icefield. The hike to the icefield is a difficult ascent which follows a steep, roughly cut and sometimes slippery route on the north side of Exit Glacier, beginning at its base. It's a five-mile, one-way hike to the icefield at 3500 feet and for reasonably fit trekkers a good four-hour hike/climb.

The all-day trek is well worth it for those with the stamina, as it provides spectacular views of not only the icefield but of Exit Glacier and the valley below. The upper section of the route is snow covered for much of the year. You pick up the trailhead at the beginning of the Lower Loop Trail.

Kayaking

Blue-water paddles out of Resurrection Bay along the coastline of the park are challenges for experienced kayakers or involve a costly drop-off, pick-up fee but reward you with almost daily wildlife encounters and close-up views of the glaciers from a unique perspective. Alaska Treks & Voyages (☎ 224-3960) rents out rigid kayaks from the Small Boat Harbor in Seward; singles/doubles are $30/40 a day and include skirts, paddles, lifejacket and storage bags. The guide company also runs a 10-day trip along the park's coastline or overnight and weekend tours.

The company books drop-off service for Fox Island Charters for those who want to skip the open water of Gulf of Alaska. It's $190 for round-trip drop-off to Aialik Bay and $250 into the more remote Northwestern Lagoon.

Aialik Bay This is the more popular arm for kayakers to paddle. Many people transported by the tour boats to near Aialik Glacier then take three or four days to paddle south past Pedersen Glacier and into Holgate Arm, where they are picked up. There are public-use cabins in Holgate Bay and on the east shore of upper Aialik Bay ($25 a night) that must be reserved in advance through the Forest Service (USFS) office in Seward. The highpoint of the trip is Holgate Glacier, an active tidewater one. Keep in mind, however, the glacier is also the main feature of all the boat tours.

Northwestern Lagoon This fjord is more expensive to reach but much more remote with only an occasional tour boat entering if any at all. The wildlife is excellent, especially the seabirds and sea otters, and there

are more than a half-dozen glaciers that can be seen, including three tidewater ones. Plan on three to four days if you are being dropped inside the lagoon (for more details see Paddling in the Wilderness chapter).

Boat Tours

For most visitors the best way to see the rugged fjords, glaciers and wildlife is on a tour boat. In the past few years, Kenai Fjords cruises have become Seward's main attraction and they all maintain a booth or office in the Small Boat Harbor, right next to the Harbormaster's Office. It always pays to shop around before booking but keep in mind there are Kenai Fjords tours and wildlife tours. The wildlife tours are just cruises inside Resurrection Bay that never get close to the glaciers and most of the wildlife is seabirds. If you want to view the national park, you're going to have to pay around $100.

Kenai Fjords Tours (☎ 224-8068 or (800) 478-8068 within Alaska) runs an eight-hour tour of the park with boats departing at 8 and 10 am and 11.30 pm daily. The fare is $85 per person and tickets may be purchased at their office on the boardwalk in Seward's Small Boat Harbor. Likewise Mariah Charters & Tours (☎ 224-8623) has a similar trip that departs at 8 am for $80 and Kenai Coastal Tours (☎ 224-7114 or (800) 770-9119) for $95 with a departure at 11.30 pm. All of these companies offer cruises to Aialik Bay, past several glaciers including Holgate and, if the sea gods are smiling on you that day, pass a variety of marine life including sea otters, a sea lion colony and even humpback or minke whales. Often the difference in price depends on whether they serve lunch or not.

Mariah and Kenai Fjords Tours also offer a four-hour wildlife tour inside Resurrection Bay with departures at 8.30 am and 1 pm for around $50. Or call Alaska Renown Charter (☎ 224-3806) which has a 2½-hour wildlife tour for $35 departing six times a day from 8.45 am to 8.45 pm. In 1993, Mariah began offering a 10-hour tour into Northwestern

Lagoon on Friday at 8 am for $105 per person.

HOPE HWY

This paved road leads almost 18 miles north to the historical community of Hope and the northern trailhead for the Resurrection Pass Trail. Hope experienced a minor stampede in 1896 when news of a gold strike bought over 3000 prospectors to the cluster of cabins and to nearby Sunrise, a tent city. Within a few years the majority had left to look for gold elsewhere and today Hope is a small village with a summer population of 225. Nothing remains of Sunrise.

Even if you are not planning to hike the Resurrection Pass Trail, Hope is a great side trip; the town is tucked away in a very scenic area and lets you step back in time. Hitchhiking is not hard, but plan on at least two days for this trip rather than a rushed overnight stop.

At *Mile 16* of the Hope Hwy is the junction to Palmer Creek and Resurrection Creek roads. Turn left (south) onto Resurrection Creek Rd and in 0.7 miles Palmer Creek Rd branches to the left. Near the junction is the unattended Hope airstrip. Four miles down Resurrection Creek Rd is the northern trailhead of the Resurrection Pass Trail.

Palmer Creek Rd is a scenic drive that leads seven miles to the USFS *Coeur d'Alene Campground* (six sites, free use). Beyond the campground, the road is not maintained but leads another five miles to alpine country above 1500 feet and ends at the ruins of the abandoned Swetmann mining camp. From the old mining buildings it is easy to scramble through the tundra to several small alpine lakes.

Hope

To reach the town of Hope, turn right on Hope Rd at *Mile 16.5* of Hope Hwy. Hope Rd first leads past the post office where across the street is the new **Hope-Sunrise Mining Museum** that was built in 1993. Then it winds past the many log cabins and some abandoned log structures that have become favorites among photographers. You end up near the waterfront at what is can best described as 'downtown Hope'. Here you'll find a gift and mining shop, the Hope Social Hall and Seaview Cafe, all quaint buildings in a scenic setting.

Places to Stay & Eat Hope has a general store, laundromat and a couple of lodges and cafés. Near the junction to Resurrection Creek Rd on Hope Hwy, there is *Henry's One Stop* (☎ 782-3222) where you can get a meal, a beer, a shower or even a room. Next door is *Bear Creek Lodge* (☎ 782-3141) where it is possible to rent restored hand-hewn log cabins along the creek. Rates begin at $60 a night for a cabin but the lodge is a scenic resort in the woods with a small restaurant, a scattering of cabins and even a replica of an old log cache.

Camping sites abound all around Hope but the USFS maintains the *Porcupine Campground* (24 sites, $6 fee), 1.3 miles beyond Hope at the end of Hope Hwy. The campground features the usual well spreadout sites, a scenic overlook to watch the tide roll in and two trailheads to Hope Point and Gull Rock. Beware, the place is often filled on weekends and sometimes even in the middle of the week. Near the campground is *Davidson Enterprises*, a general store that sells groceries, gasoline and liquor.

Gold Panning

There are about 125 mining claims throughout the Chugach National Forest but most of today's prospectors are recreational miners out there for the fun, searching their pans or sluice box for a little color. Some of the more serious ones actually make money from their time spent along the creeks, but most are happy to take home a bottle with a few flakes of gold in it.

The Hope area provides numerous opportunities for the amateur panner, including a 20-acre claim that the USFS has set aside near the Resurrection Pass trailhead for recreational mining. There are usually some regulars out there who don't mind showing newcomers how to swirl the pan. Other panning areas include Sixmile Creek

Panning for a Fortune

When panning for gold the only piece of equipment that is absolutely necessary is a gravity-trap pan, one that measures 10 to 20 inches in diameter and can usually be bought at any good Alaskan hardware or general store. Those who have panned for a while also show up with rubber boots and gloves to protect feet and hands from icy waters, a garden trowel to dig up loose rock, a pair of tweezers to pick up gold flakes and a small bottle to hold their find.

Panning techniques are based on the notion that gold is heavier than the gravel it lies in. Fill your pan with loose material from cracks and crevices in streams or around large boulders where gold might have washed down and become lodged. Add water to the pan and rinse and discard larger rocks, keeping the rinsing in the pan. Continue to shake the contents towards the bottom by swirling the pan in a circular motion and wash off the excess sand and gravel by dipping the front into the stream.

You should be left with heavy black mud, sand and, if you are lucky, a few flakes of gold. Use tweezers or your fingernails to transfer the flakes into a bottle filled with water. ∎

between *Mile 1.5* and *Mile 5.5* of Hope Hwy, and many of the creeks along the Resurrection Pass Trail.

Hiking

Gull Rock Trail From Porcupine Campground there are two fine trails to scenic points overlooking the Turnagain Arm. The first is an easy 5.1-mile walk to Gull Rock, a rocky point 140 feet above the Turnagain shoreline. The trail follows an old wagon road built at the turn of the century, and along the way there are the remains of a cabin and a sawmill to explore. You also get an occasional view of the Turnagain Arm and even Mt McKinley on a clear day during this extremely scenic trek. The round trip to Gull Rock takes from four to six hours.

Hope Point This is not a trail but more of a route that follows an alpine ridge for incredible views of Turnagain Arm. Begin at the entrance sign to Porcupine Campground and follow an unmarked trail along the right-hand side of the small Porcupine Creek. After 0.3 miles, the trail leaves the side of the creek and begins to ascend a bluff to the right, reaching an outcrop with good views of Turnagain Arm in 45 minutes or so. From here, you can follow the ridge above the tree line to Hope Point, elevation 3708 feet. Other than an early summer snowfield, there is no water after Porcupine Creek.

STERLING HWY TO KENAI

It is only 58 miles from Tern Lake Junction to Soldotna along the Sterling Hwy, not much more than an hour's drive. Yet the stretch contains so many hiking, camping and canoeing opportunities that it would take you a month to enjoy them all. Surrounded by the Chugach National Forest and Kenai National Wildlife Refuge, Sterling Hwy and its side roads pass a dozen trails, 20 campgrounds and an almost endless number of lakes, rivers and streams in which to fish or paddle.

More than anywhere else, this is Alaska's favorite playground. Despite all the campgrounds and facilities, the summer crowds that descend onto the area in July and August (both Alaskans and tourists) are crushing at times. Be prepared, if you're traveling by car at this time of year, to stop at a handful of campgrounds before finding an available site. Better yet, seek out the places away from Sterling Hwy and the main flow of traffic. And even better (for those with a backpack, tent and camp stove) hike up a trail, if only for a mile or so, to ensure that your peaceful evening is not destroyed by the constant hum of a campground full of RVers and their generators.

Mileposts along the highway show distances from Seward, making Tern Lake Junction at *Mile 37*, the start of the Sterling Hwy. The first campgrounds are eight miles west from the junction at *Mile 45*. Just past the Sunrise Motel (restaurant, bar, gas and lodging) is the Quartz Creek Rd. Follow the road south 0.3 miles to the USFS *Quartz Creek Campground* (41 sites, $6 fee) on the shores of Kenai Lake or three miles to the USFS *Crescent Creek Campground* (13 sites, $6 fee).

The **Crescent Creek Trail**, about half a mile beyond the Crescent Creek Campground, has a marked trailhead and leads 6.5 miles to the outlet of Crescent Lake and a USFS cabin (reservations needed, $25 per night). The trail is an easy walk and is beautiful in September with the colors of fall; from the cabin there is access to the high country. Anglers can fish for arctic grayling in the lake during the summer and fall. Make cabin reservations at the Chugach National Forest office (☎ 271-2599) in Anchorage. At the east end of the lake is the Carter Lake Trail to Seward Hwy, but no path connects the two trails.

Another half-mile west on Sterling Hwy is a large lookout and observation point for dall sheep in the Kenai Mountains and mountain goats in the Cecil Rhode Mountains directly across Kenai Lake. Displays explain the life cycle of the animals. The Kenai River Bridge is at *Mile 47.8* and immediately after it is Snug Harbor Rd, which leads south 12 miles to Cooper Lake and the eastern trailhead to the Russian Lakes Trail (see the Trekking section in the Wilderness chapter).

The Kenai River parallels the highway for the next 10 miles where several gravel lookouts offer good views. At *Mile 48.7* you pass through **Cooper Landing** (population 400). This service center was named after Joseph Cooper, a miner who worked the area in the 1880s. A school was built here in 1929 and the first post office was established in 1937, a year before the town was connected by road to Seward.

There is now a five-building national historic district, which includes the colorful Old Cooper Landing Store. But this town is best known as the starting point for half-day raft trips down the Kenai River. A number of companies run the trip, including Alaska

Wildland Adventures (☎ (800) 478-4100 in Alaska) and the Alaska River Co (☎ 595-1226). Expect to pay about $40 for a three to four-hour trip, which includes some white water in the Kenai Canyon.

At *Mile 50.7* of the Sterling Hwy is the USFS *Cooper Creek Campground* (27 sites, $6 fee) where there are camping sites on both sides of the highway. Several of those on the north side of the highway are scenically located on the Kenai River but like for most others, either arrive here early or find a more remote facility.

The final USFS campground is at *Mile 52.8*, 16 miles west of Tern Junction. The *Russian River Campground* (84 sites, $8) is a beautiful spot where the Russian and Kenai rivers merge and the most popular one by far. Both the Cooper Creek and Russian River campgrounds lie in prime red salmon spawning areas and the camp sites tend to fill up by noon in late summer. The Russian River Campground is so popular that they charge you $2 just to park and fish.

A mile down Russian River Campground Rd is the trailhead and parking area for the Russian Lakes Trail, while a quarter of a mile west of the campground on Sterling Hwy is the well-marked entrance to the Resurrection Pass Trail (see the Trekking section in the Wilderness chapter).

Once west of the Resurrection Pass trailhead, you leave Chugach National Forest, administered by the Forest Service, and enter the **Kenai National Wildlife Refuge**, managed by the US Fish & Wildlife Service. The impressive populations of dall sheep, moose, caribou and bear found here have attracted hunters from around the world since the early 1900s. In 1941, President Roosevelt set aside 1.73 million acres as the Kenai National Moose Range and the 1980 Alaska Lands Act increased it to almost two million acres.

Along with an abundance of wildlife, good fishing and great mountain scenery, the refuge offers some of the least used trails on the Kenai Peninsula. Hikers who want to spend a few days trekking here should first go the Kenai National Wildlife Refuge

Visitor Station at *Mile 58* of Sterling Hwy or the visitor center in Kenai and pick up a copy of the booklet *Kenai National Wildlife Refuge Hiking Trails*.

The first campground in the refuge is *Kenai-Russian River Recreational Area* (10 sites, $6) at *Mile 55* of Sterling Hwy. West of the confluence of these two salmon-rich rivers, this campground is heavily used from mid to late summer by anglers and the fee applies whether you want to camp or just park. Facilities include a pay phone and an information display on the area.

A privately owned ferry carries anglers to the opposite bank of the Kenai River here for $3, using cables and the current to propel it across the river in both directions. During the height of the salmon season a couple of hundred anglers will be lined up at 5 am to catch the first trip across the river.

The three-mile **Fuller Lake Trail** begins at *Mile 57.2* of the Sterling Hwy and ends at Fuller Lake just above the tree line. The trail, an old road blocked by logs, is marked. Halfway up the trail you reach Lower Fuller Lake, where you cross a stream over a beaver dam and continue over a low pass to Fuller Lake. At the lake, the trail follows the east shore and then branches; the fork to the left leads up a ridge and becomes the **Skyline Trail**. This trail is not maintained and is unmarked above the bush line. It follows a ridge for 6.5 miles and descends to *Mile 61* of Sterling Hwy. Those who want to hike both trails should plan to stay overnight at Fuller Lake.

Just past the Fuller Lake trailhead on Sterling Hwy is the **Skilak Lake Loop Rd** junction at *Mile 58* and the **Kenai National Wildlife Refuge Visitor Station**. The log cabin is open daily from 10 am to 7 pm and is the source of hand-outs, maps and brochures on the refuge. The 19-mile loop road, a scenic side trip to an already scenic highway, is a popular and often crowded recreational avenue. There are seven USFS campgrounds along the road, some like Hidden Lake and Upper Skilak are $6 a night, others are free. All these campgrounds are well marked and, from east to west, are:

Campground	No of Sites	Location
Jim's Landing	5	near the junction
Hidden Lake	40	*Mile 3.6*
Upper Skilak Lake	10	*Mile 8.4*
Lower Ohmer	4	*Mile 8.6*
Engineer Lake	8	*Mile 9.7*
Lower Skilak Lake	14	*Mile 14*
Bottinentnin Lake	3	*Mile 19*

The **Kenai River Trail**, 0.6 miles past the visitor station on the Skilak Lake Loop Rd, winds 6.3 miles to Skilak Lake and then turns into the **Hidden Creek Loop**. The 1.4-mile loop trail curves back to its beginning at *Mile 4.6* of Skilak Lake Loop Rd. Both trails are easy walks along level terrain.

The **Skilak Lookout Trail** begins at *Mile 5.5* of Skilak Lake Rd and ascends 2.6 miles to a knob at 1450 feet that offers a panoramic view of the surrounding mountains and lakes. Plan on four to five hours for the round trip and bring water as there is none on the trail.

The **Seven Lakes Trail**, a five-mile hike to the Sterling Hwy, begins at *Mile 9.7* of Skilak Lake Loop Rd, at the spur to Engineer Lake. The trail is easy walking over level terrain and passes Hidden and Hikers lakes before ending at *Kelly Lake Campground* on a side road off Sterling Hwy. There is fair to good fishing in Kelly and Engineer lakes.

If you choose to stay on the Sterling Hwy past the Skilak Lake Rd junction, you pass the small *Jenny Lake Campground* at *Mile 60* and a side road at *Mile 69* that leads south to the *Peterson Lake Campground* (three sites, free) and *Kelly Lake Campground* (three sites, free) near one end of the Seven Lakes Trail. The west junction with Skilak Lake Rd is at *Mile 75.3* of the Sterling Hwy.

At *Mile 81* of Sterling Hwy you arrive in the small town of **Sterling** (population 1800), where the Moose River empties into the Kenai. Sterling meets the usual travelers' needs with restaurants, lodges, gas stations and grocery stores. Affordable hostel accommodations can be reached four miles east of town off Spruce Lane at *Mile 76.5* of the highway. *Moose Range Cabins* (☎ 262-8546) has a bunkhouse for $10 a night, bedrooms for $30 and log cabins for $50. You can even camp there for $4 and facilities include kitchen, showers and laundry.

Beyond the town is the *Izaak Walton Recreation Site* (17 sites, $6 fee) at the confluence of the Kenai and Moose rivers. A display explains the nearby archaeological site where excavations suggest that the area was used by Inuit people 2000 years ago. The recreational area is heavily used all summer, as anglers swarm here for the salmon runs, while paddlers end their Swan Lake canoe trip at the Moose River Bridge. Canoe rentals and transport are available at the bridge for the Swan Lake and Swanson River canoe trails (see the Paddling section in the Wilderness chapter).

At *Mile 85* of the Sterling Hwy, Swanson River Rd turns north for 18 miles, with Swan Lake Rd heading east for three miles at the end of it. The roads are accesses to the Swanson River and Swan Lake canoe routes and three campgrounds: *Dolly Varden Lake Campground* (15 sites, free) 14 miles up Swanson River Rd; the *Rainbow Lake Campground* (three sites, free) another two miles beyond; and the *Swanson River Campground* (eight sites, free) at the very end of the road. Even without a canoe, this is a good area to spend a day or two as there are trails to many of the lakes which offer superb fishing.

Across Sterling Hwy from Swanson River Rd is the entrance to Scout Lake Loop Rd, where the *Scout Lake Campground* (14 sites, $6) and *Morgan Landing State Recreation Area* (50 sites, $6) are located. The Alaska Division of Parks Office (☎ 262-5581), also off Scout Lake Loop Rd, has hand-outs, displays and information on the remote Kachemak Bay State Park to the south.

KENAI

Kenai (population 6700) is the second-oldest permanent settlement in Alaska as it was established by Russian fur traders in 1791. It offers good views of the active volcanoes across the inlet and a little Russian history and color that often get lost in the town's massive oil industry. Kenai does not,

however, have the charm of Seward or Homer.

The town is at the mouth of the Kenai River on Cook Inlet, where you can view Mt Redoubt (the volcano that erupted stream and ash in December 1989) to the southwest, Mt Iliamna at the head of the Aleutian Range and the Alaska Range to the northwest. You reach the heart of the city by going north on Kenai Spur Rd at *Mile 94.2* of Sterling Hwy.

Information

In 1991, Kenai replaced Moosemeat John's Cabin with the impressive Kenai Bicentennial Cultural Center as its visitors center. Built to mark the city's 200th anniversary, the center houses a museum as well as an information center with the usual racks of brochures and hand-outs. The center (☎ 283-1991) is on the corner of Main St and Kenai Spur Hwy and is open Monday to Friday from 9 am to 5 pm with extended weekend hours during the summer.

Things to See

Inside the Bicentennial Cultural Center is the **Kenai Museum**, with historical artefacts and exhibits on the city's Russian heritage, wildlife displays and an audio-visual room with daily showings of videos on the state. The center and museum are open daily during the summer. Admission is free.

From the visitors center, follow Overland Ave to **Fort Kenay**, two blocks west towards Cook Inlet. Inside the fort is the **Kenai Historical Museum** with a collection of artefacts dating back to the town's Russian origins and its gold-mining days. Around the fort (constructed as part of the Alaska Centennial in 1967) are several old homes moved there for restoration. The fort and museum are open Monday to Saturday from 10 am to 5 pm; donations are accepted.

Across Mission St from the fort is the **Russian Orthodox Church**, built in 1896 and today the oldest Orthodox church on mainland Alaska. West of the church is the blue-domed **St Nicholas Chapel**, built in

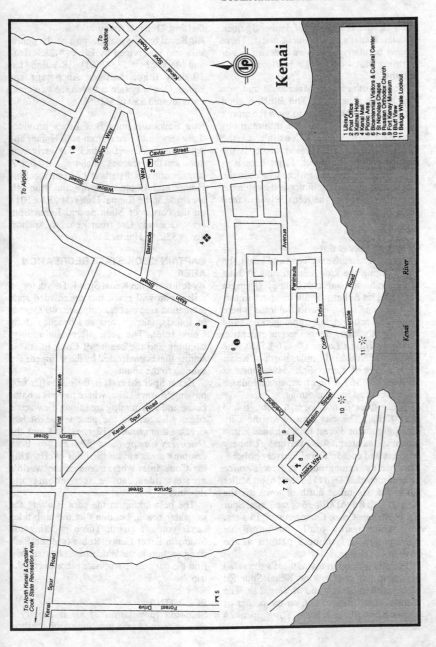

Kenai

To Soldotna

To Airport

Caviar Street

Kenai Spur Road

Frontage Way

Willow Street

Barnacle Street

Main Street

First Avenue

Birch Street

Kenai Spur Road

Spruce Street

Kenai Spur Road

Forest Drive

To North Kenai & Captain
Cook State Recreation Area

Peninsula Avenue

Overland Avenue

Cook Drive

Riverside Road

Mission Street

Alaska Way

Kenai River

1 Library
2 Post Office
3 Katmai Hotel
4 Kenai Mall
5 Picnic Area
6 Bicentennial Visitors & Cultural Center
7 St Nicholas Chapel
8 Russian Orthodox Church
9 Fort Kenay Museum
10 Bluff View
11 Beluga Whale Lookout

1906 on the burial site of Father Igumen Nicolai, Kenai's first resident priest. There are no regularly scheduled tours of either building but both are a photographer's delight.

Head south-east on Mission St and you will be traveling along **The Bluff**, a good vantage point from which to view the mouth of the Kenai River or the mountainous terrain on the west side of Cook Inlet. On the corner of Main and Mission streets is the **Beluga Whale Lookout**. From here it is possible to see groups of white whales in the late spring and early summer as they ride the incoming tides into the Kenai River to feed on salmon.

Places to Stay & Eat

Hotels in Kenai are expensive and tend to be filled during the king salmon runs in June and July; most rooms cost from $100 a night for a single. Either plan on camping in this area or head south-east to Soldotna where there is more competition among motels and thus slightly lower rates. The one exception is *Moose Haven Lodge* (☎ 776-8535). The lodge is in Nikiski, 17 miles north of Kenai at *Mile 28* of Kenai Spur Hwy but has doubles for $65 a night which includes a huge breakfast in the morning.

Sadly there is no longer a campground near Kenai. The city shut down the City Campground on Forest Dr and turned it into a picnic area after it was overrun by cannery workers and couldn't be effectively policed. The nearest campground is now *Bernice Lake Recreation Area* (11 sites, $6) on Miller Loop Rd, six miles north of town off the Kenai Loop Rd. At *Mile 36* of the Kenai Spur Rd is *Bishop Creek Campground* (15 sites, $6), while nearby you'll find affordable hamburgers and friendly patrons at the *Bishop Creek Bar*.

For cheap food in town, there's the salad and soup bar at *Carr's* on Kenai Spur Rd along with an *Arby's* and *McDonald's*. The *Katmai Hotel Restaurant*, on the corner of Kenai Spur Rd and Main St, is open 24 hours.

Getting There & Away

Air Kenai has the main airport on the peninsula and is serviced by ERA (☎ 283-3168) and MarkAir (☎ 283-2881). ERA alone has 10 daily flights between Anchorage and Kenai. One-way fare between the two cities costs around $50 to $60.

Bus Seward/Homer Bus Lines provides daily service to Kenai from both Homer and Anchorage. A northbound bus arrives at noon and then reaches Anchorage at 4 pm. A southbound bus departs at 1.55 pm, reaching Homer at 3.45 pm. Pick-ups and drop-offs are made at the Katmai Hotel (☎ 283-6101), on the corner of Main St and Kenai Spur Hwy. One-way fare from Kenai to Anchorage is $30, to Homer $17.

CAPTAIN COOK STATE RECREATION AREA

By following the Kenai Spur Rd north for 36 miles, you will reach this uncrowded state recreation area that encompasses 4000 acres of forests, lakes, rivers and beaches along Cook Inlet. The area offers swimming, camping and the beauty of Cook Inlet in a setting that is unaffected by the stampede for salmon to the south.

Kenai Spur Rd ends in the park after first passing Stormy Lake, where there is a bathhouse and a swimming area along the water's edge. Also within the park is the *Bishop Creek Campground* (12 sites, $6) and the *Discovery Campground* (57 sites, $6). Both camping areas are on the bluff overlooking the Cook Inlet where some of the world's greatest tides can be seen ebbing and flowing.

The best hiking in the park is along the saltwater beach, but don't let the high tides catch you off guard. Those paddling the Swanson River Canoe Route (see the Paddling section in the Wilderness chapter) will find the park an appropriate place to end the trip.

SOLDOTNA

Soldotna (population 3800) is strictly a service center at the junction of the Sterling

Hwy and Kenai Spur Rd. The town was born when both roads were completed in the 1940s and WW II veterans were given a 90-day preference to homestead the area. But what used to be little more than a hub for anglers hoping to catch an 80-pound-plus king salmon from the Kenai River, is now one of fastest growing commercial areas on the peninsula. The main reason for the boom in business is tourism. In a four-year period alone, from 1986 to 1990, out-of-state tourists increased 70% from 93,000 to 160,000. The Alaska Department of Fish & Game reports the Kenai River to be the most heavily fished stream in the state, as hundreds of thousands of anglers flood the area annually and congest the waterway with powerboats.

Just about all of these people (anglers, RVers and hitchhiking backpackers) have to pass through Soldotna. The reason no doubt, there's a McDonald's.

Information
Information on the town can be obtained at the Kenai Peninsula Visitor Information

Center (☎ 262-9814) in the center of town on the Sterling Hwy, just south of the Kenai River Bridge. The impressive center is built in a wooded setting along the banks of the river and outside there is a series of steps and landings that lead down to the water.

How important is sport fishing to this town? If you're unsure, go inside the visitor center where among the stuffed and mounted animals is a 94-pound king salmon that was caught in 1987 and is the fifth largest sport-caught salmon in the world. You can picnic on the decks, fish in the river or gather information on the surrounding area at the center; it is open from 9 am to 7 pm daily during the summer.

Things to See & Do
The most interesting thing to do in Soldotna is to drive onto Kalifornsky Beach Rd just after passing the bridge over the Kenai River. The road heads west at first and passes Centennial Park where in 1990 the Soldotna Historical Society opened **Historic Homestead Village** on six acres within the park. The village consists of six log buildings from early Soldotna, including a log schoolhouse, the former tourist information building and Damon Hall. Many of them now have historical displays or in the case of Damon Hall wildlife exhibits. Hours are from 10 am to 5 pm Tuesday to Sunday in the summer.

Eventually Kalifornsky Beach Rd heads north, then south after passing a junction to Kenai. It continues south for 16 miles along the Cook Inlet and offers some splendid views on the waterway and the Alaska Range before rejoining Sterling Hwy at the small settlement of Kasilof.

Opposite the Kalifornsky Beach Rd near the Kenai River is the junction to Funny River Rd. Turn left (east) here and turn right (south) immediately onto Ski Hill Rd, following it for a mile to reach the Kenai **National Wildlife Refuge Visitor Center** (☎ 262-7021). Open from 8 am to 4.30 pm weekdays and from 10 am to 6 pm weekends, the center features a good series of wildlife displays, daily slide shows and wildlife films in its theater and naturalist-led outdoor pro-

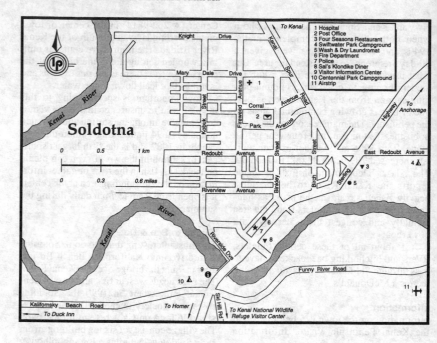

To Kenai

1	Hospital
2	Post Office
3	Four Seasons Restaurant
4	Swiftwater Park Campground
5	Wash & Dry Laundromat
6	Fire Department
7	Police
8	Sal's Klondike Diner
9	Visitor Information Center
10	Centennial Park Campground
11	Airstrip

Knight Drive

Kenai River

Mary Dale Drive

Soldotna

0   0.5   1 km

0   0.3   0.6 miles

Kobuk Street

Firweed Avenue

Corral

2

Park

Redoubt Avenue

Riverview Avenue

Kenai River

Spur Road

Avenue

Corral

To Anchorage

Highway

East Redoubt Avenue

▼ 3

4 ▲

● 5

Binkley Street

Birch Street

Sterling

Riverside Dr

✦ 6
7
▼ 8

Funny River Road

9

ℹ

10 ▲

11 ✦

Kalifornsky Beach Road

To Homer

Ski Hill Rd

To Duck Inn

To Kenai National Wildlife
Refuge Visitor Center

grams on the weekends. There are also three short trails (maps available) that begin at the visitor center and wind into the nearby woods and lakes. No admission fee.

Raining in Soldotna? Check out the **Joyce Carver Library** (☎ 262-4227), at 235 Binkley St. The facility was totally renovated in 1990 and now has pleasant sun-lit reading rooms and free typewriters in case you want to dash off a letter. On Saturday at 2 pm Alaska videos are shown. Opening hours are from 9 am to 6 pm on Monday, Wednesday and Friday; until 8 pm on Tuesday and Thursday; and from noon to 6 pm on Saturday.

Places to Stay
Camping There is the *Centennial Park Campground* (108 sites, $6 per night), on the corner of Sterling Hwy and Kalifornsky Beach Rd (near the visitor center), and the *Swiftwater Park Campground* (20 sites, $6), on East Redoubt Ave at *Mile 94* of the Ster-

ling Hwy. Both are on the Kenai River which means from late June to mid-August you'd better be there before noon to stake out a site.

B&Bs There are more than 30 B&Bs in the area and rates range from $50 to $70 for a single. Stop at the visitors center for brochures and locations of them or try *Denise Lake Lodge* (☎ 262-1789 or (800) 478-1789 in Alaska). Located 2.5 miles from downtown Soldotna on Denise Lake, the log lodge features six rooms and a cabin along with a large fireplace and a kitchen available to guests at night. A single with shared bath is $45, and a double $65. *Marlow's Kenai River B&B* (☎ 262-5218), off Scout Lake Rd on the Kenai River, has three double rooms for $40 a night.

Hotels Most of hotels are geared up for RVers and anglers and are lined up along Sterling Hwy and Kenai Spur Rd – take your pick. The *Duck Inn* (☎ 262-1849), 3.5 miles out on Kalifornsky Beach Rd, has the cheapest rooms from $60 to $70. The *Bunk House Inn* (☎ 262-4584) on the Sterling Hwy is a step up with rooms beginning at $75, which seems to be the competitive rate here.

Places to Eat

Fast (and cheap) restaurants include *Dairy Queen,* on the corner of Kenai Spur Rd and Sterling Hwy, which serves hamburgers and *McDonald's* and *Burger King* further down the Sterling Hwy. *Sal's Klondike Diner* near the bridge on the Sterling Hwy is open 24 hours and is the best diner for miles around. Breakfast begins at $5 and you can amuse yourself with the menu before the eggs and toast arrive. For something to savour between bites, try the *Four Seasons* (☎ 262-5006) at the Soldotna 'Y'. The restaurant has home-made desserts, breads and soups, nightly specials and a Sunday breakfast buffet for $8 served from 9 am to 1 pm.

All-you-can-consume deals include *Golden International Chinese Restaurant* on Sterling Hwy with a lunch buffet for $4.95 and *Godfather's Pizza,* also on the highway, with an unlimited lunch for $6. Even cheaper, *Safeway* in Soldotna is open 24 hours and has a salad bar.

Getting There & Away

Seward/Homer Bus Lines also stops at Soldotna at the King Salmon Motel on Sterling Hwy near the 'Y'. A van departs at 12.55 pm daily and heads north to reach Anchorage at 4 pm while another comes through at 1.30 pm and reaches Homer at 3.45 pm. The fares are the same as those to Kenai.

STERLING HIGHWAY TO HOMER

At Soldotna, the Sterling Hwy rambles south, hugging the coastline and opening up to grand views of Cook Inlet every so often. This stretch is 78 miles long and passes through a handful of small villages near some great clamming areas, ending at the charming village of Homer. Take your time in this area; the coastline and Homer are worth every day you decide to spend there.

Kasilof

Kasilof (population 1200), a fishing village, is at *Mile 108.8* of Sterling Hwy. Turn west on Kalifornsky Beach Rd and travel 3.6 miles to reach the Small Boat Harbor on the Kasilof River, the heart of the town. Sterling Hwy crosses a bridge over the Kasilof River a mile south of the Kalifornsky Beach Rd turn-off. On the other side of the bridge is the *Kasilof River State Wayside* (11 sites, $6 fee) on the riverbank. At *Mile 111.5* of the Sterling Hwy, the Coho Loop Rd heads north-west towards the ocean, and the Johnson Lake Access Rd heads south-east.

Just east on the Johnson Lake Access Rd from the Sterling Hwy is the **Crooked Creek Hatchery**, a state-owned salmon hatchery open to the public from 8 am to 4 pm daily. The hatchery handles silver and king salmon and steelhead trout. If you're here at the right week in July you can watch the 'egg take' (biologists removing eggs from female kings). Another 0.3 miles down the access road is the *Johnson Lake Recreation Area* (43 camp sites, $6 fee) with entry into the lake which has rainbow trout. At the end of the seven-mile access road is the *Tustumena Lake Campground* (10 sites, $6 fee), which really lies on the Kasilof River, a mile from the large Tustumena Lake.

Clam Gulch

At *Mile 117.4* of Sterling Hwy, before reaching the hamlet of Clam Gulch (population 120), you pass the junction of a two-mile gravel road. Just west on the road is *Clam Gulch State Recreation Area* which has covered picnic tables, outhouses and a campground (116 sites, $6 fee). More importantly, the road provides access to the beaches along the Cook Inlet and the start of the area's great clam digging. Of all the beaches, the Clam Gulch beach is generally thought to be the best by clammers, due to its easy access, the nearby campground and gradual gradient that makes for wide beds.

The village of Clam Gulch is less than a mile south of the gravel road on Sterling Hwy and has a post office and gasoline station. More importantly, there's *Clam Shell*

Digging for Clams

Almost all of the beaches on the west side of the Kenai Peninsula (Calm Gulch, Deep Creek, Ninilchik and Whiskey Gulch) have a good supply of razor clams, considered by mollusk connoisseurs to be a true delicacy from the sea. Not only do razors has the best flavor, but they are the largest of the mollusks gathered. The average razor clam is 3½ inches long but most clammers have their heart set on gathering clams five, six even seven inches in length.

You first have to purchase a sport-fishing licence (a one-day visitor's licence is $15, and a 14-day licence is $30). The daily bag limit is 60 clams but remember that's an awful lot of clams to clean and eat. Two dozen per person are more than enough for a meal. There is good clamming from April to August, though the best time is July, right before spawning. Wait for the tide to drop at least a foot from the high-water mark, or better still to reach its lower levels four to five feet down.

Equipment consists of a narrow-bladed clam shovel that can either be purchased or, if you don't feel like hauling it around all summer, rented at many lodges and stores near the clamming areas. You also will want rubber boots, rubber gloves, a bucket and a pair of pants you're not terribly attached to.

Look for the clam's footprint in the sand, a dimple mark left behind when it withdraws its neck. Shovel a scoop or two next to the mark (dig right below the dimple and you'll break its shell) and then reach in the sand for the clam. You have to be quick, since a razor clam can bury itself and be gone in seconds.

Once you are successful, leave the clams in a bucket of sea water for several hours to allow them to 'clean themselves'. Many locals say a handful of cornmeal thrown in helps this process. The best way to cook clams is right on the beach over an open fire while you're soaking in the mountain scenery across Cook Inlet. Use a large covered pot and steam the clams in salt water or, better still, in white wine with a clove of garlic. ■

Lodge (☎ 262-4211), where you can rent a clam shovel and then, after a morning on the beach, take a shower and do some washing. If that sounds too much like work, the lodge restaurant serves calm chowder, razor clams and steamers (also a type of clam).

Ninilchik

Halfway between Soldotna and Homer is Ninilchik, a scenic area with a Russian accent, some great clamming beaches and three state campgrounds that all have a view of those impressive volcanoes across Cook Inlet. For many travelers, Ninilchik is merely a stop for gas and a quick look at its Russian church. But this interesting little village is well worth spending a night at.

The community is actually the oldest on the Kenai Peninsula, having been settled in the 1820s by employees of the Russian-American Company. Many stayed even after imperial Russia sold Alaska to the US and today their descendants form the core of the present community.

Like so many other Kenai Peninsula

towns, Ninilchik suffered heavily during the 1964 earthquake when the village sank three feet and huge sections of land, including its landing strip, disappeared into the Cook Inlet. Subsequently, 'New Ninilchik' was built on the bluffs at *Mile 135.5* of the Sterling Hwy between the Ninilchik River and Deep Creek.

Information The Ninilchik Community Library (☎ 567-3333), on Sterling Hwy just north of Oilwell Rd, doubles up as a visitor information center.

Things to See & Do Pick up a free *Tour of Ninilchik Village* brochure at the community library and then head north and turn west on Beach Access Rd, just south of the bridge over Ninilchik River and posted with signs to the Russian Church. **Old Ninilchik Village**, the site of the original community, is a postcard scene of faded log cabins in tall grass, beached fishing boats and the spectacular backdrop of Mt Redoubt. The walking tour of the old village points out a dozen buildings, including the Sorensen/Tupper Home built in 1895 with fir logs salvaged from fish traps and the town's first Russian School House.

The most spectacular building, however, is the **Russian Orthodox church**, built in 1901 and reached from a posted footpath in the village. The historic church, topped with the unique spires and crosses of the Russian Orthodox faith, is on a wide bluff and commands an unbelievable view of Cook Inlet and volcanoes on the other side. A Russian Orthodox cemetery adjoins the church and

together they make for a photographer's delight on a clear day.

Also check out **Village Cache**, a log cabin that was built in the late 1800s and then completely dismantled and restored, log by log, in 1984. Inside is a gift shop featuring usual Russian items, not moose-nugget ear rings.

The other popular activity is Ninilchik is clamming. At low tide head to either Ninilchik Bear State Recreation Site or Deep Creek. You can either purchase a shovel at the Ninilchik General Store on Sterling Hwy

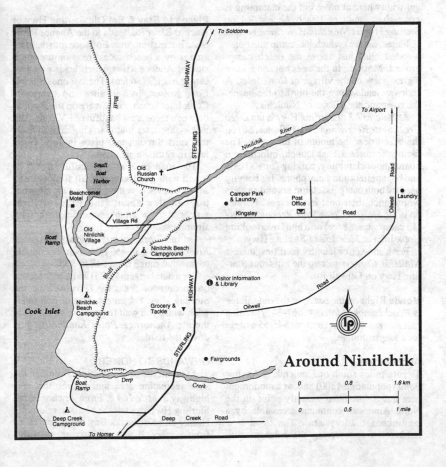

Around Ninilchik

or rent one from Banadana Bob's Tackle Shop in the old village.

The main event in Ninilchik is the Kenai Peninsula State Fair, the 'biggest little fair in Alaska' which is held annually in town near the end of August.

Places to Stay

Camping Sandwiched around the town are three public campgrounds while a fourth is just a few miles down the highway. Across the river from the old village is *Ninilchik Beach State Recreation Site* (35 sites, $6 fee), an open area along the shoreline. It can get windy here at times but the clamming is great. Just south of Beach Access Rd on Sterling Hwy is *Ninilchik View Campground* (12 sites, $8 fee) which has camp sites on a wooded bluff just above the beach campground. Most are in the trees but some have a great view of the village or Cook Inlet. A stairway leads down the bluff to the beach, the river and the village of Ninilchik.

At *Mile 137.2* of Sterling Hwy is the *Deep Creek State Recreation Site* (100 sites, $6) on the beach near the mouth of the creek. The facility features a boat launch, information board about clamming, parking for 300 cars and boat trailers and a pay phone. It's heavily used by both campers, clammers and anglers who launch their boat in the creek. Further on is the *Stariski Creek State Recreation Site* (13 camp sites, $8 fee) on a bluff overlooking Cook Inlet at *Mile 152* of Sterling Hwy.

For a shower or laundry facilities, there's *Ninilchik Corners* just up the hill from Sterling Hwy on Oilwell Rd.

Motels Right on the beach in the old village is *Beachcomber Motel* (☎ 567-3417) with a half a dozen units that rent for $45/55 a night for a single/double.

Anchor Point

Twenty miles south of Ninilchik is Anchor Point (population 1300) and, as a monument here notes, 'the most westerly point on the North American continent accessible by a continuous road system'. The town is a fishing hot spot during the summer with Anchor River renowned for its salmon, steelhead and Dolly Varden fishing. If you're bringing your rod and reel, make sure you pick up an Anchor River State Recreation Area brochure which lists the seasons and even shows the favorite fishing holes along the river. But be prepared for massive crowds here in July and through much of August.

Information At the junction of Sterling and Old Sterling highways is the Anchor Point Visitor Center, housed in a log cabin and staffed by volunteers. Summer hours are from 10 am to 4 pm weekdays.

Places to Stay & Eat Old Sterling Hwy or Anchor River Rd, leads to the Anchor River State Recreation Area. Entrance into the state area is by a beach access road on the south side of Anchor River which leads past five campgrounds ($6 fee). The last one, *Halibut Campground*, has 30 sites and overlooks Cook Inlet beach, the rest are on the river. In between them are a handful of RV parks and tackle shops, testimony to king salmon fever that runs through this place in July. Good luck in getting a site then.

The road ends at a beautiful stretch of beach with good views of Mt Redoubt and Mt Iliamna across the inlet and an information display about 'the Ring of Fire' volcanoes, on an observation deck with sighting scopes.

On the Sterling Hwy in town is *Anchor River Inn* (☎ 235-8531), which has double rooms that range from $48 to $75.

For a hamburger ($5.25) and a beer served on an outdoor deck, try *Teri Ann's* on the Sterling Hwy. For an espresso or deli sandwich while you wait for your wash to finish, there's *Anchorage Point Roadhouse* just down the road.

ONWARDS TO HOMER

The Old Sterling Hwy continues south in the state recreation area and rejoins the new highway at *Mile 164.8*. From Anchor Point, Sterling Hwy ascends the bluffs overlooking Homer and Kachemak Bay, about five miles from Homer. If you are driving, take this section slowly as there are some great viewing points that will be missed by the hasty. One of the best is 3.2 miles north of Homer.

HOMER

Arriving in Homer (population 3900) is like opening one of those pop-up greeting cards – it's an unexpected thrill. A couple of miles before town, the Sterling Hwy provides a few teasers that whet your appetite but never fully prepare you for the charming, colorful fishing village that lies ahead. As the road makes a final turn east along the bluffs, Homer unfolds completely. It's an incredible panorama of mountains, white peaks, glaciers, and the beautiful Kachemak Bay into which stretches Homer Spit, a long strip of land.

In the beginning the Spit was Homer and it has always played a prominent role in the development of the city. The town was founded, and picked up its name, when Homer Pennock, an adventurer from Michigan, landed on the Spit with a crew of gold seekers in 1896, convinced that Kachemak Bay was the key to their riches. It wasn't and in 1898 Pennock was lured away by the spell of the Klondike fields, failing to find gold there as well.

Coal first supported the fledging town and in 1899 the first dock on the Spit was built by the Cook Inlet Coal Field Company. It was later destroyed by ice. The second dock didn't come until 1938 when a combination of the CCC and local fund raising (including the Homer Women's Club which raised enough to build a warehouse) reconnected the city to the sea. When the first steamship arrived that fall, the residents celebrated the end of an era of dismal isolation.

Despite the arrival of the first gravel road to Homer in 1951, the Spit continued to be the focal point of the town. Homer switched

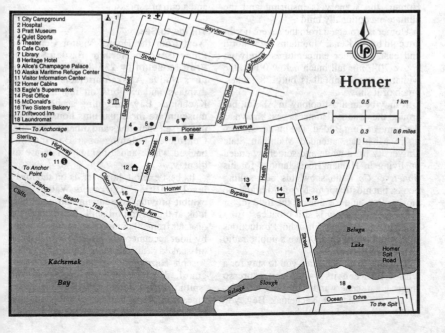

1 City Campground
2 Hospital
3 Pratt Museum
4 Quiet Sports
5 Theater
6 Cafe Cups
7 Library
8 Heritage Hotel
9 Alice's Champagne Palace
10 Alaska Maritime Refuge Center
11 Visitor Information Center
12 Homer Cabins
13 Eagle's Supermarket
14 Post Office
15 McDonald's
16 Two Sisters Bakery
17 Driftwood Inn
18 Laundromat

from a coal-based economy to fishing which is centered in the Small Boat Harbor on the Spit and today pumps $30 million a year into the area. The Spit and the town also survived the Good Friday Earthquake, which dropped the narrow peninsula by six feet and leveled most of the building. By high tide the Spit was no longer a spit but an island. Six years and almost $7 million later, the Spit and the road to it was reconstructed.

The Spit has also survived the ravages of fire and high water, political battles over land use and currently is being besieged by an onslaught of tourism. Nonetheless its unique character is still intact as is the rest of Homer.

The community is supported by both its fishing industries and a growing influx of tourism but is still recognized around the state as the arts capital of Southcentral Alaska and something of a retreat for the 1960s generation of radicals, artists and dropouts from mainstream society. It is little wonder that the graying hippies choose Homer; the scenery is inspiring and the climate exceptionally mild.

Homer is protected from the severe northern cold by the Kenai Mountains to the north and east. Summer temperatures rarely go above 70°F nor fall much below 0°F in the winter. Annual rainfall is only 28 inches, much of it snow.

It may be an artist colony in Alaska, but around the country, Homer is best known as the home of Tom Bodett. The humorist grew up in Michigan, attended Michigan State University for a while and somehow ended up living in Homer. He is famous for his *Bodett & Co* radio show, his best selling books, but mostly for his Motel 6 ads and the closing line 'and we'll leave the light on for ya'. The radio show is still broadcast from Homer from Bodett's Clearshot Productions studio and heard on the town's public radio station, KBBI-AM 890.

This is a town that lures you to stay for a while. Between its half-dozen espresso shops, great scenery and interesting side trips on the other side of Kachemak Bay, you could easily spend a week here.

Information

How popular is the Spit with tourists? The Homer Visitor Center (☎ 235-5300) was recently moved from a log cabin downtown to the end of the Spit. Opening hours are from 8 am to 8 pm from Memorial Day to Labor Day. There is also some limited tourist information at the Pratt Museum and the Alaska Maritime National Wildlife Refuge Visitor Center (see the following Things to See section).

You can take a shower ($3) and wash your clothes at the same time on the way to the Spit at Washboard Laundromat (☎ 235-6781) at 1204 Ocean Dr.

Books The Homer Public Library (☎ 235-3180), on Pioneer Ave across from Quiet Sports, is an excellent facility. Among other services, it usually has used books for sale. Hours are from 10 am to 8 pm Thursday and Tuesday and until 6 pm Wednesday, Friday and Saturday. There's also Bagdad Books & Cafe (☎ 235-8787), inside the Kachemak Mall, the place to go for a used paperback and a cup of espresso.

Things to See

West from the Homer Visitor Center on Pioneer Ave and north on Bartlett St is the **Pratt Museum** (☎ 235-8635), which features Native Alaskan artefacts, historical displays and exhibits on marine life in Kachemak Bay. Intriguing aspects of the museum are the aquariums housing octopuses, sea anemones and other marine life. Complete skeletons of a Bearing Sea beaked whale and a beluga whale are on display.

Its best exhibit, however, is on the lower level. Entitled 'Darkened Waters', the exhibit provides a stunning and emotional look at the Exxon oil spill. It considers the disaster from all points of view, has an hour-by-hour account of the effort to save just one oil-soaked seal, the radio tapes of Captain Joseph Hazelwood contacting the coastguard, displays on both protestors and 'spillionaires' – locals who made small fortunes from the spill. It is by far the best look at Alaska's worse environmental tragedy.

The museum is open daily in summer from 10 am to 6 pm and charges $3 for admission.

More natural displays can be seen nearby at the **Alaska Maritime National Wildlife Refuge Visitor Center**, on Sterling Hwy just before entering town. There is a small theater with regularly scheduled videos, a book and map counter and information on hiking and kayaking in Kachemak Bay. The center (☎ 235-6961) also hosts guided bird walks and children's programs throughout the summer. Call for a schedule or stop by from 10 am to 5 pm daily.

Art Galleries The beautiful scenery has inspired numerous artists to gather here, and the handful of galleries in town display more than the usual ivory carvings and gold nugget jewelry you see everywhere else. Most of the galleries are along Pioneer Ave, including Studio One (☎ 235-3848) which features pottery made from Cook Inlet clay and glazes. Next door is the equally impressive Ptarmigan Arts (☎ 235-5345), which features a variety of works from more than 40 artists in the area. The Pratt Museum also has an art gallery that exhibits work by artists from around the Kenai Peninsula while more remote studios are in Anchor Point and out along the Sterling Hwy.

For a map and descriptions of the galleries in town, pick up the *Downtown Homer Art Galleries* from the visitor's center. For a complete description of all the area studios, check out the *Homer Tourist Guide*, published by the Homer News.

The Spit This long needle of land is a five-mile sand bar which stretches into Kachemak Bay; during the summer it is the center of activity in Homer and the heart of its fishing industry. The Spit draws thousands of tourists and backpackers every year,

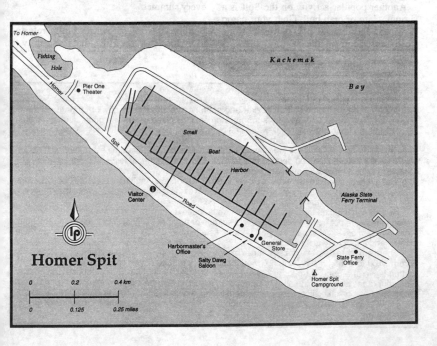

making it not only a scenic spot but an interesting mecca for fishers, cannery workers, visitors and charter-boat operators.

The hub of all this activity is the **Small Boat Harbor** at the end of the Spit, one of the best facilities in Southcentral and home base for over 700 boats. On each side of the harbor's entrance is a cannery. Nearby are boardwalks, rows of gray Cape Cod buildings that house charter-boat operators, gift shops, seafood markets and almost a dozen eateries.

The favorite activity on the Homer Spit, naturally, is beachcombing, especially at dawn or dusk while viewing the sunset or sunrise. You can stroll for miles along the beach, where the marine life is as plentiful as the driftwood, or you can go clamming at Mud Bay, on the east side of the spit. Blue mussels, an excellent shellfish overlooked by many people, are the most abundant. Locals call the clams and mussels 'Homer grown'.

Another popular activity on the Spit is a shrimp, clam or crab boil. Grab your camp stove and large metal pot, purchase some fresh seafood from the seafood markets around the Small Boat Harbor and buy a can of beer from the general store next door to the Salty Dawg Saloon. Then head down to the beach and enjoy your Alaskan feast while watching the tide roll in and the sun set. No beach fires are allowed between Land's End and the Whitney Fidalgo Access Rd.

If you're into catching your dinner rather than shoveling or buying it, try your luck at the **Fishing Hole**, posted across the road from the visitor center. The small lagoon is the site of a 'terminal fishery' in which salmon are planted and then return three or four years later to a place where they can't spawn. The enhancement program is carried out by the state's Department of Natural Resources and is strictly for shore anglers. From mid-May to mid-September, anglers bait their hooks with colorful spoons, salmon eggs or herring or shrimp under bobbers and then cast into the lagoon. More than 15,000 salmon, ranging from 40-pound kings to five-pound pinks and cohos, are caught here every summer.

Skyline Dr North of town are bluffs, referred to by locals as 'the Hill', that rise gently to

Hooking a Halibut in Homer

Homer may be the home of Tom Bodett and an intriguing arts community, but to thousands of tourists who come to Alaska every summer, Homer is the place where you go to catch a halibut.

Halibut is a bottom-dweller that, when first born, looks like any normal fish with an eye on each side of the head. But as a halibut feeds exclusively off the bottom, it flattens out and one eye moves to other side, now the top of the fish. Females are larger than males, in fact, just about every halibut more than 100 pounds is a female. And almost without fail, a 300-pound halibut is hauled out of Kachemak Bay every summer.

The average size fish, however, is closer to 30 or 40 pounds. Anglers use a large hook, usually baited with herring, and a heavy weight to take it down to the bottom of the bay where they proceed to 'jig' (raising and lowering the hook slightly) for a fish.

As you can imagine, reeling in a halibut can be quite a workout and to many anglers exciting though they are not battlers or jumpers like salmon or trout. Actually getting the fish into the boat can be the most exciting part as charter captains often use a club or even a gun to subdue their catch and a gaff to haul it aboard.

There are more than two dozen charter captains working out of the Spit and charging anywhere from $100 to $155 for a halibut trip. Most captains try to take advantage of two slack tides and often leave at around 6 am for a 12-hour trip on the bay. Pack a lunch or purchase one from a handful of restaurants that sell box lunches on the Spit. Also take warm clothing and rain gear and purchase a fishing licence (non-resident licences cost $15 for three days, $30 for 14 days).

Head to the Spit to book a charter. Just about all of them have an ad in the *Homer Tourist Guide* handed out free at the visitor center on the Spit. ∎

1100 feet. These green slopes, broken up by colorful patches of wildflowers, on a clear day provide excellent views of the glaciers that spill out of the Harding Icefield across the bay. The best views are from Skyline Dr, which runs along the bluff above Homer.

Follow Pioneer Ave east out of town where it turns into East End Rd and then turn north onto East Hill Rd up the bluffs to Skyline Dr. At the west end of Skyline Dr is Ohlson Mountain Rd which ascends 1513 feet to the peak of Ohlson Mountain. Many roads, including East End Rd, are paved and ideal for cycling (see the Homer Cycling section).

Kachemak Bay This beautiful body of water extends 30 miles into the Kenai Peninsula and features a coastline of steep fjords and inlets with the glacier-capped peaks of the Kenai Mountains in the background. Marine and bird life are plentiful in the bay, but it is best known for its rich fishing grounds, especially for halibut.

For those who have no desire to hook an 80-pound halibut, there's **Gull Island**, a group of bare rock islets halfway between the Spit and Halibut Cove. The islands are the site of thousands of nesting seabirds: tufted puffins, black legged kittiwakes, common murres, cormorants and many more species. The stench is surpassed only by the opportunities to photograph the birds up close, even if you don't have a 300-mm lens.

Both Rainbow Tours (☎ 235-7272) and Kachemak Bay Adventures (☎ 235-8206) run 1½-hour tours to the islands with a naturalists on board and maintain offices on the Spit. Rainbow departs daily at 9 am and 4.30 pm, Kachemak Bay Adventures at 10 am. The cost is $10 per person, making it possibly the best birding tour in the state.

Rainbow Tours also has a Natural History Tour, in which a full day is spent in Kachemak Bay to sight more wildlife and to include a visit to the **Center for Alaskan Coastal Studies**, a non-profit marine center in Peterson Bay. The tours depart daily at 9 am, return at 6 pm and are $49 per person. Another interesting side trip is **Halibut**

Cove, a small village of 50 people on the south shore of Kachemak Bay. In the early 1920s, the cove supported 42 herring salteries and had a population of over 1000. Today, the quaint community has a pair of art galleries that produce 'octopus ink paintings', the noted Saltry Restaurant, some cabins for rent and boardwalks to stroll on but no roads.

Danny J is the ferry that will run you across to the cove from the Spit. It departs at noon, swings past Gull Island and then at 1.30 pm arrives at Halibut Cove where you have 2½ hours to explore the 12 blocks of boardwalks and galleries or have lunch on the outdoor deck of the *Saltry Restaurant*. The ferry returns to the Spit by 5 pm and then makes an evening run to the cove for dinner at the Saltry, returning to Homer at 10 pm.

The noon tour of the *Danny J* is $35 per person, its evening trip is $17.50. Dinner at the Saltry ranges from $8 to $15 and is well worth it. To make Halibut Cove an even more interesting side trip, book a cabin at *Quiet Place Lodge* (☎ 296-2212) and spend the night. Cabins are $150 per couple and include breakfast. There is also *Halibut Cove Cabins* (☎ 296-2214) which offers a pair of cosy cabins that sleep four people (bring your own sleeping bags). You can book all of this at Central Charter Booking Agency (☎ 235-7847 or (800) 478-7847 in Alaska) which has an office on the Spit.

Festivals
Summer events in Homer begin in May with the almost month-long Spring Arts Festival. This event began as an outlet for local artists to display their work and has since evolved into a festival with dancers, musicians and craftspeople.

The Fourth of July celebration is usually a three-day event that includes a parade, a foot race, various local contests such as a grease-pole climb, and art & craft booths.

Places to Stay
Camping Beach camping is allowed in designated areas of west side of Homer Spit, a beautiful spot to pitch a tent. The nightly fee is $3 if you are pitching your tent in the

city-controlled sections near the end of the Spit; there are toilets next to the Harbormaster's Office. Keep in mind the Spit can get rowdy at times.

The *City Campground* is on a hill overlooking the town and can be reached by following the signs north up Bartlett St. There is a $4 nightly fee at the City Campground, and a 14-day limit applies at both campgrounds.

Hostels There's no official hostel in Homer but there is *Seaside Farm* (☎ 235-7850 or 235-2670), five miles from Homer out on East End Rd. The working farm has a variety of accommodations including a backpacker hostel with bunks for $15, cabins that sleep three to four people for $50 and even the 'hay barn' for $8. You can also pitch your tent $6 in a grassy pasture overlooking Kachemak Bay. The farm has an outdoor kitchen area for campers, showers, laundry facilities and cheap transport back to town. Getting low on funds? You can even trade farm work for accommodations.

B&Bs Bed & breakfast places have popped up in Homer like mushrooms in the spring, at last count there were more than 30 in the area.

Others to consider are *Lily Pad* (☎ 235-6630), at 3954 Bartlett St in the heart of town, with seven rooms and doubles for $65 and *Beach House Bed & Breakfast* (☎ 235-5945), near the airport with four rooms that begin at $50, with good views of the Spit and a jacuzzi. Then there is the *Jailhouse Bed & Breakfast*, a no-host lodge that was indeed Homer's first jail and then home of Tom Bodett's 'The End of the Road' radio show. A double is $100 a night but a triple is only $120.

Others to check out include *Brass Ring B&B* (☎ 235-5450), close to the downtown area at 987 Hillfair Court. The log cabin home features, among other amenities, an outdoor hot tub. Up on Skyline Rd with a view from an outdoor deck that's hard to beat and a bush pilot as a host, is *Ridgetop B&B*

(☎ 235-7590) with two large bedrooms for $65 a night.

Hotels There are almost a dozen hotels/motels in the area with mostly single rooms ranging from $60 to $70. All of them are heavily booked during the summer. A delightful, small hotel is the *Driftwood Inn* (☎ 235-8019 or (800) 478-8019 in Alaska), on the corner of Main St and Bunnell Ave near Bishop Beach. Single rooms without bath begin at $66, doubles at $72. Some rooms overlook Kachemak Bay while in the lounge is a fieldstone fireplace and, out the back, a barbecue area and deck. Equally charming and affordable is *Homer Cabins* (☎ 235-6768), at 3601 Main St. The individual log cabins contain kitchens and even microwaves and rent for $55 a night or $220 for the week.

Other cheap sleeps include *Road Runner Retreat* (☎ 235-3678), three miles out on East End Rd. Double rooms range from $45 to $55 including a full breakfast. Within walking distance of downtown Homer is *Ocean Shores Motel* (☎ 235-7775), at 3500 Critten Dr, with rates from $40 to $90. Right on Pioneer Ave is *Heritage Hotel* (☎ 235-7787 or (800) 478-7789 in Alaska), an historical log lodge where singles with shared bath are $45.

To treat yourself, try the new *Beluga Lake Lodge* (☎ 235-5995), at 984 Ocean Dr, overlooking its namesake lake. Double rooms begin at $90 a night.

Places to Eat

Sure, Homer has a *McDonald's* and even two *Subway* shops, but pass up the fast lane to fast food and try one of the charming and unique eateries. Spoon for spoon, no other town in Alaska has the variety in dining that Homer boasts of with the exception of the big two – Anchorage and Fairbanks.

The Spit Cheap eats at the end of the Spit consist of a *Subway* franchise, a fish and chips carry out, *Glacier Drive-In* and a couple of meals-on-wheels vans selling espresso and fresh bagels. For something a little more charming, however, drop in at *Dockside Seafood Restaurant*. Bowls of halibut chowder, seafood gumbo or a fisherman's stew with a big slice of sourdough bread is $4. They also have an interesting selection of imported beer and if the day is nice you can sit outside on a deck and watch the cannery workers ice down fish.

Equally nice is *Barb's Steak & Seafood* with a small dining room overlooking Kachemak Bay. A 12-inch pizza costs $13, a spaghetti dinner $8, and a seafood pasta dinner (your choice of halibut, scallops or shrimp) is $10. Across the road is *Addies's Paddies*, which has a dining room and bar overlooking the Small Boat Harbor. Eggs in the morning begin at $4, a baked halibut dinner is $15 and steamed tanner crab in the shell is $19.

Downtown In town, there is an assortment of cafés and bakeries, including a handful of espresso shops. You've read it right – this town of 3000 supports more than a half-dozen places where you can get a cup of cafe latte. The most interesting is *Cafe Cups* with its bizarre coffee cup exterior and its pleasant interior where each wall is an art gallery. Huge sandwiches, made with thick cuts of bread, are $6 and include several veggie models, home-made soup is $4. The café opens up at 7 am for breakfast and serves several unusual egg dishes, just what you would expect in Homer. Equally good cafe latte, baked goods, and that 1960s atmosphere can be enjoyed at *Two Sisters Espresso & Bakery* on the corner of Main and Bunnell streets. The shop is in the Old Inlet Trading Post Building and has a few tables inside and a few more outside on the porch overlooking the bay. Next door is the interesting Bunnell Street Gallery.

Interesting and affordable is *Neon Coyote*, a diner on Pioneer Ave that specializes in Southwest cooking. For dinner there's tamale pie, cornbread smothered with black beans, cheese and green chilli for $5.25. Or come in the morning for huevos rancheros, corn tortilla with beans, cheese and eggs.

Also worth mentioning downtown is

Smoky Bay Co-op and the *Strudel Factory*, both on Pioneer Ave. The Co-op is Homer's health food store but also runs a small kitchen that serves filling vegetarian dishes for lunch for under $4. The factory is a small bakery tucked away in Kachemak Center with great croissants.

All-You-Can-Eat Homer has two Chinese restaurants next door to each other on Pioneer Ave with a lunch buffet. Try *The Thai & Chinese* with a $5.95 feast for lunch and an all-you-can-eat deal at dinner for just $1 more. There is also *Pioneer Pizza* on Pioneer Ave that has all the pizza and pop you can 'scarf' from Monday to Saturday for $7.

Entertainment

Homer's most famous drinking hole is on the Spit. The *Salty Dawg Saloon*, a log cabin bar with a lighthouse tower over it, has the same claim to fame as Juneau's Red Dog Saloon, right down to the sawdust on the floor and an amazing collection of orange life-rings on the walls, each stenciled with the name of the ship from which it came. Actually the saloon is three small log structures, including a tower that was originally a water tank, relocated here after the Good Friday Earthquake of 1964. It's worth at least a look at the collection, if not a few beers while you study it.

Downtown there is *Alice's Champagne Palace*, which rocks with bands and live music almost nightly while next door is the saloon of the *Heritage Hotel*, both on Pioneer Ave. Sock hop music and other oldies are offered on the weekends at the *Waterfront Bar* across Bunnell St from the Driftwood Inn.

Homer is also blessed with entertainment that doesn't require a bar stool. *Pier One Theater* (☎ 235-7333 or 235-7951) performs live drama and comedy in a 'come as you are' warehouse next to the Fishing Hole on the Spit. Performances are Friday and Saturday at 8.15 pm and Sunday at 7.15 pm throughout the summer. There are often midweek performances as well, including Tom

Bodett's radio show of which a portion is taped live on most Wednesdays. There is also *Homer Family Theater* (☎ 235-6728) on the corner of Main St and Pioneer Ave.

Hiking
For all its natural beauty, Homer lacks good public trails. The best hiking is along the beaches, while most trails off the road system are private paths that usually lead to somebody's homestead or cabin.

Bishop Beach Hike This hike, which begins at Bishop Park and makes either an excellent afternoon stroll or a 10-mile trek north of Homer. The views of Kachemak Bay and the Kenai Mountains are superb, while the marine life seen scurrying along the sand at low tide is fascinating.

Check a tide book, available from most gasoline stations or sports stores, and leave before low tide and return before high tide. High tides cover most of the sand, forcing you to scramble onto the base of the nearby cliffs. Within three miles of the park you'll pass a sea otter rookery a few hundred yards offshore and in seven miles you'll reach

Diamond Creek. To reach Bishop Park head south on Main St, then left on Bunnell Ave and right on Beluga Ave.

Homestead Trail This new trail, developed by Kachemak Heritage Land Trust, links Rogers Loop Trail with Crossman Ridge Rd. It's best picked up at the trailhead on Diamond Ridge Rd, reached from the Sterling Hwy by turning north on West Hill Rd just west of town. From the Diamond Ridge Rd, it's 2.5 miles to the south to Rogers Loop Trail Trailhead on Sterling Hwy. To the north it's 1.6 miles to Crossman Ridge.

Cycling
The dirt roads in the hills above Homer lend themselves to some great mountain biking, Diamond Ridge and Skyline in particular, while an easy tour is to just head out East End Rd, which extends 20 miles east to the head of Kachemak Bay. Quiet Sports (☎ 235-8620), on Pioneer Ave across from the library, has mountain bike rentals for $20 a day or $12 a half day.

Rocky River The best mountain bike adven-

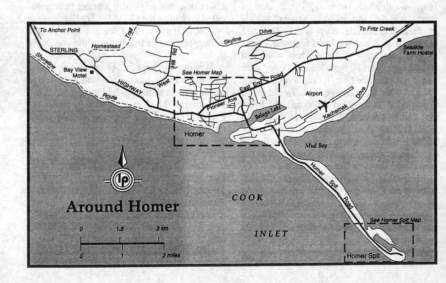

tures in the area are on the south side of Kachemak Bay where you can ride along the Jakolof-Rocky River Rd from Jakolof Bay all the way to Windy Bay. The 20-mile rough dirt road follows a river bed that cuts across the very tip of the Kenai Peninsula. There are numerous stream crossings. Beware loggers, and thus logging trucks, could be in the Windy Bay area at the end of the road. Cyclists in good shape can reach Rocky Bay and return in one day, a 30-mile ride. Otherwise plan to camp.

To reach the dock on Jakolof Bay there's Jakolof Ferry Service (☎ 235-2376) that departs the Spit daily during the summer at 10 am.

Getting There & Away

Air ERA Aviation (☎ (800) 426-0333), the contract carrier for Alaska Airlines, provides seven daily flights between Homer and Anchorage from the Homer Airport, 1.7 miles east of town on Kachemak Dr. The one-way fare is $90; a round-trip, advance-purchase ticket is $150. Homer Air (☎ 235-8591 or (800) 478-8591 in Alaska) provides an air-taxi service to Seldovia. One-way fare is $26.

Bus Seward/Homer Bus Lines (☎ 235-8280) departs from a small hut at 455 Sterling Hwy, on the edge of town, daily at 10 am for Kenai/Soldotna and Anchorage, which it reaches at 4 pm. One-way fare is $35.

Boat The state ferry MV *Tustumena* provides twice-weekly service from Homer to Seldovia and Homer to Kodiak, where once a week it continues onto Seward and the rest of the Southcentral ports. The ferry terminal (☎ 235-8449) is at the end of Homer Spit. The one-way fare from Homer to Seldovia is $16 and from Homer to Kodiak $46.

Rainbow Tours departs daily from the Spit at 11 am to Seldovia, and return at 4 pm. The trip takes 1½ hours and the fare is $36 return or $20 one way.

Hitchhiking Along with Bay Bushlines, in

which messages are swapped back and forth between isolated neighbors, KBBI-AM 890 also has a 'Rideline' for people seeking transportation out of town or passengers. Call the public radio station (☎ 235-7721) to leave a message for the show.

Car Rental To obtain an affordable rental, stop at Polar Car Rental (☎ 235-5998), at 3267 E St, just off Ocean Dr. The small dealer has subcompacts for $45 a day with the first 100 miles free.

KACHEMAK BAY STATE PARK

This park, along with the adjoining Kachemak Bay State Wilderness Park to the south, is 350,000 acres of mountainous and glacial wilderness that is only accessible by bush plane or boat. Visitor facilities include primitive camp sites, a seasonal ranger station at the head of Halibut Cove Lagoon and almost 20 miles of trails. For information on the park, contact the Alaska Division of Parks & Outdoor Recreation office (☎ 235-7024) at *Mile 168.5* of Sterling Hwy, four miles north of Homer.

Hiking

Grewingk Glacier Trail The most popular hike in the park is this 3.5-mile, one-way trail from a trailhead near *Rusty Lagoon Campground* (five sites). It is a level, easy-to-follow trek across the glacial outwash and ends at a lake with superb views of Grewingk Glacier. Camping on the lake is spectacular and often the shoreline is littered with icebergs.

Lagoon Trail Departing from the Grewingk Glacier trail is the mile-long Saddle Trail which leads to the start of the Lagoon Trail. This 5.5-mile route leads to the ranger station at the head of Halibut Cover Lagoon passing two side trails, Alpine Ridge and Goat Rope, that climb steeply into the alpine tundra.

You also pass the posted junction of Halibut Creek Trail. If Grewingk Glacier is too crowded for you, follow this trail to Halibut Creek to spend the night in a beautiful but much more remote valley. At the ranger station, more trails extend south to several lakes, Poot Peak and the Wosnesenki River.

Cabin

In 1992, the Division of Parks converted a bunkhouse that used to house trail crews into a public-use cabin. The three-room cabin has a pair of bunkbed sleeping platforms as well as electricity and water. It's at the southern end of Halibut Cove and can be reached by boat, water taxi or hiking in along the Lagoon Trail. The nightly rate is $35 for the first four people.

Make your reservations in advance if you can at the Homer Ranger Station (☎ 235-5581) at *Mile 168.5* of the Sterling Hwy or the Department of Natural Resources Public Information Center (☎ 762-2261 or (800) 770-2257 in Alaska) at 3601 C St in the Frontier Building in Anchorage.

Kayaking

You can also spend three or four days paddling the many fjords of the park, departing from Homer and making overnight stops at Glacier Spit or Halibut Cove. Think twice before crossing Kachemak Bay from the Spit. Although it's only 3.5 miles across, the currents and tides are strong and can cause serious problems for inexperienced paddlers.

Tour boats that run hikers across can also handle kayakers (see the following Getting Around section). The major headache for most travelers, however, is where to rent a boat. Quiet Sports in Homer no longer maintains a kayak rental service but will have a handle on who does in the area. You could try Kachemak Bay Seakayaking. The small guiding company runs day trips on the south side of the bay that includes kayaks, a lunch guide and transportation. The cost is $140 per person and they can be contacted through Central Charter (☎ 235-7847) or Jakolof Ferry Service (☎ 235-2376) on the Spit. You might also try Jakolof Bay Adventures (☎ 235-5271), which has guided kayaking trips on the bay. If the boats are available, either one might rent them out.

Getting Around

The state park makes an excellent side trip for anybody who has a tent, a spare day and wants to escape the overflow of RVers on Homer Spit. A number of tour boats offer drop-off and pick-up to the state park, charging $50 for a round-trip ticket. St Augustine's Charters will drop you off at Rusty Lagoon and pick you up at Saddle Trail as a way to avoid some backtracking. Book them through Inlet Charters (☎ 235-6126) on the Spit. You can also try Rainbow Tours (☎ 235-7272), while Jakolof Ferry Service (☎ 235-2376) provides transport to Jakolof Bay.

SELDOVIA

Across Kachemak Bay from Homer and in a world of its own is Seldovia (population 600), a small fishing village. The town is slow moving, sleepy and lives up to its nickname, 'City of Secluded Charm'. Although in recent years tour boats have made it a regular stop, the village has managed to retain much of its old Alaskan charm and can be an interesting and inexpensive side trip away from Alaska's highway system.

Seldovia is one of the oldest settlements along Cook Inlet and may have been the site of the first coalmine in Alaska when the Russians began operating one in the late 1700s. They also used the town as a year-round harbor and gathered timber here to repair their ships. By the 1890s, Seldovia was an important shipping and supply center for the region and the town boomed right into the 1920s with salmon canning, fur farming and a short-lived herring industry. After the Sterling Hwy to Homer was completed in the 1950s, Seldovia's population and importance as a supply center began to dwindle but it was the 1964 earthquake that caused the most rapid change in the community.

The Good Friday Earthquake caused the land beneath Seldovia to settle four feet, allowing high tides to flood much of the original town. In the reconstruction of Seldovia, much of its waterfront and beloved

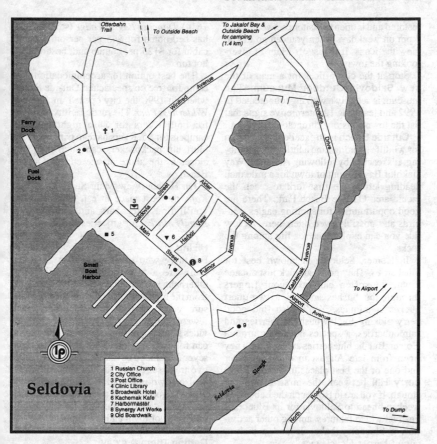

1 Russian Church
2 City Office
3 Post Office
4 Clinic Library
5 Broadwalk Hotel
6 Kachemak Kafe
7 Harbormaster
8 Synergy Art Works
9 Old Boardwalk

Seldovia

boardwalk were torn out while Cap's Hill was levelled to provide fill material.

Information

An information cache is in the Synergy Art Works on Main St across from the boat harbor. The rustic log building is a co-op for local artists to display and sell their pottery, jewelry, prints and other handcrafted items. There is also a town directory sign next to the walk-up ramp at the Small Boat Harbor while Seldovia Chamber of Commerce (☎ 234-7890) can supply information on upcoming activities and events.

Public restrooms and showers are at the Harbormaster's Office at the Small Boat Harbor. There's also Harbor Laundromat (☎ 234-7420) on Main St.

Things to See & Do

Today, a small remnant of the early boardwalk can be seen if you walk a short distance to the east of the ferry terminal. It stretches along Seldovia Slough with a number of historic houses perched on pilings nearby.

The town's most popular sight is the **St Nicholas Russian Orthodox Church**. Built in 1891, the church was recently restored and is open to visitors between 1 and 2 pm on weekdays when you can go in and view the icons. It is just off Main St, overlooking the town.

Stop at the city offices for a map of the new **Seldovia Outdoor Museum**. The museum is actually a walking tour erected in 1992 and featuring 12 interpretive signs that list the town's history chronologically.

Outside Beach is an excellent place to go for wildlife sightings and a little beachcombing. It's reached by following Anderson Way (Jakolof Bay Rd) out of town for a mile then heading left at the first fork to reach the picnic area Outside Beach Park. There are good opportunities for spotting eagles, seabirds and possibly even otters here. At low tide you can explore the sea life among the rocks.

In Homer, Seldovia is known best for blueberries. They grow so thick just outside town, you often can rake your fingers through the bushes and fill a two-quart bucket in minutes. You'll also find good berry picking for lowbush cranberries and salmonberries, a species not found around Homer. But the blueberries are the best. They ripen from late August to mid-September and one of the best places to pick is **Blueberry Hill** between the airstrip and the slough. If you are in Homer on the Labor Day weekend head to Seldovia for its Blueberry Festival which features, among other activities, a blueberry bake ale and a pick-a-cup-of-berries bicycle race.

Places to Stay & Eat

The town's hotel, *Annie McKenzie's Boardwalk Hotel* (☎ 234-7816) is on Main St across from the Small Boat Harbor and charges close to $100 a double. The hotel also offers a package that includes a room for a night, a cruise to Seldovia and a flight back with Homer Air for $149 per person and often runs specials during the summer for $119 per person.

There are also several B&Bs in town with room rates around $75 a night. They include *Crow Hill B&B*, *Gerry's Place* (☎ 243-7471) and *Seldovia Rowing Club Hotel* (☎ 234-

7614). *Dancing Eagles Lodge* (☎ 234-7627) has bedrooms for $45 per person, a chalet cabin for $125 per couple and, best of all, a hot tub.

The best option for accommodation is to camp for free on spectacular Outside Beach, where in 1990 the city opened up *Seldovia Wilderness Park*. The rustic facility has spots for both RVers for $8 a night and tent campers for $5. RVers have to park up on the bluff but backpackers can pitch their tent closer to the shore at one end of Outside Beach.

On Harbor View Main St, is *Kachemak Kafe*, the best place to eat, while in town you'll find three bars and the *Stampers Family Market* for groceries and supplies.

Hiking

For those who spend a night in Seldovia, there are a few trails in the area. The Otterbahn is a trail that was built by students from the high school to Outside Beach. Make sure you hike it at low tide. The beach towards the head of Seldovia Bay also provides hiking opportunities at low tide or you can follow a 4.5-mile logging road to reach several secluded coves along the way. These two trails start from Jakolof Bay Rd. There is also a two-mile trail to a camp site on the Tutka Lagoon, site of a state salmon-rearing facility. It departs from Jakolof Bay Rd 12 miles east of town and is signposted.

Getting There & Away

The state ferry makes a run to Seldovia twice and sometimes three times a week on a round trip from Homer. The boat to catch is the Tuesday run which leaves Homer at 5 pm, arrives in Seldovia at 6.30 pm and stays in port for 1½ hours before returning. The other services reach the town in the early hours of the morning. The ferry terminal (☎ 234-7886) is at the north end of Main St and the one-way fare from Homer to Seldovia is $16.

Several tour boats also offer trips to Seldovia and generally stay in port for two to three hours. Among them is Rainbow Tours (☎ 235-7272 in Homer) which departs daily and swings past Gull Island bird rookery as well. The round-trip fare is $36 return.

You can also fly to Seldovia. A scenic 12-minute flight from Homer passes over the Kenai Mountains and Kachemak Bay. Homer Air (☎ 235-8591 or (800) 478-8591 in Alaska) offers several flights daily to Seldovia with a one-way fare of $26.

Kodiak Island

KODIAK

South-west of the Kenai Peninsula in the Gulf of Alaska is Kodiak (population 15,575). The city is on the eastern tip of Kodiak Island, the largest island in Alaska at 3670 sq miles and the second largest in the country after the Big Island of Hawaii. Kodiak claims several other firsts. It has the largest fishing fleet in the state, with over 2000 boats, making it the second largest commercial fishing port in the USA. At one time, fishers were hauling in so much king crab, it made the city the top fishing port in the country. Residents proudly call their town the 'King Crab Capital of the World'.

Kodiak Island is home of the famed Kodiak brown bear, the largest terrestrial carnivore in the world. There are an estimated 2400 of these bears on the island and some males have reached 1500 pounds in weight.

Kodiak has some of the foggiest weather in Southcentral Alaska. Greatly affected by the turbulent Gulf of Alaska, the city is often rainy and foggy with occasional high winds. The area receives 80 inches of rain per year and has an average temperature of 60°F during the summer. On a clear day, however, the scenery is equal to that in any other part of the state. Mountains, craggy coastlines and some of the most deserted beaches accessible by road are Kodiak's most distinctive features.

The island, especially the city of Kodiak, can also claim some of the most turbulent history in Alaska. The Russians first landed

on the island in 1763 and returned 20 years later when Siberian fur trader Grigorii Shelikhov heard about the abundance of sea otters. Shelikhov sailed into Three Saints Bay on the south side of the island and brought with him his wife, the first White woman to set foot in Alaska. He also had 192 men and a cache of muskets and cannons. Shelikhov attempts 'to subdue' the indigenous people resulted in a bloodbath near what used to be the village of Old Harbor in which more 500 Alutiiq Indians were massacred and an equal number drowned in their effort to escape.

Shelikhov returned home the next year and in 1791 Alexander Baranov arrived as the manager of the colony and the Russian American Company. After an earthquake nearly destroyed the infant settlement at Three Saints Bay, Baranov moved his operations to more stable ground at a harbor at the north end which he named St Paul. Quickly it became a bustling port as the first capital of Russian America and today is the city of Kodiak. When the sea otter colonies had been wiped out, Baranov moved again, this time to Sitka in 1804.

In 1912, Kodiak had its next disaster when Mt Katmai on the nearby Alaska Peninsula erupted. The explosion not only created the Valley of 10,000 Smokes, now part of Katmai National Park, but it blanketed the then sleepy fishing village with 18 inches of ash that blotted out the sun for two days. When a 20-room log cabin caught fire and burned, people 200 feet away were unaware of the blaze it was so dark. Kodiak's 400 residents escaped to sea briefly on a ship that was in port fueling but soon returned to find ash drifts several feet high and spawning salmon choking in ash-filled streams.

Disaster struck again in 1964. The Good Friday Earthquake shook the entire island, and the following tidal wave, called a tsunamis, leveled the downtown area, destroying the boat harbor and wiping out the local fishing fleet. Processing plants, canneries and 158 homes were lost; damage cost a total of $24 million.

The natural disasters, however, are now

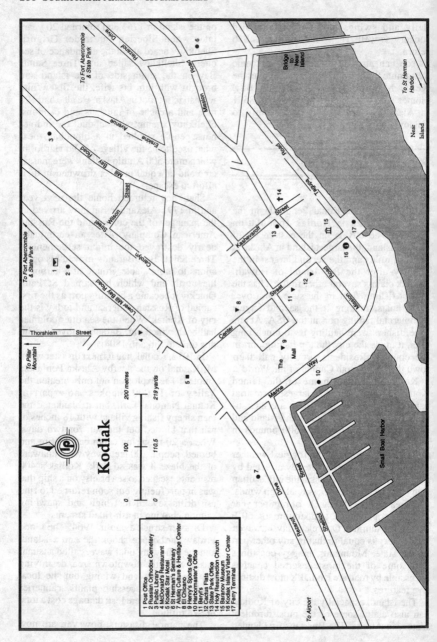

Kodiak

To Fort Abercrombie & State Park
To Pillar Mountain
Thorshiem Street
To Fort Abercrombie & State Park
Thorshiem Street
To Airport

To St Herman Harbor
Bridge to Near Island
Near Island

St Herman Harbor
Small Boat Harbor

0   100   200 metres
0   110.5   219 yards

1 Post Office
2 Russian Orthodox Cemetery
3 Public Library
4 McDonald's Restaurant
5 Kodiak Star Motel
6 St Herman's Seminary
7 El Chicano
8 Mill Bay Culture & Heritage Center
9 Henry's Sports Cafe
10 Harbormaster's Office
11 Beryl's
12 Solatti Flats
13 State Park Office
14 Holy Resurrection Church
15 Baranov Museum
16 Kodiak Island Visitor Center
17 Ferry Terminal

part of Kodiak's turbulent history and today the city thrives as the fishing capital of Alaska with 15 fish-processing plants employing thousands of people during the summer. Kodiak Island is also the site of Alaska's largest coastguard station, which occupies the old US naval base. Four large coastguard cutters patrol out of Kodiak, seizing foreign vessels that illegally fish in US waters and assisting distressed ships caught in the violent storms of the North Pacific. Kodiak Island was also affected by the Exxon oil spill, although it took a while to reach its shorelines.

But the spill's impact on the fishing pales compared with what over-harvesting did to several species, most notably the king crab. This giant of crabs is taken from especially deep areas of the ocean and can easily exceed 10 to 15 pounds – enough to feed two or three people. The record king taken in Kodiak weighed a whopping 25 pounds and had a leg span of almost five feet. Kodiak began canning king crabs in 1949 and by 1966, the peak year of the catch, the town landed 90 million pounds. Two years later Kodiak, for the first time, topped all other ports in the country in the value of fish caught with an incredible $132 million, mostly from king crab and a lucrative shrimp fishery. But the harvest of king crab went into a downward spiral after that until a moratorium halted the crab fishery in 1983. The drag fishery for shrimp was also halted two years later. The city has since rebuilt its seafood industry on bottomfish but dockside value of this fishery, most notably of halibut, was only $34 million in 1991, a far cry from the golden days of king crab.

Information

You'll reach the Kodiak Island Visitor Center (☎ 486-4782) as soon as you leave the state ferry terminal. On the corner of Center St and Marine Way, the center is open weekdays from 8 am to 5.30 pm and is the source of many free hand-outs, including a good map of the city.

The Alaska Division of Parks & Outdoor Recreation office (☎ 486-6339) is on the corner of Mission Rd and Kashevaroff St, north-east of the visitor center. The office is open weekdays from 8 am to 5 pm and is the place to go for information on hiking trails, state campgrounds or renting recreation cabins.

The Kodiak National Wildlife Refuge office (☎ 487-2600) is four miles south-west of the city, near the airport at 1390 Buskin River Rd. Open from 8 am to 4.30 pm weekdays and from noon to 4.30 pm weekends, it has information on the public-use cabins.

Things to See

Across the street from the visitor center is the **Baranov Museum** in Erskine House, built by the Russians between 1792 and 1799 as a storehouse for precious sea otter pelts. The museum contains many items from the Russian period of Kodiak's history and many fine examples of Aleut basketry. The museum is open from 10 am to 4 pm weekdays and noon to 4 pm weekends; admission is $1.

Near the museum on Mission Rd is the **Holy Resurrection Church**, which serves the oldest Russian Orthodox parish in the New World – it was established in 1794. One of the original clerics was Father Herman, who was elevated to sainthood at Kodiak in 1970 during the first canonization ever performed in the USA. His relics are kept in a carved wooden chest near the altar. Also within the church are polished brassware, several icons and rare paintings. The church doesn't keep set opening hours; enquire at the visitor center about tours of the interior. Its blue and white onion-domed features make a great photograph, if you can squeeze out the huge gas storage tank that flanks it.

More Russian Orthodox history can be explored at **St Herman's Theological Seminary** which opens its Veniaminov Research Institute Museum to the public from 1 to 4.30 pm daily. On display inside the museum are indigenous artefacts, icons and Bibles used by Orthodox missionaries on the Yukon River in the 1800s. The seminary, founded in 1973 to train orthodox readers and priests, is on Mission Rd north-east of the church.

Follow Marine Way left (west) from the ferry terminal as it curves past the **Small Boat Harbor**, the heart and soul of Kodiak. Crab boats, salmon seiners and halibut schooners cram the city docks, while more boats dock across the channel at **St Herman Harbor** on Near Island. An afternoon on the docks can lead to friendly encounters with fishermen and the chance to see catches unloaded or nets being repaired. Although no tours are available, canneries can be seen clattering and steaming around the clock during the summer on nearby Shelikof St, or you can take the bridge across the channel to St Herman Harbor to view more boats.

Relatively new in Kodiak is the **Alutiiq Culture & Heritage Center** (☎ 486-1992). It was established by the Kodiak Area Native Association in 1992 to preserve the culture of its people and to store artefacts until a museum is built on Near Island. Inside you see a growing display of Native Alaskan artefacts including bone fish hooks as well as kayaks that the Koniags used to harvest fish and marine mammals. The spruce-framed kayak and a diorama of a traditional Koniag village are especially interesting. The museum is on Rezanof Dr just west of Marine Way. Opening hours are from 9 am to 5 pm weekdays, admission is free.

Fort Abercrombie State Historical Park
This military fort was built in 1941. Its two eight-inch guns, left over from WW II, were installed by the US Army in preparation for a Japanese invasion that never came. In the end it was lousy Kodiak weather, not the army's superior firepower, that kept the Japanese bombers away from the island. Today, the fort is a state historical park, sitting majestically on the cliffs over wooded Monashka Bay. Restoration of the fort has begun with remounting of the guns and repair of the bunkers.

A self-guided tour winds through the WW II relics on Miller Point and on Sunday, Tuesday and Thursday at 2.30 pm, the park staff give a guided historic tour, beginning at the visitor center. Just as interesting as the gun emplacements are the tidal pools found

along the rocky shorelines of the park. It's best to have rubber boots if you can for an afternoon of searching for starfish and other sea creatures. The park, 4.5 miles north-east of Kodiak off Monashka Bay Rd, has 14 camping sites. Nearby is the Frank Brink Amphitheater.

Pillar Mountain The placement of a Distant Early Warning (DEW)-line site and later a communications saucer on top of this 1270-foot mountain has resulted in a road that climbs to a scenic overlook behind the city and provides excellent views of the surrounding mountains, ocean, beaches and islands. One side seems to plunge straight down to the harbor below, while the other overlooks the green interior of Kodiak Island. Pick up the bumpy dirt road to Pillar Mountain by heading north up Thorsheim St and turning left on Maple Ave, which runs into Pillar Mountain Rd.

Buskin River State Recreation Site Four miles south-west of the city on Chiniak Rd is this 90-acre state recreation area, containing 18 camping sites and access to the Buskin River. Anglers flock here for the salmon fishing, the best on this part of Kodiak Island, while nearby is the US Fish & Wildlife Service visitor center dedicated to Kodiak National Wildlife Refuge. The center has numerous exhibits and displays, as well as films on the island's wildlife including the brown bears that live there. Outside there is Buskin View Trail, a short, self-guided nature trail. The center is open from 8 am to 4.30 pm weekdays and from noon to 4.30 pm weekends.

Places to Stay
Camping There are no campgrounds in Kodiak and camping within the city limits is illegal. The closest campground is the *Buskin River State Recreation Site* (18 sites, $6 fee) four miles south-west of town on Buskin River Rd, on the way to the airport. The spot provides picnic shelters, pit toilets, trails through nearby wooded areas and good fishing on Buskin River or surf fishing in the

ocean. Nearby is the Kodiak National Wildlife Refuge headquarters and visitor center.

There is also camping at *Fort Abercrombie State Historical Park* (14 sites, $6 fee) north-east of Kodiak, the most scenic campground in which to pitch a tent, and at *Pasagshak River State Recreation Site* for 45 miles from town. All campgrounds have a seven-day limit on stays.

B&Bs There are a dozen B&Bs in Kodiak and most have rates ranging from $60 to $70 – not exactly budget accommodation. You can get a current list of them at the visitors center or contact *Kodiak Bed & Breakfast* (☎ 486-5367) which runs a referral service for many of them. Kodiak B&B is at 308 Cope St, just up the hill from the Small Boat Harbor. Other places within walking distance of the downtown area include *Wild Iris* (☎ 486-3335 or 486-2837) at 619 Lower Mill Bay Rd, *Inlet Guest Rooms* (☎ 486-4004) and *Baranov Bluff B&B* (☎ 486-5407) at 1427 Yanovosky St, which includes a beautiful breachfront view and Russian gun site. You pay for that history however.

Hotels There is no hostel in Kodiak and hotels are expensive, partly because the city hits you with a six percent sales tax and so does the borough. On a $60 room you can pay another $6 in local taxes. The slightly rundown *Kodiak Star Motel* (☎ 486-5657) on 119 Yukon St has rooms from $60, while the *Shelikof Lodge* (☎ 486-4141) at 211 Thorsheim St is slightly more. There's also *Inlet Guest Rooms* (☎ 486-4004 or (800) 478-4005), 10 blocks north of the downtown area on Mill Bay Rd. Singles or doubles before the tax are $55 a night. All hotels tend to be heavily booked during the summer.

Places to Eat
For fast food there's *McDonald's* near the busy intersection of Center and East Rezanof streets, while just down Center St towards the ferry terminal is *Subway* where small subs are $3.50 and a large seafood and crab sub is $6. There's also a *Pizza Hut* on Mill Bay Rd.

Rub elbows with locals or fishermen over early morning coffee at the *Kodiak Cafe* next to the Small Boat Harbor on Marine Way. Breakfast portions are large and the place is always open. It's where you go if the ferry arrives at 2.30 am. There's also *King's Diner* in the Lilly Lake Plaza on Mill Bay Rd. It opens daily at 5.30 am to serve sourdough pancakes while at night there are dinner specials and home-made pie.

For Mexican food, there's *El Chicano* on Center St in the mall next to the Ford Dealer. Open daily, the popular restaurant has small portions but 'grande' marguerites. It's up to you if you want to eat or drink. All of the city's Asian restaurants are near Rezanof Dr and Center St and two even have karaoke. The best deal on Chinese, however, is at *Henry's Sports Cafe* on the mall in front of the Small Boat Harbor. Its $6 Chinese lunch special, from 11 am to 3 pm, includes soup, fried rice, a main dish and tea.

You'll find health food at *Cactus Flats* on the corner of Mission and Center streets, espresso and desserts at *Beryl's* down an alley just off Center St and have a night of adventure when you drive 40 miles to *Road's End* (☎ 486-2885) for dinner or drinks.

Entertainment
Clustered around the city waterfront and Small Boat Harbor are a handful of bars that cater to Kodiak's fishing industry. At night they are interesting places, overflowing with fishers, deck hands and cannery workers drinking hard and talking lively. The *B&B* across from the harbor claims to be Alaska's oldest bar, having served its first beer in 1899. Another is the *Breakers* nearby on Center St which is almost as colorful inside as its mural outside.

For music at night, there is *Solly's Office* in the mall which is a restaurant and lounge featuring country music, while *Mecca* nearby has rock & roll music booming across its dance floor.

Festivals
Kodiak's best event, if you happen to be around in late May, is its week-long Crab

Festival featuring a parade, foot and kayak races, fishers' skills contests and a lot of cooked king crab.

There is also the State Fair & Rodeo held in mid-August at the Bell Flats rodeo grounds, a Fourth of July celebration, and the Great Buskin Raft Race in June that combines a raft race with five mandatory beer stops.

If you enjoy local pageantry, make an effort to see *Cry of the Wild Ram*, which depicts Kodiak's Russian days in a high-spirited manner complete with cannons roaring and a wooden stockade bursting into flames. It is held during the first two weeks of August in the Frank Brink Amphitheater, a magnificent outdoor theater near Fort Abercrombie. The play takes place rain or shine and tickets cost from $12 to $15 per person. Contact Kodiak-Baranof Productions (☎ 486-5291) for ticket information.

Hiking

There are dozens of hiking trails in the Kodiak area but unfortunately very few are maintained and the trailheads are not always marked along the roads. Once on the path, windfall can make following the track difficult or even totally conceal it. Still, hiking trails are the best avenue to the natural beauty of Kodiak Island. Before starting out, contact the Kodiak area ranger of the Alaska Division of Parks (☎ 486-6339) for the exact location and condition of trails. The handout, *Bear Country*, published by the Kodiak National Wildlife Refuge, also has brief, one-paragraph descriptions of all the trails and maps showing their location. Pick up a copy at the visitor center or at the refuge headquarters on Buskin River Rd.

Pillar Mountain Two trails depart from Pillar Mountain Rd. The first begins near the KOTV satellite receiver near the lower city reservoir and provides an easy walk north to Monashka Bay Rd. The second begins at the communications tower at the top of the mountain and is a descent of the south-west side. It ends at the Tie Substation, where a gravel road leads out to Chiniak Rd about a

mile north-east of the Buskin River State Recreation Site. Plan on an afternoon for either trail.

Barometer Mountain Trail This trail is popular but there's a steep climb of five miles to the 2452-foot summit. To reach the trailhead, follow Chiniak Rd south of the Buskin River Campground and turn right on the first road immediately after passing the end of the airport's runway. Look for a well-worn trail on the left. The trek begins in thick alder before climbing the hogback ridge of the mountain to provide spectacular views of Kodiak and the bays south of the city.

Termination Point Trail This is another popular hike along a five-mile trail that starts at the end of Monashka Bay Rd and branches into several trails near Termination Point. Most of the hiking is done in virgin spruce forest.

Cycling

Cyclists will find Kodiak's roads interesting to ride around, especially the 12-mile Anton Larsen Bay Rd that leads north-west from near Buskin River State Campground over the mountain pass to the west side of the island, where you will find quiet coves and shorelines to explore. Plan on two hours for the ride to Anton Larsen Bay. The ride down Chiniak Rd can be equally impressive while there is now a bike trail that begins on Beaver Lake Loop and ends at the entrance of Fort Abercrombie State Historical Park.

The Elkay Bicycle Shop (☎ 486-4219), at 122 West Rezanof St, in Kodiak handles repairs and parts or will rent you used cycles or mountain bikes for $25 a day and $125 a week.

Kayaking

With its many bays and protected inlets, scenic coastline and offshore rookeries, much of Kodiak is kayaker's dream. A scenic day trip from the downtown area is to paddle around Near and Woody island (both of which have trails on them), then onto Monashka Bay. More extensive expeditions can be put together by flying into the long bays of Kodiak National Wildlife Refuge or Shuyak Island.

Backcountry Sports & Backcountry Rentals (☎ 486-3771) has kayak rentals, including double Kleppers for $50 a day and hardshell singles for $30 a day. The shop also rents other camping gear and carries backpacking supplies and topographical maps. Kayak Kodiak Tours (☎ 486-2604) offers both a guided two-hour trip to Near Island for $35 per person and a hour-hour paddle to Monashka Bay for $65. The price includes the kayak and other equipment.

Getting There & Away

Air MarkAir (☎ (800) 478-0800) offers five flights a day from Monday to Friday from Anchorage while Alaska Airlines and its contract carrier, ERA, (☎ (800) 426-0333) offers seven flights daily. The regular, round-trip fare is around $280 but an advance purchase ticket where you stay over on Saturday is only $184. Both airlines also offer a special $95 one-way fare if you ask for it. (Keep in mind that if you travel from Anchorage to Kodiak, via bus to Homer and then take the ferry, that's going to cost you $155 as well as taking 12 hours on a bus.) The airport is five miles south of Kodiak on Chiniak Rd and the Airporter bus (☎ 486-5200) will run you into town for $5.

Boat The state ferry MV *Tustumena* stops at Kodiak three to four times a week coming from either Seward or Homer, stopping first at Port Lions, a nearby village on Kodiak Island. The ferry terminal (☎ 486-3800) is right downtown, where it's easy to walk around even if you're just in port for an hour or two. The one-way fare to Homer is $46 and to Seward is $52.

Getting Around

Car Rental There are a number of car-rental companies in Kodiak that will provide you with wheels to explore the island's outer edges. The cheapest is Rent-A-Heap where used cars cost $27 a day plus 27c a mile for a small two-door compact. The company has

two locations: the MarkAir terminal in the airport (☎ 487-4001) and Port of Kodiak Gift Shop (☎ 486-8550) downtown on the mall.

Tours Island Terrific Tours (☎ 486-4777) offers tours of the island that include the coastguard base, wildlife refuge center, Baranov Museum and Fort Abercrombie State Historical Park among other sights. The cost is $70.

AROUND KODIAK
Kodiak Island Roads

More than 100 miles of paved and gravel roads head from the city into the wilderness that surrounds Kodiak. Some are rough jeep tracks, manageable only by 4WD vehicles, but many can be driven or hitched along to isolated stretches of beach, great fishing spots and superb coastal scenery.

To the south of Kodiak, Chiniak Rd winds 47.6 miles to Cape Greville, following the edge of three splendid bays along the way. The road provides access to some of the best coastal scenery in Alaska and opportunities to view sea lions and puffins offshore, especially at Cape Chiniak near the road's southern end.

Just past *Mile 30* of Chiniak Rd you arrive

Puffin

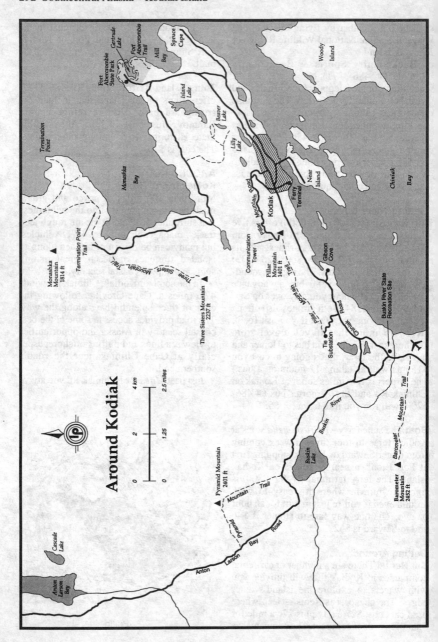

Around Kodiak

Monashka Mountain 1814 ft

Three Sisters Mountain 2237 ft

Pyramid Mountain 2401 ft

Barometer Mountain 2452 ft

Pillar Mountain 1401 ft

Termination Point

Termination Point Trail

Three Sisters Mountain Trail

Mamoshka Bay

Fort Abercrombie State Park

Fort Abercrombie Trail

Gertrude Lake

Mill Bay

Spruce Cape

Woody Island

Island Lake

Beaver Lake

Lilly Lake

Chiniak Bay

Near Island

Kodiak

Ferry Terminal

Pillar Mountain Road

Communication Tower

Pillar Mountain Trail

Gibson Cove

Tie Substation

Chiniak Road

Buskin River State Recreation Site

Buskin River

Buskin Lake

Barometer Mountain Trail

Pyramid Mountain Trail

Anton Larson Bay Road

Pyramid Road

Cascade Lake

Anton Larson Bay

0 2 4 km

0 1.25 2.5 miles

at the junction with Pasagshak Bay Rd that winds 16.4 miles due south to the *Pasagshak River State Recreation Site*. This small campground (seven sites, free) is famous for its silver and king salmon fishing as well as for a river that reverses its flow four times a day with the tides. These scenic areas, and not the city, are the true attractions of Kodiak Island. Anybody who has the time (and patience) to hitchhike or the money to rent a car (see the Kodiak Getting Around section) should explore these roads.

Kodiak National Wildlife Refuge

This 1.8 million-acre preserve, which covers the southern two-thirds of Kodiak Island as well as Ban Island and a small section of Afognak Island, is the chief stronghold of the Alaska brown bear. An estimated 2400 bears reside in the refuge and the surrounding area. The refuge is known worldwide for brown bear hunting and to a lesser degree for salmon and steelhead fishing. There are no maintained trails within the preserve and cross-country hiking is extremely hard due to thick bush. Nor can any part of the refuge be reached from the road system. Access into the park is by charter plane or boat out of Kodiak – either way can run you a tab as most of the refuge is 25 air miles away.

What most people really want to see in the refuge are the massive brown bears. Just about every air charter company in town offers a brown bear-viewing flight, in which you fly over remote shorelines in the refuge looking for bears. The length of flights and the number of times you land differ from one 'tour' to the next but generally you can count on paying from $150 to $250 per person for flights lasting from 90 minutes to two hours. For those with only a day or two in Kodiak, this is really the only feasible way you have of seeing the famous bears. Among the air services that offer bear tours are Seahawk Air (☎ 486-8282 or (800) 770-HAWK), Island

Air Service (☎ 486-6196) and Uyak Air Service (☎ 486-3407).

Cabins The US Fish & Wildlife Service administers nine free-use cabins in the refuge that should be reserved in advance. Cabin reservations are selected by four annual lotteries, each covering usage for certain months. Cabins that are not reserved can be obtained on a first-come-first-served basis. The closest units to Kodiak, Uganik Island Cabin and Veikoda Bay Cabin, are both on the ocean with good beaches nearby. If you are planning your trip, write to the Kodiak National Wildlife Refuge (PO Box 825, Kodiak, AK 99615) about reserving a cabin. If you're already in Kodiak, call the refuge headquarters (☎ 487-2600) to check if any cabins are available.

Shuyak Island State Park

Covering almost a quarter of the most northern island in the Kodiak archipelago, this park, 54 air miles north of Kodiak, features a unique rainforest of virgin Sitka spruce, rugged coastline, beaches and protected waterways. Shuyak is not large, the island is only 12 miles long and 11 miles wide, yet it contains more sheltered waterways than any other part of the archipelago, making it a kayaker's delight. Wildlife includes otters, sea lions, dall porpoises offshore and a modest population of the famous Kodiak brown bear.

The park's four cabins are on inlets and bays, and the cedar structures have bunks for eight, a wood stove, propane lights, a cooking stove but no running water. The cabins cost $20 per person per day. It's best to write for reservations before your trip to Alaska State Parks, SR Box 3800, Kodiak, AK 99615. But if you are passing through Kodiak give the Alaska Division of Parks (☎ 486-6339) a call to see if any of the cabins happen to be available.

Anchorage

Anchorage, the hub of Alaska's road system, an international air junction and home for almost half of the state's residents, is a city of prosperity and much debate. Those who live in the Anchorage area claim there is no other city like it in the world. It's Alaska's Big Apple and the state revolves around it. Everything you could possibly want is only a short hop away from the urban area which houses 237,907 people. Glaciers, mountains, hiking trails or white-water rivers to raft are only 20 minutes away from the city. Within a couple of hours' drive is the recreation paradise of the Kenai Peninsula and a handful of state and national preserves which offer unlimited camping, hiking and fishing.

Yet in Anchorage you can enjoy all the comforts and attractions offered by any large US city, including a modern performing arts center, enclosed shopping malls, major retailers (such as K-Mart, Wal-Mart and Sears that bring the lowest cost of living in Alaska to Anchorage) and bars and nightclubs that buzz late into the night.

But many of the state's residents look at the city, shake their heads and say, 'Anchorage is great. It's only 20 minutes from Alaska'. To them, everything that Alaska is, Anchorage isn't. The city is a mass of urban sprawl or, in down-to-earth terms, 'a beer can in the middle of the woods'. It has billboards, traffic jams and dozens of fast-food restaurants and, occasionally, even smog.

With the exception of New York, no other city provokes such a love-hate relationship. Without exception, no other city in any other state has such pull nor gobbles up so much of the public funds as Anchorage, an Athens in Alaska. And if you're a traveler, it is inevitable that you'll pass through Anchorage at least once, if not several times.

Anchorage has the advantage of being north of the Kenai Mountains, which shield the city from the excess moisture experienced by Southcentral Alaska. The Anchorage Bowl – the city and surrounding area – receives only 14 inches of rain annually. Nor does the area have the extreme temperatures of the Interior. The average temperature in January is 13°F, while at the height of the summer it's only 58°F. The area does, however, have more than its fair share of overcast days, especially in early and late summer.

Although Captain James Cook sailed up Cook Inlet in 1778 looking for the mythical Northwest Passage, Anchorage wasn't founded until 1914 when surveyors chose the site as the work camp and headquarters for the Alaska Railroad. In 1915 the 'Great Anchorage Lot Sale' was held when some 655 lots were sold for $225 and soon there was a tent city of 2000 people. From that point on the area's growth occurred in sudden spurts, caused by increased farming in the Matanuska Valley to the north in the 1930s, the construction of military bases during WW II, and the discovery of oil in Cook Inlet in 1957.

But two events literally reshaped and were responsible for Anchorage today. The first was the Good Friday Earthquake of 1964, the largest one ever recorded in the Western Hemisphere. It measured 9.2 on the Ritcher Scale and lasted an unprecedented five minutes. Afterwards the north side of 4th Avenue was 10 feet lower than the south side of the street. In one neighborhood, more than

100 homes slid off a bluff into the Knik Arm, some as far as 1200 feet. Nine people were killed, upwards of $50 million in damages recorded – a city lay in shambles. Then four years later, Atlantic Richfield discovered a $10-billion oil reserve at a place called Prudhoe Bay.

Though the Trans-Alaska Pipeline doesn't come within 300 miles of Anchorage, as the headquarters for the petroleum and service companies, the city gushes with oil money. Prudhoe Bay oil revitalized Anchorage and turned its downtown area into a showpiece that would be the envy of many other cities.

When a barrel of crude was more than $20 during the late 1970s and Alaska couldn't spend its tax revenue fast enough, Anchorage received the lion's share of it. The downtown area was revitalized with such projects as the Sullivan Sports Arena, the Egan Civic Center and the stunning Alaska Center for the Performing Arts. A 122-mile network of bicycle trails was paved, the Anchorage Museum of History & Art was expanded.

Today Anchorage boasts more than 75 cultural organizations, reasonably mild winters where the average temperature is above 0° and the coldest temperature rarely below -20° F, and more espresso coffee shops than all of Michigan.

The city that has stage plays and snowy peaks also has pork-barrel power. It comes from its residents who make up 40% of the state's population. Translated into political muscle, nine of the 20 state senators and 17 of the 40 state representatives represent the municipality of Anchorage. This causes problems if you don't happen to live in Anchorage.

The biggest rivalry lies between Anchorage and Fairbanks, the second largest municipality with 70,000 residents. Among other things, Fairbanks has long accused its sister to the south of trying to swipe major departments from their campus of the University of Alaska (the main one) to UA-Anchorage.

Juneau, the third largest city (population 30,000), has no love for Anchorage either,

seeing it as the power broker in an effort to move the state capital north. The capital-move issue, a raging controversy since 1976, heated up again in 1993 when Juneau residents voted to increase their city sales tax from four to six percent to finance the construction of a new state capitol. The vote is viewed by many in Anchorage as an underhanded attempt by Juneau to solidify its right as the seat of state government and prompted one legislator to introduce a bill nullifying it while two petition drives demanding another statewide vote on the capital-move question popped up.

But perhaps the animosity between this city and the rest of the state is due more to the fact that Anchorage is so un-Alaska.

What can't be debated is that Anchorage is truly the heart of Alaska and the center of the state's commerce and financial communities. Though the wide Anchorage Bowl is boxed in by the Chugach Mountains to the east and Cook Inlet to the west, the city continues to sprawl and seems to be in a constant state of rebuilding. Although the decline of oil prices in the late 1980s has slowed its economy, Anchorage is still the fastest growing city in Alaska. Love Anchorage or hate it, one thing is certain, as long as oil gushes from Prudhoe Bay or anywhere in Alaska, this city will prosper.

Orientation

If you fly into Anchorage, you'll arrive at the airport in the south-west corner of the city. If you drive in from the south on Seward Hwy or from the north on Glenn Hwy, the roads lead you through the city towards Cook Inlet. Whichever way you arrive, it's best to head for the downtown area. There is bus transport from the airport and where both highways end (or begin if you are leaving), less than a mile from each other.

Downtown Anchorage is a somewhat undefined area boxed in by 3rd Ave to the north, 10th Ave to the south, Minnesota Dr to the west and A St to the east. What is commonly referred to as Midtown Anchorage is an area that extends from east to west from Minnesota Dr to Seward Hwy and north to south from Fireweed Lane to Inter-

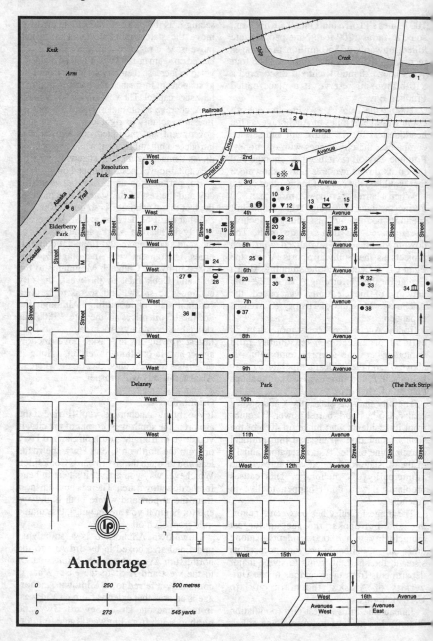

Anchorage

0   250   500 metres

0   273   545 yards

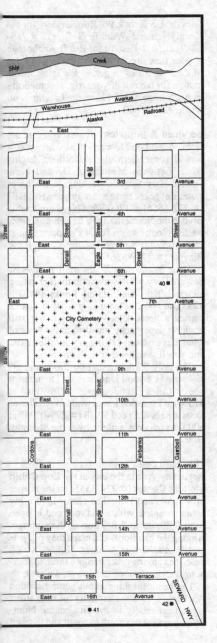

1	Ship Creek Salmon Viewing Platform
2	Alaska Railroad Depot
3	State Court Building
4	Cadastral Survey Monument
5	Sheep Creek Overlook
6	Oscar Anderson House
7	Alaska Adventures & Delights Espresso
8	Old Federal Building & Alaska Public Lands Information Center
9	Alaska Airlines
10	Alaska Booking Center
11	Gray Line & Columbia Glacier Tours
12	Downtown Deli
13	Post Office Mall
14	Post Office
15	Blondie's Cafe
16	Simon & Seaforts Saloon & Grill
17	Hotel Captain Cook
18	Imaginarium
19	Side St Espresso
20	Log Cabin Visitors Center
21	Old City Hall
22	Convention Center
23	Cyrano's Books
24	Inlet Inn
25	Alaska Center for the Performing Arts
26	Open Door Clinic
27	Oomingmak Musk Ox Producers Co-op
28	Transit Center
29	City Hall
30	YMCA
31	Library
32	Police
33	Fire
34	Anchorage Historical & Fine Arts Museum
35	Taheta Art & Culture Group Co-op
36	Anchorage International (AYH) Hostel
37	ACRO Building
38	Federal Building
39	Pioneer Schoolhouse
40	Alaskan Samovar Inn/Seward Bus Lines
41	Mulcahy Ball Park
42	Sports Arena

national Airport Rd. The heart of it is the heavily commercialized area around Northern Lights and Benson boulevards. Finally South Anchorage is generally considered to be the area south of Dowling Rd, including the Hillside residential areas on the doorstep of Chugach State Park.

Information

There are several visitor centers in Anchorage. The main one is in the log cabin (☎ 274-3531), on the corner of 4th Ave and F St, open daily from 7.30 am to 7 pm June to August, 8.30 am to 6 pm May and September, and 9 am to 4 pm the rest of the year. Along with many services and hand-outs, this center operates an Emergency Language Bank of 27 languages designed to help foreign travelers in distress. They also have the 24-hour All About Anchorage recording (☎ 276-3200) that lists current events taking place in the city that day.

There is another an information center (☎ 266-2437) at the Anchorage International Airport in the baggage claim level of the South (Domestic) Terminal. Hours are from 9 am to 5 pm. You will also find self-service information areas in the North (International) terminal, the railroad depot downtown and in the Valley River Mall in Eagle River.

Backpackers and hikers should contact the Alaska Public Lands Information Center (☎ 271-2737) in the Old Federal Building on the corner of 4th Ave and F St (diagonally opposite the Log Cabin Visitors Center) for information and hand-outs on any national park, federal refuge or state park in Alaska. This is where to head for help planning wilderness adventures and to purchase topographic maps and books. The center is like 'one-stop shopping' for information on outdoor activities and trips; 99% of your questions will be answered here, opening hours are from 9 am to 7 pm daily.

If the Public Lands office can't help you, there are several other centers that you can contact. Information on state parks can also be obtained from the Alaska Department of Natural Resources Public Information Center (☎ 762-2261 or (800) 770-2257 in Alaska) at 3601 C St. The Chugach National Forest office (☎ 271-2500) at Suite 206, 201 East 9th St, has details on any US Forest Service national forest, trail or cabin.

The Bureau of Land Management (for the Pinnell Mountain Trail) also maintains an office (☎ 271-5555) at 222 West 7th Ave, as does the US Fish & Wildlife Service (for the Kenai National Wildlife Refuge) (☎ 786-3487) at 1011 East Tudor Rd. If Anchorage is your first stop in Alaska, make good use of these agencies to gather the latest information for the rest of your trip. If somebody in Anchorage doesn't have the brochure, no one in Alaska will.

Services & Supplies Whatever you need, from a used book to a new tent stake, you'll find it somewhere along Northern Lights Blvd, between Minnesota Dr and New Seward Hwy. For backpacking, kayaking or camping gear, there's an impressive REI (☎ 272-4565) at 1200 West Northern Lights Blvd in the Northern Lights Shopping Center while a block away is Barney's Sports Chalet (☎ 561-5242) and across the street R&R Bicycle (☎ 276-8536).

There is also the Sears Mall near New Seward Hwy, a Safeway Supermarket, cheap gas and Title Wave Used Books (☎ 278-9283), at 505 Northern Lights Blvd, which carries a great selection of used but still readable paperbacks, mostly half the price of what they cost new. Bring in your used titles and you'll save another dollar or two.

The only thing missing on this commercial strip is a good laundromat. The nearest one is Coles Laundromat (☎ 276-9114) at 413 West Fireweed Lane, while in the downtown area is K Speed Wash (☎ 279-0731) at 600 East 6th Ave, a block from the Sheraton Hotel.

Things to See

Begin any visit to the city at the **Log Cabin Visitors Center** (☎ 274-3531) on the corner of 4th Ave and F St. The center is in a log cabin complete with a sod roof and is open from 7.30 am to 7 pm during the summer. Among the hand-outs and maps they provide is the *Anchorage Visitors Guide*, which describes among other things a three to four-hour walking tour of the downtown area.

The beautiful thing about getting around Anchorage is the simplicity of the street layout, especially in the city center. Numbered avenues run north to south and lettered streets east to west. The city walking tour begins by heading over to the **Alaska Public Lands Information Center**, in the Old Federal Building, open from 9 am to 7 pm. Even if you're not into backpacking or camping, the exhibits inside are excellent. Among the wildlife displays, there is a series of individual monitors that shows videos ranging in topics from glaciers and salmon in the Kenai River to Inuit whaling.

By heading north on E St, on the corner of 2nd Ave you pass the **Cadastral Survey Monument** and swing near the **Alaska Railroad Depot**. The monument notes the original 1915 town-site survey and has four etchings that trace the development of Anchorage from its first auction of public land to a current city map. The railroad depot, at the base of the hill, features historical photos and a railroading gift shop in its lobby, totem poles outside and Engine No 1 on a platform. The small locomotive was built in the 1900s for construction of the Panama Canal and was later shipped to Alaska for use on the railroad.

The tour continues west on 2nd Ave, however, pass the **Alaska Statehood Monument, Ship Creek Viewpoint** and then the start of the **Tony Knowles Coastal Trail** (see Cycling following). West on 4th Ave and half a block north on K St is the eye-catching large statue entitled *The Last Blue Whale*. Inside the adjoining building is Fred Machetanz's famous painting *The Hunt*. Nearby at the west end of 3rd Ave is **Resolution Park** and the **Captain Cook Monument**, which honors the 200th anniversary of the English captain's sailing into Cook Inlet with officers George Vancouver and William Bligh at his side.

If not overrun by a tour bus or two, this observation deck has an excellent view of the surrounding mountains, including the Talkeetnas to the north-east and the snow-covered Alaska Range to the west. On a clear day you can see Mt McKinley and Mt Foraker to the north, while to the west is Mt Susitna, known as 'The Sleeping Lady', which marks the south-west end of the Alaska Range. There is also a panorama of

Cook Inlet; often the large white caps you see are beluga whales feeding on salmon fry or smelt.

The tour continues south down to **Oscar Anderson House** (☎ 274-2336) in the delightful Elderberry Park on M St just north of 5th Ave. Anderson was the 18th person to set foot in Anchorage and his home was the first wood-frame house built in the city. Now it's the only home museum in Anchorage and is open from 10 am to 4 pm on weekdays and from 1 to 4 pm on Saturday and Sunday. There is a small admission fee.

On the corner of 6th Ave and H St is the **Oomingmak Musk Ox Producers Co-op** (☎ 272-9225). The co-operative handles a variety of garments made of arctic musk-ox wool, hand knitted in isolated Inuit villages. Outside, a mural depicts a herd of musk oxen, while inside the results of this cottage industry are sold. Those interested in the unusual garments should consider the co-op's farm tour in Palmer. East on 6th Ave on the corner of G St is the **People Mover Transit Center**, where you can pick up a local bus to any section of the city (see the Anchorage Getting Around section).

At 725 5th Ave, near the bus station, is the **Imaginarium** (☎ 276-3179), a hands-on science museum and a place to go if you have children tagging along. The award-winning center features more than 20 exhibits that explain the northern lights, earthquakes, oil exploration, bears and other Alaskan topics. You can even enter a polar bear's den or dabble your fingers in a marine life touch tank. The museum is open from 10 am to 6 pm Monday to Saturday and noon to 5 pm on Sunday. Admission is $4 for adults and $2 for children.

Diagonally across from the transit center on the north side of 6th Ave is the new **Alaska Center for the Performing Arts**, one of only 22 in the country. Alaskan artists designed the lobby and contributed a number of art pieces, including 23 Native American masks. During the summer tours are given on Monday, Wednesday, Friday and Saturday at 1 pm for a suggested donation of $1. Or you can just buy your lunch from a street vendor on 4th Ave and enjoy it on a hillside seat in **Town Square Park** that overlooks the arts center and surrounding flower beds.

Eventually, the tour leads to the **Anchorage Historical & Fine Arts Museum** (☎ 343-4326) near the corner of 7th Ave and A St. In 1984, the museum was expanded to triple its original size and now is an impressive center for displays on Alaskan history and indigenous culture as well as an art gallery featuring work by regional, national and international artists. The Alaska Gallery upstairs traces the history and people of this land in large three-dimensional exhibits. The museum is open daily from 9 am to 6 pm during the summer; admission is $4. Ask about the Alaskan films shown.

Across A St from the historical museum is **Taheta Art & Culture Group Co-op** (☎ 272-5829), a Native American arts cooperative. Inside there are several studios where you can watch artists work on ivory, soapstone and other materials. You can also purchase

such pieces here. Hours are from 9.30 am to 6.30 pm Monday to Saturday and noon to 5 pm on Sunday.

Another place to see fine Native art work is the **Heritage Library Museum** (☎ 265-2834) on the 1st floor in the National Bank of Alaska building on the corner of Northern Lights Blvd and C St. The center features an impressive collection of Native American tools, costumes and weapons, original paintings, including several by Sydney Laurence, and lots of scrimshaw. Much of the carved ivory is from the gold-rush days in Nome and was purchased by miners as proof they had been in Alaska despite not bringing any gold home. The museum is open weekdays from noon to 4 pm and there is no admission fee.

Parks Among other things, the 1964 earthquake caused 130 acres of land on the west side of the city to slip 2000 feet towards the sea. The east end of that strip was Turnagain Heights, a neighborhood where 75 homes were destroyed and three people died. The

---

The Art of Sydney Laurence

Of all the artists that have been inspired by Alaska, and the grandeur of this land has inspired a lot of them, none is more widely recognized than Sydney Laurence, the 'Painter of the North'. Born in Brooklyn New York in 1865, Laurence was exhibiting paintings by the time he was 22 and was involved in the founding of the American Fine Arts Society in 1889. But the lure of gold was a strong fever and in 1904 the painter left his wife and two children and made his way to Alaska.

For the next nine years Laurence did little painting and a lot of panning for gold in Southcentral Alaska but never found any great quantities of the precious metal. In 1913, he was commissioned by a group of Valdez businessmen to produce a painting of Mt McKinley for the Panama Pacific Exposition in San Francisco. The grand painting never made it to the expo but was added to the Smithsonian Institution collection in 1915, the same year Laurence set up a photography studio in a bustling little tent city called Anchorage.

The painter lived in Anchorage until his death in 1940 and during those years was enormously prolific. While the rest of the country may not have always recognized his name, in Alaska Laurence has become an almost mythic figure and his paintings still mesmerize thousands of people each summer. As one art critic put it in an issue of Southwest Art magazine 'the message of his work is clear; the Alaskan landscape was immeasurably greater than the deeds of the men and the women who inhabited it. Not so much hostile as indifferent, the northern landscape had the same mystique of unspoiled, seemingly limitless horizon that the American west had a half century earlier'.

Laurence's most impressive work, a six by 10-foot painting of Mt McKinley, is the centerpiece of the historical art collection of the Anchorage Museum of History & Art which has several other oils by Laurence. You can also enjoy a half-dozen more of his works, including several smaller paintings of Mt McKinley (his favorite subject), at the fine Heritage Library Museum in the NBA building on Northern Lights Blvd. ■

other end was undeveloped and today is Earthquake Park at the west end of Northern Lights Blvd on the Knik Arm (take bus No 93 from the Transit Center).

There is an interesting display at the park which details the earthquake while its power can still be seen in jagged crease that runs through the middle. The best feature of the park is the excellent panorama of the city skyline set against the Chugach Mountains. On a clear day you can see Mt McKinley and Mt Foraker to the north. The view is best seen from the Tony Knowles Coastal Trail at the lower area of the park.

Within the city center there is Delaney Park, known locally as 'The Park Strip' because it stretches from A to P streets between 9th and 10th avenues. The green strip, the site of the 50-ton bonfire that high-lighted statehood in 1959 and later where Pope John Paul II gave an outdoor mass in 1981, is a good place to lie down on a hot afternoon. Or check out Engine No 556 (a locomotive that was built in 1943 and shipped to Alaska by the US Army) in the park on the corner of 9th Ave and E St.

Russian Jack Springs is a 300-acre park south of Glenn Hwy on Boniface Parkway that can be reached by Bus No 12. The city park features tennis courts, four miles of hiking and biking trails and a picnic area. Near the entrance is the Municipal Green-house (☎ 333-8610) with tropical plants, exotic birds and fish and open from 8 am to 3 pm weekdays and until 2 pm on weekends.

Far North Bicentennial Park is 4000 acres of forest and muskeg in east central Anchorage. It features more than 20 miles of trails for hiking and mountain biking along with Hilltop Ski Area, whose chalet (☎ 346-1446) can provide you with a trail guide. In the center of the park is BLM's Campbell Tract, a 700-acre wildlife oasis where it's possible to see moose and bears in the spring. Come back in mid-September and the fall colors can be brilliant here. To reach the Hilltop Ski Area, take O'Malley Rd east to Hillside Dr and follow the road to the parking area. Buses Nos 91 and 92 go past it.

More wildlife, mostly ducks and geese, can be seen closer to the downtown area at **Westchester Lagoon Waterfowl Sanctuary**. On the corner of Spenard Rd and 19th Ave, the small preserve is a year-round home for a variety of birds and features displays and a half-mile nature trail around the small lake.

For information and a program of activities in Anchorage's parks, call the city's Department of Parks & Recreation (☎ 343-4474).

Lakes If the weather is hot enough, several lakes in the area offer swimming. The closest one downtown is **Goose Lake**, two miles south-east on Northern Lights Blvd (take bus No 3, 45 or 93). Before or after your dip, take a stroll through the **University of Alaska** at Anchorage, the largest campus in the state university system. It is connected to Goose Lake Park by footpaths. There is also swimming at **Spenard Lake**, three miles south of the downtown area on Spenard Rd and then west on Lakeshore Dr (take bus No 6, 7 or 93), and at **Jewel Lake**, 6.5 miles south-west of the city center on Dimond Blvd (take bus No 7).

Military Bases Elmendorf Air Force Base and Fort Richardson were established during WW II as the major northern military outposts for the USA, and continue today to contribute to Anchorage's economy. In the early 1940s, **Elmendorf Air Force Base** (☎ 552-5755) housed one of the nation's strongest air stations and is now home base for F-15 Eagles, T-33s and other huge aircraft.

During the summer the base offers a free tour on Wednesday that allows you to view the hangars and planes along with the rest of the facility. Call ahead to find out times and reserve a seat on the bus. There is also a log cabin **wildlife museum** (☎ 552-2282) with over 200 Alaskan mammals, fish, birds and a 10-foot-six-inch-high brown bear that misses the world record by an eighth of an inch. Opening hours are from noon to 5 pm weekdays. Take bus No 76 from the Transit Center.

Fort Richardson (☎ 384-0437) also has a **wildlife museum** with 250 specimens, along with a golf course and a salmon hatchery. The museum, Building 600, is open from 8.30 am to 5 pm weekdays, from 10 am to 4 pm Saturday and from noon to 4 pm Sunday (take bus No 45). Both museums are free.

UA-Anchorage This is the biggest college campus in the state but there is not nearly as much to do here as there is at its sister school, UA-F, to the north. Still the school is impressive and connected with bike paths to Goose Lake, Chester Creek Beltway and Earthquake Park. Stop in at the Campus Center, where you'll find an olympic-size pool with open swims, a small art gallery, and the UA-A Bookstore for some collegewear with Alaska on it. On the ground floor is the University Pub where there are affordable sandwiches and occasionally live music. Bus Nos 11, 45 and 3 swing past the campus.

Lake Hood Air Harbor Those enchanted by Alaska's bush planes and small air-taxi operators will be overwhelmed by Lake Hood, the world's busiest float-plane base (and skiplane base in the winter). Almost every type of small plane imaginable can be seen flying onto and off the lake's surface. The float-plane base can be reached by bus No 93 from the international hostel and makes an interesting afternoon trip when combined with a swim in adjoining Lake Spenard.

On the south shore of Lake Hood at 4721 Aircraft Dr is the **Alaska Aviation Heritage Museum** (☎ 248-5325). In an effort to preserve Alaska's unique approach to aviation, the museum has films, displays on such pioneer pilots as Ben Eielson, Noel Wein and Russell Merrill, vintage aircraft and an observation deck. Summer opening hours are from 9 am to 6 pm. The admission is $5.

If you're into planes, you may also want to stop in at the Reeve Aviation Picture Museum, dedicated to Alaska pioneer aviator Robert Reeve. Located downtown on the corner of 6th Ave and D St, the museum is actually a room with more than 1100 photos of the state's famous bush pilots and the story of Robert Reeve and Reeve Aleutian Airlines, which despite flying in one of the most turbulent places in the world has never lost a plane – amazing! Hours are from 9 am to 5 pm weekdays and admission is free.

Salmon Viewing From mid to late summer, king, coho and pink salmon spawn up Ship Creek, the historical site of Tanaina Indian fish camps. **Ship Creek Salmon Overlook**, a half-mile east from the Railroad Depot, is where you can watch the return of the salmon. Follow C St north as it crosses Ship Creek Bridge and then turn right on Whitney Rd.

Another good viewing is the **Elmendorf State Salmon Hatchery**. Take Bus No 45 and get off on the corner of 3rd Ave and Reeve Blvd. Head north on Reeve Blvd past the state hatchery to Post Rd where you turn right for the viewing area.

Festivals
Summer festivals include a large Fourth of July celebration, a Renaissance Faire with Shakespearean-type costumes and plays in early June at the Tudor Sled Dog Race Track, and the Mayor's Midnite Sun Marathon (call Anchorage Parks & Recreation (☎ 343-

4474) which celebrates the summer solstice with a variety of foot races.

For a small town festival, head to Girdwood on the 4 July weekend for its Girdwood Forest Fair or to Eagle River in mid-July (call 694-4702 for exact dates) for the Bear Paw Festival. A number of smaller events such as Kite Day, free concerts and arts and crafts shows, are held throughout the summer in Delaney Park. Call the All About Anchorage recorded message (☎ 276-3200) to see if anything is happening while you're passing through town.

Places to Stay

Camping The Anchorage Parks & Recreation Department (☎ 343-4474) maintains two parks where there is overnight camping. The main one is *Centennial Park*, which has 83 sites, showers and rest rooms but is 4.6 miles from the downtown area on Glenn Hwy. Take the Muldoon Rd exit south of the highway and turn west onto Boundary Ave for half a block. Bus No 75 runs past the corner of Muldoon Rd and Boundary Ave. The cost is $12 per night for either campground and there is a limit of three days. When Centennial is full, the city uses *Lion's Camper Park* in Russian Jack Springs Park as an overflow camping area. There is also *Ship Creek Landings* (☎ 277-0877) that offers 180 RV sites just off East 1st Ave. The rate is $12 per night.

Chugach State Park, which practically surrounds Anchorage also has public campgrounds but none of them is close and they always fill up fast. The nearest facilities are at Bird Creek on the Seward Hwy (see the South of Anchorage section) and at Eagle River off the Glenn Hwy (see the North of Anchorage section).

Hostels The *Anchorage International (AYH) Hostel* (☎ 276-3635) is downtown, one block south of the Transit Center at 700 H St. The cost is $12 per night for members and $15 for nonmembers. There is a four-night maximum stay unless special arrangements are made with the house

parents. Check-in is from 5 pm to midnight and check-out time is noon.

Along with sleeping facilities, there is a common room, kitchen, showers and even double rooms. Laundry facilities are available and you can store extra bags here for $1 per day. From the airport, take bus No 6 for the 5.7-mile trip into the Transit Center. This hostel is busy during the summer, so many travelers reserve a bunk ahead of time by mailing a money order for the first night's stay along with details of the number and gender of people arriving to Anchorage AYH, 700 H St, Anchorage, AK 99501.

The AYH now also has an overflow hostel on Spenard Rd in Anchorage and a list of the growing number backpacker hostels in the city. Among them is *International Backpackers Hostel* (☎ 274-3870) on the east side of the city. The hostel is actually five homes in the same neighborhood that can accommodate up to 45 people a night with two to four people per room. Facilities include sheets and blankets on the beds, a coin-operated laundry, and a fully equipped kitchen and a TV room. Rates range from $12 to $15 a night. To reach the hostel from the Transit Center take Bus No 45 to Bragaw St and Peterkin Ave and head west on Peterkin Ave for three blocks.

B&Bs B&Bs have blossomed in Anchorage! There are now several hundred residents who have opened up their spare bedrooms to summer travelers. Most places are on the fringes or in the suburbs of the city and provide a clean bed, a good breakfast and local insight into both the city and the Alaskan way of life. The going rate is a bit steeper in Anchorage than in the rest of the state as you generally pay from $65 to $75 a night. Stop at the Log Cabin Visitors Center for an entire rack of B&B brochures or call either Alaska Private Lodging (☎ 258-1717) or Stay with a Friend (☎ 278-8800) to arrange such accommodation.

In the downtown area there is *6th & B Bed & Breakfast* (☎ 279-5293), located, you guessed it, on the corner of 6th Ave and B St. The three rooms range in price from $58 to

$88 and there are even complementary bikes to use. At 327 East 15th is *Little Blue House B&B* (☎ 258-2653) with rooms beginning at $29 and $39 a night and at 1610 E St, across from the Chester Creek park strip, is *Walkabout Town B&B* (☎ 279-2918). Rooms start at $45 a night and two of them include a private entrance and share a small kitchen area. They also provide courtesy pick-up from the airport or train station.

For something different and away from the downtown area there's *The Potter's Inn* (☎ 562-5464), at 2120 Tudor Hills Court off Lake Otis Parkway and south of Tudor Rd. Along with the pottery studio, there's a large sauna and double jacuzzi. Finally, if you've just spent a week in the mountains and need to splurge and rejuvenate rent the Ivory Room at *Alaskan Frontier Gardens B&B* (☎ 345-6556), on the corner of Hillside Dr and Alatna St. It comes with a sauna, a private jucuzzi and wide-screen TV. The rate is $175 but other rooms here cost as low as $60 and courtesy transport from the airport or railroad depot is provided.

Hotels Anchorage has more than 50 hotels and motels and 4000 rooms for rent, still in the middle of the summer plan on spending a few dimes on phone calls to find a bed. Trying to find a single room for under $70 is even more challenging. Passing through the city before June or after August saves you a bundle as room rates often drop as much as $20 to $30 a night in the off season.

Airport Late night arrivals at the airport have a choice of motels that offer courtesy transportation and are nearby along Spenard Rd just north of International Airport Rd. But be prepared for Alaskan-size rates at around $100 a night. *Puffin Inn* (☎ 243-4044), at 4400 Spenard Rd, is exceptionally clean, will run out to the airport until 1 am and has complimentary muffins, coffee and newspapers in the morning. A double is $110 a night. Nearby is *Lake Shore Motel* (☎ 248-3485 or (800) 770-3000), at 3009 Lake Shore Dr. It has courtesy transport and costs slightly under $100.

The alternative is *Arctic Inn Motel* (☎ 561-1328), at 842 West International Airport Rd. It's a $6 taxi ride away and has singles/doubles for $69/79. Each room has a small stove/refrigerator and a laundry room is available from 7 to 11 pm.

Downtown The most affordable motel with the best location downtown is *Inlet Inn* (☎ 277-5541). It's across the street from the Transit Center at 539 H St and has singles/doubles for around $60/70. The motel also shares a courtesy van with several other places providing free transport from the airport.

Surrounding the downtown area are several motels with much more reasonable rates. To the west near the corner of Gambell St and 6th Ave is the *Alaskan Samovar Inn* (☎ 277-1511), where the large rooms are situated around a courtyard and the summer rates are $50/54 a single/double. Nearby is *Alaska Budget Motel* (☎ 277-0088), at 545 East 4th St, far enough away from the seedy section of 4th St for a quiet evening.

At the other end of the scale, if you want to spend your final night or two in Alaska in glorious comfort, there are a number of elegant hotels in Anchorage. The best of the Big Three (Sheraton, Hilton) is *Hotel Captain Cook* (☎ 276-6000), with an ideal location downtown on the corner of 5th Ave and K St. Rooms start at $160 but they pamper you here.

Midtown To the south is *Midtown Lodge* (☎ 258-7778) where small cubicle-like rooms with shared baths and a group kitchen are $40 a night. The lodge is at 604 West 26th Ave, just off Spenard Rd near Chilkoot Charlie's Saloon. Even further south, where Spenard Rd crosses Minnesota Dr, is *Qupqugiaq* (☎ 562-5681), at 3801 Spenard Rd. The group of houses has doubles with shared bath and a kitchen for $45 a night. A big step up is *Chelsea Inn* (☎ 276-5002 or (800) 770-5002), nearby at 3836 Spenard Rd. Singles with shared bath are $75, doubles $85 but the rooms are clean and comfortable and a continental breakfast is provided.

Elsewhere If you have a car, book a room on the outskirts of the city for better rates. For those driving in late from the north, there is *John's Motel* (☎ 277-4332) at 3543 Mt View Drive off Glenn Hwy two miles before you begin to enter the heart of Anchorage. This small motel, which also has hook-ups for RVers, has singles/doubles from $44/55. If you're heading up from the Kenai Peninsula, *The Brown Bear Motel* (☎ 653-7000), in Indian 20 minutes south of Anchorage on the Seward Hwy, has rooms that begin at $38 a night.

Places to Eat
Downtown For those on a strict budget there's a choice of fast-food places including *McDonald's* on the corner of 4th Ave and E St and *Burger King* at 520 West 5th Ave. All now compete for the breakfast trade as well as for the lunch and dinner crowd looking for a quick burger. Just as easy on the money pouch is the *Federal Building Cafeteria* off C St between 7th and 8th avenues, just across from the Anchorage Museum. It opens at 7 am weekdays and serves breakfast for around $4 as well as lunch in pleasant surroundings where you don't feel like gulping down your food. If the weather is nice, there is seating outdoors.

For food and surroundings that are a little more distinct, the downtown area of Anchorage has a wonderful selection of cafés, eateries and espresso shops. There's *Blondie's Cafe* open 24 hours on the corner of 4th Ave and D St. At the start of the Iditarod race, the bright and cheery café is loaded with sled-dog paraphernalia, including an entire sled hanging on the wall. An eggs breakfast is $4, a huge Blondie burger $5.50 and, if it's not raining, there's outdoor seating. Further west on 4th Ave is *Tito's Gyros* where you can get a large pizza for under $11 and gyro sandwiches stuffed with lamb for $5.75. Still further west on 4th is the *Downtown Deli*, unquestionably the city's best known delicatessen. Breakfasts

are great – eggs, potatoes and a lightly toasted bagel for $5 – large deli sandwiches cost from $7 to $9. There is an outdoor area where you can enjoy your cafe latte while watching the throngs of tourists head for the Log Cabin Visitors Center.

Other fine spots to enjoy lunch or dinner outdoors include *Phyllis's Cafe* on the corner of 5th Ave and D St. Art decorates the interior, a sawdust-covered courtyard is out the back. The salmon dinner costs $16 and the hamburgers (from $5.50 to $8) are excellent. Try the Bristol Bay Buffalo Burger (yes, it is buffalo meat you're eating), the Rampart Reindeer Burger or the Moose Pass Mushroom Burger. More outdoor dining with a view of the surrounding mountains is at *Club 26* at 611 West 9th Ave.

Cheap eats near the international hostel include *Wings & Things*, near the corner of I St and 6th Ave, that's open to 10 pm. Chicken wings, vegetables and sauce (try their Nuke sauce if you want to burn your mouth) are $6, whole subs start at $5.50. Next door is *Muffin Man Cafe* which opens for breakfast at 6 am. Muffins are 75c, a full breakfast $6 and, of course, there's espresso.

Those looking to make an evening out of dinner have a long list of places to choose from. One of the best is *Simon & Seafort's Saloon & Grill* (☎ 274-3502) at 420 L St between 4th and 5th avenues. The restaurant has the interesting décor of a turn-of-the-century grand saloon and a nice view of Cook Inlet where you can watch the sun set behind Mt Susitna. Dinners are expensive, plan on spending from $15 to $20 not counting your liquor, but the beer list might be the best in Alaska, try either the local Birdcreek Ale or Pete's Wicked Ale. Reservations are a must.

Two other places for an evening out are *La Mex* at 900 West 6th Ave for fajitas, chimichangas, burritos and refreshing margaritas or *Thai Cuisine* at 444 H St, between 4th and 5th Ave, where you can get excellent spring rolls, satay, Pad-Thai and noodle main dishes for $7 to $10.

Midtown Head down Northern Lights or

Benson boulevards, between New Seward Hwy and Minnesota Dr, for any fast-food restaurant you're craving for. *McDonald's* is near Arctic Blvd; *Burger King* is just down the road; while nearby is *Kentucky Fried Chicken, Taco Bell* etc. On Benson Blvd near New Seward Hwy is one of four *Skipper's* in Anchorage for all the fish, salad and chowder you can consume for $7.

There are also two interesting, and very distinct, places in the center slice of the city. *Hogg Brothers Cafe*, at 2421 Spenard Rd next to Chilkoot Charlie's, is a small but bizarre restaurant with a 'piggy' décor including a stuffed hog mounted on the wall. Breakfast is served all day and the selection is creative. You could order two eggs, home fries and toast for $2.95 but why when there are more than a dozen breakfast sandwiches like the Hogg McKinley and the Seafood Mama.

Also serving breakfast all day is *Gwennie's Old Alaska Restaurant*, at 4333 Spenard Rd, west of Minnesota Dr. The portions are big, the prices reasonable and the artefacts are so numerous that the place mat doubles up as a guide to what's on the walls. Order an omelette and then study the baleen sleds that Native Alaskans once used to haul freight, photos of the 1964 earthquake, pieces of the Trans-Alaska Pipeline or the 45,000-year-old bison head found in the Lucky Seven Mine.

To the south in the Plaza Mall, on the corner of 36th Ave and C St, is *Natural Pantry* (☎ 563-2727), a health food store and a restaurant. The restaurant is excellent: the food is healthy for you as well as being affordable. The extensive salad bar is $4.25 for all you can eat, and most sandwiches are under $5. At 2477 Arctic Rd is *Arctic Roadrunner*, the 'Local Burgerman', where you can enjoy big hamburgers while looking at the restaurant's Wall of Fame. Among those enshrined are Norma Jean, the first woman to climb Mt McKinley; Mark Schlereth, the only Alaskan-born player in the National Football League; and Bob Henderson, who once landed a 26-pound northern pike with a muskrat in its stomach.

Good Greek and Italian food are combined at *The Greek Corner* at 302 West Fireweed Lane. The mousaka plate for $12.95 will fill you up while Italian dishes range from garlic-feta spaghetti and rigatone al forno to calzone. Beer and wine are also served here.

Of the more than a dozen Chinese restaurants in Anchorage, *Peking Palace*, on East Benson Blvd across from the Sears Mall, is one of the best. It specializes in that spicy northern Chinese cuisine and can serve a full dinner for under $10, tea included. (In fact, for most people, there's enough food left over from dinner for lunch the next day.) The hot and sour soup is especially hot and spicy.

On the upswing is *Harry's* on the corner of Benson Blvd and C St, a relaxing bar and restaurant where you might feel a little self-conscious arriving in hiking boots and the T-shirt you wore for six days straight at Denali. The restaurant is dedicated to Harry Truman, the man who refused to move from his home on the side of Mt St Helens when the volcano began erupting in 1980. The seafood here is excellent but you'll also find a wide selection of pub food. Hamburgers are big and begin at $6.25, The stuffed potatoes are a meal in themselves and there are 20 beers, half of which you never knew existed, on tap.

For an evening out there are other places like *Sourdough Mining Co* (☎ 563-2272), a half-block of Old Seward Rd at International Airport Rd and Juneau St. Here you can 'dine in a gold mine' without having to own one to pay for the bill. For $19.75, you get an all-you-can-eat buffet, including ribs, chicken and salmon, 'Yukon Pappy's Sourdough Show' and a ride back to a number of major hotels in the city.

Elsewhere The best Mexican dishes are found in South Anchorage at *Mexico in Alaska*, 7305 Old Seward Hwy, just south of Dowling Rd. The menu covers traditional Mexican cuisine, the beer list from south of the border is impressive and there is an outdoor seating area if the weather is nice. It's a long way from downtown but Bus No

60 goes right past the restaurant. Coming in from the north, *Peggy's Place* on 5th Ave, right across the from Merrill Airfield is where the locals eat. The longtime favorite is open to 10 pm, usually has specials for under $7, and features 'Peggy's home-made pies' and good coffee to go with them.

Espresso Shops There's no shortage of cappuccino in this city. You can't walk more than a block or two downtown without passing a coffee shop. Kickback at *Side Street Espresso*, just off 4th Ave on G St. There's interesting selection of prints on the walls, a used-book shelf in the corner and, by the afternoon, a couple of copies of the *Daily News* spread across the tables. A large 16-ounce cafe latte is $3, a bagel and cream cheese is $1.75, and sandwiches are $5.

Another interesting place is *Cyrano's Books & Cafe*, on the corner of 4th Ave and D St. The shop is an offbeat bookstore with an excellent Alaska section as well as an espresso shop with a variety of baked goods and sandwiches. There's also *Alaska Adventures & Delights*, on the corner of K St and 4th Ave, that doubles as an espresso shop. It's a travel-book store with material on Alaska and the complete selection of Lonely Planet guides. Sip, read and dream about your next trip.

Entertainment

There's lots to do in Anchorage when the midnight sun finally sets. The best way to check out what's happening where is to pick up a copy of *Anchorage Bypass*, the offbeat weekly entertainment tabloid, which features bar and dance club listings, movie reviews and news about events and festivals in the Southcentral portion of the state. It's free and distributed at most tourist places in the downtown area.

Dancing & Music Anchorage is a city where you can hike all day in the mountains and dance all night in the bars. One of the more colorful places is *Chilkoot Charlie's*, or 'Koots' as the locals call it, at 2435 Spenard Rd in the midtown area. The bar hops at night

and features three bands, dancing, horse-shoes outside and a long bar with sawdust on the floor and rusty artefacts all over the walls. The cover charge is $3 and liquor prices are Alaskan but reasonable if you arrive before the bands do at 8 pm.

Other places for music are *Hod Rods*, a 50s nightclub at 4848 Spenard Rd; *Hellfighters Bar & Grill*, a top-40 dance club at 313 E St; and *The Whale's Tail* a lounge with live entertainment in the Hotel Captain Cook. The *Last Frontier Bar* at 369 Muldoon Rd features country (and country karaoke) and *Pierce Street Annex* at 701 East Tudor Rd is a comedy club.

Then there is *Mr Whitekeys Fly by Nite Club* (☎ 279-SPAM) at 3300 Spenard Rd. The club plays jazz, blues and early rock but is best known for its 'Whale-Fat Follies', a fun and raunchy look at Alaska that teaches you all you'll ever want to know about duck tape, spawning salmon and Alaska's official state fossil, the woolly mammoth. Tickets for the show are $10, $14 and $16 and reservations are a must.

Pubs & Bars Downtown there is a variety of low-key pubs and lively bars where you can go to cap off the evening. Locals head for *Darwin's Theory* where the popcorn is free. It's near the corner of 4th Ave and G St. *The Sports Edition Bar* in the Anchorage Hilton has 17 TVs of every size imaginable for viewing whatever game is being played that night, while nearby on E St is *Rumrunner's Old Town Pub* where yuppie Anchoragites drink and *F Street Station* across from the Old Federal Building if you're looking for a Cheers in Alaska.

Great views of the area can be obtained for the (steep) price of a drink in the *Crow's Nest*, at the top of the Captain Cook Hotel on the corner of 5th Ave and K St; or at the *Penthouse Lounge*, at the top of the Westmark Hotel at 720 West 5th Ave, where floor-to-ceiling windows let you marvel at Mt McKinley on a clear day.

Got a car? Then head out to *Mile 101* of the Seward Hwy for a night at the *Birdhouse Bar*. The log cabin saloon is where every visitor passing through feels obligated to leave something, from business cards to bras, on the walls, ceiling or beams.

The Arts Anchorage has a civic opera, a symphony orchestra, several theater groups and a concert association that brings a number of dance companies and art groups to the city every year. Big-name performers arrive more frequently now that the Alaska Center for the Performing Arts (☎ 263-2900) has been completed. Call the center for a schedule of who's in town and, if interested, then call its box office (☎ 263-ARTS) for the price and availability of tickets.

You might also check out the 4th Street Theater (☎ 257-5600) just down the street from the Log Cabin Visitors Center. Built in 1947 by Austin Lathrop, the Art-Deco theater was the first building in Anchorage to use marble lavishly inside and out. This historical landmark was recently totally restored and now is the city's most impressive theater. A variety of performances, including a dinner theater, is staged here during the summer.

For a daily report on all cultural events around the area, call the All About Anchorage phone line (☎ 276-3200) for its recorded message.

Movies & Films Those watching their funds carefully should keep in mind the free films offered around town. The Anchorage Historical & Fine Arts Museum shows Alaska films daily at 3 pm while the Alaska Public Lands Information Center has daily showings of wildlife movies. The *ACRO Theater* (☎ 263-4545), in the tallest building in the state on the corner of G St and 7th Ave, presents two free films. The first is on Alaska's development from the gold-rush to the oil era and the second is about indigenous art and culture. They are shown on Tuesday and Thursday at 2 and 3 pm.

The city has numerous movie theaters, including *Capri Cinema* (☎ 561-0064), take bus No 75; *Fireweed Theater* (☎ 277-3825), take bus No 60; and *Totem Theater* (☎ 333-8222), take bus Nos 5 and 75. *Denali Theater*

(☎ 279-2332), just off Spenard Rd at 27th Ave (bus Nos 3 and 60) has late-run movies for $2 a seat. There's also *Cyrono's Cafe* (☎ 274-1173) which shows foreign films downstairs from Thursday to Saturday.

Or for something more touristy, head to the *Alaska Experience Theater* (☎ 272-9076) on the corner of G St and 6th Ave. The theater shows a 40-minute, 70-mm film that is projected on a huge domed screen and is entitled *Alaska the Great Land*. Admission is $6. For $10 you also get to watch a second film about the 1964 Good Friday Earthquake.

Cycling

Anchorage has 121 miles of paved bicycle paths that parallel major roads or wind through many of its parks and green-belt areas. You can rent bicycles downtown at two places. Anchorage Coastal Bicycle Rentals (☎ 279-1999) is in the Adventures & Delight shop at 414 K St and has mountain bikes for $7 an hour and $25 a day. Downtown Bicycle Rental (☎ 279-5293), on the corner of 6th Ave and B St, has mountain bikes for $14 a day and single-speed bikes for $10.

If you need parts or service, head to Northern Light Blvd. On that commercial strip between Minnesota Dr and New Seward Hwy is R&R Bicycle (☎ 276-8536), The Bicycle Shop (☎ 272-5219), REI (☎ 272-4565) and Sunshine Sports (☎ 272-6444). One of them is going to have the part you need. Descriptions of some of the longer bike trips in the Anchorage bowl follow.

Chester Creek Trail One of the more popular routes is the four-mile path through the Chester Creek Green Belt from the University of Alaska and Goose Lake Park to Westchester Lagoon overlooking Knik Arm.

Tony Knowles Coastal Trail The most scenic route is the 11-mile Coastal Trail, which begins at the west end of Second Ave downtown and reaches Elderberry Park within a mile. From there it winds 10 miles west of Anchorage through Earthquake Park,

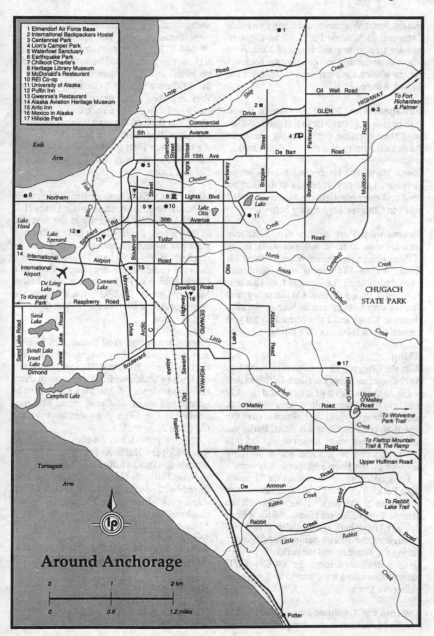

1 Elmendorf Air Force Base
2 International Backpackers Hostel
3 Centennial Park
4 Lion's Camper Park
5 Waterfowl Sanctuary
6 Earthquake Park
7 Chilkoot Charlie's
8 Heritage Library Museum
9 McDonald's Restaurant
10 REI Co-op
11 University of Alaska
12 Puffin Inn
13 Gwennie's Restaurant
14 Alaska Aviation Heritage Museum
15 Artic Inn
16 Mexico in Alaska
17 Hillside Park

Around Anchorage

0   1   2 km

0   0.8   1.2 miles

around Point Woronzof and finally to Point Campbell in Kincaid Park. Along the way you are treated to good views of Knik Arm where occasionally you can spot the backs of beluga whales. On clear days you can see the Alaska Range.

Turnagain Arm Trail This 14-mile paved path begins at Potter Marsh Refuge and then hugs the shoreline for sweeping views of Turnagain Arm until it ends at Bird Creek.

Glenn Hwy Trail Head north on this paved path out of the city. It begins at the Bartlett Pool and then parallels the highway for 14 miles to Chugiak Elementary School.

Bicentennial Park Within this 4000-acre park are more than 30 miles of trails, many of them open to mountain bikes. Hilltop Ski Area (☎ 346-1446) now rents mountain bikes daily during the summer for $18 a half day and $28 a full day. On Saturday and Sunday they hold mountain-bike orientation clinics at 10 am and 2 pm where $25 get you a rental and a lesson in trail riding.

Hiking
With the Chugach Mountains at its doorstep, Anchorage has many excellent day hikes that begin on the outskirts of the city and quickly lead into the beautiful alpine area to the east. Most of them begin in the Hillside area of the city that borders Chugach State Park, the second largest state preserve at 495,000 acres, and can be reached within walking distance on the People Mover bus system.

For trail information, contact the Chugach State Park office (☎ 345-5014) in Anchorage or stop in at the park visitor center in the historic Potter Section House at *Mile 115* of Seward Hwy. Park rangers also lead hikes throughout the area on Saturday and Sunday during the summer, and the park office maintains a recorded message (☎ 694-6391) listing what hikes are planned and where to gather for them.

To/From the Trailheads At a $1 a ride, the People Mover bus is the cheapest way to get

within walking distance of the trails. But now there is also Backpacker Shuttle (☎ 344-8775) which provides transportation right to the trailheads. The van service picks up hikers at the international hostel, REI in the Midtown area and Centennial Camper Park and then continues on to a variety of trails including Bird Creek and Crow Pass along the Seward Hwy and Ship Creek and the Eagle River trails. The fare is $5 one-way for trails like Flattop Mountain and ranges up to $10 one-way for Crow Pass and Eklutna Lake.

Maps The USGS map center, which sells topos for the entire state, is now in Grace Hall at Alaska Pacific University at the east end of Providence Dr. Hours are from 8.30 am to 4.30 pm weekdays and the center can be reached on bus No 11 or 45. Upstairs from the map center is the headquarters of Lake Clark National Park. There's also Maps, Maps, Maps (☎ 562-6277), a store on the corner of Arctic Blvd and 34th Ave, that sells USGS topos.

Flattop Mountain Trail Because of its easy access, this trail is the most popular hike near the city. The path to the 4500-foot peak is not difficult to walk and from the summit there are good views of Mt McKinley (to the north) and most of Cook Inlet. The trail begins at the Glen Alps entrance to the Chugach State Park.

Catch bus No 92 to the corner of Hillside Rd and Upper Huffman Rd. Walk 0.7 miles east along Upper Huffman Rd and then turn right on Toilsome Hill Dr for two miles. This switchback road ascends steeply to the Glen Alps park entrance, a parking lot where trailhead signs point the way to Flattop Mountain. The round trip is four miles with some scrambling over loose rock up steep sections near the top of the mountain. Plan on three to five hours for the entire hike.

Rabbit Lake Trail People Mover bus No 92 also provides transport to this trail, which leads to the beautiful alpine lake nestled under 5000-foot Suicide Peak. Leave the bus at the corner of Hillside Dr and De Armoun Rd. Extending to the east here is Upper De Armoun Rd. Follow it a mile and then turn right onto Lower Canyon Rd for 1.2 miles to reach the trailhead parking lot.

The trail begins by paralleling Upper Canyon Rd, a rough jeep track, for 3.5 miles and then continues another two miles from its end to the lake. The return trip from the corner of Hillside Dr and De Armoun Rd is 15.4 miles, or a six to nine-hour hike. You can camp on the lake's shore for a scenic evening in the mountains.

Wolverine Peak Trail This path ascends to the 4455-foot triangular peak that can be seen to the east of Anchorage. It makes for a strenuous but rewarding full-day trip resulting in good views of the city, Cook Inlet and the Alaska Range.

Take bus No 92 to the intersection of Hillside Dr and O'Malley Rd. Head east up Upper O'Malley Rd for a half-mile to a 'T' intersection and turn left (north) onto Prospect Dr for 1.1 miles. This ends at the Prospect Heights entrance and parking area of the Chugach State Park. The marked trail begins as an old homesteader road that crosses South Campbell Creek and passes junctions with two other old roads in the first 2.3 miles.

Keep heading east, and the old road will become a footpath that ascends above the bush line and eventually fades out. Make sure to mark its whereabouts in order to find it on the way back. From here it is three miles to the Wolverine Peak.

The return trip from the corner of O'Malley Rd and Hillside Dr is 13.8 miles, a nine-hour hike. Many people just trek to the good views above the bush line, shortening the trip to 7.8 miles.

Rendezvous Peak Route The trek to the 4050-foot peak is an easy five-hour round trip, less from the trailhead, and rewards hikers with incredible views of Mt McKinley, Cook Inlet, Turnagain and Knik arms, and the city far below. Take bus No 75 for 6.5 miles north-east on Glenn Hwy to Arctic

Valley Rd. Turn right (east) on Arctic Valley Rd (this section is also known as Ski Bowl Rd) and head seven miles to the Arctic Valley Ski Area at the end. From the parking lot, a short trail leads along the right-hand side of the stream up the valley to the north-west. It ends at a pass where a short ascent to Rendezvous Peak is easily seen and climbed.

The round trip from the ski area parking lot is only 3.5 miles, but it is a much longer day if you can't thumb a ride up Arctic Valley Rd.

The Ramp This is another of the many alpine summit hikes from the east side of the city that includes hiking through tranquil tundra valleys with good chances of seeing dall sheep during the summer. Begin at the Glen Alps entrance to the state park (see the previously mentioned Flattop Trail for directions to the entrance).

Instead of following the upper trail to Flattop Mountain at the parking lot, hike the lower one as it extends half a mile to the power line. Turn right and follow the power line for two miles, past 13 power poles, to where an old jeep trail crosses over from the left and heads downhill to the south fork of Campbell Creek.

The trail then crosses the creek and continues up the hill beyond it to a valley on the other side. Hike up the alpine valley to Ship Lake Pass, which lies between The Ramp at 5240 feet to the north, and The Wedge at 4660 feet to the south. Either peak can be climbed. The round trip from the Glen Alps entrance is 14 miles, or an eight to 10-hour hike.

Williwaw Lakes Trail This hike leads to the handful of alpine lakes found at the base of Mt Williwaw. The trail makes a pleasant overnight hike and many trekkers consider it the most scenic outing in the Hillside area of Chugach State Park. The hike begins on the same lower trail as The Ramp does, from the Glen Alps entrance parking lot (see the Flattop Mountain Trail for directions to the entrance).

Walk half a mile to the power line and then

turn right. This time walk only about 300 yards and then turn left on a trail marked by a Middle Fork Loop Trail sign. This trail leads down and across the south fork of Campbell Creek and then north for 1.5 miles to the middle fork of the creek. Here you reach a junction; continue on the right-hand trail and follow the middle fork of Campbell Creek until you reach the alpine lakes at its end. The round trip from Glen Alps is 16 miles, or seven to nine hours of easy hiking.

Guide Companies

Anchorage is home base for a large number of guide companies that run hiking, kayaking and rafting trips to every corner of the state. Check the Wilderness chapter for the complete list and descriptions of their expeditions, and don't be shy about calling them at the last minute. Often you not only get a place in the group but get a hefty discount as well for filling up a leftover spot. Those who don't have the time or the money for a 10-day float or a trek in the Brooks Range should not overlook the day trips out of the city.

Camp Alaska Tours (☎ 376-9438), based in Wasilla, offers tours by van (as opposed to tours by bus), where travelers sleep in a tent and donate to a food kitty. Although not quite a wilderness guide company, the air services are definitely a lot more personal and affordable than a Gray Line tour.

Among the trips they offer are a seven-day journey that includes Valdez, Columbia Glacier, Fairbanks and Denali National Park for $655 per person, and a six-day adventure through the Kenai Peninsula and Kodiak Island areas for $625. The nice thing about the Kodiak trip is that a van allows the group to see parts of the island most travelers miss.

Hugh Glass Backpacking Company (☎ 344-1340) is the longtime Anchorage guiding company that offers trips throughout the state. Their most popular trip is ocean kayaking in Kenai Fjords National Park offered 13 times during the summer. A five-day paddle is $950 and includes Klepper kayaks and a flight into the remote southern end of the park.

Chugach Hiking Tours (☎ 278-4453) offers three guided hikes into the surrounding state park, including a sunset one that begins at 6 pm and returns at 11 pm. The treks often range from two to five miles in length and include a naturalist's perspective, trail snacks and opportunities for photography going to and from the trailheads. All trips depart from the Log Cabin Visitors Center downtown and are $45 per person.

Earth Tours Inc (☎ 279-9907) is a small guiding company run by Margriet Ekvall, who speaks several languages including German, French and Dutch. She offers a wide variety of rafting, backpacking and naturalists tours in the Southcentral portion of the state including the Wrangell-St Elias area and Kachemak Bay State Park.

The best white water in the Anchorage area is Eagle River, a 15-mile run of mostly Class I water but with short stretches of Class II and even Class III. Eagle River Raft Trips (☎ 333-3001) runs the river twice daily in the summer at 11 am and 5 pm. Each trip lasts from four to five hours and the transportation from Anchorage is included in the $80 price.

Guided biking trips are also available in Anchorage. Sage Alaska Bicycle Adventures (☎ 243-2329 or (800) 770-SAGA) has day trips to Eagle River Rd and Bird Creek ($65 per person) and Portage Glacier ($95 including cruise to the glacier). They also have an eight-day trip which includes riding the Alaska Railroad to Fairbanks, a 360-mile pedal down Richardson Hwy to Valdez and a ferry trip across Prince William Sound. The cost is $400 per person.

Getting There & Away

Air Anchorage International Airport, 6.5 miles west of the city center, is one of the busiest airports in the country, handling 130 flights daily from the 14 major airlines that serve it. From here you can catch a flight to anywhere in Alaska. Alaska Airlines (☎ (800) 426-0333) and its system of contract carriers provide the most intrastate routes to travelers, with flights departing daily.

Samples of one-way fares from Anchorage are: $146 to Fairbanks, $220 to Juneau,

$190 to Kodiak and $290 to Nome. Far cheaper flights are available if you book return tickets two weeks in advance. ERA provides flights to Valdez, Homer, Cordova and Kodiak and you book them through Alaska Airlines.

Reeve Aleutian Airways (☎ 243-4700 or (800) 544-2248) offers flights throughout south-west Alaska, including Pribilof Islands and Unalaska. MarkAir (☎ (800) 478-0800) provides services to Katmai, Barrow, and Kodiak among other places and Delta Airline (☎ (800) 221-1212) has flights to Anchorage but not to Juneau. There is often information about plane tickets for sale in the classified pages of the *Anchorage Daily News*.

Bus There is now a variety of bus and van transport companies operating out of Anchorage and providing service to almost everywhere in the state. The biggies, like Gray Line Alaskon Express, you can count on but double-check on many of the smaller companies by making a phone call. You never know if they are going to survive from one summer to the next.

To Tok & Haines Alaskon Express (☎ 227-5581) departs from its office on 745 West 4th Ave as well as from a handful of major hotels on Sunday, Monday, Wednesday and Friday at 7 am for Palmer, Glennallen, Tok and Beaver Creek in the Yukon Territory where the bus stops overnight. From Beaver Creek you can make connections to Whitehorse, Haines or Skagway. The overnight stop is at your own expense and the one-way fare to Haines is $189, Skagway $199, Tok $99 and Glennallen $60.

Alaska Direct (☎ 277-6652 or (800) 770-6652) offers a similar run for a slightly smaller fare. The bus departs Anchorage Monday, Wednesday and Saturday for Glennallen, Tok and Haines Junction where you can pick up a second bus for Haines the next day at noon. One-way fare is $125 to Haines Junction, $175 to Haines, $37 to Glennallen and $65 to Tok.

To Denali & Fairbanks Moon Bay Express (☎ 274-6454) has daily van service to Denali National Park and anything in between, including trailheads. The van leaves daily from the international hostel at 8 am, reaching the park at 1 pm. One-way fare is $35, round trip $30. Once at the park you can connect with the Fireweed Express van to continue on to Fairbanks for another $25. There is also Denali Express (☎ (800) 327-7651) that runs a bus to Denali National Park.

To Kenai Peninsula Seward/Homer Bus Lines (☎ 278-0800) takes on passengers at the Samovar Inn on the corner of 7th Ave and Gambell St and departs daily at 2.30 pm for Seward, reaching the town at 5.30 pm. The one-way fare is $30. Another bus departs the motel at 9.45 am daily and reaches Homer at 3.45 am after passing through the town of Kenai, and Soldotna. One-way fare to Homer is $35.

To Valdez & Portage Caribou Express (☎ 278-5776) has departures from an office at 700 West 6th Ave at 7.30 am on Wednesday, Friday and Sunday, reaching Valdez at 2.30 pm, where it turns around for a return trip. One-way fare is $75. The company also makes a daily run to Portage at 11 am and 3 pm to meet train passengers. Round-trip fare is $25. Eagle Custom Tours (☎ 277-6228) also has a shuttle service to Portage but charges $25 one way.

Train The Alaska Railroad (☎ 265-2494) maintains its office in the depot at 421 West 1st Ave and provides services both north and south of Anchorage. To the north, the Denali Express departs Anchorage daily at 8.30 am, reaching Denali Park at 3.45 pm and Fairbanks at 8.30 pm. The one-way fare to Denali is $85 and to Fairbanks is $120. On Wednesday and Saturday a local 'Flag Stop' train departs Anchorage at 6.30 am and makes an all-stops trip to Hurricane Gulch, arriving at 11.21 am; the return fare to Hurricane Gulch is $88. On Sunday the same train departs at noon.

From Portage, the Alaskan Railroad runs four trips a day on Wednesday and Thursday and six a day the rest of the week. The daily 1.20 pm train out of Portage is the one you have to be on to catch the 2.45 pm state ferry out of Whittier for Valdez. The one-way fare to Whittier is $13.

From late May to the first week of September you can also catch a rail diesel car to Seward from Thursday to Monday. The trip is a scenic one along the Turnagain Arm and through the mountains of the Kenai Peninsula where you pass three glaciers and cross steep gorges. The train departs Anchorage at 7 am and arrives in Seward at 11 pm. There is also a special run on the Fourth of July holiday. The one-way fare is $40, and the round trip is $70.

Boat The State Marine Ferry (☎ 272-4482) doesn't service Anchorage but does have an office in the city at 333 West 4th Ave. Here you can obtain information, make reservations or purchase advance tickets. If you know the dates on which you want to make the Columbia Glacier cruise, it is highly recommended that you purchase your ticket as far in advance as possible for this popular trip.

Hitchhiking Hitching out of Anchorage can be made a lot easier by first spending $1 and hopping on a People Mover bus. Travelers heading north should take bus No 76, 78, 93 or 102 to Peter's Creek Trading Post on Glenn Hwy. If you're heading to Portage, Seward or the rest of the Kenai Peninsula, take bus No 92 or 101 and get off at the corner of De Armoun Rd and Seward Hwy.

Getting Around
To/From the Airport People arriving at the International Airport have a couple of ways to reach the city. Catch the People Mover bus No 6, which departs outside the South Terminal for the Transit Center downtown on weekdays. Departure times are 7.21 and 8.30 am and 3.50, 4.50 and 5.50 pm. The fare is $1.

Many hotels and B&Bs, mostly listed in the baggage claim area, also have courtesy van service. Finally there is an endless line of taxis eager to take your bags and your money. Plan on a $12 fare to the downtown area.

Bus Anchorage has an excellent public bus system in the People Mover and its clean buses and friendly drivers. All buses, except No 93, begin at the People Mover's downtown terminal in the Transit Center at the Municipal Building near the corner of 6th Ave and G St. Most buses pass by every half hour and there's a time schedule posted at every stop. The fare is $1 a ride or $2.50 for an all-day, unlimited ticket. If the trip requires more than one bus, ask the driver for a transfer, which allows you to ride on the connecting bus for only an additional 15c.

A full service operates from Monday to Friday, with a reduced service on Saturday; 10 buses run on Sunday, none of which goes to the International Airport. For information on any route call the Ride Line on 343-6543.

If you are planning to spend some time in the Anchorage area there are two things worth investing in. Pick up a copy of the *People Mover Timetable* for $1 at the Transit Center which details all the routes and bus times. You might also want to purchase a monthly bus pass which provides unlimited travel.

Car Rental Often when there are two or more of you, renting a used car is an affordable and ideal way to see Anchorage, the surrounding area or the Kenai Peninsula. The cheapest deal is from Affordable Car Rental (☎ 243-3370 or (800) 248-3765), at 4707 Spenard Rd and with a counter in the Anchorage Hilton downtown. They advertise some cars for as low as $24 but never seem to have any vehicles available when you call.

Better to try Rent-A-Wreck (☎ 562-5499 or (800) 478-5499 in Alaska) at 512 West International Airport Rd or Allstar Rental (☎ 561-0350 or (800) 722-6484 in Alaska) just a block down the street at 940 West International Airport Rd. Both have subcompacts for $29 a day with a 100 free miles. They will also provide courtesy transport from your motel or to the airport before or after you rent the car.

All the national concerns (Avis, Budget, Hertz, Payless, National etc) maintain a counter in the ground transportation lobby of the South Terminal at the airport. If you're hoping to rent a cheap compact, reserve a vehicle in advance if at all possible as car rentals in Anchorage can be heavily booked in the summer.

Tours A number of companies offer a city bus tour of Anchorage. Almost all of these tours are three to four hours long and include Resolution Park, Lake Hood, and the Anchorage History & Fine Arts Museum. The cheapest is Gray Line (☎ 277-5581) which charges $22.50. The rest – Alaska Sightseeing (☎ 276-1305), Far North Tours (☎ 272-7480) and Eagle Custom Tours (☎ 277-6228) – charge $25.

Perhaps a better deal is Alaska Sightseeing's full-day tour which also includes Portage Glacier and Alyeska Ski Resort. Book this trip within seven days and it's only $47.

Area Tours Gray Line offers a daily seven-hour Portage Glacier/Turnagain Arm tour for $51 which departs at 9 am and noon. The trip includes the USFS visitor center and a trip on Gray Line's *Ptarmigan* which cruises past the face of Portage Glacier. You can also do Seward and Kenai Fjords National Park in a day from Anchorage. The Alaska Railroad (☎ 265-2494 or (800) 544-0552) has a day in Seward that includes the train ride down and a half-day cruise to Bear Glacier on the edge of the national park. The fare is $169 per person and the train pulls out daily at 7 am.

Far North Tours has a Matanuska Valley tour that includes the interesting Iditarod Headquarters, Musk Ox Farm and Eklutna Historical Village. You have to be hard pressed for something to do to take the farm tour, but it departs at 8 am during the summer and the fare is $65.

Denali Express (☎ (800) 327-7651) offers a one-day tour to Denali National Park. The trip is $138 per person and includes round-trip van transportation, a ride on the park shuttle bus to Eielson Visitor Center (the best place to view the mountain) and lunch.

A better and much cheaper way to spend an afternoon is to hop on People Mover bus No 74, 76 or 78 for the scenic trip north of Anchorage along Eagle River, through Chugiak and to Peter's Creek. The 48-mile round trip takes about two hours and costs a mere $2. Those who take the first bus out in the morning have been known to occasionally spot moose between Fort Richardson and Eagle River.

Package Tours Travelers on a tight schedule will find a variety of package tours to other areas of the state available in Anchorage. They include accommodations, transport and meals, and are a way to cover a lot in a day or two if you are willing to pay the price.

The most popular trip out of the city is the cruise past Columbia Glacier to Valdez and returning to Anchorage along the scenic Richardson and Glenn highways. Both Gray Line (☎ 277-5581) and Alaska Sightseeing (☎ 276-1305) offer the tour as a two-day/one-night package with an overnight stay at a Valdez hotel. American Sightseeing's two-day trip is $345 per person, based on shared accommodation; Gray Line is cheaper at $275.

MarkAir, Grey Line and Alaska Sightseeing, along with a few other large tour companies, have package tours everywhere, shuffling tour groups to such unlikely places as Barrow and Kotzebue. If you only have a day left in Alaska and are just dying to see Kotzebue or Nome, Markair (☎ (800) 478-0800 in Alaska) will take you there and back in only 11 hours for $332.

Also offering a variety of package tours is Alaska Railroad (☎ 265-2494). Three of these tours are worth considering for those short on time. The Denali Overnight tour includes a return train trip to Denali National Park and a night's lodging in the park for

$289 per person, based on double occupancy. It does not include, however, a bus ride through the park to Wonder Lake. Eagle Custom Tours has its 'Denali Quickie', which includes an overnight stay at the park and a tundra wildlife tour into the park. The fare is $292 per person. Gray Line comes in with a two-night stay in the national park for $339 if you ride the bus up and back, or $491 if you choose their private railcars on the Alaska Railroad.

If you don't book these package tours in advance and find yourself in Anchorage near the end of your stay with too much money in your pocket, try to cut a deal on 4th Ave. Along this downtown avenue there is a number of booking and reservation centers that might have better deals for you. Two places to try are Alaska Booking & Reservation Center (☎ 277-6228) on the corner with F St and All Alaska Tours (☎ 272-8687) on G St next door to Darwin's Theory Bar.

South of Anchorage

Travelers who arrive in Anchorage and head south to the Kenai Peninsula will immediately be struck by Alaska's splendor; they no sooner leave the city limits than they find themselves following the edge of the spectacular Turnagain Arm. An extension of Cook Inlet, the arm is known for having some of the highest tides in the world while giving way to constant views of the Kenai Mountains to the south.

SEWARD HWY

The Seward Hwy, which runs along Turnagain Arm south of Anchorage, hugs the water and at times has been carved out of the mountainside; it runs side by side with the Alaska Railroad. A bike path shoulders much of the road and when completed will connect the bike trails in Anchorage with those in Girdwood.

The Seward Hwy begins as New Seward Hwy in Anchorage, on the corner of 5th Ave and Gambell St at a junction with the Glenn

Hwy. It heads south and reaches the coast near Rabbit Creek Rd. From here the mileposts on the road measure the distance to Seward. Keep in mind that people who live in Anchorage often play on the Kenai Peninsula. Add the usual RVers of the summer and on Friday afternoon you have major traffic tie-up heading south on Seward Hwy.

At *Mile 118* or nine miles south of Anchorage city center, the highway passes the first of many gravel Turnagain Arm lookouts. In a mile, the highway reaches two lookouts and a massive boardwalk out onto the **Potter Marsh Waterfowl Nesting Area**, a state game refuge. There are display signs at the lookouts where you can often marvel at arctic terns and Canada geese nesting nearby. Some 130 species of birds and waterfowl have been spotted in this refuge at Anchorage's back door.

Two miles to the south you enter Chugach State Park and pass the **Potter Section House**. Renovated and re-opened in 1986, the house used to be home for a crew of railroad workers who maintained the tracks when locomotives were powered by coal. Now the complex is a state historic site and museum with displays and railroad exhibits, including a vintage snowblower and working model train. It's open from 8 am to 4.30 pm daily during the summer except for an hour when they close for lunch. Stop here for information on outdoor activities in Chugach State Park or to use the picnic facilities. There is no admission charge.

Across the street is the posted northern trailhead for the **Old Johnson Trail**, an 11-mile path. The route was originally used by Indians and later by Russians, trappers and gold miners at the turn of the century. Today, it provides you with an easy hike and a 'mountain-goat's-eye view' of Turnagain Arm, alpine meadows and beluga whales feeding in the waters below. From Potter, the trail heads south-east and reaches McHugh Picnic Area in 3.5 miles; Rainbow (with access to Seward Hwy) in 7.5 miles; and Windy Corner at its southern end in 9.5 miles. Plan on five to seven hours for the entire walk.

In the next 10 miles, the highway passes numerous lookouts, many with scenic views of Turnagain Arm. Just beyond *Mile 112* of Seward Hwy is McHugh Creek Picnic Area (30 picnic tables) and the second access to the Old Johnson Trail followed by **Beluga Point**. The point has a commanding view of the Turnagain Arm and features telescopes and interpretive displays to assist travelers in spotting the white whales in May and August. At *Mile 103.6* is **Indian**, consisting mainly of a couple of bars and a restaurant.

Just west of Turnagain House and Indian Creek is a gravel road that leads 1.3 miles past a pump station and ends near Indian Creek, where there is parking space and the posted trailhead for the **Indian Valley Trail**, a six-mile path to Indian Pass. The trail is easy, with only an occasional ford of Indian Creek, and leads to the alpine setting of the pass. In the alpine areas of the pass, more experienced hikers can continue north to eventually reach the Ship Creek Trail which ends at Ski Bowl Rd north of Anchorage. Plan on five to seven hours for the 12-mile round trip on the Indian Valley Trail.

The **Bird Ridge Trail** starts near *Mile 102* of Seward Hwy, look for a large marked parking area to the north. From here the trail to the ridge begins with an uphill climb to a power-line access road, follows it for 0.3 miles and then turns left and climbs Bird Ridge, which runs along the valley of Bird Creek. The hike is steep in many places but quickly leaves the bush behind for the alpine beauty above. You can hike over four miles on the ridge itself, reaching views of the headwaters of Ship Creek below. Viewing points of Turnagain Arm are plentiful and make the trail a good mountain hike.

The *Bird Creek State Campground* (19 sites, $6) is just beyond *Mile 101*. The campground is scenic and known for its fine sunbathing, but is often full by early afternoon during the summer, especially on weekends. The next 10 miles after Bird Creek Campground contains 16 turn-offs, all good spots to watch the **tidal bores**. Bores (barreling walls of water that often exceed 10 feet in height as they rush 15 mph back

across the mud flats) are created twice a day by the powerful tides in Turnagain Arm.

There are more than 60 places around the world where tidal bores occur (the highest are the 25-foot bores on the Amazon basin) but the Turnagain and Knik arms are the only places in the USA where they take place on a regular basis. To avoid missing the turbulent incoming waves, get the time of low tide from the *Anchorage Daily News* and add two hours and 15 minutes. At that time the bore will be passing this particular point along the highway. Arrive early and then continue down the road after the bore passes your lookout to view it again and again.

Alyeska Access Rd
Girdwood At *Mile 90* of Seward Hwy is the junction with Alyeska Hwy, the access road which goes to Girdwood, a small hamlet of 300 residents, two miles up the side road. The junction itself now features a strip-mall housing, among other things, a 7-Eleven, a taco shop and a video-rental store in case you have a VCR in your backpack. For something less urban, pass this up for Girdwood. The town has a post office, quaint *Girdwood Cafe*, grocery store, laundromat with showers and Kinder Park (site of the town's annual Forest Fair usually held in the first week of July). The two-day event features a variety of entertainment, art and craft booths, contests and food in a delightful small-town atmosphere.

Alyeska Ski Area Another mile east of Girdwood is the Alyeska Ski Area. The ski resort hums during the winter and is also a busy place during the summer, when tour groups leave the buses to wander through the gift shops and expensive restaurants or participate in hot-air balloon flights and horse-drawn carriage rides. The best thing about the resort is the scenic lift ride to the Skyline Restaurant, 2000 feet above the valley floor. In 1993, the ski resort suspended the summer rides while they replaced the open chair lift with a tram. When they resume, your guess is as good as mine as to how much they will charge for the great views of Turnagain Arm. Still, it's easy access to good alpine hiking.

During the summer there are rooms at the resort's Nugget Inn but they tend to be overrun by tour bus groups and rates reflect that. There is also a number of restaurants at the resort that remain open year around, including *The Deli Express* in the Nugget Inn which from 11 am to 3 pm, serves soup and sandwiches for $7.

A small but charming hostel in the area can be reached by turning right onto Timberline Dr before the ski lodge and then turning right again on Alpine Rd for 0.4 miles. The *Alyeska International (AYH) Home Hostel* (☎ 277-7388) is in a cabin with wood heating, gas lighting and a kitchen area, and includes the use of a wood-burning sauna.

Unfortunately, the hostel only has six beds, so you might want to call ahead to try to secure space. It is only open from Wednesday to Sunday and the nightly fees are $12 for members and $10 for nonmembers.

Hiking

Just up the Alyeska Hwy from Seward Hwy is a Chugach National Forest ranger office (☎ 783-3242). The center is open daily during the summer and is a place to go for not only hiking trails in the Girdwood area but all over the Kenai Peninsula.

Begin the **Alyeska Glacier View Trail** by taking the chair lift to the Skyline Restaurant and then scrambling up the knob behind the sun deck. From here, you follow the ridge into an alpine area where there are views of the tiny Alyeska Glacier. The entire return hike is less than a mile. You can continue up the ridge to climb the so-called summit of Mt Alyeska, a high point of 3939 feet. The true summit lies further to the south but is not a climb for casual hikers.

Winner Creek Gorge This is an easy and pleasant hike that winds 3.5 miles through a tall spruce and hemlock forest and ends in the gorge itself. The gorge is where Winter Creek flows through a small cleft in the rocks and becomes a series of small falls and cascades on its way to emptying into Glacier Creek. You pick up the trail at Alyeska Ski Resort by parking on Arlberg Rd and walking along the bike path past the new hotel towards the bottom of the new tram. Follow the edge of a ski trail above the tram and look for the footpath heading into the forest.

Crow Creek Rd Two miles up the Alyeska Access Rd and just before Girdwood is the junction with Crow Creek Rd, a bumpy gravel road. It extends 5.8 miles to a parking lot and the marked trailhead to the **Crow Creek Trail**, a short but beautiful alpine hike. It is four miles to Raven Glacier, the traditional turn-around point of the trail, and with transport, hikers can easily do the eight-mile round trip in four to six hours.

The trail is a highly recommended trek as it features gold-mining relics, an alpine lake and usually dall sheep on the slopes above. There are also many possibilities for longer trips and a US Forest Service (USFS) cabin three miles up the trail ($25 per night) which can be reserved in advance through the USFS office in Anchorage. You can also camp around Crow Pass, turning the walk into a pleasant overnight trip. Or, you can continue and complete the three-day, 25-mile route along the Old Iditarod Trail to the Chugach State Park's Eagle River Visitor Center (see the North of Anchorage section in this chapter).

From the Alyeska Access Rd, Seward Hwy continues south-east and at *Mile 81* reaches the **Wetland Observation Platform** constructed by the Bureau of Land Management. The platform features interpretive plaques on the ducks, arctic terns, bald eagles and other wildlife that can often been seen from it.

Portage

Portage, the departure point for passengers and cars going to Whittier on the Alaska Railroad, is passed at *Mile 80* of Seward Hwy. There is not much left of Portage, which was destroyed by the Good Friday Earthquake, other than a few structures sinking into the nearby mud flats. During the summer, the shuttle train departs the loading ramp six times from Thursday to Monday at 8 and 10.45 am and 1.30, 5, 7.30 and 9.30 pm. On Tuesday and Wednesday it just departs on the four afternoon runs. The daily 1.30 pm trip connects with the MV *Bartlett*, the state ferry that cruises from Whittier to Valdez. The one-way fare from Whittier to Portage is $7.50 per adult and $32 for a car.

Portage Glacier

A mile south of the loading ramp in Portage is the junction with Portage Glacier Access Rd. The road leads 5.4 miles past three campgrounds to a visitor center overlooking Portage Glacier, which recently surpassed Denali National Park as Alaska's most visited attraction. The magnificent ice floe is five miles long and a mile wide at its face and is the Southcentral's version of the drive-in glacier. It's impressive but in 1880 it filled what is now Portage Lake. Indians and miners used the ice as a route or 'portage' between Turnagain Arm and Passage Canal. By 1890 the glacier began to retreat and today more than 2.5 miles of the lake has been exposed. Retreating at more than 300 feet per year, the glacier is now expected to reach the end of the lake by the year 2020. What it will do at this point is anybody's guess.

The glacier and the ice that clutters the west end of the lake is quite a sight and more than 700,000 people view it annually with this number raising sharply each year. This is evident during the summer as a stream of tour buses and cars is constantly passing through. But even if crowds are what you're trying to avoid, Portage Glacier is not to be missed. This is classic Alaskan imagery, while the **Begich-Boggs Visitor Center**, completed in 1986, is well worth viewing. The $8 million center houses, among other things, a simulated ice cave you can walk through to reach the Glacier Exhibit room with its displays demonstrating the formation of crevasses, as well as glacial motion and the range of glaciers today. Elsewhere you can touch an iceberg, bought in fresh daily, take a close look at ice worms or take

in the excellent movie *Voices From the Ice* shown every hour in a 200-seat theater. All around there are observation decks and telescopes to view the main attraction. During the summer the center is open from 9 am to 7 pm daily.

For those who want to get even closer to the glacier, Gray Line offers hour-long cruises on board its tour boat, *Ptarmigan*. Don't get this cruise confused with any glacier cruise along Tracy Arm in the Southeast or College Fjord in Prince William Sound; you simply motor around the lake and it's $20 per person.

If you're planning to camp in the area, take in some of the activities sponsored by the center. They include nature walks, goldpanning demonstrations and a hike to Byron Glacier to search for ice worms.

There are only two campgrounds in the area now as Beaver Pond was flooded when nature's little engineers built additional dams. Try either the *Black Bear Campground* (12 sites, $6 fee) or *Williwaw Campground* (38 sites, $6 fee). Williwaw is particularly pleasant as there is a salmon-spawning observation deck near it and a mile-long nature walk through beaver and moose habitat. Keep in mind, you never get a site late in the day at these campgrounds. With more than half a million people coming to see Portage Glacier annually, the facilities always seem to be full.

Check with the rangers about a planned trail to the face of Portage Glacier. Otherwise, hiking in the area consists of the **Byron Glacier Trail**, an easy one-mile path to the base of Byron Glacier that begins on the road to the boat tour dock. Once you reach the permanent snow in front of the glacier, look for ice worms in it. The worms, immortalized in a Robert Service poem, are black, thread-like and less than an inch long. They survive by consuming algae and escape the heat of the sun by sliding between ice crystals of glaciers and snowfields.

From Portage, Seward Hwy turns south and heads for the scenic town of Seward on Resurrection Bay, 128 miles from Anchorage (see the Southcentral chapter).

North of Anchorage

GLENN HIGHWAY

The 189-mile Glenn Hwy begins at the corner of Medfra St and 5th Ave *(Mile 0)*, just west of Merrill Field Airport in Anchorage, and extends to Glennallen and the Richardson Hwy. The first 42 miles heads north-east to Palmer, the trade center of the Matanuska Valley, and recently has been turned into a true highway – four lanes enabling motorists to pass road hogs in their RVs. Just west of Palmer the Glenn Hwy forms a major junction with the George Parks Hwy. The George Parks Hwy heads to Fairbanks. Glenn Hwy curves more due east for Glennallen (see the Interior chapter). Mileposts on the highway show distances from Anchorage.

On the first eight miles north-east from Anchorage, you pass the exits to Elmendorf Air Force Base, Centennial Campground and Arctic Valley Rd to Fort Richardson (see the Anchorage Things to See section). At *Mile 11.5* of Glenn Hwy is the turn-off to *Eagle River State Campground* (50 sites, $12 fee), just up Hiland Rd. The scenic campground is in a wooded area on the south bank of the Eagle River. The spot is popular and has a four-day limit. Don't drink the glacier-fed water of the Eagle River. Also, don't depend on getting a tent space if you arrive late. Because of its proximity to Anchorage, this is one of the busiest campgrounds in the state.

At *Mile 13.6* of Glenn Hwy is the exit to Eagle River (population 9000) and Eagle River Rd. This 12.7-mile road is paved and a beautiful side trip into the Chugach Mountains. It ends at the **Eagle River Visitor Center** of the Chugach State Forest. The log cabin center (☎ 694-2108) is open daily from 11 am to 7 pm and features wildlife displays, hand-outs for hikers, naturalist programs and telescopes with which to view dall sheep in the surrounding mountains.

There is also a outdoor picnic area with more telescopes and a stunning view of the Chugach Mountains. Two trails depart from here. One is the easy Rodak Nature Trail, a loop of less than a mile that passes a series of interpretive panels and an impressive observation deck straddling a salmon stream. Albert Loop Trail is a three-mile hike through a boreal forest and along Eagle River.

The visitor center also serves as the northern trailhead for the **Old Iditarod Trail**, a 26-mile historical trail. The route was used by gold miners and dog-sled teams until 1918, when the Alaska Railroad was completed from Seward to Fairbanks. Today, it is a three-day hike through excellent mountain scenery and up to Crow Pass, where you can view nearby Raven Glacier and Crystal Lake. From here you hike down the Crow Creek Trail and emerge on Crow Creek Rd, seven miles away from the Seward Hwy (see the South of Anchorage section in this chapter).

Dog Sled Team

Top: King Mountain & the Matanuska River (DS)
Bottom: Sheep Mountain in Fall, Chugach Range (DS)

Top: Winter in Interior Alaska (DS)
Left: Fall colours, Mentasta Range, Interior Alaska (DS)
Right: Birch trees in winter, Fairbanks (DS)

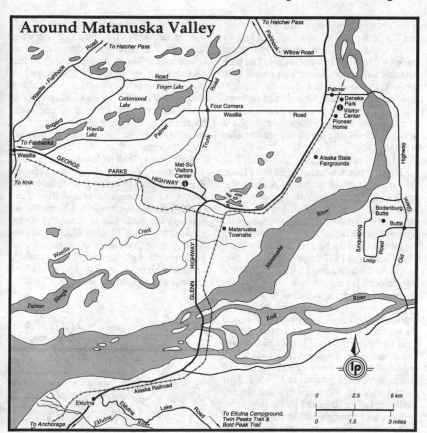

Around Matanuska Valley

Although this route involves fording several streams, including Eagle River itself, and some climbing to Crow Pass, it is an excellent hike – one of the best in the Southcentral and Anchorage regions. It is also a way to bypass Anchorage for those who want to avoid big-city hassles and head straight for the Kenai Peninsula. Backpackers in Anchorage can reach the junction of Eagle River Rd on People Mover buses Nos 74, 76 and 78 and from there hitch to the visitor center. Bring a stove as campfires are not allowed in the state park.

Northbound on Glenn Hwy, the Thunder-bird Falls exit is reached at *Mile 25.2* and leads 0.3 miles to a parking area and the trailhead for the **Thunderbird Falls Trail**. The mile-long trail is a quick uphill climb to the scenic falls formed by a small, rocky gorge. At the end is an deck with benches overlooking the cascade, a great place to enjoy lunch.

Eklutna Lake

The Indian village of Eklutna (population 25 or so) is reached by taking the Eklutna Lake Rd exit at *Mile 26.5* of Glenn Hwy and heading west. Dating back to 1650, Eklutna is the oldest continually inhabited Athabascan site in the region. Much of that history can be seen at the **Eklutna Village Historical Park** (☎ 276-5701 in Anchorage). The park contains a Heritage House with displays on the indigenous lifestyle and art, the St Nicholas Russian Orthodox Church, a hand-hewn log chapel, and brightly colored spirit houses in a cemetery nearby. Hours are from 8 am to 8 pm daily during the summer, admission is $3.50.

Eklutna Lake Rd bumps and winds east for 10 miles to the west end of Eklutna Lake, the largest body of water (at seven miles long) in Chugach State Park and one of the most scenic as it is surrounded by peaks. Here you'll find the *Eklutna Lake State Recreation Area* (50 sites, $6 fee). Skirting along the north side of the lake is **Lakeshore Trail**, an old road until 1977 when numerous washouts turned it into a route for hikers, horses, mountain bikers and, unfortunately, those on motorized all-terrain vehicles (ATVs).

There is a separate parking lot for the trailhead with a trail information kiosk and telescopes for viewing dall sheep. Lakeside Trail begins on the other side of Twin Peaks Creek and is an easy one-way walk of 13 miles. There are even mile markers and backcountry campgrounds at *Mile 8.8*, *Mile 11* and *Mile 12*. They are free and feature vault toilets, fire rings and picnic tables.

If you are hoisting a pack to stay overnight at one of them, plan on hiking to Cottonwood Campground at *Mile 12*. Motorized ATVs aren't allowed at the facility and you will be near the trailhead for **Eklutna Glacier Trail**. The 0.75-mile trail ends at interpretive panels and a view of the glacier. Also nearby is **East Fork Trail** at *Mile 10.5*, just before Lakeside Trail crosses a bridge over the East Fork of the Eklutna River. East Fork Trail is a 5.5-mile walk up the river to a glacial lake surrounded by the highest peaks of the Chugach Mountains.

Heading in the opposite direction of the Lakeshore Trail is **Twin Peaks Trail**. The trail is another abandoned road that heads 3.5 miles above the tree line to the passes between Twin Peaks. It is well marked in the

beginning and halfway up you can lie out and soak up the views of the lake and valley and some sun, if it's shining that day (chances are it won't be). Above the tree line, the trail becomes steeper and more challenging to follow. At this point, scrambling in the alpine area is easy and the views of Eklutna Lake below are excellent. Plan on several hours for the hike, depending on how far you go above the tree line, and keep a sharp eye out for dall sheep.

Bold Peak Trail is another good hike which starts 5.5 miles along the Lakeshore Trail. The 3.5-mile trail is a moderately hard hike to the alpine area below Bold Peak (7522 feet) and begins with a steep ascent, reaching the bush line in 1.5 miles. Great views of the valley, Eklutna Glacier and even Knik Arm of Cook Inlet are obtained here, while people with the energy can scramble up nearby ridges. Plan on two hours to climb the trail and an hour for the return. To actu-

Dall Sheep

ally climb Bold Peak requires that you have mountaineering skill and equipment.

PALMER

From Eklutna Lake Rd, the Glenn Hwy continues north, crosses bridges over the Knik and Matanuska rivers at the northern end of Cook Inlet, and at *Mile 35.3* reaches a major junction with the George Parks Hwy. At this point, Glenn Hwy curves sharply to the east and leads into Palmer (population 3000), seven miles away.

Although a railroad station was built here in 1916, the town was really born in 1935, when it was selected for an unusual social experiment during President Franklin Roosevelt's New Deal relief programs. Some 200 farming families, hit hard by the Great Depression in the US Midwest, were moved north to raise crops and livestock in the Matanuska and Susitna valleys.

The failure rate was high within this transplanted agricultural colony, but somehow Palmer survived and today it is the only community whose economy is based primarily on farming. The farms of the Matanuska

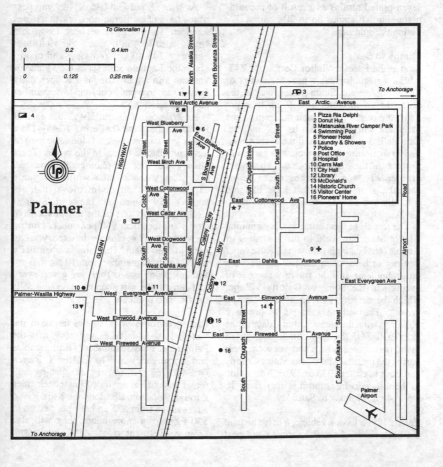

Big cabbages

Valley grow the 60-pound cabbages and seven-pound turnips as a result of the midnight sun that shines up to 20 hours a day during the summer.

Things to See

Stop at the **Palmer Visitor Center** (☎ 745-4493), a rustic log cabin near the corner of Fireweed Ave and South Valley Way in the center of town. Open from 9 am to 6 pm daily, the center has a small museum in the basement with relics from its 'colony' era. Outside is a picnic area and the **Matanuska Valley Agricultural Showcase**, a garden of flowers and the area's famous oversized vegetables. To see cabbages the size of basketballs or radishes that look like red softballs, you have to come from late July to late August.

The town's biggest attraction is its annual Alaska State Fair, held in the last week of August (see Festivals following). But even if you're not here when the fair is, the state fairgrounds are still the site of a number of events and the home of **Colony Village**, which began in 1975 as a Bicentennial project. The village attempts to preserve buildings from the area's 'colony' days of the late 1930s. Of the five buildings, four of them, two houses, a barn and a church, were part of the original Matanuska Valley Colony and built in either 1935 or 1936. Admission to the village is free, and it is open from 10 am to 4 pm Monday to Saturday.

Farms If you have a vehicle, a drive around the back roads of the Palmer area and past the farms makes an interesting afternoon. To view a few of the colony farms that survived along with the original barns built, head north-east nine miles on Glenn Hwy and exit onto Farm Loop Rd.

Old Glenn Hwy, which departs from the present highway right before the bridges across the Knik and Matanuska rivers and rejoins it in Palmer, can also provide views of the area's farms, especially on Bodenberg Loop Rd that runs off it, west from Butte. Keep an eye out for vegetable stands if you're passing through the area from mid to late summer.

At *Mile 11.5* of Old Glenn Hwy you pass near a farm of a different sort, one that raises reindeer. Turn onto Bodenberg Loop and within a mile you'll reach the **Reindeer Farm** (☎ 745-4000). You view and photograph the Lapland animals as they graze or you can join a tour. The farm is open daily from 10 am to 6 pm from June to September and admission is $3.

At *Mile 50* of Glenn Hwy, just east of Palmer, is the **Musk Ox Farm** (☎ 745-4151), where you can see the only domestic herd of these prehistoric beasts in the world. Tours allow you to view and photograph more than 100 shaggy musk oxen while the guide explains how their qiviut (down hair) is combed and woven into the world's rarest cloth – probably one of the most expensive cloths at more than $60 per ounce. During the tour, you get so close to the oxen, you can pet and feed them. The farm is open daily from May to September from 10 am to 6 pm and admission is $6. Tours are given every half-hour and a gift shop displays and sells the finished products.

Riding Stables With all the farms in the valley, it shouldn't be surprising that the Palmer area boasts a number of riding stables and horse ranches. The Rafter T Ranch (☎ 745-8768; call to get exact turn-by-turn directions) offers unguided horseback rides through wooded trails along the Knik River. Rates range from $35 an hour per person to $30 for two or more hours; they will also arrange overnight rides. Also check with

Motherlode Lodge (☎ 746-1464) in the Hatcher Pass area north of Palmer which maintains a small stable of riding horses.

Festivals

The best reason to stop in Palmer is the Alaska State Fair, an 11-day event that ends on Labor Day. The fair features produce and livestock from the surrounding area, horse shows, a rodeo, a carnival and the largest cabbages you'll ever see. Within the state fairgrounds is the outdoor Borealis Theater and during the third week of July it is the site of a bluegrass festival, worth attending if you are passing through. Those in Anchorage should check with the Alaska Railroad (☎ 265-2494) which occasionally runs special trains to Palmer for these events.

Places to Stay

Camping Camping in town is possible at *Deneke Park*, where there is a large grassy area for people to pitch tents. The park also has tables and coin-operated showers. The nightly fee is $5. From the visitor center, head north along South Valley Way and turn right into East Cottonwood Ave just past the Alaska State Troopers office. The park is on the corner of East Cottonwood Ave and South Denali St.

B&Bs Outside the Palmer Visitor Center is a rack for the local B&Bs and you'll find almost a dozen in the area. Most of them are a drive out of town. The exception is *Jean's Bed & Breakfast* (☎ 746-4373) at 317 Independence St, a 15-minute walk from the visitor center. Rooms are clean and comfortable and priced at $45 a double.

Hotels There is no hostel in Palmer. The cheapest hotel in town is the *Pioneer Motel* (☎ 745-3425) on the corner of North Alaska and Arctic streets, where a double room is $43 per night. Also in Palmer, and a definite step up, is the *Fairview Motel* (☎ 745-1505) across from the state fairgrounds which has singles/doubles for $50/60.

Places to Eat

Palmer now has a *McDonald's* and a *Subway* near the intersection of the Glenn and Palmer-Wasilla highways. For something a little more personal, try *Pizza Ria Delphi*, a Mexican-Greek-Italian restaurant as strange as that might sound, on the corner of South Alaska St and West Arctic Ave, a block south of Glenn Hwy. Pasta dinners begin at $7, pizzas at $9 and burritos and enchiladas at $8.

Practically next door is *The Donut Hut* where the coffee starts pouring at 6 am from Monday to Saturday and the refills are free. Or try the *Round House Cafe* in the Valley Hotel at 606 South Alaska. They serve homemade pies and soup 24 hours a day.

There are two large farmers' markets in the area. Both are near the junction of the Glenn and George Parks highways. North towards Fairbanks is *Bushes Bunches* and east towards Palmer is *Matanuska Farm Market*, open until 7 pm in the summer.

Hiking

The best hike near Palmer is the climb to the top of **Lazy Mountain**, elevation 3720 feet. The 2.5-mile trail is steep at times, but makes for a pleasant trek that ends in an alpine setting with good views of the Matanuska Valley and its farms below. From the Glenn Hwy in Palmer, head east on Arctic Ave, the third exit into town, which turns into Old Glenn Hwy. After crossing the Matanuska River, turn left onto Clark-Wolverine Rd and then left after half a mile at a 'T' junction. This puts you onto the unmarked Huntly Rd, and you follow it for a mile to the Equestrian Center parking lot at its end. The trailhead, marked Foot Trail, is on the north side of the parking lot. Plan on three to five hours for the return hike.

McRoberts Creek Trail is a backcountry hike up McRoberts Creek valley and provides an easy approach to climbing Matanuska Peak (6119 feet). The trail reaches the tree line in 2.5 miles and 3880-foot Summit Ridge in nine miles. The trek to Matanuska Peak would be a 18-mile hike. To reach the trailhead, take Old Glenn Hwy from Palmer toward Butte and turn left onto Smith Rd at *Mile 15.5*. Follow Smith Rd for 1.4 miles until it curves into Harmony Ave. There is no parking at the South Fork Trailhead so leave the car at the bend in the road.

Tours

Want to see a glacier? Knik Glacier Scenic Tours (☎ 373-2628 or 745-6183) offers jet-boat tours three times a day from Knik River Landing at *Mile 5.5* of Old Glenn Hwy of the three-mile long glacier. It's $80 for the tour. For something less motorized, NOVA Riverrunners (☎ 745-5753) offers a Lions Head float on the Matanuska River to the impressive Matanuska Glacier. The raft trip last four hours and comes with lunch and plenty of white water. The cost is $60 per person.

HATCHER PASS

Just north of Palmer, via the Fishhook-Willow Rd off Glenn Hwy, is the Hatcher Pass area, an alpine paradise filled with panoramas of the Talkeetna Mountains, foot trails, gold-mine artefacts and even some unusual lodging possibilities. The area is probably the most photographed in the Mat-Su Valley and can be entered from either Wasilla, Willow or Palmer but the drive from Palmer is the shortest and especially scenic as it follows the Little Susitna River through a vertical-walled gorge. It also has the most traffic, making hitching a lot easier for those without a set of wheels.

The pass itself is 22 miles out of Palmer and, at 3886 feet, is an alpine area of meadows, ridges, steep drops and a beautiful body of water known as Summit Lake. It's also a popular destination for parasailing and, on most calm evenings, you can sit on a ridge and watch the daredevils strap themselves to the colorful sails and glide with the wind.

Independence Mine State Historical Park

This fascinating 272-acre state historical park, 18 miles north of Palmer, is entirely above the tree line. Within the beautiful bowl-shaped valley of the park are the remains of 16 buildings that were built in the 1930s by the Alaska-Pacific Mining Company which for 10 years was second only to Juneau's A-J Mine as the leading hardrock gold mine in Alaska.

Gold was first discovered in the area by a pair of Japanese prospectors shortly after 1900 and the rough nature of the gold was an indication to many miners that there was a 'motherlode' waiting to be found higher in the Talkeetna Mountains. Robert Lee Hatcher discovered and staked the first lode claim in Willow Creek valley in 1906 and within a few years mining took off. From 1906 until 1950 more than 50 gold mines were worked the Hatcher Pass area, but the two most productive were the Alaska Free Gold Mine on Skyscraper Mountain and Independence Mine on Granite Mountain.

In 1938, the two mines were consolidated by Alaska-Pacific, which controls a block of 83 mining permits, 1350 acres and 27 structures. In is peak year of 1941 APC employed 204 workers, blasted almost 12 miles of tunnels and recovered 34,416 ounces of gold that was worth $1.2 million. Today that gold would be worth almost $18 million.

WW II shut down the Independence Mine in 1943. It reopened in 1948 and briefly in 1950 before being finally abandoned in 1955. Now a state park, seeing Independence Mine and the company town that was built around it makes for a fascinating afternoon in anybody's trip to Alaska.

Begin at the Manager's House which has been converted into a visitor center. There are video interviews of the old miners, displays on the different ways to mine gold (panning, placer mining and hardrock) and even a simulated mining tunnel. The visitor center (☎ 745-2827) is open from 11 am to 7 pm daily and can provide a walking-tour map of the park, a list of area hikes. It even conducts guided tours.

From the center, you follow Hardrock Trail past the buildings, including bunkhouses and the mill complex that is built into the side of the mountain and looks like an avalanche of falling timber. Make an effort to climb up the trail to the water tunnel portal where you get a great overview of the entire complex and a blast of cold air pouring out of the mountain.

Hiking
Gold Mint Trail This is one of the easiest hikes in the Hatcher Pass area. It begins from a parking lot across from Motherlode Lodge at *Mile 14* of the Fishhook-Willow Rd. The trail follows the Little Susitna River into a gently sloping mountain valley. Within three miles you can spot the ruins of Lonesome Mine. Keep trekking and you will eventually reach the head of the river at Mint Glacier.

Reed Lakes Trail A mile past Motherlode Lodge, a road to Archangel Valley splits off from Fishhook-Willow Rd and takes you to the trailhead of Reed Lakes. The trail begins as a wide road and is soon climbing to the crest of the valley. Lower Reed Lake is reached within a quarter mile after reaching the crest, Upper Reed Lake follows after a bit more climbing.

Craigie Creek Trail This trail, posted along the Fishhook-Willow Rd west of Hatcher Pass, actually starts out as a road that an occasional four-wheeler will use. The trail follows a valley up to the head of the creek where it's possible to cross a pass into the Independence Mine Bowl. The road climbs

gently for four miles past several abandoned mining operations and then becomes a very steep trail for three miles to Dogsled Pass.

Places to Stay & Eat
At *Mile 14* of Fishhook-Willow Rd is *Motherlode Lodge* (☎ 746-1464), that was originally built in the 1930s as part of the local mining operation. Today it's been totally renovated and has rooms for $75 a night including breakfast. There is also a dining room here with superb view of the mountains from every table and a bar where you can sit out on the deck and take in more panoramas. Across the road, the lodge offers gold panning and horseback riding.

Closer to the pass itself and within Independence Mine State Park is *Hatcher Pass Lodge* (☎ 745-5897) where small cabins are $95 a night per couple and rooms cost $58. Both include breakfast. The lodge also has a restaurant and bar where you can enjoy your favorite brew at 3000 feet above sea level as well as a sauna built over a rushing mountain stream.

Getting Around
Other than renting a car in Wasilla or hitching, the only other way to get to Hatcher Pass and Independent Mine is to join a tour. Mat-Su Tours (☎ 376-3608) offers a full-day tour that begins in Wasilla and includes the Musk Ox Farm and the state park for $60. They also throw in lunch but the price still seems steep.

The Interior

At the Fairview Inn in Talkeetna the house rules are easy to understand and even easier to read. They're posted right above the hotel's horseshoe bar:

- All firearms must be checked in with the bartender before drinks are ordered.
- Dogs must be left outside.
- The bartender is the only one allowed to stoke the wood-burning stove.
- Profanity is discouraged.

Welcome to Interior Alaska, that 'great, big, broad land way up yonder' between Anchorage and Fairbanks that has been searched over by miners, immortalized by poets such as Robert Service, and is immediately visualized when somebody says 'the Last Frontier'. The images are of dog sleds and gold pans, roadhouses and fish wheels, a moose on the side of the road and a seemingly endless stretch of pavement that disappears into the mountains.

The Interior, in fact, is bordered by dramatic mountain chains, with the Alaska Range lying to the south and the Brooks Range to the north. In between is the central plateau of Alaska, a vast area of land that gently slopes to the north and is broken up by awesome rivers such as the Yukon, Kuskokwim, Koyukuk and Tanana. It is the home of Mt McKinley, the highest peak in North America (20,320 feet) and of Denali National Park & Preserve, the best known attraction in the state for hiking, camping and wildlife-watching opportunities. It is the stomping grounds for brown bear, moose, caribou and dall sheep, whose numbers are unmatched anywhere else in the country.

The Interior can be enjoyed by even the most impecunious traveler because it's accessible by road. The greater part of Alaska's highway system forms a triangle which includes the state's two largest cities, Anchorage and Fairbanks, and allows cheap travel by bus, train, car or hitchhiking.

The George Parks Hwy leaves Anchorage and winds 358 miles to Fairbanks, passing Denali National Park along the way. The Glenn Hwy spans 189 miles between Anchorage and Glennallen and then continues another 125 miles to Tok in a section known as the Tok Cutoff. The Richardson Hwy passes Glennallen from Valdez and ends at Fairbanks, 368 miles away. Dividing the triangle from east to west is the Denali Hwy, 136 miles long and at one time the only road to Denali National Park.

All four roads are called highways, though they are rarely more than two-lane roads. All of them pass through spectacular scenery, offer good possibilities of spotting wildlife and are lined with turn-offs, campgrounds and hiking trails. For the most part, the towns along them are small, colorless service centers with gasoline stations, motels and cafés, although a few have managed to retain their rustic gold-rush and frontier flavor. The real attraction of the Interior is not these service centers but what lies in the hills and valleys beyond the highway.

In this region of mountains and spacious valleys, the climate varies greatly and the weather can change appreciably from one day to the next. In the winter, the temperatures drop to -60°F for days at a time; in the summer, they can soar above 90°F. The norm for the summer is long days with warm tem-

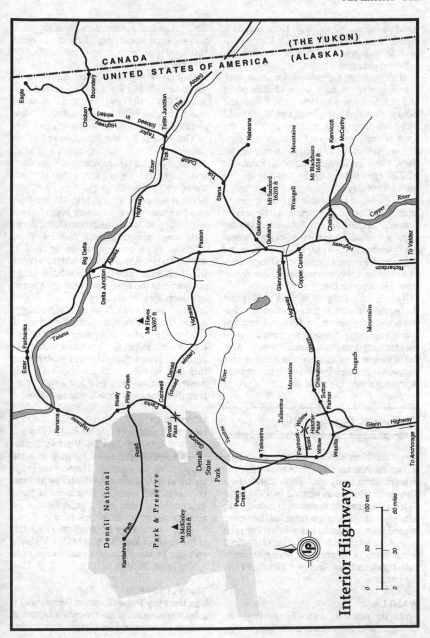

Interior Highways

peratures from 60 to 70°F. However, it is common for Denali National Park to experience at least one snowfall in the lowlands between June and August.

Here, more than anywhere else in the state, it is important to have warm clothes while still being able to strip down to a T-shirt and hiking shorts. Most of the area's 10 to 15 inches of annual precipitation comes in the form of summer showers, with cloudy conditions common, especially north of Mt McKinley. In Denali National Park, Mt McKinley is hidden by the weather for two out of three days.

Bus transport is available on every highway except the Denali, and there is a train service between Anchorage and Fairbanks (see the Getting Around chapter or the Getting There & Away sections in this chapter). Bus routes and even the companies themselves change often in Alaska, so it pays to double-check bus departures with a phone call.

The hitchhiking is surprisingly good during the summer, as the highways are cluttered with the stream of RVs and summer tourists arriving from down south. Avoid backtracking if you can, even if it means going out of your way on an alternative route. All the highways offer their own roadside scenery that is nothing short of spectacular.

George Parks Hwy

Many travelers and most overseas visitors arrive in Alaska through Anchorage and venture north along the George Parks Hwy. The road, which was opened in 1971, provides a direct route to Denali National Park while passing through some of the most rugged scenery Alaska has to offer. The road begins at a junction with the Glenn Hwy 35.3 miles north of Anchorage. Mileposts indicate distances from Anchorage and not from the junction.

WASILLA
From its junction with Glenn Hwy, the George Parks Hwy heads north and, for the first 20 miles, passes through a jungle of tacky tourist stops, strip malls and as many fast-food restaurants as you'll see in all of the Southeast. The ultimate in this stretch of seemingly out-of-place tourist traps is at the junction with Big Lake Rd where you have several discount fireworks stands, including one that has a huge gorilla balloon floating overhead and the Batmobile out front.

The reason for the development is the caravan of RVers heading north to Denali National Park, a steady stream of consumerism that everybody is trying to tap into, and the town of Wasilla (population 3700) just seven miles from the junction. At one time, this community was a mining supply center and in the 1970s was little more than a sleepy little town servicing local farmers. From 1980 to 1983, the population of Wasilla doubled when Alaskans who wanted to work in Anchorage but live elsewhere began moving into the town making it an Anchorage dormitory community.

There was even talk of building a bridge across the Knik Arm to shorten the drive to Anchorage, while shopping centers and businesses have mushroomed along the highway. This is all a bit ironic because many feel that Wasilla, with its strip malls and convenience stores, is now just a slice of the big city that others were trying to escape.

Information
Near the junction of George Parks Hwy and Trunk Rd is the Mat-Su Visitors Center (☎ 746-5002) open from 7.30 am to 6 pm daily during the summer. The new log lodge sits on a small rise and along with bathrooms, postcards and racks of brochures, it has a small outdoor deck with a great view of the mountains surrounding Knik Inlet.

The Dorothy Page Museum (☎ 376-2005) in the town of Wasilla, just off the highway on Main St, doubles as the visitor center and is also open daily.

Things to See
The **Dorothy Page Museum** (see above) is a both museum and an interesting historical village of preserved buildings, each loaded

with artefacts. Named after 'the mother of the Iditarod', the museum is open daily year-round from 9 am to 6 pm and admission is $3. The museum is packed with artefacts, including tools and other relics from the early farmers, and mining displays in the basement. In the historical village there are half a dozen buildings, mostly classic log cabins. One is Wasilla's first public sauna that was opened in 1942 with men and women using it on alternate days of the week. Another is the Capital Site Cabin, erected in Wasilla as a reminder of an issue that had split the state. If you have already traveled through Juneau and picked up the residents' fear at the thought that the state capital might move, now you are in Wasilla where for a brief time in the late 1970s, the residents were drooling in anticipation of all that political pork coming north.

What was once a Palmer attraction, is now part of Wasilla as the **Museum of Alaska Transportation & Industry** (☎ 376-1211) moved from the state fairgrounds to a new location off the Richardson Hwy in 1992. Turn off at *Mile 46.5* and follow the signs for less than a mile to see such transportation relics as a C-123 plane and tractors of the first Mat-Su farmers to the first diesel locomotive used in Alaska. There is also a picnic area and tours. The museum is open from 10 am to 6 pm Monday to Saturday. There is an admission fee.

Sled Dogs & the Iditarod
Wasilla serves as the second starting point for the famous 1049-mile Iditarod race to Nome, while Knik, the home for many Alaskan mushers, is checkpoint No 4 on the route. For more on this uniquely Alaskan race, stop in at the **Iditarod Headquarters** (☎ 376-5155) at *Mile 2.2* of Knik Rd. The log cabin museum is open daily during the summer from 8 am to 5 pm and has one room that is laden with historical displays, photos of past champions and racks of race para-phernalia – jackets, hats and shirts for sale. The most unusual exhibit is Togo, the famous sled dog that lead his team across trackless Norton Sound on the last leg in

delivering the serum to diptheria-threatened Nome in 1925, which gave raise to today's Iditarod. He's been stuffed and is now on display.

In another room, an excellent video on sled dogs and the race itself is shown. But almost as impressive is the checkpoint-by-checkpoint leader board of the last race that is posted on the wall, telling you who made it and whose team couldn't endure the challenge of 1000 miles. This is a small but interesting museum and, best of all, it's free.

If you want more information on dog mushing and racing, continue south along Knik Hwy to *Mile 13.7* and the **Knik Museum & Sled Dog Musher's Hall of Fame**. The museum, a pool hall at one time, is on the original townsite of Knik, which at the turn of the century had a population of more than 500 while Anchorage was nowhere to be found. Inside you'll find displays on the Iditarod Trail, early Alaskan mushers and, of course, the Canine Hall of Fame. Outside there is an Indian graveyard nearby. Hours are from noon to 6 pm Wednesday to Sunday and admission is $1.

Places to Stay
Still want more on mushing? Can't get that Iditarod blood out of your system? Then book a room at *Yukon Don's Bed & Breakfast* (☎ 376-7472), 1.5 miles down Fairview Loop Rd and posted along George Parks Hwy. Within this converted barn are five guest rooms, including the Iditarod Room filled with memorabilia of the famous race including a dog sled above your bed. Nightly rates begin at $55.

There are quite a few hotels and B&Bs in the Wasilla area but the most convenient place to stay is the *Windbreak Hotel* (☎ 376-4484), a mile south of town on George Parks Hwy. The hotel has singles/doubles for $45/55 and a good café that isn't part of a national chain, a rarity in Wasilla. Also check the *Mat-Su Resort* (☎ (800) 376-3229) on the shores of Wasilla Lake. The resort has rooms and cabins, some with kitchenettes if you plan to stay for a while, along with a restaurant, lounge and an assortment of rowboats and paddleboats for rent on the lake. Room rates begin at $80.

The nearest place to camp is *Lake Lucille Park*, a Matanuska-Susitna Borough park near the Iditarod Headquarters on Knik Hwy. The park has a campground (46 sites) along with rest rooms, a shelter and a network of trails. There is also access to the lake which is stocked annually with silver salmon and rainbow trout.

Places to Eat

It's mind boggling the variety of fast-food restaurants found in Wasilla, mostly surviving on the highway trade. In this town of under 4000 residents, you'll find a *Little Ceasar's Pizza*, *McDonald's*, *Burger King* and *Taco Bell*. The only one missing from this group is the Colonel. To gorge yourself for practically nothing, there's *Pizza Hut* with its $4.99 lunch buffet.

Head further north on the highway for restaurants that don't have a clown or play area for the kids. You'll find *Golden Palace* for Chinese, *Kahim Inn* and my favorite as a budget-conscious traveler, *Chepo Mexican Restaurant*.

Big Lake

From Wasilla, the George Parks Hwy continues in a westerly direction for the next 10 miles and then curves north, reaching Willow at *Mile 69*. Before entering the small village, you pass two side roads to the west that lead to state recreation areas offering lakeside campgrounds and canoe trails.

At *Mile 52.3*, where the George Parks Hwy curves north, is the junction with Big Lake Rd. Head 3.3 miles down the road and turn right at the gasoline station; in half a mile you will reach the *Rocky Lake State Campground* (10 sites, $6 fee). A few hundred yards further along Big Lake Rd is a fork known as 'Fisher's Y' where the town of Big Lake (population 2300) has sprung up. The right fork leads 1.6 miles to the *Big Lake North State Campground* (150 sites, $6), the left fork 1.7 miles to the *Big Lake South State Campground* (13 sites, $6 fee).

Big Lake is connected to several smaller lakes by dredged waterways, making it possible to paddle for miles, though you have to share the lake with powerboats. Another possible trip (if you can figure out how to get back) is to paddle Fish Creek, which begins in Big Lake and flows into the Knik Arm. The start of this canoe trail is where the left fork of Big Lake Rd crosses the creek. The trip is a 13-mile paddle and ends at the Knik Rd bridge west of Knik (see the following Nancy Lake State Recreation Area section for information on canoe rental).

Nancy Lake State Recreation Area

The George Parks Hwy continues north-west from Big Lake Rd, passes the village of Houston (population 800) and *Little Susitna River City Campground* (86 sites, $6 fee), and reaches the junction with Nancy Lake Parkway at *Mile 67.2*. The parkway leads to the northern portion of the Nancy Lake State Recreation Area, one of Alaska's few flat, lake-studded parks that offers camping, fishing, canoeing and hiking.

Although it lacks the dramatic scenery of the country to the north, the 22,685-acre state park with its 130 lakes is still a scenic spot and one worth stopping at for a couple of days if you have the time. Within a mile or so on the parkway you come to the State Recreation Area office (☎ 496-6273). It's unmarked from the road so most people just pass it by but it is the place to stop for information or to reserve a cabin. Nancy Lake Parkway extends 6.6 miles to the west and ends at the *South Rolley Lake Campground* (106 sites, $6 fee). The rustic campground has secluded sites and is so large that the chances are good that there will be an open site, even on the weekend. Within the campground is a canoe-rental shed if you're interested in an easy paddle on the small lake. The only other vehicle campground in the park is *Nancy Lake Campground* (30 sites, $6 fee) just off the George Parks Hwy and just south of the entrance to the parkway. This is not nearly as nice as setting up your tent at South Rolly Lake.

Hiking For those without a canoe, you can

still reach the backcountry by one of two trails. The **Chicken Lake Trail** begins at *Mile 5.7* of the parkway and extends three miles south to the lake and another 2.5 miles to the east shore of Red Shirt Lake. A round-trip hike on the trail is an 11-mile overnight trek but count on wet conditions from time to time.

More popular, and drier, is the **Twin Shirt Lakes Trail** that begins near the campground at the end of the parkway. Built in 1986, the trail leads 3.5 miles south primarily on high ground and ends at the northern end of Red Shirt Lake. Along the way you pass Red Shirt Overlook with its scenic views of the surrounding lake country and the Chugach Mountains on the horizon. You end at a group of backcountry camp sites with a vault toilet, situated along the lake.

There are also two short hikes in the park to stretch your legs. At *Mile 2.5* of the parkway is **Tulik Trail**, a one-mile, self-guided nature trail that takes you past ponds and bogs via boardwalks and viewing platforms. Near South Rolly Lake Campground there is also a half-mile trail to North Rolly Lake.

Paddling The most popular canoe trail is the **Lynx Lake Loop**, a two-day, 16-mile trip that passes through 14 lakes and over an equal number of portages. The trail begins and ends at the posted trailhead for the Tanaina Lake Canoe Trailhead at *Mile 4.5* of the parkway. The portages are well marked and many of them are planked where they cross wet sections. The route includes 12 backcountry camp sites, accessible only by canoe, but bring a camp stove because campfires are prohibited in the backcountry.

The largest lake on the route is Lynx Lake and you can extend your trip by paddling south on it where a portage leads off to six other lakes and two more primitive camp sites on Skeetna Lake. You can rent canoes at Tippecanoe Rentals (☎ 495-6688) which has an office on the George Parks Hwy just south of the parkway and a rental shed in South Rolly Lake Campground. Rates begin at $5 an hour or $40 for two days, $50 for

three and $60 for four or to seven days. They will also provide free drop-off and pick-up transport within a 15-mile radius of Willow.

Cabins The state recreation area has 12 cabins scattered along the shorelines of four lakes. They can be rented for up to three nights and most hold six people and cost $20. A few are larger and cost $25 a night. Four of the cabins are on Nancy Lake, and three of these can be reached after a short hike in from the Nancy Lake Parkway. Four more cabins are on Red Shirt Lake which require a three-mile hike in and then a short canoe paddle. This is possible because Tippecanoe keeps some canoes stashed on the lake and rents them to cabin users. The other four cabins are on the Lynx Lake Canoe Route with three on Lynx Lake and one on James Lake.

The cabins are relatively new, most of them were built in 1988, and have plywood sleeping platforms, a wood stove and screens on the windows. As you can imagine, they are very popular. Try to reserve them ahead of time by writing to: Division of Parks & Outdoor Recreation, PO Box 107001, Anchorage, AK 99510; or call (907) 561-2020.

Getting There & Away The state recreation area can be reached from the Alaska Railroad by taking the local train from Anchorage to Willow and then hitchhiking or walking 1.8 miles south on George Parks Hwy to the junction of the Nancy Lake Parkway.

WILLOW

Willow (population 500) at *Mile 69* of the George Parks Hwy is a sleepy little village that became famous in the 1970s as the place selected for the new Alaskan capital that was to be moved from Juneau. The capital-move issue was put on the back burner in 1982, however, when funding for the immense project was defeated in a general state election.

To many travelers heading north, Willow is often their first overwhelming view of Mt McKinley. If the day is clear 'the Great One' dominates the Willow skyline. Actually just about anything would dominate the skyline of this sparse little village. The Alaska Railroad stops in Willow and you'll find the usual visitor facilities such as a gasoline station, restaurant and grocery store.

More Sled Dogs

Willow, like many towns along this stretch, owes it existence to gold and the Alaska Railroad that came through in the early 1920s to serve the Hatcher Pass mines. Today the town calls itself 'Dog Mushing Capital of the World', though Wasilla, Tok and a few other communities would surely dispute that. The area does, however, have its share of mushers and, in the 1993 Iditarod, 13 teams from the Willow area competed and 10 finished the 1049-mile event. Five teams even finished in the top 20 to bring home a slice of the purse.

Several of the kennels offer informal tours. Call first, but try Bomhoff's Alaskan Sled Dog Kennel (☎ 495-6470) at *Mile 80* which also has a gift shop and an Iditarod Checkpoint Display. Nearby is Masek Racing Kennel (☎ 495-6820), but be forewarned; Alaskan huskies are so friendly you might end up bringing one home.

Places to Stay & Eat

Heart of Willow Cafe is right on the highway and is where the locals like to go for a fresh-baked cinnamon roll and a cup of coffee. *Willow Trading Post* (☎ 495-6457) is just off the highway across from the train platform and has cabins, RV and tent spaces, a café, bar, showers, laundry, liquor store, just about everything you need to recuperate from a week in the wilderness.

Two miles north of Willow is the junction to Fishhook-Willow Rd that leads 31.6 miles to the Independence Mine State Park, via Hatcher Pass, and eventually to Glenn Hwy. By driving just 1.3 miles up this road you reach the *Willow Creek State Campground* (17 sites, $6 fee).

To spend a night in a rustic cabin or for a great piece of home-made pie, stop at the *Sheep Creek Lodge* (☎ 495-6227) at *Mile 88*

of the George Parks Hwy. The lodge has four log cabins, some with private baths and some without, that begin at $40 a night. Inside the main lodge is a restaurant, lunch counter and a bar.

TALKEETNA

At *Mile 98.7* of George Parks Hwy, a side road heads off to the north and leads 14.5 miles to Talkeetna (population 600), the most interesting and colorful town along the highway. Located near the confluence of the Susitna, Talkeetna and Chulitna rivers, Talkeetna is a Tanaina Indian word meaning 'river of plenty'.

Gold bought miners to the Susitna River in 1896 and by 1901 Talkeetna was a miner's supply center and eventually a riverboat station. But its real growth came in 1915 when Talkeetna was chosen as the headquarters of the Alaska Engineering Commission responsible for building the railroad north to the Tanana River at Nenana. When the railroad was finished in 1923, President Warren G Harding arrived in Alaska and rode the rails to the Nenana River, where he hammered in the golden spike. In Talkeetna, they swear (with a grin on their face) that he stopped here on the way home, had numerous drinks in the local hotel and wound up dying in the San Francisco less than a week later. For a long time residents of this off-beat little town boasted that 'President Harding had been poisoned at the Fairview Inn'.

Talkeetna peaked out with a 1,000 residents before the mining slowed down and WW I dramatically decreased its population. In 1964, new life flowed into Talkeetna when a 14-mile spur road connected the town to the Parks Hwy, drawing the interest of anglers, hunters and others with the recreational opportunities of the area. But the group who were most interested in Talkeetna were climbers, who used the town as a staging area for ascents of Mt McKinley, and its bush pilots who provide transportation to the mountain.

Talkeetna has managed to retain much of its early Alaskan flavor with its narrow dirt roads that are lined by log cabins and clap-

Scaling the Mountain

More than any other place in Alaska, much more than the entrance area of Denali National Park itself, Talkeetna is associated with climbing the highest peak in North America, Mt McKinley.

The first attempt to scale the mountain was undertaken by James Wickersham, the US District Judge in Alaska. After moving his court from Eagle to Fairbanks in 1903, the judge took a couple of months off that summer and treked overland more than a 100 miles to reach the 7,500-foot mark of the 20,320-foot peak. Though his party was unsuccessful in its bid to be the first on top, they created a summit fever that would rage on for more than decade until the peak was finally conquered.

In 1906, Dr Frederick Cook returned for his second attempt at the peak and this time attacked it from the south. His party disbanded after a month of slogging through the heavy brush and tussock but then in September Cook and a companion sent a telegram to New York claiming that they had reached the peak and even sent along a photo showing the good doctor holding a flag at the top. The climbing world immediately disputed the claim and four years later Belmore Brown located the false peak and duplicated Cook's photo. Not only was the 8000-foot peak a lot shorter than Mt McKinley, it was more than 20 miles from the true summit. Despite all the evidence, the controversy over Cook continued right into the 1970s when his daughter wrote to Ray Genet for his opinion on the 1906 feat and photo. Both the letter and Genet's reply are now on display at the Talkeetna Museum.

The next serious attempt came in 1910 when four Fairbanks miners decided Alaskans should be the first to conquer the peak, not outsiders. Dubbed the Sourdough Expedition, they headed straight for the peak visible from Fairbanks. Remarkably they climbed the final 11,000 feet and returned to their base camp in 18 hours. Even more remarkable they carried only a thermos of hot chocolate, a bag of donuts and a 14-foot spruce pole. Imagine then their shock when they reached the top of the North Peak only to realize that it was 850 feet lower than the South Peak and thus not the true summit.

Success finally came in 1913 when an expedition of Hudson Stuck, Henry Karstens, Robert Tatum and Walter Harper reached the top on 7 June. The foursome would have made it in May but they spent three weeks hewing a three-mile staircase through a mass of jumbled ice caused by the 1912 eruption and earthquake of Katmai 300 miles away. When they reached the top they saw the spruce pole on the North Pole to verify the claims of the Sourdough Expedition.

The most important date to many climbers, however, is 1951. That year Bradford Washburn, the director of the Boston Museum of Science, arrived and pioneered the West Buttress route, by far the preferred avenue to the top. Not long after Talkeetna's two most famous characters – Ray Genet and Don Sheldon, began to impact the climbing world. Genet was an Alaskan mountain climber who made a record 25 climbs to the summit of Mt McKinley, including being a part of the first successful winter ascent. Sheldon was a bush pilot who pioneered many of the routes used today to carry climbers to Mt McKinley.

The two men worked closely together in guiding climbers to the top and, more important, rescuing them when they failed. Their rescue attempts are legendary and a sample of these stories can be read in the Talkeetna Museum. Sadly, the town unexpectedly lost both men within four years. Sheldon, the most famous of all Alaskan bush pilots, died in 1975 at the age of 56 years due to cancer. The Pirate died at the age of 48 in Nepal. After reaching Mt Everest, the highest peak in the world, Genet froze to death in his sleeping bag on the descent.

The High One (as the Athabascan people called to Mt McKinley) and the colorful legends of both these men add considerably to the mountaineering atmosphere that is felt, seen and heard in Talkeetna during the summer, especially during the climbing season of May and June. The vast majority of climbers use the West Buttress route, which means flying in ski planes from the town's airstrip to a base camp on the Kahiltna Glacier. From here, at 7200 feet, they begin climbing for the South Peak, passing a medical/rescue camp maintained by mountaineering clubs and the National Park Service at 14,220 feet.

Roughly 1000 climbers attempt the peak each year spending an average of three weeks on the mountain. Expeditions carry roughly 120 pounds of food and gear per person for the ascent. Ironically, due to the multiple trips in shuttling gear to higher camps, successful climbers actually climb the mountain twice.

In a good season, when storms are not constantly sweeping across the range, 50% of those attempting the summit will be successful. In a bad year, several people will die – in 1992 the mountain claimed the lives of 11 climbers. ■

board business premises. Main St, the only paved road in the village, begins with a 'Welcome to beautiful downtown Talkeetna' sign at the town park and ends at the banks of the Susitna River. With the recent popularity of the Northern Exposure television series, Talkeetna often becomes the mythical Cicley, Alaska many tourists come looking for. Thus the reasons for its numerous gift shops. There are almost a dozen of these shops and what's even more amazing is that every one of them sells moose-nugget items: nugget ear rings, nugget Christmas ornaments, moose nugget on a stick called 'Lollipoop'.

This love of moose scat can be traced back to 1974 when the town first began holding its annual Moose Dropping Festival on the second weekend of July. The three-day event has the usual: a parade, live entertainment and a beer tent they call a 'Tee Pee'. And then there are bizarre things you will only find in Talkeetna: a Moose Dropping Toss Game (or how far can you throw a moose turd), an opportunity to kiss a moose and the Mountain Mother Contest, where single women compete in various skills: wood chopping, water hauling, fire building etc, in front of a panel of eligible bachelors. The festival is a good time and every effort should be made to attend it if you are in the area. But beware – more than 5,000 people now pack Talkeetna during the event.

Things to See & Do

A block south of Main St is the **Talkeetna Historical Society Museum** (☎ 733-2487), a small complex that consists of four restored buildings. In the town's 1936 schoolhouse is a exhibit devoted to Don Sheldon (the bush pilot who pioneered landing climbers high on Mt McKinley's glaciers for a better shot at the peak) as well as artefacts on trapping and mining. There is also a fully furnished trapper's cabin and a railroad depot. But the most fascinating building by far is the Section House. Inside you'll find a 12-foot by 12-foot relief model of Mt McKinley and its climbing routes in a room where it's surrounded with Bradford Washburn's famous mural-like photos of the mountain – impressive. The history of climbing and a exhibit devoted to the town's most famous climber, Ray 'The Pirate' Genet, is also on display.

The museum is open daily during the summer from 10 am to 5 pm and admission is $1. You can also pick up a map of the town's historical walking tour here. The walk weaves you through Talkeetna, past 16 historical buildings, each featuring a plaque with the history and stories behind the structure.

There is a **mountaineering ranger station** (☎ 733-2231) on Main St to handle the numerous expeditions to Mt McKinley during the summer. It has a small display outside on the mountain. You can also get a sense of the adventure at the main airport just down Talkeetna Spur Rd in an area posted as East Talkeetna. Here during May and June several small aircraft, utilizing wheel-and-ski planes, fly the climbers up to the 7000-foot level.

Perhaps the most solemn way to experience the effect of the mountain on this town and experience how the residents grieve

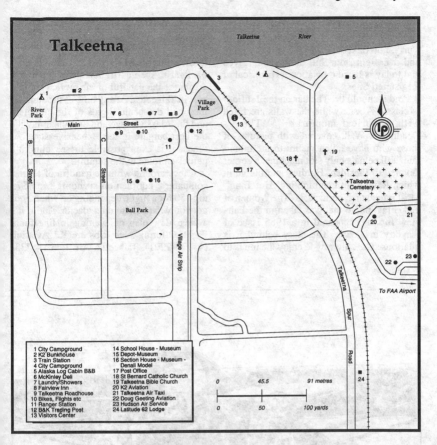

Talkeetna

1 City Campground
2 K2 Bunkhouse
3 Train Station
4 City Campground
5 Alaska Log Cabin B&B
6 McKinley Deli
7 Laundry/Showers
8 Fairview Inn
9 Talkeetna Roadhouse
10 Bikes, Flights etc
11 Ranger Station
12 B&K Trading Post
13 Visitors Center
14 School House - Museum
15 Depot-Museum
16 Section House - Museum - Denali Model
17 Post Office
18 St Bernard Catholic Church
19 Talkeetna Bible Church
20 K2 Aviation
21 Talkeetna Air Taxi
22 Doug Geeting Aviation
23 Hudson Air Service
24 Latitude 62 Lodge

when climbers are lost is to visit the **Talkeetna Cemetery**, just off the Spur Rd across from the airport. The most impressive grave is Sheldon's with the mounted ice axe and his epitaph of 'He wagered with the wind and won'. There is also a Mt McKinley Climber's Memorial including a stone for Genet despite the fact that his body was never removed from the slopes of Mt Everest. The most emotional sight, however, is a simple bulletin board that lists the names and ages of all the climbers who died on Mt McKinley over the years. Some were as young as 18 years.

The town also has two privately owned museums, attached to giftshops. **Museum of the Northern Adventure** (☎ 733-3999), right on Main St, consists of 24 large dioramas of historical events on two floors. It's open daily from 11 am to 7 pm but admission is $3.50 – a little steep for what you see. The other gift shop museum is at **B&K Trading Post**, Talkeetna's historical general store.

Even more interesting is the **Fairview Inn**, not an official museum but it might as well be. The hotel was built in 1923 to serve as the overnight stop from Seward to Fairbanks on the newly constructed Alaska Railroad.

Unfortunately, Anchorage, not Seward, was chosen as the start of the northerly trip so Curry, not Talkeetna, was the halfway point and overnight stop. Still the hotel survived and today is listed on National Historical of Registered Sites.

And it should be. The bar on the 1st floor is classic Alaska while the walls are filled with historical memorabilia. There's Deadman's Wall, covered with pictures of those who have fallen victim to the mountain, Talkeetna's only slot machine, a corner devoted to President Harding and the ad in which Ray Genet is promoting 'Hot Tang'. Most interesting, perhaps, is 'The Women of Talkeetna' photo that was taken in the Fairview Inn and appeared in a 1985 issue of Playboy magazine. The story behind it is hilarious. The only way to enjoy the inn is to belly up to the bar, order a schooner of beer and take in the décor.

Scenic Flights With Mt McKinley in their backyard, scenic flights have become a staple for the handful of air service companies in Talkeetna. At any time of the summer they will do scenic flights of the mountain and the Alaska Range and on a clear day it's the best bargain in this expensive state. At times, it is even possible to see climbing parties en route to the summit.

Check around with the handful of charter companies, but plan on spending from $75 to $150 for a flight, depending on whether or not you want to land on a glacier. And if it's a clear day, plan on waiting in line for a flight. Offering such trips are K2 Aviation (☎ 733-2291), Talkeetna Air Taxi (☎ 733-

Bush Pilots

2218) and Doug Geeting Aviation (☎ 733-2366).

Places to Stay

There are numerous hotels, motels, roadhouses and B&Bs in Talkeetna along with a public campground. The *City Campground* is split with sites at the end of Main St and others with a boat launch and a shelter across the tracks from railroad shelter. The fee is $5 a night.

A block off Main St near the river is the *K2 Bunkhouse* (☎ 733-2291). The hostel-style bunkhouse is primarily for climbers but others are welcome to stay if there is room. Inside there are 18 bunks, showers and a large kitchen. The rate is $12 a night.

There is also the *Fairview Inn* (☎ 733-2423), on Main St, where singles/doubles are $35/42 per night. There are seven rooms and a shared bath but remember that on the weekends the band in the bar just below you plays until 2.30 am. The *Talkeetna Roadhouse* (☎ 733-1351) is just up Main St with equally small rooms and shared bath for $35/50 a single/double. Of the handful of motels in town, try the *Latitude 62 Lodge* (☎ 733-2262) on the Talkeetna Spur Rd where single rooms with private bath begin at $50.

How about renting a log cabin? Hey, why not, this is Alaska. Call *Alaska Log Cabin B&B* (☎ 733-2668) two blocks from the Talkeetna River or *Trapper John's B&B* (☎ 733-2354), a 1920's cabin and outhouse at the south end of the Village Airstrip.

Places to Eat

The best place for a hearty meal is the *Talkeetna Roadhouse* on Main St, where eggs, toast, potatoes and sausage are $5.75 and the climber's breakfast (three eggs and an extra order of toast) is $7.75. Dinners cost around $9 or $10, hamburgers are $5. Try their Cheese Browns – hash browns cooked with cheese and served with salsa.

Across the street is *McKinley Deli & Espresso Bar*, open to 11 pm daily during the summer. Sandwiches and subs run from $6 to $7, small pizza is $11. The cinnamon rolls

are more than enough to keep you going in the morning.

Biking & Canoeing

Bikes, Flights, Etc... (☎ 733-2692) on Main St has mountain bikes for rent for $4 an hour or $15 a day. One possibility is to rent one for several days and then hop on the train to Denali National Park and explore the park road by pedaling. The small shop also doubles up as a booking agency and will arrange everything from scenic flights and raft trips to fishing guides.

Alaska Camp & Canoe (☎ 733-CAMP), operates a small camp just outside Talkeetna and offers tent cabins, complete with cookstove, lights and a table, for $40 a night for two people or $65 a night for four. They also rent canoes for $25 a day and will arrange drop-off and pick-up service.

Getting There & Away

The express train of the Alaska Railroad stops daily in Talkeetna from late May to mid-September on both its northbound and southbound runs from Anchorage to Fairbanks. The northbound train from Anchorage, heading for Denali National Park, arrives at noon; the southbound train arrives at 4.30 pm and reaches Anchorage that night at 8.30 pm. On Wednesday, Saturday and Sunday during the summer, the local train passes through Talkeetna before it turns around at Hurricane Gulch.

DENALI STATE PARK

This 324,420-acre reserve, the second largest state park in Alaska, is entered when you cross the southern boundary at *Mile 132.2* of the George Parks Hwy. The park covers the transition zone from low coastal environment to the spine of the Alaska Range and provides numerous views of towering peaks, including Mt McKinley and the glaciers on its southern slopes. The park is largely undeveloped but does offer a handful of turn-offs, trails and one campground that can be reached from the George Parks Hwy which runs through the preserve.

It may share the same name and a border

with the renowned national park to the north, but Denali State Park is an entirely different experience. Because of its lack of facilities, you need to be more prepared when you arrive for hiking and backpacking adventures. There are no rangers here describing routes nor an information center selling maps and guidebooks. But this may be the park's blessing for this preserve also lacks the crowds, long waits and tight regulations that irk many backpackers to the north in Denali National Park. At the height of the summer season, experienced backpackers may want to consider the state park as a hassle-free and cheaper alternative to the national park.

Less than three miles from the southern boundary of the park at *Mile 135.2* of George Parks Hwy is **South Denali Viewpoint**, where the Ruth Glacier is less than five miles to the north-west. Displays at the paved lookout also point out Mt McKinley, Mt Hunter, Moose Tooth and several other glaciers. *Lower Troublesome Creek State Recreation Site* (10 sites, $6 fee) at *Mile 137.3* and *Byers Lake State Campground* (66 sites, $6 fee) at *Mile 147* of George Parks Hwy provide tables, outhouses and are close to nearby trails. Byers Lake Campground also has access to Byers Lake.

At *Mile 156* of Parks Hwy, is *Chulitna River Lodge* (☎ 733-2521), the only facility within the state park. The lodge has a small café, gas and log cabins for $50 to $80 a night. It's also near the Ermine Hill Trailhead, an emergency trail that accesses the Kesugi Trail in the state park.

Hiking

There are several trails and alpine routes in the park and interested hikers should contact the Alaska Division of Parks office in Anchorage (☎ 762-2261 or (800) 770-2257 in Alaska) about possible closures (due to bears) and location of trails. Keep in mind that no fires are allowed in the backcountry so you must pack a stove.

Troublesome Creek Trail The trailhead is posted and in a parking area at *Mile 137.6* of

the George Parks Hwy. The trail ascends along the creek until it reaches the tree line where you move into an open area dotted with alpine lakes and surrounded by mountainous views. From here, it becomes a route marked only by rock cairns as it heads north to Byers Lake.

Byers Lake Campground is a 15-mile backpacking trip of moderate difficulty or, for the more adventurous, continue onto the Little Coal Creek Trail, a 36-mile trek above the tree line. The views from the ridges are spectacular. Keep in mind numerous black bears feeding on salmon is the reason for the creek's name and that often in July and August the trail is closed to hikers.

Byers Lake Trail This is an easy five-mile trek around the lake. It begins at the Byers Lake State Campground and passes six hike-in camp sites on the other side of the lake that are 1.8 miles from the posted trailhead.

Kesugi Ridge Trail This is actually a route that departs from the Byers Lake Trail and ascends its namesake ridge and then follows it to Little Coal Creek Trail at the north end of the park. The route is well marked with cairns and flags to provide a 27.4-mile route to George Parks Hwy via Little Coal Creek Trail.

Little Coal Creek Trail At *Mile 163.9* of the George Parks Hwy, there is the trailhead and parking area for the Little Coal Creek Trail, which ascends to the alpine areas of Kesugi Ridge. From there, you continue to the summit of Indian Mountain, an elevation gain of about 3300 feet, or continue along the ridge to either Byers Lake or Troublesome Creek. Little Coal Creek is the easiest climb into the alpine area as you emerge above the tree line in three miles. It's a nine-mile round-trip trek to Indian Peak and 27.4 miles to Byers Lake.

BROAD PASS TO DENALI NATIONAL PARK

The northern boundary of the Denali State Park is at *Mile 168.6* of George Parks Hwy, and nine miles beyond that is the bridge over Honolulu Creek where the road begins a gradual ascent to **Broad Pass**. Within 18 miles of the creek you begin viewing the pass and actually reach it at *Mile 203.6*, where there is a paved parking area.

Broad Pass (elevation 2300 feet) is the point of divide where rivers to the south drain into Cook Inlet and those to the north empty into the Yukon River. The area is worth stopping in for some hiking. The mountain valley, surrounded by white peaks, is unquestionably one of the most beautiful spots along the George Parks Hwy or the Alaska Railroad line, as both use the low gap to cross the Alaska Range.

From the pass, the George Parks Hwy begins a descent and after 6.3 miles comes to the Cantwell Post Office just before *Mile 210* at the junction with Denali Hwy. The rest of **Cantwell** (population 100) lies two miles west on the Denali Hwy. Another scenic spot is reached at *Mile 234* on the east side of the highway, where there are fine views of **Mt Fellows**, elevation 4476 feet. The mountain is well photographed because of the constantly changing shadows on its sides. The peak is especially beautiful at sunset.

The entrance to Denali National Park & Preserve is at *Mile 237.3* of George Parks Hwy and just inside the park are two campgrounds. The next public campground is in Fairbanks. The highway before and after the park entrance has become a tourist strip of private campgrounds, lodges, restaurants and other businesses, all feeding off Alaska's most famous drawcard.

Denali National Park

Call it the Dilemma in Denali: 'we love the wilderness and wildlife so much we're overrunning what is unquestionably Alaska's best known attraction'. In 1993, this park attracted more than 800,000 visitors for the first time, and topping a million is probably just a few seasons away.

Yet Denali has carefully imposed barriers and protection for its delicate wilderness. There are shuttle buses; backcountry zones are still in place, which means more people are showing up every summer having to wait longer and longer to do what they came for, whether it's to go backpacking or to camp at Wonder Lake. All the paperwork and permits, long lines at the visitors center, and crowds at the entrance area create something of a bizarre atmosphere of people hustling and pushing just for an opportunity to get away from it all in the wilderness.

For many, this is not the Alaska they came looking for so they leave in search of quieter areas. Others join them because their itinerary can not spare the minimum of four to five days needed to tour the park. But if you have the time and, more importantly, the patience, Denali National Park is still the great wilderness that awed so many of us 10 or 20 years ago. The entrance may have changed and maybe even the kind of visitors have, but a brown bear meandering on a tundra ridge still provides the same quiet thrill as it did when the park first opened in 1917.

Although generations of Athabascans had wandered through the area that is now Denali, they never set up permanent settlements. This came in 1905 when gold was discovered and a miners' rush resulted in the town of Kantishna. A year later, naturalist and noted hunter Charles Sheldon arriving in the area was stunned by the beauty of the land and horrified at the reckless abandon of the miners and others in hunting the caribou and other big game. Sheldon returned in 1907 and with guide Harry Karstens traveled the area in an effort to set up boundaries for a proposed national park.

He then launched a campaign for a Denali National Park but politics being politics and Ohio having a particular strong delegation of senators, it emerged as Mt McKinley National Park. Karstens became the park's first superintendent and in 1923, when the railroad arrived, 36 visitors enjoyed the splendor of Denali.

As a result of the 1980 Alaska Lands Bill, the park was enlarged by four million acres, redesignated and renamed. Today, Denali

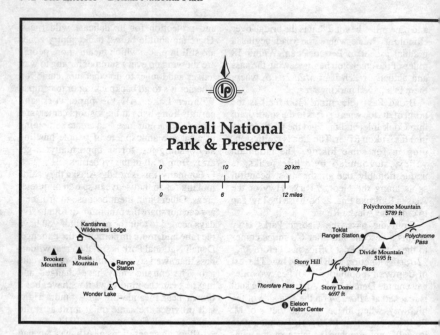

Denali National Park & Preserve

0   10   20 km

0   6   12 miles

Polychrome Mountain
5789 ft

Toklat
Ranger Station

Polychrome
Pass

Kantishna
Wilderness Lodge

Divide Mountain
5195 ft

Brooker
Mountain

Busia
Mountain

Ranger
Station

Stony Hill

Highway Pass

Thorofare Pass

Stony Dome
4697 ft

Wonder Lake

Eielson
Visitor Center

comprises six million acres or an area slightly larger than the state of Massachusetts and is generally ranked as Alaska's second most-visited attraction after Portage Glacier.

Situated on the northern and southern flanks of the Alaska Range, 237 miles from Anchorage and about half that distance from Fairbanks, Denali is the nation's first subarctic national park and a wilderness that can be enjoyed by those who never sleep in a tent. Within it roam 37 species of mammals, ranging from lynx, marmots and dall sheep to foxes and snowshoe hares; while 130 different bird species have been spotted, including the impressive golden eagle. Most visitors, however, want to see four animals in particular: the moose, caribou, wolf and brown bear. If you see all four from the shuttle bus – it's a rare 'grand slam' according to the drivers.

There are an estimated 200 to 300 brown bears in the park and another 200 black bears, most of them west of Wonder Lake. It's everybody's favorite, the brown or grizzly bear, that is almost always seen while you're on the shuttle bus. Since Denali's

Snowshoe hare

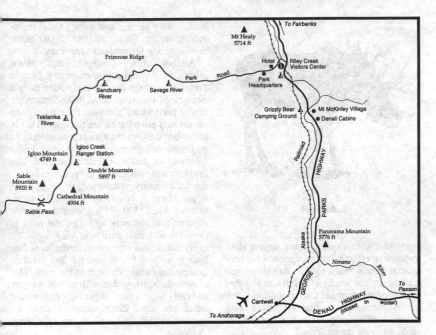

streams are mostly glacially fed, the fishing is poor so subsequently the diet of the bears is 85% vegetable materials. This accounts for their small size. Most males range from only 300 to 600 pounds while their cousins on the salmon-rich coasts can easily top 1000 pounds.

All the caribou in the park belong to the Denali herd, one of 13 herds in Alaska, which fluctuates between 2500 and 3000 animals. Since the park has been enlarged, the entire range of the herd, from its calving grounds to where it winters, is now in Denali. The best time to spot caribou is often late in the summer when the animals begin to band into groups of six to a dozen in anticipation of the fall migration. The caribou is easy to spot, the racks of a bull often stand four feet high and look out of proportion with the rest of the body.

Most visitors will sight their moose on the eastern half of the park road, especially along the first 15 miles. Moose are almost always found in stands of spruce and willow shrubs (their favorite food) and often you have a better chance of seeing a moose hiking the Horseshoe Lake Trail then you do in the tundra area around Eielson Visitor Center. There are roughly 2000 moose on the north side of the Alaska Range and the most spectacular scene in Denali comes in early September when the bulls begin to clash their immense racks over breeding rights to a cow.

The wolf is the most difficult of the 'grand slam' four to see in the park. There is a stable population of 160 wolves and during much of the summer when small game is plentiful, the packs often break down and wolves become more solitary hunters. The best bet for most visitors is witnessing a lone wolf crossing the park road.

Due to fact that hunting has never been allowed in the park, professional photographers refer to animals in Denali as 'approachable wildlife'. That doesn't mean you can actually approach them, though

Bull moose

every year visitors and photographers alike try to in an effort to get that photo-of-a-lifetime. It means bears, moose, dall sheep and caribou are not nearly as skittish as in other regions of the state and tend to continue their natural activities despite 40 heads with camera lens hanging out of a yellow bus 70 yards away on the park road.

Despite the excellent wildlife-watching opportunities, the park's main attraction is still Mt McKinley – an overwhelming sight if you catch it on a clear day. At 20,320 feet, the peak of this massif is almost four miles high, but what makes it stunning is that it rises from an elevation of 2000 feet. What you see from the park road is 18,000 feet (almost three miles) of rock, snow and glaciers reaching for the sky. In contrast, Mt Everest, the highest mountain in the world at 29,028 feet, only rises 11,000 feet from the Tibetan Plateau.

Combine the park's easy viewing of wildlife and the grandeur of Mt McKinley with its wilderness reputation throughout the world and suddenly the crowds are easy to understand. From late June to early September, Denali National Park is a busy and popular place. Riley Creek Campground overflows with camper vans, nearby Morino Campground is crowded with backpackers, and the park's hotel is bustling with large tour groups. The pursuit of shuttle-bus seats,

backcountry permits and campground reservations at the Visitor Access Center often involves long Disneyland-type lines.

Although crowds disappear once you are hiking in the backcountry, many people prefer to visit the park in early June or late September to avoid them. Mid-September can be particularly pleasant, for not only are the crowds gone but so are the bugs. This is also when the area changes color and valleys go from a dull green to a fiery red, while the willows turn shades of yellow and gold. The problem is the shuttle buses (your ticket into the backcountry) stop running around 10 September. A four-day vehicle lottery follows when 300 private cars a day are allowed into the park and then the road is closed to all traffic until next May.

By late September, however, the snow has usually arrived for the winter and another backpacking season is over in the park. The crowds do begin to diminish in late August and early September but getting coupons for the shuttle bus, a campground site or backcountry permit will still be an agonizing challenge.

Your best bet is to include some extra days for your trip. If all you want to do is camp at the entrance and take the shuttle bus out the road one day, a minimum of four days is needed at the park, possibly five if you arrive at the height of the season. If you want to spend two or three days backpacking or staying in the interior campgrounds, you'll need from seven to 10 days.

There's no getting around it. You'll waste one day alone on the outside of the park waiting to get into the Riley Creek area. Another two days can be used up waiting for a campground or backcountry area to become available. The exception to this are those who manage to reserve the shuttle bus or campground in advance at either Public Lands Information offices in Anchorage or Fairbanks (see the Shuttle Bus or Park Campgrounds sections following).

In the end, however, if you are patient and follow the system, you will get into the backcountry and then, thanks to the rules and permit limits you were cussing just a day before, you will enjoy a quality wilderness experience.

What price is that in today's world?

Information & Fees

There is an admission fee now, though it should hardly stop anybody from visiting the park. A $4 per person fee is charged to all visitors traveling beyond the check point at Savage River Campground or $8 per family. The fee is good for seven days in the park and is collected when you obtain a shuttle bus coupon at the Riley Creek Visitor Access Center. You pay it the first time you pick up coupons and after that bus is free. Keep in mind this is an entrance fee and you will still have to pay to stay in the park's campgrounds.

The new Visitor Access Center, or VAC for short, near the entrance of the park is the place to organize your trip into the park and pick up permits and coupons as well as pur-

chase topographic maps and books. The center is open daily during the summer from 7 am to 6 pm and lines begin forming outside the door at 6 am. At the height of the summer, there will often be more than 100 people in line and it's something of a stampede when the door is open. This is necessary because shuttle bus coupons and camp sites are handed out only two days in advance, for backcountry permits it's one day. That's why you can't arrive at the park at midday and plan you stay. It's almost imperative you be at the visitor center before 7 am to be able to book anything at all.

Within the VAC there is a bookstore; staff counters for backcountry permits, shuttle buses and camp sites; a video theater with shows 10 and 40 minutes after the hour; and rest rooms. There is also an information area on other parks in Alaska in case the Denali hassle is too much for you. Outside there is an information board with all park activities,

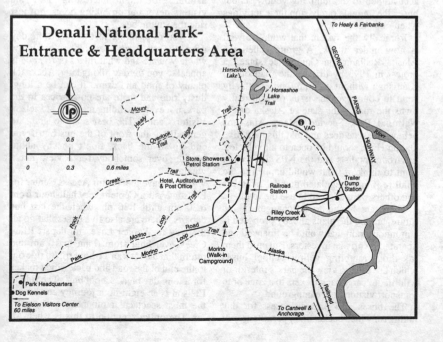

a monitor that gives you a basic rundown on park procedures and storage lockers that are big enough to handle a backpack.

Eielson Visitor Center is a smaller center at *Mile 66* of the park road and features limited displays, a small bookstore and a great observation deck overlooking Mt McKinley. The ranger staff hold their own hikes and naturalist programs. Eielson is open daily during the summer from 9 am to 6.30 pm.

Shuttle Bus

What makes the park and its wildlife so accessible is the park road that runs the length of the preserve and the free shuttle buses that use it. The shuttle-bus service began in 1972 after the George Parks Hwy was opened and attendance in the park doubled in a single season. Park officials then put a ban on private vehicles to prevent the park road from becoming a highway of cars and RVers and today the wildlife is so accustomed to the rambling yellow school buses the animals rarely stop their activities when one passes by.

Ironically, the system that works so well is now under attack. A group called the Alaska Reclamation Committee staged a protest in 1993 by driving the road out to Kantishna without a permit and eventually went to court over the issue of who really owns the road – the state of Alaska or the National Park Service? Many Alaskans believe the state does and that this road, like Dalton Hwy, should be open to all vehicles. Environmentalists and the NPS don't even want to think of what would happen to the wildlife if an unregulated number of RVers and others were allowed to use the road.

There are bound to be changes in the future, among the plans already proposed is a monorail train that would be financed and operated by private investors. But until then, it's those rambling yellow school buses which are used to view the park's interior or wildlife, to carry backpackers to a zone or to transport visitors to a campground.

The buses also provide access for day hiking for which backcountry permits are not needed. Once in the backcountry, you can stop a bus heading in either direction on the park road by flagging it down for a ride back or further into the park. Some photographers ride the bus only until wildlife is spotted. Changing buses several times each day is a practice commonly referred to as 'shuttle bus surfing'. By all means get off the buses, it's the only way you will truly see and experience the park but remember you can only get back on if there is an available seat. No one is ever left out in the backcountry against their will but it's not too uncommon at the height of the season to have to wait two or three hours as the first four buses that pass by are full.

While riding the buses, passengers armed with binoculars and cameras scour the terrain for wildlife. When something is spotted, the name of the animal is called out, prompting the driver to slow down and most often stop for viewing and picture taking. The driver also doubles as a park guide and naturalist for a more interesting trip. Some visitors never put on hiking boots, but just ride the shuttle bus.

If you're planning just to spend the day riding the bus, carry a park map so you know where you are and what ridges or river beds appeal to you for day hiking later. Also pack plenty of food and drink. It can be a long, dusty ride and there are no services in the park, not even a vending machine at Eielson Visitor Center. The best seats to grab are generally at the front of the bus but if you end up in the back, don't be shy about leaning over somebody for a view out a window.

Buses leave the Visitor Access Center for Eielson Visitor Center every half-hour from 6.30 am until 1.30 pm when the last bus departs. There are also five buses that go all the way to Wonder Lake and depart Riley Creek ever hour from 6 am to 10 am and return that day. It's an 11-hour trip to ride out to the end of the road and back which makes for a long day on a 'school bus'. The ride to Eielson is an eight-hour journey and passes the most spectacular mountain scenery by far. The only exception to this is when Mt

McKinley is out then the ride to Wonder Lake is 11 of the most scenic hours you'll ever spend on a bus of any kind.

On the flip side, the last bus from Wonder Lake leaves at 4 pm, the last one from Eielson Visitor Center at around 5.25 am. Unless you're prepared to go backpacking, don't miss them!

Use of the buses is free, but there is a heavy demand for the 40 seats on each one. Demand is so heavy, that park officials hand out bus coupons for available seats. The coupon guarantees you a seat on a particular bus and in theory it should work.

The problem is the popularity of the park. Boarding coupons are available up to two days in advance of a particular bus departure. Throughout much of the summer, the coupons for all the buses the next day are gone by mid-morning. At the peak of the tourist season in July and early August, people are lining up at the VAC at 6 am, an hour before it opens, to be ensured of getting a coupon for a bus two days later. If you don't have a coupon, don't bother showing up for a bus, hoping somebody oversleeps. Generally no-shows account for 15% of the tickets but drivers leave the seats empty in order to pick up backpackers returning from a trek. All this is a bit of a shame as many visitors now don't dare leave the bus, even for a few hours for a hike in the backcountry, for fear of not getting a seat on the way back.

The exception to this is picking up your coupons at the Public Lands Information Center in Anchorage or Fairbanks. The two centers receive 10% of the bus coupons and you can begin picking them up 21 days in advance of the date they are issued for. In fact you almost have to because they tend to be snapped up by both locals and knowledgeable travelers the morning they become available.

Tour Bus The park concessionaire operates a wildlife bus tour along the park road. The bus departs from the Denali National Park Hotel daily as often as there is demand for the seats. The six-hour tour, designed primarily for package-tour groups, costs $45 per person and goes to Stony Hill when the mountain is out, to the Toklat River when it isn't. Reserve a seat the night before at the Denali National Park Hotel (☎ 276-7234) reservation desk or by calling in advance.

Along the Park Road

The park road begins at George Parks Hwy and winds 91.6 miles through the heart of the park, ending at Kantishna, an old mining settlement and the site of three wilderness lodges. Travelers with vehicles can only drive to a parking area along the Savage River at *Mile 14*, a mile beyond the Savage River Campground unless you have a special permit, that's nearly impossible to obtain.

Most of the free shuttle buses run from Riley Creek to the Eielson Visitor Center at *Mile 66* and then turn around. The round trip takes eight hours. Five buses drive all the way to Wonder Lake Campground, *Mile 84*, a 11-hour round trip.

Mt McKinley is not visible from the park entrance or the nearby campgrounds and hotel. Your first glimpse of it comes between *Mile 9* and *Mile 11* of the park road, if you are blessed with a clear day. The park's weather, despite its Interior location, is cool, with long periods of overcast conditions and drizzle during the summer. The rule of thumb stressed by the National Park Service rangers is that Mt McKinley is hidden two out of three days. Keep in mind that, while the Great One might not be visible for most of the first 15 miles, this is the best stretch to spot moose because of the cover of spruce and especially willow, the animal's favorite food.

From Savage River, the road dips into the Sanctuary and Teklanika river valleys, and Mt McKinley disappears behind the foothills. Both these rivers make for excellent hiking areas, and three of the five backcountry campgrounds are situated along them. Sanctuary River Campground is the most scenic of the three and at *Mile 22* it is a good base camp to explore Primrose Ridge, an excellent hiking area.

Equally scenic and just as small (seven sites) is the Igloo Creek Campground at *Mile*

34 of the park road in a spruce woods along the creek. This camp allows you to make an easy day hike into the Igloo and Cathedral mountains to spot dall sheep.

After passing through the canyon formed by the Igloo and Cathedral mountains, the road ascends to **Sable Pass** (elevation 3880 feet) at *Mile 38.5*. The canyon and surrounding mountains are excellent places to spot dall sheep, while the pass is known as a prime habitat for Toklat brown bears. From here, the road drops to the bridge over the East Fork Toklat River at *Mile 44*. Hikers will enjoy treks that lead from the bridge along the river banks both north and south. By hiking north, you can complete a six-mile loop that ends at the **Polychrome Pass Overlook** at *Mile 46.3* of the park road.

The pass is a rest stop for the shuttle buses and a popular spot for visitors. This scenic area has an elevation of 3500 feet and gives way to views of the Toklat River to the south. The alpine tundra above the road is good for hiking as you can easily scramble up ridges that lead north and south of the rest area shelter.

The park road then crosses two single-lane, wooden bridges over the Toklat River and ascends near **Stony Hill** (elevation 4508 feet) at *Mile 61*. This is perhaps the finest place to view Mt McKinley in the stretch to Eielson Visitor Center. Another quarter of a mile down the road is a lookout for viewing caribou and from here a short scramble north takes you to the summit of Stony Hill.

After climbing through Thorofare Pass (elevation 3900 feet) the road descends to the **Eielson Visitor Center** at *Mile 66*. The center is known for its excellent views of Mt McKinley, the surrounding peaks of the Alaska Range, and Muldrow Glacier. It offers a few interpretive displays and conducts a series of its own programs, including a tundra hike daily at 1.30 pm, an hour-long walk from the center. Catch a shuttle bus by 9 am at Riley Creek to make it to the Eielson Visitor Center for the walk. Several day and overnight hikes are possible from the center, including one around Mt Eielson (see the Trekking section in the Wilderness chapter) and another to Muldrow Glacier.

Past the Eielson Visitor Center the park road drops to the valley below, passing at *Mile 74.4* of the park road a sign for **Muldrow Glacier**. At this point, the glacier lies about a mile to the south, and the terminus of the 32-mile ice floe is clearly visible though you might not recognize it. The ice is covered with a mat of plant life. If the weather is cloudy and Mt McKinley and the surrounding peaks hidden, the final 20 miles of the bus trip will be a ride through rolling tundra and past numerous small lakes known as kettle ponds. Study the pools of water carefully to spot beavers swimming or a variety of waterfowl.

Wonder Lake Campground is at *Mile 84* of the park road. Here the beauty of Mt McKinley is doubled on a clear day, with the mountain's reflection in the lake's surface. Ironically, the heavy demand for the 28 sites at Wonder Lake and the numerous overcast days caused by Mt McKinley itself prevent the majority of visitors from ever seeing this remarkable panorama. If you do experience the reddish sunset on the summit reflecting off the still waters of the lake, cherish it as a priceless moment.

The campground is on a low rise above the lake's south end and is only 26 miles from the mountain. First the shuttle bus stops at a bus shelter near the campground and then drives to the edge of the lake for half an hour or so before turning around and heading back. Those who come on the early buses can gain another hour at the lake by getting off and picking up a later one for the trip back. Keep in mind that those famous McKinley-reflecting-in-the-lake photos are taken along the north-east shore two miles beyond the campground. The historic mining town of Kantishna is six miles from where the shuttle bus stops.

Camping in the Park

The only way you can reserve a camp site before arriving at the park is through the Public Lands Information Center in Anchorage and Fairbanks. Like with the bus coupons, the centers have a very limited number of sites available 21 days in advance and these tend to be snapped up quickly. Otherwise the campgrounds are filled on a first-come-first-serve basis at the Riley Creek Visitor Access Center two days in advance.

The key to getting into the campground of your choice, like Wonder Lake, is just getting into a campground, any campground. That includes either Morino or Riley Creek. Once in, you can secure a guaranteed site for the next 14 days wherever there is an opening. With this system, you can still get to Wonder Lake even during the busiest time of the year if you are willing to camp elsewhere in the park for four or five days. This is especially easy for walk-ins who can immediately pitch a tent in Morino then return to the VAC that afternoon to book other campgrounds as soon as there are openings. The limit on staying in one campground or a combination of them is 14 days.

Due to the popularity of the shuttle buses, the park has set up a camper bus system which uses the same yellow school buses but with a third of the seats removed to facilitate hauling in backpacks and mountain bikes. Four camper buses leave the VAC daily at 7 and 10.30 am and 1.30 and 3.30 pm and they are free. If you get a camp site or backcountry permit, there is no hassle or wait to get a coupon on the camper bus.

Riley Creek The campground at the main entrance of the park is Riley Creek, the largest and nicest facility in Denali as well as the only one open year-round. A quarter of a mile west of Parks Hwy, Riley Creek has 102 sites, piped-in water, flush toilets and evening interpretive programs. The nightly fee is $12. Popular with RVers, in fact overrun by RVers, this is the only campground where sites are assigned at the visitor center.

Morino Near the railroad depot, Morino is a walk-in campground for backpackers without vehicles. It provides only two metal caches to keep your food away from the bears, piped-in water and vault toilets. Though its capacity is listed at 60 persons,

it's rare for anybody to be turned away. During much of the summer, however, this place can be packed and rangers are very strict about not allowing people to pitch a tent beyond the campground. The nightly fee is $3 per person (note that's per person not per site) and you self-register after pitching the tent.

Savage River Despite its name, Savage River is at *Mile 13* a mile short of the actual river but is only one of two campgrounds with a view of Mt McKinley. It has 34 sites that can accommodate both RVs and tents and has water, flush toilets and evening interpretive programs. Those with a vehicle can drive to this campground. The nightly fee is $12.

Sanctuary River This is the next campground down the road, at *Mile 23* on the banks of a large glacial river. There are seven sites for tents only and no piped-in water. It's a free facility, however, in a great area for day hiking. You can either head south to hike along the Sanctuary River or make a day out of climbing Mt Wright or Primrose Ridge to north for an opportunity to see and photograph dall sheep.

Teklanika River At *Mile 29*, Teklanika has 50 sites for either RVs or tents, piped water, evening programs and a $12 per night fee. You must book this one for a minimum of three days due to the fact that you are allowed to drive to the campground. Registered campers are issued a road pass for a single trip to the facility and then must leave their vehicle parked until they are ready to return to Riley Creek.

Igloo Creek This is another free and waterless facility located at *Mile 34* with only seven sites limited to tents. The day hiking in this area is excellent, especially the numerous ridges around Igloo Mountain, Cathedral Mountain and Sable Pass that provide good routes into the alpine area.

Wonder Lake The jewel of Denali campgrounds is Wonder Lake, at *Mile 85* of the park road, due to the immense views of Mt McKinley. The facility has 28 sites for tents only but does feature flush toilets and piped-in water. The nightly fee is $12. If you are lucky enough to reserve a site, book it for three nights and then pray that the mountain appears during one of them. Also pack in plenty of insect repellent and maybe even a head net. In midsummer the bugs are vicious.

Places to Stay

Inside the Park Those opposed to sleeping in a tent have few alternatives at the main entrance of the park. The *Denali National Park Hotel* (☎ 683-2215 in the summer) only offers rooms at $125 for two people per night. Back in the early 1980s there was more inexpensive lodging in the form of original Pullman sleepers of the Alaska Railroad and a youth hostel situated nearby in railroad cars, but all have long since been condemned and removed by the National Park Service.

At the western end of the park road are three places that are as close to wilderness lodges as you'll ever find on a road. Their rates tend to shock most budget-concious backpackers but include round-trip transportation from the railroad depot, meals and guided activities.

Camp Denali (☎ 683-2290 or 603-675-2248 during the winter) offers several different types of accommodations, most with fixed arrival and departure dates. The camp is more of a resort and definitely not just a place to sleep as it offers a wide range of activities including wildlife observation and photography, rafting, fishing, gold panning and, of course, hiking. Plus your best view of the 'High One' (Mt McKinley) is obtained from here.

Its North Face Lodge offers rooms for $530 for two nights per adult, $795 for three nights and $1060 for nights which includes transportation from the Denali railroad depot, all meals, guided expeditions and trips and use of recreational equipment. Its Camp Denali costs slightly less but this is for longer stays. They also have Hawk's Nest cabins. Located a mile from Wonder Lake, the main cabin sleeps four people, a smaller one sleeps two. Rates for the housekeeping units are for $200 a night for one to four people, $250 for five or six.

Nearby is the *Kantishna Roadhouse* (☎ 733-2535 or (800) 942-7420) with cabin accommodation that starts at over $150 a night. The wilderness resort also has gold panning, hiking, photographic activities during the day and a hot tub and sauna to enjoy at night. Keep in mind that these places will most likely be booked long before you arrive in Alaska. If you want to treat yourself (and escape the crowds at Riley Creek), write to the lodges in advance – six months in advance is not overdoing it. Write to: Camp Denali, PO Box 216, Cornish, NH 03746, or Kantishna Roadhouse, PO Box 130, Denali National Park, AK 99755.

The newest end of the road accommodation is the *Denali Backcountry Lodge*

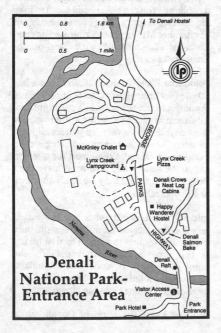

Denali National Park-Entrance Area

To Denali Hostel

0   0.8   1.6 km

0   0.5   1 mile

GEORGE PARKS HIGHWAY

Nenana River

McKinley Chalet

Lynx Creek Campground

Lynx Creek Pizza

Denali Crows Nest Log Cabins

Happy Wanderer Hostel

Denali Salmon Bake

Denali Raft

Visitor Access Center

Park Hotel

Park Entrance

(☎ 683-1341 or (800) 841-0692). The resort offers 24 cabins grouped together along with a lodge with a dining room and lounge. Standard rates are $500 for two people. But the resort also has a 'standby rate' when you book 72 hours before arriving with a cabin for two costing $340 per night.

Outside the Park For a park of six million acres, Denali occasionally stuns visitors who arrive late in the afternoon or the early evening to find that there is no place to stay. They are informed by National Park Service rangers of individuals offering private accommodation outside the park, and these people can make a living just from the overflow.

Included among these are several private campgrounds where you can expect to pay from $10 to $15 for a camp site. The closest is the *Lynx Creek Campground* (☎ 683-1240) a mile north of the park entrance on George Parks Hwy. Camp sites are $15 a night for tents, $20 for full hook-up and include showers. There is a store and pub on site.

Six miles south of the park entrance is the *Denali Grizzly Bear Campground* (☎ 683-2696) which offers camp sites for $15 a night, tents for rent, cabins with cooking facilities and coin-operated showers. Near Healy, a small town 11 miles north of the park entrance, there is the *McKinley KOA* (☎ 683-2379), which has tent sites, a store and provides bus rides to the Riley Creek Visitor Center.

If there are three or four in your party, consider booking a cabin in advance. At *Denali Cabins* (☎ 683-2643 during the summer) you can get a large cedar cabin for one to four people with outdoor hot tub for $90 per night. The cabins are a mile north of the park entrance at *Mile 238* of George Parks Hwy but there is a free shuttle bus service to the entrance. At *Mile 238.5* of the George Parks Hwy is *Denali Crow's Nest Log Cabins* (☎ 683-2723), looking like a Swiss alpine village on the edge of Horseshoe Lake. Rates are the same.

There is also a pair of backpacker's hostels

near the park. *Denali Hostel* (☎ 683-1295) is in Healy and has bunks for $22 a night along with kitchen facilities, showers and transport back to the park. If you arrive on the train, there will be a Denali Hostel van at the depot. *The Happy Wanderer Hostel* (☎ 683-2690 or 683-2360) is closer to the park entrance at *Mile 238.6* of the George Parks Hwy and offers eight beds for $15 a night.

Finally for those with a RV, van or even a car, who arrive late, there are large gravel pull-outs north of the park entrance on the both sides of George Parks Hwy where you can stop and spend the night at a pinch. There are almost a dozen of them between Healy and the park entrance and throughout the summer, you'll see from eight to 10 vehicles there every night.

Places to Eat

Inside the Park There are two restaurants and one bar in the park, all off the lobby of the Denali National Park Hotel. The *Denali Dining Room* serves full meals in pleasant surroundings but is overpriced for most budget travelers. Breakfast after 7 am, however, can be a leisurely and reasonable $6 affair; it is pleasant to sit around drinking fresh coffee for a spell. Occasionally they also have an all-you-can-eat lunch buffet for $10. The *Whistle Stop Snack Shop*, also off the lobby, is open from 5 am until 7 am to provide early shuttle-bus passengers with breakfast or the opportunity to purchase a box lunch. It's then open from 8 am to 11 pm. Hamburgers and sandwiches are priced from $4 to $6, a cup of coffee and a large sweet roll around $4.

The *Gold Spike Saloon*, two lounge cars side by side, is the hotel's bar that hops at night with an interesting mixture of climbers, hikers, visitors and park employees. An even more interesting gathering of travelers can be found in the hotel lobby itself whenever it rains or snows – you'll find retired couples dragging large suitcases, foreign tour groups being herded here and there, and backpackers munching on dried banana chips from their day pack.

McKinley Mercantile, a block from the

hotel, sells a variety of fresh and dried food, some canned goods and other supplies. The selection is limited and highly priced. Your best bet is to stock up on supplies in Fairbanks or Anchorage before leaving for the park. The small park grocery store is open daily from 8 am to 11 pm and has showers ($2) behind it. Once you leave the main entrance area, there are no more visitor services in the park.

Outside the Park The best food outside the park is at *Lynx Creek Pizza* (☎ 683-2547) near the McKinley Chalets, north of the entrance at *Mile 238.6*. The log cabin restaurant has excellent pizza along with Mexican dishes, deli sandwiches and an impressive selection of beers. A small pizza that will feed two people or one backpacker just out of the mountains is $11 with a couple of items.

Practically across the highway is *Denali Salmon Bake* where $15 gets you the usual Alaskan salmon dinner. You get a single serving of salmon but everything else is all-you-can-consume. South of the park entrance at *Mile 224* is *The Perch* (☎ 683-2523), one of the best restaurants in the area. Steak and seafood dinners begin at $13 but they also have a home-made soup and a salad bar for $7.50. Breakfast is also a good time to arrive as they bake fresh breads and giant cinnamon rolls daily.

Visitor Programs
The Visitor Access Center offers a variety of programs during the summer, all of them free. One of the most popular is the sled dog demonstration. Denali is the only national park that keeps the sled dogs for winter maintenance and during the summer holds demonstrations daily at 10 am, 2 and 4 pm at the kennels, 3.5 miles west of the entrance on the park road. The 40-minute talks explain the current and historical use of the dogs and then a team pulls a ranger on a wheeled sled. A free bus leaves the visitor center half an hour before each demonstration and 20 minutes before from the park hotel.

The VAC also offers daily nature walks and longer hikes throughout the park (see the following Hiking section) while the auditorium behind the park hotel is the site of daily slide or film programs. An afternoon program begins at 1.30 pm with tours posted in the hotel lobby and at 8 pm is a slide program that covers the history, wildlife or mountaineering aspects of the park. There are also daily campfire programs at Riley Creek, Savage River and Teklanika River campgrounds at 8 pm which are open to anybody. Finally Naturalist's Choice programs involve park interpreters and could range from a bird walk, a children's activity or a sampling of wild berries. They take place daily at Eielson at 3 pm and at the VAC at various times and locations around the park entrance area.

Hiking
Even for those who have neither the desire nor the equipment for an overnight trek, hiking is still the best way to enjoy the park and to obtain a personal closeness with the land and its wildlife. The best way to undertake a day hike is to ride the shuttle bus and get off at any valley, river bed or ridge that takes your fancy. No backcountry permit is needed. There are few trails in the park as most hiking is done across open terrain. When you've had enough for one day, return to the road and flag down the first bus going in your direction.

You can hike virtually anywhere in the park that hasn't been closed because of the impact on wildlife. Popular areas include the Teklanika River south of the park road, the Toklat River, the ridges near Polychrome Pass and the tundra areas near the Eielson Visitor Center. On a day hike, always take piped water with you, as water found in the park must be boiled or treated before drinking (see the Health Section in the Facts for the Visitor chapter for information on water purification).

There are numerous guided walks in the park for those unsure of entering the backcountry on their own. Naturalist's Walks are easy two-hour hikes in the entrance area of

Top: View from Broad Pass near Cantwell, Alaska Range (DS)
Bottom: Trans-Alaska Pipeline crossing, Tanana River (DS)

Top: Junk Wagon, Fairbanks Golden Days Festival, Fairbanks (DS)
Bottom: Fishing trawler at Dutch Harbor in the Aleutian Islands (DP)

the park. They begin at either the park hotel or VAC and a list of them with times is posted at both places. Taiga Hikes are moderately hard walks on the entrance-area trails that last three to four hours. They are held at 12.30 pm daily and meet at the park hotel auditorium.

In the backcountry, there are Discovery Hikes where a naturalist leads groups of up to 16 people for a three to five-hour trek that can cover anywhere from three to six miles. These hikes can range from moderately difficult to strenuous climbs up ridges. You have to sign up for Discovery Hikes at the VAC one or two days in advance and then obtained the necessary shuttle-bus coupon for a ride out to where the hike begins on the park road. Examples of these adventurous treks are hiking Hogan Creek up to Primrose Ridge, following the West Branch of Toklat River or exploring the tundra around Eielson Visitor Center for an old miner's cabin.

At Eielson there is also a Tundra Walk offered daily at 1.30 am and lasting from 30 minutes to an hour. The few maintained trails in the park are found around the main entrance area – descriptions follow.

Horseshoe Lake Trail This trail is a leisurely 1.5-mile walk through the woods to an overlook of the oxbow lake and then down a steep trail to the water. The trailhead is 0.9 miles on the park road where the railroad tracks cross. Follow the tracks north a short way to the wide gravel path.

Morino Loop Trail This leisurely walk of 1.3 miles can be picked up in the back of Morino campground as well as the park hotel parking lot and offers good views of Hines and Riley creeks.

Taiga Loop Trail This is another easy hike that begins off the parking lot of the park hotel and loops 1.3 miles through the taiga forest.

Mt Healy Trail Veering off the Taiga Loop Trail is the trail for the steep hike up Mt Healy. The trail is 2.5 miles long, ascends 1700 feet and offers fine views of the Nenana Valley. Plan on three to six hours for the round trip.

Rock Creek Trail This moderate 2.3-mile walk connects the hotel area with the park headquarters and dog kennels area. The trail begins just before the park road crosses Rock Creek but doesn't stay with the stream. Instead it climbs a gentle slope of mixed aspen and spruce forest, breaks out along a ridge with scenic views of Mt Healy and the Parks Hwy and then begins a rapid descent to the service road behind the hotel and ends on the Taiga Loop Trail. It's far easier hiking the trail to the hotel as all the elevation is gained with the drive up the park road.

Backpacking

For many, the reason to come to Denali, to endure the long lines at VAC, is to escape into the backcountry for a true wilderness experience. Unlike many parks in the Lower 48, Denali's rigid restrictions ensure that you can trek and camp in a piece of wilderness that you can call your own, even if it's just for a few days.

The park is divided into 43 zones and in 37 of them only a regulated number of backpackers is allowed into each section at a time. You have to obtain a permit for the zone you want to stay overnight in, and that usually means waiting two days or more at Riley Creek until something opens up.

All of this is done at the Visitor Access Center where at the Backcountry Desk you'll find two wall maps with the zone outlines and a quota board indicating the number of vacancies in each unit. Permits are issued only a day in advance and at first glance most backpackers are horrified to find most units full for two or three days in a row.

Like getting into the campgrounds, the key to obtaining a permit is first getting into the backcountry. Once you're in, you can book a string of other units throughout the park for the next 14 days. Units that are easier to obtain include Nos 1, 2, 3 and 24 because they surround the park entrance and are heavily wooded. Spend a night or two here and then jump on a shuttle bus for a more favorable place deeper in the park. At the opposite end of the park are most of the zones with unlimited access. These tend to be areas of extensive tussock where the trekking is extremely difficult or involves a major fording of the McKinley River, a difficult feat even when the river is low. Again by camping here, you can enter the backcountry immediately and then book other units as they open, bypassing the one-day-in-advance restriction.

Although any regulated zone can be filled, you'll generally find the more popular ones to be Nos 12, 13 and 18 in the tundra area south of Eielson Visitor Center; Nos 8, 9, 10 and 11 which include both branches of the Toklat River and tundra area south of Polychrome Pass; No 27 north of Sanctuary Campground and No 15, the unit just west of Wonder Lake.

The first step in the permit process is to watch the Backcountry Simulator Program in a video booth in the VAC. It's an interactive video that covers such topics as dealing with bears and backcountry travel. Then check which units might be closed due to bear activity or recent wolf kills. Check the quota board for an area that you can access within a day and finally approach the ranger behind the desk to outline your entire backcountry itinerary.

Along with your permit, you'll receive a Bear Resistant Food Container, free of charge, for food storage in the backcountry. The containers are bulky but they work. Since they were first introduced in 1986, bear encounters in the park have dropped by 90%. Next shuffle over to the shuttle bus counter and sign up for a camper bus and finally head over to the bookstore to purchase whatever topographical maps you will need at $2.50 each for the 1:63,000 scale topos.

It's important to realize that Denali is a trail-less park and the key to successful backcountry travel is being able to read a topographical map. You must be able to translate the contours (elevation lines) on the map into the land formations in front of you.

River beds are easy to follow and make excellent avenues for the backpacker but they always involve fording. Pack a pair of tennis shoes for this.

Ridges are also good routes to hike if the weather is not foul. The tree line in Denali is at 2700 feet, above that you usually will find tussock or moist tundra – humps of grass with water between to make for sloppy hiking. In extensive stretches of tussock the hiking has been best described as 'walking on basketballs'. Above 3400 feet you'll encounter alpine or dry tundra which generally makes for excellent trekking.

Regardless of where you are headed, five miles of backcountry in Denali is a full day for the average backpacker. For the best overview of the different units in the park purchase the book *Backcountry Companion for Denali National Park* by Jon Nierenberg (Alaska National History Association, 605 West 4th Ave, Anchorage, AK 99501; 94 pages, $8.95). It's available at both the VAC and park hotel gift shop.

Mountain Biking

An increasingly popular way to explore the park road is on a mountain bike. No special permit is needed to ride your bike on the road but you are not allowed to leave the road at any time. Most bikers book a campground site at the VAC and then carry the bike on the camper bus, using it to explore the road from there. You can even book a string of campgrounds and ride with your equipment from one to the next. The nearest place to rent a mountain bike is Mountain Bike Rentals (☎ 683-1295), next door to the Denali Hostel on Otto Lake Rd. Rental rates are $25 for a day and $17 for a half day. You can also rent mountains bikes in Talkeetna and take them on the train (see the previous Talkeetna section).

Rafting

The Nenana River and the impressive gorge it carves is a popular white-water rafting area. The most exciting stretch of the river begins near the park entrance and ends 10 miles north near the town of Healy. Here the river is rated Class III as rafters sweep through standing waves, rapids and holes with names like 'Coffee Grinder' that are situated in sheer-sided canyons. South of the entrance the river is much milder but to many it's just as interesting as it swings away from both the highway and the railroad increasing the opportunities of sighting wildlife.

Several rafting companies offer daily floats during the summer and the Nenana is easily one of the most rafted rivers in Alaska. Of the companies that run the river, Denali Raft Adventures (☎ 683-2234) has been around the longest (17 years) and seems the most organized. Its office is at *Mile 238* of the highway but they will provide free transport from the railroad depot inside the park or most campgrounds and motels outside. Their Canyon Run through the gorge is $36 and is offered at 8.30 am and 4 and 7.30 pm daily. The milder McKinley Run is also $36 and offered at 9 am and 1.30 and 7.30 pm or you can do them both on the four-hour Healy Express for $56. It departs daily at 1.30 pm. You can contact also McKinley Raft Tours (☎ 683-2392) or Owl Rafting (☎ 683-2215) for similar trips.

Getting There & Away

Bus Both north and southbound bus services are available from Denali National Park. If heading south, there is Moon Bay Express (☎ 274-6454 in Anchorage) whose van departs from the Visitor Access Center daily in the summer at 3 pm, reaching the Anchorage International Hostel at 8 pm. This is a great little company which will also arrange in-between pick-ups and drop-offs in case you want to spend a day in Sunshine or Caswell on the way down. One-way fare to Anchorage is $35, bikes cost another $10. Heading north is Fireweed Express Van Service (☎ 488-7928 in Fairbanks), which swings by both the VAC and park hotel at 4 pm and then arrives at Fairbanks Visitor Center at 6.30 pm. One-way fare is $25.

Other bus companies that make the run to Denali (everybody does) include Alaska Direct (☎ (800) 770-6652), Denali Express (☎ 274-8539 or (800) 327-7651) and Gray

Line. Of the three, Denali Express tends to be the cheapest but the service is not nearly as good as Moon Bay Express.

Train The most enjoyable way to arrive at the park is aboard the Alaska Railroad (see the Train section in the Getting Around chapter) with its viewing-dome cars that provide sweeping views of Mt McKinley and the Susitna and Nenana river valleys along the way. All trains arrive at the railroad depot between the Riley Creek Campground and the park hotel, and only stay long enough for passengers to board.

You can only arrive at Denali on the express train; the northbound train leaves Anchorage at 8.30 am daily from late May to mid-September arriving in Denali at 3.45 pm and reaching Fairbanks at 8 pm. The southbound train leaves Fairbanks at 8.30 am, arrives in Denali at 12.15 pm (or so they say) and arrives in Anchorage at 8.30 pm. The one-way fare from Denali National Park to Anchorage is $85; the fare to Fairbanks is $45. If heading south, consider getting off at Talkeetna for a day. The town is a classic but, being 14 miles off the George Parks Hwy, can't be reached by bus or van service.

Getting Around

Courtesy Buses There is free transportation into and around the park entrance and to just about anywhere you want to go. The park has the blue courtesy buses that run every half-hour from 6.30 am to 9 pm. They begin at the VAC and their loop includes the park hotel, the railroad depot, Riley Creek Campground and points in between. The park also runs free buses to the sled dog demonstrations that depart the VAC a half-hour before each show.

To head to the campgrounds and cabins outside of the park entrance, look for the cream colored buses at the park hotel. They are up and running by 5 am and don't stop until 11 pm. A schedule is posted in the hotel. If you want to go to Lynx Pizza Parlor, the Salmon Bake or anywhere north of the entrance, grab the bus for the McKinley Chalets; to the south jump on the one for

McKinley Village. Also keep in mind that the rafting companies, hotels and Denali Hostel will also send their own van out or meet you at the depot when you arrive.

North of Denali National Park

Just north of the park entrance is the town of Healy with restaurants, grocery stores and accommodations. Didn't see any bears in Denali? Try the Healy landfill. It's best just before sunset and you will probably be joined by the locals who sit in their cars and watch the black bears come prowling at close range.

Continuing north the George Parks Hwy in the next 50 miles parallels the Nenana River, providing many viewing points of the scenic river. One of them is the June Creek

Rest Area at *Mile 269*, where a gravel road leads down to the small creek and a wooden staircase takes you up to fine views of the area. Also provided are outhouses, picnic tables and shelters.

Nenana

The only major town between Denali National Park and Fairbanks is Nenana (population 540) which you reach at *Mile 305* of George Parks Hwy before crossing the Tanana River. Nenana was little more than the site of a roadhouse until it was chosen as the base for building the northern portion of the Alaska Railroad in 1916. The construction camp quickly became a boom town that made history on 5 July 1923 when President Warren G Harding arrived to hammer in the golden spike on the north side of the Tanana River.

The sickly Harding, the first president to ever visit Alaska, missed the golden spike the

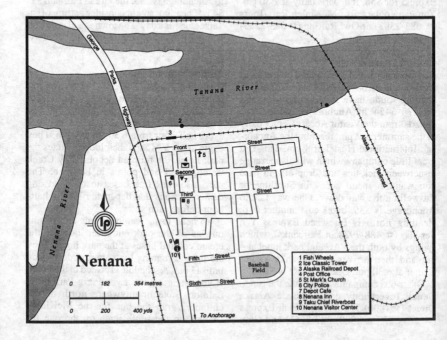

Nenana

1	Fish Wheels
2	Ice Classic Tower
3	Alaska Railroad Depot
4	Post Office
5	St Mark's Church
6	City Police
7	Depot Cafe
8	Nenana Inn
9	Taku Chief Riverboat
10	Nenana Visitor Center

0   182   364 metres
0   200   400 yds

To Anchorage

first two times, or so the story goes, but finally drove it in to complete the railroad. Less than a month later the president died in San Francisco, prompting the citizens of Talkeetna to claim he was 'done in' when he stopped at their Fairview Inn for a drink on the ride home.

In preparation for the president's arrival, the Nenana depot was built in 1923 at the north end of A St, extensively restored in 1988, and is now on the National Register of Historic Places. It's an impressive building and includes the **Alaska State Railroad Museum** (☎ 832-5500), which houses railroad memorabilia and local artefacts. Hours are from 9 am to 6 pm daily and admission is free. East of the depot, a monument commemorates when President Harding drove in the gold spike marking the completion of the Alaska Railroad.

An equally interesting building is the **Nenana Visitor Center** (☎ 832-9953), a log cabin with a sod roof that during the summer is planted with colorful flowers. It's on the corner of the George Parks Hwy and A St and features a few displays on the Nenana Ice Classic, the town's noted gambling event, as well as local information. Outside the visitor center is the *Taku Chief* river tug, which once pushed barges along the Tanana River. The

Breaking the Ice in Nenana

Railroads may have built Nenana but the town's trademark today is its annual gamble, the Nenana Ice Classic. The lottery event has Alaskans all over the state trying to guess the exact time of ice break-up on the frozen Tanana River. The first movement of river ice in April or May is determined by a tripod, which actually has four legs and stands guard 300 feet from shore. Any surge in the ice dislodges the tripod which tugs on a cord which in turn stops a clock on shore. The exact time on the clock determines the winner.

Crazy? Sure, but what else is there to do at the end of a long Alaskan winter? The tradition began in 1917 when Alaska Railroad surveyors, stir crazy with cabin fever, pooled $800 of their wages and made bets when the ice would move out. Today that same excitement swells in the small town, and through most of Alaska for that matter, as breakup in Nenana triggers visions of $100,000 payouts everywhere else.

Tickets are $2 for each guess and must be made by 1 April. What you win is determined by how many other people had the same guess as you did. In 1993, the jackpot was $240,000 but only had to be split three ways after the tripod tripped at 1.01 pm on 23 April for the second earliest breakup ever. Often so many people have the same guess that the winners take home only a few hundred dollars.

You can see a replica of the Ice Classic tripod and the 1974 book of guesses – a 12 by 18-inch volume that is almost four inches thick, at the Nenana Visitors Center. You can see the real tripod even if you're not getting off the train. When not on the ice, it's on the banks of the Tanana River near the depot and can be seen from the left side of trains heading north.

You can enter the contest even if you are basking in the sun in southern California. Frost bitten toes is not a requirement to lay down your bets. Just send a $2 money order and include the date, hour and minute you think the ice will go out to: Ice Classic Office, PO Box 272, Nenana, AK 99760. The office will then send you a photocopy of your guess and keep the original in case you are the winner. ■

center is open daily during the summer from 8 am to 6 pm.

Travel down Front St, parallel to the river in town, or cross to the north side of the bridge to view **fish wheels** at work, best seen in late summer during the salmon runs. The wheels, a traditional fish trap, scoop salmon out of the water as they move upstream to spawn.

Places to Stay & Eat *Nenana Inn* (☎ 832-5238), on the corner of 2nd and A St, is open 24 hours and has a laundromat and showers even if you're just camping off in the woods. Rooms begin at $65.

There are also two interesting B&Bs. In town there is the *Nenana Bed & Maybe Breakfast* (☎ 832-5272), on the 2nd floor of the depot, right above the Alaska State Railroad Museum. At *Mile 302* of the Parks Hwy, 2.5 miles south of Nenana, is *Finnish Alaskan B&B* (☎ 832-5628), with three rooms and a Finnish log sauna for guests. Rates range from $50 to $75 per room.

For a bit to eat, try the *Depot Cafe* on the corner of 1st and A streets and open daily from 6 am to 10 pm. The giant cinnamon rolls are all you need for breakfast.

Ester

From Nenana, the George Parks Hwy shifts to a more easterly direction, passes a few more scenic turn-offs and arrives at the old mining town of Ester (population 200) at *Mile 351.7*. The town was established in 1906 when a sizeable gold strike was made at Ester Creek, and at one time Ester was a thriving community of 15,000 with three hotels and five saloons. The town was revived in the 1920s when the Fairbanks Exploration Company began a large-scale mining operation. Most of Ester's historical buildings are from that era and were either built by the company or moved from Fox.

Gold mining still takes place in the hills surrounding Ester today. But the town is best known as the home of the Cripple Creek Resort and its Malemute Saloon. The restored mess hall and bunkhouse of the mining camp are a regular stop for every tour

bus out of Fairbanks. If you can hold off from rushing into Fairbanks, an evening here can be enjoyable, but only after 5 pm. Nothing happens in this town until the evening, even the two gift shops don't open their doors until the magic hour of 5 pm.

Places to Stay & Eat Rooms at the *Cripple Creek Hotel* (☎ 479-2500), an old miner's bunkhouse, are 'historically proportioned' (small) but affordable. Singles are $46 a night, doubles $64. There is also a RV campground at the resort where sites with water and showers are available for $9 a night.

Dinner is an all-you-can eat feast at the hotel and is served in dining-hall fashion. The regular buffet is excellent and includes halibut, chicken, reindeer stew, corn-on-the-cob and great biscuits among other things. The price is $13.95, not cheap but worth it if you've just spent a week living off freeze-dried dinners at Denali.

Entertainment The *Malemute Saloon* is one of those classic Alaskan bars – sawdust on the floors; junk, err excuse me, mining artefacts in the rafters; patrons tossing peanut shells everywhere. You can go in there and have a beer anytime but the saloon is famous for its stage show which combines skits, songs, Robert Service poetry and the Sawdust String Band. This is one of the best, and funniest, shows in Alaska that is guaranteed to leave you rolling in the sawdust and peanut shells by the end of the night. Show time is 9 pm, from Monday to Saturday while in July a second show at 7 pm is added from Wednesday to Saturday. Tickets are $9.

Nearby is *Firehouse Theatre*, where Leroy Zimmerman presents 'The Crown of Lights', an award-winning photo symphony. The show combines panoramic photography of the northern lights on a 30-foot screen with classical music.

Some people marvel at this type of show, others fall asleep. One thing for sure, if you're not going to see the real aurora borealis, this is the next best thing. Shows are at 7 and 8 pm daily. Admission is $5.

Getting There & Away From Ester, it is seven miles to Fairbanks, the second largest city in Alaska, at the end of George Parks Hwy at *Mile 358* (see the Fairbanks chapter). A taxi will run you from Ester to the airport for $12 and to the downtown area for around $20. There is also the Cripple Creek Shuttle Bus which provides round-trip transport from the major hotels in Fairbanks (Bridgewater, Westmark, etc) to Ester every evening for $4.

The Alcan

Travelers heading north along the Alcan (also called the Alaska Hwy) reach the US/Canadian border at *Mile 1189.5* from Dawson Creek in British Columbia. The spot is marked by a observation deck and plaque, while a half-mile further along the highway is the US Customs border station. On the US side of the highway you will notice mileposts at almost every mile. These posts were erected in the 1940s to help travelers know where they were on the new wilderness road. Today, they are a tradition throughout Alaska and are still used for mailing addresses and locations of businesses. They measure the mileage from Dawson Creek, *Mile 0* on the Alcan.

Your first opportunity for information and free hand-outs comes at *Mile 1229*. The **Tetlin National Wildlife Refuge Visitor Center** (☎ 883-5312) is a sod-covered log cabin with a cache and a huge viewing deck overlooking the Scotty and Deeper creeks drainage areas with Mentasta and Nutsotin mountains in the distance. Inside, the cabin is packed with interpretive displays (on wildlife and mountains) and racks of brochures. Opening hours are from 7 am to 7 pm daily during the summer.

You also pass two US Fish & Wildlife campgrounds (free!) along the Alcan before you reach Tok. At *Mile 1249.4* is the *Deadman Lake Campground* (15 sites) that has a boat ramp on the lake and a short nature trail but no drinking water. At *Mile 1256.7* is

the *Lakeview Campground* (eight sites) on beautiful Yager Lake, where on a nice day you can see the St Elias Range to the south. It's also a free campground with no piped-in water.

TOK

Although you enter Alaska just north of Beaver Creek in the Yukon, Tok serves as the gateway to the 49th State. The town of 1200, 125 miles beyond the US/Canadian border, is at the major junction between the Alcan (Alaska Hwy) that heads north-west to Fairbanks 206 miles away, and the Tok Cutoff, an extension of the Glenn Hwy that ends in Anchorage 328 miles to the south-west.

Tok was born in 1942 as a construction camp for the Alcan. Originally, it was called Tokyo Camp near Tokyo River, but WW II sentiment caused locals to shorten it to Tok. Today, the town is a trade and service center for almost 4000 residents in the surrounding area. If you're arriving in Alaska, this is your first chance to gather up information and brochures for the entire state.

Information

If nothing else, Tok is a town of information, maps and brochures because of its role as 'the Gateway to Alaska'. Near the corner of the Tok Cutoff (Glenn Hwy) and the Alcan is the Tok Visitors Center. The massive log building was built in 1992 to celebrate the 50th anniversary of the Alaska Hwy to the tune of $450,000. Inside there is regional and local information, outside a sign shows the temperature extremes the town suffers every year. Hours are from 7 am to 9 pm daily during the summer.

Next door is the Alaska Public Lands Information Center (☎ 883-5667), open daily in the summer from 8 am to 8 pm. The center offers a mountain of travel information and hand-outs along with free coffee, a large floor map and rest rooms. The small museum features wildlife displays – mounted heads and skins along with an impressive exhibit on plant succession based on the Tok fire of 1990. The center also has films on Alaskan wildlife shown hourly from 9 am to 5 pm.

The most important item in the center for many backpackers is the message board. Check out the board or display your own message if you are trying to hitch a ride through Canada along the Alcan. It is best to arrange a ride in Tok and not wait until you reach the international border. In recent years, the Canadian customs post at the border has developed a reputation as one of the toughest anywhere. With a new 'zero tolerance' attitude, it's not unusual see hitch-hikers, especially Americans, turned back at the border.

Directly across the highway from the visitor centers is the **US Fish & Wildlife Service Office** (☎ 883-5312) with information about various USFW refuges in northern Alaska including Tetlin National Wildlife Refuge. Hours are from 8 am to 4.30 pm Monday to Friday.

Things to See

Tok, along with a half-dozen other towns, considers itself the 'Sled Dog Capital of Alaska' as it is estimated one of every three people in the area is involved with the sport in one way or another – most of them by raising dogs. Ask at the visitor center about local dog-sled demonstrations that are usually held in town throughout the summer.

If you are staying overnight in Tok, by all means don't miss the showing of *Spirit of the Wind*, a movie that was made and produced in Alaska and covers the life of one of the state's most famous dog-sled racers. The music in this film, alone, is worth the admission. It's shown nightly at the Westmark Inn.

Places to Stay

Camping The closest private campground is the *Golden Bear Motel* (☎ 883-2561) just a third of a mile south of town on Tok Cutoff. The motel has tent spaces for $10 a night with showers, but it is the first of many tourist traps in the state set up to catch the steady stream of RVers passing through. The closest public campground is the *Tok River State Recreation Site* (25 sites, $8 fee), a

scenic spot with access to the river at *Mile 1309* of the Alcan, five miles east of town.

Hostels Probably the most affordable place to stay in town is at the *Tok International (AYH) Hostel*, a mile south on Pringle Dr at *Mile 1322.5* of the Alcan. That puts it nine miles west of the town, but it provides 10 beds in a big army tent along with tent sites in a pleasant wooded area. Those biking it to Alaska should note that Tok's bike trails pass near the hostel before ending at Tanacross Junction at *Mile 1325.8* of the Alcan. The rate per night at the hostel is $5.50 for members and $8.50 for nonmembers. There is no phone at the hostel, but the Tok Visitor Center can supply information about it.

Hotels Those travelers bussing up north from Haines or Skagway will find themselves stopping overnight in Tok. There are nine hotel/motels in the area; many of them are around the junction of the two highways. The cheapest one is the *Snowshoe Gateway Motel* (☎ 883-4511 or (800) 478-4511 in Alaska or the Yukon) across the Alcan from the visitor center. The motel has rooms with shared baths from $30 a single. Just about everything else in town begins at $50 for a single.

Getting There & Away

Tok can be difficult for hitchhikers. If you can't score a ride, even after pleading with motorists at the visitor center, keep in mind that Alaskon Express has a bus headed where you most likely want to go. The buses leave from the Westmark Inn (☎ 883-2291). On Sunday, Monday, Wednesday and Friday a bus leaves at 4 pm and overnights in Beaver Creek, reaching Whitehorse, Haines or Skagway the next day. On Tuesday, Wednesday, Friday and Sunday a bus departs at 11 am and reaches Anchorage by 7.15 pm that day. There is also a bus that runs to Fairbanks, daily except Tuesday at 3 pm. The one-way fare from Tok to Anchorage is $99, to Fairbanks $60, to Glennallen $54, to Haines $134 and Skagway $154.

The Alaska Direct bus (☎ (800) 770-

6652) passes through Tok almost daily during the summer. Once on its way to Whitehorse and Haines, it pulls in Monday, Wednesday and Saturday at 2.30 pm and then continues on to Beaver Creek. Westbound buses depart at 3 pm on Tuesday, Friday and Sunday with one heading for Glennallen and then Anchorage and another going to Fairbanks. The one-way fare from Tok to Anchorage is $65, to Fairbanks $40.

TOK TO DELTA JUNCTION

Within 10 miles west of Tok on the Alcan you are greeted with views of the Alaska Range which parallels the road to the south. The *Moon Lake State Campground* (15 sites, $8 fee) is at *Mile 1332*, 18 miles west of Tok. This state wayside offers tables, outhouses and a swimming area in the lake where it is possible to do backstroke while watching a float plane land nearby.

Although there are no more public campgrounds until Delta Junction, travelers often stop overnight at the *Gerstle River State Wayside*, a large lookout at *Mile 1393* of the Alcan. The scenic spot provides covered tables and outhouses but no piped-in drinking water. Nearby is the trailhead for the **Donna Lakes Trail**, a trek of 3.5 miles to Big Donna Lake and 4.5 miles to Little Donna Lake. Both are stocked with rainbow trout.

DELTA JUNCTION

This town (population 1300) is known as the 'End of the Alcan', as the famous highway joined the existing Richardson Hwy here to complete the route to Fairbanks. The community began as a construction camp and picked up its name from the junction between the two highways. Delta Junction is a service center not only for travelers but also for the growing agricultural community in the surrounding valleys and the 1200 military personnel and their families stationed at nearby Fort Greely.

Information

The log cabin which houses the Delta Junction Visitors Center is in the 'Triangle', the area where the Alcan merges into the Richardson Hwy and the town's unofficial 'downtown.' Just outside the visitor center is the large white milepost for *Mile 1422* of the Alcan, marking the end of the famous highway.

The visitor center (☎ 895-9941), open daily from 8.30 am to 7.30 pm in the summer, is the usual source of local information, hand-outs and free coffee. There is also a display of local crafts and furs while those who have just completed the journey on the Alcan from Dawson Creek can purchase an End-of-the-Highway certificate.

Things to See

There isn't a lot to do in Delta Junction unless you wander in during the Deltana Fair (giant vegetables, livestock shows and parades) on the first weekend in August. Even if you miss the fair, Delta has a **Farmer's Market**. Enquire at the visitor center for the days and hours it's open.

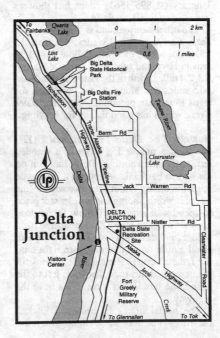

If you have the time, head three miles south of Delta Junction down Richardson Hwy to the scenic lookout across from the FAA facility. The mountainous panorama with the Delta River in the foreground is spectacular from this spot. On a clear day you can easily spot Mt Hayes (13,832 feet) in the center and Mt Moffit (13,020 feet) to the left, as well as several other peaks.

Check out the **Delta Junction Public Library** (☎ 895-4102) behind the city hall in the center of town if you have run out of reading material after the long haul on the Alcan. The library is open afternoons until 4 pm from Monday to Saturday in the summer and runs a paperback swap for travelers.

Places to Stay

Camping There are two public campgrounds in the area. The closest is the *Delta State Campground* (24 sites, $6 fee), a mile north of the visitor center. Two blocks north of the campground is Delta Self Service Laundry (☎ 895-4561) which has showers and is open to 10 pm daily.

The other campground is the *Clearwater State Campground* (18 sites, $6 fee), 13 miles north-east of town. Follow the Richardson Hwy and turn right on Jack Warren Rd, 2.4 miles north of the visitor center. Head 10.5 miles east along the road and look for signs to the campground, along Clearwater Creek which has good fishing for grayling.

Hostels The *Delta International (AYH) Hostel* is a unique log cabin in a wooded retreat 10 miles north of Delta Junction on the way to Fairbanks. Although it is a hassle to get out there without your own vehicle, the hostel is worth finding and is a pleasant place to spend a day or two. Follow Richardson Hwy six miles to *Mile 272* as measured from Valdez, and turn right onto Tanana Loop Rd. Head a mile down the road, turn right onto the Tanana Loop Extension and then look for the unmarked dirt road that leads left to the hostel; the building is three miles from the highway.

The hostel offers 10 beds and kitchen facilities but has no phone. You can,

however, call 895-5074 for more information. Rates are $5 for members and $7 for nonmembers.

Hotels There are a number of hotel/motels within Delta Junction. The *Evergreen Inn* (☎ 895-4666) is across from the visitor center and has rooms from $40 to $60. *Kelley's Motel* (☎ 895-4667) is nearby, on the west side of the highway, and offers singles/doubles for $50/60. Also consider the *Silver Fox Roadhouse* (☎ 895-4157), 18 miles south-east of Delta Junction on the Alcan, where there are cabins.

Richardson Hwy

The Richardson Hwy, Alaska's first highway, begins in Valdez and extends north 266 miles to Delta Junction, where the Alcan (Alaska Hwy) joins it for the final 98 miles to Fairbanks. The road was originally scouted in 1919 by Captain W R Abercrombie of the US Army, who was looking for a way to link the gold town of Eagle with the warm-water port of Valdez. At first it was a telegraph line and footpath, but it quickly turned into a wagon trail following the gold strikes at Fairbanks around the turn of the century.

Today, the road is a scenic wonder; it passes through the Chugach Mountains and the Alaska Range while providing access to Wrangell-St Elias National Park. Along the way it is highlighted by waterfalls, glaciers, five major rivers and the Trans-Alaska Pipeline, which parallels the road most of the way.

VALDEZ TO DELTA JUNCTION

The first section of the Richardson Hwy from Valdez, *Mile 0*, to the junction with the Glenn Hwy, *Mile 115*, is covered in the Richardson Hwy to Glennallen section in the Southcentral chapter. The next 14 miles from Glennallen to the junction of the Tok Cutoff, which includes the campgrounds at the Dry Creek State Recreation Site and Gulkana, is covered in the Tok Cutoff section following in this chapter. Mileposts along the highway show distances from old Valdez, four miles from the present city which is the new beginning of the Richardson Hwy.

Glennallen to Sourdough Creek

At *Mile 112.6* of the highway, just north of Glennallen, is a turn-off with an interpretive display on the development of transport in Alaska. Even more appealing is the view from a bluff nearby where you can view several peaks of the Wrangell Mountains which lie in Wrangell-St Elias National Park. The highest mountain is Mt Blackburn at 16,300 feet.

Once past Gulkana, the highway parallels the Gulkana River for the next 35 miles through land that is owned by the Ahtna Native Corporation. Fishing for king and red salmon is excellent in this river from mid-June to mid-July, and for rainbow trout and grayling most of the summer. In order to fish off the shore, you must have a permit ($10), issued at the Ahtna Corp Building in Gulkana. During the popular salmon runs the permits are also sold along the highway.

At *Mile 147.6* the road reaches the Bureau of Land Management *Sourdough Creek Campground* (47 sites, free), which provides access into the Gulkana River for canoeists and rafters. Since 1991 the campground has been closed for a $2 million facelift. When the BLM unveils it in late 1994 or 1995, it will be a stunning facility. The campground will include a new boat launch and entrance, trails that lead to a river observation shelter and a fishing deck. Best of all, the BLM plans putting in a walk-in camp site so that no matter how many RVers cram into the campground, there should always be a few sites open for tenters.

On the other side of the highway there used to be the Sourdough Roadhouse, one of the most colorful of a vanishing breed of accommodations for travelers in Alaska. Established in 1903 when the old Valdez Trail to Eagle ran behind it, the roadhouse became a national historical site and was the oldest existing roadhouse in Alaska until it caught fire in December 1992 and burnt to the ground. There are a set of interpretive panels in the Sourdough Campground detailing its history.

Gulkana Canoe Route

This trip along the Gulkana River from Paxson Lake, *Mile 175* of the Richardson Hwy, to where the highway crosses the river at Gulkana is a popular canoe, kayak and raft route of 80 miles. The first 45 miles is only for experienced white-water paddlers or rafters, as it involves several challenging rapids, including Canyon Rapids, Class IV white water. Although there is a short portage around Canyon Rapids, rough Class III waters follow. The final 35 miles from Sourdough Creek BLM Campground to Gulkana is a pleasant one or two-day paddle in mild water that can be enjoyed by less hard-core canoeists.

All land from the Sourdough Creek Campground south is owned by the Ahtna Native Corporation, which charges boaters to camp on it. The exception, three single-acre sites, are signposted along the river banks and have short trails leading back to the highway.

Alaska Range Foothills to Black Rapids Glacier

Ten miles north of Sourdough Creek, the Richardson Hwy enters the foothills of the Alaska Range. Gradually there are sweeping views of not only the Alaska Range to the north but the Wrangell Mountains to the south and the Chugach Mountains to the south-west. More splendid views follow; you can see the large plateau to the west where the headwaters of the Susitna River form and the Glennallen area to the south. At *Mile 175* of Richardson Hwy is the gravel spur that leads 1.5 miles west to the recently upgraded *Paxson Lake BLM Campground* (50 sites, $6). The lakeshore campground now has walk-in sites for tenters that cost only $3 a night.

The junction with the Denali Hwy is at *Mile 185.5*, where the small service center of **Paxson** is. Five miles north of Paxson, look for the parking area by the Gulkana River on the west side of the highway, where there are litter barrels and picnic tables. This scenic spot provides views of Summit Lake and the Trans-Alaska Pipeline. From mid to late summer this is also a good spot to watch the salmon spawn.

After passing Summit Lake, the bridge over Gunn Creek is reached at *Mile 196.7* of Richardson Hwy and provides views of **Gulkana Glacier** to the north-east. From here, the highway begins climbing to its highest point at **Isabel Pass**, elevation 3000 feet. The pass is at *Mile 197.6* and is marked by a historical sign dedicated to General Wilds Richardson, after whom the highway is named. From this point you can view Gulkana Glacier to the north-east and Isabel Pass pipeline camp below it.

Three miles north of the pass at *Mile 200.5* of Richardson Hwy, a gravel spur leads 1.5 miles to *Fielding Lake Wayside*, where you can camp (seven sites, free) in a scenic area above the tree line at 2973 feet. This high up in the Alaska Range, the ice often remains on the lake until July. The highway and the pipeline parallel each other north from Fielding Lake, and there are several lookouts to view the monumental efforts to move oil. One of the best is at *Mile 205.7*, where the pipeline can be photographed on an incline up a steep hill.

At *Mile 225.4* of Richardson Hwy, there is a viewpoint with picnic tables and a historical marker pointing out what little ice remains of **Black Rapids Glacier** to the west. The glacier is known as the 'Galloping Glacier' for its famous three-mile advancement in the winter of 1936 when it almost engulfed the highway. Across from the marker, the easy **Black Rapids Lake Trail**, 0.3-miles long, winds through wildflowers to Black Rapids Lake.

Donnelly Creek to Delta Junction

The last public campground before Delta Junction is just before *Mile 238* of Richardson Hwy, where a short loop road leads west of the highway to the *Donnelly Creek State Campground* (12 sites, $6 fee). This is a great

place to camp as it is seldom crowded and is extremely scenic with good views of the towering peaks of the Alaska Range. Occasionally, the Delta bison herd can be seen from the campground.

Two interesting turn-offs are passed in the final 25 miles before reaching the Alcan. The first is at *Mile 241.3* and overlooks the calving ground of the Delta buffalo herd to the west. Twenty-three bison were transplanted here from Montana in 1928, for the pleasure of sportsmen, and today there are almost 400 bison. The animals have established a migratory pattern in the area which includes summering and calving along the Delta River. There is an interpretive display at the turn-off where often you can spot up to 100 animals. Since the herd is two to three miles away, binoculars are needed for clear views.

The other turn-off is just before *Mile 244* and has spectacular views of the pipeline and three of the highest peaks in the Alaska Range to the south-west. From south to west you can view Mt Deborah (12,339 feet), Hess Mountain (11,940 feet) and Mt Hayes (13,832 feet).

The highway passes Fort Greely just beyond *Mile 261* and then arrives at the Delta Junction Visitor Center on the 'Triangle', where the Alcan merges with the Richardson Hwy at *Mile 266*. From here it is 98 miles to Fairbanks.

DELTA JUNCTION TO FAIRBANKS

From Delta Junction, the Richardson Hwy merges with the Alcan for the remaining 98 miles to Fairbanks and passes the most interesting attraction in the Delta Junction area at *Mile 275*. **Big Delta State Historic Park** (☎ 895-4201), a 10-acre historical park, preserves Rika's Landing, an important crossroad for travelers, miners and the military on the Valdez to Fairbanks Trail from 1909 to 1947.

The centerpiece of the park is Rika's Roadhouse which has been renovated and now contains historical displays and a gift shop. The roadhouse began as little more than a cabin in 1904 when John Hajdukovich came along and constructed most of the buildings within the park before trading them to a young Swedish woman in 1923, reportedly for $10 and her back wages. The roadhouse is named after Erika Wallen, who ran it until the late 1940s and lived there until her death in 1969. Of the 30 roadhouses that once stretched along the rutted and muddy Valdez-to-Fairbanks Trail (now the Richardson Hwy), only Rika's and the one in Copper Center remain.

Today guides in period dress lead tours through the complex which includes a blacksmith's shop museum, Signal Corp station, and the Packhouse Pavilion where local artisans work on spinning, weaving, quilting and willow carving. The roadhouse is open daily during the summer from 9 am to 8 pm and guided tours are offered every two hours from 11 am to 5 pm. There is also a restaurant in the Packhouse Pavilion.

Just beyond the state historical site, you pass through the farming village of **Big Delta** (population 300) at *Mile 275.3*. From the town's bridge across the Tanana River you can look east for an impressive view of the Alaska Pipeline suspended over the water or look west for equally impressive views of the Alaska Range.

The junction to the *Quartz Lake State Campground* (16 sites, $6 fee) is at *Mile 277.7* of Richardson Hwy. Turn east at the posted road and head 2.8 miles to the campground along the shores of the scenic lake which provides good fishing for rainbow trout. A trail from the campground leads over to nearby Lost Lake, where there are two more camp sites.

For the next 20 miles, the highway passes a handful of lookouts where there are spectacular views of both the Tanana River in the foreground and the Alaska Range behind it.

The spur that leads to *Harding Lake State Campground* (89 sites, $6 fee) is at *Mile 321.5*. The campground, which has a ranger office near the entrance, has picnic shelters and drinking water as well as swimming and canoeing opportunities in the lake.

From the campground, it is 43 miles to Fairbanks, and there are two public camp-

grounds along the way. At *Mile 346.7* of Richardson Hwy is *Chena Lakes Recreation Area* (78 camp sites, $6), and three miles north of here is the *North Pole Public Park* with a few tent sites. The Richardson Hwy reaches Fairbanks at *Mile 363*.

Tok Cutoff

The Tok Cutoff is often considered to be the northern half of the Glenn Hwy, but mileposts along the road show distances from Gakona Junction and not from Anchorage, as they do once you pass Glennallen.

TOK TO GLENNALLEN

From Tok, it is 328 miles to Anchorage, which is reached by first traveling the Tok Cutoff 139 miles south-west to Glennallen at the junction of Richardson and Glenn highways. From there, it is another 189 miles to Anchorage via the Glenn Hwy.

The first of only two public campgrounds on the Tok Cutoff is reached at *Mile 109.3*. The *Eagle Trail State Campground* (40 sites, $8 fee) is near Clearwater Creek and provides drinking water, toilets, rain shelter and fire pits. The historical **Eagle Trail**, which at one time extended to Eagle on the Yukon River, can still be hiked for a mile from the campground. Look for the posted trailhead near the covered picnic shelters.

The second campground is another 45 miles south-west along the highway just before *Mile 64.2*. The *Porcupine Creek State Recreation Site* (12 sites, $6 fee) is set in a scenic spot along the creek and provides tables, toilets and drinking water. An historical marker and splendid views of Mt Sanford, a dormant volcano with an elevation of 16,237 feet, is a mile north along the highway.

Nabesna Rd

At *Mile 59.8* of Tok Cutoff is the junction with Nabesna Rd. The 45-mile side road extends into the Wrangell-St Elias National Park (see the Wrangell-St Elias National

Park section in the Southcentral chapter) and ends at **Nabesna**, a mining community of less than 25 residents.

The side trip is a unique experience off the highways; the road is only one of two that lead into the heart of the national park. At the beginning of the road is **Slana**, a small village of 40 residents or so. Slana has a Native Alaskan settlement on the north banks of the Slana River and fishing wheels can still be seen working during the salmon runs. There is also a National Park Service ranger station that can assist with information on Wrangell-St Elias National Park. Hours are from 8 am to 5 pm daily from June to September. *Huck Hobbit's Homestead* is a campground and retreat in Slana with cabins for rent, hostel accommodations and canoes available. There is no phone at this homestead, ask at the ranger station how to reach it.

The first 30 miles of Nabesna Rd is manageable gravel road but after that the surface is extremely rough with several streams flowing over it. There is a lodge with gas at *Mile 28.6* but no other tourist facilities beyond that or in Nabesna. There are also no campgrounds along the way. Good camping spots, however, along with scenic lakes and inviting ridges for backpackers, lie from one end of this road to the other.

Gakona Junction

Officially, Tok Cutoff ends at Gakona Junction, 125 miles south-west of Tok, where it merges with the Richardson Hwy. The village of **Gulkana** (population 200) is two miles to the south and you can camp (voluntary fee) along the Gulkana River by the bridge in town. There is also *Bear Creek Inn* (☎ 822-5095), a B&B with a sauna and a good view of the Wrangell Mountains, two miles south of Gakona Junction at *Mile 126* of the Richardson Hwy. For an interesting meal, try the dining room of the *Gakona Lodge* (☎ 822-3482). The roadhouse opened in 1905 as Doyle's Ranch near the junction of the Eagle and Fairbanks cutoffs. In 1929, a larger lodge was added on and the original one was made into a carriage house. Today

it's listed on the National Register of Historical Places and the carriage house has been turned into a dining room. There is also a bar inside, natural food store and rooms are available.

From the roadhouse at Gakona Junction, the eastern end of the Glenn Hwy is 14 miles south via Richardson Hwy.

Glenn Hwy

The Glenn Hwy runs west from Glennallen to Anchorage with the mileposts along the road showing the distance from Anchorage, *Mile 0*.

GLENNALLEN

Glennallen (population 500), referred to by some as 'The Hub' of Alaska's road system, is a service center on Glenn Hwy, two miles west from the junction with the Richardson Hwy. Because of its strategic location, the town provides a wide range of facilities and services, and is the major departure point to the Wrangell-St Elias National Park. It is also the home base for many fishing and hunting guides; otherwise, it looks like a RV park and there is little reason to linger here.

Places to Stay

Camping The closest public campground is the *Dry Creek State Campground* (58 sites, $6 fee), five miles north-east of town on the Richardson Hwy between the junction with the Glenn Hwy and the Tok Cutoff to the north. Hitchhikers who get caught in Glennallen overnight, however, never have to walk far to find a place to pitch a tent.

Motels The only motel in town, *Caribou Motel* (☎ 822-3302) is right on Glenn Hwy and the lack of competition shows. Rooms are $100 a night.

Getting There & Away

Bus Glennallen is notorious among hitchhikers as a place for getting stuck in, especially at the Glenn Hwy junction when trying to thumb a ride north to the Alcan.

The *Hub of Alaska* (☎ 822-3555), a Tesoro service station at the junction of the Richardson and Glenn highways, also has a log-cabin visitor center which will provide you with the latest information on what bus is headed where. The center is open from 8 am to 7 pm daily and it's wise to double-check with them as the meagre system of buses is always in a constant state of flux. However, you can count on Gray Line's Alaskon Express passing through almost daily headed either for Anchorage or Tok. On Sunday, Monday, Wednesday and Friday a bus departs north at 12.30 pm and on Tuesday, Wednesday Friday and Sunday a bus heads south at 2.30 pm. One-way fare to Anchorage is $60, to Tok $54.

The Caribou Cafe (☎ 822-3656), next door to the Caribou Hotel in Glennallen, serves as the pick-up point for these buses along with the vans from Backcountry Connection (☎ 822-5292 or (800) 478-5292). Backcountry Connection has vans departing for McCarthy on Monday and Wednesday at 1.15 pm; Thursday, Friday and Sunday at 8 am and on Saturday at 10.45 pm. On Monday and Wednesday at 8 am there is also a van that heads south for Valdez. One-way fare to McCarthy is $55, to Valdez $40.

GLENNALLEN TO PALMER

The Glenn Hwy runs west from Glennallen through a vast plateau bordered by the Alaska Range to the north and the Chugach Mountains to the south. This is an incredibly scenic section that extends for almost 150 miles west; it is also a good area for spotting wildlife. Moose and caribou roam the lowlands and the timbered ridges are prime habitat for black bears and grizzlies. On the slope of both mountain ranges and often visible from the highway, are dall sheep.

Tolsona Creek to Little Nelchina River

The first public campground west from Glennallen is the *Tolsona Creek State Campground* (10 sites) at *Mile 172.7* on the south side of the Glenn Hwy. There is no fee for staying in this state campground, but there's no drinking water either. The creek is a good spot to fish for grayling.

Nearby is the *Tolsona Wilderness Campground* (☎ 822-3865), a private facility with 45 sites that border the river. The fee is $8 a night for a site but here you have water, coin-operated showers and laundry facilities. In the morning, if you're really hungry, stop at the *Tolsona Lake Lodge* (☎ 822-3433) at *Mile 170.5* of Glenn Hwy for their all-you-can-eat sourdough-pancake breakfast.

The next public campground along the highway is the *Lake Louise State Recreation Area* (46 sites, $6 fee) which provides shelters, tables, water and swimming in the lake. The scenic campground is 17 miles up Lake Louise Rd which leaves the Glenn Hwy at *Mile 160*. A mile up Lake Louise Rd from the Glenn Hwy is a turn-off with good views of Tazlina Glacier and Carter Lake.

The *Little Nelchina River Campground* (11 sites, free) is just off Glenn Hwy at *Mile 137.5*. The 35 miles between these three campgrounds is a hiker's delight, as several trails go from the highway to the nearby mountains and lakes.

A lookout with litter barrels marks the trailhead for the **Mae West Lake Trail**, a short hike at *Mile 169.3* of Glenn Hwy. This mile-long trail leads to a long, narrow lake fed by Little Woods Creek.

The trailhead for the **Lost Cabin Lake Trail** is on the south side of the highway at *Mile 165.8*, where a pair of litter barrels has been placed. The trail winds two miles to the lake and is a berry picker's delight from late summer to early fall.

At *Mile 138.3* of Glenn Hwy, or 0.8 miles east of the Little Nelchina River Campground for those camping there, is the trailhead for the **Old Man Creek Trail**. This trail leads two miles to Old Man Creek and nine miles to Crooked Creek, where you can fish for grayling. It ends at the old mining area of Nelchina, 14.5 miles from the highway. Here it merges into the old Chickaloon-Knik-Nelchina Trail, a gold miner's route used before the Glenn Hwy was built.

Today, the Chickaloon-Knik-Nelchina route is an extensive system of trails that extends beyond Palmer, with many posted access points along the north side of the highway. The system is not maintained regularly and hikers attempting any part of it should have good outdoor experience and the right topographic maps. Also keep in mind you'll have to share the trail with off-road vehicles.

Eureka Summit to Palmer

From Little Nelchina River, the Glenn Hwy begins to ascend, and views of Gunsight Mountain (you have to look hard to see the origin of its name) come into sight. At Eureka Summit, you can not only see Gunsight Mountain but the Chugach Mountains to the south, the Nelchina Glacier spilling down in the middle and the Talkeetna Mountains to the north. This impressive unobstructed view is completed to the west, where the highway can be seen dropping into the river valleys separating the two mountain chains. Eureka Summit (elevation 3322 feet) is at *Mile 129.3* of the Glenn Hwy; it is the highway's highest point.

The trailhead for the **Belanger Pass Trail**, at *Mile 123.3* on Martin Rd across from the Tahneta Lodge, is marked by a Chickaloon-Knik-Nelchina Trail sign. For the most part it is used by miners and hunters in off-road vehicles for access into the Talkeetna Mountains, and at times the mining scars are disturbing.

The views from Belanger Pass, a three-mile hike, are excellent and well worth the climb. From the 4350-foot pass, off-road-vehicle trails continue north to Alfred Creek, another 3.5 miles away, and eventually they lead around the north side of Syncline Mountain past active mining operations.

Two miles west of the Belanger Pass trailhead is **Tahneta Pass** at *Mile 121* of the Glenn Hwy and half a mile further is a scenic turn-off where you can view the 3000-foot pass. To the east of the turn-off lies Lake Liela, and Lake Tahneta beyond it.

The **Squaw Creek Trail** is another miners' and hunters' trail that begins at *Mile 117.6* of

Glenn Hwy and merges into the Chickaloon-Knik-Nelchina Trail. It begins as an off-road-vehicle trail marked by a Squaw Creek Trail sign. It extends 3.5 miles to Squaw Creek and 9.5 miles to Caribou Creek after ascending a low pass between the two. Although the trail can be confusing at times, the hike is a scenic one with the Gunsight, Sheep and Syncline mountains as a backdrop.

From here, the Glenn Hwy begins to descend and the scenery becomes stunning as it heads towards the Talkeetna Mountains, passing an oddly shaped rock formation known as the Lion's Head at *Mile 114*. A half a mile beyond it, the highway reaches the first view of Matanuska Glacier. To the north is Sheep Mountain, properly named as you can often spot dall sheep on its slopes.

At *Mile 113.5* of Glenn Hwy is the *Sheep Mountain Lodge* (☎ 745-5121), which is affiliated with Alaska Youth Hostels. The lodge is 70 miles east of Palmer and has no kitchen facilities but does feature a café, bar and liquor store along with 12 beds. There is also a sauna, hot tub and great hiking nearby. The hostel charges $8 a night for a bunk and is open from April to September. The lodge also has comfortable cabins for $75 a night if you're not up for a bunk. There's also a restaurant that serves excellent home-made soups and sandwiches for $5 to $7.

There is also inexpensive lodging just two miles west down the road at *Mile 111.5* of the Glenn Hwy, which raises the question why good accommodations are always next door to each other? The *Bunk 'n Breakfast* (☎ 745-5143) offers a bunk for $10.50 per night and a bunk and breakfast for $15.50. Bring your sleeping bag and your binoculars to search for dall sheep on Sheep Mountain just across the highway.

At *Mile 101* you reach the *Matanuska Glacier State Campground* (12 sites, $6 fee). The area has sheltered tables, water and trails and viewing decks along a nearby bluff that provide good viewing points of the glacier. It is a beautiful campground but, for obvious reasons, a popular one so there is a three-day limit here.

Matanuska Glacier is a stable ice floe that is four miles wide at its terminus and extends 27 miles back into the Chugach Mountains. Some 18,000 years ago, it covered the area where the city of Palmer is today. If you want to drive near the glacier's face, swing into the *Glacier Park Resort* (☎ 745-2534), *Mile 102* of Glenn Hwy, and pay $5 to follow its private road to within 400 feet of the ice. At this point some people just walk to the face, others spend a whole day on the ice. For another $2.50 you can also camp at this 540-acre resort which features a café and limited supplies.

The **Puritan Creek Trail** is just before the bridge over the creek (also known as Puritan) at *Mile 89* of the Glenn Hwy. There is a short dirt road that heads north of the highway and then east, passing an off-road-vehicle trail that ascends a steep hill to the north. The trail is a 12-mile walk to the foot of Boulder Creek, though the final seven miles consist mainly of trekking along the gravel bars of the river. The scenery of the Chugach Mountains is excellent and there are good camping spots along Boulder Creek.

From Boulder Creek, it is possible to climb to Chitna Pass and down to Caribou Creek and more sections of the Chickaloon-Knik-Nelchina Trail, a system that parallels the Glenn Hwy. The adventurous backpacker who is experienced with a map and compass could hike for days, exiting at a number of trailheads, including Belanger Pass and Squaw Creek.

In the next 13 miles, the Glenn Hwy passes three public campgrounds. The first is *Long Lake State Campground* (nine sites, free) at *Mile 85.3*. Along with toilets and fire pits, the campground offers access to a grayling fishing hole that is a favorite with Anchorage's residents.

Two miles west of the Long Lake Campground is a gravel spur road that leads to the *Lower Bonnie Lake State Campground* (eight sites, free), a two-mile side trip from the highway. The third campground is the *King Mountain State Recreation Site* (22 sites, $6 fee) at *Mile 76* of the Glenn Hwy. This scenic campground is on the banks of

the Matanuska River, with a view of King Mountain to the south-east. Just outside the campground is *King Mountain Lodge* for your burger and beer along with a small market for other supplies. Across the highway is the office for Nova (☎ 745-5753), a rafting company which runs the Matanuska River daily. They offer a mild 3½-hour run at 10 am for $50 per person and wilder one, that features Class IV rapids around Lionshead Wall, at 9 am and 2 pm for $70. All this, the scenery, the rafting and the beer store, makes the state campground a good place to pull up, or stop hitching, for a day or two.

Just before passing through Sutton (population 850) at *Mile 61*, you come to **Alpine Historical Park** (☎ 745-7000). The park has several buildings, including the Chickaloon Bunkhouse and the original Sutton post office which now houses a museum. Inside the displays are devoted to the Athabascan people, the 1920 coal-boom era of Sutton and the building of the Glenn Hwy. The park is open from 10 am to 7 pm daily during the summer and admission is $2.

Beyond Sutton, you come to the last public campground before Palmer. The *Moose Creek State Recreation Area* (12 sites, $6 fee) is a small campground on the creek at *Mile 54.5* of Glenn Hwy which has sheltered tables, outhouses and drinking water. There is also a trail that leads up the creek for anglers. Five miles beyond Moose Creek is the junction to the Fishhook-Willow Rd which provides access to the Independence Mine State Park (see under Hatcher Pass in the Anchorage chapter). The highway then descends into the agricultural center of Palmer.

From Palmer, Glenn Hwy merges with the George Parks Hwy and continues south to Anchorage, 43 miles away (see the Anchorage chapter).

Denali Hwy

With the exception of 21 miles that is paved at its east end, the Denali Hwy is a gravel road extending from Paxson on the Richardson Hwy to Cantwell on the George Parks Hwy, just south of the main entrance to Denali National Park.

When the 135-mile route was opened in 1957 it was the only road to the national park, but it became a secondary route after the George Parks Hwy was completed in 1972. Today, the Denali Hwy is only open from mid-May to October. Most of it runs along the foothills of the Alaska Range to the north and through glacial valleys where you can see stretches of alpine tundra, enormous glaciers and braided rivers. The scenery is spectacular but the road itself can be a disaster at times. This, say most travelers, is the worst road in Alaska. Plan on at least six hours to drive it from end to end.

There are numerous trails into the surrounding backcountry but none of them is marked. Also in the area are two popular canoe routes. Ask locals at the roadhouses for information and take along topographic maps that cover the areas you intend to trek or paddle.

There are no established communities along the way, but four roadhouses provide food and lodging and two of them, at *Mile 20* and *Mile 81* have gasoline for sale. If

driving, it is best to fill up with gasoline at Paxson or Cantwell.

From Paxson, *Mile 0*, the highway heads west and passes the mile-long gravel road to Sevenmile Lake at *Mile 7*. From here, the terrain opens up and provides superb views of the nearby lakes and peaks of the Alaska Range. Most of the lakes, as many as 40 in the spring, can be seen from a lookout at *Mile 13* of the Denali Hwy.

The **Swede Lake Trail** is near *Mile 17* of the highway and leads south three miles to Swede Lake after passing Little Swede Lake in two miles. Beyond here, it continues to the Middle Fork of the Gulkana River but the trail is extremely wet at times and suitable only for off-road vehicles. Anglers fish the lakes for trout and grayling. Enquire at the Tangle River Inn (☎ 895-44439) at *Mile 20* for directions to the trail and an update on its condition. The inn has a café, gas, canoe rentals, showers and rooms that begin at $40 a night.

The paved portion of the Denali Hwy ends just beyond *Mile 21*, and in another half-mile the highway reaches the Bureau of Land Management (BLM) *Tangle Lakes Camp-*

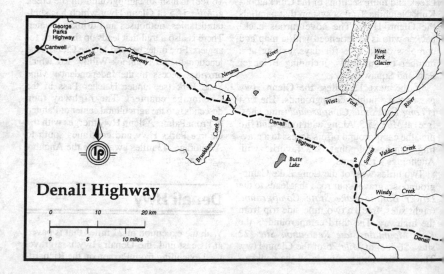

Denali Highway

ground (13 sites, free) to the north, on the shores of Round Tangle Lake and features displays explaining the archaeological digs in the area. A second BLM campground, *Upper Tangle Lakes* (seven sites, free), is a quarter-mile down the road on the south side. Both campgrounds serve as the departure point for two scenic canoe routes and nearby Tangle River Inn provides canoe rentals. Caribou are occasionally spotted in the surrounding hills.

Paddling

The **Delta River Canoe Route** is a 35-mile paddle which begins at the Tangle Lakes BLM Campground north of the highway and ends a few hundred yards from *Mile 212.5* of Richardson Hwy. Begin the canoe route by crossing Round Tangle Lake and continuing to Lower Tangle Lake, where you must make a portage around a waterfall. Following the waterfall is a set of Class III rapids that must either be lined for two miles or paddled with an experienced hand. Every year, the BLM reports of numerous canoeists who damage their boats beyond repair on these rapids and are forced to hike 15 miles

back out to the Denali Hwy. The remainder of the trip is a much milder paddle.

The **Upper Tangle Lakes Canoe Route** is easier and shorter than the Delta River route but requires four portages, none of which is marked but they are easy to figure out in the low bush tundra. All paddlers attempting this route must have topographic maps. The route begins at Tangle River and passes through Upper Tangle Lake before ending at Dickey Lake, nine miles to the south. There is a 1.2-mile portage into Dickey Lake.

From here, experienced paddlers can continue by departing Dickey Lake's outlet to the south-east into the Middle Fork of the Gulkana River. For the first three miles, the river is shallow and mild but then it plunges into a steep canyon where canoeists have to contend with Class III and IV rapids. Most canoeists choose to either carefully line their boats or make a portage. Allow seven days for the entire 76-mile trip from Tangle Lakes to Sourdough Campground on the Gulkana River off Richardson Hwy.

At *Mile 25*, the Denali Hwy crosses Rock

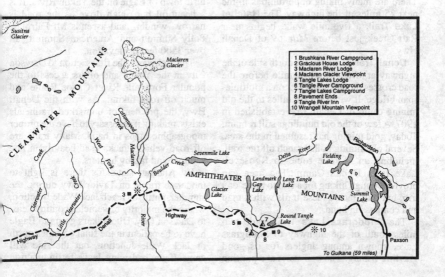

Creek Bridge, where the **Landmark Gap Trail** leads north three miles to Landmark Gap Lake, elevation 3217 feet. You can't see the lake from the highway but you can spot the noticeable gap between the Amphitheatre Mountains.

A parking lot on the north side of the highway at *Mile 32* is the start of the three-mile **Glacier Lake Trail**.

From here, the highway ascends **MacLaren Summit** (elevation 4086 feet) one of the highest highway passes in the state. The summit is reached at *Mile 35.2* and has excellent views of Mt Hayes, Hess Mountain and Mt Deborah to the west and MacLaren Glacier to the north.

The MacLaren River is crossed at *Mile 42* of Denali Hwy on a 364-foot multiple-span bridge. Another bridge crosses Clearwater Creek at *Mile 56*, where nearby there are camp sites and outhouses. Beginning at *Mile 69* is the first of many hiking trails in the area; all are unmarked and many are nothing more than old gravel roads. Enquire at the Gracious House Lodge, a roadhouse at *Mile 82*, for the exact location of the trails.

Hiking

There are many hiking opportunities in the next 25 miles of the highway. The **Hatchet Lake Trail**, a five-mile walk, begins near Raft Creek just before *Mile 69* of Denali Hwy.

Denali Trail begins on the north side of the highway at *Mile 79*, a half-mile before the road crosses the Susitna River on a multiple-span bridge. It winds for six miles to the old mining camp of Denali, first established in 1907. A few of the old buildings still remain. Today, gold mining has resumed in the area. Several old mining trails branch off the trail, including an 18-mile route to Roosevelt Lake from Denali Camp. The area can provide enough hiking for a two to three-day trip, but only tackle these trails with a map and compass in hand.

The **Snodgrass Lake Trail** leads two miles south of the highway to Snodgrass Lake, known among anglers for its good grayling fishing. The trail starts at a parking

area between *Mile 80* and *Mile 81* of the Denali Hwy.

The **Butte Lake Trail**, an off-road-vehicle track, leads five miles south to Butte Lake, known for its large lake trout, often weighing over 30 pounds. The trailhead is at *Mile 94*.

The *Gracious House Lodge* (☎ 333-3148) at *Mile 82* has rooms, a café and gas while at *Mile 104.3* is the *Brushkana River BLM Campground* (17 sites, free). The campground has a shelter, drinking water and a meat rack for hunters who invade the area in late summer and fall. The river, which the campground overlooks, can be fished for grayling and Dolly Varden. From here, it is another 20 miles to where the Denali Hwy merges with the George Parks Hwy. The entrance to Denali National Park is 17 miles north of this junction on George Parks Hwy.

Taylor Hwy

The scenic Taylor Hwy extends 161 miles north from Tetlin Junction, 13 miles east of Tok on the Alcan (Alaska Hwy), to the historic town of Eagle on the Yukon River. It is a beautiful but rough drive as the road is narrow, winding and ascends Mt Fairplay, Polly Summit and American Summit, all over 3500 feet in elevation.

The highway is the first section to Dawson City in the Yukon and offers access to the popular Fortymile River Canoe Route and much off-road hiking. As with the Denali Hwy, the problem of unmarked trailheads exists, making it necessary to have the proper topographic maps in hand. Many trails are off-road-vehicle tracks used heavily in late summer and fall by hunters.

By Alaskan standards there is light to moderate traffic on Taylor Hwy during the summer, until you reach Jack Wade Junction, where the majority of vehicles continue east to Dawson City. Hitchhikers going to Eagle have to be patient in the final 65 miles north of Jack Wade Junction, but the ride will come. If you're driving, leave Tetlin Junction with a full tank of gasoline because roadside services are limited along the route.

From Tetlin Junction, *Mile 0*, the highway heads north, and within nine miles begins to ascend towards Mt Fairplay, elevation 5541 feet. A lookout near the summit is reached at *Mile 35* and is marked by litter barrels and an interpretive sign describing the history of Taylor Hwy. From here, you are rewarded with superb views of Mt Fairplay and the valleys and forks of the Fortymile River to the north. The surrounding alpine area offers good hiking for those who need to stretch their legs.

The first Bureau of Land Management (BLM) campground is at *Mile 49* on the west side of the highway. *West Fork BLM Campground* (25 sites, free) has outhouses but no drinking water; all water taken from nearby streams should be boiled or treated first (see the Health section in the Facts for the Visitor chapter for information on water purification). Travelers packing along their gold pans can try their luck in West Fork River which is the first access point for the paddle down Fortymile River.

CHICKEN

After crossing a bridge over the Fortymile River's Mosquito Fork at *Mile 64.4*, the Taylor Hwy passes the old **Chicken Post Office** on a hill beside the road, at *Mile 66.2*. The post office, still operating today, was originally established when Chicken was a thriving mining center. **Old Chicken**, the original mining camp, is now privately owned but can be viewed during a daily walking tour that begins at the Chicken Creek Cafe. Among the buildings you will see is the schoolhouse of Ann Purdy, who later wrote the novel, *Tisha*, based on her days as a school teacher here.

The community of Chicken itself (population between 30 and 50) is 300 yards to the north on a spur road that leads to an airstrip, grocery, the *Chicken Creek Cafe* and gasoline station. The town's name, according to one tale, originated at a meeting of the resident miners in the late 1800s. When trying to come up with a name for the new tent city,

Ptarmigan

somebody suggested Ptarmigan, since the chicken-like bird existed in great numbers throughout the area. All the miners liked it but none of them could spell it. The town's name has been Chicken ever since.

Just north of the spur to the village is Chicken Creek Bridge, built on tailing piles from the mining era. If you look back to the left, you can see the **Chicken Dredge** which was used to extract gold from the creek between 1959 and 1965. Most of the forks of the Fortymile River are virtually covered from one end to the other by active mining claims and often you can see suction dredging for gold from the highway.

Views of the old town site of Chicken, now in the hands of a mining company, can be obtained at *Mile 67.3* by looking to the west. At *Mile 75.3* is the bridge over South Fork and the most popular access point for the Fortymile River Canoe Route.

FORTYMILE RIVER CANOE ROUTE

The historic Fortymile River, designated as the Fortymile National Wild River, offers an excellent escape into scenic wilderness for paddlers experienced in lining their canoes around rapids. It is also a step back into the gold-rush era of Alaska as paddlers will view such abandoned mining communities as Franklin, Steele Creek and Fortymile while undoubtedly seeing some present-day mining. The best place to start is the bridge over South Fork, because access points south of here on Taylor Hwy often are too shallow for an enjoyable trip.

A common trip is to paddle the 40 miles to the bridge over O'Brien Creek at *Mile 113* of Taylor Hwy. This two to three-day trip involves three sets of Class III rapids. A greater adventure is to continue past O'Brien Creek and paddle the Fortymile River into the Yukon River and from here head north to Eagle at the end of the Taylor Hwy. This trip is 140 miles long and requires seven to 10 days to cover, along with lining several sets of rapids in the Fortymile River. The planning and organizing for such an expedition has to be done carefully before you leave for Alaska (see the Eagle section in this chapter about paddling the Yukon River).

WALKER FORK TO AMERICAN CREEK

At *Mile 82* of Taylor Hwy is the *Walker Fork BLM Campground* (18 sites, free) which lies on both sides of the highway and has tables, firewood and a short trail to a limestone bluff overlook.

A lookout is reached at *Mile 86* of the highway, where you can view the **Jack Wade Dredge**, which operated from 1900 until 1942. For most of its working days the dredge was powered by a wood-burning steam engine which required 10 to 12 cords of wood per day. The old Jack Wade mining camp is passed four miles north of the dredge; after being abandoned for 30 years the mine is now being reworked as the result of higher gold prices.

The Jack Wade Junction is at *Mile 95.7* of Taylor Hwy, and here the Top of the World Hwy (also known as the Dawson Hwy)

winds 3.5 miles to the Canadian/US border and another 75 miles east to Dawson City. The Taylor Hwy continues north from the junction and ascends **Polly Summit**, elevation 3550 feet. The summit is reached at *Mile 105*, and five miles beyond it is a scenic lookout where you can view the Fortymile River.

From the summit, Taylor Hwy begins a steep descent; drivers must take this section slowly. Along the way there are numerous lookouts with good views as well as a variety of abandoned cabins, old gold dredges and mine tailings. Primitive camping is possible at *Mile 134* of Taylor Hwy on the south side of a bridge over King Solomon Creek. This is a former BLM campground which has not been maintained in years. Holiday prospectors should try their luck in the nearby creek. Eagle is another 27 miles to the north.

EAGLE

The historic town of Eagle (population 160) had its beginnings in the late 1800s and today is one of the best-preserved boom towns of the mining era in Alaska.

The original community, today called Eagle Village, was established by the Athabascan Indians long before Francois Mercier arrived in the early 1880s and built a trading post in the area. A permanent community of miners was set up in 1898. A year later, the US Army decided to move in and build a fort in its effort to maintain law and order in the Alaskan Interior. A federal court was established at Eagle in 1900 by Judge Wickersham, and the next year President Theodore Roosevelt issued a charter that made Eagle the first incorporated city of the Interior.

Eagle reached its peak at the turn of the century when it had a population of over 1500 residents and the overland telegraph wire was completed from Valdez in 1903. Some residents even went as far as to call their town the 'Paris of the North', though that was hardly the case.

Other gold strikes in the early 1900s, most notably at Fairbanks, began drawing residents away from Eagle and caused the removal of Judge Wickersham's Court to the

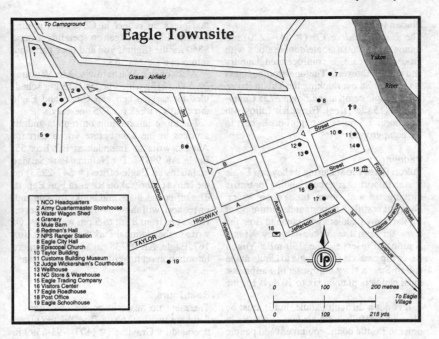

Eagle Townsite

To Campground

Grass Airfield

Yukon River

Street

Street

TAYLOR

HIGHWAY

Avenue

4th

3rd

2nd

B

A

Jefferson Avenue

Adams Avenue

Front Street

1st

1 NCO Headquarters
2 Army Quartermaster Storehouse
3 Water Wagon Shed
4 Granary
5 Mule Barn
6 Redmen's Hall
7 NPS Ranger Station
8 Eagle City Hall
9 Episcopal Church
10 Taylor Building
11 Customs Building Museum
12 Judge Wickersham's Courthouse
13 Wellhouse
14 NC Store & Warehouse
15 Eagle Trading Company
16 Visitors Center
17 Eagle Roadhouse
18 Post Office
19 Eagle Schoolhouse

0   100   200 metres
0   109   218 yds

To Eagle Village

new city in the west. The army fort was abandoned in 1911, and by the 1940s Eagle's population had dwindled to 10. When the Taylor Hwy was completed in the 1950s, however, the town's population increased to its present levels.

Things to See

If you're spending a day in Eagle, the best way to see the town and learn its history is to be in front of **Judge Wickersham's Courthouse**, on the corner of B St and 1st Ave, at 10 am. The courthouse, now a museum managed by the Eagle Historical Society, offers a walking tour of the town daily during the summer, beginning at the front porch. The tour is $2 per person and covers such historical buildings as the **Eagle City Hall**, where the city council continues to hold regular meetings, the **Customs Building Museum** and the **Eagle Post Office** on the corner of A St and 1st Ave, where a plaque commemorates explorer Roald Amundsen's visit to Eagle.

The Norwegian explorer hiked overland to Eagle in 1905 after his ship froze in the Arctic Sea off Canada. From the town's telegraph office he sent word to the waiting world that he had just navigated the Northwest Passage. Amundsen stayed two weeks in Eagle and then mushed back to his sloop. Nine months later, the ship reached Nome completing the first successful voyage from the Atlantic to the Pacific Ocean across the Arctic Ocean.

To the north of town is **Fort Egbert**, which can be reached from Taylor Hwy via 4th Ave. The Bureau of Land Management has been involved in restoring the old army fort, which once contained 37 buildings; several are now open to visitors during the summer. The restored mule barn, carriage house, dog house and officers' quarters are clustered together in one section of the fort.

Places to Stay

The *Eagle Trading Co* (☎ 547-2220) has rooms for $50/60 a single/double along with groceries, a café, a coin-operated laundry and public showers. The one-stop business is on Front St, overlooking the Yukon River. Most people camp at the *Eagle BLM Campground* (15 sites, free). To reach it, follow 4th Ave north 1.5 miles through Fort Egbert to the campground.

Paddling

Yukon River Float During its heyday, Eagle was an important riverboat landing for traffic moving up and down the Yukon River. Today, it is still an important departure point for the many paddlers who come to float the river through the Yukon-Charley Rivers National Preserve. The 150-mile Yukon River trip extends from Eagle to Circle at the end of Steese Hwy north-east of Fairbanks; most paddlers plan on six to 10 days for the float.

It is not a difficult paddle, but it must be planned carefully with air-taxi operators in order to shuttle boats, equipment and people from Circle. Floaters and paddlers should come prepared for insects and can usually camp on open beaches and river bars where winds keep the bugs down. Paddlers also need to be prepared for extremes in weather; freezing nights can be followed by daytime temperatures of 90°F.

Tatondak Outfitters in Eagle rent rafts for $400 per week but in 1994 the company was switching owners. Call Eagle Trading Co (☎ 547-2220) to see who has taken it over. The guide company also arranged air service

that picks up rafters in Circle and returns them to Eagle. Budget on spending around $360 for the flight if you and your party can return in a Cessna 185.

Also check Warbelow's Air Ventures (☎ 547-2213) which began offering scheduled air service between Circle and Eagle three days a week for $95 one-way.

For more information on rentals and air services in the area before you depart for Alaska, write to Tatondak at PO Box 55, Eagle, AK 99738. The National Park Service maintains an Eagle office (☎ 547-2233) on the banks of the Yukon River in Fort Egbert. The office has maps and books for sale and, on request, will show a video on the preserve. Hours are from 8 am to 5 pm weekdays. Or write to the National Park Service (PO Box 167, Eagle, AK 99738) in advance for more information on traveling the Yukon River.

Boat Tours

There are no buses in or out of Eagle but there are two tour boats. The *Yukon Queen*, operated by Grayline (☎ (403) 993-5599 in Dawson, the Yukon Territory), makes the trip from Dawson as part of a package tour. But the operators will also sell round-trip and one-way tickets in either town to fill up the empty seats.

New in 1994 is the Alaska Yukon Sternwheeler Company (☎ 455-4320, Fairbanks), whose sternwheeler will pass through during summer. Deck passage costs $125 per day. It's a steep price but this isn't transportation, but rather an historical cruise on the Yukon River.

Fairbanks

Fairbanks (population 77,720) goes by a lot of names and descriptions. It's often referred to as the 'Golden Heart City' because of its location in the center of the state and, I suspect, the willingness of the residents to help each other out during those long, cold winters. It's also been labeled the 'Hub of the Interior' for the role it plays as the transportation center for The Bush. But perhaps the best description for Fairbanks was a slogan its Convention & Visitors Bureau came up with one summer. Fairbanks, according to the ad campaign, was 'extremely Alaska'. Oh, is it ever. Extremes are a way of life in the state's second largest city.

At first glance, Fairbanks appears to be a spread-out, low-rise city with the usual hotels, shopping malls, McDonald's and a university tucked away on the outskirts of town. A second look reveals that this community is different, that the people and the place are one of a kind, even for Alaska.

Fairbanks has log cabins, lots of them, from the heart of town to those hidden among the trees on the back roads. It has a semiprofessional baseball team that plays games at midnight without the aid of artificial lights. It also has a golf course that claims to be the 'world's most northernmost', a college campus where if the day is clear students can view the highest mountain in North America and there are more sled dogs living here than there are horses in the bluegrass state of Kentucky.

'Extremely Alaska' is the only way to describe Fairbanks' weather. During the summer, it is pleasantly warm with an average temperature of 70°F and an occasional hot spell in August where the temperature breaks 90°F. The days are long with more than 20 hours of light from June to August, peaking at almost 23 hours on 21 June.

In the winter, however, Fairbanks is cold. The temperature stays below 0°F for months and can drop to -60°F or even lower for days at a time. The days are short, as short as three or four hours, and the nights are cold. It's so cold in the winter that parking meters come equipped with electric plugs because cars have heaters around the transmission, oil pan and battery. When it's -60°F unprotected fingers become numb in seconds, beards and moustaches freeze and turn into icicles in minutes and a glass of water thrown out of a 2nd-floor window shatters as ice when it hits the ground.

When it's -60°F, planes don't fly into Fairbanks for fear that landing gear will freeze up, the mail isn't delivered, state employees are not required to go to work and, perhaps most unusual, tires freeze. This strange phenomenon is known as 'square tires' because the bottom of tires molds to the flat surface of the road. When you take off, they're simply pulled off the rims.

Consider the city's boom-or-bust economy for extremes. Fairbanks was founded in 1901 when E T Barnette was heading up the Tanana River with a boat load of supplies and was swept up by the fast waters of the Chena River. When the river became too shallow, he stepped ashore at the present site at the corner of 1st Ave and Cushman St and decided to stay and set up his trading post. Barnette could have been just another failed merchant in the Great White North but the following year an Italian prospector named Felix Pedro struck gold 12 miles north of Barnette's trading post. A boom town sprang to life amid the hordes of miners stampeding into the area and by 1908 there were more than 18,000 people living in the Fairbanks Mining District.

But retrieving the gold proved far more challenging here than elsewhere in Alaska due to the permafrost. Gold pans and sluice boxes were of little use here because the ground firstly had to be thawed before the mineral-rich gravel could be recovered. Early miners cuts trees to thaw the ground with fires but timber was scarce this far north and eventually other gold rushes drained the city of its population. By 1920, Fairbanks had a population of a little more than 1000.

Ironically, the city's gold mining industry outlasted any other in the state. After the Alaska Railroad reached Fairbanks in 1923, major mining companies, with money to invest in materials and machines, arrived and brought with them three-story mechanized dredges. But the key to reaching the gold was a new process that utilized needle-nose pipes to thaw the ground. Hundreds were driven into the ground by hand and then water was forced through an opening at the end of the pipes into the frozen ground. Once the ground was thawed, the dredges worked nonstop extracting the gold and turning the terrain into mincemeat.

More than $200 million in gold has been extracted from the mining district where dredges still operate today. The most famous one, however, was Gold Dredge No 8, that operated from 1928 to 1959 in recovering 7.5 million ounces of the precious metal. Eventually it was listed as a National Historical Site and today is probably the most viewed dredge in the state.

When the mining slowed down, Fairbanks' growth slowed to a crawl. WW II and the construction of the Alcan (Alaska Hwy) and military bases produced the next booms in the city's economy, but neither affected Fairbanks like the Trans-Alaska Pipeline. After oil was discovered in Prudhoe Bay in 1968, Fairbanks was never the same. From 1973 to 1977, the town burst at its seams as the principal gateway to the North Slope, where construction of the Trans-Alaska Pipeline was at its height.

Workers, who came from all over the country and the world looking for four-digit weekly pay checks, filled every hotel room and tent site for miles around. Prices soared, lines at the supermarket became unbearable, and suddenly there were traffic jams in a town that had none before. During this boom everybody tried to profit; this was truly a 20th-century 'gold rush'.

The aftermath of the pipeline construction was just as extreme. The city's population shrank and unemployment crept towards 25% through much of 1979. The oil industry bottomed out in 1986 with the declining price of crude and Fairbanks, like Anchorage, suffered through more hard times.

But like the weather, Fairbanks' residents endured all this, and will endure more busts or booms if oil companies are allowed to drill the Arctic National Wildlife Refuge. Perhaps more so than any town south of the Arctic Circle, Fairbanks' residents are a hardy and independent breed because they have to be. That, more than the log cabins or the midnight sun, is the city's trademark. The residents tend to be more colorful than most Alaskans, maybe a bit louder and a degree more boastful. They exemplify to the fullest the Alaskan theme of 'work hard, play hard, drink hard'.

Whether you enjoy Fairbanks or not depends on where you're coming from and your perceptions. If you've just spent 10 days paddling the Noatak River in the Brooks Range, Fairbanks can be an extremely hospitable place to recoup. And an affordable one at that. Generally you'll find tourist-related businesses – hotels, taxis, restaurants etc – to be much more reasonably priced than in Anchorage. If, however, you've just arrived from such places as Homer or Juneau, the charming aspects of these towns surrounded by mountains, glaciers and the sea might blind you to what is so unique – and so extreme – about Fairbanks.

Orientation

Fairbanks, the transport center for much of the Interior is a spread-out town that covers 31 sq miles. 'Downtown' is hard to describe and even harder to recognize sometimes. Generally, it is considered to be centered around Golden Heart Park on the corner of 1st Ave and Cushman St and spreads west to Cowles St, east to Noble St, north across the Chena River to the railroad depot and south along Cushman St as far as you want to walk. Cushman St is the closest thing Fairbanks has to a main street.

Several miles to the north-west is the university area, sprawling from the hilltop campus of UA-Fairbanks to the bars, restaurants and other businesses along University Ave and College Rd that make a living serving the college crowd. The city's other major commercial district is along Airport Way, between University Ave and Cushman St where you'll find most of the fast-food chain restaurants, malls, and Fred Meyers store as well as many motels.

If you arrive by train, motels, B&Bs and restaurants in the downtown area are a 15-minute walk away. If you arrive by bus, you can usually get dropped off either along the Airport Way stretch or downtown. Fly in and the only way to get out of the airport (see Getting Around) is by taxi. The downtown area is a $7 fare away.

Information

The main source of information is the Convention & Visitors Bureau Log Cabin (☎ 456-5774) which overlooks the Chena River near the corner of 1st Ave and Cushman St. The many services offered include a recorded telephone message (☎ 456-INFO) that lists the daily events and attractions in town; racks of brochures and information, courtesy phones to call up motels and B&Bs and a fairly knowledgeable staff. They also have a walking-tour map of the downtown area that begins and ends at the cabin and winds through Old Fairbanks, including the Line, the city's infamous red light district in the 1930s.

The log cabin is open daily during the summer from 8.30 am to 8 pm. Other visitor centers are in the Railroad Depot (open before and after each train arrival), Alaskaland and there's a limited one near the baggage claim of the Fairbanks International Airport.

Head to the Alaska Public Lands Information Center (☎ 451-7352) on Cushman St, two blocks south of the Chena River, for brochures, maps and information on state and national parks, wildlife refuges and recreation areas. You can also obtain shuttle bus coupons and campground reservations for Denali National Park 21 days in advance. Doing this can save a lot of headaches once you arrive at the park. But beware, the coupons and campground sites go on the first couple of days they are available. The center has exhibits and video programs on a variety of topics along with a small theatre that shows nature films at 10 am, noon and 4 pm and interpretive programs daily at 2 pm. Hours for the center are from 9 am to 6 pm daily during the summer.

Pools & Showers For those needing a shower and some clean clothes, there's B&D Laundromat (☎ 479-2696) in the Campus Corner Mall on the corner of College Rd and University Ave near UAF. It's open to 10.30 pm daily and showers are $2.50. In the downtown area head north of the Chena River to B&L Laundromat (☎ 452-1355), in the Eagle Plaza on Third St, a block east of Steese Hwy.

You can also get a shower and a swim at the four indoor pools in the Fairbanks area. Lathrop High School's Hamme Pool (☎ 459-1085 recording or 459-1086) is at 901 Airport Way, Mary Siah Recreation Center (☎ 459-1081 recording or 459-1082) is nearby at 1025 14th Ave, Wescott Pool (☎ 488-9401 recording or 488-9402) is on 8th Ave in North Pole and Patty Gym Pool (☎ 474-7205) in on the UAF campus. Swim sessions range from $2 to $3. Call for the exact times and different swims.

Things to See

Next to the visitor bureau is the **Golden**

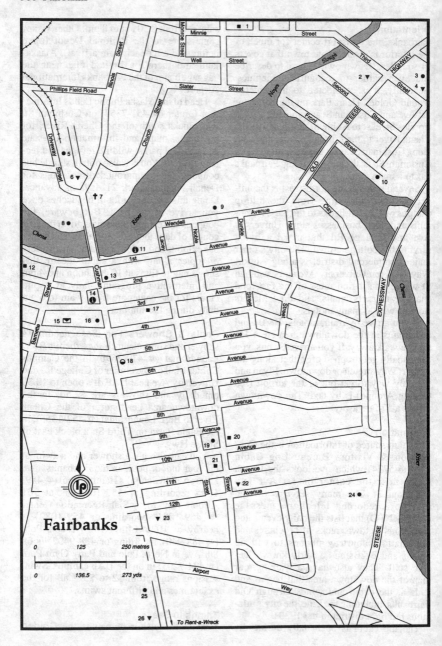

Fairbanks

| 0 | 125 | 250 metres |
| 0 | 136.5 | 273 yds |

Heart Plaza, a pleasant riverside park that is truly the center of the city. Showcased in the middle is the impressive bronze statue, *The Unknown First Family*, that was dedicated in 1986 and depicts an Inuit family struggling against all odds.

The **Immaculate Conception Church**, just across the Chena River Bridge from the plaza, was built in 1904 and was moved to its present location in 1911. The church is a national historic monument and features beautiful stained glass windows. **St Matthew's Episcopal Church**, at 1035 1st Ave, is a unique log church built in 1905 and rebuilt in 1947 immediately after it burned down.

The excellent **Noel Wien Library** (☎ 459-1020), on the corner of Airport Way and Cowles St, is a long walk from the visitor bureau (take the Metropolitan Area Commuter Service (MACS) Blue Line bus). Along with a large Alaskan section, the library has a selection of more than 50 paint-ings and prints, many by Alaskan artists, and a stone fireplace, so it can be a warm place to be on a rainy day. Hours are Monday to Wednesday from 10 am to 9 pm, Thursday and Friday from 10 am to 6 pm, Saturday from 10 am to 5 pm and Sunday from 1 to 5 pm.

Don't overlook Fairbanks' outdoor art as you walk around town. In 1979, local artists painted murals, ranging from abstract art to wildlife scenes, on 20 buildings as part of a beautification program. Most of them can be seen in a four-block section beginning at the visitor center.

Alaskaland The city's largest attraction is this 44-acre pioneer theme park created in 1967 to commemorate the 100th year of American possession of Alaska. Inside are such historical displays as the *Nenana*, a former sternwheeler of the Yukon River fleet, the railroad car that carried President Warren Harding to the golden spike ceremony in 1923, the home of Judge James Wickersham and a century-old carousel that still offers rides to the young and young-at-heart. Also inside is Gold Rush Town, a street of relocated log cabins with many of them converted into giftshops, the Pioneer Air Museum and the Pioneers Museum which depicts the settlement of Alaska.

At the back of the park, you'll find the Native Village Museum and Mining Valley, with displays of gold-mining equipment. A miniature 30-gauge train, the Crooked Creek & Whiskey Island Railroad, will take the kids around the park, while at night there's entertainment at the Palace Saloon and one of the best salmon bakes in the state.

The entrance to Alaskaland is off Airport Way near Peger Rd. A free shuttle bus, made to look like a train, makes hourly runs each day between the visitor center and major hotels to the park from 4 am to 9 pm. You can also reach the park on a MACS Blue Line bus. Alaskaland (☎ 459-1087) is open daily from 11 am to 9 pm. Some visitors find a theme park in Alaska a little corny, while others think it is an enjoyable step back into Alaska's history. Whatever you may think, you can't beat the price – there is no admission fee to enter.

University The University of Alaska-Fairbanks (UAF) is the original and main campus of the statewide college and an interesting place to wander around for an afternoon. It was incorporated in 1917 as the Alaska Agricultural College and School of Mines and began its first year with six students. Today it has more than 8,000 students and 70 degree programs despite the cold winters. The school is four miles west from the center of Fairbanks in a beautiful and unusual setting for a college; it is on a hill that overlooks the surrounding area, and on a clear day it is possible to view Mt McKinley from marked vantage points.

Stop at the Wood Center in the middle of campus first to pick up a map of the college. The building is the student center and general meeting place on campus, as it provides a cafeteria, pizza parlour, games rooms, outdoor patio, and an information desk for all activities on the campus. There is also a ride board here for those trying to hitchhike to other parts of the state or the Alcan. Nearby is Constitution Hall where territorial delegates drafted a constitution for statehood. Now it's the site of, among other things, the University Bookstore where UAF and Nanook (school mascot) sweatshirts can be purchased.

The main attraction of UAF is the excellent University Museum, which sits splendidly on top of a grassy ridge overlooking the Tanana Valley. The museum is generally regarded as one of the best in the state, rivaling the state museum in Juneau and definitely the best attraction in Fairbanks. Inside it is divided into regions of the state with each section examining the geology, history and unusual aspects of that area. Its most famous exhibit is Blue Babe, the fully restored 36,000-year-old bison that was found preserved intact, thanks to the permafrost, by Fairbanks-area miners. Even more impressive, however, is the state's largest public gold display with nuggets large enough to make you run out and buy a gold pan. The museum is open daily in the summer from 9 am to 7 pm during the summer and to 5 pm in May and September. The admission fee is $4 but well worth it if you have the better part of an afternoon to thoroughly enjoy each exhibit.

Ask at the Wood Center information desk for the when and wheres if you are interested in a free tour of the university. Also on Wednesday during the summer you can take in films on Alaska's mining heritage at 2 pm in the Brooks Building. The films include *Permafrost Frontier* and *Alaska's Gold* and admission is free.

On the outskirts of the campus is the Agricultural Experiment Farm (☎ 474-7627), where the university dabbles in growing vegetables of mythical proportions as well as such small grains as barley, wheat and oats that seem best suited for the short Alaskan growing seasons. Ironically because of the grain fields, the station is an ideal place to spot sandhill cranes, an endangered species in the rest of the country. The station is open for self-guided tours from Monday to Friday from 8 am to 8 pm and guided tours are offered at 2 pm on Friday. To reach the station take Tanana Dr west from the lower campus, bear left at the fork and continue for a mile on Sheep Creek Rd.

The UAF's Large Animal Research Station which focuses on unique adaptations of animals to a sub-Arctic climate, is off Farmer's Loop Rd. Best known as a musk ox farm, the station also features colonies of reindeer, caribou and experimental hybrids of the two called 'reinbou' and 'carideer'. Platforms outside the fenced pastures provide visitors with a place to view the herds but bring binoculars if you have them as the animals aren't always cooperative by grazing nearby. Viewing is free but tours, offered during the summer at 1.30 and 3 pm on Tuesday and Saturday, are $5 for adults. The station also has a gift shop that sells, among other things, raw qiviut from the musk ox. To reach the station head north from the campus on Farmers Loop Rd, turn left on Ballaine Rd and then left again on Yanovich Rd.

Because of its lofty perch, the campus is the best place in Fairbanks to view Mt McKinley on a clear day. A turn-off and marker defining the mountainous horizon is at the south end of Yukon Dr. You can also attend special shows at the Geophysical Institute if you're curious about the center of the earth. Call the UAF Relations office (☎ 474-7581) for more information and details. Reach the campus by taking MACS Red or Blue Line buses right to Wood Center.

Pipeline The closest spot to view the Trans-Alaska Pipeline, where some 1.5 million barrels of oil flow daily on their way to Valdez, is at the Alyeska Visitor Center, eight miles north of the city on Steese Hwy. The turn-off is at Goldstream Rd. The center is open from Memorial Day to Labor Day from 8 am to 6 pm daily.

Sled Dogs Like a handful of other towns in Alaska, Fairbanks bills itself as the dog mushing capital of the world. It's hard to argue with them. Snow and temperatures begin dropping in early October and sled dog racers enjoy a season that often exceeds five months. The city even has a 'musher's race track'. Jeff Studdert Racegrounds is at *Mile 4* on Farmers Loop and consists of a system of groomed trails ranging in length from three to more than 20 miles.

Fairbanks is the home of the North America Sled Dog Championships, a three-day event where mushers, some with teams as large as 20 dogs, compete in a series of races. This is not the Iditarod. Speed, not endurance, is the key as the races range from 20 to 30 miles. The Alaska Dog Mushers Association, which hosts the championships, recently moved its Dog Mushers' Museum (☎ 456-6874) downtown to Courthouse Square, just above the Public Lands Information Center. Open daily from 10 am to 6 pm during the summer, the museum features exhibits on sled dog racing, of course, and videos of races and dogs in training. Among the equipment on display are the sleds used by Susan Butcher and Martin Buser to win the Iditarod as well as the sled

Sonny Kinder used to become the first musher to run both the Iditarod and the Yukon Quest, a pair of 1000-mile races, in the same year.

Though the Iditarod is the best known dog-sled event in Alaska, it's only one of two long-distance races. The other is the Yukon Quest, a 1000-mile run between Fairbanks and Whitehorse that was organized in 1983 along many of the early trails used by trappers, miners and the postal service. Many will argue that the Quest is by far the tougher of the two races. Mushers climb four mountains more than 3000 feet in elevation and run along 200 miles of the frozen Yukon River. While the Iditarod has 25 checkpoints racers must stop at, the Quest has only six.

The race headquarters is at the Yukon Quest General Store (☎ 451-8985), just south of the visitor bureau on the corner of Cushman St and 2nd Ave. The store is open from 9 am to 7 pm daily and inside you'll find race memorabilia and souvenirs.

Gold Panning Those who are inspired by the huge gold nuggets at the University Museum, can try their own hand at panning in the Fairbanks area. If you're serious about panning, start out at Alaskan Prospectors & Geologists Supply (☎ 452-7398) which stocks and sells all the necessary equipment for recreational prospecting. The store also has books, pamphlets and video tapes to help you strike it rich and even offers panning instructions. Hours are from 10 am to 5 pm Monday to Saturday.

The next stop should be the Alaska Public Lands Information Center to research where you can pan and where you can't. Popular places in the area include Pedro Creek off the Elliott Hwy near the Felix Pedro monument and the Chatanika River off the Steese Hwy.

For the not so serious there are three gold mining attractions that include a part of panning as part of the tour. At *Mile 9* of Old Steese Hwy is Gold Dredge No 8 (☎ 457-6058), which includes gold panning as part of its $10 tour (see the Steese Hwy section).

Tours are held from Monday to Saturday from 9 am to 8 pm and on Sunday until 5 pm.

Further up the Steese Hwy at *Mile 27.5* is FE Gold Camp (☎ 389-2414) where you can pan at a trough for $5. Finally the Little El Dorado train (☎ 479-7613) has a two-hour train tour on a mile-long narrow gauge track that winds through a reconstructed mining camp and culminates with visitors panning gold-laden dirt and helping the owner work a sluice box. The train departs daily at 10 am and 2.30 pm from *Mile 1* of the Elliott Hwy and tickets are $20 per person.

The Northern Lights Fairbanks' best attraction is also its highest one; the aurora borealis or better known as the northern lights. In the simplest of all explanations, the aurora is a phenomenon of physics that takes place 50 to 200 miles above the earth's surface. Solar winds flow across the earth's upper atmosphere, hitting molecules of gas so they light up much like the high-vacuum electrical discharge of a neon sign.

What you end up with is a solar-powered light show where waving, curtain-like light streaks across the night sky. In the dead of winter, the aurora often fills the sky with the dancing light lasting for hours. Other nights 'the event', as many call it, lasts less than 10 minutes with the aurora spinning into a giant green ball and then quickly fading. Milky green and white are the most common colors, red auroras are the rarest. In 1958, the northern sky was so bloody with brilliant red auroras that fire trucks were rushing out to the hills surrounding Fairbanks only to discover their massive forest fires were just the northern lights.

This polar phenomenon has been seen as far south as Mexico but Fairbanks is the undisputed aurora capital. Whereas somebody in upper Minnesota might witness less than 20 events a year and someone in Anchorage will see around 150, in Fairbanks you can see the lights on an annual average of 240 nights. Heading north the number begins to decrease. At the North Pole, somebody would see the lights less than 100 nights a year.

From May to mid-August, there is too much daylight in Alaska to see 'an event'. But generally by the second week of August, the aurora begins to appear in the Interior and can be enjoyed if you're willing to be awake at 2 am. By mid-September the lights are knocking your socks off and people are already asking 'did you see the lights last night'?

The best viewing in Fairbanks is in the outlying hills to distance yourself from the city lights. UAF is also a good spot to view the lights and you'll find a permanent aurora exhibit in the University Museum while its Geophysical Institute sells a informative booklet, *Understanding the Aurora* for $1.25.

At Chatanika FE Gold Camp (☎ 389-2414), *Mile 27.5* of the Steese Hwy, there is a 'aurorium', a 40-foot octagonal building with a glass front and partial glass roof, built especially for staying warm while watching the lights. If you're not staying at the lodge, admission is $10.

If you're passing through June or July, you're out of luck. In that case you might want to head to Ester where Leroy Zimmerman presents his *The Crown of Light*. The photo symphony show features panoramic slides of the northern lights projected on a 30-foot screen and accompanied by classic music. It's the best view of the aurora you can get indoors. Shows are at 7 and 8 pm daily at the Firehouse Theater. Admission is $5.

Festivals & Events
Golden Days has grown to be Fairbanks' largest celebration of the summer. Staged during the third week of July, the festival commemorates Felix Pedro's discovery of gold with parades, games, booths, a boat parade on the Chena River and numerous special events such as the Hairy Legs Contest and locking up unsuspecting visitors in the Golden Days Jail. The summer solstice is also well celebrated on 21 June, when the sun shines gloriously for almost 23 hours. Events include foot races, speedboat races, art & craft booths and the traditional Midnight Sun

Midnight Sun

baseball game pitting the Goldpanners against another Alaska rival in a night game in which no artificial lights are used.

Around the second week in August, the Tanana Valley Fair is held at the fairgrounds on College Rd. Alaska's oldest fair features the usual sideshows, a rodeo, entertainment, livestock shows and large produce.

Places to Stay

Camping The only public campground in the Fairbanks area is the *Chena River State Campground* (51 sites, $12 fee), off University Ave just north of Airport Way. The campground has tables, toilets, fire places and water, and being right on the river, a boat launch. It can be reached by MACS Blue Line bus.

If you just want to park the van or RV and don't need facilities or a hook-up, there's *Alaskaland* (☎ 459-1087) on the corner of Airport Way and Peger Rd, where spending the night in its parking lot costs $7. Even better is the *Fred Meyers* store just west along Airport Way. It's become a common practice since the store arrived, for RVers and others to just spend the night in the parking lot. The store is open to 10 pm daily for restocking your supplies and there is no fee for spending the night.

Out in the university area is *Alfonsi Memorial Campground* (☎ 474-6027), in a wooded area in the north-west corner of the UAF campus. Sites are $4 a night and you can use the showers and laundry facilities in the basement of the Wood Center.

The other campgrounds in the city are private and charge from $15 to $20 per night to camp. They include the *Norlite Campground* (☎ 474-0206 or (800) 478-0206 in Alaska), on Peger Rd just south of Airport Way and the entrance to Alaskaland. Norlite has showers, laundry facilities, a small store and even a special $7.50 rate for single backpackers but its sites are open and close together. There's also *River's Edge RV Park* (☎ 474-0286 or (800) 288-9799), at 4140 Boat St near the corner of Airport Way and University Ave, which charges $15 for tents and $19 for hook-ups. The campground is on the Chena River and has showers, laundry facilities, shuttle service and has access to the city's bike trail system. Finally *Tanana Valley Campground* (☎ 456-7956), near the fairgrounds on College Rd, has $10 tent sites and free showers.

Hostels The best thing to happen to Fairbanks is the arrival of backpacker's hostels that offer inexpensive, bunkroom-type lodging. There is an official international hostel here but it's been on the move ever since the local chapter was opened in the early 1980s. Presently the *Fairbanks Hostel* (☎ 456-4159) is a home hostel with eight beds. You reach it from College Rd by turning south on Aurora Dr and then east on Willow St. The MACS Red line bus passes near it and the nightly fee is $6.

Even better is *College Bunkhouse* (☎ 479-2627), three blocks south of College Rd on Westwood Way. The place is clean, provides showers, kitchen, and a small picnic and barbecue area and is near both a MACS Red Line bus stop and a bike trail. There is also free coffee in the morning and the option of having a homecooked meal for around $5 to $10 extra. The rate for a bunk is $14.95 a night. Nearby is *Billie's Backpacking Hostel* (☎ 479-2034), on Mack Rd which intersects Westwood Way. This hostel has the same facilities plus a sun deck while the rate is $13.50 a night. Both places offer courtesy pick-up and drop-off to the airport and train station.

Also check out *Alaska Heritage Inn* (☎ 451-6587), an ex-bordello known as Ruthies Place, which has seven bunks for $12 a person, rooms that begin at $40 and tent sites in the backyard for $10 a night. The inn is in the south Fairbanks area at 1018 22nd Ave, off South Cushman St.

B&Bs Fairbanks has more than 100 B&Bs

and most of them have a brochure in the visitors center downtown. A courtesy phone there lets you check who has a room and who's filled for the night. The Fairbanks Association of Bed & Breakfast also publishes a brochure with more than 30 members listed in it and a map showing their locations. Pick it up at the visitors center or write in advance to the Fairbanks Association of Bed & Breakfast, PO Box 73334, Fairbanks, AK 99707.

If you're arriving by train or bus, there are several downtown places that are within easy walking distance of the depot. On the corner of Cowles St and 4th Ave, there is *Cowles Street B&B* (☎ 452-5252) and next door *Ah, Rose Marie* (☎ 456-2040). Between them they have nine rooms and will refer guests back and forth to find a bed. Both places include a full breakfast though Cowles St B&B is slightly more affordable with singles/doubles that start at $50/60. Further to the west is *Thompson's Bed & Breakfast* (☎ 452-5787) at 1315 Sixth Ave. Singles/doubles are $35/$45 and the hosts are friendly.

If you have a vehicle, try the *North Woods Lodge* (☎ 479-5300) reached from the Pump House Rd on Chena Pump Rd by heading north on Roland Rd and then east on Chena Hills Dr. The variety of rooms in the log lodge includes bedrooms that begin at $30, a sleeping loft with two double beds for $50 a night and a bedroom with a jacuzzi bath tub for $75. There is also a small cabin with twin beds that rents as a single for $25 a night and as a double for $40.

Hotels Most hotel/motel rooms in Fairbanks are not as expensive as those in Anchorage but still be prepared to pay $70 per night during the summer. The few with reasonable rates are less than desirable or are a considerable distance from the city center. With the handful of places clustered downtown on the east side of Cushman St check out the room before handing over your money.

The cheapest in the downtown area is the *Fairbanks Hotel* (☎ 456-6440) at 3rd Ave. But even with singles at $45, I would think twice before staying there. A slightly better choice downtown is *Alaskan Motor Inn* (☎ 452-4800) at 419 4th Ave. Rooms begin at $59 and the ones on the top floor are the best. The *Tamarac Inn* (☎ 456-6406), on the north side of the Chena River, is within easy walking distance from the railroad depot at 252 Minnie St. Singles/doubles cost $62/68; some units have cooking facilities.

By heading away from the city center you can find better rates and cleaner rooms. Try *Noah's Rainbow Inn* (☎ 474-3666) at 700 Fairbanks St, reached by heading west on Geist Rd from University Ave or by jumping on the MACS Blue Line. Rooms are small but begin at $35 a night and the inn features shared baths and kitchen as well as having a coin-operated laundry on site. The *Golden North Motel* (☎ 479-6201 or (800) 447-1910) at 4888 Airport Way has rooms with cable TV, rolls and coffee in the office and free van service within the city. Rooms tend to be on the small side and rates in the summer begin at $69. Closer to the downtown area at 1909 Airport Way is *Super 8 Motel* (☎ 451-8888) with clean, big rooms that cost $86/99 a single/double.

Finally, if you've just spent 10 days in the Bush and want to splurge, check into the *Bridgewater Hotel* (☎ 452-6661), downtown at 723 1st Ave. The hotel was totally renovated and is now the one of the nicest in Fairbanks and certainly has the best location overlooking the Chena River. Singles/doubles cost $100/110 a night.

Places to Eat

Downtown A relatively inexpensive breakfast, two eggs and toast for $4, a hamburger or even dinner is available at the grill in *Woolworth's* at 302 Cushman St. If you need to catch the morning train, there's *June's Cafe*, right in front of the railroad depot on Illinois Ave for good lunch-counter breakfasts served anytime and home-made soup. The café opens up at 6 am. Nearby on the north side of the Chena River is *Souvlaki* at 112 North Turner for gyros, spinach cheese pie, stuffed grape leaves and lunch specials that start at $4.75.

More interesting places include *Soapy Smith's* at 543 2nd Ave. Despite the fact that Smith is a Skagway character and never set foot in Fairbanks, the restaurant has good hamburgers, including a half-pounder for $6, as well as deli sandwiches and salads served in a saloon atmosphere. The full menu is often posted in Golden Heart Plaza. Next door to Bridgewater Hotel on 1st Ave but with an entrance on 2nd Ave is *Gambardella's Pasta Bella*, for home-made pasta dinners that begin at $10 as well as pizza. Its outdoor café is a delight during Fairbanks' long summer days. For your espresso-fix, there's *Café de Paris* on the north side of the Chena River, just west of the Daily News Miner at 801 Pioneer Rd. Open from 11 am to 3 pm, the café is in a 65-year-old home featuring a large outdoor deck.

By walking 15 minutes south on Cushman St, you'll reach several more restaurants. *Peking Gardens* is on the corner of 12th and Noble St and has a daily lunch buffet special for $7 and dinners ranging from $8 to $10. Nearby on Gaffney Rd, just off Cushman St is *Carr's*, the city's best supermarket that is open 24 hours. Besides produce and groceries, you'll find an excellent salad and soup bar priced at $3.29 a pound as well as a deli, bakery and their 'Orient Express' counter. The store also has seating inside and outside on an enclosed deck. It's the best deal in town, especially if you do a load of washing – there's a laundromat right across the street.

Airport Way This is Fairbanks' answer to your craving for fast food just like you eat at home. Between Cushman St and University Ave, you have McDonald's, Pizza Hut with a lunch buffet, Sizzler's, Skipper's Seafood with its own $6 lunch buffet, Burger King, and a Denny's that will even give you a souvenir card saying you ate in the 'Farthest North Denny's in the World'. Hungry souls should take in the *Alaskaland Salmon Bake* (free shuttle bus from major hotels, including the Bridgewater), where for $17 you not only get grilled salmon but halibut, spareribs and salad.

Along Airport Way as well as the Bentley

Mall and South Cushman St is the *Food Factory* which has cheap subs and other sandwiches that can be enjoyed with your favorite beer. The best Mexican restaurant is *Los Amigos*, near the corner of 28th Ave and Cushman St, south of Airport Way.

University Area More food chains can be found around UA-Fairbanks area but also some unique eateries. *Hot Licks* on the corner of College Rd and University Ave has delicious home-made ice cream at $2 a scoop, home-made soups and cinnamon rolls and an espresso bar. It's open until 11 pm from Monday to Saturday for that late night cappuccino. Below it is *Whole Earth Grocery & Deli* for natural foods, organic produce and a lunch menu of vegie sandwiches and salads.

Just south on University Ave you can have good sourdough pancakes anytime of the day at *Sam's Sourdough Cafe* as well as lunch and dinner that can be enjoyed in an outdoor eating area. Across the street is *Hunan Garden* in the old Dairy Queen. Its all-you-can-eat lunch buffet is only $5.95 and dinners range from $6 to $8. To the west at the fairgrounds on College Rd the *Tanana Valley Farmer's Market* is held throughout much of the summer from noon to 5 pm on Wednesday and 9 am to 4 pm on Saturday. Come in late August and you can buy a 20-pound cabbage, enough for a month's supply of coleslaw.

Fine Dining The best place around town to turn dinner into an evening is the *Pumphouse* (☎ 479-8452), two miles from downtown on Chena Pump Rd. The Pumphouse, once used in the gold-mining era, is now a national historical site that houses a restaurant and saloon. The atmosphere is classic gold rush; inside and out there are artefacts and relics from the city's mining era. Dinners cost from $17 to $25, or you can go there simply to enjoy a drink while taking in the boat traffic on the Chena River. The MACS Blue Line bus includes the restaurant in its run.

Another enjoyable spot for fine dining is *Two Rivers Lodge* (☎ 488-6815), 16 miles

out on Chena Hot Springs Rd. The lodge offers a rustic décor in a natural setting away from town with the drive out being almost as pleasant as the meal itself. If you don't have a car, call about shuttle bus service.

Entertainment

The bar rooms are the best place to meet locals in Fairbanks, and it seems you never have to travel far to find one. Rowdy saloons that are throwbacks from the mining days are the area's specialty. The *Palace Saloon* (☎ 456-5960) at Alaskaland is alive at night with honky-tonk piano, turn-of-the-century can-can dancers and other acts in the 'Golden Heart Revue' performed on its large stage. Show time is at 8 pm nightly and admission is $9.50.

The *Malemute Saloon*, seven miles west of Fairbanks in Ester, also offers music, skits and vaudeville acts and its ritual of reading Robert Service poetry. The bar is a classic while the show is perhaps one of the best locally produced acts in Alaska. They'll have you laughing in the sawdust by the end of the evening. Showtime is at 9 pm daily and during July a second show is added at 7 pm. Admission is $9 per person. There's bus transport from Fairbanks that stops at the visitors center and major hotels, including the Bridgewater. Or you can make it an evening by booking a room and a meal at the Cripple Creek Hotel (see Ester in the Interior chapter).

Other lively establishments on the outskirts of Fairbanks are *Senator's Saloon* at the Pumphouse on Chena Pump Rd; the new *Crazy Loon Saloon* on Parks Hwy just north of Ester; and the *Howling Dog Saloon* in Fox, at the intersection of the Steese and Elliott highways 12 miles north of the city center. All these places have live music or entertainment. The Howling Dog has rock & roll bands and as well as volleyball games and horseshoes played out the back under the midnight sun.

If you're here in September, live music and a college atmosphere are found at the *University Pub* in the Wood Center at UAF once classes are in session. In the city center, try *The Big I Bar*, the local hang-out for city workers and reporters from the *Daily News-Miner*. The bar is north of the Chena River near the railroad depot on North Turner Rd. Another spot to meet locals is *LA*, the bar downstairs from Los Amigos restaurant near the corner of 28th Ave and Cushman St south of Airport Way.

Have no wheels? Call Go Shuttle Service (☎ 474-3847) which runs a 'Alaska Saloon Tour'. Is this Fairbanks or what? The tour lasts from 9.30 pm to 1.30 am and covers the Howling Dog, Crazy Loon Saloon and Fox Roadhouse. The cost is $12 per person and they need a minimum of five drinkers to run it – not usually a problem in Fairbanks.

The Goldpanners baseball team is Fairbanks' entry in a semipro league made up of teams of top college and amateur players from around the country which compete each summer. More than 80 professionals, including Tom Seaver, Dave Winfield and Barry Bonds, have played in what began as an all-Alaska baseball league but now includes teams from Hawaii, Nevada and other states as well. Games are played at Growden Memorial Park on the corner of Wilbur St and 2nd Ave. Games start at 7.30 pm.

Want a little culture in the Far North? Then check out the *Fairbanks Shakespeare Theatre* (☎ 457-POET). During July the group performs a Shakespeare classic downtown at the Riverfront Field, on the north side of Chena River behind the Immaculate Conception Church, with the audience arriving with lawn chairs, blankets or sleeping bags. Performances are staged on various days throughout the month and begin at 9 pm. Tickets are $10 per person.

Fairbanks' largest movie house is *Goldstream Cinema* (☎ 456-5113), on the corner of Airport Way and Lathrop St, and features eight screens.

Hiking

Unlike Anchorage or Juneau, Fairbanks does not have outstanding hiking on its door step. The best trail for an extended backpacking trip is the impressive **Pinnell Mountain Trail**

at *Mile 85.5* and *Mile 107.3* of Steese Hwy (see the Trekking section in the Wilderness chapter for information on the trails). For a variety of long and short hikes head to the Chena River Recreation Area. Neither area, however, is served by public transportation though hitching to the state recreation area would be fairly easy.

For information on Pinnell Mountain Trail or Summit Trail, part of the White Mountain Trail system, stop at the Public Lands Information Center or the Bureau of Land Management office (☎ 474-2200) on the corner of Airport Way and University Ave. Practically next door to the BLM office is Division of Parks for the Alaska Natural Resources (☎ 451-2695) for information on the Chena River Recreation Area.

You can pick up topographical maps at the Public Lands Information Center but they handle primarily the larger scale 1:250,000 maps. For 1:63,000 maps for anywhere in Alaska stop by the US Geological Survey office (☎ 456-0244) in the Federal Building at 101 12 St, east of Cushman St. Hours are from 8 am to 5 pm Monday to Friday.

Creamer's Field Trail A self-guided, two-mile trail winds through Creamer's Field Migratory Wildlife Refuge, an old dairy farm that has since become an Audubon bird-lover's paradise, as more than 100 species of bird pass through each year. The refuge is at 1300 College Rd (MACS Red Line bus) and the trailhead is in the parking lot adjacent to the Alaska Department of Fish & Game office (☎ 452-1531), where trail guides are available. The trail is mostly boardwalk with an observation tower along the way and lots of bugs. The flocks of geese, ducks and swans move onto nesting grounds by late May but sandhill cranes can be spotted throughout the summer.

Chena Lakes Recreation Area This facility opened in 1984 as the last phase of an Army Corps of Engineers flood control project prompted by the Chena River's flooding of Fairbanks in 1967. Two separate parks, Chena River and Chena Lakes, make up the recreational area which is 18 miles southeast from Fairbanks past North Pole, off the Laurance Rd exit of Richardson Hwy. The Chena River park contains a 2.5-mile self-guided nature trail. The Chena Lakes park offers swimming as well as canoe, sailboat and paddle-boat rentals. Between the two parks there are three campground loops providing 78 sites. The day-use fee is $3 and the overnight camping fee is $6.

Granite Tors Trail Along with the Chena Dome Trail, a 29-mile backpacking adventure (see the Wilderness chapter for a description), there are several other good treks in Chena River State Recreation Area. The Granite Tors Trail is a 15-mile loop that provides access into the alpine area and to the unusual rock formations. The trailhead is across the road from Tors Trail State Campground, at *Mile 39* of the Chena Hot Springs Rd, and can be reached by following the levee for a short distance on the west side of the stream.

Tors are isolated pinnacles of granite popping out of the tundra. The first set of tors is six miles from the trailhead; the best group lies two miles further along the trail. The entire hike is a five to eight-hour trek in which you gain 2500 feet in altitude.

Angel Rocks Trail This 3.5-mile loop trail leads to Angel Rocks, large granite outcrops near the north boundary of the Chena Recreation Area. It's an easy day hike with the rocks less than two miles from the road. The posted trailhead is just south of a rest area at *Mile 49* of the Chena Hot Springs Rd. Practically across the street is southern trailhead for the Chena Dome Trail.

Paddling
Fairbanks offers a wide variety of canoeing opportunities, both leisurely afternoon paddles and overnight trips, into the surrounding area. There are also several places to rent boats. The most convenient is 7 Bridges Boats & Bikes (☎ 479-0751), downtown off Cushman St just on the north side of the Chena River. They also have boats at

Alaska's 7 Gables B&B, just off the river at 4312 Birch Lane. They provide both canoes and a pick-up and drop-off service. Canoes are $30 a day, transport is a $1 a mile. You can even arrange to paddle down the Chena River and bike back to the downtown area.

There's also Independent Rental (☎ 456-6595), at 2020 South Cushman St, which rents canoes for $30 a day and $150 a week, and Beaver Sports (☎ 479-2494) which, at 3480 College Rd, is no longer conveniently located near water. For help in transportation, you can check out Backcountry Logistical Services (☎ 457-7606) at 469 Goldmine Trail.

Around Town An afternoon can be spent paddling the Chena River; the mild currents let you paddle upstream as well as down. You can launch a canoe from almost any bridge crossing the river, including the Graehl Landing near the north side of Steese Hwy where locals like to paddle upstream and then float back down.

From either of the 7 Bridges Boats & Bikes locations you can drop a canoe in the Chena River, head downstream and into the quiet Noyes Slough and complete the loop by paddling east back into the river. The round trip is a 13-mile journey.

Chena & Tanana Rivers Those looking for an overnight, or even longer paddle, should find out about a float down the Chena River from the Chena River Hot Springs Rd east of Fairbanks (see the Paddling section in the Wilderness chapter) or a pleasant two-day trip down the Tanana River. The popular Tanana River trip usually begins from the end of Chena Pump Rd and finishes in the town of Nenana, where it is possible to return with your canoe to Fairbanks on the Alaska Railroad. This 60-mile trip can be done in a single day but would require 10 to 12 hours of paddling.

Chatanika River The Chatanika River can be paddled for 28 miles west from Cripple Creek BLM Campground at *Mile 60* of Steese Hwy. The river runs parallel to the road to Chatanika River State Campground at *Mile 39*. From here, the trip can be extended another 17 miles to a bridge at *Mile 11* of Elliott Hwy.

The river is not a difficult paddle but this trip requires considerable driving because you have to shuttle boats and people between Fairbanks and the two highways. Many locals get around this by only paddling the upper portion of the river that parallels Steese Hwy and by leaving a bicycle chained at the end of the route so they can get back to their car.

Cabins

Fred Blixt Cabin This public-use cabin is off *Mile 62* of Elliott Hwy, 10 miles before the junction with Dalton Hwy. A short spur leads from the road to the cabin, which should be reserved in advance through the BLM office (☎ 474-2200) in Fairbanks. The rental fee is $20 per night.

Cripple Creek Cabin This old trapper's cabin, renovated by the BLM in 1972, is at *Mile 60.5* of Steese Hwy. It is between the highway and the Chatanika River and is reached by a short trail. The cabin, available only from mid-August to mid-May, does not offer a truly isolated setting because Cripple Creek Campground and a YCC Camp are nearby. Still, the surrounding area is scenic. The rental fee is $20 and the cabin should be reserved in advance through the Fairbanks BLM office.

Lee's Cabin In the White Mountains National Recreation Area, the relatively new Lee's Cabin is accessed from the Wickersham Creek Trail at *Mile 28* of the Elliott Hwy. It's a seven-mile hike in to the cabin, which features a large picture window overlooking the White Mountains and a loft to comfortably sleep eight people. Rental fee is $25 and the BLM (☎ 474-2250) is the place to reserve it in advance.

Guiding Companies

Check the Wilderness chapter for a list of the many outfitters based in the Fairbanks area.

For a mild float, call Chena River Rafts (☎ 479-0007), which runs a three-hour raft trip through Fairbanks on the Chena River for $25 per person and a far more scenic one on the Upper Chena River for $45 which includes lunch and fishing for grayling.

Getting There & Away

Air The Fairbanks International Airport was expanded in 1984 and serves as the gateway for supplies and travelers heading into the Brooks Range and Arctic Alaska. The airport is almost four miles south-west of the city off Airport Way.

Alaska Airlines (☎ 474-0481) provides eight daily flights to Anchorage, where there are connections to the rest of the state, as well as a direct flight from Fairbanks to Seattle. The one-way standard fare (the most expensive) to Anchorage is normally around $190 but air fare wars have pushed it to as low as $55 at times. The other intrastate airline is MarkAir (☎ (800) 478-0800), though you have to wonder how long the financially troubled carrier will remain flying. Delta Air Lines (☎ (800) 221-1212) also offers a handful of flights between the two cities while Air North Canada (☎ 474-3999) provides service to Dawson City with a connecting flight to Whitehorse.

For travel into Arctic Alaska, there's Frontier Flying Service (☎ 474-0014) and Larry's Flying Service (☎ 474-9169) with offices/terminals next door to each other off University Ave on the east side of the airport. There's a regularly scheduled flight to more than 30 villages, including Nome, Kotzebue and Galena. The round-trip fare to Bettles, to access Gates of the Arctic National Park, costs from $180 to $200; to Fort Yukon $165 and Nome $400.

Bus From Fairbanks, Alaskon Express (☎ 452-2843) stops at Delta Junction, Tok and then overnights at Beaver Creek in the Yukon. The next day you can make connections onto Haines or Whitehorse. Buses depart from the Westmark-Fairbanks at 820 Noble St in the city center at 9 am Sunday, Monday, Wednesday and Friday during the summer. One-way fare from Fairbanks to Delta Junction is $45, to Tok $60 and to Haines $165 (lodging at Beaver Creek is not included).

Alaska Direct Busline (☎ (800) 770-6652) also makes the run to Haines from Fairbanks with a bus departing at 9 am on Monday, Wednesday and Saturday and reaching the Southeast that night around midnight. They seem to move their pick-up point every summer so call them to find out what hotel they are presently working out of. One-way fare to Haines is $150, to Whitehorse $120.

Van service is the cheapest way to reach Denali National Park other than hitching. Fireweed Express (☎ 488-7928) offers daily transport to the park with a van departing the visitors center at 8 am and Hot Licks coffee shop at Campus Corners on College Rd and University Ave at 8.15 am. The van arrives at the park's Visitor Access Center at 10.30 am, two hours before the train does. One-way fare is $25, round-trip $45. It also connects with the Moon Bay Express van at Denali, meaning you can travel from Fairbanks to Anchorage for $60. Also offering van service is Denali Express (☎ (800) 327-7651), which departs Fairbanks at 6 am and arrives at the park at 8.15 pm but one-way fare is $45.

Train The Alaska Railroad (☎ 456-4155) has an express train that departs Fairbanks daily at 8.30 am from late May to mid-September. The train reaches Denali National Park around noon and Anchorage at 8.30 pm. The railroad depot is at 280 North Cushman St, a short walk from the Chena River. The one-way fare to Denali National Park is $45 and to Anchorage $120. If you plan to take the train, arrive at the depot a few minutes early to take in the model train that is maintained by the Tanana Valley Railroad Club. It's as extensive a model train as you'll see, complete with mountains, tunnels, entire towns and, this being Alaska, a glacier. The display fills a room of its own at the depot.

Hitchhiking Thumbing is made much easier by jumping on a MACS bus first. Hitchhikers heading towards Denali National Park and Anchorage on George Parks Hwy should take the Blue Line bus and get off on the corner of Geist St and the George Parks Hwy. To head down Richardson Hwy towards Delta Junction and the Alcan, jump on the Green Line Bus for the Santa Claus House on Richardson Hwy in North Pole.

Getting Around
To/From the Airport There's no Metropolitan Area Commuter Service (MACS) bus to the airport; the closest stop is a 1.5-mile hike to the University Center on the corner of Airport Way and University Ave. GO Shuttle Service (☎ 474-3847) will transport you from the airport to anywhere in the city for $5 but needs a minimum of three people. A taxi from the airport to downtown costs around $7.

Bus MACS provides local bus transport in the Fairbanks area from 6.25 am to 7.45 pm Monday to Friday with limited services on Saturday and none on Sunday. Transit Park, on the corner of Cushman St and 5th Ave, is the central terminal for the system as all buses pass through here. There are now three runs with a Green Line heading from the Transit Park downtown out to North Pole on Richardson Hwy. The Blue Line runs from the Transit Park west via Airport Way and the university. The Red Line goes from the hospital on the south side of Airport Way, through the city and to the university via College Rd.

The fare is $1.50, although you can purchase an unlimited day pass for $3. For more information call the Transit Hotline (☎ 459-1011) which gives daily bus information.

There is also the Alaskaland Tram which runs daily from 11.30 am to 9 pm and passes the visitor center and a few of the major hotels (Westmark Inn, Golden Nugget) every hour. It heads west along 1st Ave to Alaskaland before heading back to the city center along Airport Way and Cushman St. It's limited transport but it's free.

Car Rental For two or three travelers, often splitting the cost of a used-car rental is the best and the cheapest way of getting around the city and outlying areas such as Chena Hot Springs. What the operators won't let you do, however, is drive the rough Steese, Elliott or Dalton highways, to visit such places as the Circle or Manley Hot Springs. In fact you might have to search around to find anybody that will take a rental 'out the road'.

Rent-A-Wreck (☎ 452-1606) at 2105 Cushman St, south of Airport Way, has compacts for $38 per day with 100 free miles. Likewise Allstar Rent-A-Car (☎ 479-4229), at 4415 Airport Way just north of the airport, has cars for the same rate and provides courtesy pick-up at major hotels. You can also check with Affordable Car Rental (☎ 452-4279) and U-Save Auto Rental, at Chevron Stations at 3245 College Rd (☎ 479-7060) and near downtown at 333 Illinois St, (☎ 452-4236) before calling the expensive national companies. Like in most other cities in Alaska, it's hard to score a rental car in Fairbanks at the last minute.

Bicycle Like so many other towns, Fairbanks is well on its way to putting together a fine network of posted bike routes in and around the city. Bike paths begin at 1st Ave and Cushman St and extend all the way past Alaskaland, across the Chena River and to UAF and Parks Hwy. Shoulder bikeways lead you out of town.

You can pick up a free *Fairbanks Area Bicycle Map* at the visitors center and then cross the Chena River and rent a single or 10-speed from 7 Bridges Boats & Bikes (☎ 479-0751) for $10 a day. One of the more popular rides is to head north on Illinois St and then loop around on College Rd and Farmers Loop Rd for a ride of 17 miles.

Tours Both Gray Line, which leaves from the Westmark Fairbanks (☎ 452-2843), and Alaska Sightseeing, which departs from the Captain Bartlett Hotel (☎ 452-8518), offer a three-hour city tour for $22 that includes the university, Gold Dredge No 8 on Steese Hwy and the Trans-Alaska Pipeline. The tour is scheduled twice daily at 9 am and 2.30 pm. For a more personal tour, or to escape the hoard of Grayline senior citizens, call Raven Tours (☎ 452-8459). The small, personally guided tours can include what you really want to see, whether it's gold camps, hot springs or dog teams.

You can travel the Chena River on the historic sternwheeler Discovery (☎ 479-6673) if you're up to parting with $34 for the four-hour trip. Along the way the boat stops at a replica of an Athabascan village and there's a demonstration with a dog musher and her team. The boat departs twice daily at 8.45 am and 2 pm in the summer from Discovery Landing, off the Dale Rd exit at *Mile 4.5* of Airport Way. Alaska Yukon Sternwheeler Co (☎ 455-4320) is another sternwheeler option. The company began operating on the Yukon River in 1994 with runs between Dawson City and Circle City, transfering passengers in and out of Fairbanks by bus and plane (see Circle City following).

If for some strange reason you're not heading south but still want to experience Denali National Park, the Alaska Railroad (☎ 456-4155) has an overnight excursion to the park. The fare is $199 per person, based on double occupancy, and includes a return ticket, accommodation for one night and a three-hour tour along the park road.

The Arctic Circle may be an imaginary line, but it's fast becoming one of Fairbanks' biggest draws. Small air-charter companies are now doing booming business flying travelers across the Arctic Circle, landing in a small village for an hour or two and then heading back. Fort Yukon is probably the most popular destination for such a quick trip. Larry's Flying Service (☎ 474-9169) offers a round-trip flight and a one-hour tour of the village for $178 per person. Along the way they point out the Arctic Circle, which has been conveniently clear-cut so you can't miss it, and then award you with a certificate stating that you have indeed crossed it.

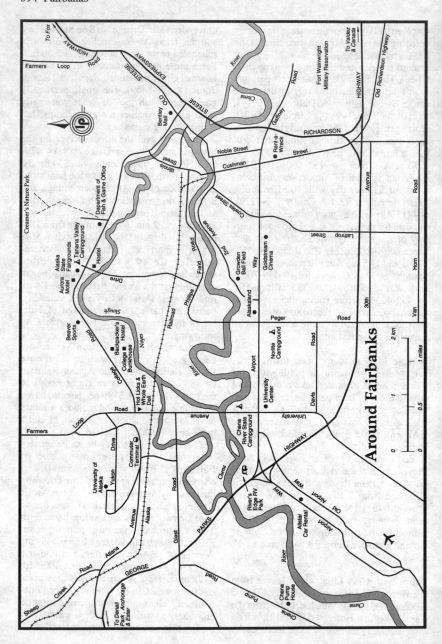

Around Fairbanks

Around Fairbanks

NORTH POLE

Back in the 1940s, a group of residents was kicking around names for their crossroad hamlet south-east of Fairbanks and somehow 'Mosquito Junction' just wasn't very appealing. So they settled on North Pole, Alaska. While the name hasn't brought in any Fortune 500 companies, a steady stream of camera-toting tourists has been wandering through ever since.

Today the funky little town keeps up the Christmas theme year-round with holiday decorations and trimmings even if it's 80 °F in July. You can wander down streets named Kris Kringle Dr and Mistletoe Lane or do your wash at Santa's Suds Laundromat. The town comes alive in December when radio stations from around the world call City Hall with disc jockeys asking what the tempera-ture is or if 'Santa Claus really lives there'? And at the North Pole Post Office, at 325 South Santa Claus Lane, bundles of letters and cards arrive from people wanting the North Pole postmark on their Christmas cards. Hundreds of other items of mail are simply addressed to 'Santa Claus, North Pole, Alaska'.

The biggest attraction in town is **Santa Claus House**, a sprawling barn-like store that claims to be the 'largest theme gift shop in Alaska'. Here you'll find endless aisles of Christmas ornaments and toys, the largest Santa in the world and the 'North Pole' a candy-striped post. It's on the Richardson Hwy between the North Pole exits and is open until 8 pm daily. There's also **Jesus Town**, a sod-roofed log cabin community that surrounds KJNP, the 'Gospel Station at the Top of the Nation', off the Richardson Hwy off Mission Rd. A half-mile to the north is the Chamber of Commerce Log Cabin

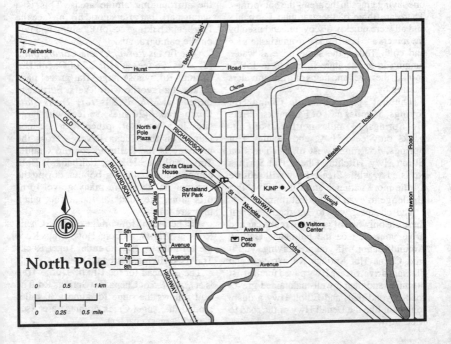

North Pole

Writing to Santa

Want to send a letter to Santa? The correct mailing address is: Santa Claus, North Pole, AK 99705-9998. Every December the town's small post office gets swamped with such letters as well as Christmas cards from people who want the North Pole postmark.

Most of the Santa letters are given to Happiness Inc, an organization of children at North Pole Middle School who try to send off answers to children around the world. In 1992, they answered more than 10,000 letters. There are also Santa response centers in Anchorage and Juneau. ■

(☎ 488-2242) for information while free camping is available at the city's 5th Ave Campground.

The town is about 15 minutes south of Fairbanks and reached on the MACS Green Line. Gimmicky? Sure, but if you have nothing else to do on an afternoon in Fairbanks, why not?

HOT SPRINGS

Back around the turn of the century, when gold prospectors were stooping in near-freezing creeks panning for gold, there was one saving grace in the area – the hot springs. There are three of them around Fairbanks and all were quickly discovered and used by the miners as a brief escape from Alaska's ice and cold. Today, the same mineral water, ranging in temperature from 120 to 150°F, soothes the aches and pains of frigid travelers passing by.

The hot springs include Chena Hot Springs, 56 miles east of Fairbanks; Circle Hot Springs, 135 miles north-east of Fairbanks on Steese Hwy; and Manley Hot Springs, 152 miles west of Fairbanks on Elliott Hwy. Hitching Chena Hot Springs Rd is easy, while Steese Hwy will require a little more patience and Elliott Hwy is a challenge to even the hottest thumb.

The cheapest way to get there, even if there are only two of you, is to rent a car and drive yourself (see the Fairbanks Getting Around section). If you are driving, you'll find Chena Hot Springs Rd a paved and pleasant drive; Steese Hwy paved for the first 40 miles and then a well-maintained gravel road beyond that; and Elliott Hwy a dusty long haul like the Denali Hwy or the road to McCarthy.

CHENA HOT SPRINGS RD

Chena Hot Springs Rd extends 56 miles east off Steese Hwy to the hot springs of the same name. The road is paved and in good condition. The resort, the closest of the three hot-spring resorts to Fairbanks, is also the most developed as it has been turned into a year-round facility offering downhill skiing in the winter.

From *Mile 26* to *Mile 51*, the road passes through the middle of the **Chena River State Recreation Area**, a 254,080-acre preserve containing the river valley and the surrounding alpine areas. This is a scenic park that offers good hiking (see the Fairbanks Hiking section), fishing and two public campgrounds.

The first is *Rosehip State Campground* (25 sites, $6 fee) at *Mile 27* of Chena Hot Springs Rd, whose large, flat gravel pads makes it a favorite with RVers. Further to the east at *Mile 39.5* is *Tors Trails State Campground* (20 sites, $6 fee) with large sites in a stand of spruce with a canoe launch on the Chena River. Across the highway is the trailhead for the Granite Tors Trail (see Hiking, Fairbanks). Both campgrounds tend to be popular during the summer but there are many gravel turn-offs along the road for the nights when they are full.

Just before the fifth bridge over the Chena River at *Mile 49* of Chena Hot Springs Rd is the turn-off for the 3.5-mile Angel Rocks Trail (see Hiking, Fairbanks).

The trailhead for the **Chena Dome Trail** is at *Mile 50.5* of Chena Hot Springs Rd. The trail follows the ridge for almost 30 miles around the Angel Creek drainage area (see the Wilderness chapter).

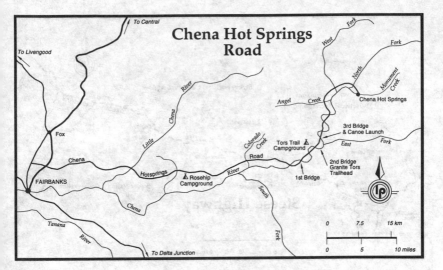

Chena Hot Springs Road

To Central
To Livengood
To Delta Junction
West Fork
Fork
North Fork
Monument Creek
Chena Hot Springs
Angel Creek
3rd Bridge & Canoe Launch
East Fork
Tors Trail Campground
Colorado Creek
Road
2nd Bridge Granite Tors Trailhead
1st Bridge
Rosehip Campground
River
Chena
Fox
Little
Chena
Hotsprings
FAIRBANKS
Chena
Tanana
River
South Fork

0   7.5   15 km
0   5   10 miles

Chena Hot Springs

At the end of the Chena Hot Springs Rd is the Chena Hot Springs Resort (☎ 452-7867), which recently updated its already fine facilities. The springs themselves were discovered by gold miners in 1905 and first reported by the US Geological Survey field teams two years later. By 1912, Chena Hot Springs was the premier place to soak for residents in the booming town of Fairbanks. It still is. The busy season for this resort, by far, is winter and often during midweek in the summer you can score on some impressive 'slow season discounts'.

The springs are at the center of a 40-sq mile geothermal area and produce a steady stream of water that's so hot, at 156°F, it must be cooled before you can even think about a soak. The most popular activity is hot-tub soaking, done indoors where there are two jacuzzis, a pool and a hot (very hot) tub. The resort has a restaurant, a bar and a huge fireplace in the lounge. Hotel rooms and rustic cabins begin at $80 per couple per night.

If the accommodation seems highly priced, take heart. If there are a lot of you, large cabins with sleeping lofts holding up to

10 people are $110 a night. If there are only one or two of you, head for the campground, where a site is $8 per night. The use of the hot tubs is extra for campers; $8 for unlimited day use; $6 after 7 pm.

Getting There & Away

Hitchhiking is not the grand effort it is on the Elliott Hwy because of the heavy summer usage of the Chena River State Recreation Area. Or call the resort for its shuttle van service. Round-trip transport is $50 per person, with a minimum of two persons per trip.

STEESE HWY

Circle Hot Springs lies off the 162-mile long Steese Hwy, once a miner's trail, where today you can still see the signs of old mining camps as well as new ones. The road is paved for the first 44 miles and then consists of a good gravel base to Central then in the final 30 miles narrows and becomes considerably rougher. The excellent scenery along the highway and the good accommodations at Circle Hot Springs make this side trip well worth the time and money.

The Steese Hwy starts in Fairbanks, *Mile*

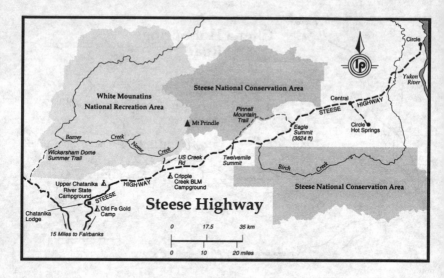

0, at the junction of Airport Way and Richardson Hwy. From there, it passes the beginning of Chena Hot Springs Rd at *Mile 4.6* and then Elliott Hwy at *Mile 11* near Fox, a small service center and your last opportunity to purchase beer, other supplies and gas at a reasonable price. The golden past of Steese Hwy can first be seen at *Mile 9.5*, where it passes the Goldstream Rd exit to **Gold Dredge No 8**, a five-deck, 250-foot dredge built in 1928 and named a national historical site in 1984. The dredge operated until 1959 and before it was closed had displaced 1065 tons of pay dirt from Pedro, Engineer and Goldstream creeks. No 8 is still making money, it's probably the most visited dredge in Alaska. Tours, which include actually stepping onto the dredge and panning for gold afterwards, are $10 per person.

At *Mile 16.6*, on the east side of the highway, is the **Felix Pedro Monument**, commemorating Felix Pedro whose discovery of gold nearby resulted in the boom town that was to become Fairbanks. Amateur gold panners are often in the nearby stream 'looking for color' or you can go another 10 miles to see a much more serious attempt at obtaining the metal. At *Mile 27.9* you take a

sharp turn up a hill to reach the old gold camp at **Chatanika**. The support center was built in 1925 for the gold dredging that went on from 1927 to 1957 and removed an estimated $70 million in gold at yesterday's prices.

Today, the *Old FE Co Gold Camp* (☎ 389-2414) is another national historical site and lodge with singles/doubles for $45/55. The camp also has a great sourdough breakfast served from 9 am to 2 pm Saturday and Sunday. For $12 you get an all-you-can-eat buffet with sourdough pancakes (of course), sourdough biscuits, eggs, French toast, potatoes, sweet rolls – the list goes on – in a mining-camp dining room with a 12-foot-long wood stove.

Another mile up the road is *Chatanika Lodge* (☎ 389-2164), another log lodge with moose heads, bear skins and mining artefacts hanging all over the walls of the dining room and saloon. Hungry? Friday to Sunday from 4 to 10 pm they have family-style all-you-can-eat dinners.

The first public campground along the Steese Hwy is the *Upper Chatanika River State Campground* (25 sites, $6 fee) on the river at *Mile 39*. Water and firewood are usually available, but have your bug dope handy – this is mosquito country. Those with a canoe can launch their boat here and the fishing for grayling is generally good. The next campground is the *Cripple Creek BLM Campground* (21 sites, $6 fee) at *Mile 60*, the site of the uppermost access point to the Chatanika River Canoe Trail (see the Fairbanks Paddling section in this chapter). The campground has tables, water and a nature trail nearby.

Access points for the Pinnell Mountain Trail (see the Trekking section in the Wilderness chapter) lie at *Mile 85.6* and *Mile 107* of Steese Hwy. The first trailhead is Twelvemile Summit, and even if you have no desire to undertake the three-day trek, the first two miles is an easy climb to spectacular views of the alpine area and past some unusual rock formations.

The **Birch Creek Canoe Route** begins at *Mile 94* of Steese Hwy, where a short road leads down to a canoe launch on the creek. The wilderness trip is a 140-mile paddle to the exit point at *Mile 147* of the highway. The overall rating of the river is Class II, but there are some Class III and Class IV parts that require lining your canoe. More details on the trip can be obtained from the Fairbanks BLM office (☎ 474-2200). Ask for their brochure entitled *Alaska's River Trails – Northern Region*.

Eagle Summit (3624 feet) is at *Mile 107*, where you'll find a parking area and a display for the second trailhead of the Pinnell Mountain Trail. A climb of less than a mile leads to the top of Eagle Summit, the highest point along the Steese Hwy and a place where the midnight sun can be observed skimming the horizon around the summer solstice on 21 June. The summit is also near a caribou migration route. The next 20 miles, from Eagle Summit to the town of Central is a scenic stretch of the Steese Mountains with the exception being the streams and creeks. Practically every one of these mountains has been marred and eroded by piles of rubble and tailings due to gold mining. Most of the operations are small and involve sluicing the rock with water from the creek. It's amazing how much of a creek bed or hillside the

miners will chew up in their quest to find the precious metal. To environmentalists and others unaccustomed to active mining, it's repulsive.

Central
At *Mile 127.5*, the highway reaches Central (population 800 in the summer) where it's briefly paved and there are gasoline and groceries, a post office and various places to stay including a motel and cabins for rent. Originally referred to on maps as Central House, the town began as a supply stop on the trail from Circle City to the surrounding creeks of the Circle Mining District. Central became a town in the 1930s, thanks largely to the Steese Hwy that was built in 1927, and then in the late-1970s and early 1980s experienced something of a second gold rush. With the price of the metal bouncing between $300 and $400 an ounce, miners were suddenly making a fortune sluicing the streams. One miner alone, Jim Regan, recovered 26,000 ounces of gold between 1979 and 1986 from the Crooked Creek area. Even more interesting was a diamond that was recovered by gold miners in 1982. Nicknamed 'Arctic Ice', it was the first diamond ever recovered from Alaska.

Although the mining activity has dwindled in recent years and most efforts are now small family operations, the miners' distrust of anybody or any agency threatening their right to make a living still looms throughout the town. All you have to do to see it is pull up to Crabb's Corner Cafe and read the sign outfront ('government workers and environmentalist do not enter'). Ironically across the street from the café is the BLM zone headquarters.

Things to See & Do
One of the best museums in any small Alaskan town is the **Circle District Museum** (☎ 520-1893), right on the Steese Hwy in Central. Established in 1984, the main portion of the museum is a large log lodge that houses a miner's cabins, exhibits on early mining equipment and dog-team freight and mail hauling and the Yukon

Press, the first printing press north of Juneau which produced Interior Alaska's first newspaper. But by far the most interesting display is the museum's collection of gold nuggets and gold flakes, recovered and donated by local miners. This, more than anything else, will help you understand why they continue to tear away at the hills and streams in an effort to find the precious metal.

Outside in a large barn is a collection of dog sleds and other large artefacts including an unusual covered wagon – covered with metal, not cloth. The museum also has a small video area with tapes on mining and other topics, a gift shop, and a visitor's information area. Most amazing, it's open and staffed daily from noon to 5 pm during the summer. Admission is $1.

One of the things the museum sells is gold pans but be aware, before you go splashing around in the local creeks trying to find nuggets of your own, that most streams are staked and to wander uninvited onto somebody's claim is asking for a nasty encounter with a miner or even worse – having a few pot shots aimed at your head. If you are swept up by the gold fever of this town, the safest place to pan is wherever the Steese Hwy crosses a creek or stream.

Places to Stay & Eat
In town is the *Central Motor Inn* (☎ 520-5228) which has it all – rooms, camp sites, showers, café, gas, you name it. Rooms are $38 for two people and showers are $3 per person. The café is perhaps the best place to eat anywhere on the Steese Hwy. Three eggs with toast and potatoes is less than $4 and at night they often have an all-you-can-eat special for around $10. If the bugs are not too vicious you can enjoy the meal on an outdoor deck under the midnight sun.

Groceries and other supplies can be purchased at Crabb's Corner which also has a café.

Circle Hot Springs
Just beyond Central, the Circle Hot Springs Rd heads south and in six miles passes the *Ketchem Creek Campground* (seven sites,

free). The BLM campground is rundown and unmarked along the road but it's still the best place to pitch a tent in the area. Two miles beyond the creek is *Circle Hot Springs Resort* (☎ 520-5113), a popular spot with Fairbanks residents.

The springs were first used by Kutchin Indians and then miners began soaking in the naturally hot water at the turn-of-the-century. The resort followed 30 years later when Frank Leach arrived and made the development of the springs his lifelong obsession. Leach started by building Alaska's first runway specifically designed for airplanes in 1924 and then followed this by building his impressive three-story hotel in the early 1930s, hauling most of the materials down the Yukon River to Circle City and then overland by wagon to the springs.

Now listed on the National Register of Historical Sites, the hotel is a classic. Inside the lobby and lounge there are artefacts everywhere including a safe where gold was once stored, photos and clippings on the wall illustrating the early mining era, and a poker table that looks as natural here as it would in Las Vegas. Outside is a string of small log cabins, each with some old mining equipment out the front and a moose rack over the doorway.

The water from the hot springs is piped into an Olympic-sized pool in which 139°F mineral water is pumped through at a rate of 231 gallons a minute. Spend 20 or 30 minutes soaking here and you won't have sore muscles or a care in the world. There is also a restaurant and miner's saloon on site. The hotel rooms with shared baths begin at $45 while on the 3rd floor are hostel accommodations for $20 a night. They also rent the rustic cabins, some with no running water, and other more deluxe cabins with kitchens and hot tubs. If you're camping down the road it's $7 to soak in the pool that's open until midnight.

Circle
Beyond Central, the Steese Hwy passes the exit point of the Birch Creek Canoe Route at

Mile 147 and ends at Circle (population 90) at *Mile 162*.

Circle is an interesting little wilderness town that lies on the banks of the Yukon River and was the northernmost point you could drive to before the Dalton Hwy was opened up. A large sign in the center of town still proclaims this fact. The town is 50 miles south of the Arctic Circle, but miners who established it in 1896 thought they were near the imaginary line and gave Circle its present name.

After gold was discovered in Birch Creek, Circle was a bustling log-cabin city of 1200 with two theatres, a music hall, eight dance halls and 28 saloons. It was known as the 'largest log-cabin city in the world' until the Klondike reduced the town significantly and the Steese Hwy reduced its importance even more. For most part, Central has now replaced Circle City as the supply center for area miners.

Much of the original town has been devoured by the Yukon River but you can get a feeling for the town's history by walking to **Pioneer Cemetery** which has headstones dating back to the 1800s. To find it, head upriver along the gravel road. Beyond a barricade is a trail that leads into dense underbrush and the graves are off to the left.

A city-operated campground at the end of Steese Hwy consists of tables, outhouses and a grassy area along the banks of the Yukon River where you can pitch your tent. Nearby is the **Yukon Trading Post**, which includes a general store with Arctic Alaska prices, a café, bar and motel. The bar is an especially important spot because this is the only place you can go at night (other than your car) to escape the wave of mosquitoes.

Getting There & Away

Needless to say, hitchhiking is more difficult on Steese Hwy than on Chena Hot Springs Rd but it's not as difficult as it might appear. There is a fair amount of traffic moving between the communities and Fairbanks and people this far north are good about stopping. Still, you have to consider your time schedule and patience level before attempting this road.

You can also reach the area renting a vehicle in Fairbanks but will have to look around. Most car-rental companies, including the discount ones like Rent-A-Wreck and All-Star, do not allow their vehicles to be driven on the Steese Hwy.

The newest way to reach Circle City is the oldest way. In 1994, the Alaska Yukon Sternwheeler Company began operations between Circle and Dawson City, stopping at Eagle along the way, a trip of 265 miles. The sternwheeler has both berths and deck passage and has a season from late May to early September. There are both three-day and five-day cruises and the fare for deck passage only is $125 a day. You can write to the new company in advance at PO Box 75097, Fairbanks, AK 99707; or call (907) 455-4320.

ELLIOTT HWY

From the crossroad with the Steese Hwy at Fox north of Fairbanks, the Elliott Hwy extends 152 miles north and then west to Manley Hot Springs, a small settlement near the Tanana River. This is by far the roughest road out of Fairbanks. The first 28 miles of the highway are paved and the rest is gravel; sections past the junction with Dalton Hwy are so narrow and steep you could get stuck behind a RVer for days. At *Mile 28* of Elliott Hwy is the trailhead, parking lot and information box for the White Mountain Trail to Borealis-Le Fevre and Lee's cabins (see the Trekking section in the Wilderness chapter and Cabins in Fairbanks). Lee's is a seven-mile hike in and Borealis-Le Fevre is a hike of 19 miles over the Summit Trail.

An old Bureau of Land Management (BLM) campground, no longer maintained, is passed at *Mile 57* of Elliott Hwy where a bridge crosses the Tolovana River. There is still a turn-off here and the fishing is good for grayling and northern pike, but the mosquitoes are of legendary proportions. Nearby is the start of the **Colorado Creek Trail** to Windy Gap BLM Cabin. Check with the

BLM office (☎ 474-2200) in Fairbanks about use of the cabin during the summer.

At *Mile 71* is the service center of **Livengood**, where you will find a small general store. At this point Elliott Hwy swings more to the west and in two miles passes the junction of the Dalton Hwy (see the Dalton Hwy section in the Bush chapter). From here, it is another 78 miles south-west to Manley Hot Springs.

Manley Hot Springs

The town, which has a summer population of 150 or so, is on the west side of Hot Springs Slough and provides a public campground ($2 per night fee) near the bridge that crosses the slough. The town was first homesteaded in 1902 by J F Karshner just as the US Army Signal Corps arrived to put in a telegraph station. Frank Manley arrived a few years later and built a four-story hotel at the trading center which was booming with miners from the nearby Eureka and Tofly mining areas. Most of the miners have gone

now but Manley left his name on the village and today it's a quiet but friendly spot known for its lush gardens, a rare sight this far north.

Just before entering the village you pass the *Manley Hot Springs Resort* (☎ 672-3611) up on a hill, where most of the serious bathing is done. The resort has 24 rooms that range from $65 to $90, a restaurant, a bar and, of course, a mineral hot springs pool. It's $5 just to walk and use the hot springs. They also have showers, a laundromat and run tours up the Tanana River to see a fish camp or to go gold panning.

In town is the *Manley Roadhouse* (☎ 672-3161) offering singles/doubles for $50/$60 and cabins that sleep up to four people for $65. This classic Alaskan roadhouse was built in 1906 and today features antiques in its restaurant, bar and lounge. You will find groceries, gas, liquor and the post office at the *Manley Trading Post* or you can wander around town and usually purchase vegetables from some of the residents. The produce here is unbelievable.

The Bush

The Bush, the wide rim of wilderness that encircles Anchorage, Fairbanks and all the roads between the two, constitutes a vast majority of the state's area, yet only a trickle of tourists ventures into the region for a first-hand look at rural Alaska.

Cost, more than the great mountains or the mighty rivers, is the barrier that isolates the Bush. For budget-minded travelers who reach the 'Great White North', what lies out in the Bush is usually beyond the reach of their wallets. Apart from a few exceptions, flying is the only way to reach a specific area. Once you're out there, facilities can be sparse and very expensive, especially if you don't arrive with a tent and backpacker's stove.

Those who do endure the high expense and extra travel are blessed with a land and people that have changed far less than the rest of the state. The most pristine wilderness lies in the many newly created national parks and preserves found away from the road system – parks where there are no visitor centers, campgrounds or shuttle buses running trips into the backcountry. Only nature in all its grandeur is encountered. Traditional villages, where subsistence is still the means of survival, and hearty homesteaders, as independent and ingenious as they come, lie hidden throughout rural Alaska.

There are three general areas in Bush Alaska. Southwest Alaska consists of the Alaska Peninsula, the Aleutian Islands and the rich salmon grounds of Bristol Bay. The Alaska Peninsula extends 550 miles from the western shore of Cook Inlet to its tip at False Pass. From there the Aleutian Islands, a chain of over 200 islands, curve another 1100 miles west into the Pacific Ocean.

Southwest Alaska is characterized by more than 60 active and dormant volcanoes, a treeless terrain and the worst weather in the state. Alaska's outlying arm is where the Arctic waters of the Bering Sea meet the warm Japanese Current,

causing considerable cloudiness, rain and fog. Violent storms sweeping across the Pacific Ocean contribute to high winds in the area. The major attractions of the region are Katmai National Park & Preserve at the beginning of the Alaska Peninsula, Lake Clark National Park & Preserve across Cook Inlet from Homer, and McNeil River State Game Sanctuary.

Western Alaska is a flat, treeless plain that borders the Bering Sea north of the Alaska Peninsula to beyond Kotzebue and the Arctic Circle. This flatland is broken up by millions of lakes and slow-moving rivers such as the Yukon, while the weather in the summer is cool and cloudy with considerable fog and drizzle. The most visited parts of this region are the towns of Nome and Kotzebue, and the Pribilof Islands, north of the Aleutian Islands in the Bering Sea and the location of seal-breeding grounds and bird rookeries.

The third area in the Bush is Arctic Alaska, also known as the North Slope, which lies north of the Arctic Circle. Here the Brooks Range slopes gradually to the north and is eventually replaced by tundra plains that end at the Arctic Ocean. The harsh climate and short summers produce 400 species of plants in the treeless tundra that are often dwarfed versions of those further south. Wildlife in the form of polar bears, reindeer, caribou,

Polar bear

wolves and brown bears have adapted amazingly well to the rough conditions.

Arctic Alaska is characterized by nightless summers and dayless winters. In Barrow, Alaska's northernmost village, the midnight sun doesn't set from May to August. Surprisingly, the Arctic Alaska winters are often milder than those in the Interior. The summers, however, are cool at best and temperatures are rarely warmer than 45°F. Barrow attracts a small number of tourists each summer, and backpackers have discovered that the Gates of the Arctic National Park & Preserve, an intriguing place for a wilderness adventure, is becoming more accessible and more affordable with every passing summer.

Although many places are geared for tourists, with formal accommodation available most of the time, it is best to be completely self-sufficient whether you are venturing into a new wilderness preserve or into a traditional village set in its ways.

Don't just pick out a village and fly to it. It is wise to either have a contact there (someone you know, a guide company or a wilderness lodge) or to travel with somebody who does. Although the indigenous people, especially the Inuit, are very hospitable people, there can be much tension and suspicion of strangers in small, isolated rural communities.

Southwest Alaska

There are two ways to see a small part of the Bush without flying. One of them is to drive the Dalton Hwy (also known as the North Slope Haul Rd). The other is to hop onto the State Marine Ferry when it makes its special run five times each summer along the Alaska Peninsula to the eastern end of the Aleutian Islands. Around 14 May, 18 June, 24 July, 20 August and 17 September (the dates vary slightly from year to year), the MV *Tustumena* continues west to Sand Point, King Cove, Cold Bay and Dutch Harbor/Unalaska, and possibly several other small villages, before backtracking to Kodiak.

This is truly one of the best bargains in public transportation. The scenery is intriguing. You'll pass the perfect cones of Pavlof and Pavlof's Sister (a pair of volcanoes on the Alaska Peninsula), the treeless but lush green mountains of the Aleutians, and distinctive rock formations and cliffs. The wildlife is even better. Passing through Barren Islands on the way to Kodiak passengers often spot two dozen whales at a time. Sea lions, otters and porpoises are commonly sighted and then there are the birds. More than 30 species of seabirds nest in the Aleutians and 250 species of bird pass through. Diehard birders are often on board sighting such species as albatrosses, auklets, cormorants and puffins. Even if you don't know a puffin from a kittiwake, naturalists from the US Fish & Wildlife Service ride the boat, pointing out birds and giving programs through the trip on other aspects of the Aleutians.

All the wildlife and scenery are dependent, however, on the weather. This can be an extremely rough trip at times, well deserving of its title 'the cruise through the cradle of the storms'. On the runs in fall, 40-foot waves and 80-knot winds are the norm and no matter when you step aboard, you'll find 'barf' bags everywhere on the ship – just in case.

The smoothest runs are from June to

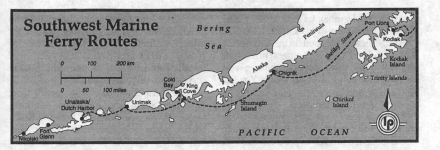

Southwest Marine Ferry Routes

August. A state room is nice but not necessary. There are no lounge chairs in the solarium but a sleeping pad and bag work out nicely. You'll find both free showers on board and free coffee and hot water. The hot water is especially nice, allowing you to stock up on cup-a-soup and tea to avoid spending a small fortune in the dinning room where lunch will cost $7 and dinner from $8 to $13. And bring a good book. On days when the fog surrounds the boat there is little to look at but the lapping waves along the side.

The MV *Tustumena*, a 290-foot vessel which holds 230 passengers, is the only ferry in the Alaskan fleet rated as an ocean-going ship, thus its nickname, 'Trusty Tusty'. It leaves Kodiak on Friday, returns early Wednesday morning and continues on to Seward that day. The boat docks at the villages only long enough to load and unload (from one to two hours), but in Dutch Harbor/Unalaska it stays in port from five to six hours. Still, spending just an hour in most of these villages is more than sufficient time to get off for a quick look around. On board are state rooms, a dining room and a bar.

Round-trip fare for walk-on passengers to Dutch Harbor from Kodiak is $400; if you begin in Homer and end in Seward, it is $488. For those who want to spend more time in Dutch Harbor/Unalaska, Reeve Aleutian Airways (☎ 243-4700 in Anchorage), Mark-Air and Peninsula Airways (☎ 243-2323 in Anchorage) provide services to the Aleutian Islands as well as the Pribilof Islands and other destinations on the Alaska Peninsula.

The other way to spend more time on land and reduce the cost of the trip is to leave the ferry early and then wait for it on its return run. King Cove is ideally situated for this but the place is little more than a company town. The best place by far is False Pass, a small village surrounded by snow-covered peaks. But carefully check to see if the ferry is stopping at the town both on the way out and back. If it doesn't, it could be a long wait until the next time the MV *Tustumena* is passing through.

KING COVE
This town of 700 residents is a commercial fishing base at the western end of the Alaska Peninsula near the entrance of Cold Bay. Surrounded by mountains, King Cove supports a hotel, a restaurant and a busy harbor during the summer as well as a market and laundromat. Those thinking of stepping off and just pitching a tent out the road, beware. Brown bears wander into town frequently here. Reeve Aleutian Airways charges $278 for a one-way ticket to King Cove from Anchorage purchased 14 days in advance.

COLD BAY
On the west shore of Cold Bay is the town of the same name. The 160 residents are mostly government workers as the town is a major refueling stop for many flights crossing the Pacific to or from the Orient. Russian explorers also used the bay and most likely spent the winters here on their first trips along the coast. Before they departed, Count Feodor

Lutke named Izembek Lagoon in 1827 after a doctor aboard one of his ships.

A huge airstrip was built in the area during WW II; today it's the third longest in the state and is why the town serves as the transport center for the entire Aleutian chain. You can still see Quonset huts and other remains from the WW II military build-up.

The town also serves as the gateway to the **Izembek National Wildlife Refuge**, which was established in 1960 to protect some 142 species of bird, primarily the black brant. Almost the entire North American population of brant, some 150,000 of them, arrive in spring and fall to feed on large eelgrass beds during their annual migration.

A 10-mile road runs from Cold Bay to the Izembek Lagoon; otherwise, travel in the refuge is by foot or plane. Contact the Wildlife Refuge office in Cold Bay (Pouch 2, Cold Bay, AK 99571) for more information. Within town, accommodation, meals and groceries are available. Reeve Aleutian Airways (☎ 532-2380 or (800) 544-2248) services the community and charges $217 for a one-way, advance purchase ticket from Anchorage.

UNALASKA & DUTCH HARBOR

Unalaska on Unalaska Island and its sister town Dutch Harbor on Amaknak Island, are at the confluence of the North Pacific Ocean and the Bering Sea, one of the richest fisheries in the world. Dutch Harbor is the only natural deep water port in the Aleutians and more than 400 vessels call there each year from as many as 14 countries. The two towns lie deep into Unalaska Bay and are connected to each other by a 500-foot bridge. During the summer, the population of the area can easily exceed 3000 due to the influx of cannery workers who process seafood, most notably crab. Dutch Harbor also serves as a transport center for much of the Bristol Bay salmon fishery. In 1978, the towns earned more from fishing than any other port in the country and today are usually in the top five for value of fish processed.

Unalaska was the first headquarters for the Russian-American Company and a corner-stone in the lucrative sea-otter fur trade in the 1700s. It was also an important harbor for miners sailing to the golden beaches of Nome. In 1939, the USA built navy and army installations here and at one time 60,000 servicemen were stationed there.

In June 1942, the Japanese opened their Aleutian Islands campaign by bombing Dutch Harbor, and then took Attu and Kiska islands in the only foreign invasion of US soil during WW II. The attack on Dutch Harbor had a silver lining in it for the USA. A fallen Zero fighter plane was retrieved near the harbor and, for the first time since the war began, the Americans could closely study Japan's most devastating weapon.

The bombing also resulted in heavy fortification of the islands as well as areas around Kodiak and Seward, in anticipation of future attacks and to regain control of the Aleutians. The campaign to retake the two islands was a bloody one and included a 19-day battle on Attu in which US forces recaptured the plot of barren land but only after suffering 2300 casualties and 549 deaths. The Japanese lost even more lives.

Today Dutch Harbor is the site of the canneries and fish-processing plants, something of an industrial park. Unalaska is where everybody lives and, despite the large influx of transient workers, can be a charming and friendly town, if you have the time to enjoy it. Unfortunately, those returning on the ferry really don't. To stay longer you can either splurge on an expensive airline ticket or be reckless and arrive hoping to pick up a cheaper one in town. Either way, a few days in Unalaska can be a refreshing cure for anybody who is suffering from an overdose of RVers and Alaska crowded with tourists and tour buses.

Things to See & Do

Unalaska is dominated by the **Church of the Holy Ascension**, the oldest Russian-built church still standing in the country today. It was first built in 1825 and then was enlarged in 1894 when wings were attached to change its floor plan from a 'vessel' to a 'pekov' or one in the shape of a crucifix. On Broadway

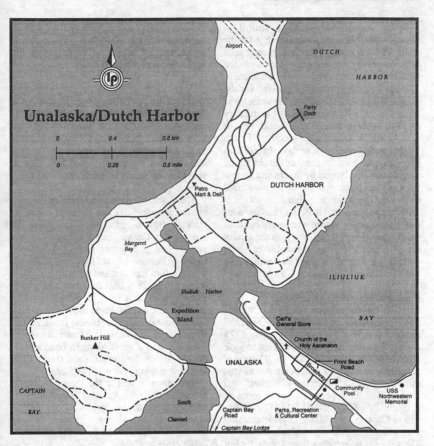

and overlooking the bay, the church with its onion domes is a photographer's delight. Outside is a small graveyard with the largest marker belonging to the Baron Nicholas Zass. Born in 1825 in Archange, Russia, he eventually became bishop of the Aleutian Islands and all of Alaska before dying in 1882. Next door is the **Bishop's House**; both buildings are being restored.

Military relics still remain around Dutch Harbor and Unalaska though in recent years the communities have begun an effort to clean them up. On the road from the ferry terminal and airport to Unalaska, you pass one concrete pillbox after another. **Bunker Hill** is an easy place to see the remains of the Aleutian campaign. Known to the military as 'Hill 400', it was fortified with 155-mm guns, ammunition magazines, water tanks, 22 Quonset hut bunkers and a concrete command post at the top. You can hike to the peak of Bunker Hill along a gravel road, picked up just after crossing the bridge to Amaknak Island. Along the way you see many of the Quonset huts while at the top the gun turrets still remain along with the ammunition magazines and the command post. The view from the top on a clear day is excellent.

More war history can be found in Unalaska by following Front Beach Rd to the south end of town. There's a picturesque hillside graveyard along the bay with the **USS Northwestern Memorial**. Launched in 1889 as a passenger and freight ship for the Alaska Steamship Company, the vessel was retired in 1937 then repaired by the military in 1940 to serve as a floating bunkhouse. It was bombed during the attack of Dutch Harbor and burned for five days. In 1992, as part of the 50th anniversary of the event, the propeller was salvaged by divers and is now part of the memorial to those who died during the Aleutian campaign.

If it's raining in Unalaska, and it does more than 250 days of the year, head to Community Pool (☎ 581-1649) in the school complex on Broadway. A number of swim periods are offered daily and the facility also includes a sauna. Admission is $3 per person.

Places to Stay & Eat

In 1993, the *Grand Aleutian Hotel* (☎ 581-3844) opened up in Dutch Harbor near the airport but unless you're willing to pay $175 a night for a double, you might want to look elsewhere for accommodations. There are actually a number of lodges in the towns, most catering to the cannery workers and fishers. The best place to get a room is *Captain Bay Lodge* (☎ 581-1825) near the end of Captain Bay Rd, the first intersection after crossing the bridge to Unalaska Island. The lodge is three miles from Unalaska but has singles/doubles for $60/70 a night. There is also a restaurant where fishermen, construction workers and others feast on an all-you-can-eat breakfast for $6 and dinner for $12. Add $15 to your room rate and you can have a bed and three meals a day.

There is also *Jackie's Bed & Breakfast* (☎ 581-2964) in downtown Unalaska or you can camp practically anywhere outside the towns.

In Unalaska, there is *Storm's Pizza* which also serves Mexican dinners and *Carl's*, a large general store which includes groceries. Both are on Broadway. Near the Grand Aleutian Hotel there is *Petro Mart & Deli* where

more supplies can be purchased as well as fresh sandwiches for $6 to $7. There is also a nice, but rather expensive, restaurant and bar in the airport terminal.

Hiking

Within Dutch Harbor there is the Sitka Spruce Plantation, six trees the Russians planted in 1805 that have somehow survived when all other foliage can't. That's it for trees on Unalaska Island and because of the treeless environment, hiking is easy here. Nor do you have to worry about bears – there are none.

There are few developed trails in the area but an enjoyable day can be spent hiking to Uniktali Bay, a round trip of eight to 10 miles. From Captain Bay Rd, turn east on a gravel road just before passing Westword Cannery. Follow the road for a mile to its end where a foot trail continues along a stream. In two miles, the trail runs out and you'll reach a lake in a pass between a pair of 2000-foot peaks. Continue south-east to pick up a second stream that empties into Uniktali Bay. The bay is an undeveloped stretch of shoreline and a great place to beachcomb. From time to time even glass floats from Japanese fishing nets wash ashore.

You can also trek to the top of Ballyhoo Mountain behind the airport to look at more artefacts from the military build-up, including tunnels that allowed gunners to cart ammunition from one side of the mountain to the other.

Getting There & Around

Both the ferry terminal and the airport are on Amaknak Island, about three miles from Unalaska. The most amazing thing about this place is the number of taxi vans available. There are literally dozens of them running around on the dirt and gravel roads. Blue Checker Cab Company (☎ 581-2186) is the largest operation but you can't walk more than five minutes here without a taxi driver asking if you need a ride. It doesn't matter where you go or how far; all rides are $5 per person.

If you arrive on the ferry and are returning

on it, the $10 you dish out for two taxi rides is money well spent to see as much of Unalaska as possible. If you're staying for a day or two, however, it's easy enough to hitchhike. Another way to get around is to rent a mountain bike from the Unalaska Parks, Recreation & Cultural Department (☎ 581-1297), in the back of the community center on Broadway. Bikes are $10 for the day or $3 for three hours with helmets.

Other than the once-a-month ferry, the only other way of getting out of Unalaska/Dutch Harbor is flying. The town is serviced by MarkAir (☎ 581-1727 or (800) 478-0800 in Alaska), Reeve Aleutian Airways (☎ 581-1202) and Peninsula Airways (☎ 581-1383). MarkAir flies in a jet here, but is more likely to be turned back by bad weather. Either pay the going rate ($330 for an advance purchase, one-way ticket to Anchorage) or check around town for somebody trying to unload a ticket. The bulletin boards at Carl's are a good place to start.

WOOD-TIKCHIK STATE PARK
At 1.6 million acres, Wood-Tikchik is the largest state park in the country. It's 30 miles north of Dillingham, the service and transport center for Bristol Bay. The park preserves two large systems of interconnecting lakes that are the important spawning grounds for Bristol Bay's salmon which enter the area through the Wood River.

With the exception of five fishing lodges which only offer packaged stays at $2000 to $3000 a week, the park is totally undeveloped. There are no campgrounds, trails, ranger stations or shelters. In short, it is an ideal place for a wilderness canoe or kayak trip. Traditional trips include running the Tikchik or Nuyakuk rivers or floating from lake to lake.

Information
For park information during the winter contact Wood-Tikchik State Park (☎ (907) 842-2375); PO Box 3022, Dillingham, AK 99576. During the summer call (907) 345-5014.

Woods River Lakes These are the lakes in the southern half of the park connected to one another by shallow, swift moving rivers. For that reason most parties are flown in and paddle out, returning to Dillingham via the Wood River. A popular spot to put in is Lake Kulik and then you paddle to Dillingham, a trip of close to 140 miles requiring from seven to 10 days in a kayak or canoe.

These lakes are attractive to many as they eliminate the additional air time you need to be picked up. They also are an easy paddle for most intermediate canoeists. But keep in

mind that three of the five fishing lodges are here and all use their powerboats extensively to get around the lakes.

Tikchik Lakes In the northern half of the park, and much more remote, are these six lakes. The most common trip consists of being dropped onto Nishlik or Upnuk lakes and leaving them by traveling along the Tikchik River into Tikchik Lake. Either you can be picked up here or you can continue your journey by floating the Nuyakuk River and then the Nushagak River to one of several Native Alaskan villages where air charter is available back to Dillingham.

Keep in mind the Allen River, which drains from Chikuminuk Lake into Lake Chauekuktuli on another route to Tikchik Lake, requires a series of portages around Class V rapids. Likewise the upper Nuyakuk River, just below the Tikchik Lake outlet has a white-water stretch that will require you to make a portage. The upper lakes are more challenging and more costly to experience. But the scenery – mountains, pinnacle peaks and hanging valleys surrounding the lakes – is the most impressive in the park and there will be far less motorboat activity if any at all.

The paddling season is from mid-June when the lakes are finally free of ice and snow until early October when they begin to freeze up again. Be prepared for cool and rainy weather and pack along plenty of mosquito repellent. On the open lakes you have to be cautious as sudden winds can create white-cap conditions, and white water may exist on many of the streams connecting the lakes.

Highlights of any such adventure, besides the wilderness, are the possibilities of spotting brown and black bears, beavers, moose, foxes and maybe even wolves. The fishing for arctic char, rainbow trout, Dolly Varden, grayling and red salmon is excellent in late summer.

Dillingham Services

There are a number of hotels and lodges in Dillingham but you'll find the price of accommodations here on the high side. At the top end is *The Bristol Inn* (☎ 842-2240) while slightly more affordable and in the center of town is *Dillingham Hotel* (☎ 842-5316) with singles/doubles for $88/102.

Near the airport in the Tackle Shop is *Bristol Bay Rafters* (☎ 842-2212). This outfitter specializes in unguided trips into the state park and will provide canoe or raft rentals as well as other camping equipment or arrange for drop-off and pick-up service.

Getting There & Away

To reach Dillingham from Anchorage, book an air ticket in advance through Alaska Airlines (☎ (800) 426-0333) or MarkAir (☎ (800) 478-0800 in Alaska); a round-trip ticket costs from $300 to $350.

A 24-mile road extends from Dillingham to the village of Aleknagik on the south end of the Wood River Lakes system. Otherwise Contact Yute Air (☎ 842-5333) in Dillingham about chartering a float plane but expect to pay around $250 an hour for the flight in. Also ask if they need a second trip to haul your canoe in.

KATMAI NATIONAL PARK

In June 1912, Novarupta Volcano erupted violently and along with the preceding earthquakes rocked the area now known as Katmai National Park & Preserve. The wilderness was turned into a dynamic landscape of smoking valleys, ash-covered mountains and small holes and cracks (fumaroles) fuming with steam and gas. In only one other eruption in historic times, on the Greek island of Santorini in 1500 BC, has more ash and pumice been displaced.

If the eruption had happened in New York City, people living in Chicago would have heard the explosion; it was 10 times greater than the 1980 eruption of Mt St Helens in the state of Washington. For two days, people in Kodiak could not see a lantern held at arm's length and the pumice, which reached half the world, lowered the temperature in the Northern Hemisphere that year by two degrees. In history books, 1912 will always be remembered as the year without a summer. But the most amazing aspect of this eruption, perhaps the most dramatic natural event in the 20th century, was that no-one was killed.

The National Geographic Society sent Robert Grigg to explore this locality in 1916, and standing at Katmai Pass the explorer saw for the first time the valley floor with its thousands of steam vents. He named it the Valley of 10,000 Smokes. Robert Grigg's adventures revealed the spectacular results of the eruptions to the rest of the world and two years later the area was turned into a national monument. In 1980, it was enlarged to 3.9 million acres and redesignated a national park and preserve.

Although the fumaroles no longer smoke and hiss, the park is still a diverse and scenic wilderness, unlike any in Alaska. It changes from glaciated volcanoes and ash-covered valleys to island-studded lakes and a coastline of bays, fjords and beaches. Wildlife is abundant with more than 30 species of mammals including large populations of brown bears, some of which weigh over 1000 pounds. Katmai is also a prime habitat for moose, sea lions, arctic fox and wolves. The many streams and lakes in the park are known around the state for providing some of the best rainbow trout and salmon fishing.

The weather in the park is best from mid-June to the end of July. Unfortunately, this is also when mosquitoes, always heavy in this part of the state, are at their peak. The best time for hiking and backpacking trips is from mid-August to early September, when the colors of fall are brilliant, the berries ripe and juicy, and the insects scarce. However, be prepared for frequent storms. In fact be ready for rain and foul weather any time in Katmai and always pack warm clothing. The summer high temperatures are usually in the low 60s°F.

Information

Katmai is not a place to see at the last minute. Because of the cost involved in reaching the park, most visitors plan to spend at least four days or more to justify the expenses.

To contact the park beforehand write to:

Katmai National Park, PO Box 7, King Salmon, AK 99613; or call on (907) 246-3305. In the USA, use the toll-free numbers to MarkAir (☎ (800) 426-6784) and Katmailand (☎ (800) 544-0551) for advance reservations. Katmailand is the concessionaire that handles the lodge and canoe rentals.

King Salmon

King Salmon and its runway is the transportation hub that you pass through on your way to Katmai National Park. Most people see little more than the terminal building where they pick up their luggage and the float dock where they catch a flight to Brooks Camp in the park, which is fine. King Salmon is a village of 600 residents, almost all of them either federal employees (National Park Service or US Fish & Wildlife Service) or military personnel scheduled to be pulled out in the near future.

Occasionally you get stuck in King Salmon for a few hours or even a day. If that's the case, head to the **King Salmon Visitor Center** (☎ 246-3339), right next door to the terminal and open daily during the summer from 8 am to 5 pm. The center is staffed by both the NPS and USFWS and inside there is an excellent selection of books and maps for sale, a growing number of displays and a small video room where they will show you a variety of videos on subjects ranging from brown bears to the creation of the park.

Just up the road from the terminal on the way to the town of Naknek is the King Salmon Mall (no kidding, it even has a Radio Shack) with the headquarters of Katmai National Park on the 2nd floor. It's open from 8 am to 4.30 pm Monday to Friday and is a good place to ask questions but there is little else for visitors there.

Nearby in the mall is a bar and restaurant, a large general store that also sells groceries and *King Ko Inn* (☎ 246-3377) where rooms run from $60 to $80 for a single in case, heavens forbid, you need to spend a night here. Better but more expensive accommodations can be found at *Quinnat Landing Hotel* (☎ 246-3000) where you can expect to pay close to $150 a night. Others just wander down the road away from town and set up camp on the banks of the Naknek River. Just remember that winds can be murderous here, the real reason for the lack of trees in the region, and you'd best have a tent that can withstand strong gusts.

If you are struck for a day in King Salmon, consider giving Tundra Tours (☎ 246-4218) a call. It offers a personalized van tour of the area, including the village of Naknek for a look at rural Alaska, a salmon cannery and a hike along the Bering Sea. The tours run from three to four hours and cost $32.50 per person, a minimum of three people.

Brooks Camp

The summer headquarters for Katmai National Park is Brooks Camp, on the shores of Naknek Lake, 47 miles from King Salmon. The camp is best known for Brooks Falls where thousands of red sockeye salmon attempt to jump every July, much to the interest of both bears and tourists. In the middle of the wilderness, this place crawls with humanity during July, when sometimes as many as 300 people will be in Brooks Camp and the surrounding area in a single day.

When you arrive at the camp, you are immediately given a 'bear orientation' by a ranger as the bruins are frequently seen – often strolling down the beach, between the lodge and cabins and the float planes pulled up the sand. From here you can head straight to a visitors' center, open from 8 am to 6 pm daily, to find out the status of available sites in the campgrounds or to fill out backcountry permits. You can also purchase books or maps at the center while rangers here run a variety of interpretive programs, including a daily walk to an Inuit pit house at 1 pm. At 8 pm nightly they also have programs or slide shows at a nearby auditorium.

Bear Watching

Katmai has the largest population of non-hunted brown bears in world as more than 2000 live in the park. At Brooks Camp they congregate around Brooks River to take advantage of the easy fishing for salmon.

Most of this takes place in July when it is almost impossible to get a camp site, a cabin or sometimes even a spot on the observation decks without planning months in advance. The bear activity then tapers off in August when the animals follow salmon up into small streams but it increases in September as the bears return to congregate in the lower rivers to feed on spawned-out fish. In reality, a few brown bears can be spotted in the Brooks Camp area through much of the summer as there always seem to be a couple of younger ones hanging around.

There are two established viewing areas. From Brooks Lodge a dirt road leads to a bridge over the river and a large observation deck. From here you can spot the bears feeding in the mouth of the river or swimming in the bay. Continue on the road to the Valley of 10,000 Smokes and in half a mile a marked trail winds to Brooks Falls. It's another half-mile walk to the falls where there is a second observation deck. This is a prime viewing area. Right above the falls, you can photograph both salmon making those spectacular leaps over the rushing water or a big brownie at the top of the cascade waiting with open jaws to grab the fish.

At the peak of the salmon run, there are usually eight to 12 bears, two or three of them on the falls themselves. The observation deck, however, will be crammed with 30 to 40 photographers. You can imagine how heated it gets there with people trying to squeeze in their open tripods for the photo-of-a-life-time and professionals with two-foot-long lens battling it out with amateurs and their instamatics. For those reasons the NPS institutes a number of rules and limits your stay at the site to an hour or less. It's the only way to keep a 35-mm war from breaking out on the deck.

Bus Tours

The only road in Katmai is 23 miles long and ends at Overlook Cabin, where there is a sweeping view of the Valley of 10,000 Smokes. Katmailand, which runs the lodge, also has a bus that makes a daily run out and

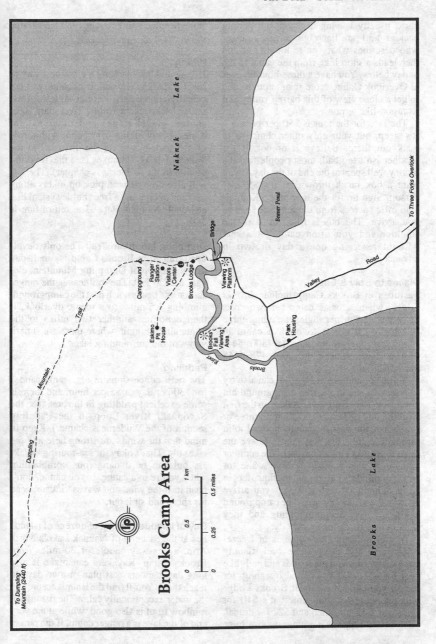

Brooks Camp Area

back, usually leaving at 9 am and getting back at 4.30 pm. Each bus carries a ranger who describes what you're looking at and then leads a short hike from the cabin to the valley below. You have a three-hour layover at Overlook Cabin, more than enough time to get a close view of this barren valley and its moon-like terrain.

The fare for the tour is $50 per person – it's steep, but your only other choice is to walk out there. Believe it or not, if the weather isn't too bad, most people feel it's money well spent at the end of the day. If you want a box lunch thrown in, it's $57 per person. Sign up for the tour at the Katmailand office across from the lodge as soon as you arrive. The bus is filled most of the summer and you often can't get a seat without reserving one a day or two in advance.

Places to Stay & Eat
Facilities in Brooks Camp include *Brooks Lodge*, where a basic cabin for two costs $120 per person per night, including three full meals. It's best to book a cabin in advance through Katmailand (☎ (800) 544-0551 outside Alaska or (800) 478-5448 inside Alaska).

If you are coming in July you can also try to reserve a site in the free campground but good luck. Reservations are taken on the first working day of January, and within three or four hours, the sites are usually booked solid throughout July, the best month to see the bears at Brooks Falls. The rest of the summer you might also want to reserve a site for peace of mind by calling the headquarters in King Salmon (☎ 246-3305). If you arrive unannounced, don't worry. The campground hosts are very accommodating and they usually find room for everybody.

A store sells limited supplies of freeze-dried food and camp-stove fuel, fishing equipment, flies and other odds and ends like beer for $3 a can. You can also sign up for the all-you-can-eat meals at Brooks Lodge without being a cabin renter; it's $10 for breakfast, $12 for lunch and $22 for dinner. Also in the lodge is a lounge with a huge

stone fireplace, soft couches and bar service in the evening.

Hiking
Hiking and backpacking are the best way to see the park's unusual backcountry. Like Denali National Park, Katmai has few formal trails; backpackers follow river bars, lake shores, gravel ridges and other natural routes. Many hiking trips begin with a ride on the park bus along the dirt road to the Valley of 10,000 Smokes (see the Trekking section in the Wilderness chapter). The bus will also drop off and pick up hikers along the road but it is not a free shuttle system like at Denali National Park. The return fare is $60.

Dumpling Mountain Trail The only developed trail from Brooks Camp is a half-day trek to the top of Dumpling Mountain, elevation 2520 feet. The trail leaves the ranger station and heads north past the campground, climbing 1.5 miles to a scenic overlook. It then continues another two miles to the mountain's summit, where there are superb views of the surrounding lakes.

Paddling
The park concessionaire also rents canoes for $30 per day or $5 per hour, and there is some excellent paddling in the area (see the Savonoski River Loop in the Paddling section of the Wilderness chapter). Keep in mind that the winds are strong here and the lakes big. That's okay for sea-touring kayakers but can be a dangerous combination when you're in a canoe. If you canoe, don't push it. If the wind and waves kick up, head for shore and sit it out.

Bay of Islands A group of dozens of islands lies at the east end of Naknek Lake's North Arm, a one-way paddle of 30-miles from Brooks Camp. Kayakers can make it in a long day, canoers best plan on two days to reach them. You'll find the islands scenic and the water exceptionally calm. The fishing for rainbow trout is also good, while at the very end of the lake is a ranger cabin. If the ranger is not in, paddlers are welcome to use the cabin and it makes a nice break from your tent. This is a good four to five-day paddle, depending on how much time you want to spend in the islands.

Margot Creek Along the south shore of the Iliuk Arm of Naknek Lake is the mouth of this creek where you will find both good fishing and lots of bear activity. It's a 10-mile paddle from Brooks Camp and, in ideal conditions, you can reach it in under five hours. But for most people it's a good overnight trip as you can camp on islands nearby to minimize encounters with bears.

Getting There & Away
Although the park is closer to Kodiak or Homer, to get there from Anchorage to Katmai you first have to fly to King Salmon. There is a variety of ways to reach the park. A round-trip ticket on Alaska Airlines to King Salmon is $250 while MarkAir (☎ 243-1414 in Anchorage) will sell you a round trip to King Salmon and a flight into Brooks Camp on it own float plane for $370. Also check with Peninsula Airways (☎ 243-2323 in Anchorage) which offers service from Anchorage to King Salmon.

Once you're in King Salmon, a number of air taxi companies will fly out to Brooks Camp, including Katmai Air (☎ 246-3079 or (800) 478-3079 within Alaska) which charges $124 for a round trip. You can also take a jet boat from King Salmon to Brooks Camp on the *Katmai Lady*. The daily service is run through Quinnat Landing Hotel (☎ 246-3000) with the boat departing in the morning and then making a return trip to King Salmon in late afternoon from Brooks Camp. One-way fare is $25 per person.

McNEIL RIVER
The McNeil River State Game Sanctuary, just north of Katmai National Park on the Alaska Peninsula or 200 miles south-west of Anchorage, is famous for its high numbers of brown bears from July to August. The majority of the bears gather a mile upstream from the mouth of the river where falls slow

down the salmon and provide an easy meal. This spot is world renowned among wildlife photographers and every great bear-catches-salmon shot you've ever seen was most likely taken from either here or the Brooks River. Often there are 20 or more brown bears feeding together below the McNeil River Falls and up to 80 have been seen congregated here at one time.

The fishing is so easy, that by the end of the summer, the bears get picky. Many feel for the egg sack of a female salmon, eat the raw caviar and then discard the rest of the fish to waiting seagulls, eagles and other birds. Male salmon are often just dropped back in the river.

The Alaska Department of Fish & Game has set up a viewing area and allows 10 visitors per day to watch the bears feed. From a camp, park guides lead you on a two-mile hike across sedge flats and through thigh-deep Mikfik Creek to the viewing area on a bluff. There you can watch the bears feed less than 20 yards away in what is basically a series of rapids and pools where the salmon gather between leaps. Though an expensive side trip, for most visitors, viewing and photographing giant brown bears this close is an once-in-a-lifetime experience.

That's the reason for the permit system. You need to pull a permit – lottery style – to be one of the 185 people who state officials allow into the park from July to August, the prime season for bear watching. In 1993, more than 2000 applications were received from around the world.

Permits
Visits to the game sanctuary are on a permit basis only and your odds of drawing a permit from the lottery are less than one in 10. Write to the Alaska Department of Fish & Game, Wildlife Conservation Division, 333 Raspberrry Rd, Anchorage, AK 99518 for an application; or call (907) 267-2180. Return your application with $50, of which $10 is non-refundable, by 1 April for a May lottery drawing. Permits are drawn for only 10 people a day from July to 25 August. If your name is drawn, by all means take advantage

of this rare opportunity in wildlife photography.

Getting There & Away

Most visitors depart for McNeil River from Homer. Kachemak Air Service (☎ 235-8924) is based in Homer and offers a return fare of $300 to McNeil River. It makes the trip whether the plane is filled to capacity (12 seats) or carries only one passenger – the plane lands in a tidal area during high tide. Even if you don't have a permit, check with the air service as they stay in constant touch with rangers at the state game area. Occasionally, cancellations or no-shows will create last-minute openings in the sanctuary's permit system.

LAKE CLARK

Apart from backpacking enthusiasts and river runners in Southcentral Alaska, few people knew about Lake Clark National Park & Preserve, 100 miles south-west of Anchorage, until recently. Yet it offers some of the most spectacular scenery of any of the newly created parks in the state. It is within this 3.6 million-acre preserve that the Alaska and Aleutian ranges meet. Among the many towering peaks are Mt Iliamna and Mt Redoubt, two active volcanoes clearly seen from Anchorage and the western shore of the Kenai Peninsula.

Much of the park's obscurity changed in January 1990 when Mt Redoubt erupted. After 25 dormant years, the volcano roared back to life sending ash into the air and creating a cloud that could be seen along the western shore of the Kenai Peninsula. The spreading ash closed the Anchorage International Airport and oil terminals in the area, while 10,000 face masks were distributed to the residents of central Kenai Peninsula worried about inhaling the fine powder.

If you are contemplating a wilderness trip into the area, check with the park headquarters (☎ 271-3751) in Anchorage before departing. Since most recreational activities take place in the western half of the park, chances are the eruption will have little effect on your travel plans.

Along with its now famous volcanoes, the park also features numerous glaciers, spectacular turquoise lakes (including Lake Clark, the park's centerpiece) and three designated wild rivers that have long been havens for river runners.

Wildlife includes brown and black bears, moose, red foxes, wolves and dall sheep on the alpine slopes. Caribou roam the western foothills, while the park's watershed is one of the most important producers of red salmon in the world, contributing 33% of the US catch. The weather in the western section of the preserve, where most of the rafting and backpacking takes place, is generally cool and cloudy with light winds through much of the summer. Temperatures range from 50 to 65°F from June to August, with an occasional heat wave of 80°F.

Hiking

Lake Clark is another trail-less park for the experienced backpacker only. Most extended treks take place in the western foothills north of Lake Clark, where the open and

Red fox

Wolf

relatively dry tundra provides ideal conditions for hiking.

Less experienced backpackers are content to be dropped off at the shores of the many lakes in the area, camp and undertake day hikes. Popular destinations for backpackers include Telaquana, Turquoise and Twin lakes. An excellent cross-country route is to hike from Turquoise south to Twin Lakes, where there is usually a ranger stationed. Experienced backpackers can travel between the two lakes in a day.

There is a summer ranger station at Port Alsworth (☎ 781-2218), but it is best to contact the park headquarters (☎ 271-3751) in Anchorage regarding desirable places to hike and camp. You can also write to them before departing for Alaska at: Lake Clark National Park, 4230 University Dr, Suite 311, Anchorage, AK 99508.

Rafting

Float trips down any of the three designated wild rivers are spectacular and exciting since the waterways are rated from Class III to IV. Raft rentals are usually available in Port Alsworth. Contact the ranger to ask who is providing the service.

Chilikadrotna River Beginning at Win Lakes, this river offers a good adventure for intermediate rafters. Its steady current and narrow course winds through upland spruce and hardwood forest, draining the west flank of the Alaska Range. From the lakes to a take out on the Mulchatna River is a 60-mile, four-day float that involves some Class III stretches.

Tlikakila This fast but small glacial river flows from Summit Lake to upper Lake Clark through a narrow, deep valley within the Alaska Range. The 46-mile trip requires three days and hits a few stretches of Class III water. The hiking in tundra around Summit Lake is excellent and from there you make a portage to the river.

Mulchatna River Above Bonanza Hills, this river is a shallow rocky channel from its headwaters at Turquoise Lake with stretches of Class III rapids. Below the hills the Mulchatna is an easy and leisurely float. Plan on two days to float from the lake to the end of Bonanza Hills while the entire river is a 220-mile run to the Nushagak River.

Getting There & Away

Access into the Lake Clark region is by small charter plane which makes the area tough to visit on a limited budget. The cheapest way to reach the park is to book a week in advance through Alaska Airlines (☎ (800) 426-0333). A return ticket between Anchorage and Iliamna, a small village 30 miles south of the park, is $206. ERA Aviation, a contract carrier of Alaska Airlines, makes the flight twice a day. From Iliamna, you have to charter a plane to your destination within the park through air-taxi operators such as Iliamna Air Taxi (☎ 571-1248).

Western Alaska

PRIBILOF ISLANDS

The Pribilof Islands are in the Bering Sea, 300 miles west of Alaska's mainland and 900 miles from Anchorage. They are desolate, wind-swept places where the abundance of wildlife has made them tourist attractions despite the inhospitable weather. The four islands have two communities: St Paul (population 600) and St George (population 200) consisting mostly of Aleut Indians and government workers.

Although the Pribilof Islands are the home of the largest Aleut villages in the world, seals are the reason for the tourist trade. Every summer the tiny archipelago of rocky shores and steep cliffs becomes a mad scene

Baby seal

when a million fur seals swim ashore to breed and raise their young. The seals spend most of the year at sea between California and Japan, but each summer they migrate to the Pribilofs, becoming the largest group of mammals anywhere in the world.

Many visitors also venture to the islands to view the extensive bird rookeries. About 2.5 million birds, made up of 200 species, nest at the Pribilofs, making it one of the largest seabird colonies in North America. The cliffs are easy to reach and photograph, and blinds have been erected on the beach to observe seals.

Because of strict regulations and limited facilities, most travelers choose package tours in order to visit the Pribilof Islands. Gray Line (☎ 277-5581 in Anchorage) offers a three-day tour of St Paul that departs Anchorage on Tuesday and Thursday. The tour, which includes accommodation, meals, air fares and transport to the beaches and rookeries, costs $840 per person. Reeve Aleutian Airways (☎ (800) 544-2248) also runs tours to St Paul and offers longer stays including four days for $989, six days for $1291 and even an eight-day trip for $1593. This includes round-trip air fare, hotel and sightseeing transport but not meals.

If you do have an extra $1000 to spend, a more unique experience, while still seeing the immense amount of wildlife, is to travel independently to St George, a smaller and much less visited island. You can stay at the *St George Hotel*, a recently designated national historical landmark, where rooms are $89 person per night and you can cook your own meals in the kitchen downstairs.

Since the island isn't that big (only five miles wide) hiking to within view of the wildlife is possible. Call St George Tanaq Tours (☎ 562-3100) in Anchorage to reserve a room at the hotel. Then contact Peninsula Airways (☎ 243-2323) to book a flight to St George; the return fare is $840.

NOME

In 1898, the 'Three Lucky Swedes' Jafet Lindberg, Erik Lindblom and John Brynteson found gold in Anvil Creek. By that winter the news reached the gold fields of the Klondike and the following year the tent city that miners initially called Anvil City had a population of 10,000. More gold was found on the beaches nearby that summer and when the news finally made its way to Seattle in 1900 it set off yet another stampede of hopeful miners to Alaska. By the end of that year, there were 20,000 people in the town that was now called Nome – a place that would forever be associated around the world with gold and quick fortunes. At the height of the gold rush, Nome was declared

Alaska's largest city when the US Census recorded a permanent population of 12,488 in 1900 and listed one-third of all non-native Alaskan residents as living in the city.

Nome has had its fair share of natural disasters, like much of Alaska, as fires all but destroyed the town in 1905 and 1934 and a Bering Sea storm overpowered the sea walls in 1974. Though little of its gold-rush architecture remains, the city survived and today it has a population of 4500 and even a little frontier façade along historical Front St.

Nome serves as the transport center for

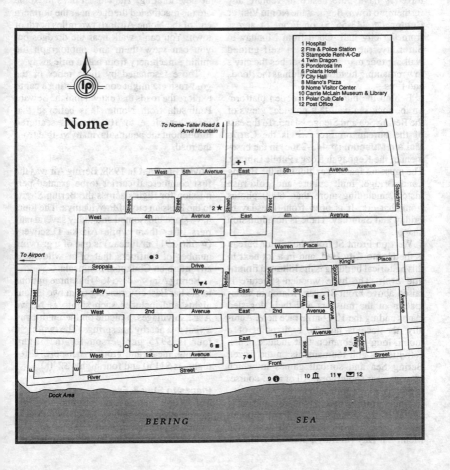

Nome

To Nome-Teller Road &
Anvil Mountain

To Airport

1 Hospital
2 Fire & Police Station
3 Stampede Rent-A-Car
4 Twin Dragon
5 Ponderosa Inn
6 Polaris Hotel
7 City Hall
8 Milano's Pizza
9 Nome Visitor Center
10 Carrie McLain Museum & Library
11 Polar Cub Cafe
12 Post Office

BERING   SEA

much of Western Alaska and during the summer, ocean-going barges unloading offshore are a common sight. A surge in gold prices in recent years has also given new life to the mining industry, and the lure of gold still draws people to Nome. However, it's summer tourists rather than miners who contribute to Nome's economy these days, especially with the growing tours of Eastern Siberia.

Things to See & Do

Nome's sights are along Front St and most travelers have little desire to venture any further into town. Begin at the **Nome Visitor Center** (☎ 443-5535) on Front St across from the city hall. Open from Monday to Saturday, the bureau has a self-guided walking tour map which describes the city's few remaining historical buildings the floods and fires.

Behind the bureau is a wooden platform on the rock sea wall that provides views of the Bering Sea and Sledge Island. To the east of the bureau on Front St is the **Carrie McLain Museum** (☎ 443-2566) in the basement of the Kegoayah Kozga Public Library. The museum features exhibits on the Bering Land Bridge, Inuit culture and gold-rush history, including more than 6000 photos from that era. It is open from Tuesday to Friday and Saturday. There is no admission charge.

West on Front St from the visitor bureau is the **Nome City Hall**, and in a lot next to this historical building is the **Iditarod finish-line arch**. The huge wooden structure is raised above Front St every March in anticipation of the mushers and their dog-sled teams ending the 1049-mile race here. Actually, the race is just the high point of a month-long celebration that includes such activities as golf tournaments on the frozen Bering Sea and softball games in which players wear snowshoes. All of it, of course, is merely a cure for cabin fever.

Nome's **public beach** is nearby, and in the height of the summer a few local children may be seen playing in the 45°F water. On Memorial Day (in May), 20 to 30 residents participate in the annual Polar Bear Swim by plunging into the ice-choked waters. A warmer swim can be obtained in the public pool (☎ 443-5717) at the Nome Public School. The admission charge is $2 per session.

At night, stop in at the *Board of Trade Saloon*, the oldest bar on the Bering Sea, on Front St. It's a good place to meet the locals.

Gold Dredges There are 44 gold dredges in the area surrounding the city, some of which are still being used today while many others lie deteriorating. The closest ones to Nome are the reactivated dredges near the northern end of the Nome Airport, two miles north of town. You can't walk near the dredges but you can view them and photograph the mining machinery from half a mile away.

Those fascinated by these relics of the gold-rush era might consider renting a car to explore the roads that extend into the Seward Peninsula from Nome. It is believed that there are close to 100 dredges scattered throughout the peninsula, many visible from the road.

Soviet Far East In 1988, Bering Air was the first commercial carrier to be granted permission for flights across the Bering Straits to the Russian city of Provideniya. The tours have since blossomed and today several carriers offer them while Alaska Discovery (☎ 586-1911 in Juneau) is one of a growing number of outfitters that offer wilderness adventure on Chukotka Peninsula.

Bering Air (☎ 443-5464) has three options to the Far East city, ranging from two to four nights and includes such sights as Native Alaskan villages, a picnic on the tundra and a visit to a nearby hot springs. The two-night tour is $975 per person for the flight, lodging, meals and ground transport. Three nights is $1150 and four nights $2400.

Places to Stay & Eat

The visitor bureau has information about camping on the public beach which is a common practice in Nome. There are also nine hotels and B&Bs. The old section of the

Gold Mining in Nome

Recreational mining is allowed on Nome's beaches without a permit for those using a gold pan, small rocker box or portable dredge with an intake of less than two inches. But before you sell your return ticket home to make your fortune on the beaches of Nome consider this – the amount of gold in a cubic yard is small and amounts of gravel that must be washed out to make a living extremely large.

Before 1961 the average gold-bearing gravel mined in Alaska yielded from 35c to 75c per cubic yard. Today, because of the higher prices of gold (generally around $350 an ounce) that value ranges up to $15 per cubic yard. But a cubic yard of gravel is 180 large panfuls and even for a sourdough miner it usually takes five minutes of steady, careful panning to work down the concentration of a pan without losing it.

Still want to sell the farm? Try this first – take a No 2 round-pointed shovel generously filled with fine gravel or sand and place it in your pan. Stir in some iron filling or small buckshot to simulate gold. Start separating it. How long did it take you to reach the buckshot? Now multiply that by 180 and you've just earned $10 or $15 on the beaches of Nome. You'll probably make more flipping burgers at McDonald's. ■

Polaris Hotel (☎ 443-2000) has singles with shared bath at $40 per night and doubles with private bath at $80. The *Ponderosa Inn* (☎ 443-5737) has singles/doubles for $64/75 and is nicer. There is also a handful of B&Bs that generally charge $50/60 a single/double. Try *Betty's Igloo* (☎ 443-2419), *June's B&B* (☎ 443-5984) or *Oceanview Manor* (☎ 443-2133).

Locals eat at the *Polar Cub Cafe* on Front St. Pizza is available at *Milano's Pizzaria*, across the street and there is even Chinese available here at *Twin Dragon* on the corner of Bering St and Alley Way.

Around Nome

Extending from Nome are three major roads that are maintained by the state and well traveled during the summer. Each is an adventure in itself but they offer absolutely no services whatsoever, especially gas stations. There are four places in Nome to rent a car, all of them offering unlimited mileage in an area of the state where there is very limited mileage. Stampede Rent-A-Car (☎ 443-3838) has Ford Escorts for $60 a day and a 'Miner's Special', a room and a vehicle for $125 a day. Bonanza (☎ 443-2221) has pick-ups for $65 a day and 4WD vehicles for $80.

Nome-Council Rd This is a 72-mile route that heads north-east to the small Native Alaskan village of Council. For the first 30 miles the road follows the coast, where during the salmon season you'll see fish drying from driftwood racks. At *Mile 13* the road reaches Cape Nome, which offers a panoramic view of the Bering Sea, and then heads inland and passes through Solomon at *Mile 34*. The community was once prosperous and even boasted of having its own railroad. Today it's a ghost town and what's left of the Solomon Railroad will be seen before entering the town. Council is a town of 30 to 40 people during the summer and can only be reached after fording a small river. Otherwise head downriver to a launch and catch a ride with a resident crossing over in a boat.

Kougarok Rd This is also known as Nome-Taylor Rd and leads 83 miles north through the heart of the Kigluaik Mountains. The drive will allow you to see more artefacts from the gold-rush days, including old miner's cabins, dredges and railroad bridges and tracks. At *Mile 40* you pass Salmon Lake Campground while a mile trek inland from the road is a public cabin managed by the city of Nome in the Mosquito Pass area. In the summer you can hike into the pass by leaving the road near the confluence of the Hudson Creek and the Nome River and heading west. The cabin is at the confluence of the Windy Creek and Sinuk River. Another 19 miles

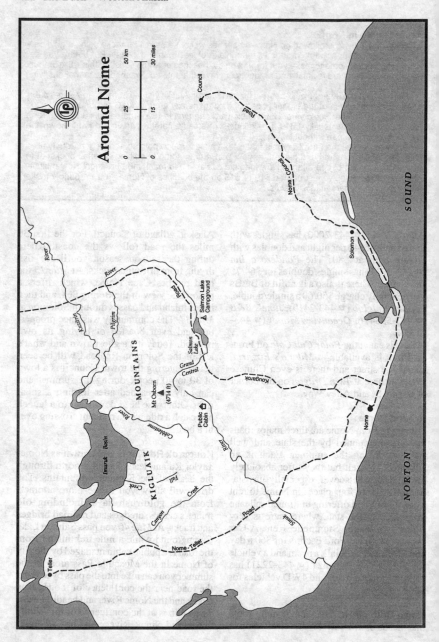

north of Salmon Lake at *Mile 65* is Pilgrim River Rd which leads west to Pilgrim Hot Springs.

Nome-Teller Rd This road leads 73 miles to Teller, a village of 200 with a gift shop and a small store but no other tourist facilities.

Getting There & Away
Air Nome is serviced by Alaska Airlines, which offers three daily flights to the town from Anchorage. A return ticket, booked two weeks in advance, costs $450.

Tours Most people visit Nome and Kotzebue on package tours which are usually cheaper than even round-trip tickets to the city. Gray Line (☎ 277-5581 in Anchorage) offers a two-day package tour that begins in Anchorage, spends a day in Kotzebue and then overnights in Nome for $419. The price is based on shared accommodation and includes air fare, lodging and meals. Alaska Airlines (☎ (800) 468-2248) has the identical trip plus one that spends three days in the two cities for $484 and a one-day tour of Nome for $315.

KOTZEBUE
Situated 26 miles north of the Arctic Circle, Kotzebue has one of the largest communities of indigenous people in the Bush; over 80% of its 3600 residents are Inuit. Kotzebue is on the north-west shore of the Baldwin Peninsula in Kotzebue Sound, near the mouths of the Kobuk and Noatak rivers. Traditionally, it serves as the transport and commerce center for Northwest Alaska.

More recently, it has experienced an increase in tourism mostly through the efforts of NANA, a Native American corporation, and as the departure point into the new national preserves and parks nearby. NANA also manages a reindeer herd, numbering over 6000 head, on the Baldwin Peninsula. Many residents still depend on subsistence hunting and fishing to survive.

The majority of travelers to Kotzebue are either part of a tour group or are just passing through on their way to a wilderness expedition in the surrounding parks. The community is extremely difficult to visit for an independent traveler on a limited budget.

Things to See & Do
The town is named after Polish explorer Otto von Kotzebue, who stumbled onto the village in 1816 while searching for the Northwest Passage for the Russians. Much of the town's history and culture can be viewed at one of two museums. The **Ootukahkuktuvik City Museum** features artefacts of the indigenous people and early settlers, including a rain parka made of walrus intestine. Independent travelers wanting to view the museum on Kotzebue Way near Tundra Way must first contact Kotzebue City Hall (☎ 442-3401).

Most tour groups visit the **Museum of the Arctic**, where 2nd and 3rd avenues meet at the western end of town. The center is owned and operated by NANA, which offers a two-hour program of indigenous culture, demonstrations in Inuit handicrafts, a visit to the adjoining jade factory and a traditional blanket toss. Independent travelers can join the museum tour, if they want to part with $25, by contacting the NANA office (☎ 442-3301). Or you can just visit the museum to view the wildlife exhibits and displays on the unique natural history of Northwest Alaska; it is open daily during the summer and there is no admission charge.

Perhaps the most interesting thing to do in Kotzebue is just stroll down **Front St** (also known as Shore Ave), a narrow gravel road only a few yards from the water at the northern edge of town. Here you can see salmon drying out on racks, fishing boats crowding the beach to be repaired and locals preparing for the long winter ahead. This is also the best place to watch the midnight sun roll along the horizon, painting the sea reddish gold in a beautiful scene of color and light reflecting off the water. Beginning in early June, the sun does not set for almost six weeks in Kotzebue.

In the center of town there is a large **cemetery** where spirit houses have been erected over many of the graves.

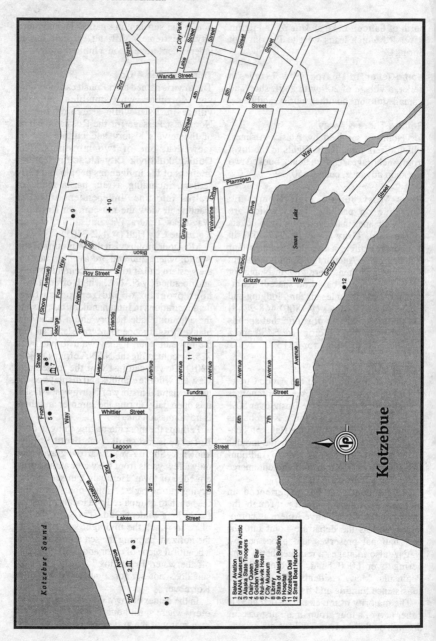

Kotzebue

Kotzebue Sound

Swan Lake

To City Park

Wanda Street
Turf Street
Ptarmigan
Grizzly Way

1 Baker Aviation of the Arctic
2 NANA Museum of the Arctic
3 Alaska State Troopers
4 Dairy Queen
5 Golden Whale Bar
6 Nul-luk-vik Hotel
7 City Museum
8 Library
9 State of Alaska Building
10 Hospital
11 Kotzebue Deli
12 Small Boat Harbor

Places to Stay & Eat

There is no hostel or public campgrounds in Kotzebue. The only hotel, *Nul-luk-vik* (☎ 442-3331), has rates from $120 per night for singles. It is a common practice among backpackers, however, to hike south of town (a quarter of a mile past the airport) and pitch their tents on the beach. Keep in mind that much of the beach around Kotzebue is difficult to camp on because it is narrow and sloping or is privately owned.

As out of place as it may seem, there is a *Dairy Queen* in town, undoubtedly the northernmost of the chain, on the corner of 2nd Ave and Lagoon St. Along with hamburgers and ice cream, it serves steaks and seafood. A cheaper place is the *Hamburger Hut* on Front St, where you can get a hamburger for around $8. There is also a *Pizza House*, and *Arctic Dragon* for Chinese.

Paddling

Kotzebue provides access to some of the finest river running in Arctic Alaska. Popular trips include the Noatak River, the Kobuk River and Salmon River (which flows into the Kobuk), and the Selawik River (which originates in the Kobuk lowlands and flows west into Selawik Lake).

Trips along the Kobuk National Wild River consist of floats from Walker Lake 140 miles downstream to the villages of Kobuk or Ambler, where there are scheduled flights to both Kotzebue and Bettles, another departure point for this river. Bering Air Service (☎ 442-3943) charges $100 for a one-way flight from Kobuk to Kotzebue and $100 from Ambler. Most of the river is rated Class I, but some lining of boats may be required just below Walker Lake and for a mile through Lower Kobuk Canyon. Paddlers usually plan on six to eight days for the float.

The Noatak National Wild River is a 16-day float of 350 miles from Lake Matcharak to the village of Noatak, where Bering Air has scheduled flights to Kotzebue for $60 per person one way. However, the numerous access lakes on the river allow it to be broken down into shorter paddles. The entire river is rated from Class I to II.

The upper portion in the Brooks Range offers much more dramatic scenery and is usually accessed from Bettles (see the Gates of the Arctic section following). The lower half, accessed through Kotzebue, flows through a broad, gently sloping valley where hills replace the sharp peaks of the Brooks Range. The most common trip here is to put in at Nimiuktuk River where within an hour of paddling you enter the 65-mile-long Grand Canyon of the Noatak, followed by the seven-mile-long Noatak Canyon. Most paddlers pull out at Kelly River where there is a ranger station with a radio. Below the confluence with the Kelly River, the Noatak becomes heavily braided.

For more information contact the National Park office (☎ 442-3890) in the Museum of the Arctic at Kotzebue, which is open Monday to Friday from 8.30 am to 5.30 pm in the summer, or write to the National Park Service (NPS) at PO Box 287, Kotzebue, AK 99752 before you depart for Alaska.

Canoes can be rented in Kotzebue (check with the NPS for names of people renting them) or in Ambler from Ambler Air Service (☎ 445-2121), which can also supply transport up the Kobuk River. It is possible to book a return supersaver flight from Anchorage to Ambler, stopping at Kotzebue ($670) and from there rent boats from Ambler Air Service. See the list of guide companies at the end of the Wilderness chapter.

Getting There & Away

Alaska Airlines offers a round-trip ticket to Kotzebue, if booked two weeks in advance, for $386 from Anchorage. You can also purchase a round-trip ticket from Anchorage with stopovers in both Nome and Kotzebue for $471. Alaska Airlines also offers a one-day tour of Kotzebue from Anchorage for $315 as does Gray Line.

Arctic Alaska

DALTON HIGHWAY

Although officially called the Dalton Hwy,

this road is best known in Alaska simply as the 'Haul Rd'. This stretch of gravel winds 416 miles north from Elliott Hwy to Deadhorse at Prudhoe Bay, the community that houses the workers of what is believed to be the largest oil reserve in the USA. Prudhoe Bay is the start of the Trans-Alaska Pipeline that carries oil 800 miles to the ice-free port of Valdez on Prince William Sound.

After the road was completed in 1978, all but the first 56 miles of the highway to the Yukon River was kept closed to the public. In 1981, after a bitter battle in the state legislature, the public was allowed to drive 211 miles along the road to Disaster Creek. This section of the highway takes you into the Brooks Range and near the borders of Kanuti and Yukon Flats national wildlife refuges and the Gates of the Arctic National Park & Preserve north of them.

To travel past Disaster Creek you need a permit from the Department of Transportation (☎ 451-2249) which does not issue them to 'tourists, sightseers or hunters' – technically that is, but every summer travelers just keep heading north right up to Prudhoe Bay. *Mile 0* of Dalton Hwy is at the junction with Elliott Hwy, 73 miles north of Fairbanks. The beginning is marked by an information center that covers the route north. At *Mile 25*, there is a lookout with good views of the pipeline crossing Hess Creek. It is possible to camp around the creek, the color of which draws an occasional amateur gold panner.

The highway begins to descend to the Yukon River at *Mile 47*, and shortly you will be able to view miles of pipeline. At *Mile 51* of Dalton Hwy, a rough road leads east 5.4 miles to the Yukon River. There is a boat launch maintained by the Bureau of Land Management on the north side of the river.

The **Yukon River Bridge** is at *Mile 56*. The wooden-decked bridge was completed in 1975 and is 2290 feet long. On the north side of the bridge is Yukon Ventures (☎ 655-9001), one of two places to purchase supplies and gasoline. They also have rooms for $50 per person while east of the highway is a rough camping area with litter barrels. Just

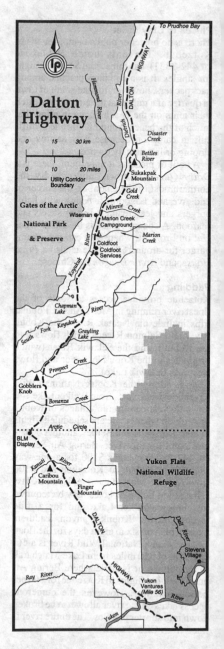

beyond *Mile 91* is a lookout with a scenic view of the road and the pipeline to the north.

At *Mile 96*, the highway ascends above the tree line into an alpine area where there is good hiking and berry picking. The road stays in this alpine section for the next five miles before the terrain turns rugged and you pass many impressive rock outcrops and views of the surrounding mountains.

The **Arctic Circle**, near *Mile 115* of Dalton Hwy, is the site of an impressive BLM display that was installed in 1992. The exhibit includes a large, brightly colored circumpolar map of the imaginary line and four information panels explaining the basis for the seasons and what it means to Arctic plants and animals. There is also a viewing deck, picnic tables and, someday in the future, a BLM campground will be here. But why wait? Camp anyhow and watch the sun set at 12.30 am and then rise 45 minutes later.

From the turn-off, the road passes six streams and the small Grayling Lake, in the next 64 miles, all of which offer superb grayling fishing.

Coldfoot Services (☎ 678-5201), a lodge and restaurant that also sells gasoline and groceries, is at *Mile 175*. The restaurant is open 24 hours and the food is surprisingly good. Rooms begin at $90 for singles with shared bathroom, camp sites are $7.50 for two people and showers are $3.50. In another five miles north is the spur to the *Marion Creek Campground*. The road is now near the boundaries of Gates of the Arctic National Park and the scenery is at its best. Wildlife is plentiful, especially dall sheep high on the mountain slopes.

After passing *Mile 186* there is a lookout where you can view the historical mining community of **Wiseman**, west of the road across the Koyukuk River. Buildings from the town's heyday in 1910 still stand, but all are private property – only a handful of people remain in Wiseman.

More spectacular mountain scenery begins around *Mile 193* of Dalton Hwy, with the first views of Sukakpak Mountain to the north and Wiehl Mountain to the east, both 4000 feet in elevation. Poss Mountain (6189

feet) comes into view to the east after another 2.5 miles, and the Koyukuk River, a heavily braided stream, is seen near *Mile 201*.

Just before *Mile 204* is a lookout with a half-mile trail leading to Sukakpak Mountain. The mounds between the road and the mountain were formed by ice pushing up the soil and vegetation.

Another lookout is passed after *Mile 206*, where there are good views of Snowden Mountain (5775 feet), 10 miles to the northwest. Six miles north of the lookout is Disaster Creek and the turnaround point. If you do continue on to the end of the road, keep in mind that the *Prudhoe Bay Hotel* (☎ 659-2449) has double rooms for $65 to $85 without meals and $75 to $85 with meals.

Getting There & Away
Car Finding somebody to rent you a car in Fairbanks for travel on the Dalton Hwy would be a major challenge. Don't even bother with the used-car rentals (see the Fairbanks Getting Around section in the Fairbanks chapter). If you're driving, remember that the road is used heavily by tractor-trailer rigs driving at high speeds. Never stop in the middle of the road to observe wildlife or scenery, as the trucks have limited braking ability.

Gasoline at about $1.70 a gallon, tire-repair services and limited food supplies are available where the road crosses the Yukon River, 141 miles north of Fairbanks, and at Coldfoot, 37 miles south of the turnaround point.

Tours There are now a number of tours available in Fairbanks for a trip up the highway. Northern Alaska Tour Company (☎ 474-8600) offers three including a daily bus tour to the Arctic Circle and back for $85 and another with a flight back to Fairbanks for $145. The company also has a two-day trip to Prudhoe Bay for $395 that includes lodging at Wiseman, some meals and a flight back.

Princess Tours (☎ 479-9660) and Grayline (☎ 456-5816) have three-day, two-night tours to the oil fields priced at $679.

GATES OF THE ARCTIC

The Gates of the Arctic National Park & Preserve, one of the finest wilderness areas in the world, straddles the Arctic Divide in the Brooks Range, 200 miles north-west of Fairbanks.

The entire park covering 8.4 million acres, extends 200 miles from east to west and lies totally north of the Arctic Circle. The park extends from the southern foothills of the Brooks Range, across the range's ragged peaks and down onto the North Slope. Most of the park is vegetated with shrubs or is tundra, and is a habitat for grizzly bears, wolves, dall sheep, moose, caribou and wolverines. Fishing is considered superb for grayling and arctic char in the clear streams and for lake trout in the larger, deeper lakes.

Within this preserve, you have dozens of rivers to run, miles of valleys and tundra slopes to hike and, of course, the Gates themselves. Mt Boreal and Frigid Crags are the gates that flank the North Fork of the Koyukuk River. It was through these landmark mountains that Robert Marshall found an unobstructed path northward to the Arctic coast of Alaska. That was in 1929 and Marshall's naming of the two mountains has remained ever since.

Hiking in the Arctic

The park is a vast wilderness containing no National Park Service facilities, campgrounds or trails. Many backpackers follow the long, open valleys for extended treks or work their way to higher elevations where open tundra and sparse shrubs provide good hiking terrain. Regardless of where you hike, trekking in the Arctic is a challenge and not for anybody who's only used to the posted trails of the Lower 48. Hiking across boggy ground and tussock, inevitable on any trip in the Gates of the Arctic, has been described by one guide as 'walking on basketballs'. A good day's travel in the Arctic is covering five or six miles.

It's also important to remember how fragile the Arctic ecosystem is. Its delicate balance of tundra, tussock plains and spruce boreal forests can be easily impacted on by the most sensitive backpackers and require years to regenerate due to permafrost and the short growing season. For these reasons the NPS puts a six-person limit on trekking parties. Try to avoid forming trails by traveling in a fan pattern whenever possible and by never marking routes.

Camp-site selection is your most important decision in an effort to minimize impact. Gravel bars along rivers and creeks are the best choice due to their durable and well-drained nature. If you must choice a vegetated site, select one with a hardier species such as moss or heath rather than the more fragile lichens. And avoid building fires at all costs. Tree growth in the Arctic is extremely slow, a spruce only inches in diameter may be several hundred years old.

Most backpackers enter the park by way of charter air-taxi out of Bettles, which can land on lakes, rivers or river bars. Extended treks across the park require outdoor experience and good map and compass skills. One of the more popular treks is the four to five-day hike from Summit Lake through the Gates to Redstar Lake. Less experienced backpackers often choose to be dropped off and picked up at one lake and from there explore the surrounding region on day hikes. Lakes ideal for this include Summit Lake, the Karupa lakes region, Redstar Lake, Hunt Fork Lake or Chimney Lake.

The lone exception to chartering a plane is the trek beginning from the Dalton Hwy into several different areas along the eastern border of the park. First stop at the Coldfoot Information Center for advice and assistance in trip planning. Then continue north to your access point into the park. The further north you travel on the highway, the quicker you get into the tundra and the spectacular scenery. Many backpackers stop at Wiseman, however, which provides access to several routes including the following two.

Nolan/Wiseman Creek Area Just before

Mile 189 of the Dalton Hwy, head west at the Wiseman exit and continue hiking along the Nolan Rd which passes through Nolan, a hamlet of a few families, and ends at Nolan Rd. This will provide access to Wiseman Creek and Nolan Creek Lake which lies in the valley of Wiseman and Nolan creeks at the foot of three passes: Glacier, Pasco and Snowshoes. Any of these passes provides a route to Glacier River which can be followed to the North Fork of the Koyukuk for a more extensive hike. The USGS topos that cover this area are Wiseman B-1, B-2, C-1 and C-2.

Lower Hammond River Area From Wiseman continue north by hiking along the Hammond Rd which can be followed for quite away along the Hammond River. By following the river, you can further explore the park by following one of several drainage areas including Vermont, Canyon and Jenny Creek, which heads east to Jenny Creek Lake. The topos that cover this area are Chandlar C-6 and B-6 and Wiseman C-1 and B-1.

Paddling
Floatable rivers in the park include the John, the North Fork of the Koyukuk, the Tinayguk, the Alatna and the Middle Fork of the Koyukuk River from Wiseman to Bettles. The headwaters for the Noatak and Kobuk rivers are in the park.

The waterways range from Class I to III in difficulty. Of the various rivers, the North Fork of the Koyukuk River is one of the most popular because the float begins in the shadow of the Gates and continues downstream 100 miles to Bettles through Class I and II waters. Canoes and rafts can be rented in Bettles and then floated downstream back to the village.

Upper Noatak The best known river and the most popular for paddlers is the upper portion of the Noatak. Part of the reason is the excellent scenery as you float through the sharp peaks of the Brooks Range. Part is because it is a relatively mild river that can

be handled by intermediate canoeists on an unguided trip.

The most common trip is a 60-mile float that begins with a put-in near Portage Creek and ends at a riverside lake near Kacachurak Creek, just outside the park boundaries. This float is often covered in five to seven days but does involve some Class II and possible Class III stretches of rapids towards the end. Also keep in mind that during the summer you will most likely see other canoeing or rafting parties on the water.

Guide Companies
A number of guide companies run trips through the Gates of the Arctic National Park, including Sourdough Outfitters (☎ 692-5252 in Bettles) which charges $1350 for a seven-day canoeing expedition on the North Fork of the Koyukuk River and $2,250 for an 11-day paddle on the headwaters of the Noatak River. Also check with Arctic Treks (☎ 455-6502) if you are passing through Fairbanks. Both guide companies have been around for years and offer a variety of trips in the park or elsewhere in the Brooks Range.

Canoes and rafts can be rented from Sourdough Outfitters which offers unguided expeditions with arranged drop-off and pick-up air services for independent backpackers. A six-day backpacking adventure from Summit Lake to Chimney Lake is $350 per person for a party of two, and to turn that into a two-week adventure with a paddle down the North Fork of the Koyukuk is $400. The company has a wide range of other unguided trips and rents canoes for $25 a day and rafts for $35 to $50 depending on their length.

Getting There & Away
Access to the park's backcountry is usually accomplished in two steps, with the first being a scheduled flight from Fairbanks to Bettles. Check out Frontier Flying Service (☎ 474-0014) or Larry's Flying Service (☎ (800) 478-5169) in Fairbanks which makes regular flights to Bettles for $180 round trip. The increase of regularly scheduled flights to Bettles over the past few years

is amazing. Frontier Flying now offers three flights a day from Monday to Friday during the summer. Keep your eye on the weight of your pack. The charter companies allow you 40 pounds after that it's 43c a pound.

The second step is to charter an air-taxi in Bettles to your destination within the park. A Cessna 185 on floats holds three passengers and costs around $225 per hour. Most areas in the park can be reached in under two hours of flying time from Bettles. If you're in Bettles, check with Brooks Range Aviation (☎ 692-5444) or Bettles Air Service (☎ 692-5111) for air charters out of Bettles.

The alternative to expensive air chartering is to begin your trip from the Dalton Hwy. Travelers with time but little money can hitchhike the highway. A trickle of cars and a couple of hundred trucks use the road daily. While trucks will not stop to pick you up on the roadside, it is often possible to pick up a ride with one at the Hilltop Cafe, a truck-stop and gasoline station at *Mile 5.3* of Elliott Hwy.

BETTLES

This small village of 40 residents serves as the major departure point to the Gates of the Arctic National Park. Originally Bettles was six miles down the Middle Fork of the Koyukuk River. It was founded by Gordon C Bettles in 1900 at a trading post. Riverboats would work their way up the Koyukuk and unload their supplies in Bettles from where it was transported to smaller scows and horse-drawn barges. The smaller boats would then take the cargo to the mining country further upriver.

WW II brought a need for a major airstrip in Arctic Alaska and the Civil Aviation Agency (now the FAA) chose to construct one on better ground upriver. Eventually the entire village moved to the airstrip and today has the distinction of being the smallest incorporated city in Alaska.

Information

The National Park Service maintains a ranger station (☎ 692-5494) at Bettles, just beyond the airstrip next door to Sourdough

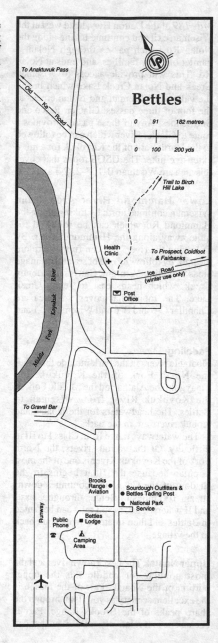

Bettles

To Anaktuvuk Pass

Old Ke — Road

Middle Fork Koyukuk River

Trail to Birch Hill Lake

Health Clinic ✚

To Prospect, Coldfoot & Fairbanks

Ice — Road (winter use only)

Post Office ✉

To Gravel Bar

Brooks Range Aviation ●

Sourdough Outfitters & Bettles Trading Post ●

National Park Service ●

Runway

Public Phone ☎

Bettles Lodge

Camping Area

0   91   182 metres

0   100   200 yds

Outfitters. During the summer the station is open daily and inside there are a stack of handouts, a small library of books and videos relating to the park, and usually somebody who can answer questions about trips into the park.

Places to Stay & Eat

Camping is allowed behind the Bettles Flight Service building off the runway and at the north edge of the aircraft parking area where you'll find barbecue grills. It would also be just as easy to pitch a tent on the gravel bars along the Middle Fork of the Kuyukuk River that the town overlooks.

A variety of lodging is available at the *Bettles Lodge* (☎ 692-5111), just off the runway. Actually everything in Bettles is just off the runway. The inn is a classic Alaskan log lodge with a rooms, a restaurant, a small tavern and bush pilots constantly wandering through in their hip boots. Singles/doubles are $60/95 a night, and a bed in a bunkhouse is $15. *Sourdough Outfitters* (☎ 692-5252) also has a bunkroom and showers for rent.

The restaurant is open from 8 am to 7 pm and has breakfasts for $7, hamburgers $6.50 and the single entree (main course) at dinner for $11. Sign up for dinner if you plan to eat there. The other option for food is the *Bettles Trading Post*, which is run by Sourdough Outfitters and has the usual Bush Alaska selection and prices to match.

Hiking

If you find yourself with an unexpected day in Bettles, something that can easily happen in August, take a hike up to Birch Hill Lake. The trailhead is unmarked but located by first heading to the Evansville Health Clinic. Next to it is a small brown house and the trail can be found just to the right of it. It's a three-mile trek to the lake and can get swampy. It's best to wear rubber boots.

BARROW

Barrow (population 3000) is the largest Inupiat Inuit community in Alaska and one of the largest in North America. Although the residents enjoy such modern-day conve-

niences as a local bus system and gas heating in their homes from the nearby oil fields, they remain very traditional in their outlook on life and seasonal events; this is symbolized by the spring whale hunts.

The town, the northernmost community in the USA, is the place where US humorist Will Rogers died in 1935 when the plane carrying him and Wiley Post stalled and crashed into a river, 15 miles south of Barrow, during their trip from Fairbanks to Siberia. Barrow is 330 miles north of the Arctic Circle and less than 1200 miles from the North Pole.

Barrow became front-page news around the world in the fall of 1988 after several residents discovered that three grey whales had become entrapped by ice during their migration south to warmer waters off the coast of Mexico. The Inuit, wielding chainsaws, spent long hours cutting holes in the ice to allow the mammals to breathe.

When the news media caught wind of the

Inuit child

story, Barrow was flooded by reporters and television crews. The Top of the World Hotel was booked solid, there was a 30-minute wait to be seated at Pepe's North of the Border Mexican Restaurant and somebody was selling souvenir T-shirts (your choice of commemorative logos) on the streets of Barrow.

The unusual ordeal lasted almost two weeks and more than a $1 million was spent keeping the whales alive before a Soviet icebreaker finally cleared a path through the ice to open water. Two whales swam to freedom, one died and Barrow returned to its normal lifestyle after the media left. 'It was a good experience,' said an employee of a local restaurant, 'but we're glad to see it over with'.

Most people visit the town to say they've been at the top of the world or to view the midnight sun, which never sets between 10 May and 2 August. Otherwise, there is little reason to make the expensive side trip to Barrow. The return air fare from Fairbanks can be as low as $309 if you book it 21 days in advance on Alaska Airlines, but rooms in the town's three hotels begin at over $100 per night for a single. Barrow is not geared for tourism as much as Nome or Kotzebue and occasionally independent travellers can feel a bit of tension between them and the locals.

Getting There & Away

For those set on seeing Barrow, by far the best and most economical way is to book a package tour. Gray Line (☎ 456-5816) in Fairbanks offers a 12-hour trip to the community for $399. MarkAir Tours (☎ (800) 478-0800 in Alaska) has both a one-day trip and an overnighter from Fairbanks for $405 which includes a room at the Top of the World Hotel. Alaska Airlines (☎ (800) 468-2248) offers similar tours for the same price. You can also book these tours from Anchorage.

Index

MAPS

TEXT

Map references are in **bold** type.

Keep in touch!

We love hearing from you and think you'd like to hear from us.

The Lonely Planet Newsletter covers the when, where, how and what of travel (AND it's free!).

When...is the right time to see reindeer in Finland?
Where...can you hear the best palm-wine music in Ghana?
How...do you get from Asunción to Areguá by steam train?
What...should you leave behind to avoid hassles with customs in Iran?

To join our mailing list just contact us at any of our offices (details below).

Every issue includes:

- *a letter from Lonely Planet founders Tony and Maureen Wheeler*
- *travel diary from a Lonely Planet author - find out what it's really like out on the road*
- *feature article on an important and topical travel issue*
- *a selection of recent letters from our readers*
- *the latest travel news from all over the world*
- *details on Lonely Planet's new and forthcoming releases*

Also available: Lonely Planet T-shirts. 100% heavyweight cotton (S, M, L, XL)

LONELY PLANET PUBLICATIONS
Australia: PO Box 617, Hawthorn 3122, Victoria (tel: 03-819 1877)
USA: Embarcadero West, 155 Filbert St, Suite 251, Oakland, CA 94607 (tel: 510-893 8555)
UK: 10 Barley Mow Passage, Chiswick, London W4 4PH (tel: 081-742 3161)
France: 71 bis rue du Cardinal Lemoine – 75005 Paris (tel: 46 34 00 58)

Guides to the Americas

Argentina, Uruguay & Paraguay – a travel survival kit
This guide gives independent travellers all the essential information on three of South America's lesser-known countries. Discover some of South America's most spectacular natural attractions in Argentina; friendly people and beautiful handicrafts in Paraguay; and Uruguay's wonderful beaches.

Baja California – a travel survival kit
For centuries, Mexico's Baja peninsula – with its beautiful coastline, raucous border towns and crumbling Spanish missions – has been a land of escapes and escapades. This book describes how and where to escape in Baja.

Bolivia – a travel survival kit
From lonely villages in the Andes to ancient ruined cities and the spectacular city of La Paz, Bolivia is a magnificent blend of everything that inspires travellers. Discover safe and intriguing travel options in this comprehensive guide.

Brazil – a travel survival kit
From the mad passion of Carnival to the Amazon – home of the richest ecosystem on earth – Brazil is a country of mythical proportions. This guide has all the essential travel information.

Canada – a travel survival kit
This comprehensive guidebook has all the facts on the USA's huge neighbour – the Rocky Mountains, Niagara Falls, ultramodern Toronto, remote villages in Nova Scotia, and much more.

Central America on a shoestring
Practical information on travel in Belize, Guatemala, Costa Rica, Honduras, El Salvador, Nicaragua and Panama. A team of experienced Lonely Planet authors reveals the secrets of this culturally rich, geographically diverse and breathtakingly beautiful region.

Chile & Easter Island – a travel survival kit
Travel in Chile is easy and safe, with possibilities as varied as the countryside. This guide also gives detailed coverage of Chile's Pacific outpost, mysterious Easter Island.

Colombia – a travel survival kit
Colombia is a land of myths – from the ancient legends of El Dorado to the modern tales of Gabriel Garcia Marquez. The reality is beauty and violence, wealth and poverty, tradition and change. This guide shows how to travel independently and safely in this exotic country.

Costa Rica – a travel survival kit
Sun-drenched beaches, steamy jungles, smoking volcanoes, rugged mountains and dazzling birds and animals – Costa Rica has it all.

Ecuador & the Galápagos Islands – a travel survival kit
Ecuador offers a wide variety of travel experiences, from the high cordilleras to the Amazon plains – and 600 miles west, the fascinating Galápagos

Islands. Everything you need to know about travelling around this enchanting country.

Hawaii – a travel survival kit
Share in the delights of this island paradise – and avoid its high prices – both on and off the beaten track. Full details on Hawaii's best-known attractions, plus plenty of uncrowded sights and activities.

La Ruta Maya: Yucatán, Guatemala & Belize – a travel survival kit
Invaluable background information on the cultural and environmental riches of La Ruta Maya (The Mayan Route), plus practical advice on how best to minimise the impact of travellers on this sensitive region.

Mexico – a travel survival kit
A unique blend of Indian and Spanish culture, fascinating history, and hospitable people, make Mexico a travellers' paradise.

Peru – a travel survival kit
The lost city of Machu Picchu, the Andean altiplano and the magnificent Amazon rainforests are just some of Peru's many attractions. All the travel facts you'll need can be found in this comprehensive guide.

South America on a shoestring
This practical guide provides concise information for budget travellers and covers South America from the Darien Gap to Tierra del Fuego.

Trekking in the Patagonian Andes
The first detailed guide to this region gives complete information on 28 walks, and lists a number of other possibilities extending from the Araucanía and Lake District regions of Argentina and Chile to the remote icy tip of South America in Tierra del Fuego.

Also available:
Brazilian phrasebook, **Latin American Spanish** phrasebook and **Quechua** phrasebook.

Lonely Planet Guidebooks

Lonely Planet guidebooks cover every accessible part of Asia as well as Australia, the Pacific, South America, Africa, the Middle East, Europe and parts of North America. There are five series: *travel survival kits*, covering a country for a range of budgets; *shoestring guides* with compact information for low-budget travel in a major region; *walking guides*; *city guides* and *phrasebooks*.

Mail Order

Lonely Planet guidebooks are distributed worldwide. They are also available by mail order from Lonely Planet, so if you have difficulty finding a title please write to us. US and Canadian residents should write to Embarcadero West, 155 Filbert St, Suite 251, Oakland CA 94607, USA; European residents should write to 10 Barley Mow Passage, Chiswick, London W4 4PH; and residents of other countries to PO Box 617, Hawthorn, Victoria 3122, Australia.

Indian Subcontinent
Bangladesh
India
Hindi/Urdu phrasebook
Trekking in the Indian Himalaya
Karakoram Highway
Kashmir, Ladakh & Zanskar
Nepal
Trekking in the Nepal Himalaya
Nepali phrasebook
Pakistan
Sri Lanka
Sri Lanka phrasebook

Africa
Africa on a shoestring
Central Africa
East Africa
Trekking in East Africa
Kenya
Swahili phrasebook
Morocco, Algeria & Tunisia
Arabic (Moroccan) phrasebook
South Africa, Lesotho & Swaziland
Zimbabwe, Botswana & Namibia
West Africa

Central America
Baja California
Central America on a shoestring
Costa Rica
La Ruta Maya
Mexico

North America
Alaska
Canada
Hawaii

Europe
Baltic States & Kaliningrad
Dublin city guide
Eastern Europe on a shoestring
Eastern Europe phrasebook
Finland
France
Greece
Hungary
Iceland, Greenland & the Faroe Islands
Ireland
Italy
Mediterranean Europe on a shoestring
Mediterranean Europe phrasebook
Poland
Scandinavian & Baltic Europe on a shoestring
Scandinavian Europe phrasebook
Switzerland
Trekking in Spain
Trekking in Greece
USSR
Russian phrasebook
Western Europe on a shoestring
Western Europe phrasebook

South America
Argentina, Uruguay & Paraguay
Bolivia
Brazil
Brazilian phrasebook
Chile & Easter Island
Colombia
Ecuador & the Galápagos Islands
Latin American Spanish phrasebook
Peru
Quechua phrasebook
South America on a shoestring
Trekking in the Patagonian Andes

The Lonely Planet Story

Lonely Planet published its first book in 1973 in response to the numerous 'How did you do it?' questions Maureen and Tony Wheeler were asked after driving, bussing, hitching, sailing and railing their way from England to Australia.

Written at a kitchen table and hand collated, trimmed and stapled, *Across Asia on the Cheap* became an instant local bestseller, inspiring thoughts of another book.

Eighteen months in South-East Asia resulted in their second guide, *South-East Asia on a shoestring*, which they put together in a backstreet Chinese hotel in Singapore in 1975. The 'yellow bible' as it quickly became known to backpackers around the world, soon became *the* guide to the region. It has sold well over half a million copies and is now in its 7th edition, still retaining its familiar yellow cover.

Today there are over 130 Lonely Planet titles in print – books that have that same adventurous approach to travel as those early guides; books that 'assume you know how to get your luggage off the carousel' as one reviewer put it.

Although Lonely Planet initially specialised in guides to Asia, they now cover most regions of the world, including the Pacific, South America, Africa, the Middle East and Europe. The list of *walking guides* and *phrasebooks* (for 'unusual' languages such as Quechua, Swahili, Nepali and Egyptian Arabic) is also growing rapidly.

The emphasis continues to be on travel for independent travellers. Tony and Maureen still travel for several months of each year and play an active part in the writing, updating and quality control of Lonely Planet's guides.

They have been joined by over 50 authors, 60 staff – mainly editors, cartographers & designers – at our office in Melbourne, Australia, at our US office in Oakland, California and at our European office in Paris; another five at our office in London handle sales for Britain, Europe and Africa. Travellers themselves also make a valuable contribution to the guides through the feedback we receive in thousands of letters each year.

The people at Lonely Planet strongly believe that travellers can make a positive contribution to the countries they visit, both through their appreciation of the countries' culture, wildlife and natural features, and through the money they spend. In addition, the company makes a direct contribution to the countries and regions it covers. Since 1986 a percentage of the income from each book has been donated to ventures such as famine relief in Africa; aid projects in India; agricultural projects in Central America; Greenpeace's efforts to halt French nuclear testing in the Pacific and Amnesty International. In 1993 $100,000 was donated to such causes.

Lonely Planet's basic travel philosophy is summed up in Tony Wheeler's comment, 'Don't worry about whether your trip will work out. Just go!'.